The Entertaining Cookbook

Evelyn Rose is well known for her writing and broadcasting on food. She is cookery editor of the *Jewish Chronicle* and writes a monthly food column for *Decanter*. A regular contributor to 'Women's Hour', she has also appeared on BBC1's 'Look North'. She is active in consumer affairs and is a member of the Consumer's Committee of the Meat and Livestock Commission. Her previous books include *The Complete International Jewish Cookbook, Cooking and Eating for Health, More Fun With Your Food* (for the British Medical Association), and two booklets of recipes from 'Look North'.

D1079020

Evelyn Rose

The Entertaining Cookbook

Fontana/Collins

First published by Robson Books Ltd 1980
First issued in Fontana Paperbacks 1982

Copyright © Evelyn Rose 1980

Printed in Great Britain by
Richard Clay (The Chaucer Press) Ltd,
Bungay, Suffolk

To our family and friends who have shared our table over the years. Without them this book would not have been written.

Author's Acknowledgements

Food is a subject of universal interest, and it is impossible to write about it without making use of the knowledge and experience of very many different people. In my case these have included—besides my family and friends—readers, viewers, listeners and professional colleagues, all of whom have generously given me their advice and practical assistance. I would like to mention in particular the following people who have given me specific assistance: Sula Leon who helped me to test and select the recipes; my daughter Judi, who helped me to develop some of the recipes and to refine the seasoning of many others; my husband, Myer, who helped me with recipe research abroad, and with taste-testing at home, as well as giving me immense practical assistance in preparing the book for publication; my assistants, Pamela Waters and Mary Bagnall, who prepared the typed manuscript from an often illegible original; my editor, Liz Rose, of Robson Books,who gave me tremendous support and encouragement.

I have not acknowledged individual recipes, as in almost every case I have changed or amended them, and I therefore take full responsibility for all the recipes as they appear in this book.

Home economist: Lucille Barber

Contents

Appendix:

Introduction

In earlier times, when it was extremely difficult to obtain any kind of refreshment except under the domestic roof, offering a guest some food and drink was not merely a courtesy born of custom, but an absolute necessity. However, except on the most formal occasions, extra places would be set at the family table, and the guest would be invited to share in the normal household meal.

Today, though no longer a necessity, the custom of welcoming guests into our homes with delicious food and well-chosen drink remains. In some ways, because of the variety and quantity of food now available whatever the time of year, it has never been so easy to provide refreshment for our guests. On the other hand, because there is so little uncommitted time left in our busy modern lives, entertaining presents new problems unknown to a less hurried age, and must therefore become what it was in the old days: an extension of family living, rather than something quite separate from everyday life for which the time for special preparations must somehow be found.

Of course, there are many occasions when it's delightful to invite friends to a very special meal – and in this book I have given what I hope is the kind of practical guidance which is most useful in the context of the way we live now. But it can be equally pleasant to set a few extra places at the family table and serve favourite family dishes, albeit with a little extra shine on them. That is why, in addition to the special occasion luncheons, dinners and supper parties, the celebration teas and the formal drinks parties, I have given suggestions for many delicious alfresco meals which can be prepared on a sudden impulse in very little time, as well as a whole chapter of 'family plus' meals which, with a few imaginative touches, can end up as memorable occasions.

I have compiled *The Entertaining Cookbook* in two parts. The second part is a complete cookbook in itself. The first part is devoted to various kinds of entertaining occasion, with general advice on organizing and catering for each, and a number of seasonal or special menus which I have devised with many different factors in mind: the type of occasion, the season, the

9

amount of time and assistance available, as well as special circumstances such as catering for foreign visitors, vegetarians, large crowds, family or business friends. In addition, I have tried to balance the different foods within each menu so that colour, texture and taste blend with and complement each other in the most successful way.

However, the menus are only suggestions; the recipes can be used in any way and in any combination. My sole aim has been to help keep alive the true spirit of hospitality which, at its best, gives pleasure to both host and guest in equal measure.

EVELYN ROSE

Part 1

NOTE: In each menu
F denotes a dish that can be prepared and frozen in advance.
R indicates any ingredient or a complete dish that can be prepared and refrigerated up to 24 hours in advance (unless a different time scale is given in the 'pointers to success' or the recipe itself).
L (used infrequently) indicates the length of time a dish may be kept in the larder.

The Luncheon Party

The luncheon party usually takes place of necessity at the weekend, but this often means that it can prove to be one of the most relaxed forms of entertaining – the guests arrive after an unhurried morning and can sit long over the table as the afternoon stretches lazily ahead of them.

As the atmosphere is usually less formal than at a dinner party, simple seasonal food seems best; in any case, few people welcome elaborate or heavy dishes at this time of day. Most of the menus included here have therefore been planned for particular times of the year, though I have also suggested menus for vegetarians as well as for those who are watching the calories. In addition, for the single-handed host or hostess, I have planned a buffet brunch with just one hot dish, with quantities for 6 or 16 guests, as preferred. I think this is the ideal way to entertain when there is only one pair of hands. But perhaps the nicest kind of luncheon is the impromptu one; then the emphasis must be on food that can be found in the freezer, or bought quickly and conveniently. I have planned most of the menus for between 6 and 8 guests, though of course there are times when there could be as few as two, or very many more. Instructions on how to adapt the quantities are therefore given where appropriate.

I like to see a luncheon table looking fresh and friendly rather than sophisticated in appearance, so this is the time for cotton print cloths or woven mats, pottery, and chunky glassware, with a simple centre-piece of garden flowers.

Pre-luncheon drinks allow guests to relax while the cook adds the finishing touches, and also helps to sharpen the palate for the delicious food to come. So unless they are being served as the first course of the meal, keep any titbits offered with the drinks as light and simple as possible: for example, garlic or calamata olives, radishes with salt, or sliced pickled cucumbers, speared on cocktail sticks.

With each menu I have suggested an appropriate drink, usually a light wine of some kind. However, you may prefer to serve cider, beer, chilled fruit juices such as apple or grape, or simply a large jug of orange cordial, slightly sharpened with lemon juice and given a more interesting flavour with a dash of fruit syrup such as raspberry, cherry or grenadine.

A Lunch in Spring (6-8)

Smooth, pale green soup contrasts with the crunchy brown topping on grilled fish. The richness of an ice-cream bombe is counterbalanced by the tartness of a fresh fruit compote and crisp, orange-flavoured biscuits.

F	**Cream of Watercress Soup, cream garnish**	p.179
F	**Croûtons**	p.160
	Plaice with Crusty Cheese Topping	p.206
	Baked New Potatoes, butter	p.307
	Minted Peas	p.178
F	**Rum and Raisin Bombe**	p.391
F	**Melon and Mandarin Cocktail**	p.130
F	**Orange Crisps**	p.445

Suggested wine: A light, dry white, e.g. Riesling or Muscadet.

Pointers to success:

★ Early in the season, use frozen petit pois instead of garden peas.

★ The ice-cream mixture should be frozen in a glass bowl or bombe mould, then turned out any time up to 24 hours beforehand and decorated with whipped cream, glacé cherries and chopped nuts. Return to freezer. Just before the meal is served, slip on to a serving dish and leave to soften slightly in the refrigerator.

★ At the table, pour a thin thread of single cream on to the surface of each bowl of soup.

A Lunch in Summer (6-8)

A chilled soup makes a refreshing start to a summer meal. Salmon trout is equally delicious hot or cold; a herb-flavoured sauce makes a perfect accompaniment. Custard sponge puddings have a tender topping which adds a little substance to the delicate custard beneath. Choose either pineapple or lemon flavour.

F	Chilled Cucumber and Mint Soup	p.172
	Melba Toast and butter	p.160
F/R	Poached Salmon or Salmon Trout, Herb Cream Sauce	p.217
R	Swiss Potato Salad	p.325
R	Mixed Salad in the Greek Fashion	p.318
F	Brown Bread and butter	p.499
R	Individual Fruit Custard Sponge Puddings	p.384
F	Raspberry Sorbet garnished with whole berries	p.401
F	Lemon Drops	p.446

Suggested wine: A light, dry white, e.g. Alsatian Riesling, Orvieto Secco.

Pointers to success:
★ Chill the soup in a jug then, just before the meal, pour into soup cups arranged at each place.
★ For a small number like this, present the salmon trout whole, then carve at the table.
★ For maximum effect, serve the sorbet in tall wine glasses (flutes).
★ If available, offer Crème de Framboises (raspberry liqueur) for each guest to pour on his sorbet.

A Lunch in Autumn (6-8)

A satisfying egg starter contrasts with a light main course of chicken livers in a subtly-flavoured sauce. The salad adds an interesting crunchiness. Streusel takes the place of a top pie crust for a lighter apple pie.

R Eggs with Tuna Mayonnaise, anchovy, pickled
      cucumber, calamata olive garnish   p.155
    French or Vienna Bread
F Spaghetti with Chicken Liver Sauce   p.283
R Spiced Mushrooms with Celery and Green
      Peppers   p.329
F Streusel Apple Pie   p.409
R Fresh Pineapple Compote   p.349

Suggested wine: A light red, e.g. Bardolino, Valpolicella, Beaujolais.

Pointers to success:
★ The tuna mayonnaise tastes better if made early in the day. Store the egg whites in an airtight plastic container meanwhile.
★ Put the French bread in the oven, turn to Gas No.6 (400°F, 200°C) for 7 or 8 minutes or until crisp. Cool, then slice diagonally.
★ Make the spiced mushrooms the day before to allow them to soak up the dressing. Add the celery and peppers on the day to keep them crisp.
★ For maximum flavour serve the apple pie warm, but never hot.

A Lunch in Winter (6-8)

A hearty rustic salad goes well with coarse-grained granary bread. Brown rice helps soak up the savoury juices from a lamb casserole. A cool fruit dessert makes a refreshing end to the meal.

R Tuna and Bean Hors d'Oeuvre   p.153
F Granary Loaf   p.500
F Turkish Lamb Casserole   p.254
R Brown Rice Pilaff   p.312
    Boiled Bean Sprouts
R Bananas in White Wine   p.343

Sugested wine: A dry, full-bodied red, e.g. Côtes du Rhône; Rioja.

Pointers to success:
★ It is essential to let the salad stand overnight in the fridge so that the beans can absorb the dressing and the raw onion soften in it.
★ The casserole improves enormously in flavour if left to stand overnight. Refrigeration also facilitates the removal of any excess fat.
★ Use slightly under-ripe bananas: ripe, brown-speckled ones become mushy when cooked.

A Family Celebration Lunch in Spring or Summer (6-8 or 12-16)

Delicate salmon trout is the highlight of this special lunch which starts with chilly button mushrooms in a spicy sauce and ends with a truly refreshing fruit and cream gâteau, as well as a fruit slice made from puff pastry with a juicy, fresh apricot filling.

R	Champignons à la Greque	p.146
F	Buttered Brown Bread	p.499
	Baked Salmon Trout in Riesling	p.219
	New Potatoes in Parsley Butter	p.309
	Chicory, Cucumber and Watercress Salad	p.318
F	Carmel Cloud Gâteau garnished with straw-berries	p.357
	Apricot Slice	p.423

Suggested wine: A light, dry white, e.g. Riesling, Alsatian or Yugoslavian Sylvaner.

Pointers to success:
★ All the quantities can easily be doubled for 12-16 guests. Use a larger salmon or bake two fish side by side.
★ As mushrooms have very little taste in themselves, it is essential to leave them overnight to absorb the flavours of the poaching liquor.
★ A home-made, a ready-mix, or even a bought sponge are equally successful as a basis for the gâteau which gets most of its flavour from the fruit juice and liqueur with which it is moistened. Only a very few strawberries are needed for garnish but they do

17

give a 'special occasion' air to the cake, particularly when used out of season.

★ The apricot slice is nicest if baked fresh on the day and served slightly warm.

A Family Celebration Lunch in Autumn or Winter (6-8 or 12-16)

The musky taste of the cantaloup type of melon partners smoked salmon to perfection. Rice moulded in a ring makes an unusual 'container' for green peas or beans to accompany the veal main dish. A fruity savarin is offered as one sweet, a banana mousse that is equally good when made with non-dairy cream, the other.

Suggested wine: A dry, full-bodied red, e.g. St. Emilion (claret), Barolo.

Pointers to success:

★ Chill both the salmon and the melon for 2 hours before serving.

★ Provided it is never allowed to boil, the veal is a good-tempered dish which can be kept hot or reheated without spoiling.

★ As the banana sweet is accompanied by a fruit salad, it is not necessary to fill the savarin with fruit as well. If preferred, the savarin can be made with best margarine instead of butter.

★ Double all quantities given in recipes for 12-16. For speed use 2 pans to cook the veal for the larger number of guests.

A Vegetarian Lunch (6-8)

A mixture of Mediterranean vegetables cooked in olive oil makes a delicious starter to serve hot or cold. In contrast, paper-thin pastry rolled round a creamy herb and cheese filling makes a light but satisfying main course, which is perfectly partnered by a fruity salad. An unusual mousse which uses avocado purée instead of cream finishes this light but sustaining meal.

Suggested wine: A dry, medium-bodied white, e.g. Rhine wine; or rosé, e.g. Anjou; or sparkling apple or grape juice.

Pointers to success:

★ Brown rolls can be made very satisfactorily from a mix. To get a really crusty finish (to contrast with the soft ragoût), brush with salty water before baking and then again when half-cooked. Do the same with commercial par-baked rolls.

★ A special pastry cloth will make it easier to roll out the puff pastry to the necessary paper-thinness.

★ The mousse looks very pretty set in demi-tasse cups or petit pots and decorated with pistachio nuts.

A Lunch for the Weight-Conscious (6-8)

This delicious lunch consists of dishes whose calorie content has been carefully considered. It may not cause the diners to lose weight, but it will not cause them to gain it!

Suggested wine: A dry, full-bodied red, e.g. Claret, Beaujolais, Bardolino.

Pointers to success:
★ If possible add a pea-sized piece of fresh yeast with the usual squeeze of lemon juice and a few drops of Worcestershire sauce when shaking the tomato juice cocktail. This makes it very sustaining.
★ Make individual holders for the crudités from half an orange emptied of its fruit (reserve for a fruit salad).

A Dairy Lunch for the Weight-Conscious (2-3)

This menu is particularly suitable for a women's lunch as it has a very light main course. However, when low fat white cheese is added to eggs – whether scrambled or in an omelette – it makes them much more sustaining and tasty.

Suggested wine: A rosé, e.g. Tavel; or a dry, light white, e.g. Soave.

Pointers to success:
★ Chill the watermelon several hours beforehand to ensure that the texture is icy and crisp. Serve it whilst the omelette is cooking so that it can be eaten as soon as it's ready.
★ Sprinkle the fresh peaches with lemon juice and leave for 2 hours at room temperature for the juices to flow. Chill only half an hour before serving.

A Brunch (6-8 or 12-16)

This light buffet meal is ideal for the single-handed to prepare and serve. There is only one hot dish, and the guests can help themselves to the cheeseboard, salads and relishes.

F   Feuilleton aux Champignons   p.436
    Cheeseboard
R   Cream Cheese Dip   p.514
    Celery sticks, calamata olives
    Mixed Green Salad   p.317
R   Danish Cucumber Salad   p.323
F   Granary Bread   p.50ͻ
    Bought or home-made savoury biscuits (crackers)
    Melon cubes on sticks
F   Warm Danish pastries

Suggested wine: A dry, light white, e.g. Muscadet, Frascati.

Pointers to success:
★ The feuilleton can be prepared the day before, refrigerated, then baked just before the guests arrive. Cook either in a flan dish or (for a larger number) in slices, as directed in the recipe. Serve warm rather than hot.
★ Slice the bread and serve on a tray or in baskets, leaving some on a board to cut if necessary. Have butter in blocks rather than individual pats for this kind of informal meal.
★ Danish pastries should be warmed in a slow oven. Serve in wicker baskets.
★ Have good-sized coffee cups set out and if possible leave the coffee on a hot plate for guests to pour themselves. Slightly whipped cream would add to the glamour of the occasion.

An Impromptu Lunch in Spring or Summer (6-8)

All the fresh food for this lunch can be bought quickly, whilst the soup and ice-cream can be found in the freezer. A soup could, of course, be made fresh if there was an extra pair of hands. A mackerel pâté takes seconds to make in a blender or food processor.

Suggested wine: A dry, full-bodied white, e.g. Gewurtztraminer, Hock.

Pointers to success:
★ The soup takes little longer to make than mashed potatoes; however, it does need a fresh or dried herb to flavour it – if tarragon is not available, use dried fines herbes. As this is a cheap soup to make, do use fresh cream in it – it makes all the difference.
★ Half a pound (225g) of rich cream cheese mixed with a tablespoon of snipped chives makes a delicious addition to the cheeseboard. Serve in a small, deep pottery dish.

An Impromptu Lunch in Autumn or Winter

One of the many varieties of melon which are superb at this season is marinated in a mint-flavoured syrup. A good-tempered dish of creamed eggs goes well with a coarse brown bread and a crisp coleslaw of Chinese leaves which are sliced rather than shredded.

Cinnamon Whipped Cream p.149
Fresh Fruit

Suggested wine: A medium-dry white, e.g. Sylvaner, Oppenheimer; or dry cider.

Pointers to success:
★ If time is limited, simply slice the melon then over each slice pour some of the mint syrup an hour or two beforehand.
★ The egg casserole can be prepared several hours in advance (or even overnight) then heated up in a quick oven.
★ Chinese leaves can always be kept in stock for winter salads as they keep crisp under refrigeration for up to 3 weeks.

An Impromptu Lunch from Stock or Shop (any number)

All the ingredients for this lunch could be in stock, or quickly purchased locally. However, each ready-made food has something extra added to give it an individual flavour. Canned soup is enriched with fresh herbs, sherry and cream; a pizza has its topping augmented, and even a commercial sorbet is given a fresh-fruit flavour which makes it taste home-made.

    Cream of Mushroom Soup
    Toasts
F **Pizza**
    Coleslaw
F **Lemon Sorbet**
    Home-made-style packeted biscuits (cookies)

Suggested wine: A dry, full-bodied red, e.g. Chianti, Valdepenas.

Pointers to success:
★ Use condensed soup, diluted with equal quantities of milk and water. Bring slowly to steaming point then add 2 teasp each of chopped parsley and medium sherry, a pinch of ground nutmeg and 4 tbsp evaporated milk or single cream.
★ To cook the pizza, first grease a baking tray with olive oil then

23

put in the oven to heat as it comes up to the temperature recommended on the package (this gives the pizza a crisp rather then a bready base). To the pizza, add a thin smear of extra tomato purée, a sprinkling (say, 1/2 teasp) of dried Italian herbs, 2 oz (50g) of sliced olives or a can of anchovies. Finally top generously with ready-grated Parmesan and sprinkle lightly with olive oil. Bake on the pre-heated tray according to directions.

★ Add a few raisins, roasted peanuts and a cubed apple to bought coleslaw.

★ Soften the lemon sorbet slightly then mix with the grated rind and juice of 1 lemon (do this quickly so it doesn't melt completely and spoil the texture). Freeze in a glass serving bowl.

The Dinner Party

To the Athenians of 500 B.C., the seal of an evening's wining and dining would really be set by the excellence of the 'symposium' that followed: a period of stimulating conversation and lively discussion which is still the aspiration of the host of today. The achievement of this ambition depends on careful thought and planning, with due consideration given to several factors; but I cannot emphasize too strongly that, with so much contingent upon the correct 'orchestration' of the meal, it is essential to allow sufficient time for working out timetables and procedures beforehand.

The number of guests

I have planned all the menus for 6-8 guests as I have come to consider this the optimum number, both from the point of view of social intercourse and the practicalities of preparation and service. With extra help it is, of course, possible to serve more people, even if they are seated at two tables. But I have had in mind the single-handed hostess who may have help in the kitchen, but only for clearing or washing up.

The setting

Whether the table is set with pottery or porcelain, chain-store glass or cut crystal, an effect of harmony and elegance can be achieved by anyone prepared to give a little time and thought to it. The ambiance in which a meal is served can greatly enhance the enjoyment of the guests and add an indefinable extra to the pleasure gained from the food itself. But however the table is set, do be sure that the dining chairs are comfortable and that a minimum of 21 inches (53cm) of table space is allowed for each place setting.

Serving the food

Unless it is a formal dinner party, it is usual for the hostess to serve, assisted as necessary by a member of the family. It is convenient to have the first course (other than a hot soup) set ready on the table before the guests sit down, and the dessert (other than a hot or a frozen one) laid on a trolley or sideboard for service by the hostess. The main course is usually served by the hostess (preferably from a hot plate or heated trolley), and she can either serve the accompaniments as well or set them on the table for the guests to help themselves.

The food

All the menus in this chapter consist of three courses, as I feel this is the optimum number for a dinner party at home. This allows the cook to devote full attention to each course and the guests to savour fully the different flavours. In composing the menus, besides taking into consideration the time of year and the occasion, and the balance of colour, texture and temperature, I have tried to ensure that the hostess-cook need not be absent too long from the dinner table in between courses. Many of the dishes can be kept hot without spoiling, and special thought has been given to ensuring that vegetables are crisp and fresh with the minimum of last-minute attention.

Drinks before dinner

If guests are invited 30-45 minutes before the dinner is to be served, there will be ample time for them to meet their fellow-diners and enjoy one or two pre-prandial drinks. Rather than being vague about what time to arrive, I prefer the formula 'Come at 7.30 for dinner at 8', which leaves guests in no doubt about what time you actually intend to sit down to dine.

Drinks during the meal

With each menu I have suggested an appropriate type of wine to serve, but this is only intended as a guide. A good wine merchant might well have other – and equally suitable – ideas. Even at a formal dinner party, it is advisable to have a selection of soft drinks at hand, as many people do not drink alcohol in any form.

Coffee

Elsewhere in the book I have gone into great detail about the different methods of making coffee. While some people enjoy making a ritual of coffee at the end of a meal, I honestly feel that after a varied menu it takes an acute palate to distinguish between a freshly-made brew and that made from a freshly-opened container of top-quality, freeze-dried, instant coffee.

A Dinner Party in Spring (6-8)

A delicate golden lentil soup is followed by chops baked in a sweet and sour sauce. A beautiful lemon ice-cream is served with caramelized oranges.

F	Lentil Soup	p.167
F	Croûtons	p.160
	Lamb Chops with Barbecue Sauce	p.243
	Whole Fried New Potatoes	p.309
	Danish Caramelized Carrots	p.300
F	Frozen Lemon Slice	p.394
R	Caramel Oranges Italian Style	p.347

Suggested wine: Dry, full-bodied red, e.g. Chianti, Barolo, Côtes du Rhône.

Pointers to success:
★ Soak the lentils overnight so that they will 'melt' into the soup without being puréed.
★ Some butchers cut a 'double' shoulder chop which makes an excellent serving.
★ If preferred the ice-cream can be set in individual coffee cups, in which case serve it with a sponge finger or similar crisp biscuit (cookie).
★ As they are to be served as an accompaniment to the ice-cream, make a compôte of the oranges as described in the recipe, rather than serving them whole.

A Dinner Party in Summer (6-8)

Sweet red peppers are grilled then served Italian-style in an olive
oil dressing. Fillets of white fish are stuffed with mushrooms and
poached in a delectable cider sauce. A delicately-perfumed pale
pink syllabub is served with a crisp butter biscuit (cookie).

R	Italian Pepper Salad	p.151
F	Hot Herb Bread	p.507
	Stuffed Fish Fillets in Cider Sauce	p.212
	New Potatoes in Parsley Butter	p.309
	Fresh Green Beans	p.292
F	Raspberry Cloud	p.353
F	Almond Butter Crisps	p.443
	Fresh Peaches	

Suggested wine: Dry, full-bodied white, e.g. Pouilly Fuissé or
Yugoslav Riesling; or dry cider.

Pointers to success:
★ The herb bread can be prepared and frozen for up to a week
beforehand, then baked as directed on the day.
★ The fish dish can also be prepared in advance – but on the
morning of the day. Then it will only need a brief reheating and
browning under the grill as directed and it will taste freshly
cooked.
★ The raspberry cloud is at its best made on the morning of the
dinner party. It should be very cold, though the raspberries used
for garnish taste better if left at room temperature for an hour
before serving.
★ Buy the peaches a day or so beforehand to allow them to ripen
fully at room temperature.

A Dinner Party in Autumn (6-8)

Really ripe tomatoes are used to make a superb fresh-tasting soup,
which is followed by a tender joint of braised veal with herb
stuffing, served with a richly-flavoured sauce made from the
braising liquor. Pears cooked until amber in spiced cider provide
a suitably autumnal ending to the meal.

F	Fresh Tomato Soup	p.165
	Braised Veal with Lemon and Herb Stuffing	p.235
	Roast Potatoes	p.307
	Courgettes (Zucchini) Sauté	p.298
	Green Beans with Toasted Nuts	p.294
R	Spiced Pears in Cider	p.349
F	Fresh Peach Pie	p.410

Suggested wine: Full-bodied dry or medium-dry white, e.g. Macon Blanc, Mersault; or light to medium-bodied red; e.g. Bordeaux Rouge, Valpolicella.

Pointers to success:

★ The flavour of the soup will be infinitely better if made the day before. However, add a little extra chopped fresh basil when it is reheated.

★ Allow the cooked veal to stand in a warm place for about 20 minutes to facilitate carving.

★ Spiced pears will keep for up to 3 days in the refrigerator. After that they tend to become a little flabby in texture.

A Dinner Party in Winter (6-8)

A quickly-prepared pâté made with bottled cod's roe has a cool, smooth taste in contrast to a chicken casserole which is highly seasoned in the Provençale fashion and garnished with black olives. Courgettes (Zucchini) chipped and fried like potatoes provide an unusual contrast in taste and flavour. Tart cherries are baked with an almond topping in a crust of meltingly-tender texture. Passion fruit sorbet (made with bottled juice) refreshes the palate at the end of the meal.

R	Smoked Cod's Roe Pâté	p.135
	Hot toast or cold melba toasts	p.160
F	Chicken Provençale	p.272
	Courgette (Zucchini) Crisps	p.298
F	Savoury Rice	p.311
F	Cherry Frangipane Flan	p.418
F	Passion Fruit Sorbet	p.400

Suggested wine: Dry, light-bodied red, e.g. Beaujolais or Corbières; or dry, light-bodied white, e.g. Orvieto Secco.

Pointers to success:
★ The pâté looks particularly effective if piped into small soufflé dishes or cocottes, using a ¹/₂ inch (1.5cm) plain pipe.
★ Make the chicken casserole the day before to allow the flavours to mingle. If it is to be frozen in advance, cook only until barely tender to avoid the chicken falling to pieces when it is reheated.
★ The tart is nicest served slightly warm (definitely not hot). Dredge with icing (confectioners') sugar just before serving.
★ The sorbet looks especially attractive served in individual glasses. Divide it among the glasses just before the meal, then refrigerate. This will allow it to soften slightly before it is eaten.

A Vegetarian Dinner (6-8)

A beautiful, smooth yellow soup, sweet with carrots, is followed by an unusual casserole of fried aubergines (eggplants), eggs and both soft and hard cheeses. A celery salad is dressed with a fruit mayonnaise to provide a refreshing contrast. Both honey and brown sugar are used in the desserts, one to flavour an unusual ice-cream, the other to give a welcome depth of flavour to poached pears.

Suggested wine: Medium-dry white, e.g. Oppenheimer or Piesporter; or sparkling apple juice.

Pointers to success:

★ Deep red carrots produce a soup with the best colour.

★ The moussaka can be made in the morning, then reheated when required. This actually gives it a firmer texture which can be portioned more easily.

★ Fresh dates are in season for most of the year. They should always be kept under refrigeration until used.

★ For the ice-cream choose bananas with brown-speckled skins. This means they are very ripe and sweet.

★ All poached pears take on a beautiful translucent texture if refrigerated overnight before they are served.

★ The hazelnut biscuits (cookies) should be kept in an airtight container for several days to allow their flavour to develop fully. They can then be used or frozen for later.

A Dinner for the Weight-Conscious (6-8)

This menu cuts out the 'empty' calories which do not add positive enjoyment to a meal. However, it is not calculated to provide a specific number of calories, merely to prevent a reducing diet being too disastrously compromised.

A high-protein salad appetizer is followed by a satisfying but completely clear soup. A beef casserole is made entirely without added fat but with plenty of flavour in the savoury sauce. Potatoes boiled in their skins are optional, but the lightly-cooked, crunchy spring cabbage can be enjoyed by all. A delicious fresh fruit salad completes a meal which leaves the guests satisfied but not sated.

F	Salad Niçoise	p.152
F	Consommé	p.166
F	Slimmer's Paprika Beef	p.252
	Potatoes Boiled in their Skins	p.309
	Greenhearted Spring Cabbage	p.295
R	Melon Celebration Cup	p.345

Suggested wine: Dry, full-bodied red, e.g. Rioja or a Burgundy.

Pointers to success:

★ If preferred, make individual salads, and serve low calorie and normal dressings, both of which should include plenty of fresh herbs.

★ Make sure the consommé is piping hot and really deep in flavour by topping it up if necessary with an extra beef cube and a judicious amount of sherry.

★ Omit the sugar from the fruit cup; instead pour on a small bottle of low calorie ginger ale 30 minutes before serving. Pass a bottle of liqueur round at the table for the non-dieters.

A Family Holiday Meal in Spring or Summer (6-8)

Hard-boiled eggs coated with a delicate mayonnaise stimulate the appetite for a traditional lamb roast which is boned and stuffed for easy carving. There is a choice of a pie made from early pink rhubarb or, for heartier eaters, a pineapple pudding topped with a golden caramel glaze. A bowl of seasonal fresh fruit – or it could be fresh cherries on ice – rounds off the meal.

R	Eggs with Herb Mayonnaise	p.155
F	Brown Bread	p.499
	Roast Stuffed Shoulder of Lamb	p.233
	Mint Jelly	p.495
	Roast Potatoes	p.307
	Crumbed Cauliflower	p.300
	Carrots and peas	
F	Spring Rhubarb Pie	p.413
F	Pineapple Upside-Down Pudding, Pineapple Sauce	p.379
	Fresh fruit in season	

Suggested wine: Dry, light-bodied red, e.g. Bordeaux Rouge, Medoc or Rioja.

Pointers to success:

★ If you prefer to use ready-made mayonnaise, whether home-made or bought, add finely chopped herbs and a squeeze of lemon juice. However, it will not have the even green colour produced by the original recipe.

★ If rhubarb is not available, use fresh apricots in the pie instead.

★ Pineapple canned in its own juice has a flavour much nearer to the fresh fruit than when canned in syrup. Any left-over sauce can be thinned down with a little extra orange-juice and used as the basis of a fresh fruit salad.

A Family Holiday Dairy Dinner in Spring or Summer (6-8)

A savoury Middle Eastern pâté of aubergines (eggplants) precedes a crisp cheese strudel. The mainstay of the meal, however, is a superb dish of salmon steaks in a gentle sour cream sauce, followed by a dessert of bananas in a fruit and spice sauce.

R	Aubergine (Eggplant) Caviar with Challah	p.133
F	Savoury Cream Cheese Strudel	p.439
	Salmon Steaks in Sour Cream Sauce	p.219
	New Potatoes	p.309
	Buttered Fresh Peas	p.293
	Mixed Salad with Avocado	p.318
R	Hot Spiced Bananas	p.377

Suggested wine: Dry, full-bodied white wine, e.g. Graves, Sancerre or Rudesheimer.

Pointers to success:

★ Challah keeps fresh for several days because of its oil and egg content. If not available, use pitta (Middle Eastern) or French bread.

★ The strudel should be served warm rather than hot. It will keep crisp for up to 30 minutes in a low oven (Gas No. 1, 275°F, 140°C).

★ If preferred, omit the avocado and add half a large red pepper, finely shredded, instead.

A Family Holiday Dinner in Autumn (6-8)

Whole melons, their musky flavour lightened with a little lemon juice, decorate the table when the guests sit down. Then comes a hearty meat soup followed by aubergines (eggplants) stuffed with minced (ground) meat and simmered in a fruity sauce. As a counterpoint, a crispy chicken slice is served as an accompaniment. A frozen pavlova – with apple compote for those who prefer a less sweet dessert – ends the meal on a refreshing note.

Suggested wine: Dry or medium-dry, full-bodied red, e.g. Chianti, Rioja or Côtes du Rhône.

Pointers to success:

★ The melons can either be served in grapefruit glasses, or arranged on a large leaf on a glass or pottery plate.

★ If the soup has thickened after standing overnight, simply dilute to a thin cream consistency with extra stock. Watch carefully to see that it a does not 'catch' on the bottom of the pan as it is reheated.

★ The easiest procedure is to make the aubergines (eggplants) the day before. Set the oven to a high temperature, cook the chicken slice, keep it hot in a warming oven, then put the aubergine into the oven, immediately turn down to moderate and reheat to bubbling. If necessary, the slice can be put back into the oven with the aubergines while the first course is being served.

★ Transfer the gâteau from freezer to fridge during the meal – this will allow the ice-cream in it to soften slightly.

A Family Holiday Dinner in Winter (6-8)

A traditional roast turkey meal but with a delicious home-made pâté instead of the appetite-deadening soup which is often served. A rich British Christmas pudding is paired with a Russian wine sauce, with a refreshing Italian fresh orange presentation to round off the meal.

Suggested wine: Full-bodied red, e.g. Burgundy (Côte d'Or) or Bordeaux (St. Emilion).

Pointers to success:

★ Make the pâté two days beforehand then refrigerate to allow the flavours to mature. The turkey can be prepared ready for the oven (including the stuffing) the night before, provided it can be refrigerated—or stored at refrigerator temperature (40°-47°F; 4°-7°C) until 2 hours before roasting.

★ Peel the chestnuts then cook and freeze in advance, or freeze them raw until required. This greatly simplifies the making of the stuffing, particularly on a busy day.

★ Chill the whole oranges for several hours, then prepare as described in the recipe about an hour beforehand and leave at room temperature for the juices to flow. When served the Venetian oranges should be cool but not chilly.

A Family Celebration Dinner in Spring or Summer (6-8)

A rich cream soup is followed by fish with a pepper and herb topping, accompanied by an unusual dairy dish of noodles and cream cheese. The dairy theme is continued in the fruit custard flan and the butterscotch-flavoured ice-cream.

F Super Cream of Mushroom Soup	p.177
F Croûtons	p.160
R Sole Créole	p.210
Noodle and Cream Cheese Puff	p.187
French Peach or Apple Flan	p.417
F Butterscotch Walnut Ice-cream	p.392
R Caramel Syrup	p.490

Suggested wine: Rosé wine from Provence (Tavel); or medium-dry white Bordeaux, e.g. Entre Deux Mers.

Pointers to success:
★ Don't chop the mushrooms for the soup too finely – it has more interest if one can actually see some slices of mushroom. A good idea is to chop half the mushrooms finely in a food processor, and then slice the rest.
★ Use a sweet but crisp eating apple for the flan.
★ The fish can be very conveniently prepared first thing in the morning and refrigerated until baked.

A Family Celebration Dinner in Autumn or Winter (6-8)

A delicate fruit cocktail is followed by a light but richly-flavoured chicken soup. Crisp joints of chicken are served with a smooth sauce. Tart raspberries contrast with a smooth almond sponge in a sweet pastry case, with light fruited soufflés offering an interesting contrast. Fresh dates with an unusual-flavoured filling accompany the coffee.

Suggested wine: Dry, full-bodied white wine, e.g. Alsatian Riesling or Sauvignon.

Pointers to success:

★ Be sure the fruit cocktail is tart rather than sweet – remember it is a starter not a dessert. Add extra lemon juice just before serving if necessary.

★ Make the stock for the soup from the chicken's giblets plus cubes – a little beef bouillon will give it extra depth of flavour.

★ Fresh chickens can be completely coated then frozen. Defrost completely before putting in the oven.

★ Offer the soufflé either in tiny soufflé dishes or in tall flutes. Chill thoroughly – they can even be put in the freezer for 30 minutes before dinner.

A Formal Dinner in Spring or Summer (6-8)

The delicate flavour of fish pickled in the Swedish style sets the scene for an elegant dinner which deserves to be served with panache. A main course of veal and walnuts is simple yet sophisticated, as is the deep purple sorbet elegantly served with a dash of a matching liqueur.

Suggested wine: With gravlax: dry, full-flavoured white, e.g. Gewurztraminer or white Burgundy; with schnitzels: dry, light-bodied red, e.g. Bordeaux Rouge from the Medoc.

Pointers to success:

★ Gravlax can be bought but, given a good fishmonger who will fillet the fish, it is very easy to make oneself – and of course it is then far more economical.

★ If the walnuts look at all dusty, pour boiling water over them and drain well before using.

★ As you are seasoning the drained noodles be sure to taste them to get the balance of flavours right, and toss thoroughly, preferably with a wooden salad spoon and fork, so that the pasta is evenly coated with the herbs.

★ If Créme de Cassis (blackcurrant liqueur) is not available, stew a few blackcurrants, add brandy to taste, then spoon over each serving like a sauce.

A Formal Dinner in Autumn or Winter (6-8)

Whole aubergines (eggplants) stuffed then stewed gently in a rich sauce make an impressive beginning to this meal, in which special attention is paid to the presentation. Choice lamb cutlets baked in a fruity sauce are accompanied by an eye-catching presentation of rice in a ring filled with beans. But the most dramatic dish is left till last – a smooth ice-cream slice, accompanied by whole caramelized oranges, each nestling on a slice of fresh pineapple. For a final touch, little clusters of chocolate ginger are offered with the coffee.

Suggested wine: With Cumberland Cutlets: dry, light-bodied red, e.g. Beaujolais or Bardolino; with dessert: sweet white, e.g. Sauternes or Barsac.

Pointers to success:
★ Have the aubergines (eggplants) well chilled (this makes them taste a little less rich). The pitta (Middle Eastern) bread should be briefly warmed before serving.
★ The nicest green beans are no wider than a shoe lace. They must be cooked only until barely tender so that there is still some 'crunch' left in them.
★ If Chinese leaves are not available, use a Webb lettuce or finely shredded white cabbage instead.
★ Do not chill the pineapple slices but arrange them on a large serving platter. Just before the meal, top each slice with a chilled orange and spoon some of the caramel syrup over it.

A Dinner of Choice British Produce in Spring or Summer (6-8)

For the benefit, perhaps, of a visitor from abroad, the finest British food in season is cooked by traditional methods which develop and conserve the essential flavour. Thus fat sticks of asparagus are cooked with meticulous care until barely tender then served with the simplest of butter sauces. Alternatively, young peas (fresh or frozen) are used to make an exquisite pale green soup. Salmon is cooked lightly then served with a choice of accompaniments which complement its delicate flavour without overwhelming it. Finally, summer fruits are used to make two of Britain's best desserts – a superb syllabub and a meltingly tender tart in the Yorkshire fashion.

Suggested wine: Dry white English or dry, full-bodied quality white Burgundy.

Pointers to success:

★ The butter for the asparagus sauce should be of a creamy consistency slightly thinner than mayonnaise. Do not let it get too hot or it will become oiled. The best method is to leave it near a gentle source of heat – the cooker or warming drawer – and when it begins to soften give it a good stir so that it does not separate. If at all possible do not warm over direct heat as it is then very difficult to achieve the correct texture. A microwave oven, set to warm, is, however, excellent.

★ The soup purée freezes to perfection. However, it should be defrosted overnight and made into the finished soup early in the day. It will then have a chance to develop its full flavour.

★ The salmon can be portioned and set out on a dish 2 or 3 hours in advance. It must, however, be tightly covered with film. Add the cucumber garnish only shortly before serving, as it may otherwise make the fish a little damp.

★ Use only the tender pale green heart of the lettuce for this kind of meal. The outer leaves can be used for a soup.

★ Buy the tomatoes slightly under-ripe then leave on the windowsill (no need for direct sun) for 2 days beforehand. They will then have a superb sweetness of flavour.

★ The biscuits (cookies) should be put out only shortly before dinner to conserve their delicate crispness.

A Dinner of Choice British Produce in Autumn or Winter (6-8)

Scotch smoked salmon and finest British beef are the stars of this meal which uses only fresh food and embodies all that the visitor from abroad thinks of as British food cooked in the traditional fashion. For example, our sprouts and parsnips cannot be equalled, and our wild blackberries have a winey flavour unknown in more exotic fruits.

Fresh Scotch Smoked Salmon with fine brown bread	p.499
Traditional Rib Roast of Beef with Gravy	p.229
Extra Crisp Individual Yorkshire Puddings	p.231
Roast Potatoes and Parsnips	p.307
Brussels sprouts	
Crumbed Cauliflowerets	p.300
Old-fashioned Apple Pie with Brambles	p.408

Suggested wine: Dry, full-bodied red, e.g. Burgundy or Rhône wine such as Châteauneuf du Pape.

Pointers to success:
★ If there is a waitress, the salmon can be served from one large platter. Otherwise have it ready on individual dishes at each place, with thick slices of lemon to squeeze on it.
★ It is important to order the meat at least 2 weeks beforehand as it must hang a minimum of 14 days in the butcher's cold room to be really tender.
★ If wild brambles (blackberries) are not available, by all means: use fresh or frozen cultivated ones. However, you may need to use a tbsp extra lemon juice. Raspberries or loganberries could also be substituted.

A Debut Dinner in Spring or Summer (6)

A menu for the novice cook – composed to take all the worry out of preparing a meal! Thus the unusual dip is quickly and easily made in advance and left to chill. Nothing can harm the fish dish as it gently bakes in the oven, as it is cooked in cream rather than a complicated sauce. The difficulty of timing vegetables is avoided as the potatoes are cooked with the fish and a salad is substituted for green vegetables. Only the ability to handle a sharp knife is necessary in the preparation of the fruit for the dessert, while the melt-in-the-mouth biscuit (cookie) recipe has been specially chosen for its simplicity. Anyone who can use a paintbrush or a lipbrush can prepare the eye-catching grape garnish.

Suggested wine: Dry, light-bodied white wine, e.g. Muscadet or Graves.

Pointers to success:

★ It's a good plan to make a timetable of when each dish is to be prepared. The cooking itself is minimal in this menu.

★ The dip can be prepared the day before, the biscuits (cookies) a week before (shortbread does not need freezing when kept for up to a month). The grapes can be prepared and refrigerated overnight too. (Keep in a tin.)

★ To save the hassle of scraping and cooking new potatoes, use finest quality canned potatoes but rinse well to remove the canning liquor. Assemble the fish dish completely and refrigerate until it is time to put it in the oven. Start heating the grill whilst the dip is being eaten with drinks, then brown the fish in between courses when you can keep an eye on it.

A Debut Dinner in Autumn or Winter (6)

The new cook will find this menu equally easy and certain of success. A simple but unusual salad starter is followed by a chicken casserole of superb flavour which can happily be made the day before. Rice makes the simplest of main dish accompaniments as it can easily be kept hot in the oven without spoiling, while the green vegetable cooked ahead in the French manner needs the minimum of last minute attention. The dessert is a simple but delicious fruit salad, artistically arranged, and the accompanying petits fours require practically no cake-making technique yet are moist and luscious to eat.

Suggested wine: Dry, light-bodied white, e.g. Alsatian Sylvaner or Yugoslav Riesling.

Pointers to success:
★ The success of the starter will depend on the quality of the avocado – so cradle it in your hands and make sure it gives *all over* to gentle pressure – best policy is to buy the avocados 4 days in advance, and if they reach ripeness before the day, refrigerate until required (don't freeze!).
★ For simplicity buy a variety of chicken joints. This will avoid the need to cut up a bird – a daunting prospect for a new cook. If possible, however, buy fresh rather than frozen portions as the flavour is so much superior.
★ Buy a good quality long grain rice. The easiest to cook is the par-boiled American rice, which never goes mushy whatever you do. Follow packet instructions.
★ Frozen petit pois are dearer but they are generally sweeter than regular peas.
★ As with the avocados, unless you have a superb greengrocer, buy the melons and ripen them for several days at home – with this kind of simple dessert only the ripest and best quality fruit will do.
★ Cook the brownies only as long as recommended – they should still be moist inside. For this recipe a soft margarine is actually better than butter as it gives a moister texture, and the flavour is completely masked by the chocolate.

A Quick and Easy Dinner in Spring or Summer (6-8)

The food only needs putting together as the ingredients come ready from shop or freezer. Fat canned pimentos make a luscious salad starter in the Italian manner, accompanied by freshly-crisped French bread and butter. An unusual herb and anchovy sauce is quickly made from bought mayonnaise to accompany

43

bought cooked salmon (or the fish can be baked with the utmost simplicity at home). The vegetables come from a can, and the luscious gâteau is quickly assembled from a bought spongecake and canned marron purée. A delicious cheeseboard, garnished with fruit in the Danish fashion, rounds off the meal.

Suggested wine: Slightly sparkling Portuguese rosé; or medium-dry white French table wine.

Pointers to success:

★ To serve French bread at its best, turn on the oven to a moderate temperature, put in the uncovered bread and leave for 5-7 minutes or until the crust feels really crisp. Allow the bread to cool, then serve within an hour.

★ To cook salmon with as little effort as buying it, bake wrapped in foil in the oven. This can be done 2 days in advance, and the fish refrigerated until it is time to portion it.

★ The dressing tastes infinitely better if allowed to mature for 24 hours. It will then keep for a week under refrigeration.

★ A memorable cheeseboard can make a meal. As the main part of the meal has required so little time, concentrate on making the cheeseboard a work of art, with some cheese in wedges, some in slices, some in small cubes, and the appropriate fresh fruits in season as colour and texture contrast. The simpler the actual cheeseboard – perhaps wood or glass, the more dramatic the presentation will look.

A Quick and Easy Dinner in Autumn or Winter (6-8)

Requires the minimum of cooking, most of the food comes ready from shop or freezer. Creamy-textured avocado halves are filled with a quickly-made tuna salad. Chicken portions are simmered in a canned sauce, accompanied by packeted rice, mixed with nuts and raisins. A beautiful fruit salad is enlivened by a very few out-of-season strawberries, and a home-made or bought sorbet is accompanied by imported French biscuits (cookies).

Suggested wine: Dry, full-bodied red wine, e.g. Rioja or Beaujolais.

Pointers to success:

★ If a stock of vinaigrette dressing is kept in the refrigerator, it takes only minutes to make the tuna salad. Taken from stock, you can be sure that the dressing will have had time to mature – fresh herbs can be added as required.

★ It's only necessary to season the chicken joints very well, then fry until golden before simmering them in a canned sauce made for the purpose. The best of these sauces produce a really fine dish, and are particularly convenient for the small household with a limited stock of seasonings.

★ Buy the best quality pack of celery you can find.

★ When it comes to dessert, if time is of the essence it's worth investing in superb, well-flavoured fruit which need the minimum of preparation. To preserve the delicate texture of the berries, make the fruit salad freshly on the day.

★ If you use bought sorbet rather than the home-made recipe, top each serving with a sprinkle of one of the orange-flavoured liqueurs – Aurum, Cointreau, Curaçao or Grand Marnier. Many people would say the flavour is actually better than when the liqueur is incorporated in the sorbet. For a quick presentation, pile scoops of sorbet into a tall, narrow glass bowl, then leave in the refrigerator during dinner – the texture will be just right, smooth and creamy.

A Dinner for Two in Spring or Summer (2)

Slightly warm artichokes are served with a gentle but well-flavoured dressing. Trout is served in a delicious but uncomplicated butter sauce, accompanied by two refreshing salads. A section from a superb Brie cheese is followed by fresh strawberries folded into a subtle orange cream, accompanied by meltingly-tender biscuits.

R	Artichokes with Herb Cream Sauce	p.142
	Trout in Brandy and Cream Sauce	p.202
	New Potatoes	p.309
	Swedish Cucumber Salad	p.324
R	Mixed Green Salad	p.317
	Brie and biscuits (crackers)	
R	Strawberries in Orange Cream	p.353
F	Vanilla Kipferl	p.453

Suggested wine: A dry, fruity white wine, e.g. German Riesling or Graves.

Pointers to success:

★ For a speedy version of the sauce, mix together half a 5 fl oz (150 ml/⅔ cup) carton of soured cream with an equal amount of a mild mayonnaise (about 4 tbsp), then stir in the herbs suggested in the recipe.

★ Depending on the degree of intimacy of the diners, choose between keeping the trout hot, and making the sauce just before serving, or cooking the fish fresh, chatting meanwhile.

★ Make sure the Brie is really ripe – it should be beginning to run a little at the sides. At this stage, the top crust is usually speckled with brown. Try to have it cut fresh on the day.

★ The strawberries for the sweet can be small, but they must be well-flavoured. Taste one before buying.

A Dinner for Two in Autumn or Winter (2)

The famous Middle Eastern appetizer of hummus (chick peas) and tahina (sesame seed paste) is served with hot pitta (Middle Eastern) bread. As excellent 'instant' packs of this mixture are now available, all that is necessary is to season it judiciously with garlic, lemon and olive oil to have a most intriguing starter. Tender scallops of veal are served with a pilaff of brown rice and a juicy pepper stew. The meal ends with a delicately-flavoured fruit ice-cream.

	Hummus and Tahina with Pitta (Middle Eastern) bread	
	Veal Scallops with Mushrooms	p.246
R	Brown Rice Pilaff	p.312
R	Peperonata	p.302
F	Apricot Ice-cream with Apricot Brandy	p.396

Suggested wine: Full-bodied, dry white, e.g. a Burgundy; or dry, medium-bodied red, e.g. Bordeaux from the Medoc.

Pointers to success:

★ To a 15 oz (425g) tin of instant hummus and tahina, add 3 tbsp lemon juice and olive oil, a crushed clove of garlic, and salt and pepper to taste. You will have to judge the amounts needed for packets or cans of a different size. Leave for several hours for the flavours to blend. Serve as individual dips with the hot pitta (Middle Eastern) bread. Refrigerate any left-overs as this size of tin will probably be more than you will need for two.

★ If you have made the veal dish earlier to reheat it, make sure it is thoroughly hot but do not let the sauce boil vigorously as this will toughen the meat.

★ Peperonata reheats to perfection, so make it beforehand.

★ For two it's best to scoop the ice-cream into individual glasses in the kitchen, rather than serving it from a large dish, as the left-over ice-cream will melt and lose its texture before it can be refrozen.

Family Plus Meals: Setting Some Extra Places at the Table

How do you find the time to entertain close friends when you're out at work all day? Of course there is always the weekend, but another solution – if you've got the temperament for it – is to set some extra places at the table and serve family-style food spiced with a pinch or two of imagination. It's almost as quick to make a familiar family dish for 6 or 8 as it is for 3 or 4, and you know, because you've made it so many times, that it's going to work!

Most people nowadays don't bother with a first course for everyday eating, but when guests join the family circle, you can add a touch of glamour with even simple dishes such as raw vegetables with a garlic or mustard mayonnaise, or an avocado and cream cheese dip. A salad starter is another idea – perhaps celery, apple and walnut, bound together with orange-flavoured mayonnaise and then topped with chopped hazelnuts or salted peanuts. That's particularly good with warm wholemeal bread or rolls, whether home-made or fresh from the local baker.

When melon is in season (and it's often particularly cheap on a Saturday) serve it in boats, that is, slices cut free from the skin but left in place and then divided into easy-to-handle, one-inch pieces. The important thing is to sprinkle the fruit with a little sugar and lemon juice about an hour beforehand then leave it at room temperature for the juices to flow, before refrigerating for the last 30 minutes. But perhaps best and easiest of all the starters is a really good soup. If you keep a stock in the freezer, it will only need reheating and re-seasoning, but even freshly-made soup is convenient because it actually tastes better when made the day before.

For the main course, serve with a casserole or beefburgers, or even a savoury soufflé, but add a few extras such as spicy tomato sauce, cream, or wine instead of water, and accompany it with

48

a special vegetable such as sautéed courgettes (zucchini), carrots in a shiny glaze, or sweet and sour red cabbage.

And finally, for the sweet, don't despise family favourites such as ice-cream with a fruity sauce, a really good tart, baked apples or a fruity sponge.

A Meal With Meat in Spring (6-8)

Lamb chops of the most economical cut available are cooked on a bed of potatoes, simmering in a savoury gravy. The first gooseberries of late spring (or last season's frozen ones) are stewed to serve with individual sponge puddings.

R	Tomato Juice Cocktail	*below*
	Lamb Chops and Potato Braise	p.243
	Perfect Frozen Peas	p.295
F	Hot Feather Sponges with Gooseberry Compote	p.378

Pointers to success:

★ Add 2 teasp lemon juice and 1 teasp Worcestershire sauce to a can of tomato juice, then chill for several hours. Serve with a long strip of carrot as a 'stirrer'.

★ Cook the chops in the oven (rather than top-of-stove) to utilize it to the full.

★ If individual tins are not available, bake the sponge mixture in a 10 or 11 inch (25-27.5cm) flan dish, then cut it like a cake.

★ Hot canned damsons or plums may be substituted for the gooseberries.

A Meal with Poultry in Spring (6-8)

A crisp starter of raw vegetables with a mustardy dip is followed by a richly-flavoured chicken casserole in which sweet and tart are evenly balanced. The first forced rhubarb is used to make a crunchy-topped, lightly-spiced and refreshing pudding.

R	Crudités with Mustard Mayonnaise	p.510
F/R	Southland Barbecued Chicken	p.270

F/R	Fried Rice	p.312
	Carrots and peas	
F/R	Rhubarb and Ginger Crumble	p.376

Pointers to success:

★ Use young carrots and celery for the crudités, as green peppers will be dear. The vegetables can be washed and film-wrapped several hours in advance, then cut in fingers just before using. The mustard mayonnaise can be based on a top-quality mild commercial mayonnaise.

★ The casserole is infinitely richer in flavour if made one or two days in advance, then reheated until bubbling.

★ Rice from the freezer can be fried and will taste delicious. For convenience and economy use commercial frozen cubed green peppers.

★ The crumble can be prepared up to 2 days before and refrigerated, then cooked just before the meal. If rhubarb is too dear, use with an equal quantity of apples or use apples alone (see p.376).

A Meal with Fish in Spring (6-8)

Chilled fruit juice with a very subtle flavour precedes a quickly-made fish casserole complete with its own vegetables. The first tart gooseberries contrast with a very crisp yet flaky pastry.

	Apricot Nectar	*below*
	Fisherman's Casserole	p.207
	Peas and New Potatoes	p.309
F	Green Gooseberry Tart with Vanilla Ice-cream	p.411

Pointers to success:

★ Bottled apricot juice has a very deep flavour as it is made from tree-ripened fruit. Make sure, however, that it is well-chilled. Add a dash of lemon juice to counteract the sweetness if preferred.

★ Do not let the fish boil as this toughens it. The liquid should barely simmer until the flesh of the fish loses its glassy appearance and it can be easily flaked with a fork. If using canned potatoes, rinse them thoroughly before reheating in the sauce.

★ The pastry for this tart keeps fresh for several days, so the tart can be made the day before and reheated, loosely covered with foil, for 20 minutes in a moderate oven. Serve warm rather than hot. For everyday use, commercial dairy ice-cream is quite adequate unless you have some home-made ice-cream in the freezer.

A Dairy Meal in Spring (6-8)

A fresh-tasting yet satisfying salad starter precedes a rich but economical hot soufflé accompanied by a herb-flavoured hot bread. Fresh apricot compote is used as the basis of a delicately-flavoured fruit salad accompanied by biscuits (cookies) so easy a child can make them.

F	**Carrot and Raisin Slaw**	p.323
	Mushroom Soufflé	p.191
F/R	**Hot Herb Bread**	p.507
R	**Fresh Apricot Fruit Salad**	p.343
	Liqueur Cream	*below*
F	**Orange Crisps**	p.445

Pointers to success:

★ If you have time, plump the raisins by bringing them to the boil in water to cover, then draining well before combining with the other ingredients.

★ The soufflé can be fully prepared up to an hour before it is put in the oven. Keep it covered with a large basin during the waiting time.

★ To make the liqueur cream, whisk ¼ pt (150ml/⅔ cup) whipping cream until it has started to thicken, then add 2 teasp fruity liqueur such as Cointreau, Curaçao, or Amaretto (almond flavoured) with 2 teasp caster (superfine) sugar. Taste, and add a teasp more liqueur if necessary, but remember there should only be a hint of the liqueur. Chill well before serving.

51

A Meal with Meat in Summer (6-8)

Beefburgers, whether bought or home-made are given a special flavour with a herb and tomato sauce. Fresh or frozen brown rice makes the perfect flavour and texture complement, with a crisp green salad to freshen the palate. The first early strawberries are given heightened flavour by soaking in a hot sugar syrup, and are accompanied by light-as-air lemon-flavoured biscuits (cookies).

Pointers to success:
★ A quick pizzaiola sauce can be made by simmering a can of ready-to-use tomato sauce for a few minutes with the garlic and herbs specified in the recipe.
★ For speed, the sugar topping can be omitted from the lemon drops, but they won't have the same crunchy appearance.

A Meal with Poultry in Summer (6-8)

Crisply-fried slices of chicken or turkey breast are accompanied by two easy-to-make but flavourful salads. An unusual two-fruit tart completes the meal.

Pointers to success:

★ If preferred, and to save time, the chicken can be left unboned and cut into smaller portions. It is nicest served not more than an hour or two after frying but, if necessary, can be refrigerated overnight.

★ Left-over rice pilaff (whether from the freezer or refrigerator) can form the basis of this extremely tasty but quickly-made salad.

★ Tomatoes can be ripened by leaving in a dish in the kitchen (there is no need for direct sunlight).

★ Vary the proportion of the two fruits according to their price and availability.

A Meal with Fish in Summer (6-8)

A refreshing cold soup precedes mackerel grilled with a piquant topping, accompanied by courgettes (zucchini) cooked in a quickly-made sauce. Fresh peaches are left, during the meal, to soak up the flavour of a delicious cider marinade.

R	Chilled Yoghurt Soup	p.171
	Tremadoc Bay Grilled Mackerel	p.204
R	Courgettes (Zucchini) in Tomato and Herb Sauce	p.299
	Parsleyed New Potatoes	p.309
	Peaches in Cider	p.340

Pointers to success:

★ The soup can be drunk from cups or sipped from a spoon, as convenient. Make sure it is well chilled before serving.

★ As the fish needs no basting it can safely be left to cook under a moderately hot grill while the soup is drunk.

★ The courgettes (zucchini) can be made in advance and served hot or cold with the fish, depending on the weather. The potatoes can also be cooked beforehand, but are best served hot, reheated in parsley butter.

A Dairy Meal in Summer (6-8)

A satisfying main-dish egg casserole is accompanied by brown rolls and a green salad which is given an unusually nutty flavour by the addition of slices of raw courgettes (zucchini). Fresh raspberries are served over ice-cream, either as whole sugared fruit or as a delicious purée. Little lemon cakes soaked in syrup in the Greek fashion bring the meal to a satisfying close.

R	Creamed Eggs in Corn and Cheese Sauce	p.183
F	Granary Rolls and butter	p.500
R	Mixed Salad with Raw Courgettes (Zucchini)	p.317
R	Herb Vinaigrette Dressing	p.332
F	Ice-cream with sugared raspberries	
F/R	*or* Fresh Raspberry Sauce	p.375
F	Little Lemon Cakes	p.481

Pointers to success:

★ The egg casserole can be made in advance, then reheated (covered), in the oven or micro wave. Use the grill to crisp the topping.

★ If really fresh courgettes (zucchini) are not available, use cucumber instead. Always have some basic vinaigrette dressing in the fridge. If chopped fresh herbs are also kept there in a plastic container, the two can be combined very quickly to make a fresh-tasting dressing.

★ Add a dash of lemon juice to enliven raspberry purée. There is no detectable difference between frozen and freshly-made purée, so even in the summer it's a good idea to make and freeze a large batch when the price is right.

A Meal with Meat in Autumn (6-8)

Spicy wedges of melon are served before a very savoury casserole which is given added interest by an unusual vegetable. Hot and crisp fruit fritters finish the meal.

	Honeydew Melon Wedges in Ginger Sauce	p.131
F/R	Beef Braised in the Italian Style	p.250

Pointers to success:

★ At this time of year it is useful to keep a melon always in stock, as the storage period can be used to ripen it, and it can then be refrigerated until required.

★ This casserole actually improves if made ahead (say, 1-2 days in advance) and refrigerated until it is reheated. It also keeps its flavour well in the freezer.

★ Cook the peppers until they are softened but still have a little 'bite' left. They can then also be reheated if more convenient.

★ Fritters are essentially a family dish as they must be made fresh, though the batter can be made well in advance, even the day before.

A Meal with Poultry in Autumn (6-8)

A smooth soup precedes a delicious chicken mixture in the Chinese style, served either as a stuffing for crisply-fried pancakes or on a bed of rice. Apples are simmered in a spicy syrup for a light but flavourful dessert.

Pointers to success:

★ Pancakes freeze well whether plain or stuffed. They are useful both as a main dish or as a snack after the cinema or theatre. If left to get quite cold before stacking they will not stick together.

★ The compote is particularly delicious made with eating apples (e.g. Cox, Golden Delicious) rather than cooking apples. It is then much easier to keep the apple slices whole.

A Meal with Fish in Autumn (6-8)

A richly-flavoured tuna and pasta casserole is accompanied by a tomato salad that uses the last of the season's fresh basil. Plums are used as a filling between pastry and crumble.

	Apple or orange juice	
F/R	**Tuna Lasagne**	p.215
	Italian Tomato Salad	p.327
F/R	**Crunchy Plum Slice with Pouring Cream or Ice-cream**	p.412

Pointers to success:
★ Make the lasagne the day before and reheat it when required. In this way it acquires the traditional texture and cuts into neat squares.
★ Serve the plum slice warm rather than hot: the plums will have a softer, less acid flavour.

A Dairy Meal in Autumn (6-8)

A savoury vegetable starter is served with warm granary bread. Pancakes layered with spinach and cheese make a casserole accompanied by a coleslaw in the Israeli fashion. A pale green jelly mousse, sharpened with lime juice, completes the meal.

F/R	**Aubergine (Eggplant), Green Pepper and Tomato Ragoût**	p.151
F	**Granary Bread and butter**	p.500
	Spinach and Cheese Bake	p.185
R	**Coleslaw of Chinese Leaves**	p.322
R	**Avocado Lemon/Lime Mousse**	p.364

Pointers to success:
★ Allow plenty of time to fry all the vegetables: it can be done ahead and reheated.
★ If there are frozen pancakes in the freezer, this dish can be prepared in minutes.
★ Chinese leaves can be dressed even 24 hours in advance as, though they are delicate in texture, they do not go soggy like shredded lettuce.

★ The mousse is as simple to make as a jelly and is an excellent way to utilize a very ripe avocado.

A Meal with Meat in Winter (6-8)

A fresh grapefruit cocktail starts a meal whose main course is a richly-flavoured meat loaf that is equally delicious hot or cold. The upside-down cake has a caramel topping that makes it especially appealing to young palates.

R	Fresh Grapefruit Cup with Grapes	p.128
F	Picnic Loaf	p.260
	Mashed Potatoes	p.304
	Carrots and peas	
F/R	Pineapple Upside-Down Pudding, Pineapple Sauce	p.379

Pointers to success:

★ The grapefruit in syrup can be left for up to 48 hours under refrigeration. However, it is better to add the grapes shortly before serving to preserve their crispness.

★ Apart from the ketchup (which acts as a binder), the seasonings for the meat loaf can be varied to suit the family's taste. I recommend using the soy sauce, which helps to bring out the flavour of the other ingredients.

★ The pudding reheats to perfection – most easily in the microwave. Otherwise, cover it loosely with foil and reheat in a moderate oven until it feels warm. A heavy, non-stick frying pan makes an ideal cake 'tin' (if the handle is not heatproof, wrap it in foil).

A Meal with Poultry in Winter (6-8)

A boiling fowl provides the basis of both the delicious soup and the main course pie. Red cabbage is simmered in the oven to accompany it, but the delicious Swiss potato pancake must be cooked freshly. A simple fresh fruit jelly ends the meal on a refreshing note.

Pointers to success:

★ Cook the bird the day before to allow the soup to deepen in flavour. If possible, reheat the soup in the oven as this also helps to improve the taste.

★ The cabbage can be reheated, and will keep under refrigeration for up to 3 days.

★ For the fruited jelly, use an ordinary packet jelly (gelatin mix) but replace some of the water with the juice of a whole orange and a lemon and flavour with 1 tbsp apricot jam. When syrupy, stir in whatever fruits are available – tangerines, bananas, pears, etc.

A Meal with Fish in Winter (6-8)

A delicately-flavoured soup is followed by a simple but richly-flavoured casserole. Ice-cream is topped with a superb hot orange sauce to make a light, refreshing dessert.

Pointers to success:

★ If possible use the stringless celery from Israel as this makes a smoother soup.

★ The fish dish can be prepared whenever convenient during the day, then baked as required.

★ If preferred, use one of the ready-to-serve bottled fruit sauces or your own frozen raspberry, strawberry or cherry sauce with a dash of liqueur.

A Dairy Meal in Winter (6-8)

A smooth and satisfying vegetable soup is followed by a layered casserole of aubergines (eggplants), cheese and potatoes served with a crisp mushroom pasty. Baked apples provide a simple fruity end to the meal.

Pointers to success:

★ If the soup is freshly made, always leave it to stand for several hours to allow the flavours to develop. It can then be thinned with extra milk or water.

★ This casserole reheats extremely well. Top it with extra cheese and little nuts of butter, and bake till bubbly.

★ The filling for the feuilleton can be made the day before but the pastry is best when baked just before serving.

★ Although the dry salad greens can be refrigerated in a tea towel for up to 24 hours, the dressing should only be added just before serving.

★ Baked apples should be served warm rather than hot.

The Supper Party

No matter what the occasion, whether it's six close friends invited back after the theatre or fifty members of a club happily enjoying cheese and wine, all supper parties have one thing in common: the informality of the food and the way it is served. That is why it is probably one of the most popular methods of entertaining today. Depending on time and inclination, the hostess can choose to serve a simple, economical menu built round a cheeseboard, or go for a more ambitious assortment of casseroles, salads and desserts. However, in both cases the food is likely to be served buffet-style, so that this kind of party can be organized with the very minimum of assistance – and that usually from other members of the family. In this chapter, therefore, I have suggested a wide variety of menus, ranging from a series of seasonal suppers, to meals after the theatre, to holiday buffets, wine and cheese parties and meals particularly suited for the single- handed host or hostess.

Most of the menus are for twelve guests, but there are some devised for both smaller and larger numbers. In each case I have indicated what quantities of the suggested dishes should be served. However, if you are entertaining smaller or greater numbers, it is a matter of simple arithmetic to alter the quantities you will find the chapter on Cooking for Fifty very helpful in this connection. It should be remembered, however, that as a buffet menu usually consists of a greater number of dishes than a formal meal, the guests are likely to eat less of each individual dish. That is why in some cases I have not suggested double quantities of a recipe for twice as many guests.

The menu pattern
The main dish of a supper party is usually a hot casserole, a savoury pastry, or some kind of cold meat, poultry or fish.

Increasingly, however, there is a tendency to centre the menu on a cheeseboard which is offered with a variety of salads and fish pâtés or dips. This kind of 'cheese-plus' menu is particularly useful when preparation time is short, as all the 'etceteras' can be frozen in advance, leaving only the cheese to be purchased and the salads freshly prepared. Although only two courses are normally served, several of the menus do include a first course to be served with drinks – this is usually some kind of savoury dip, which is particularly useful if the hostess needs to spend a few last minutes in the kitchen.

The drinks

As with the food, the accent should be on informality, with cider, wine cups and hot punches particularly welcome. If wine is served, it is usually a table wine which can be bought in litre bottles. It is useful to have the drinks table set up away from the food, so that as the evening progresses the guests can help themselves.

The service

It is best to set cold foods, together with the plates and cutlery, on one centrally-placed table, with the hot dishes on an adjacent hot plate or trolley. Guests help themselves to the main course, with some assistance with hot dishes, and then the dessert is wheeled round on a trolley, or served from a sideboard together with the coffee. Accompanying drinks are served by the host.

With willing help from family or friends, plus a dishwasher, there is no need for extra help for numbers up to twelve. But for larger numbers, it is useful to have one person in the kitchen for assistance with hot dishes, preparing the coffee and clearing away.

A Supper Party in the Spring (12)

Crudités and crisps with a delicately flavoured garlic mayonnaise are offered with the drinks before supper. Then the guests help themselves to an unusual dish of fish in a tomato and green pepper sauce, accompanied by a fluffy quiche, a crisp mixed salad and a crunchy herb bread. A cheeseboard precedes an exquisite cream cheese and fruit gâteau and a fresh fruit ice-cream.

Pointers to success:

★ *Äioli with crudités.* Use quantities given in recipe.

★ *Fillets of sole in Provençale sauce.* Use two fillets of fish per person and 1½ times the quantity of sauce given in recipe. Serve the fish at room temperature rather than chilled.

★ *Stuffed olive quiche.* Use quantity of filling given in recipe but bake it in a 12 inch (30cm) pastry case. Serve the quiche slightly warm – slip it into the oven where the bread is crisping for 5-10 minutes, or until warm to the touch.

★ *Herb bread.* Double the recipe, using two loaves.

★ *Mixed salad with avocado.* Double the recipe.

★ *Lancashire, Wensleydale and Brie cheese with biscuits (crackers).* If the cheese is bought the day before, keep it wrapped in a plastic container in a cool larder or the least cold part of the refrigerator. Arrange it an hour before supper, but keep it loosely covered with film or greaseproof paper until required. This will prevent it drying out.

★ *Morello (sour red) cherry gâteau.* Use quantities given in recipe. Serve the gâteau straight from the refrigerator.

★ *Apricot ice-cream.* Use quantities given in recipe. Transfer ice-cream from the freezer to the refrigerator half an hour before supper.

A Supper Party in Summer (12)

A crisp and savoury onion tart from Alsace is offered first. The guests then help themselves to cold salmon with its accompanying salads and two kinds of mayonnaise. Summer berries make a delectable filling for a pavlova. Fresh peaches are poached and served with ice-cream.

Pointers to success:

★ *La tarte à l'oignon.* Make two tarts. The tart will reheat but will not be quite as puffy as when freshly made. In either case serve very hot rather than warm.

★ *Salmon.* Allow 8 oz (225g) per person of whole salmon, 6 oz (175g) of cleaned fish. A whole fish looks more dramatic but it is more convenient for serving to divide it into fillets beforehand and arrange on a platter on a bed of lettuce, decorated with the eggs.

★ *Curried eggs.* Allow 1 per person.

★ *Cucumber salad.* Use quantities given in recipe.

★ *Whole egg mayonnaise and green herb mayonnaise.* Use quantities given in recipe. Mayonnaise soon dries out on the surface so keep closely covered with cling film until just before serving.

★ *Italian tomato salad.* Use quantities given in recipe but with 2 lb (1 kg) tomatoes.

★ *Mixed green salad.* Double the recipe.

★ *Red berry party pavlova.* Use quantities given in recipe. If the pavlova has been frozen in advance, leave to thaw in the refrigerator during the day. By evening it will have defrosted but will still be well chilled.

★ *Peaches in apricot sauce.* Use quantities given in recipe, but allow 1 peach per person. Be sure the peaches are well covered with the syrup (or basted with it at intervals) so that they do not go brown.

★ *Vanilla ice-cream.* Use quantities given in recipe.

A Buffet Supper in Autumn (12)

Guests have their drinks accompanied by a savoury avocado dip. The hostess serves the piping hot onion soup, and then the guests help themselves to the hot dishes and the accompanying rice and crisp green salad. A delicate lemon ice-cream accompanies a satisfying dessert of apples in a crisp tender pastry.

Pointers to success:

★ *Guacamole with crisps and crudités.* Use quantities given in recipe.

★ *Onion soup.* Make double the recipe. Serve the soup plain without the cheese topping, which is unnecessary in such a varied menu. Any left-over soup can be frozen.

★ *Sweet and sour chicken.* Use quantities given in recipe. The chicken is best kept hot over a candle or spirit heater or on an electric hot plate or trolley.

★ *Romanian meatballs.* Make $1\frac{1}{2}$ × the quantities given in recipe.

★ *Savoury rice.* Make $1\frac{1}{2}$ × the quantities given in recipe.

★ *Salad of Chinese leaves, green pepper and cucumber.* Double the recipe. Dress the salad an hour or two in advance, then refrigerate it – it is most refreshing when served well chilled.

★ *Lemon ice-cream.* Use quantities given in recipe. The ice-cream can be frozen in a deep, narrow container and served in scoops, or frozen in a cake tin, turned out, and served in wedges like a cake.

A Buffet Supper in Winter (12)

A rich beef casserole is served over a dish of crunchy brown rice and accompanied by an unusual stuffed loaf and a crisp salad. Guests are offered a choice of a rich chocolate ice-cream or a seasonal fruit salad, with meringue kisses.

F/R	Southern Beef Casserole	p.250
F/R	Brown Rice Pilaff	p.312
F	Savoury Sausage Loaf	p.531
	Chicory, Cucumber and Watercress Salad	p.318
F	Chocolate and Rum Bombe	p.391
R	Orange and Chestnut Salad	p.348
F/R	Golden Meringue Kisses	p.451

Pointers to success:

★ *Southern beef casserole.* Double the quantity using 5 lb (2.25kg) meat. Fry the meat in one pan and the vegetables in the other, then combine in a casserole with the liquids and seasonings.

★ *Brown rice pilaff.* Make $1^{1}/_{2}$ × the quantity given in recipe.

★ *Savoury sausage loaf.* Double the recipe, but using loaves about 15 inches ($37^{1}/_{2}$cm) long. This will give more meat per serving in relation to the bread.

★ *Chicory, cucumber and watercress salad.* Double the recipe.

★ *Chocolate and rum bombe.* Use the larger quantity given. Freeze in a bowl as described on p.388.

★ *Orange and chestnut salad.* Double the recipe, but use only 9 oranges.

★ *Golden meringue kisses.* Use quantities given in recipe, serve plain without cream.

Holiday Supper Party in Winter to Freeze Ahead (12)

When a party is planned for the middle of a holiday season, it is convenient to have a menu consisting mostly of dishes that can be frozen or refrigerated in advance. Thus there is a delicious pâté maison, a hearty beef casserole, meat turnovers and cold meat. Even the dessert can be frozen, leaving only the salads to be made on the day.

Pointers to success:

★ *Pâté maison, pickled gherkins.* Use quantities given in recipe. If frozen, remove 24 hours in advance and transfer to refrigerator. Leave at room temperature for 1 hour before serving from terrine in which it was cooked.

★ *Boeuf bourguignonne.* Make 1½ × the quantities given in recipe. If you do not want to open a second bottle of wine, make up the difference with extra stock.

★ *Turkish turnovers.* Use quantities given in recipe. Serve freshly cooked, as the puff pastry tends to dry up when reheated.

★ *Spiced pickled tongue.* Use quantities given in recipe. Can be sliced up to 2 hours in advance then plated and left tightly covered with foil or film.

★ *South Island salad.* Double the recipe. This is nicest served in a long, fairly shallow container so that there is a large surface to cover with the nuts.

★ *Brandy mincemeat squares.* Use quantities given in recipe. For a non-dairy version, use margarine instead of butter and mix with water instead of milk. The pastry will be crisp rather than cakey in texture.

New Year's Eve Fork Supper Party with Meat (12)

A delicious but simple soup is followed by a sandwich buffet with one hot dish and two salads. Mince pies and fresh fruit salad complete this easily-prepared menu which makes use of food that may have been cooked for other holiday meals.

Pointers to success:

★ *Tomato soup with noodles.* Make 1½ × the quantity given in recipe. Turkey stock can be used if available.

★ *Pickled pastrami sandwiches.* Half a large sliced loaf and 6-8 oz (175-225g) meat will make 12 half-slice sandwiches. They can be made several hours in advance, as can the pâté sandwiches, but be sure to cover them tightly with film.

★ *Chicken liver pâté sandwiches.* Half a large sliced loaf and 8 oz (225g) pâté will make 12 half-slice sandwiches. They are especially delicious made with sliced rye bread.

★ *Meat strudel.* Double the recipe. For a buffet, slice the strudel before arranging on the serving plate.

★ *Green bean salad.* Make 1½ × the quantity given in recipe. Whole beans are particularly nice.

★ *Warm mince pies.* Use quantities given in recipe. Serve warm rather than hot.

★ *Pineapple, peach and lychee salad.* Follow quantities given in recipe but use 1 large whole pineapple (8-10 slices, according to size). Offer an assortment of fruit liqueurs for guests to add to their salad if they wish.

New Year's Eve Supper Party with Dairy Food (12-16)

Guests are welcomed with two unusual savouries – little cheese puffs and a delicate aubergine (eggplant) dip. After a smooth cream soup they are then offered salmon and a quiche, accompanied by both a fruity and a more hearty fish salad. There is a cheeseboard decorated with fruit, followed by a choice of two superb desserts, including a syllabub and a meringue cake. The New Year is welcomed in with a sparkling wine accompanied by hot Danish pastries.

Pointers to success:

★ *Petites gougères.* Use quantities given in recipe. Freeze ahead, then reheat from frozen when guests arrive.

★ *Aubergine (eggplant) herb dip with crackers.* Make quantity for 12. It does not freeze very well, but is excellent if refrigerated in advance.

★ *Potage Parisien.* Make 1½ × the quantity given in recipe. As a New Year's Eve supper is usually served rather later than usual – about 9 p.m., guests may well be hungry and will welcome a creamy soup. Serve if possible from a hot plate.

★ *Salmon mayonnaise and garnish.* Use quantities given in recipe. Allow one egg per person.

★ *Tuna and bean hors d'oeuvre.* Follow quantities given in recipe, but use an extra can of tuna and enough dressing to moisten.

★ *Asparagus quiche.* Make 2 ten inch (25cm) quiches.

★ *South Island celery and apple salad.* Double the recipe.

★ *Cheeseboard with tangerines.* Allow approx. 3 oz (75g) per head of cheese of three different varieties.

★ *Buttered French and wholemeal bread.* Allow 1 French stick (heated in quick oven for 4 minutes or until crust feels crisp) and 1 small granary or wholemeal loaf. It's a good idea to slice a little of the brown bread, then leave on a board with a knife for guests to cut extra if required.

★ *Avocado and lime syllabub.* Make 3 × the quantities given in recipe. This looks very atttractive served in tiny coffee cups or individual soufflé dishes.

★ *Chestnut and liqueur pavlova cake.* Make the 6 egg white version.

★ *Nutty butter crisps.* Use quantities given in recipe.

★ *Sparkling wine and Danish pastries.* Allow ⅓ bottle and ½-1 Danish pastry (according to size) for each guest.

A Fork Supper for New Year's Day (12)

This is a relaxed meal to serve to a group of close friends. Two salads in the Italian style are served with hot herb bread, and the Italian theme is carried on with the unusual tuna and pasta casserole. A crisp cheese strudel is accompanied by refreshing salads, and there is a platter of cheese and fruit to add a decorative touch to the table. Two fruity desserts round off the meal.

R	Aubergine (Eggplant) Caviar	p.133
R	Italian Pepper Salad	p.151
F/R	Hot Herb Bread	p.507
F/R	Tuna Lasagne	p.215
F	Savoury Cream Cheese Strudel	p.439
R	Green and Gold Salad	p.329
R	Carrot and Raisin Slaw	p.323
R	Cheese and Fruit Platter	p.535
R	Lemon Bavaroise with Cherry Sauce	p.364
R	Party Sponge Flan	p.360
F	Lemon Sorbet	p.402

Pointers to success:

★ *Aubergine (eggplant) caviar.* Use quantities given in recipe. It is important to allow several hours for the flavour to develop.

★ *Italian pepper salad.* Follow quantitites given in recipe, but use 8 canned pimentos.

★ *Hot herb bread.* Make 2 loaves. Serve warm rather than hot.

★ *Tuna lasagne.* Double the quantities given in recipe, using only 3 cans of tuna. Find a dish large enough to hold the full amount

– a roasting tin, the outside covered with foil before being put on the table, would be excellent. (The dish should measure approx. 14 × 8 × 3 inches/35 × 20 × 7.5cm)

★ *Savoury cream cheese strudel.* Make 1¹/₂ × the quantity given in recipe – 3 strudels in all. Make the lasagne the day before, then reheat it after the strudel has been baked and is being kept hot. Alternatively bake the strudel in advance then reheat during the latter part of the lasagne's cooking time.

★ *Green and gold salad.* Make 1¹/₂ × the quantity given in recipe, but use 2 cans of corn.

★ *Carrot and raisin salad.* Use 1¹/₂ × the quantities given in recipe.

★ *Cheese and fruit platter.* Allow 3 oz (75g) per head cheese, using firm rather than creamy varieties to contrast with the strudel.

★ *Lemon bavaroise, cherry sauce.* Use quantities given in recipe.

A Cheese and Wine Supper Party for 50

The cheese is augmented with savoury pastries and dips, and a selection of special desserts is offered. A hot wine cup goes particularly well with this kind of informal supper.

Pointers to success:

★ *Äioli.* Make quantity for 25-50.

★ *Crudités.* Use 1 very large pepper, 2 large carrots, 1 heart of celery. Also 2 jars stuffed olives, 3 large (3.8 oz/100g) packs crisps, 4 packets assorted savoury biscuits, ½ lb (225g) each salted peanuts and raisins.

★ *Cheese.* Allow 3 oz (75g) per person, approx. 9 lbs (4kg) in total. Cut it in ¾ lb (350g) pieces and arrange on 2-3 cheeseboards.

★ *Bread, biscuits (crackers), butter.* Allow 5 French sticks, 2 brown loaves and a tin of assorted biscuits for cheese. Allow 2 lb (1kg) butter.

★ *Syrian cheese puffs.* Make quantity for 50. They can be kept hot in warming oven for up to 30 minutes.

★ *Avocado dip.* Make quantity for 50, for guests to use as a spread on bread or biscuits.

★ *Smoked mackerel spread.* Double the recipe.

★ *Chinese leaves in vinaigrette dressing.* Use 6 medium heads of Chinese leaves and 1 pt (575ml) dressing. Can be dressed well in advance.

★ *Cherry and chocolate gâteau.* Make two gâteaux.

★ *Lemon pavlova cake.* Make two 6-egg pavlova cakes.

★ *Melon cubes.* Use 8 medium melons. Cut fruit in cubes and spear on cocktail sticks.

★ *Mince tarts.* Use 1½ × the quantities given in recipe.

★ *Glühwein.* Make quantity for 50. Serve from hot plate if possible.

A Cold Table in Spring or Summer (12)

Nothing hot is served for this delightful supper which is very practical when the weather is warm or the hostess is single-handed. An avocado dip is offered with pre-supper drinks, and then the guests can help themselves to a smoked fish platter, egg mayonnaise, a cheeseboard and vegetable salads. A pastry and a sponge dessert round off the meal.

R	Guacamole, crisps and biscuits (crackers), cala-mata olives	p.513
R	Smoked Mackerel Fillets with Tartare Sauce	p.141
F	Buttered brown bread (bought or home-made)	p.499

Pointers to success:

★ *Guacamole.* Make quantity given for 12. Divide between two small pottery bowls and surround with the crisps and biscuits to use as dippers. The calamata olives (these can be bought most economically in tins) look attractive in small soufflé dishes.

★ *Smoked mackerel fillets with tartare sauce.* Use quantities given in recipes, allow 1 fillet per person.

★ *Buttered brown bread.* Allow 2 loaves, as some will be used to accompany the cheese. Leave some bread uncut for guests to help themselves if necessary.

★ *Cheeseboard.* Allow 3 oz (75g) cheese per serving.

★ *Mushroom, celery and pepper salad.* Follow quantities given in recipe but use ¾ lb (350g) mushrooms.

★ *French tomato salad.* Follow quantities given in recipe but use 2 lb (1kg) tomatoes.

★ *Apricot slice.* Double the recipe.

★ *Persimmon cream gâteau.* Make 1 gâteau. If persimmons are not available use any fleshy fruit such as plum or peach, or use canned peaches or guavas.

A Cold Table in Autumn or Winter (12)

When everything has to be prepared in advance, it is useful to have a menu that includes no hot dishes. At this time of the year, however, soup will be welcome. The main dish is a delightful fish salad served in avocado halves and accompanied by a varied selection of relishes and salads. It is followed by a fluffy apple cake and fresh fruit.

F/R	Granary bread and butter (home-made or bought)	p.500
R	Peppers in the Style of Piedmont	p.147
R	Cheeseboard, Celery Curls	p.195
F/R	Home-made Digestive Biscuits (Graham Crackers)	p.447
R	Cream Cheese Dip	p.514
R	Mixed Green Salad	p.317
F/R	Apple Kuchen with Streusel Topping	p.460
R	Cinnamon Whipped Cream	p.149
R	Fresh dates, satsumas	

Pointers to success:

★ *Cream of cauliflower soup.* Double the recipe. If more convenient, serve in cups.

★ *Avocado hagalil.* Make 1½ × the quantity given in recipe, with 6 good avocados. They should give to gentle pressure but not feel really soft as for a dip.

★ *Granary bread and butter.* Allow 2 bought loaves or quantity given in recipe.

★ *Peppers in the style of Piedmont.* Use 1½ × the quantities given in recipe, with 12 squat peppers.

★ *Cheeseboard.* Allow 2-3 oz (50-75g) per person of hard and blue cheeses such as Cheddar, Cheshire, Danish Blue, Stilton. These will contrast with the creamy dip.

★ *Home-made digestive biscuits (Graham crackers).* Use quantities given in recipe.

★ *Cream cheese dip.* Use quantities given in recipe. Leave overnight if possible for the flavours to develop fully.

★ *Mixed green salad.* Use 1½ × the quantities given in recipe. Keep the dried greens wrapped in a tea towel until shortly before supper, then tear into bite-sized pieces and turn in the chosen dressing.

★ *Apple streusel kuchen.* Use quantities given in recipes.

★ *Fresh fruit.* Allow 2 dates and 1 satsuma for each serving.

After the Theatre Supper in Spring or Summer (6-8)

There is no need to do anything but sit down and enjoy this meal after the theatre – everything can be left ready beforehand.

R	Chilled Avocado Soup	p.170
	Melba Toast	p.160
F/R	Tuna or Salmon Quiche	p.431
R	Mixed Salad in the Israeli Fashion	p.320
F/R	Crusty Brown Rolls	p.505
F/R	Vanilla Ice-cream (bought or home-made)	p.390
	Pineapple Compote on the Half Shell, Kirsch	p.349

Pointers to success:

★ Leave the soup in a jug in the fridge. Pour into soup cups just before serving.

★ The quiche is slightly more interesting if it is served warm rather than at room temperature. Put in oven and turn to moderate as soon as you come in.

★ Cut the pineapple in half through the tufts, remove the flesh and make the compote. Chill the shells, then refill with the compote before leaving for the theatre. Offer the kirsch for guests to sprinkle on their compote.

After the Theatre Supper in Autumn or Winter (6-8)

The guests satisfy their immediate hunger with pâté on toast, whilst the hostess heats the prepared casserole. A crisp salad accompanies it, followed by a delicious winter version of blackcurrant rödgröd.

R	Chicken Liver Pâté with French Toasts	p.136
F/R	Sweet and Sour Pineapple Beef with New Potatoes	p.252
R	Chicory, Cucumber and Watercress Salad	p.318
R	Rödgröd (winter version)	p.368
F	Lemon Drops	p.446

Pointers to success:

★ As ready-spread toasts would get soggy, have the pâté ready in a shallow dish so that guests can help themselves while sipping a drink.

★ Meanwhile add a large can of drained new potatoes to the ready-cooked casserole and reheat until bubbly, top of stove.

A Supper of Cheese Fondue for the Single Host or Hostess (6-8)

This is an ideal way for the single-handed to entertain a small number of close friends. It is possible to buy everything on the menu; alternatively the pâté, fondue and the dessert can all be home-made.

F/R	Smoked Cod's Roe Pâté on Toast	p.135
R	Garlic Olives	p.535
R	Fondue (bought or home-made)	p.192
F	French Bread	
F/R	German Apple Cake with pouring cream or	p.461
F	Warm Danish pastries	
R	Strawberries or frozen raspberries with orange slices	*below*

Pointers to success:

★ Leave the guests to enjoy a drink with the pâté on toast while you finalize preparations for the fondue, and once it is in position on its heater, invite them to the table.

★ Allow one large or 2 small Danish pastries per person. Heat them for 5 minutes in a warm oven (Gas No. 3, 325°F, 160°C) just before supper then leave in a warm place (or covered with foil) until required.

★ The fruit is simply 1 lb (450g) fresh or frozen berries, sprinkled with caster (superfine) sugar 1 hour in advance. Add 4 sliced skinned oranges just before serving.

A Casserole Supper for the Single Host or Hostess (12)

F/R	Harold's Hearty Casserole	p.253
R	Pickled Cabbage or Red Cabbage Slaw	p.322
F	Rye Bread (bought or home-made)	p.501
R	Spiced Canned Pears	p.350
F	Honey and Spice Cake (bought or home-made)	p.471

Pointers to success:

★ *Red cabbage slaw*. Double the recipe.

★ *Rye bread*. Buy 1 large loaf, or use quantities given in recipe. The home-made version does not need to be either frozen or freshly baked – it can be left in the bread drawer for several days beforehand and actually improves in flavour.

★ *Spiced canned pears*. Double the recipe.

★ *Honey and spice cake*. Make one cake. If possible allow it several days to mature before it is cut.

Parties for Tots to Teens

No matter what *you* might suggest, it's the kind of party that's currently in fashion that your children, whatever their age, will want to give for their friends. That is why I have done no more than give details of some parties that have proved popular in the recent past for children of different age groups. Food is not of supreme importance at these kind of parties – the main thing is that it should conform in quantity and style to the current pattern. Thus all the menus are low key in content. I have given some indication of the quantities the different ages are likely to eat, as this varies enormously, probably being highest in the early teens, at least among boys. At mixed parties the food is relegated to being just another factor that makes up the magic formula for a successful evening.

The degree of adult participation that is acceptable also varies among age groups, and I have suggested that, though the parents are in complete charge at a party for the younger children, by the early teens, the young host and hostess should gradually take over – even doing some of the cooking if they wish – but that parents stay within earshot or easy reach until the children reach their majority.

A Birthday Party for 5-9-Year-Olds

Simplicity and imagination are the best ingredients to put on the menu for this age group. Uncomplicated, easy to handle sandwiches are the most popular (open, and therefore with the contents visible for 5-plus, closed and more substantial for older children). Cakes should be small, non-sticky and attractive to the eye, with cream kept to a minimum, particularly for the very young. And however good the baking, chocolate biscuits (cookies) are likely to be the favourite. The birthday cake will probably prove more popular if based on a firm sponge rather than a fruit cake mixture, and will be appreciated more if served towards the end of the party rather than with the tea. For a refreshing end to the meal serve fruit and jelly, but separately, as many children don't like them mixed together. A home-made or packeted fruit-flavoured cream or milk whip also goes down well. Orange squash is served in plastic cups, with ice lollies kept in reserve for later in the party.

> **Open sandwiches on thinly sliced French bread or soft bread rolls** or
> **Closed sandwiches, crusts removed and cut into small squares or triangles**
>
> *Fillings* (select any four):
> **Cream cheese**
> **Mashed sardine or tuna fish**
> **Processed cheese spread**
> **Honey**
> **Chocolate spread**
> **Peanut butter**
> **Yeast extract savoury spread**
> **Mashed hard-boiled egg**
> **Chocolate biscuits**

F	**Brandy Snaps (bought or home-made), preferably without cream**	p.445
F	**Golden Meringue Kisses**	p.451
F	**Little Jaffa cakes**	p.480
	Canned mandarin oranges or fruit cocktail	
	Jelly in waxed cups with cream and cherry topping	
F	**Fruit Cream Dessert (bought or home-made)**	p.366
F	**Birthday Cake (bought or home-made)**	p.436
	Orange squash	
	Ice lollies	

Quantities: Allow per head:

4-6 assorted sandwiches	1-1½ portions jelly and fruit cream dessert
1½-2 small cakes	1 ice lolly
1-2 chocolate biscuits	2-3 glasses fruit squash

78

Fillings: For 20 rounds of French bread or 40 quarter-slice closed sandwiches, allow:

$^1/_4$ lb (125ml/$^1/_2$ cup) cream cheese	3 mashed hard-boiled eggs
1 × 7$^1/_2$ oz (200g) tin mashed sardine or tuna fish	8 oz (225g) pack sweet or savoury spread
6 oz (175g) pack processed cheese spread	

Bread: Calculate approx 30 slices per large loaf (60 quarter-slice sandwiches). French bread varies in length: consult your baker.

Jelly and fruit cream dessert: Each pint (575ml/2$^1/_2$ cups) will yield 6-8 servings.

Mandarin oranges or fruit cocktail: 2 × 11 oz (600g) cans or 1 × 20 oz (575g) can will yield 6-8 servings.

Pointers to success:

★ Bind canned fish and egg spreads with a nut of butter and a little salad cream. This will help to hold the mixture firmly on the bread.

★ Keep garnishes to a minimum as many children prefer their sandwiches plain. For decoration, arrange cress or parsley sprigs in between the sandwiches on the plate.

★ Sandwiches can be made up to 4 hours in advance, plated and tightly covered with film until tea time. Left-overs can be refrigerated overnight (stored in airtight plastic containers) or (with the exception of egg) frozen for up to 3 months. Freeze open sandwiches on trays until firm, then pack in an airtight container with paper between the layers. Freeze closed sandwiches in piles of 6-8 wrapped in film, foil, or in plastic containers.

★ Most young children prefer brandy snaps and meringue kisses crisp and plain. If you wish to fill them with cream do this not more than an hour before tea time.

★ With younger children, it is often better to light the candles on the birthday cake, sing 'Happy Birthday', blow out the candles, then parcel it for each guest to take home.

★ As young children enjoy looking even more than eating, it's a good idea to put all the sandwiches, biscuits and cakes on the table, with the birthday cake in the centre. Let the children see the spread in its full glory then remove the sweet things until the savouries have been eaten. Keep the jellies, the fruit cream, the squash and paper cups on a side table.

A Simple Birthday Buffet for 10-12-Year-Olds

As this age group scorns a tea party as 'babyish', a simple buffet of finger or fork food is much more welcome. When the children arrive in the late afternoon or early evening, they are offered kebabs of fruit and cheese, or salted nuts and raisins. At supper-time, they help themselves from an assortment of savoury foods, a simple jellied dessert and easy-to-handle cakes and biscuits. Drinks offered include fizzy lemonade, squash and a limited amount of sweet cider. Just before the end of the party, the birthday cake is brought in.

R	Cheese and Fruit Kebabs or	p.535
	Salted nuts and raisins	
F/R	Hot dogs on sticks with mustard and tomato ketchup as dips	p.528
	Crisps	
	Crispy Noodles	p.536
	Baked Beans	
F/R	Individual Chicken Pies or	p.277
F/R	Turkish Turnovers	p.264
	Canned peaches in jelly	
F	Chocolate Cupcakes	p.480
F	Ginger Gems	p.481
	Chocolate biscuits	
	Lemonade, squash, sweet cider	
	Birthday Cake or	p.482
	Raspberry Ice-cream Meringue Gâteau	p.398

Quantities:
For cheese and fruit kebabs, hot dogs on sticks, crispy noodles, follow quantities given in recipes.
Baked beans: 4 oz (125g) per serving
Crisps: 1-1½ oz (25-40g) per serving, plus reserve
Individual chicken pies or Turkish turnovers: 1½-2 per serving
Peaches in jelly: 1 pt (575ml) jelly and 1 × 20 oz (575g) jar sliced peaches per 6 servings
Cakes and biscuits: 2-3 per serving
Drinks: ¾-1 pt (425-575ml, 2-2½ cups) per serving

Pointers to success:

★ It is much more economical to buy raisins and salted nuts separately than in a mixed pack.

★ Be sure to *simmer* the hot dogs in water for 5 minutes to ensure they are heated through. The heat can then be turned down and the water left at *steaming point only* until required.

★ To make the peaches in jelly, drain off the syrup from the fruit, add it to the jelly dissolved in a little water, together with the juice of a lemon, then make up to the quantity of liquid required. Fold in the peaches (sliced bananas can be added as well) only when the jelly is half set otherwise the fruit will sink to the bottom.

★ If possible have a small hot plate for the hot food, then leave plates, cutlery and plenty of napkins on the table. Let the children help themselves (though the baked beans may need some assistance) and find a place to perch in the room. Fruit jelly and cakes are best on a separate table or sideboard. At this age, independence is valued so leave the children to themselves as much as possible, albeit under unobtrusive surveillance.

A Buffet Supper for Teenagers

Between the ages of 13-17, food has to compete with the attractions of the opposite sex, so it should be simple, tasty and easy to eat. Any number from 12 to 24 may be at the party, so the menu is planned to be eaten with only a fork, standing up if necessary, though this age group prefers the floor as seating accommodation. An ice-cream dessert seems to suit both boys and girls and drinks should include shandy, coke and cider.

F	Meat Strudel	p.264
F	(raw) Fried Chicken Titbits	p.528
F/R	Savoury Rice	p.279
	Baked beans	
R	Coleslaw (bought or home-made)	p.322
	Crisps	
	Pickled cucumber strips	
F	Lemon Ice-cream Meringue Gâteau	p.399
	Soft drinks, cider and shandy	

Quantities:
For meat strudel, fried chicken titbits, savoury rice, coleslaw and lemon ice-cream meringue gâteau, follow quantities given in recipe. If necessary consult chapter on Quantities for 50 (pp.112-13ff).
Coleslaw: 2-3 oz (50-75g) per serving
Crisps: 1-1½ oz (25-40g) per serving, plus reserve
Drinks: ¾-1 pt (425-575ml, 2-2½ cups) per serving

Pointers to success:
★ As the meat strudel is served hot, serve the chicken titbits just warm, or cold if more convenient.
★ The rice can be kept hot in a low oven for at least 30 minutes (Gas No.½, 250°F, 120°C) without spoiling.
★ For this age group the food is best placed on the table, with plates, cutlery and napkins, and the adults should then leave, letting the guests serve themselves. However, it is wise to stay within earshot in case any assistance is required. A drinks table should be left well-stocked, but with a strictly controlled quantity of the alcoholic drinks such as cider and shandy. The guests may, however, bring in bottles as gifts.

An Eighteenth Birthday Party Supper for 50

For a first adult party, the menu follows the pattern of a conventional supper party, albeit with simple (though equally delicious) food, all of which can be made by teenagers. There is a selection of dips to serve with drinks, followed by poultry pies served with a spicy rice dish and a cool salad. Fruited sponge flans and ice-cream with sauce are desserts that can easily be made in quantity. The birthday cake can either be based on a conventional recipe or made out of meringue layered with a liqueur and chestnut filling. A mixture of soft drinks, beer and cider, or a cider punch may be served, with a sparkling cider or wine to serve with the cake.

R	Aubergine Herb Dip	p.512
F	Avocado Dip	p.513
R	Crudités	p.510
	Salted peanuts and raisins	

Hot crisps

Quantities:
For the dips, rice, pies, coleslaw, ice-cream and the sauce, follow quantities given in recipes.
Crisps: 1 oz (25g) per person, plus a reserve
Fruited sponge flans: 4
Chestnut and liqueur pavlova cake: Make a 12 egg white pavlova, shape into a rectangle about 12 × 10 inches (30 × 25cm), and use double the filling given for the 6 egg white pavlova
Cider punch: Use 4 × the recipe, plus other drinks

Pointers to success:
★ Everything on the menu can either be frozen in advance or made and refrigerated the day before.
★ Dips should be distributed about the room in several small bowls rather than one or two large ones, as these act as 'ice-breakers' when guests arrive.
★ Crisps should be heated until warm (about 5 minutes in a moderate oven), then served to accompany the hot dishes rather than as a 'nibble'.
★ To serve the main dishes for this large number, it is a good idea to recruit several helpers to stand behind a long table, from which the guests can collect their supper. This is much more speedy than a help-yourself buffet.
★ The sweet should be kept quite separate, and can be passed round from a trolley circulating in the room, or served to the guests as they are ready.

An Informal Teenage Coffee Evening – Summer or Winter

Teenage cooks can offer refreshments that need a little cooking skill or none at all, according to their preference. In summer a sweet fondue is excellent for 8-10 people, while in colder weather soup can be followed by something hot and cheesey, with flapjacks and coffee to round off the meal.

Menu for spring or summer (8-10):

R **Chocolate Fondue** or   p.386
R **Caramel Fondue (Sauce)**   p.376
   Banana slices
   Apple slices
   Marshmallows
   Canned pineapple cubes or mandarin slices
   Coffee

Quantities:
For both fondues use the quantities given in the recipes.
Bananas: 4
Apples: 2
Marshmallows: ½ lb
Tinned fruit: 20 oz (575g) tin

Pointers to success:
★ Although the fondue can be made in advance, then reheated in front of the guests, it is more fun if it is made there and then. The ingredients should be left ready on a tray, then heated together in a fondue dish. If this is not available, heat in the kitchen, then transfer to a candle warmer to keep hot.
★ The guests will enjoy sitting on cushions round a low coffee table.

Menu for autumn or winter (8-12):

   **Vegetable tomato soup (canned or packeted) with
      Parmesan Cheese**
R **Syrian Cheese Puffs**   p.521
R **Hot Cheese Crisps**   p.522
F **Flapjacks**   p.448

Quantities:
Syrian cheese puffs and hot cheese crisps: Follow quantities given
in recipe.
Soup: Cream soup: 5 fl oz (150ml/²/₃ cup) per serving. Clear or
vegetable soup: 8 fl oz (225ml/1 cup) per serving

Pointers to success:
★ Both canned and packeted soup tastes better if heated to
simmering point, then held there for 10 minutes. A little cream
spooned into each bowl adds a glamorous touch. Let guests
sprinkle on their own cheese.
★ The puffs can be held in a low oven for 20 or 30 minutes, but
the cheese crisps should be eaten hot off the pan. They are,
therefore, more suitable for a smaller number of guests, while the
puffs are not really worth making for less than twelve.

A Tea-party for 200 Children and 200 Adults

There are occasions connected with school, club or place of
worship when children and their parents have to be entertained on
a large scale. Here the food is incidental to the occasion, and the
main concern of the organizers is the method of procedure and the
logistics. Below I give the plan of organization I have devised over
many years.

The menu:

> **Open sandwiches on French bread or finger rolls**
> **spread with egg, cream cheese and pinapple, and**
> **tuna: (bind fish and egg spreads with a little salad**
> **cream to hold the mixture firmly on the bread)**
> **Crisps**
> **Assorted small cakes, bought or home-made:**

Brandy Snaps	p.445
Golden Meringue Kisses	p.451
Flapjacks	p.448
Chocolate Cupcakes	p.480
Little Jaffa Cakes	p.480
Ginger Gems	p.481

> **Orange squash (individual packs if available**
> **Ice lollies**

Adults:
    Danish pastries (bought)
    Remainder of children's sandwiches and cakes
    (Parents sit down to tea while children have games or other entertainment)

Quantities:
Allow 4 sandwiches and 1½-2 cakes per child; ½-1 Danish pastry (according to size) per adult.

The shopping list:

3½ lb (1.675kg) butter
5 doz large eggs
12 × ½ lb (225g) cans tuna
20 oz (575g) jar salad cream
Smallest bottle of vinegar
Salt and pepper
2 lb (1 kg) full fat cream cheese
3 lb (1.5kg) very firm tomatoes
    (for garnish)
9 boxes cress (for garnish)
1½ lb (675g) tea
12 pints (7 litres) milk
4 lb (2kg) sugar
6 lb (approx 3kg) crisps – 24 large
    3.8 oz (100g) packs

35 doz medium-sized finger rolls
    or approx 20 long French sticks
    (800 slices, 40 slices to the loaf)
30 doz small cakes (bought or
    home-made)
300 individual bottles orange
    cordial
18 doz ice lollies
200 paper napkins
150 doilies
Large packet film (for covering
    sandwiches)

Assistance:
Morning: 12 volunteers to make fillings, spread sandwiches, plate cakes, set table.
Afternoon: 4-6 helpers to make tea and supervise, plus 8-10 teenagers to assist children and help a clear. 4 washers up.

Eating out of doors

So great is the variety of occasions for eating out of doors, that the only common denominator is likely to be the sky above. For instance, one can enjoy a do-it-yourself family picnic, or a 'fête champêtre' with pâté and champagne. One can relish hot dogs and baked beans cooked on a makeshift grill over an open fire, or enjoy a luxurious meal of baby lamb grilled in the Greek fashion on a sophisticated barbecue with an electrically-driven spit. So this chapter is really made up of several little chapters, and I have given the advice appropriate to each section with the relevant menu. But whatever the occasion, remember it should be different and it should be fun.

The Barbecue

In prehistoric times the returned hunters would skewer their kill on to branches and grill it in the glowing embers of the fire. Today the barbecue can be a simple home-made arrangement consisting of a metal grill supported by bricks with a charcoal fire beneath it, or one of an enormous range of sophisticated manufactured devices, circular or rectangular, with any number of optional extras such as shelves, rotating grills and trolleys. Since there are innumerable books and magazine articles offering detailed advice on how to choose the barbecue for your particular purpose, I will confine myself to setting out the basic requirements common to all kinds.

The size
Make sure the cooking area is large enough, especially if it is to

be used for party rather than only family meals. Circular grill barbecues generally offer a larger grilling area than rectangular ones and are not necessarily more expensive. The minimum width for 8 people should be approx 218 inches (45cm), but an expert barbecue cook of my acquaintance specifies his ideal as 36 × 24 inches (90 × 60cm) with a grill that can be adjusted to different levels from the source of heat (the most effective way of controlling the fierceness of the cooking). In addition, the firepan should be easy to take out for cleaning and – for dedicated barbecue cooks – there should be a hood which can be brought down to convert the grill to an oven. More important, perhaps, is the grill height: 24-28 inches (60-70cm) – about mid-thigh height – is most convenient. A spit is also useful, particularly if it is used in conjunction with a battery-driven motor to turn the spit and thus ensure that the food cooks evenly. A shelf above or below the firebox for keeping food hot is handy, too.

But whatever type of barbecue you use, its success will probably depend on the observance of one simple rule: start the fire in good time. This should be 30-45 minutes before you want to cook on it (it takes less time to heat up when it is windy). You will see a layer of grey ash on the coals when it is hot enough. To test that it is ready, hold your hand above the charcoal and you should feel the heat. If you can hold it there for 5 seconds, it is not hot enough. If you can hold it there for only 2-3 seconds, it should be just right.

Basting
It is essential to baste both meat and fish with oil or an oil-based sauce, otherwise it will stick to the grill, and in the case of lean meat and fish, dry out.

Cooking times
They are roughly similar to those when using an ordinary grill, but allowance must be made for the heat of the fire and the distance the food is set away from it. (See specific recipes.)

Cooking tools
Charcoal grilling is hot work, so it's wise to invest in tools that help you keep your distance: for instance, long-handled forks and spoons, tongs and a paint brush for basting purposes.

Insulated gloves are essential to pull hot potatoes and other foil-baked vegetables out of the fire and to turn skewered foods during the cooking.

Skewers should be flat rather than round (to prevent food slipping on them as they are turned) and long rather than short – don't go for ordinary butcher's skewers, which are the wrong shape and size. If you should come by some packets of short bamboo skewers, dampen them, then use to grill well-dried canned fruit such as pineapple or apricots which have been rolled in lemon juice and brown-sugar – they only take about 5 minutes, which isn't long enough for the bamboo to char.

A fish holder and a steak holder are also extremely useful.

A Fish Barbecue (6-8)

Mackerel and sardines both develop a special flavour when grilled over a barbecue. They are particularly nice when accompanied by baked potatoes and a cool cucumber relish. There's also a tasty quiche and a cooked vegetable salad. Summer is celebrated with a delicious variation on strawberries and cream and a fruit tart in the Yorkshire style. Besides the usual drinks, there's a jug of sweetened fresh lemon juice served over ice.

	Barbecued Mackerel with Mustard Butter or	p.205
	Sardines with Lemon Wedges	p.206
	Baked Potatoes with	p.306
R	Avocado Herb Topping	p.307
F/R	Stuffed Olive Quiche	p.432
R	Greek and Gold Salad	p.329
R	Cyprus Cucumber Salad (Talathouri)	p.325
F	Granary Bread and Butter (bought or home-made)	p.500
R	Strawberries with sugar and cream	p.344
F	Yorkshire Bilberry Tart	p.413
R	Citron Pressé	p.552

Pointers to success:

★ If you start your barbecue in really good time, and you have the room, potatoes will bake in foil in just over an hour. However, I think it's probably more practical to do them in the regular kitchen oven and then transfer them to the barbecue when you start to cook the main course outside. Choose only medium-sized potatoes – firm-skinned new potatoes are ideal – as they are going to be eaten in the hand.

★ The avocado topping is especially practical on a sunny day as it does not melt as butter would.

★ The quiche can either be warmed up in the oven after the potatoes have been cooked, or served at garden temperature. Alternatively, when you start to cook the fish, put it on the warming shelf of the barbecue, if there is one.

★ Only bring out the salads when you are ready to eat, as both are best served cold. (They can be prepared the day before and refrigerated.)

★ If bilberries are not in season – they are most plentiful towards the middle of August – use rhubarb, blackcurrants or raspberries instead.

★ Squeeze as many lemons as you will need well in advance, then chill in a jug. Or use a good quality bottled lemon juice. Freeze plenty of ice, and store in a plastic bag until required. An insulated picnic bag will help to keep it from melting outdoors.

A Meat Barbecue (6-8)

Whilst the barbecue is heating up, the guests drink a chilly orange concoction which is both refreshing and sustaining. The food for this meal has a strong Greek influence, the main dish being skewered lamb in the Greek fashion, served on rice with a mixed salad that includes black olives and scissored fresh herbs. There's also a cold meat loaf, with a fruited dessert accompanied by a very satisfying fruit cake.

R	Minty Orange Frost	p.551
	Souvlakia (Skewered Lamb, Greek Style)	p.241
R	Picnic Loaf	p.260
F/R	Basmatti Rice cooked Indian Style	p.312
R	Mixed Salad in the Greek Fashion	p.318
R	Danish Cucumber Salad	p.323
F	Rye Bread (bought or home-made)	p.501
R	Rödgröd	p.367
F	Farmhouse Fruit Cake	p.474

Pointers to success:

★ Use concentrated frozen orange juice to make the minty orange frost; however, dilute it with slightly less water than instructed on the pack. This gives it a more intense fresh fruit flavour.

★ If there is limited room on the barbecue, cook the rice indoors. It can be brought out and kept hot on a corner of the barbecue without disturbing the cooking of the meat.

★ For 8 guests, use 4-5 lbs (2-2½ kg) boned and cubed meat and the same amount of the other ingredients except for an extra teasp rigani and salt. If you like the lamb cooked rare, push the cubes of meat close together on the skewer; for medium or well done, leave a little space between them to allow the heat to circulate. Calamata olives come in 1 kilo tins, and are packed in olive oil, vinegar and brine. Once opened they can be decanted into a glass jar for storage in the refrigerator, where they will keep for weeks.

★ In a typical Greek salad, the herbs (which are in sprigs rather than finely chopped) are added to the greens rather than to the dressing. This gives it a very fresh-tasting flavour.

★ While one wouldn't serve a fruit cake with rödgröd at a dinner party, it does seem to suit outdoor eating – and the hearty appetites fresh air produces.

Barbecues for a Crowd

Once you have organized the logistics of the occasion, a communal outdoor 'nosh up' can be a winner, because it has appeal for every age group: there can be tables for those who like to sit, open spaces for those who prefer to roam. There can be a lucky dip and all the other fun of the fête, or you can just stand and chat with your friends. And an evening barbecue can also be combined with a disco. However, you must get your food and drink plans made well in advance.

First, get a good group together, preferably including both men and women – men make excellent barbecue cooks and, in any case, it can be hot and heavy work. Try to include one or two people who are already experienced at barbecues. *Next*, decide on the timing of the party: either lunch-time (for family groups) or evenings (for teenagers or adults). *Then* plan your menu and go for a few simple dishes, served in generous amounts, as well as an assortment of drink which can be included in the price of the ticket or sold at cost. *Finally*, organize your equipment. Either hire the barbecues, allowing (for a large crowd) one catering size for every 50 people, or (for a smaller party up to 75) ask a few people (about one for every 12-15 guests) to bring their own barbecue and do the cooking on it. Provide the charcoal. The price of the tickets will depend on the estimated cost of food, drink and hire of equipment, and also on whether or not you wish to make a profit.

Setting the scene
You will need assistance – either the night before (for a lunch-time barbecue) or in the afternoon (for an evening one) – to set out all the chairs and tables and equipment.

Pre-preparation
Do as much of the cooking as possible the day before, including the salads, desserts, sauces and dips. Depending on numbers this can be done at a central point with a team of workers, or the preparations can be split up and done in individual homes. Again, on the day of the barbecue it depends on the cooking facilities available whether all the food is cooked on the spot, or whether some of the more portable food, such as baked potatoes and sausages, is brought from home ovens and then kept hot on the barbecues.

On the day of the barbecue
Make sure you have enough serving tables laid out at strategic points. These will be needed near the barbecues for raw foods, and away from them for hot accompaniments and desserts. You will also need a table for paper plates, cutlery and napkins and one for glasses and drinks.

Each guest picks up his plate and cutlery, goes to be served at the barbecue and then goes to the other serving table for the rest of his meal. Be sure to have large, plastic-lined bins for used plates, plastic cups, cutlery and other rubbish.

Light the barbecues so that they are at cooking heat by the start of the party. Have plenty of drinks and crisps to serve whilst people are waiting for the food to cook.

Divide up the duties as follows: 1 person to be in charge of refuelling the barbecues; 1 person per barbecue to dip the food in the sauce or grilling liquid, season and cook it; plus as many people as you have to handle the dishing and serving of the rest of the menu, not forgetting the clearing away.

Chicken for a Crowd (50)

This is an excellent menu for a communal barbecue, combined perhaps with a garden fête. I give quantities for 50, but it's not too difficult to multiply them, to serve 200 if necessary.

Pointers to success:

★ For this number, use ready-cut chicken portions and brush them with oil and lemon juice rather than putting them in a marinade.

★ Allow 45 minutes for large barbecues to come to the correct heat and 30 minutes for smaller ones. Allow 30 minutes for each chicken portion to cook through (pierce the leg – colourless liquid will come out if it is cooked, slightly coloured liquid if it is not). If there is a very large number of portions to cook, it's as well to start them off in the oven (if available) and then put them on the barbecue to finish browning and keep hot. In any case, it's a good idea to keep a stock of ready-cooked portions in the oven, in case everyone wants to be served at once, and there aren't enough portions ready-cooked on the barbecues. It's also a good idea to have some of the barbecues very hot to brown the portions, and then others less hot where the cooking process can be completed. If all the barbecues are too hot, the birds may brown before they are cooked through.

★ When making large quantities of salads, use plastic washing-up bowls, or plastic bins lined with bin-liners.

★ Make 2 cakes if each person is to be served with one slice, 3 cakes if you are prepared to offer seconds.

A Meat Barbecue for a Crowd (75)

This menu is particularly suitable for an evening barbecue/disco, and that is why I have based it on 75 guests – the number one would hope to attract to such an event at, for example, a tennis club. However, smaller or larger numbers can be catered for by adjusting the quantities. The level of price you wish to set for the tickets will determine whether steaks or beefburgers are to be served, but the rest of the menu – the salad, baked potatoes and the variety of desserts each made by a different volunteer – can remain the same. For this number use 5 domestic-size barbecues, each manned by one volunteer.

	Barbecued Steaks or	p.237
F	Lizzie's Beefburgers	p.255
R	Barbecue Sauce	p.243
R	Easy Coleslaw	p.563
	Baked Potatoes	p.306
F/R	Mustard Butter	p.491
	Baked Beans	
	Crisps	

Assorted sweets, each serving a minimum of 8, e.g.:

F	Caramel Oranges Italian Style	p.347
R	Peach, Berry and Pineapple Salad	p.347
F	Carmel Cloud Gâteau	p.357
R	Avocado Lemon/Lime Mousse	p.364
F	Lemon Pavlova	p.370
F	Chestnut and Liqueur Pavlova Cake	p.371

White, red and rosé wine, beer, lemonade and squash

Quantities:
Beefburgers: 3 × the quantity given in the recipe.
Steaks: Allow 6-8oz (175-225g) steak per head.
Sausages: Allow 18 lb (8.5 kg).
Barbecue sauce: Double the larger quantity specified in the recipe.
Easy coleslaw: Follow the method given in the recipe but with these ingredients:

10 × 12 oz (350g) cartons	green peppers
coleslaw	red apples
3 small heads celery	1/4lb (125g/3/4 cup) sultanas

Potatoes: Allow 1 per head.

Mustard butter: Double the quantities given in recipe.
Baked beans: Allow 4 lb (2 kg).
Crisps: Allow 6 lb (3kg).
Desserts: Allow nine each serving 8-12.
Drinks: The following are approximate quantities sufficient for an entire evening. It is best if they can be bought on a sale or return basis.

11 litres white wine	8 litres lemonade
8 litres rosé wine	65 pints beer
6 litres red wine	1 bottle squash

Charcoal: Allow 6lb (3kg).

Pointers to success:
★ *Timing*: To start cooking at 9 p.m.: If 5 people have brought their barbecues, light 2 barbecues at 8 o'clock and the remainder at 8.15.
★ If steaks are served, let guests choose their own and put on barbecue. This gets them interested and involved at once.
☆ For remainder of procedures, follow general instructions for running a communal barbecue on pp.91-92.

A Simple Alfresco Lunch (6-8)

This menu has been devised for a garden lunch arranged at short notice. A cold soup (either from the freezer or quickly made that morning) – or alternatively, wedges of fresh watermelon – is followed by a cheeseboard served with savoury fish and cheese pâtés, a variety of salads and good bread. The meal is completed by a great bowl of soft fruits in season and some buttery biscuits (cookies).

F	**Dairy Borscht** or	p.170
R	**Chilled Yoghurt Soup** or	p.171
R	**Watermelon Slices**	p.131
R	**Cheeseboard**	p.195
F/R	**Cream Cheese Pâté**	p.515
R	**Italian Tomato Salad**	p.327
R	**Smoked Cod's Roe Pâté (bought or home-made)**	p.135
R	**French Cucumber Salad**	p.324

Pointers to success:

★ Serve the soup in cups or mugs as neither soup needs a spoon.

★ Buy a total of 2 lb (1 kg) cheese in 8 oz (225g) pieces. Be sure to keep the board and the cheese covered with film or foil until required, particularly if it is laid out in the garden. Bring the pâtés from the fridge at the last moment.

★ Make the pepper salad easily with canned pimentoes; however, try to make it early to allow the flavour to develop.

★ For a garden meal it is best to cut the bread only as it is needed, to prevent it drying out.

★ Have a jug of orange juice and a bowl of sugar for guests to add to their fruit as they wish. Soft fruit looks delightful in a pottery bowl. If you have had to buy the fruit the day before, don't wash or sugar it, simply clean, discard any bruised fruit, then leave in an airtight plastic container until just before lunch. Only then should it be washed and placed in the bowl. In this way it will keep its texture as if freshly picked.

The Technique of the Family Picnic

A joint family picnic, with two families or even two generations pooling their resources for a day out, can be the most enjoyable and relaxed form of party. Because the best picnics are usually planned at the last minute, it's advisable to have a picnic kit always ready except for fresh food and drink.

Here are my suggestions:

A folding table and chairs; wipeable plastic cloth. This makes an enormous difference to the enjoyment of the food. It is most uncomfortable to eat food sprawled on a rug.

A capacious, spongeable bag or wicker basket. This is for packing everything except perishable food.

An insulated bag for food. This isn't absolutely necessary but is most useful on a very hot day, particularly for keeping butter and other perishable foods cool.

Small plastic containers. These are invaluable for butter, jam, cheese, sandwich spreads, etc.

Two or three larger containers. If you plan to cook on a spirit stove, these are excellent for beating eggs, or for diluting condensed soups.

Stainless steel cutlery. It's worth investing in a set once and for all as it lasts for ever and makes food taste much better than plastic cutlery.

Plates, cups. These can be of plastic or paper, as preferred.

Pen knife (or small fruit knife), can opener, salt and pepper. Keep these always in the kit; don't be tempted to take them out or you'll forget to replace them.

Spirit stove, non-stick frying pan, milk pan, kettle. These are optional but can be extremely useful particularly for a spring or autumn picnic, when hot soup or a fry-up is especially welcome. If you have a kettle, you don't need to take an insulated container for hot water.

Plastic bags. Essential for the disposal of rubbish.

The food
It's not necessary to make stacks of sandwiches *before* you set out on the picnic. Far easier – and much more fun – is to take the ingredients with you and let everyone make their own on the spot. Buy long crunchy French bread on the way, or take buttered rolls ready to be filled by each member of the picnic party. Crispbread and digestive biscuits (Graham crackers) are also useful.

Carry a selection of sandwich fillings in small plastic containers, together with a long plastic container packed with tomatoes, lengths of cucumber and thoroughly dried lettuce. (Or you could take a mixed salad in a plastic bowl fitted with a lid.) Cakes and biscuits (cookies) should be firm and crisp. Avoid those that crumble easily.

Here are some suggestions from which to choose your menu, some put together just before you leave, others that will need pre-preparation the day before.

R	Tuna Sandwich Spread	p.521
R	Egg and Olive Butter	p.516
R	Cream Cheese Pâté	p.515
R	Cream Cheese and Pineapple	p.516
R	Cream Cheese and Walnut	p.516
R	Smoked Mackerel Mousse	p.135
	Honey, savoury sandwich spread, peanut butter	
R	Chicken Liver Pâté	p.136
F	Picnic Loaf	p.260
R	Chicken or Turkey Schnitzel	p.274
R	Sesame Chicken	p.273
R	Wiener Backhendl	p.272
R	Cold Roast Chicken	p.277
	Tomatoes, cucumber, lettuce	
	Jar of Vinaigrette	p.332
	Jar of Mayonnaise	p.333
	Fresh fruit	

Portable cakes and biscuits (cookies)

F	Ginger Gems	p.481
F	Honey and Spice Cake	p.471
F	Farmhouse Fruit-cake	p.474
F	Family Fruit-cake	p.475
F	Chocolate Cupcakes	p.480
F	Crunchy Date Bars	p.448
F	Flapjacks	p.448
F	Margaret's Shortcake Fingers	p.456

Soft drinks in cans, instant coffee, tea bags, hot water or facilities for boiling it.

The Grand Occasion Picnic (6-8)

The occasion may be an opera or a concert in the country, or perhaps a 'fête champêtre' at a member's house, organized by a society or a club. I am really devising a portable meal of luxurious cold food rather than a light-hearted do-it-yourself picnic. A table and chairs, a tablecloth and an insulated bag are essential for this meal, and normal cutlery, china and glasses may well be brought to complement the food. It is, of course, quite possible to purchase all the food ready-to-eat (and some specialist stores will lend you the picnic basket as well), but even if you don't want to prepare the entire meal at home, it is very rewarding to make one or two of the special dishes – such as the chicken and the fruit and wine dessert. As this is an informal open-air party, all the food can be served direct from the plastic containers in which it has been carried, though there is no reason why certain items that are unlikely to spoil cannot be brought on conventional plates, albeit well-protected with foil or film.

A creamy pâté is spread on toasts. There is then a most unusual dish of poached chicken masked in a nutty sauce, accompanied by a rice salad and a green salad. The meal is completed with a refreshing fruit compote accompanied by light sponge biscuits.

F/R	Pâté Maison, Gherkins	p.137
	Melba Toast	p.160
R	Circassian Chicken	p.289
R	Pineapple Rice Salad	p.331
R	Mixed Salad in the Greek Fashion	p.318
F	French bread or rolls	
R	Cherry Wine compote	p.344
F	Prelatoes or bought sponge fingers	p.453
	Fresh peaches	

Suggested wine:
A rosé, such as Portugese or Tavel.

Pointers to success:
★ Bring the pâté in the dish in which it was cooked, then provide each guest with a knife to help themselves.
★ If preferred, serve plain rice dressed only with a vinaigrette, and then bring along another spicy salad such as **Green and Gold** (p.329).

★ Bring the ingredients for the Greek salad ready in a bowl (except for the olives which should be added just before serving). Bring the dressing in a jar, and blend into the salad when the meal is served.

★ The cherry wine compote can be made with sweet cherries, but in that case increase the wine to $1/2$ pint (275ml/$1^1/4$ cups) and decrease the water accordingly.

Tea and Coffee Parties

Talking over the tea – or coffee cups – is one kind of entertaining that is popular in every culture, and every milieu. I can recall sipping Earl Grey tea in a villa in Istanbul, enjoying an old-fashioned farmhouse tea, complete with hot buttered scones, in the English Lakes, drinking mint tea and eating Oriental sweet-meats in the Negev desert of Israel, attending a formal tea-party on the West Coast of the United States and a traditional British tea-party at a Country Club in Cyprus; each occasion conducted according to its own conventions and each with its own very special atmosphere and flavour.

Alas, the tea-party is losing favour today, mainly because many people no longer want to eat between meals, particularly the cakes and biscuits (cookies) that are usually on the menu. However, there are occasions when this form of entertaining seems to be just right – when friends drop in unexpectedly, when the different generations of a family gather together, when there is a special celebration, or when a good cause needs support. These are the kinds of tea-parties I have in mind in this chapter.

Drop in for a Cuppa . . .

Despite the informality of this kind of invitation, some kind of preparation is necessary, even if it is only making sure there is an adequate stock of tea and coffee in the house, and that there are a variety of 'cut and come again' cakes and simple biscuits (cookies) in the freezer or larder cupboard. And, if you frequently invite guests to drop in, then it's also wise to have one or two savoury dips or spreads as well as cheese and biscuits (crackers) ready for those who prefer savoury things.

101

Bear in mind the following points when deciding what to cook for this kind of casual entertaining:

Is it quick and easy to make?

Will it keep well, either in the freezer or (more conveniently) in airtight containers stored in a larder cupboard?

If only a portion of a cake is eaten, will the rest keep fresh for another day?

Can it be portioned after baking so that only as much as is required for a single occasion needs to be put out at any one time?

In addition, it's useful to have a selection of recipes for last-minute cakes or scones, always to hand.

Here are some of my suggestions:

Cakes, pastries and quick breads
Note: All these cakes will keep for at least 3 months in the freezer and up to a week in an airtight container at room temperature (for exceptions, see special comments in individual recipes).

Plain or buttered

Cut-and-come-again cakes

Quickly made cakes

To portion before storage
Brandy Mincemeat Squares Cut in squares when baked, then store in plastic containers either in the freezer or larder cupboard. p.420
Autumn Apple Slices Portion as above, but more perishable, so store in the refrigerator, or keep in the freezer and thaw or microwave as required. Nicest served slightly warm. p.420

Easy-mix biscuits (cookies)
All these biscuits keep well in a tin for at least 2 weeks, and can always be 'refreshed' by crispening in a moderate oven for 10 minutes and then allowing to go quite cold before they are served. However, I like to keep a 'stock' in the freezer, and refill the tins from it each week. They are all very quickly made.
Treacle or Syrup Crisps Very quickly made, as the fat is melted and the biscuits are formed by being rolled into balls. p.442
Lemon Drops Very quickly made as based on oil. Formed by dropping from a teaspoon. p.446
Orange Crisps 'Fork' biscuits so easy a child can make them. p.445
Margaret's Shortcake Fingers Unlike most shortbread, these do not need to be rolled out. Melting in texture. p.456

The Family Tea-Party

It is a matter of personal preference whether one sits round the laden tea-table, or whether the food is set on an occasional table, and passed around among the guests while the tea is served from a trolley. Simple sandwiches may be served, but usually the refreshments consist of a variety of cakes, biscuits and buttered breads. The cakes will probably have been made specially for the tea-party but are the kind that do not stale easily and can be used up later in the week. The tea breads may well be spread with cream cheese or home-made or bought preserves. The cakes usually include one that is iced, and others which are spicy and fruity rather than rich and filled with cream. They are all easily made but with more varied and probably more expensive ingredients than those made as insurance against the unexpected guests. As a rough

103

guide I would make or buy one variety of scone or tea bread for buttering; 3 kinds of cake; and two kinds of biscuits. Here are my suggestions (all can be frozen):

To butter
Farmhouse Scones Pale brown and crumbly – lovely with jam.   p.463
Sugar and Spice Rings Children love the sticky filling.   p.270

Spreads
Lemon Curd Tart and fruity.   p.493
Whole Apricot Preserve Delicious on scones with unsweetened whipped cream.   p.492
Uncooked Strawberry Jam Lovely even on bread and butter.   p.496

A variety of cakes
Iced
Marble Cake with Coffee Fudge Icing Firm textured cake, crisp buttery icing.   p.465
Mocha Sandwich A real milk chocolate flavour.   p.466

Spicy
Farmhouse Fruit Cake Moist and nutty. Very filling.   p.474
Raisin Spice Cake Delicate in taste and texture.   p.477
Honey and Spice Cake A strong honey flavour.   p.471
Ginger Loaf A deep ginger flavour.   p.469

Fruity
German Apfel Kuchen Lovely flavour of buttered apples.   p.461

A variety of biscuits
Almond Butter Crisps Rich but quickly made.   p.443
Crunchy Date Bars Interesting contrast of juicy filling with crisp oatmeal mixture.   p.448
Crunchy Hazelnut Biscuits For nut lovers.   p.444
Orange Crisps Melting texture, fruity flavour.   p.445
Syrup Crisps Lovely butterscotch flavour.   p.442
Stuffed Monkey A rich almond flavour.   p.421

A Traditional Celebration Tea (20-24)

The occasions don't occur very often, but when they do, a tea-party is often the best way to celebrate, whether it is an engagement, a confirmation, an 80th birthday or a reunion of old friends.

With the exception of the elderly, most guests will help themselves from a buffet and probably stand up to eat and drink, though it is infinitely more comfortable if seating can be arranged. However, if the guests have to stand, then the food must be small and dainty, the equivalent of the 'finger food' at a drinks party. So offer small, colourful open sandwiches on slices of French bread, and tiny rolled sandwiches enclosing asparagus or savoury spreads. Avoid large cakes and gâteaux; instead serve small cubes of luscious cake, individual 'fancies' and extravagant biscuits arranged on platters in decorative rows.

R Smoked Salmon Sandwich Spread	p.517
R Egg and Olive Butter	p.516
R Cream Cheese Pâté	p.515
R Cream Cheese and Pineapple Spread	p.516

All on buttered slices of French bread garnished with sliced, stuffed olives, anchovy fillets, cucumber and tomato.

R Asparagus Rolls	p.518
F Apfel Kuchen with Streusel Topping, garnished with whipped cream	p.460
F Cheesecake, American-style, with peach topping	p.473
F Chocolate Éclairs	p.468
Golden Meringue Kisses, filled with coffee-flavoured whipped cream	p.451
Celebration Fruit Cake	p.477
F Nutty Butter Crisps	p.452

Quantities:
These allow for approx 5 open sandwiches, 2 rolled sandwiches and 2 cakes per person, but it is impossible to be exact, and it is always better to have some left-overs (which can be refrigerated or frozen) than be left with the feeling that people could have eaten more.

1 can green asparagus
1 large brown sliced loaf
3 long (15 inch/37cm) French sticks or 4 shorter ones (12 inch/30cm)
1/2 lb (225g) butter
5 hard-boiled eggs

1/2 lb (225g) quantity smoked salmon mix
1/2 lb (225g) quantity cream cheese pâté
4 oz (125g) quantity cream cheese and pineapple spread

For garnish: 6 tomatoes; 1/2 cucumber; 1 can anchovy fillets; 4 oz (125g) stuffed olives.

Quantity given in recipe for Apfel Kuchen with Streusel Topping

1 1/2 × recipe for Cheesecake

4 egg recipe for Chocolate Éclairs

1 1/2 × recipe for Golden Meringue Kisses, using 5 egg whites, 10 oz (275g/1 1/4 cups) sugar

1 1/2 × recipe Nutty Butter Crisps

Pointers to success:

★ Arrange the food on a buffet table, accessible from all sides, with piles of tea plates and napkins arranged at each corner. The sandwiches can be made and plated up to 4 hours in advance, then tightly covered with film until required.

★ Keep the service of the tea quite separate from that of the food, arranging the cups, saucers and teaspoons on a sideboard or trolley. Pass the sugar separately.

★ Use two family-size teapots and 3-4 hot water jugs, if possible including 1 or 2 insulated hot water jugs which can be filled in advance.

★ Thirty minutes before you wish to serve the tea, fill the hot water jugs and pour some boiling water in each teapot. Stand them on a hot plate (or ceramic hob set at 2) to get thoroughly warm.

★ Make strong tea, and then dilute with water as required, always having one hot water jug in hand to fill up the teapot. It will probably be necessary to make only one complete fresh brew.

Alternative suggestions for the menu

Baking for Charity – The Coffee or Tea-party

An effective and easy way for a charity group to raise money is to organize a 'bake in' of home-made cakes and savoury tarts. Individual members of the organization make their own favourite recipes at home, donating the ingredients. However, it is best for one person to price them and to organize the packaging, for the way the goods are presented will affect their saleability. Have a realistic pricing policy. Compare shop prices, but also make allowance for the high quality ingredients and the time and labour expended.

As a 'shop window' for the food, it is usual to organize a tea or coffee party for which tickets are sold. The refreshments at the party itself are usually very simple, either bought or home-made biscuits with a good cup of tea or coffee.

Suggestions for biscuits to serve with coffee or tea
These are all quickly and easily made, economical, and easy to eat standing up. All can be frozen for up to 3 months or kept in an airtight container at room temperature for up to two weeks.

Pointers to success:
★ *Quantities for 50*:
Instant coffee: 1 × 4 oz (113g) jar
Single (light) cream: 1½ pints (850ml/4 cups)
Demerara sugar: 1 lb (450g)
Tea bags: 6 oz (175g/2 cups)

Milk: 3 pints (1.75 litres/7½ cups)
Granulated sugar: 1 lb (450g)

★ Most convenient for brewing coffee are jugs of 3 pint (1.75 litres/7½ cups) capacity each holding 12 × 5 oz (150ml/²/₃ cup) cups of coffee. They will each need 3 level tbsp instant coffee.

★ Most convenient for tea are pots of ½ gallon (2.5 litres/10 cups) capacity each holding 16 × 5 oz (150ml/²/₃ cup) cups of tea. They will need 2 oz (50g/²/₃ cup) tea bags (allows for second cups). Have extra hot water in insulated or ordinary jugs or electric kettles for adjusting the strength of the tea.

★ Have the serving table for the tea and coffee well away from where the cakes are being sold, so that the goods are not obscured by people waiting to be served.

★ For ease in serving, arrange biscuits on a few large trays or wicker baskets rather than on a number of smaller serving plates, and pass them round as the guests drink and chat.

Suggestions for items to bake for sale
Quiches: These are popular because they are easy to carry and can provide an evening meal for the family.

Cakes: All these cakes are easy to carry and keep well with or without a freezer.

Pointers to success:
★ Place the cakes and quiches on paper or foil plates and cover neatly with film. It is worth buying attractive labels on which to write the description and price.

★ Always indicate on the label whether the quiche or cake has been freshly baked or frozen.

The Drinks Party

The drinks or cocktail party is one of the most versatile ways in which to entertain, as it can be equally successful as an impromptu get-together for a dozen close friends, or as a formal reception for as many guests as space will allow. Therefore I have not specified the number of guests, for each menu can be adapted for greater or smaller numbers.

What you serve will depend to a great extent on the assistance available, so besides giving menus a seasonal flavour, I have also divided them into those which need extra help and those which can be managed alone. Advice is also given on how much of the different foods to allow for each guest and how to adjust specific recipes accordingly.

I think that two hours is the maximum time that it is comfortable to stand and chat, and would suggest a morning drinks party from 11 a.m. to 1 p.m., or from noon to 2 p.m. if you are providing more substantial food that can take the place of a meal. For an evening party, from 6 to 8 p.m. or from 8.30 to 10.30 p.m. can be equally successful.

The question of assistance will depend to a large extent on the formality of the occasion and the number of guests. It is quite easy to cater for up to 50 guests with family help alone. Beyond that, professional assistance of some kind is really essential. If the room is large and refreshments are laid out on a buffet, then help will only be needed to pass round hot foods. If, however, there is a larger crowd and no room for a table, waitresses will be needed to circulate with trays of titbits. If there is food to be freshly fried or baked, then it is advisable to engage freelance staff who specialize in this type of party. They will often be able to give you guidance on quantities, and will help with both the pre-preparation and the service of food, as well as the clearing up afterwards.

A competent amateur can run a bar for up to 50 guests, but beyond that number a professional barman is essential. He will also be able to advise on the amount of drink to order, and may have a contact from whom you can borrow or hire glasses and order the drinks on a sale or return basis.

Part of the charm of a drinks party lies in the fact that it is easy to pass from one group to another. So the room should be as clear of furniture as possible, with chairs and sofas pushed into the corners for those who want to have a brief sit down. Don't ask more guests than the room will hold, for, while it is essential to have enough guests to fill the room comfortably, there must also be enough space for them to move round easily.

The drink is a matter of taste, but from a practical point of view, it is much simpler to serve one basic drink such as a sparkling wine cocktail, red, white or rosé wine, kir or pink champagne (see p.553), with short drinks, soft drinks and fruit and vegetable juices for those who prefer them.

Whether it is hot or cold, elaborate or simple, the food should always be easily held in the hand. To follow the savouries, it is nice to serve something fruity and something sweet, and, if numbers allow, a cup of coffee is also very welcome.

Drink – A Guide to Quantities

If possible, arrange to have the drinks on a sale or return basis – many wine merchants will do this if the quantity is large enough – so that you can always have a comfortable reserve. The quantity drunk will depend on many different factors – the time of the year, the temperature of the room, the kind of food served and the age of the guests. However, as a rough guide, allow 1/3-1/2 bottle of wine per person.

Drinks for 50

Here is a guide I have found reliable for a party serving a sparkling wine cocktail or white, red or rosé wine as the main drink.

For champagne, or sparkling wine cocktails

15-18 bottles
1 bottle 3 star brandy
1 bottle angostura bitters
lb (450g) sugar lumps

1 jar (8oz/225g) maraschino
  cherries
6 oranges (for garnish)

Red, white or rosé wine
The price, as well as personal preference, will probably guide your choice.
18-20 bottles

General drinks

1 bottle whisky
1 bottle gin
1 bottle vodka
1 bottle brandy
12 bottles ginger ale
12 bottles bitter lemon

6 bottles tonic water
6 cans beer
2 bottles cordial
2 × 43 oz (1075ml) cans tomato
  juice
Soda water

Etceteras

100 cocktail sticks (extra as
  needed for food on sticks)
8 dozen cocktail-size paper
  napkins
Large pack each oval dish papers

  and doilies
7 dozen champagne flutes (borrow
  from wine merchants)
Assorted glasses for short and
  long drinks

Food – A Guide to Quantities

Number of items of food to allow for each guest
As with the drink it is impossible to give precise quantities for this kind of party. However, from experience I have worked out the following rule of thumb. For each guest allow:

4-5 canapés and closed sandwiches and 2 small rolled sandwiches.

2-3 hot snacks (depending on size) as well as assorted dips and nibbles.

2-3 biscuits or pastries (depending on size).

Remember that almost all freshly-made food can be frozen if extra to requirements.

To work out the quantity of food required for any particular menu

Follow quantities given in specific recipes, adjusting them according to the number of guests. Many of the recipes used in this chapter are given for either 12 or 50 guests, so it is not difficult to adapt them. For further guidance see chapter on Cooking for 50, p.555ff.

For canapés and sandwiches, work out the total number required according to the number of guests, then adjust the quantity of spreads or toppings accordingly.

The following information may be helpful

1 long French stick (18 inches/45cm) cuts into 50-60 slices.
1 × 7 oz (200g) packet of savoury crackers contains 40-50.
1 large sliced loaf contains approx. 25-30 slices, according to thickness.
A spread containing 6-8 oz (175-225g) of cream cheese, minced fish or liver is enough for 40-50 canapés.
$1/2$-$3/4$ lb (225-350g) sliced meat or poultry and 1 large sliced loaf makes approx. 50 tiny closed sandwiches ($1/4$ of a large slice).

To make canapés and sandwiches in advance

Always cover tightly with film or foil and refrigerate or leave in a cool place.
Open French bread canapés: Make up to 4 hours in advance.
Closed sandwiches: Make up to 4 hours in advance.
Savoury cracker or toast canapés: Make up to 1 hour in advance.
Rolled sandwiches: Make not less than 2 hours but up to 12 hours in advance (in which case cover with foil).

If you do not wish to follow the menus suggested in this chapter, here is a selection of 'finger foods' listed under their different categories:

Dips, all with crudités

Canapés
Cream Cheese Pâté or Spread p.515
Cream Cheese and Pineapple Spread p.516
Cream Cheese and Walnut Spread p.516
Egg and Olive Butter p.516
Gaffelbiter, Tomato and Cucumber p.516
Smoked Salmon Sandwich Spread p.517
Smoked Salmon with Lemon p.517
Smoked Mackerel Sandwich Spread p.517
Salmon Mayonnaise p.221

Rolled sandwiches
Asparagus Rolls p.518
Egg and Olive Rolls p.516
Mackerel, Kipper or Smoked Salmon Rolls p.517
Smoked Salmon Rolls using slices of fish p.517

Closed sandwiches
Pastrami or Tongue on white or rye bread p.520
Chicken p.520
Chicken Liver Pâté p.520
Turkey p.521
Tuna p.521

Hot and cheesey
Syrian Sesame Cheese Puffs p.521
Hot Cheese Crisps p.522
Petites Gougères p.525

Savoury tartlets
Petites Quiches Lorraines p.523
Olive and Anchovy p.523
Cheese and Onion p.524
Miniature Pizza p.524

Other hot snacks
Stuffed Aubergine (Eggplant) or Courgette (Zucchini) Slices p.526
Chinese Chicken Bites p.527
Fried Chicken Titbits p.528
Pasteles p.528
Spanish Fried Pies p.529

A Drinks Party in Spring or Summer with help in the Kitchen (any number)

A variety of tiny open sandwiches is complemented by slivers of crisp fried fish, hot cheese puffs and miniature pizzas. There are fruit kebabs to refresh the palate and delicious biscuits and pastries are served with coffee.

F **Miniature Pizzas**   p.524
R **Melon and Grape Kebabs**   *below*
F **Nutty Butter Crisps**   p.452
F **Chocolate Nut Fingers**   p.450
F **Syrian Date Cakes**   p.426

Pointers to success:

★ See pp.111-13 for a guide to quantities.

★ Arrange the äioli in small bowls and place around the room with crudités and other nibbles. For a large party, arrange bolws on platters, surround with crudités and crisps, and pass round.

★ Have anchovies, tomatoes, cress, fresh and pickled cucumber for garnishing the canapés.

★ A fine textured loaf is much easier for rolled sandwiches than one with a coarse, open texture. The rolls keep better if made and refrigerated several hours in advance (or even overnight).

★ Goujonettes must be served not more than 15 minutes after they have been fried (though they can be kept hot for half an hour in a low oven), so it is essential to have help in the kitchen.

★ Petites gougères taste best if heated from frozen (as described in the recipe) and served within 30 minutes.

★ Miniature pizzas are nicest served warm as they are difficult to eat when too hot.

★ Melon and grape kebabs: Allow 1 large ripe melon and ¼lb (125g) grapes for each 12 guests. Remove the rind, cut in 1 inch (2.5cm) cubes and spear on cocktail sticks alternately with halved and de-seeded (or seedless) grapes.

★ Arrange the biscuits and Syrian date cakes in concentric circles on trays.

A Drinks Party in Spring or Summer without help in the Kitchen (any number up to 50)

As there is no extra help, all the food is either served cold or briefly reheated in the oven. A variety of canapés are made with either French bread or savoury biscuits (crackers). Home-made cheese biscuits (crackers) are served instead of crisps or other nibbles. There is a sweet ending with individual fruit meringues, warm Danish pastries, and meltingly tender nut biscuits served with coffee.

F Cheese Twists   p.536
   Nuts and raisins
   Calamata olives

Canapés
   R Cream Cheese and Pineapple   p.516
   R Cream Cheese Dip   p.515
   R Smoked Cod's Roe Pâté   p.135
   R Egg Spread with Anchovy   *below*
   R Gaffelbiter, Tomato and Cucumber   p.516
   R Petites Quiches Lorraines   p.523
   F Individual Berry Pavlovas   p.372
   F Vanilla Kipferl   p.453
   F Bought Danish pastries

Pointers to success:
★ See pp.111-13 for a guide to quantities.
★ The gaffelbiter is especially nice on savoury biscuits (crackers).
★ Omit the olives from the egg and olive butter (p.516). Instead, garnish the canapés with strips of anchovy.
★ The pastry for the petites quiches lorraines can be rolled and cut in advance, then frozen, or refrigerated for up to 2 days in advance (separate each layer with greaseproof paper or film). Make the filling, then fill and bake the quiches earlier in the day so that they will need only brief reheating before being served. Of course, if you have someone to watch the oven, by all means make them fresh.
★ Follow the recipe for the individual berry pavlovas, but shape the meringue into individual 'cups' each about 2½ inches (4cm) in diameter, with sides about 1 inch (2.5cm) high and hollowed in the centre. This can be done using a pastry bag and a coarse rose tube or with two spoons. Bake the cases for 40-45 minutes at the temperature given – when ready, they will be crisp and come easily off the greased tray. Fill with the berry syllabub.
★ If you wish to make the vanilla kipferl well in advance, store in an airtight tin at room temperature for 3 or 4 days to develop the flavour and then freeze.

A Drinks Party in Autumn or Winter with Help (any number)

A variety of hot savouries are cooked fresh, to augment dainty closed sandwiches. An unusual touch is added by miniature potato fritters served on cocktail sticks. Cubes of fresh pineapple make a refreshing contrast to the mince tarts.

R	Guacamole with crisps and savoury biscuits (crackers)	p.513
	Salted nuts	
R/F	Pastrami Sandwiches on rye bread	p.520
F	Pickled Tongue Sandwiches on white bread	p.520
R	Chicken Liver Pâté on toast squares	p.520
	Chinese Chicken Bites	p.527
	Stuffed Aubergine (Eggplant) or Courgette (Zucchini) Slices	p.526
F	Latkes on Sticks	p.558
	Fresh Pineapple with	
F/R	Raspberry Sauce	*below*
F	Warm mince tarts	p.426

Pointers to success:

★ See pp.111-13 for a guide to quantities. As they are so small, count two chicken bites as one savoury.

★ As guacamole is a rather soft dip, it needs a scoop like a crisp or biscuit (cracker) rather than a dipper like raw vegetable sticks.

★ As neither the chicken bites nor the vegetable slices need to be served hot off the pan, frying can start as soon as the guests arrive.

★ Latkes on sticks should be served freshly cooked. Start to fry them when the party is well under way.

★ *Fresh pineapple with raspberry sauce*: For 20 people, you will need 1 large pineapple and ½ pint (275ml/1¼ cups) of raspberry purée. Cut the pineapple into chunks and arrange on cocktail sticks. Pass round on a tray with a bowl of the raspberry sauce (purée with a squeeze of lemon or tablespoon of kirsch).

A Drinks Party in Winter without Help in the Kitchen (any number up to 50)

This menu is built round a variety of meat and poultry sandwiches, with two easy-to-serve hot dishes – little meat pies and chicken in pastry cases. Fresh fruit and a delicious honey cake provide a refreshing yet satisfying contrast.

R	Green Goddess Dressing with	p.335
	Crudités and crisps	p.510
	Salted peanuts and raisins	
	Assorted savoury nibbles (bought)	
R	Tongue and Pickled Cucumber Sandwiches	p.520
R	Turkey and Cranberry Jelly Sandwiches	p.520
R	Chicken Liver Pâté Sandwiches or Toasts	p.520
F/R	Pasteles (meat pies)	p.528
	Bouchées with Sherried Chicken Filling	p.583
	Bowl of grape clusters and small crisp apples	
	Tiny squares of Honey and Spice Cake	p.471

Pointers to success:
★ See pp.111-13 for a guide to quantities.
★ Both the pasteles and the chicken filling for the bouchées can be reheated together in a moderate oven (make sure the filling is in a covered dish). Alternatively, the filling can be reheated in a double saucepan on top of the stove. Start to reheat the bouchée cases only when the filling has heated up – they will only need 5 minutes, and another 5 minutes to heat together with the filling.

An Impromptu Drinks Party (any number)

This menu has been planned for the minimum of work – say 2 or 3 pairs of willing hands and 3 hours' preparation.

	Stuffed and calamata olives, mixed salted nuts, cheesey nibbles	
R	Cheese, Pineapple and Cherry Kebabs	p.535
R	Cheese, Mandarin and Cherry Kebabs	p.535
F/R	Avocado Dip with Smoked Mackerel, crisps and crudités	p.513

	Canapés of French bread or savoury crackers	p.515
	Gaffelbiter, tomato and cucumber	p.516
R	Tuna garnished with stuffed olives	p.535
R	Cream Cheese and Pineapple Spread	p.516
R	Asparagus Rolls	p.518
	Celebration Fruit Cake or bought cake cut in squares	p.477
	Large bowl of satsumas	
	Coffee and whipped cream	

Pointers to success:

★ See pp.111-13 for a guide to quantities.

★ The cheese for the kebabs can be cut in cubes the day before, then packed in an airtight plastic container until required.

★ Recrisp French bread that has been in the freezer by putting it in a quick oven (it can still be frozen) until it feels crisp. Allow to cool completely before cutting into slices.

★ Make the asparagus rolls before the other sandwiches so that they have a chance to 'set' in a cool place.

★ Canned fruit cake is excellent to keep in stock for the impromptu party.

★ Use whipping cream for the coffee – double cream has too high a fat content. Whip the cream only until it hangs on the whisk – don't let it go buttery.

A Drinks Party Before a Dance, Theatre or Dinner Party (8-12)

This is an informal meal of savoury titbits that is suitable for a smaller group who are then going on to another event. The guests help themselves to hot savouries, cold pâté and dips, with choice of fresh fruit in season. This menu can also serve as a first course before a visit to a restaurant.

R	Olive and Anchovy Tartlets	p.523
F	Petites Gougères	p.527
F	Spanish Deep-Fried Pies	p.529
R	Smoked Mackerel Mousse	p.135
F/R	Avocado Dip, crudités	p.513
R	Aubergine (Eggplant) Herb Dip, crisps	p.512

119

R   **Spiced Mushrooms**   p.329
      French bread and butter
      Fruit in season – grapes, cherries, plums,
         satsumas

To drink:
      Kir   p.553

Pointers to success:
★ See pp.111-13 for a guide to quantities.
★ Reheat the gougères and the tartlets just before the guests are expected. They do not need to be piping hot when served.
★ If there is someone in the kitchen, the Spanish pies can be fried when convenient; otherwise fry them just before the guests arrive, and keep them hot in a low oven as suggested in the recipe.
★ Pile the mackerel mousse into one pottery bowl. The guests scoop out a portion on to their plates and eat it with the French bread – with the help of a knife to spread it.
★ Serve only small fruit that can be eaten with the fingers and does not need a knife.
★ The kir should be made up in a large jug and chilled well. Keep some chilled wine in the fridge and a measure to hand so that more can be quickly made up if required.

Part 2

How to Use the Recipes

Solid measures are first given in spoons, pounds and ounces.
Liquid measures are first given in spoons, pints or fluid ounces. In the brackets the first figure given is the metric equivalent and the second figure given is the American equivalent measured in cups, e.g.
3 oz (75g/¹/₃ cup) – solid measure
¹/₄ pint (150ml/²/₃ cup) – liquid measure

American equivalent ingredients are given in brackets e.g.
glacé (candied) cherries
double (heavy) cream

Temperatures are first expressed as a gas number and then in degrees, e.g. **Gas No. 3, 325°F, 170°C.**

Measurements are first given in inches and then in centimetres, e.g. **2 in (5cm).**

Spoon measures As I find the use of millilitres to express spoon capacity unnecessarily complicated, I have used household tablespoons and teaspoons throughout. All spoon measures are level. As the difference in volume is so small I have assumed British and American spoons to be interchangeable. However, some adjustment in the quantity of seasonings may be necessary to suit individual tastes.

Note on metric equivalents used in the book In calculating the metric equivalents, I have worked out the *exact* equivalent and then rounded it up or down to the nearest multiple of 25, e.g.

Ounces to Grammes

Imperial oz	Exact conversion grams	Metric equivalent grams	+ − grams
4	113.40	125	+11.60
8	226.80	225	−1.80

Fluid Ounces to Millilitres

Imperial fl oz	Exact conversion millilitres	Metric equivalent millilitres	+ −
6	170.46	175	+4.54
10	284.10	275	−9.10

In all cases there is less than ½ ounce or ½ fluid ounce difference between the imperial and metric measures. This is not enough to make other than a trifling difference (in, for example, seasoning) to the recipe. *However, it is not advisable to mix imperial and metric measures in the same recipe, as this may cause an imbalance in the proportions of solid to liquid ingredients.*

Use of dairy and non-dairy ingredients Some people, whether for religious or dietary reasons, may not wish to mix dairy and non-dairy dishes in the same meal, or indeed to use dairy products at all. For this reason, wherever it is applicable, I have given non-dairy equivalents for dairy foods. For example, margarine or oil in place of butter, non-dairy cream instead of whipping cream. In some cases, where an adjustment of the recipe itself is necessary I have given both a dairy and a non-dairy version of the particular dish.

Use of artificial sweeteners Providing the sugar in a recipe is not essential to the texture of the finished dish (as for example it is in most cakes and biscuits) artificial low calorie sweeteners can often be satisfactorily substituted. They are particularly successful in salad dressings, soups and drinks. Follow the manufacturer's guide to quantities.

Note: In each recipe

F   indicates a dish that can be prepared and frozen in advance.

R   indicates any ingredient or a complete dish that can be prepared and refigerated in advance (unless a different time scale is given in the 'pointers to success' or the recipe itself).

L   (used infrequently) indicates length of time a dish may be kept in the larder.

The Hors d'oeuvre or tasty starter

The invention of the hors d'oeuvre is generally credited to the ancient Romans, who discovered that the oil which is a main ingredient of many recipes (and is still evident in the cold dressed vegetables served in Italian restaurants today) can form an effective barrier to the too rapid absorption of pre-prandial alcohol. A similar reason motivated the development of the Russian 'zakuski' and the German 'forspeise', the cold tables that preceded the vodka and schnapps party in Imperial times. More recently, however, the tasty starter has become recognized as an appetite stimulant. For this reason it is important that it should only form the prelude to the main course, but never overwhelm it either in flavour or quantity.

A successful starter must tease the eye as well as the palate, so presentation is of supreme importance, and I have given detailed advice on this in each case.

In this chapter there is a wide variety of hors d'oeuvre, including the traditional pâtés, smoked fish and dressed vegetables, as well as the more 'modern' salad and fruit starters in the North American tradition.

With very few exceptions (mainly savoury mousses and pâtés), the hors d'oeuvre does not take kindly to freezing, but if it is to be served cold, it does need a period under refrigeration to mature in flavour.

Fruity Beginnings

A sweet/sour fruit starter is a welcome beginning to a rich main course, as the tartness clears the palate for the more complicated flavours to follow.

The Grapefruit

The characteristic blend of tartness and sweetness which has made the grapefruit so popular as a breakfast food also makes it delicious as a starter for a winter's night meal. For family-style eating it can be a simple grapefruit on the half shell, grilled till bubbly under a light coating of brown sugar or apricot conserve, or the peeled fruit segmented and slightly sweetened in a fruit cup. For a dinner party, however, the shells can be enriched with sherry or liqueur and the segments blended with fruit of a contrasting flavour and texture. In all cases, however, grapefruit should be served chilled but not iced: one hour under refrigeration is all that is required.

The selection of the fruit

If you are great grapefruit eaters – or have a friendly neighbour to go halves with you – it makes good sense to buy your grapefruit by the case. Order it in advance so that your greengrocer can bring it fresh from the market on the appointed day. Most greengrocers will split the difference between the wholesale and retail price. Do specify the size you require: the largest grapefruit (which are packed 40 to the case) are ideal for cutting into segments; but for more general use the slightly smaller '48s' are probably better value – the ratio of skin to flesh does seem a little higher on the larger fruit. Keep a week's stock of fruit in the larder cupboard and the remainder of the stock under cooler conditions – a dry garden shed or the bottom of the refrigerator are ideal as they duplicate the temperature (about 5°C) at which the fruit is shipped.

The knife for the job

This year I have been experimenting with cutting the fruit into segments, a job for which an especially sharp and convenient-sized knife is essential. The best one I have found is a 'tomato' knife made by the Swiss firm of Victorinox. This has a 4½ inch (12cm) serrated blade of incredible sharpness and comes complete with its own protective plastic sheath. The knife is not cheap but it's made from a very high grade of stainless steel and is likely to last at least a generation.

To peel the fruit

If the fruit is to be cut into segments, every bit of the peel and in particular the bitter pith must be removed. The most effective way to do this is to remove both at once by using your knife in a circular sawing motion round and round the fruit. To remove the segments, lay the fruit on a board, hold it firmly with one hand then cut into each section between the pith. The sections will drop out cleanly, completely free of pith

A compote made in this way is vastly superior to the canned variety.

To sweeten it
For calorie watchers the fruit is quite sweet enough to eat as it is, or with the addition of a few sections of orange or tangerine. But really to bring out the flavour I think it is better marinated in a light syrup of sugar and water. Alternatively the fruit can be very lightly powdered with icing (confectioners') sugar (to dissolve without added water), and then sweetened with fresh orange juice just before serving.

Fresh Grapefruit Cup with Grapes

Serves 8 F 4 months (leave ½ inch/1 cm headroom in plastic container)

4 grapefruit	4 oz (125g/½ cup) sugar
¼ pint (150ml/⅔ cup) water	8 oz (225g) sweet grapes

Put the sugar and water into a small pan and heat until the sugar dissolves. Leave to cool whilst the grapefruit are peeled and segmented. Put the fruit into a bowl and pour over the syrup. Leave at room temperature, then 1 hour before serving add the halved and pipped grapes. Chill. Serve in glass dishes.

Note: A tablespoon of maraschino liqueur (*not* the synthetic juice from cocktail cherries) is an excellent addition.

Grapefruit and Tuna Cocktail

This uses the segments but in a delicious salad starter instead of a syrup.

Serves 6-8
4 grapefruit
Shredded Chinese leaves

128

Tuna salad:

2 × 7 oz (200g) cans best quality
  tuna
4 stalks celery, finely sliced
4 level tbsp each mild mayonnaise
  and soured cream (use
  home-made mayonnaise
otherwise check jar contents
list as you do not want it
vinegary)
Pinch of salt and pepper
Good pinch of curry powder

Peel and segment the grapefruit (one orange may be included for
extra colour). Blend the mayonnaise with the soured cream and
seasonings, then add the drained and flaked tuna (keep it a little
chunky for texture) and the celery. Taste, and add more
mayonnaise or seasoning if you feel it necessary ... the tuna
should be well moistened but not sloppy.

Arrange a bed of shredded Chinese leaves at the bottom of six
or eight shallow glass bowls, salad bowls or on plates. Divide the
salad between them and surround it with grapefruit sections. Just
before serving garnish with a sprig of fresh watercress, a stuffed
olive or a sprinkle of paprika.

The Melon

There is a huge variety of melons available, each with a
characteristic flavour derived from the soil of its native land.
Whatever the variety, however, a melon must be fully ripe before
it is cut, for once opened it will not mature further. Some melons,
such as the honeydew, can be tested for ripeness by gentle
pressure on the neck (or blossom) end, which gives gently when
fully ripe. Others, like the Galia, turn from green to yellow; whilst
yet others of the cantaloup type – such as the Ogen and Charentais
– develop a glorious musky odour. To be on the safe side always
purchase melons at least 2 days before they are needed. Once
ripened, they can be held for several days under refrigeration.
However, they should never be served *over-chilled,* as this will
destroy the delicate flavour.

Whole Ogen, Galia, Cantaloup or Charentais-type Melons

As these have a thin skin and a naturally small circumference, you
should allow 1 melon per person. The ideal fruit is the size of a
grapefruit, and is sold 12 to the box. Allow 1 large orange for each
6-8 servings.

Take a sliver of rind off the bottom of each melon so it will sit evenly on the plate. Take off a small 'cap' of rind (if possible vandyke it with zig-zag cuts), scoop out the seeds and put them with any free juice into a sieve over a bowl, reserving the juice. Sweeten this juice with a sprinkle of caster (superfine) sugar and a squeeze of lemon juice, and divide among the melons, replacing the cap and propping it up at an angle with a thick section of orange-on-the-skin. Chill 1 hour.

Arrange on individual glass plates, if possible sitting on a large leaf or with a delicate garland of flowers.

Minted Melon Cocktail
Serves 8 F

1 large Ogen or honeydew melon (6 to a box size)
Juice of 1 lemon
2-3 level tbsp caster (superfine) sugar

4 mint leaves, chopped
For garnish: Fresh sprigs of mint, 16 loganberries or raspberries

Halve the melon and remove the seeds, then scoop out the flesh with a ball-maker and put in a bowl. The flesh near the skin which cannot be made into balls should be scooped out and put in a separate bowl. Juice the lemon, add the sugar and chopped mint, and heat until the sugar has dissolved, then pour over the melon balls. Leave at room temperature for an hour for the juices to flow, stirring once or twice. Taste, and if juice is not sweet/sour enough add more lemon juice or sugar as required. Refrigerate the melon.

Just before serving, divide the melon *pulp* between 8 glass dishes – avocado dishes are ideal – then cover with the melon balls and syrup. Garnish with a sprig of fresh mint and two berries.

VARIATION 1
Melon and Mandarin Cocktail:
Add 1 can drained mandarins to the melon balls.

VARIATION 2
Melon and Grape Cocktail:
Add the juice of 1 orange to the lemon juice and 1 lb (450g) seedless or de-seeded grapes to the melon balls (½ lb/225g each of black and green grapes are especially pretty).

Serve in stemmed glasses.

Honeydew Melon Wedges in Ginger Sauce

It is better to buy 1 large rather than 2 small honeydew melons as the ratio of fruit to rind is much greater. A really superb honeydew melon needs no embellishment as the flavour is very satisfying in itself, but other less succulent fruit will benefit from the following treatment which helps to draw out the natural juices of the fruit.

Serves 6-8

1 large ripe honeydew melon	2 teasp ground ginger
3 tbsp caster (superfine) sugar	Sweet black grapes for garnish

Cut the melon into 6 or 8 wedges and discard the seeds. Take each wedge in turn and with a sharp serrated knife, cut between the flesh and the skin, then cut vertically into 1 inch (2.5cm) slices, leaving on the skin. Arrange the wedges on a serving plate in a sunburst pattern.

Mix the sugar and ginger and divide between the slices, sprinkling it in an even layer. Leave 1 hour at room temperature, then chill for $\frac{1}{2}$-1 hour before serving.

Decorate with small bunches of black grapes.

Watermelon Basket

This is delicious and refreshing on a very hot day as the melon has a water content of 92 per cent.

Slice off the top of a watermelon and scoop out the flesh in as large sections as possible. Vandyke the edge of the melon by cutting a serrated edge with a sharp knife all the way round. Use a melon ball scoop, or cube the flesh, and place in a bowl, removing as many seeds as you have patience for. Sprinkle with lemon or lime juice and very little caster (superfine) sugar. Return to the decorated shell and chill very well, for several hours.

Serve either in bowls or with cocktail sticks for each guest to spear a ball or cube for himself.

ALTERNATIVE PRESENTATION
Halve the melon, cut in slices $\frac{1}{2}$ inch (1.5 cm) thick and remove the skin. Lay on a flat platter, sprinkle with lemon juice and sugar and chill thoroughly. Serve speared with cocktail sticks.

Even more simply, cut in thick sections, leave on skin, chill thoroughly, then let each person get on with it (a presentation only suitable for outdoor eating!).

Pineapple and Mango Cocktail with Kirsch

A refreshing starter to a hearty main course. This can also be served as a dessert, using a sweet liqueur such as Amaretto or Curaçao instead of the dry kirsch.

Serves 6-8

1 large, ripe pineapple	Approx 2 tbsp kirsch (maraschino
2 large, very ripe mangos	may be substituted)

Cut a thin slice off the bottom of the pineapple so that it can be held upright on a board, then use a sharp knife (a breadknife is ideal) to remove the peel, cutting from top to bottom. You should now have a cube of solid pineapple. Cut this in half and remove the core, then cut the flesh first into ¼ inch (0.5cm) slices and then into ¼ inch (0.5cm) cubes. Peel the mango and cut into cubes of the same size.

Combine the two fruits then stir in the liqueur. Taste, and add more liqueur if required. Only add sugar if absolutely necessary as a really ripe pineapple should have sufficient natural sweetness for a starter. The kirsch flavour should be there but not so strongly as to overwhelm the flavour of the fruit.

Chill well, then serve in glass bowls, garnished with a sprig of mint.

Pâtés and Savoury Mousses

Although liver and poultry pâtés have been popular for many years (at least in restaurant cookery), the savoury mousse is a more recent idea which, emanating from countries such as Greece, Turkey and Israel, has become in the space of a very few years almost a culinary cliché. However, as it stimulates the appetite with its spicy flavour and pleases the eye with its lovely pastel colourings, it does make one of the best of all beginnings for a special meal.

When preparing this kind of dish it is important to pay equal attention to both the consistency and the taste. It is vital therefore, once the right *texture* has been achieved, that the food is most carefully *tasted*, and if necessary re-seasoned, until the blend is just right. I have done this when developing the recipes, but your taste may be different.

The presentation of what is essentially a shapeless cream is especially important and I have indicated in each recipe how I think it is best served, whether in miniature soufflé dishes or cocottes, as a 'cocktail', or with salad accompaniment. All the recipes in this section can, however, also be served more informally as a dip with crudités, or on biscuits or 'toasts' as an accompaniment to drinks.

Aubergine (Eggplant) Caviar – Serbian Style

This unusual vegetable pâté (known as Patliçan Salatasi in Turkey, Chatzilim in Israel) is made all over the former Ottoman Empire, where it is served as an accompaniment to grills and kebabs as well as a first course. In the traditional recipe the vegetables are grilled over charcoal, giving a characteristic 'smoky' flavour to the dish. However, I find an electric or gas grill, or even oven-baking, gives very satisfactory results.

Choose firm, glossy aubergines (eggplants) as dull and soft ones are sure to be stale. Refrigerate, wrapped tightly in foil or film, and they will then keep well for up to a week. Once cut, however, use immediately as they quickly oxidize and become discoloured.

Note: I do not advise *blending* this mixture as the texture becomes too smooth. If care is taken not to over-chop, one can use a food processor. Otherwise, use a large cook's knife or hachoir (a chopper with handle).

Serves 6-8 as a starter, 12 as a dip

2 large (1¹/₂ lb/675g) aubergines (eggplants)	3 tbsp olive oil
	1 level teasp salt
1 large or 2 medium green peppers	¹/₄ teasp black pepper
1 clove of garlic, crushed	2 tbsp finely chopped parsley
Juice of ¹/₂ lemon	

Bake the aubergines (eggplants) and the peppers (Gas No.7, 425°F, 220°C) for 30 minutes, or until the aubergines collapse and offer no resistance when pierced with a sharp knife (smaller aubergines may take less time). Wrap the vegetables in a tea towel or paper towel for 10 minutes, when the skin can easily be removed. Chop the pepper finely (discarding seeds and pith), then add the aubergine pulp and chop that. Add all the remaining ingredients gradually, blending and chopping them until you have a thick creamy purée. Spoon into a dish about 1 inch (2.5cm) deep and chill.

Serve garnished with sliced tomatoes and black olives.

Quantities for 25 as a dip

4 large aubergines (eggplants) –
   about 3 lb (1.25 kg)
2 medium cloves of garlic
2 level teasp salt

$^{1}/_2$ teasp black pepper
2 level tbsp chopped parsley
3-4 tbsp lemon juice
6 tbsp olive or corn oil

Avocado Pâté with Smoked Mackerel

This beautiful pale green pâté is given an unusual piquancy by the addition of slivers of smoked mackerel. Alternatively, the fish can be omitted and the pâté served with a mixture of crudités, such as carrot, celery and pepper sticks.

Note: Avocados that are to be puréed should feel very soft to gentle pressure when cradled in the hand. Most varieties will have brown spots – like bananas. If purchased while still hard, allow 4 days at room temperature (36 hours in airing cupboard) to ripen.

Serves 6-8 F 2 months (without fish)

$^{1}/_4$ onion (or 2 shallots) and 1
   green pepper, finely chopped
3 medium or 2 large fully ripe
   avocados, peeled, skinned and
   mashed to a purée
$^{3}/_4$ lb (350g/1$^{1}/_2$ cups) low fat
   cream cheese
3 tbsp lemon juice

1 level teasp salt, plenty of black
   pepper
1 tbsp chopped parsley
2 tbsp snipped chives
4 tbsp soured cream
6 oz (175g) (1 fat fillet) smoked
   mackerel, skinned and cut in
   bite-sized pieces

By hand: Beat all ingredients together (except fish) until well blended. By food processor: Chop onion and pepper, then add remaining ingredients (except fish) and process until well blended. The vegetables should retain some texture.

Stir in the skinned fish cut in ½ inch (1.25cm) slivers. Taste and add more seasoning if required. The texture should be like thick whipped cream.

Spoon into individual soufflé dishes or glass avocado bowls, or serve as a 'cocktail' on a bed of shredded Chinese leaves. Garnish with a lemon twist.

Smoked Cod's Roe Pâté

This is a simplified version of taramasalata that starts with a cod's roe paste instead of the unskinned smoked roe. Serve in tiny cocottes (pottery butter dishes are ideal) with hot pitta (Middle Eastern) bread. The pâté can also be mixed with the hard-boiled yolks when used as a stuffing for eggs.

6 oz (175g) cod's roe paste from a jar
½ clove of garlic
6 tbsp olive oil
1½ tbsp lemon juice
2 tbsp finely chopped parsley
¼ small onion
Black pepper to taste

Blender or food processor method: Put parsley, onion, garlic, pepper and lemon juice into the machine and process until the parsley is chopped, then add the cod's roe paste followed by the oil, a tablespoon at a time. Blend until like thick mayonnaise.

By hand: Chop onion and parsley finely. Crush the garlic to a paste. Put the cod's roe paste into a bowl and beat in half the oil until creamy, then add the lemon juice and the remaining oil a little at a time, whisking until creamy after each addition. Finally stir in the onion, garlic, parsley and black pepper.

Smoked Mackerel Mousse with Crudités

This has an unctuous texture and delicate flavour with just a little bite provided by the horseradish to contrast with the richness of the mackerel. It will keep for 3-4 days under refrigeration but I do not advise freezing because of the sour cream content.

The mousse:

2 large fillets smoked mackerel
(12 oz/350g)
1 carton (5 fl oz/150 ml/²⁄₃ cup)
soured cream
4 oz (125g/¹⁄₂ cup) cream cheese

2 oz (50g/¹⁄₄ cup) soft butter
1 tbsp lemon juice
2 teasp horseradish relish
10 grinds black pepper

Remove the skin from the fish and flake into a blender or food processor. Add all the remaining ingredients, and blend or process until smooth. Divide between individual soufflé dishes or cocottes. Cover with film and chill.

Just before serving, garnish with sliced stuffed olives and serve with buttered French bread and crudités.

The crudités:
Cut 2 large carrots, 2 green peppers and the heart of a celery into strips about 2 inches (5cm) long and ³⁄₈ inch (1cm) wide. Wrap in film or foil and chill well.

Serve a selection in a juice glass to each guest, or arrange individual glass dishes with the mousse en cocotte.

Chicken Liver Pâté

This is a creamy pâté that is very quickly made. It will keep for 3 days under refrigeration and gets better all the time. Rendered chicken fat can be made by leaving the fat from a boiling fowl in a low oven until liquid and then decanting into a glass jar. Store under refrigeration.

Serves 8

1 large (8 oz/225g) onion, finely
chopped
1 medium clove of garlic, crushed
2 oz (50g/¹⁄₄ cup) soft margarine,
or 3 tbsp rendered chicken fat
5-10 grinds (1 teasp) sea salt

20 grinds black pepper
Good pinch ground nutmeg
1 lb (450g) chicken livers
(quartered)
3 hard-boiled eggs, plus 1 extra
egg for garnish

This kind of liver pâté *can* be made with a mincer, but to get the right texture it should be made in a blender or (preferably) a food processor.

136

Hard-boil the eggs for 10 minutes then leave in the pan covered with cold water. Fry the onion and the garlic gently in the fat until a rich brown (this is important if the right depth of flavour is to be achieved). As the onion cooks, sprinkle it with the sea salt. Lift out onto a plate. In the same fat fry the livers until they are cooked through but do not allow them to become crisp. If preferred, grill the whole livers instead. Shell the 3 eggs and cut in half.

Put the onion and the garlic with their juices into the blender or food processor and process until smooth, then add the remaining ingredients and process again until smooth. Taste, and add more seasonings if necessary but remember the flavours will intensify over the next few hours. Turn into a terrine or oval gratin dish or divide between individual cocottes. Chill, covered with film, preferably overnight. Refrigerate the extra egg.

One hour before serving, remove the pâté from the refrigerator and leave at room temperature.

Just *before* serving, grate the remaining egg and use it to decorate the top of the pâté. Serve with warm French bread or slices of challah (Jewish plaited bread).

Pâté Maison

This is a smooth delicate pâté that is nicest accompanied with pickled gherkins and olives in the French manner. Serve it in scoops from the terrine, or turn out in a loaf shape and decorate with the stuffed olives and gherkins. Aim to make it 48 hours before it is required to allow the flavours to mature and blend together.

Serves 8 with second helpings F 2 months

2 oz (50g/¹/₄ cup) margarine, *or* 3 tbsp rendered chicken fat (see recipe above)

1 medium onion (5oz/125g) thinly sliced

¹/₂ lb (225g) each chicken and calf's (or lamb's) liver

2 tbsp brandy or medium sherry

1 medium clove of garlic, crushed

1 level teasp salt and 20 grinds black pepper

Pinch of allspice

2 medium bayleaves

Sauce:

½ pint (225ml/1¼ cups) chicken stock   4 tbsp flour
1 oz (25g/2 tbsp) margarine   2 eggs

Have chicken livers quartered, the other liver skinned and thinly sliced. Heat fat and cook the onion until golden then add the liver and continue to cook until the onion is caramelized (a rich brown) and the liver cooked through. If preferred, grill the liver and then add to the caramelized onion. Reserve.

Put all the sauce ingredients except the eggs into a pan and whisk together until smoothly thickened. Allow to bubble for 3 minutes, whisking constantly, then remove from the heat and drop in the two eggs, whisking briskly to incorporate them into the sauce without curdling. Put the liver mixture, the sauce, the seasonings (except the bayleaf) and the brandy or sherry into the blender or food processor and process until smooth.

Turn into a greased 2 lb (1kg) loaf tin or glazed earthenware terrine. Smooth level, then lay the bayleaves on top. Cover tightly with foil or a lid. Stand the dish in a baking tin containing 2 inches (5cm) of very hot water. Cook for 1½ hours at Gas No.2 (300°F, 150°C) until the pâté is firm to gentle touch and has begun to shrink away from the sides.

Cook well, then chill until required.

Salmon and Other Delicate Smoked Fish

Smoked fish of any kind makes a particularly beguiling start to a meal; it can also make one that is extremely expensive, as the freshly smoked Scotch salmon (still the finest in the world) commands a higher price than most expensive steak. However, nothing makes a meal more special than an hors d'oeuvre of hand-carved smoked salmon, with no more embellishment than a squeeze of lemon juice, a grind of black pepper and a plateful of paper-thin, very fresh brown bread spread with unsalted butter.

For such a presentation the salmon must be both fresh and fine, and as it has a shelf life of only 12 days, it is essential to buy it from a shop with a large and constant turnover, and then use it on the day of purchase. Though not to be compared (in my opinion) with the fresh, many brands of frozen smoked salmon do have an excellent flavour and are perfectly adequate served as part of a mixed hors d'oeuvre.

If the salmon is to be served alone, allow 1½-2 oz (40-50g) per serving; and 1 oz (25g) per serving as part of a mixed hors d'oeuvre.

Smoked Salmon and Ogen Melon Platter

This combines two incomparable flavours for a truly luxurious hors d'oeuvre.

Serves 8

2 large, very ripe, very fragrant Ogen (or the similar Galia) melons
2-3 fine slices smoked salmon per person (about 1-1½ oz/40-50g in total)

Lemon juice
Lemon wedges
Brown bread and butter

Slice the melon in crescents about ½ inch (1.5cm) thick and remove the seeds and skin. Sprinkle the salmon with lemon juice and leave for half an hour while the melon is chilling.

To serve – on each plate arrange 3 crescents of melon and 2-3 slices of smoked salmon. Garnish with lemon wedges, and serve with fine brown bread and butter.

Gravlax – Swedish Pickled Salmon

If you have a river teeming with salmon at the bottom of the garden, it might be feasible to smoke your own fish. However, for most people a far simpler and much more practical proposition is to pickle the salmon instead – a process which gives a very similar (though rather more delicately flavoured) result.

*If the salmon is pickled at the height of the season it is possible to achieve a very similar result at approximately a quarter the cost of commercial smoked salmon. Gravlax freezes extremely well. Serve it fresh with a delectable **Dill and Mustard Sauce** (see below).*

F 3 months   R 1 week

4 lb (1.75kg) fresh salmon (weight
    when filleted – approx 5½
    lb/2.5kg gross)
4 oz (125g) sea salt
4 oz (125g/½ cup) granulated
    sugar

40 white peppercorns
Olive oil
4 tbsp brandy (optional but
    delicious)
¼ pint (150ml/⅔ cup) chopped dill

Ask your fishmonger to clean, scale and fillet a fish. Do not wash, but wipe well.

Mix the salt, sugar, pepper and dill in a bowl.

Put a very large piece of double foil on a board, then lay the salmon fillets side by side, skin down. Brush the flesh of both fillets with olive oil. Cover one side of the salmon with an even layer of the salt mix – it should be half an inch (1cm) thick – if not then make some more. Moisten evenly with the brandy. Lay the second fish fillet carefully on top but with the shoulder part to the tail. In this way the thick part of the upper fillet will be resting on the thin part of the lower fillet so that the complete salmon will be an even thickness all the way through. Wrap firmly in the foil to make a compact package. It is advisable to lay foil package on a tray in order to catch any drips of brine that may come out of the parcel.

Put in refrigerator, away from the ice compartment, or in a cool larder – weighted down if possible with bricks – for 72 hours, turning after 24 hours. Unwrap and drain well.

To serve – cut like smoked salmon, but slightly thicker, with dill and mustard sauce.

To freeze Gravlax
Cut left-over salmon into ½ lb (225g) or 1 lb (450g) pieces as preferred. Wrap tightly in foil, then overwrap in a plastic bag.

Dill and Mustard Sauce

R 1 month

4 rounded tbsp mayonnaise (¼
    pint/150ml/⅔ cup)
1 level tbsp Dijon mustard
1 level tbsp clear honey

2 teasp soy sauce
⅛ teasp white pepper
2 teasp chopped dill (or more to
    taste as preferred)

Put the mayonnaise in a bowl and stir in all the remaining

ingredients. Leave covered for several hours for flavours to mingle and develop.

Serve with Gravlax. Also excellent as dip for crudités.

Note: If no mayonnaise is available, make sauce by mixing mustard with thick cream, sugar and cut up dill.

Smoked Mackerel Fillets with Avocado Mayonnaise

Allow one juicy smoked mackerel fillet (weight about 4 oz/125g) per serving. Do *not* use kippered mackerel, which needs cooking before it can be eaten. Keep tightly wrapped and refrigerated. One hour before serving, arrange on a platter (or individual plates) garnished with lemons cut in sixths. Serve with **Tartare Sauce** (see p.336) or this delicious sauce:

Avocado Mayonnaise

2 large very ripe avocados	3 tbsp lemon juice
2 tbsp mayonnaise	1 level teasp salt, speck pepper
2 tbsp thick cream, soured cream	$1/2$ level teasp sugar
or natural yoghurt	$1/2$ clove of garlic, crushed
3 tbsp oil	

Peel and stone the avocados, and cut each into four. Put into the blender or food processor with all the remaining ingredients and blend or process until smooth (about 30 seconds). By hand, mash the avocados with a fork, then gradually beat in all the remaining ingredients. Taste, and add more seasonings if required. Turn into a bowl, cover tightly with film and chill until required. May be made 2 or 3 days in advance.

VARIATION
Serve with this Quick Horseradish Sauce

5 oz (150ml/^{2}/3 cup) soured cream	Pinch of salt, 5 grinds black
4 tbsp prepared horseradish relish	pepper
$1/2$ teasp Worcestershire sauce	

Combine all the ingredients in a serving dish, cover and refrigerate for at least 1 hour.

Vegetables Choice and Whole

There are still a few choice vegetables which have only a limited season yet can meet any competition from their frozen counterparts. Cooked with care and partnered with a sauce or dressing designed to bring out their special flavour, these make one of the most unusual (if expensive) hors d'oeuvres. As taste and texture is of supreme importance, only the freshest vegetable of the choicest quality should be bought, and the cooking should be carried out with minute attention to detail. The result will be a superb and unmatched marriage of flavour and aroma.

As freshness is of the essence, I do not recommend freezing any dishes in this section.

Artichokes with Herb Cream Sauce

For this presentation choose the rounded French artichokes rather than the slimmer, more pointed Italian (or indeed Breton) ones which are more suitable for eating young and whole.

Choice artichokes feel weighty in the hand and the stalk should look green and fresh. They may be stored raw for several days if tightly wrapped in film before refrigeration.

To prepare: Two hours before serving, bend the stalk so that it breaks off and pulls out the coarse filaments at the base, which may then need to be trimmed level with a knife. Turn the artichoke on its side on a board and cut off the top ⅔ inch (2cm) using a strong sharp knife. Trim off the points of the remaining leaves with a pair of scissors. Wash well, and put into a very large pan of salted, boiling water. Simmer with the lid half-on for 35-40 minutes or until a leaf can be easily plucked out of the artichoke.

By now, the artichokes will have acquired their characteristic dark green colour. Drain thoroughly and cover with foil until required. (The artichoke should not be hot but tepid when served in this way.)

To serve, place each artichoke on a separate plate (special grooved artichoke plates are ideal), and serve with individual dishes of dressing. This can be as simple as creamily melted (but not oiled) butter (4 oz/125g/½ cup butter serves 8) acidulated with a squeeze of lemon juice, a vinaigrette similar to that served with **Avocados on the Half Shell** (p.149), or this:

Herb Cream Sauce

This is similar in texture to mayonnaise with a lovely colour and delicate flavour.

Serves 6-8

1 egg
2 tbsp wine vinegar
6 fl oz (175 ml/³/₄ cup) corn oil
4 tbsp scissored dill or a mixture of parsley, chives and a few sprigs of fresh tarragon
¹/₂ teasp sea salt

¹/₂ teasp dry mustard
Pinch of white pepper
5 fl oz (150ml/²/₃ cup) soured cream or half the quantity fresh cream, whipped
Lemon juice if required (if fresh cream is used)

Using a blender or food processor, put the egg, herbs, seasonings and vinegar into the container and process until thoroughly mixed and the herbs are finely chopped.

Start adding a third of the oil in a thin stream and when this has been thoroughly incorporated add the remainder of the oil then briefly beat in the soured or whipped cream. Taste, and add lemon juice if required – the flavour should be delicate.

Note: If the sauce is made by hand, use 2 egg yolks and a hand whisk, chopping the herbs separately. Any leftover sauce will keep for 4 days and is delicious with poached fish of any kind.

To serve: Put each artichoke on a large plate. The leaves are plucked out one at a time, dipped in sauce, then sucked to remove the flesh at the base. When all the leaves have been pulled out, the thistle-like 'choke' will be revealed. This must be cut off with a sharp knife to reveal the tender heart, which is then cut up with a knife and fork and dipped into the sauce.

Asparagus

Choice asparagus has a brief, expensive season, so it is worth taking great care in its selection and preparation, which is well repaid by its exquisite flavour and texture.

Choose a bundle with thick, green-tipped stalks, firm and fresh-looking. Allow 6-8 fat stalks per serving, more if they are thin. Untie the bundle and wash it, tips down, in a bowl under cold running water, then gently scrub it with a soft brush to remove the sand which clings to the tips. Break off the woody lower 2 inches (5cm) of the stalk – it seems to snap at just the right place, about 2 inches (5cm) below the green stem.

Scrape away the last inch (2.5cm) of scales on the lower stem using a small sharp knife, then re-tie the asparagus into a bundle of even length, using soft string. If you have no asparagus pan, leave a loop of string to make it easy to lift the cooked bundle from the pan.

Asparagus must be cooked 'al dente' – that is, it must have a tender head with a slightly chewy stalk, so that one can almost suck the juices out of it. To achieve this, it is necessary to steam the tender heads, whilst boiling the tougher stalks.

The pan: You can buy a special asparagus pan – a cylindrical pan with a perforated inner section that lifts out like a double boiler. But for most households, a percolator without the coffee container works just as well and is far cheaper (but as this vegetable has a characteristic and lingering odour, keep it only for asparagus!).

To cook: Put 4 inches (10cm) of boiling water into a pan, add the bundle of asparagus, tips to the top, close the lid and simmer for 15 minutes. To test whether done, taste one stalk – the tip should be tender without being mushy.

The sauce: While the asparagus is cooking, it is as well to get ready the sauce and the dish. The simplest sauce, and I think the best, is plain melted butter, although hollandaise sauce is often served.

Melted Butter Sauce

4 oz (125g/^{1}/$_2$ cup) butter   Few grains cayenne pepper
  (preferably unsalted)   Squeeze of lemon juice

Put the butter into a sauce boat and leave in a warm place (the warming oven or the side of the stove) so that the butter becomes liquid without oiling. Just before serving add the cayenne and lemon juice.

The asparagus dish: This can be as elaborate as a specially-designed entrée dish with a built-in tray on which the cooked asparagus is placed to drain; or it can be as simple as a flat platter with a linen napkin liner to hold excess moisture. I also use a rectangular terrine which, because it is deep and narrow, keeps the asparagus hot until the last stalk has been served.

To serve: Lay the steaming bundle of asparagus on the dish, untie the string and serve at once. Tepid asparagus is horrid. Six to seven flat stalks are quite sufficient for one serving, with a slice of French bread for mopping up the combined juices and the butter sauce.

Imam Bayeldi

The tale has been told often enough of the origins of this dish, but there is no doubt that when it is made with fresh, choice aubergines (eggplants), the dish is delicious enough to make an Imam swoon! It is essential to use olive oil and to allow the dish to rest overnight so that the aubergine absorbs the glorious flavours of the stuffing and sauce.

R

6-8 medium-sized oval aubergines (eggplants) (^{1}/$_2$ lb/225g)
3 tbsp currants
1 level teasp ground allspice, or a pinch of cinnamon
1 level teasp salt and 10 grinds of black pepper

2 tbsp chopped parsley
2 large onions
4 tbsp oil
Whole tomatoes drained from a 15 oz (425g) can

Sauce:

Olive oil and water to half-cover the aubergines (eggplants)
Juice of a large lemon (3 tbsp)

1 tbsp soft brown sugar
1 fat clove garlic and 1 bayleaf

Cut a deep slit lengthwise in the centre of each aubergine (eggplant), sprinkle inside with coarse salt and leave for one hour. Squeeze out any black juices, rinse under the cold tap and dab dry. Chop the onions finely, then sauté gently in the 4 tbsp oil until golden brown. Add the tomatoes, currants, allspice, salt and pepper and simmer gently until the mixture is thick but still juicy. Add the parsley. Cool, then use to stuff the slits in each aubergine.

145

Arrange the aubergines side by side in a shallow casserole, slit side up. Add oil and water to half cover the vegetables (use half and half of each). Pour over the lemon juice and sprinkle with sugar, adding the garlic and bayleaf to the liquid. Cover the dish and simmer very gently, either top of stove or in the oven (Gas No.3, 325°F, 160°C) for one hour, or until quite soft. Chill, preferably overnight.

To serve, lift from the sauce, spoon a little of it over each vegetable, and serve with bread or toast.

Champignons à la Grecque

There are many variations of the classic recipe, and this is a particularly delicious one. It is fragrant with herbs and spices and the mushrooms are bathed in a highly reduced aromatic sauce. To extract the maximum flavour from the herbs and spices it is a good idea to crush them coarsely using either the end of a rolling pin or a mortar and pestle.

Serves 8 (12 as part of a mixed hors d'oeuvre)

1¹/₂ lb (750g/9 cups) very white and fresh, firm button mushrooms	1 teasp coriander seeds, crushed
	1 crushed clove of garlic
	1 large bayleaf
6 tbsp olive oil	Good pinch of fennel
6 tbsp water	Large sprig each of parsley and
2 tbsp lemon juice	thyme (or pinch of dry thyme)
2 tbsp wine vinegar	¹/₂ teasp salt
2 teasp tomato purée	¹/₂ teasp sugar
12 crushed peppercorns	15 grinds of black pepper

Wipe the mushrooms with a damp cloth and cut the stalks level with the caps. (Keep these for other use.) Crush the seasonings (as described above) and put them with all the remaining ingredients except the mushrooms into a pan, bring to the boil, cover and simmer for 5 minutes. Uncover, put in the mushrooms (sliced only if too large), spoon the liquid over them, cover and simmer for 8-10 minutes, or until just tender. Remove the mushrooms to serving dish, using a slotted spoon. Boil the juice down till thick – there should be about 6 or 8 tbsp. Strain over the mushrooms and leave overnight. Serve in little saucers or gratin dishes.

Peppers in the Style of Piedmont (Peperoni alla Piemontese)

The peppers blend deliciously with the tomatoes and anchovies. They can be served with rye or brown bread, but are equally delicious as a 'relish' to serve with cold meat or fried fish.

Serves 6-8 **R**

8 medium squat green peppers
8 tomatoes, peeled, de-seeded and
   quartered; *or* 8 well drained,
   canned plum tomatoes
2 cans flat fillets of anchovies

2 medium cloves of garlic,
   crushed
6 tbsp olive oil
Chopped parsley

Cut peppers in half lengthwise. Remove all the seeds and white pith and arrange on a flat baking dish. Chop the anchovies finely and mix with the crushed garlic and the oil. Put two quarters of tomato in each pepper and spoon some of the oily mixture on top. Bake for 40 minutes at Gas No. 4 (350°F, 180°C) until softened but still slightly firm. Chill well. Sprinkle each pepper with chopped parsley.

Avocados on the Half Shell

Avocados that are to be served on the half shell should give only slightly to gentle all-over pressure when they are cradled in the hand. At this stage of ripeness, the flesh will be soft on the tongue, but will still have sufficient firmness of texture to enable it to be scooped out of the skin with a spoon. Riper avocados are too creamy for this kind of service and are better reserved for those recipes that require them to be puréed. (See **Avocado Pâté with Smoked Mackerel,** *p.513.)*

To be sure that the avocados are at the correct degree of ripeness, it is good policy to buy them well in advance – 3 or 4 days before they are required. If they are then fully ripe for the purpose, they can be refrigerated immediately; if not, they can be ripened at home in the fruit bowl and then refrigerated until they are required. Either method will ensure that they are in perfect condition when they are served, for once it is cut an avocado will not continue to ripen.

The Fuerte and Hass varieties are particularly suitable for serving on the half shell as they are oval in shape with a firm skin and buttery flesh.

Walnut oil (huile de noix) marries particularly well with the flavour of the avocado, but as it is very expensive and rather strong in flavour, it is best to combine it in the dressing with a cheaper, tasteless oil such as corn oil.

Avocado on the Half Shell with Herb and Walnut Oil Vinaigrette

Make the dressing several hours before it is required to allow the flavour to mature.

Serves 6-8

3-4 large, oval avocados

Dressing:

4 tbsp wine vinegar or cider vinegar

2 tbsp lemon juice

4 fl oz (125ml/½ cup) corn oil and 2 tbsp walnut oil, *or* 5 fl oz (150ml/⅔ cup) corn or mild olive oil

1 fat clove of garlic, crushed

2 level teasp caster (superfine) sugar

1 teasp Dijon mustard

2 tbsp very finely chopped shallots, spring onion (scallion) bulbs or mild onion

2 tbsp chopped fresh mixed herbs – parsley, chives, tarragon

1 level teasp sea salt

20 grinds black pepper

Put all the dressing ingredients into a large screw-top jar and shake together until thoroughly blended and thickened (about 1 minute). Leave at room temperature until required.

Half an hour before serving, cut the avocados in half and remove the stones. Spoon a little dressing into the stone cavity and then spread some on the surrounding flesh to prevent discolouration. Refrigerate.

Serve in avocado dishes from a platter or on individual dishes lined with fresh leaves. Pass the dressing at the table. The flesh is scooped out with an oval teaspoon. Serve with fine buttered brown bread or thinly sliced buttered French bread.

Avocado with Tuna on the Half Shell

In this presentation the flesh is scooped out in one piece, then cubed and marinated in the dressing with tuna and stuffed olives. It can then be served in the shell, spooned directly into avocado dishes, or in glasses on a bed of shredded lettuce.

Serves 6-8

3-4 medium avocados 2 × 7 oz/200g cans tuna, drained and roughly flaked
$^1/_4$ pint (150ml/$^2/_3$ cup) vinaigrette dressing (as for **Avocado on the Half Shell**, p.149)

2 level tbsp very finely chopped onion
4 oz (125g) sliced stuffed olives
2 tbsp lemon juice

Cut the avocados in half and remove the stones, then carefully scoop out the flesh. Cut into $^3/_8$ inch (1cm) chunks and put into a bowl with the tuna and olives. Measure the dressing into a small bowl then add the extra lemon juice and the onion. Stir carefully through the tuna mixture. Leave for several hours to chill. Refill the skins or serve as described above, garnished with a slice of lemon and half a stuffed olive.

Avocado Hagalil (Avocado on the Half Shell with Fish Salad)

The fish in its tart and herby dressing makes a delicious contrast to the smooth richness of the avocado flesh.

Serves 6-8

3-4 avocados
1 tbsp lemon juice
Gherkins or stuffed olives for garnish
1 lb (500g) haddock, cooked in the following:

Cold water to cover the fish
4 thin slices onion
1 level teasp salt
Pinch pepper
1 level teasp sugar

Bring to boil in a shallow lidded pan.

Simmer the fish, covered for 20 minutes, cool for 5 minutes, then lift out with a slotted spoon and drain any liquor back into the pan. Remove the skin and bone, and flake coarsely with a fork.

Dressing for the fish:

5 fl oz (150ml/²/₃ cup) soured
   cream and the same amount of
   lemony mayonnaise
2 generous tbsp chopped parsley
¹/₂ clove of garlic, crushed

10 grinds black pepper
Pinch of salt
Pinch of cayenne
2 oz (50g/¹/₂ cup) chopped walnuts

Blend all the dressing ingredients together until evenly mixed then gently stir through the fish.

An hour before serving, cut the avocados in half and twist to separate. Remove the stone and sprinkle a little lemon juice in its place. Fill with the salad, heaping it up well. Garnish with sliced gherkin or olives.

Cool and Crisp

As it is usual to put it in place before the guests sit down, a salad starter can be treated as an integral part of the table decoration. The vivid reds, yellows and greens of such ingredients as tomatoes, peppers and avocados can be skilfully blended with flowers and candles to set the scene.

Avocado, Tomato and Lemon Hors d'Oeuvre

A simple but tasty starter which depends for its flavour on the combination of ripe avocado with a subtly flavoured dressing.

Serves 6-8

3 large or 4 small, ripe avocados
4 large, ripe but firm tomatoes
3 lemons
4 tbsp olive oil

Good pinch of salt, caster
   (superfine) sugar and 10 grinds
   black pepper
Shredded lettuce or Chinese
   leaves
1 tbsp snipped chives

To make the dressing: Grate half the rind and squeeze all the juice from one lemon and put into a jar with the oil, seasonings and chives. Screw on the lid then shake until thick (about one minute).

Peel the zest and pith from the other lemons and cut into thin segments. Halve, peel then cut the avocados into ¼ inch (0.5cm) thick slices. Cut each tomato into eight and remove the seeds. Arrange the avocado slices, tomatoes and lemons on top of the shredded greens, and moisten with the dressing. Chill half an hour, then serve with brown bread and butter.

Italian Pepper Salad

This is typical of the wonderful salads of dressed vegetables such as mushrooms, aubergines (eggplants) and courgettes (zucchini) which you will be offered in any authentic Italian restaurant. The olive oil is acidulated with only the merest touch of lemon juice, while garlic and parsley are always prominent in the seasonings. I find canned pimentos (sweet red peppers) are excellent. If fresh peppers are used, they should be grilled until the skin is black and charred. Rub it off, then proceed as in the recipe (6-8 red peppers should be used).

Serves 6-8

1 × 14 oz (400g) can sweet red peppers, drained
5 tbsp olive oil
1-2 cloves garlic, crushed to a paste
1 tbsp finely chopped parsley
Squeeze of lemon juice
½ teasp sea salt
10 grinds black pepper

Cut the peppers into long strips about 1 inch (2.5cm) wide, place in a mixing bowl and cover with the remaining ingredients, turning the peppers over to coat them thoroughly. Leave for an hour at room temperature, then chill until required.

Serve as part of a mixed hors d'oeuvre or in individual dishes, garnished with sliced ripe tomatoes. Delicious with rye or coarse brown bread.

Aubergine (Eggplant), Green Pepper and Tomato Ragoût

This is delicious both hot with roasts or grills, and cold as an appetizer with pitta (Middle Eastern) or brown bread. The olive oil is essential, particularly when cold, as it combines with the vegetables to give a succulent texture.

Serves 6-8

2 medium aubergines (eggplants) (1 lb/450g), peeled and cut in 1/4 inch (1cm) cubes

6 tbsp oil

1 medium onion (5 oz/150g), halved then sliced paper thin

2 fine green peppers (about 12 oz/350g), sliced 1/4 inch (1cm) thick, seeded and cored

4 canned tomatoes, well drained (half a medium can); or 1/2 can (4 fl oz/125ml) tomato juice

2 teasp tomato purée

Plenty of black pepper

1/2 teasp salt

1 tbsp chopped parsley

1 level teasp dried herbes de Provence

Put the peeled and cubed aubergines (eggplants) in a colander and sprinkle with salt. Leave 1 hour, then squeeze well to extract the bitter juices, rinse and dry thoroughly.

Put the oil in a heavy lidded saucepan and heat gently for 3 minutes, then add the onions and cook until soft and pale gold in colour. Add the aubergines and fry until golden on both sides, then add the pepper and cook gently for another 5 minutes, stirring well. Finally add the tomatoes (or juice) and the purée, and season with the pepper and the salt. Simmer uncovered for about 20 minutes until the vegetables are quite tender and the mixture is the consistency of a thick stew. Stir in the herbs and season to taste.

Salad Niçoise

This has a glorious blend of textures and flavours yet is very suitable for a low calorie meal (substitute a low calorie dressing as well, if you prefer). The use of Chinese leaves instead of the more traditional lettuce allows one to dress the vegetables in advance without losing any of the crispness of the greens.

Serves 6-8 as main dish

6 firm tomatoes, quartered

1 medium cucumber

1/2 lb (225g) sliced or whole fresh or frozen French beans

1 large green pepper

Bunch of spring onions (scallions) (optional)

2 × 7 oz (175g) cans tuna

1 small can anchovy fillets (optional but tasty)

3 oz (75g) sliced stuffed green or black olives

4 hard-boiled eggs

Approx 8 inch (15cm) section Chinese leaves

Dressing:

6 tbsp salad oil, preferably olive
2 tbsp wine vinegar
1 tbsp lemon juice
1 level teasp each sea salt, Dijon
   mustard and caster (superfine)
   sugar

1 clove of garlic, halved
10 grinds black pepper
2 teasp chopped parsley and
   chives

Make the dressing early in the day by putting all the ingredients
into a screw-top jar and shaking for a minute until thickened.
  Refrigerate.

To prepare the vegetables: Quarter the tomatoes and remove the
seeds. Cut the cucumber in ½ inch (1.25cm) chunks – peel only if
the skin seems tough. Put in a colander, sprinkle with coarse salt,
leave 1 hour, then rinse and dry well.
  Cook the beans until barely tender. Plunge into cold water to set
the colour, then drain. Finely slice the spring onions (scallions),
if used. Put all into a bowl.
  Several hours before serving, shred the Chinese leaves and put
into a deep narrow glass salad bowl. Pour half the dressing over
the vegetables, mix well, then arrange on top of the greens.
Refrigerate. Just before serving, decorate with the flaked tuna,
halved eggs, the anchovies and olives. Mix gently at the table to
blend, passing extra dressing.

Tuna and Bean Hors d'Oeuvre (Tonne e Fagioli)

*This Tuscan salad is extremely sustaining so can also be served as
a luncheon dish or as part of a cold buffet. If you prefer, use fresh
beans, soaked overnight, then cooked until tender in boiling salted
water. A mixture of white and red beans is especially attractive.*

Serves 8

2 × 1 lb 2 oz (500g) tins of Italian
  white beans or red kidney beans
  (or butter or haricot beans if not
  available)

2 × 7 oz (200g) cans tuna fish
1 onion, very thinly sliced

Dressing:

1/4 pint (150ml/2/3 cup) oil (olive
    for preference)
2 tbsp wine vinegar
1 tbsp lemon juice
1 level teasp caster (superfine)
    sugar

1 level teasp salt
10 grinds black pepper
1 large clove of garlic, crushed
2 tbsp chopped parsley or chives
    or 1 teasp fines herbes
1 teasp Dijon mustard

Garnish:

Shredded lettuce or Chinese
    leaves
2 lemons

Chopped parsley
Few paper-thin slices of onion

Drain the beans and rinse thoroughly in cold water. Leave in a
colander while you drain the tuna fish and break it into large
chunks. Put beans and tuna into a large bowl with the finely sliced
onion.

Make the dressing by putting all the ingredients into a screw-top
jar and shaking until thickened (about 1 minute). Stir it through the
bean/tuna mixture with a wooden fork (this avoids crushing the
beans), adding just enough to moisten the mixture thoroughly.
Leave overnight for the dressing to be absorbed, and the raw onion
to mellow.

To serve: Arrange a bed of shredded lettuce or Chinese leaves at
the bottom of 8 sturdy wine goblets or on 8 small salad plates.
Divide the mixture between them. Garnish each serving with one
or two paper-thin slices of onion and a sprinkle of parsley. Serve
with a quarter of lemon and plenty of coarse brown bread and
butter.

Eggs with Herb Mayonnaise

*This makes a delicious individual hors d'oeuvre, with the eggs
garnished with pickled cucumbers, black olives and tomatoes. Or
the halved eggs can be set on a large platter as an accompaniment
to fried fish or boiled salmon.*

Note: If you like 'oeufs mollets', with a set white but a creamy
yolk, then cook for 6 minutes only. In any case, the eggs should

be gently lowered into simmering water, and the cooking time counted from when simmering recommences – putting the eggs in will obviously lower the temperature for a few seconds. When cooking time is up, immediately put under the cold tap to stop further cooking.

1 hard-boiled egg per person
1/2 pint (275ml/1 1/4 cups) herb
   mayonnaise (enough for 6-8 eggs)

Herb Mayonnaise

This is made in the blender or in a food processor, which makes the mayonnaise and chops the herbs at the same time.

8 fl oz (225ml/1 cup) oil (half corn oil and half olive oil is ideal, otherwise use all corn oil)
1 tbsp wine vinegar or lemon juice
1 level teasp each of mustard, sugar and salt

1 tbsp each of roughly cut chives and parsley
1 whole egg
Pinch of garlic salt or half a small clove garlic

If you prefer you can omit the herbs and add a pinch of curry powder instead. Put the vinegar or lemon juice, the egg, seasonings and herbs into the blender goblet or bowl of food processor, and blend for half a minute. Add 4 tablespoons of the oil and blend for a further half a minute. Pour in the remaining oil through the hole at the top, blending all the time. Taste and re-season. Coat the halved hard-boiled eggs with the mayonnaise. Any leftover keeps extremely well in the refrigerator, and can be served instead of ordinary mayonnaise as required.

VARIATION
Eggs with Tuna Mayonnaise

8 hard-boiled eggs (as above)
Shredded Chinese leaves or crisp lettuce
1/2 pint (225ml/1 1/4 cups) plain mayonnaise (see p.335)

7 oz (200g) can tuna
Juice of 1 lemon
1 can anchovy fillets
10 grinds black pepper

Halve the eggs lengthwise and arrange yolk-side down on a bed of finely shredded Chinese leaves or crisp lettuce, set on a large oval platter or individual plates.

Reserve 4 anchovy fillets, cut in two lengthwise and keep for decoration. Put the rest together with all the remaining ingredients into a blender or food processor, and process until absolutely smooth. Use to coat the egg halves, decorating with a curl of anchovy and a little chopped parsley or paprika pepper. Chill for half an hour.

Serve with fresh rolls or crispbread and butter.

Note: The tuna mayonnaise can be prepared up to 48 hours beforehand and stored in an airtight container. Thin to coating consistency if necessary with a little cream or top of milk.

Soups and Garnishes

Because there is such a very wide variety of recipes, from the clear broth that provokes the appetite, to the hearty vegetable purée that satisfies it, a bowl of soup can provide a suitable and delicious first course for almost any kind of meal, whether a formal dinner party or an alfresco luncheon. And from the point of view of the cook, it is also a very convenient food because not only can it be prepared well in advance of a meal, it actually improves in flavour in the meantime. Indeed, as almost all soups can be kept frozen for 2 to 3 months after preparation, they offer an excellent form of 'insurance' against the arrival of unexpected visitors.

To mature soup: All soups, without exception, improve in flavour if they are allowed to mature overnight, or at least from the morning until the evening of the day on which they are to be served. As soon as they are cool, cover and refrigerate, or in the case of acid soups (such as tomato) which do not sour easily, they may be kept in a cool larder. Any soup that has not been refrigerated should be brought to the boil if it has not been served within 24 hours. Stored in this way, any soup will keep sweet for up to 3 days. If a soup tastes even slightly off or appears bubbly on the surface, throw it away.

To freeze soup: Store in either plastic or glass containers, allowing 1 inch (2.5cm) of headroom for expansion, between the surface of the liquid and the lid.

If you wish to make and store soup in bulk – an excellent idea when preparing for a large party – take a tip from the commercial soup makers and freeze the *concentrate* rather than the soup. This concentrate can be either a flavoured vegetable purée (as in **Cream of Green Pea Soup**) or an extra-strong version of a regular soup recipe (for instance, **Consommé**) which can be diluted to taste with stock or water when it is required. May be frozen for 3 months.

To defrost soup: Thaw the soup overnight in the refrigerator. If time is short, however, it can be thawed from frozen as follows: cover the bottom of the soup pan with a 1/4 inch (1/2cm) layer of the appropriate liquid (water, milk or stock), add the frozen block of soup, cover and reheat (preferably in the oven to prevent scorching) until bubbly. Always carefully re-season frozen soup, paying special attention to herbs which may have lost some of their flavour in the freezer.

A note on quantities: As a rule of thumb, allow 8 fl oz (225ml/1 cup) of a thin soup, and 5 fl oz (150ml/2/3 cup) of a thick cream soup for each serving. However, my recipes have been worked out to err on the generous side, to allow for some second helpings.

Herbs, Spices and Other Flavourings

The subtle use of herbs and spices can make all the difference between a dull soup and a memorable one, and I have suggested in each recipe with what particular blend of flavourings this can be best achieved. However, the following ingredients are used in so many different soups that I think they are well worth keeping in stock.

Dried herbs
Fines herbes; Italian herb mixture; basil; powdered or individual bouquets garnis; chives; bayleaf; mint; parsley; tarragon: as the flavour of dried herbs diminishes with time, buy only enough to last you for the next three months; and if the smell does fade, be ruthless and throw them away.

As they need a longer cooking time than fresh herbs to release their flavour, they are usually added to the soup from the start of its preparation.

Fresh herbs
Basil; chives; dill; garlic; mint; parsley (both chopped and in sprigs); tarragon: whether they are from the greengrocer or the garden, fresh herbs are much crisper and stay sweet longer, if they

are washed, dried, then refrigerated in a covered container for several hours before use. Treated this way they will keep fresh and ready for immediate use for up to a week. Once they begin to smell like old grass cuttings, it is time to throw them away. Frozen fresh herbs (see p.488) which may not have retained enough crispness for salads are excellent in soup. Sprigs of herbs such as parsley and mint are usually simmered in the soup and then discarded, but chopped herbs are best added just before serving, so as to conserve their bright colour and freshness of flavour.

Flavouring vegetables

Carrot; celery; leek; onion; shallot; tomato and tomato pureé: these are used to flavour home-made stocks, to provide texture to a smooth pureé, and to add colour, depth and flavour to a delicate cream soup. Onion which has been first gently sautéed in butter or oil will sweeten and mellow the flavour of any soup as its starch content is changed to sugar in the initial cooking process.

Spices

Coriander; nutmeg; mace; black and white peppercorns: these are used whole or powdered according to the recipe. They add a piquancy of flavour which, however, should not be too obtrusive, so use by the pinch rather than by the spoonful.

Stock

Beef; chicken; vegetable or onion bouillon in cubes, concentrated beef, chicken and vegetable pastes; canned or powdered beef consommé: in the majority of soup recipes the choice of chicken, meat or vegetable stock is not as important as its intensity and depth of flavour. However, always use a *light*-coloured stock – chicken, veal or vegetable – for a delicate cream or cold soup.

Some of the best *commercial stocks* are very good indeed, but they can only be discovered by trial and error. Besides being dissolved in water to form the basis of a soup, they can also be used to deepen the flavour of home-made stock, and conversely, can have *their* flavour heightened by simmering them with home-cooked beef and chicken bones, or vegetable cooking liquor.

Home-made stocks are most quickly prepared in a pressure cooker, though for a large quantity (for freezing or party use) it is more convenient to simmer it either on top of the stove or (for better colour and flavour) in the oven.

To ensure that the stock is free from fat, always prepare it the day before it is needed, then refrigerate overnight so that the solidified fat can be easily removed from the surface. If the stock is not for immediate use, boil it down to concentrate it (to conserve storage space), then freeze or refrigerate it until required.

Storage time: **F** 2 months; **R** 3 days.

Garnishes

Vermicelli, rice
These may be cooked in stock or water, then added to the soup just before serving, to provide a texture contrast, or they may be cooked in the soup as both a garnish and a thickener.

Evaporated milk, fresh and soured cream
In some recipes these are added to the soup to enrich and thicken it. Alternatively they may be swirled on the top just before serving to provide a colour contrast.

Croûtons, melba toasts
It is most convenient (and equally satisfactory) to buy packeted melba toast, but croûtons are easily made at home.

Croûtons for 8 **F** 3 months
These crunchy morsels can be fried, baked or toasted. Start by placing 4 large slices of white or brown bread on top of each other and cutting into ½ inch (1cm) cubes using a very sharp knife.

To fry: In a large frying pan heat 2 oz (50g/¼ cup) butter and 1 tbsp oil until the butter foams (or use hot oil only). Add the bread cubes and bubble gently until a golden brown, tossing frequently in the pan to ensure even browning. Turn out onto crumpled tissue or kitchen paper.

To bake: Turn oven to Gas No. 4, 350°F, 180°C, and put in a baking tray with the chosen fat on it (see above). After ten minutes add the bread cubes and toss well to coat with the fat. Leave in the oven until a rich golden brown, shaking tin once or twice – it will take about 10-15 minutes. When the croûtons are ready they will have absorbed all the fat and be very crisp.

To toast: Put in the oven as above but without any fat, except for a thin coating of oil on the baking tray. Bake until golden brown, tossing once or twice.

Croûtons can be served immediately, or refrigerated or frozen and then reheated.

To serve, allow approx 1 generous tbsp croûtons for each serving. Add to the soup as it is served, or pass round the table for guests to help themselves.

Fresh vegetable garnishes
Green pepper, cucumber or celery in cubes or slices: for convenience, these may be prepared several hours in advance, then wrapped in film or foil. They can be stirred into the prepared soup or floated on the top of individual servings.

Meat and bone stock

Makes approx 3 pints (1.75 litres/7½ cups) **F** 3 months

3-4 lb (1.5-2kg) beef bones cut in 3 inch (7.5cm) lengths; *or* 2 lb (1kg) meaty veal bones
1 lb (450g) shin beef
Green part of a fat leek
Leaves from a head of celery
1 onion
2 squashy tomatoes *or* 1 tbsp tomato purée

Bouquet garni, *or* 1 bayleaf, 10 peppercorns, and large sprig of parsley
2 teasp salt
10 grinds black pepper
2 quarts (2.25 litres/10 cups) water (3 pints/1.75 litres/7½ cups in pressure cooker)

Put all ingredients into the chosen pan and cover with the cold water.

In a pressure cooker: Pressure at 15 lb for one hour.

Top of stove: Bring slowly to simmering point, skin with a spoon dipped in cold water, then simmer for 3-4 hours.

In the oven: Choose a pan or casserole with heatproof handle or lugs (otherwise cover with foil). Simmer at Gas No. 2, 300°F, 150°C for 3-4 hours. Strain out all the vegetables. Reserve the meat for other use (e.g. shepherd's pie, or as a soup garnish).

Chicken stock

For maximum flavour make the stock from a halved boiling fowl with its giblets. The bird can be lifted out when it is tender (after about 2 hours), the flesh removed and reserved for other use and the carcase returned to the pan for a further 2 hours. Otherwise use the cooked carcase from a roast bird with as many giblets as possible (at a pinch use giblets only. Stockpile these in the freezer when cooking roast or casseroled birds).

Makes 2 pints (1.25 litres/5 cups) **F** 3 months

3 pints (1³/4 litres/7¹/2 cups) water
2 level teasp salt
10 grinds black pepper
1-2 ripe tomatoes; or 1 teasp purée
1 bayleaf
1 large onion
2 fat carrots

2 tbsps celery leaves
1 sprig parsley or 1 teasp dried parsley
3 inches (7.5cm) green part of a fat leek
1-2 chicken stock cubes (optional but they do intensify the flavour)

Wash the fowl (if used) and the giblets. Break up the cooked carcase (if used). Put in a large pan and cover with the water, adding the salt and pepper. Bring to the boil slowly, then remove any froth from the top.

Add all the remaining ingredients and simmer very gently for 4 hours (preferably in the oven) or for 20 minutes in a pressure cooker. Pour through a sieve. Save the giblets for other use or strip off the meat from the bones, and put in the soup. Discard the vegetables – their flavour is now in the stock. Refrigerate overnight, then remove the fat and discard it.

Vegetable stock

If possible use water from cooked vegetables as the basis; otherwise use water.

Makes approx 2 pints (1 litre/5 cups) stock **F** 3 months

2 carrots
¹/2 onion
2 stalks celery
2¹/4 pints (1.25 litres/6 cups) water
1 teasp salt
¹/4 teasp white pepper

Large sprig of parsley
1 bayleaf
Few peppercorns
Good pinch of fines herbes
Few drops monosodium glutamate or other flavouring extract

Chop the vegetables finely, by hand, or in a blender or food processor. Put in a pan with the remaining ingredients. Bring to the boil, simmer with the lid partly on for ¾ hour. Strain and use as required.

Soups with a Hearty Flavour

Whether they are thick or clear all the following soups depend for much of their flavour on the excellence of the meat or chicken stock from which they are made, and all are soups to serve at an informal winter dinner or supper party.

Cock-a-Leekie Soup

This clear but satisfying soup depends for most of its flavour on the excellence of the chicken stock from which it is made. If possible use stock made from a boiling fowl (see p.162).

Serves 6-8 F 3 months

8 large prunes (soaked in water to cover overnight)
3 pints (1.75 litres/7½ cups) strong chicken stock
2 tbsp medium dry sherry (optional)
1 tbsp chopped parsley for garnish
The white parts of 2 fat leeks

Put the stock into the soup pan and bring to the boil. Taste and strengthen with a bouillon cube if necessary. Split the leeks lengthwise, wash thoroughly, then cut across in ½ inch (1cm) pieces. Add to the boiling stock with the prunes, reduce the heat, cover and simmer for 30 minutes. Stir in the sherry and parsley. Serve piping hot.

Chicken and Tomato Soup

A simple soup but with a very rich flavour. Use home-made chicken stock or a stock made with cubes.

Serves 6-8 **F** 3 months

3 pints (1.75 litres/7^1/2 cups)
  chicken stock
1 can (15 oz/425g) peeled plum
  tomatoes
Juice of a large lemon

2 level tbsp brown sugar
4 level tbsp canned or tubed
  tomato purée
2 level tbsp rice – any variety

Put all the ingredients except the rice into a soup pan. (Sieve the tomatoes or not, as you prefer.) Bring to the boil, then add the rice. Cover and simmer for 30 minutes. Taste and add additional sugar or lemon juice if necessary.

Onion Soup Gratiné

This is the famous French recipe, more a main dish than a soup. Use any stock you prefer, as the colour and the flavour of the soup depend almost entirely on the thorough, patient browning of the onions.

Serves 6-8 **F** 3 months

1 lb (450g) onions
1 oz (25g/2 tbsp) butter or
  margarine
2 teasp oil
1 level teasp sugar
Salt and pepper
1 oz (25g/4 tbsp) flour

3 pints (1.75 litres/7^1/2 cups) stock
4 fl oz (125ml/^{1}/2 cup) dry white
  wine or vermouth
French bread
Grated cheese
1 tbsp melted butter or margarine

Peel, then slice the onion thinly. Melt the butter or margarine with the oil and as soon as it stops foaming add the onion and turn to coat in the butter. Cover and cook gently for 15 minutes. Uncover, add the sugar, salt and pepper and continue to cook for another 20 minutes, until the onions are a rich golden brown. Sprinkle in the flour and continue to cook for another 3 minutes, then add the hot stock. Stir in the wine or vermouth. Simmer half covered for 1 hour. Put in deep heat-proof serving bowls and float a slice of bread on each. Sprinkle with cheese, dredge with butter and put under the grill until the bread topping is golden.

Fresh Tomato Soup

This is a light, fresh-tasting soup with delicate orange-flavoured undertones. If really ripe fresh tomatoes are not available, use a 28 oz (800g) can plum tomatoes (drained) instead. If possible chill the soup overnight before use so that any solidified fat can be removed. This is especially important when meat balls have been added (see Variation).

Serves 8 F 3 months

1 large onion, thinly sliced
1½ lb (0.750g) deep red and ripe tomatoes (or canned)
1 small clove of garlic
Bare ounce (25g/2 tbsp) butter or margarine
2 pints (1¼ litres/5 cups) vegetable or chicken stock
½ pint (275ml/1¼ cups) tomato juice

4 strips of orange peel (½ × 2 inches/1 × 5cm)
1 small bayleaf
Large sprig of parsley
1 teasp salt
Plenty of black pepper
3 level teasp brown sugar
2 teasp cornflour (cornstarch)
2 teasp canned tomato purée
1 level tbsp chopped fresh basil, *or* 1 teasp dried basil

Melt the fat in a heavy pan and add the thinly sliced onion, the crushed garlic and the quartered tomatoes. Add the sugar, salt and pepper, cover and simmer until the tomatoes are soft. Push through a sieve or vegetable mill, discarding the skins and any onion that won't go through. Return to the pan and add the stock, juice, orange peel, liquid from canned tomatoes (if used), bayleaf, parsley and purée. Simmer very gently for at least half an hour.

Discard the parsley, orange peel and bayleaf. Slake the cornflour (cornstarch) with a little water then add to the pan. Simmer 3 minutes, then add the herbs.

VARIATION

With Noodles: Make the soup as directed, but do not thicken with cornflour (cornstarch). Ten minutes before it is ready, add a handful of fine noodles or vermicelli (about 2 oz (50g/¾ cup)) and allow to simmer until tender. The pasta will slightly thicken the soup.

165

Consommé

This consommé, which has a deliciously satisfying flavour, is an excellent standby when entertaining friends on a diet. Whilst it is not quite as crystal-clear as consommé clarified with egg whites in the classic manner, it is far simpler to make and, unlike powdered or canned consommé, it contains no artificial additives or preservatives. To intensify the flavour even further use home-made stock instead of water.

Serves 8-10 **F** 3 months

1½-2 lb (750g-1kg) shin beef (the more the better)
3-4 lb (1.5-2kg) beef bones (cut in 3-4 inch/7.5-10cm lengths)
2 peeled onions, halved
2 fat carrots, scrubbed and quartered
Oil
2 level teasp salt

2 celery stalks
1 unpeeled garlic clove
Sprig of parsley
1 bayleaf
1 level teasp powdered bouquet garni
2-3 tbsp medium sherry
2 teasp parsley

Put a smear of oil in the bottom of a shallow roasting tin. Dry the bones and meat thoroughly, then put them in the tin with the vegetables. Brown for 30-40 minutes in a hot oven (Gas No. 7, 425°F, 220°C) turning occasionally. (If browned on top of the stove, they must be watched continuously.)

Take the tin from the oven, and pour off any fat that may have accumulated. Put all the ingredients except the flavourings, sherry and parsley into a large soup pan. Pour about ½ pint (275ml/1¼ cups) cold water into the roasting tin, stirring well, then put on a low heat to loosen any coagulated juices. Add this liquid to the soup pan. Add cold water to cover the ingredients by at least an inch (2.5cm), then put in the flavourings.

Now bring the pot to the simmer and remove any scum using a wet spoon. Partially cover the pan and simmer for 4-5 hours. Do this if possible in the oven, as you will get an even better flavour and colour. *Do not let the soup boil*, or it will become cloudy instead of remaining beautifully clear.

Strain the soup and remove the meat. Discard the bones and vegetables. When cool, refrigerate overnight. Next day, remove any surface fat carefully. Bring to the simmer and taste. You may like to add a good spoonful of tomato purée and a meat bouillon cube to deepen the flavour and colour further.

If you like a vegetable garnish, simmer a couple of tbsp diced carrot and leek in the soup for a further ¾ hour until tender.

The meat may be cut in small pieces and returned to the soup or used for another purpose, e.g. shepherd's pie.

Just before serving, stir in sherry to taste and the parsley.

Lentil Soup

This smooth and satisfying soup is equally delicious made with meat or vegetable stock.

Serves 6-8 **F** 3 months

1 large onion, roughly chopped	4 pints (2 litres/10 cups) meat or
2 carrots, roughly chopped	vegetable stock
3 sticks celery, roughly chopped	10 grinds black pepper
2 oz (50g/¼ cup) margarine or	½ level teasp fines herbes
butter	2 teasp chopped parsley
½ lb (225g/l cup) orange lentils	Croûtons for garnish

The day before, put the lentils in a large bowl and cover with twice their depth of cold water. Next day, tip the lentils into a sieve and rinse under the cold tap until the water runs clear. Leave to drain while you proceed as follows:

Melt the margarine or butter in a heavy-based soup pan, add the vegetables, turn in the fat, then cover the pan and cook for 5 minutes until the vegetables are softened and have absorbed the fat. Add the lentils and stir well with the vegetables, then add all the remaining ingredients except for the parsley and the croûtons. Bring to the boil, then reduce to a simmer, cover and continue to cook for 2 hours. Put in the blender or push through a fine sieve. Reheat in the pan, taste and adjust seasoning, then add the parsley. Serve with croûtons.

Polish Winter Soup

This is the soup par excellence 'like mama used to make'. Indeed for Russian and Polish peasants of the 19th century it was also their main dish of the day as the pulses and cereals it contains make it extremely nourishing, though cheap. However, its blend of ingredients also gives it a superb flavour and one capable of infinite variation. For example, butter (lima) beans can be substituted for haricot (dried white) beans, pot barley for pearl barley, brown lentils for red lentils. The consistency of the soup can also be easily adjusted by boiling it down, or diluting with extra stock.

Serves 8 **F** 3 months

$1/2$ lb (225g/1 cup) green split peas
$1/4$ lb (125g/$1/2$ cup) red lentils
2 level tbsp pearl barley
4 level tbsp haricot (dried white) beans
1 lb (450g) shin beef
4 pints ($2^1/4$ litres/10 cups) meat stock
2 level teasp salt
10 grinds black pepper

1 level teasp dried fines herbes
2 stalks celery, diced into $1/2$ inch (1cm) cubes
2 large carrots, diced into $1/2$ inch (1cm) cubes
1 large carrot, coarsely grated
White part of a fat leek, well washed and thinly sliced
Large sprig of parsley

The day before making the soup, put the split peas, lentils, barley and beans into a large bowl, cover with twice their depth of cold water and leave to soak and swell overnight. Next day, put the meat and the stock with the salt into a large soup pan and bring to the boil. Skim with a wet metal spoon. Tip the cereals into a fine sieve to remove any excess soaking-water, then put under the cold tap and rinse thoroughly until the water that drains from them is quite clear. Add to the soup pan with the seasonings and all the vegetables except the grated carrot. Bring back to the boil, then reduce heat until the mixture is barely bubbling. Cover and simmer for 2 hours. Uncover and add the grated carrot. Continue to cook for a further hour, stirring the pan occasionally to make sure the soup does not stick to the pan as it thickens. When the soup is ready, the lentils and split peas will have turned into a purée. Taste and add more seasonings if required. Remove the sprig of parsley.

Jerusalem Artichoke Soup

This soup has an unusually 'nutty' flavour.

Serves 6-8 **F** 3 months

2 lb (1kg) Jerusalem artichokes

1 oz (25g/2 tbsp) butter or 2 tbsp oil

1 medium onion

2½ pints (1.5 litres/6 cups) vegetable or chicken stock (home-made or from cubes)

1 medium clove garlic

½ teasp salt

10 grinds black pepper

2 bayleaves

Large sprig of parsley

½ (275ml/1¼ cups) milk (omit for non-dairy version)

4 tbsp cream (omit for non-dairy version)

2 tbsp chopped fresh basil for garnish

Put the artichokes into a pan, cover with water, bring to the boil and simmer for 15 minutes. Drain and when cool enough to handle, peel off the skin. I find this is easier than peeling the raw vegetable. In a heavy soup pan, melt the butter or oil, and cook the onion, covered, until soft and golden (about 10 minutes). Uncover, add the peeled artichokes, stirr well to mix, cover and cook a further 5 minutes. Uncover, then add the stock, garlic, salt and pepper, bayleaves and parsley. Bring back to the boil, cover and simmer for 15 minutes, or until the artichokes are absolutely tender. Remove the bayleaves. Liquidize in 2 or 3 batches, then return to the pan together with the milk (if used). Bring to simmering point. Just before serving add the cream (if used) and the chopped basil.

Cold Soups

A cold soup sounds a contradiction in terms, yet it is a mid-summer favourite in places as far apart as Denmark, Yugoslavia and Israel. The soup should be of the consistency of single (light) cream and the right mixture of delicate herbs is essential in most recipes.

Cold soups will keep under refrigeration for up to 3 days, and their flavour definitely matures with time. However, do not freeze any soup containing yoghurt or soured cream as they tend to separate at very low temperatures.

As the soup is so smooth, it is essential to contrast it with something crisp, such as cucumber strips, radish slices or toasts.

To serve: The soup can either be sipped from a spoon in the conventional manner or drunk from a cup – especially practical when served out of doors.

Chilled Avocado Soup

This beautiful pale green soup is a favourite both in the USA (where it would be made with chicken stock) and Israel (where a vegetable stock or chicken-flavoured vegetable bouillon would be used to satisfy the laws of kashruth). As the soup is very rich, serve only small portions, accompanied by crisp toasts.

Serves 8

3 medium, or 2 large very ripe
  avocados, peeled, halved and
  stoned.
1½ pints (850ml/4 cups) chilled
  light stock
1 tbsp snipped chives, more for
  garnish

1 teasp chopped fresh tarragon
  leaves; or pinch dried tarragon
1½ cartons (8 fl oz/225ml/1 cup)
  soured cream
1½ tbsp lemon juice
6 drops Tabasco sauce; or a
  cautious pinch of cayenne

Blend or process all the ingredients until smooth. Chill thoroughly.

Serve in small soup cups, garnishing each serving with a sprinkle of chives.

Dairy Borscht

This makes a refreshing and sustaining summer 'cocktail'. As the colour is quite beautiful, it is the ideal starter for a 'pink' summer lunch of salmon and strawberries. It is equally delicious heated to steaming point (do not boil or it will curdle), then served piping hot with a garnish of baby new potatoes.

As strained beet juice will keep for up to 4 days in the refrigerator (3 months in the freezer), it is convenient to make it well in advance. It can then be thickened with the eggs, chilled overnight and enriched with the soured cream just before serving.

Serves 8 F (unthickened juice only) 3 months

1 each medium onion and carrot,
  peeled
2 bunches raw young beets or 1½
  lb (675g) raw old beets
  (according to season)
3 pints (1.75 litres/7½ cups) water
  or light stock
3 tbsp lemon juice or ½ teasp

(approx) tartaric or citric acid
2 level tbsp sugar
2 level teasp salt
Good pinch white pepper
2 whole eggs
5 fl oz (150ml/²/₃ cup) soured
  cream

170

Wash new beets (removing stalks and greenery) and peel old beets with a potato peeler, keeping the beets on kitchen paper to avoid staining the counter or chopping board. (If this happens, wipe over with very dilute bleach.) Cut all the vegetables in rough chunks, then grate by hand (very tedious), in a food processor, or by partially liquidizing with some of the measured stock. Put the sugar, salt, pepper and stock into a large soup pan, add the vegetables, then bring slowly to the boil. Cover and simmer for 45 minutes. Pour the entire contents of the pan through a coarse sieve into a bowl. Discard the vegetables. Return the clear liquid to the pan, or refrigerate or freeze until required.

To thicken the borscht: Beat the eggs in a basin until the yolks and white are thoroughly blended. Bring the beet juice to the boil and add the lemon juice or the tartaric or citric acid. It will immediately turn a glorious claret colour. Gradually pour a cupful of the hot juice onto the beaten eggs whisking vigorously (a batter-whisk or a hand-held electric mixer are both excellent). Then return this mixture to the soup pan. Still whisking, reheat the soup until it is steaming and slightly thickened. *Do not boil* or the soup will curdle. Taste, and add more sugar and lemon juice if necessary to balance the sweet/sour flavour. Chill thoroughly.

To serve: Whisk well (as it may have separated in the refrigerator), then stir in the soured cream and serve in soup cups or wine glasses.

Alternatively, do not *stir in* the cream but *top* each serving with a spoonful of it, sprinkled with a pinch of paprika pepper.

Chilled Yoghurt Soup

This delicious and sustaining soup depends for much of its flavour on a good mixture of herbs. It will keep for several days and makes an excellent light lunch with buttered brown bread and a hunk of cheese, and some fresh fruit.

Serves 6. Do not freeze.

1/2 pint (275ml/1 1/4 cups) milk
1 pint (575ml/2 1/2 cups) natural
  unsweetened yoghurt; or 3/4 pint
  (425ml/2 cups) yoghurt and 1/4
  pint (150ml/2/3 cup) soured
  cream
1/2 cucumber
15 radishes

2 tbsp chives
2 heaped tbsp fresh dill or 1
  heaped tbsp fresh parsley
Few leaves of fresh tarragon, or
  1/2 teasp dried herbs
6 leaves fresh mint or 1/4 teasp
  dried herbs

Mix the milk, yoghurt and the cream (if used). (The cream is richer but less cooling on a hot day.) Peel the cucumber and cut into matchsticks, finely slice the radishes, snip the chives and dill (if used), and chop the fresh parsley (if used) and the tarragon. Stir into the yoghurt mixture all the remaining ingredients. If too thick, thin with milk (it should be the consistency of whipping cream). Serve cold.

Chilled Cucumber and Mint Soup

A pale green, gently minted soup that is perfect for a lovely June day. It can also be served hot. This is an excellent way to use home-grown cucumbers and mint.

Serves 8 F 3 months

1 oz (25g/2 tbsp) butter
1 small sliced onion
1 large cucumber
1 pint (575ml/2 1/2 cups) water or
  light stock
12 stalks of fresh mint
1/2 level teasp salt

Speck of white pepper
1 level tbsp cornflour (cornstarch)
1/2 pint (275ml/1 1/4 cups) milk
1 carton (5 oz/150ml/2/3 cup)
  soured or single (light) cream
2 teasp fresh, chopped dill or
  chives

In a large, heavy saucepan, melt the butter without allowing it to brown and then add the onion. Toss to coat it with the fat, then cover and cook gently until softened but unbrowned (5-6 minutes). Meanwhile, peel the cucumber, but keep a 2 inch (5cm) piece unpeeled for garnish. Chop the peeled part roughly and add to the onion, followed by the water or stock, mint leaves, salt and pepper. Cover and simmer for 20 minutes or until the cucumber and onion are absolutely tender. Push through a fine sieve or (preferably) put in a blender or food processor, until smooth.

172

Return to the pan and add the cornflour (cornstarch), mixed to a cream with the milk. Bring to the boil, stirring, then simmer for 3 minutes to cook the cornflour. Turn off the heat, then stir in the cream and the herbs. Taste and add more salt and pepper if required. Chill overnight in the refrigerator.

Serve in soup bowls garnished with very thin slices of the unpeeled cucumber.

Cream Soups

The best cream soups have a gentle but satisfying flavour and a rich creamy texture, which can be smooth as satin or pleasantly rough on the tongue, as preferred. The flavour depends in the main on the use of very fresh but fully ripe vegetables, and the judicious blending of fresh herbs and the more delicate spices. However, the final texture of the soup will depend entirely on the particular kind of machine in which you choose to prepare the purée.

With a hand sieve or food mill (moulin à legumes), you will get a soup with a grainy texture; with a food processor, one which is smoother but not completely homogenized. But if you want a soup that is completely smooth without any suggestion of fibre, then you must choose a blender or liquidizer, and run it until each batch of mixture resembles pouring cream.

Cream of Cauliflower Soup

As this soup should have a very delicate flavour, it is essential to use a really fresh cauliflour – that is, one with creamy-coloured, tightly curled flowerets and a very green stalk. (Once a cauliflower has staled it develops a very strong, unpleasant taste.)

Serves 6-8 F 3 months

1 very fresh medium-sized cauliflower	2 sticks celery
1 oz (25g/2 tbsp) butter	1 onion

Sauce:

1 oz (25g/2tbsp) butter
1 oz (25g/^{1}/4 cup) flour
1^1/4 pints (725ml/3 cups) light
  stock

1 pint (575ml/2^1/2 cups) milk
1 teasp salt
^{1}/4 teasp white pepper
Pinch of nutmeg

To finish:

4 tbsp single (light) cream
1 tbsp snipped chives

Divide cauliflower into flowerets, then cook in boiling salted water for 8 minutes, drain. Reserve 2 tbsp for garnish.

In a small pan, melt the 1 oz (25g/2 tbsp) butter and sweat the sliced onion and celery – covered – for 5 minutes. Add the cauliflower, toss to coat in the buttery juices, put on the lid and simmer a further 5 minutes or until the cauliflower is absolutely tender.

Sieve, liquidize or process the vegetables using some of the measured stock. Make the sauce by putting the butter, flour and milk together with the remaining stock into a pan. Add the seasonings and bring to the boil, whisking all the time. Add the vegetable purée and leave to simmer for 5 minutes. If possible leave several hours before serving. Reheat, re-season, add the cream, chives and reserved flowerets.

Cream of Celery Soup

The true flavour of the celery (especially the bleached variety) is in the 'root' to which the stalks are attached, so after removing the discoloured ^{1}/4 inch (0.5cm) which has been in the soil, use all the remainder in the soup. Some varieties of celery are stringless; others may need to be sieved as well as puréed to remove the strings.

Serves 8 **F** 3 months

1 fat head of celery including
  'root' and leaves
1 medium onion (5 oz/150g), thinly
  sliced
1 oz (25g/2 tbsp) butter
1^1/2 pints (850ml/4 cups) light
  stock
1 bayleaf
1 level teasp salt

10 grinds black pepper
1 pint (575ml/2^1/2 cups) milk
^{1}/4 teasp ground mace or nutmeg
1^1/2 oz (40g/3 tbsp) butter
1^1/2 oz (40g/6 tbsp) flour
^{1}/4 pint (150ml/^{2}/3 cup) single (light)
  cream or evaporated milk
Chives for garnish

174

Melt the butter in a soup pan and add the finely sliced onion. Cover and simmer for 5 minutes while you slice the celery, root, stalks and leaves, as thinly as possible – a food processor is excellent. Add to the onion together with the stock, bayleaf, salt and pepper. Bring to the boil, cover and simmer for 30 minutes until tender. Tip into a basin, then liquidize (in two portions if necessary).

Put the milk, flour and butter into the soup pan with the mace and bring slowly to the boil, whisking all the time. Add the celery purée and continue to simmer for another 3 or 4 minutes. If possible leave to stand for several hours to develop the flavour. Remove the bayleaf, add the cream or evaporated milk and bring to the simmer. Serve garnished with chives.

Cream of Green Pea Soup

This beautiful pale green soup can be served at any time of the year as it is equally successful with fresh or frozen peas.

Serves 6-8 F 3 months

1½ oz (40g/3 tbsp) butter
½ a large onion (3oz/75g)
2 lb (1kg) fresh peas (12-15 oz/350-425g shelled), *or*
1 lb (450g) frozen peas
1¼ pints (725ml/3 cups) water or light stock

1 teasp dried mint or small bunch fresh mint
1 teasp salt
Speck of white pepper
1 teasp fines herbes (dried)

To finish:

1 pint (575ml/2½ cups) milk
1 level tbsp cornflour (cornstarch)

4 tbsp single (light) cream
2 teasp chives or parsley

In a saucepan with a heavy base, melt the butter, add the finely chopped onion, and cook with the lid on until soft and golden, then add the finely sliced celery. Cover and cook a further 3 minutes. Add the peas and stir well, then add the water or the stock, the seasonings and herbs. Cover and simmer until quite tender – about 20 minutes. Sieve or put in blender or food processor until absolutely smooth. Put the cornflour (cornstarch) into the soup pan and mix with the milk until smooth, then add the purée. Bring

175

to the boil and simmer for 3 minutes. If possible leave to stand for several hours to develop the flavour. Just before serving, reheat, stir in the cream and sprinkle with 2 teasp cut chives or chopped parsley.

Serve with croûtons (p.160).

Note: Purée freezes well, or can be frozen as soup, but will need re-seasoning.

Garden Lettuce Soup

This makes use of those mature lettuces which have an excellent flavour even though they may be too coarse for salad use. The fresh tarragon adds to the subtlety of flavour of this very economical soup.

Serves 6-8 **F** 3 months.

1 medium onion (4-5 oz/125g), finely chopped
2 oz (50g/¼ cup) butter
3 medium potatoes (about ¾ lb/350g), peeled and thinly sliced
2 pints (1.25 litres/5 cups) light stock

The leaves from 1 large lettuce *or* the coarse outside leaves of 3 lettuces, coarsely shredded
½ teasp salt
10 grinds black pepper
¼ teasp nutmeg
2 teasp fresh tarragon leaves (optional)

To finish:

¼ pint (150ml/⅔ cup) single (light) cream or evaporated milk
1 tbsp snipped chives

Melt the butter without colouring in a heavy soup pan, add the onion, toss well to coat with butter, then cover and cook 10 minutes. Uncover and add the potatoes, re-cover and cook a further 10 minutes. Uncover and add the stock. Bring to the boil, then add the lettuce. Boil uncovered for 5 minutes (this conserves the colour), then liquidize until absolutely smooth. Return to the pan, add the seasonings, cream and chives.

Serve hot with croûtons.

Cream of Carrot Soup

A richly coloured soup with an excellent blend of flavours. As it is made from low cost vegetables that are available all the year round, it is an excellent soup to make in quantity. For 25 servings use four times the ingredients but omit the potato. Instead, add a 5 oz (150g) packet of instant potato to the steaming milk, then finish the soup as directed in the recipe.

Serves 6-8 F 3 months

3/4 lb (350g/2 cups) carrots
White part of 2 fat leeks
1 onion
2 stalks of celery, sliced
1 medium potato (8 oz/225g)
Good sprinkle of garlic salt; or 1/2
   clove of garlic, crushed
1 1/4 pints (725ml/3 cups) water

1 pint (575ml/2 1/2 cups) milk
2 oz (50g/1/4 cup) butter
1 level teasp salt
8 grinds black pepper
Pinch of sugar
4 tbsp cream
1 tbsp cornflour (cornstarch)
1 level tbsp chopped parsley

Melt the butter in a heavy pan, add the sliced leeks and onion, toss to coat in the fat, cover and sweat them for 10 minutes. Uncover and add the sliced carrots, celery and potato, cover for 5 minutes. Uncover and add the water (vegetables should be barely covered). Season with salt, pepper, sugar and garlic. Cover and simmer until vegetables are absolutely tender – about 40 minutes. Purée in a liquidizer or food processor. In the same pan, heat the milk until steaming, then stir in the vegetable mixture and the cream mixed smoothly with the cornflour (cornstarch). Allow to simmer for 10 minutes.

    Just before serving, stir in the chopped parsley.

Super Cream of Mushroom Soup

This is a very rich soup with a most intriguing taste. For maximum flavour, the mushrooms can be either sliced paper-thin (in a food processor) or coarsely – rather than finely – chopped.

Serves 6-8 F 3 months

2 oz (50g/¼ cup) butter
1 small onion, finely chopped
½ lb (225g/3 cups) pinky
  mushrooms, coarsely chopped
  or thinly sliced

1 small clove of garlic, crushed
2 level tbsp chopped parsley
½ pint (275ml/1¼ cups) water
1 vegetable stock cube

For sauce base:

2 oz (50g/¼ cup) butter
2 oz (50g/¼ cup) flour
2 pints (1 litre/5 cups) milk
1 teasp salt
¼ teasp nutmeg

¼ teasp white pepper
Good pinch herb salt or 'accent'
1 glass medium sherry (optional)
4 tbsp cream (optional)

Melt the butter in a soup pan, add the onion, cover and simmer for 5 minutes. Uncover, add the mushrooms, re-cover and cook for a further 5 minutes, then add the water, stock cube, parsley and garlic.

Turn into a basin. In the same pan put the butter, flour, milk, salt, nutmeg, white pepper, herb salt or 'accent'. Bring slowly to the boil, whisking all the time with a batter whisk. Bubble for 5 minutes, then stir in the mushroom mixture. Cool, then refrigerate several hours or overnight to develop the flavour. When ready to serve, bring back to the simmer. It should be the consistency of thin cream. If too thick, thin down with a little water. When steaming hot, taste, add extra seasonings if necessary, then stir in the sherry and cream (if used).

Potage Parisien

The addition of a sweet, green or (preferably) red pepper adds an extra flavour dimension to this typical French family soup.

Serves 8 F 3 months

2 fat carrots
White part of a fat leek
1 large onion
1 medium green or red pepper
1 medium potato (about 8 oz/225g)
1 pint (575ml/2½ cups) milk
1 pint (575ml/2½ cups) water
1½ oz (40g/3 tbsp) butter

1 bayleaf
Pinch powdered mace or nutmeg
2 level teasp salt
¼ level teasp white pepper
1 tbsp chopped parsley or snipped
  chives
4 tbsp cream

Peel the carrots, onion and the potato. Halve the pepper, remove the seeds and pith. Cut the leek down the centre and wash well to remove grit. Slice all the vegetables very finely (or chop in food processor). In a heavy pan, melt the butter without allowing it to brown. Add all the vegetables except the potato. Stir well to mix with the fat, cover and cook very gently for 10 minutes. Uncover, add the potato, water, bayleaf, mace or nutmeg, salt and pepper. Bring to the boil, then cover and simmer for 20 minutes or until absolutely tender. Blend or process until almost smooth (I prefer a little bit of texture). In the same pan, bring the milk to the boil, then add the vegetable mixture. Bring slowly to the simmer. Turn off the heat and leave. Just before serving reheat with the cream and herbs.

Cream of Watercress Soup

Watercress has more 'bite' than any other salad green, which makes the flavour of this soup an exception to the normal bland cream soup. It can be served hot or well chilled.

Serves 8 **F** 3 months

2 bunches very fresh watercress	1 oz (25g/2 tbsp) butter
1 medium onion, finely chopped	1 lb (450g) potatoes, thinly sliced
1 bayleaf	2 pints (1.25 litres/5 cups) water
1/2 pint (275ml/1 1/4 cups) milk	with 1-2 vegetable stock cubes
1 teasp salt	4 tbsp single (light) or whipping
10 grinds black pepper	cream

If watercress is to be kept overnight, stand unwashed in a jug of cold water and refrigerate.

Trim off the bottom 1/2 inch (1cm) of each bunch, then wash thoroughly in cold running water. Cut off the leaves from one bunch only and put aside for garnish. Roughly chop the remaining leaves and stalks. Melt the butter in the soup pan and the minute it has become liquid add the onion, toss well to coat, then cover and simmer for 5 minutes, until softened and golden. Uncover and add the potatoes, and turn to coat them with the buttery onion.

Now add the water and stock cubes, bayleaf, salt and pepper. Bring to the boil, reduce to a simmer, cover and simmer for 25 minutes or until the potatoes are absolutely tender. Add the chopped watercress, bring back to the boil and simmer for *1 minute only*. This preserves the characteristic green colour. Take off the heat and purée until absolutely smooth. In the same pan heat the milk until steaming then add the watercress purée. Bring to simmering point. Remove from heat and leave for several hours to mature in flavour (can be refrigerated overnight). Just before serving, reheat until simmering and stir in the reserved leaves, very finely chopped. Top each serving with 2 teasp of cream.

Dairy Main Dishes

Dairy and vegetable main dishes have always been popular in countries with a poor supply of fresh meat. It's only recently, however, that the growing interest in health and vegetarian food has given an impetus to their more general acceptance. They make excellent main courses for luncheons and family dinners, as well as adding substance to lighter dishes such as cold poached fish and summer salads.

Such a dairy dish depends for its success on the use of really fresh but mature vegetables and very careful if delicate seasoning, as well as some quality of crispness, usually in the topping, to counteract the otherwise 'custardy' texture.

Single (light), whipping and soured cream all have an important role to play in dairy dishes. Follow the individual recipes in making your choice. Evaporated milk can make a very successful substitute for single (18% butterfat) cream (light cream), as being canned it can always be kept in stock, while its sterilized taste is not evident in a savoury dish. Either use by the spoonful to enrich a sauce, or, when a single cream is specified as a main ingredient, use half and half (undiluted) with ordinary milk.

Main Dish Eggs

Making a meal from eggs gives you a bargain in food value, taste and money, for each egg has the body-building capacity of 3 oz (75g) of meat at a fraction of the cost, and the flavour permutations are endless. For main dish meals, buy the largest, freshest eggs you can find, then refrigerate them for up to a week, but keep each day's supply at room temperature for even cooking and ease in whisking and blending with other ingredients.

181

The following simple visual test is useful to ensure that you are getting the freshest possible eggs from your source of supply. Crack the egg on to a saucer. When the egg is fresh, the yolk will be exactly central to a viscous band of white which thins out near its perimeter. If the egg is stale, however, the yolk will have moved to one side and its profile will have flattened, whilst the surrounding white will be thinner and more watery in appearance.

Cream Cheese Omelette Soufflé

Add curd or cottage cheese to your eggs, and you've got one of the most satisfying, low-calorie main dishes I know. Double the ingredients and use a 10-inch (25cm) pan if you want a monster version.

Serves 2-3

3 large eggs, separated
$^1/_4$ lb (125g/$^1/_2$ cup) cottage cheese
  or the same quantity of low fat
  (single cream) cheese
1 level tbsp chopped chives, *or* 1
  teasp dried chives or fines
  herbes

$^1/_2$ oz (15g/1 tbsp) nut of butter
Good pinch of salt and a few
  grinds of black pepper
• Pinch of cayenne or mustard

This omelette is fried, then finished off under a gentle grill. Have ready a 7 or 8 inch (17-20cm) frying pan. Separate the eggs and beat the yolks and cheese together until thoroughly blended, then beat in all the seasonings and herbs. Whisk the whites in another bowl with a good pinch of salt until they just hold peaks (don't overbeat until dry or they won't blend well). Now gently pour the yolk mixture on top and cut and fold together (using a metal spoon) until of an even golden colour. Heat the pan empty for 2 minutes (this prevents sticking), drop in the butter, and the minute it turns a pale fawn, pour in the egg mixture, smoothing it level. Cook gently (slower than for an ordinary omelette) until puffed on top and golden underneath (about 5 minutes), then transfer to the grill and cook until set and golden.

Serve at once in wedges. Good accompaniments: black bread, tomato, cucumber and pepper salad.

Spanish Omelette (Frittata)

This delicious omelette is first fried on top of the stove and then finished under the grill to make it brown and puffy. It is served straight from the pan, cut in wedges like a cake. Almost any vegetables can be used, and the omelette can be cooked in oil or butter as preferred. It is important to season the ingredients highly, as the eggs themselves are very bland.

Serves 6

6 eggs
1/2 level teasp salt

10 grinds black pepper
1 tbsp water

Whisk the above ingredients together with a large fork until the yolks and whites are evenly blended.

The filling:

1 1/2 oz (40g/3 tbsp) butter or oil
1 medium onion, finely chopped
1 small clove of garlic, crushed
4 oz (125g/2 cups) mushrooms,
    thinly sliced
1 large red pepper, halved,
    de-seeded, and cut in thin strips

4 large canned (or fresh, skinned)
    tomatoes
1/2 teasp sea salt
10 grinds black pepper
1 tbsp chopped parsley
1 teasp dried herbes de Provence
3 oz (75g/3/4 cup) grated sharp
    cheese

Melt the butter in a 9 inch (23cm) heavy frying pan and the minute it stops foaming add the onions, garlic, mushrooms and pepper. Cook gently until the onion is a rich golden brown, then add all the remaining ingredients (except the egg mixture). Cook until the tomatoes have softened and the mixture is thick but still juicy. Pour on the egg mixture, and cook, tilting the pan, until no free egg remains on top (about three minutes). Sprinkle thickly with the grated cheese and put under a very hot grill until golden brown and well puffed.

Serve at once, straight from the pan.

Creamed Eggs in Corn and Cheese Sauce

This is a very satisfying low-cost supper dish, which is equally convenient to make either for supper à deux, or for six hungry people. I give the quantities for both 6-8 and those for 2.

For 6-8	*For 2*
9 eggs	4 eggs
1 × 11 oz (300g) can corn with peppers	1/2 × 7 oz (200g)

Sauce:	
1 pint (575ml/2 1/2 cups) milk	1/4 pint (150ml/ 2/3 cup)
1/4 pint (150ml/2/3 cup) single (light) cream or evaporated milk	2 tbsp
2 oz (50g/1/4 cup) butter	1/2 oz (15g/1 tbsp)
4 level tbsp flour	1 level tbsp
1 teasp salt	1/4 teasp
10 shakes ground nutmeg	3 or 4 shakes
1 tbsp Dijon or English made mustard	1 teasp
20 grinds black pepper	5 grinds
6 oz (175g/1 1/2 cups) grated sharp cheese	2 oz (50g/1/2 cup)

Topping:	
3 level tbsp dry breadcrumbs	1 level tbsp
3 level tbsp finely grated cheese	1 level tbsp
1 1/2 oz (40g/3 tbsp) butter, cut in little bits	1/2 oz (15g/1 tbsp)

Simmer the eggs in their shells for 10 minutes, then plunge into cold water. Put the cold milk, flour, butter, salt, nutmeg, mustard and pepper into a pan and whisk over gentle heat until bubbling. Bubble for three minutes, still stirring, then whisk in the cream or evaporated milk and the grated cheese. Turn off the heat and continue to whisk until the cheese has melted and the sauce is quite smooth.

Select a 1 1/2 pint (1 litre) dish (1/2 pint/275ml dish) about 1 1/2 inches (3.75cm) deep, or use 6-8 (or 2) individual casseroles. Butter each dish well, and cover with the drained corn. Spread about a quarter of the sauce on top, then arrange the shelled and halved hard-boiled eggs on top, cut side down. Spoon over the remaining sauce, then cover with the breadcrumbs and cheese mixed together. (If you do not have breadcrumbs available you can use just cheese). Dot with the butter. Either grill very slowly for 10 minutes until bubbly and richly brown, or put in a quick oven (Gas No. 5, 375°F, 190°C) for 15 minutes until bubbly, then grill quickly for 2-3 minutes until the topping is a rich golden brown.

Serve at once with wholemeal bread.

Dairy Casseroles

All these casseroles make ideal main dishes to serve to vegetarian friends, as they are equally nourishing and tasty as meat or fish. They are all of Israeli origin and were developed shortly after the foundation of the State at a time when there was very little meat or fish available. The production of dairy foods is now one of the biggest export food industries in Israel, but the recipes were given to me in the first place by Israeli housewives.

Spinach and Cheese Bake

Layers of tender pancakes are filled with a rich cheese and spinach sauce. The dish is then baked under a savoury topping of soured cream.

Serves 6-8
Pancake batter:

2 whole eggs	4 oz (125g/1 cup) flour
8 oz (225ml/1 cup) milk	Pinch of salt and white pepper
1 tbsp melted butter	

Blend or process until a smooth batter. Leave to stand for one hour before making into approx twelve 7 inch (17cm) pancakes.

Filling: Cheese sauce made from:

8 fl oz (225ml/1 cup) milk	Pinch mustard
1 oz (25g/2 tbsp) butter	6 oz (175g/1½ cups) grated
1 oz (25g/4 tbsp) flour	Cheddar cheese
½ level teasp salt, speck white pepper	Pinch nutmeg

Whisk all ingredients (except cheese) over gentle heat until thick and smooth. Bubble 3 minutes. Add cheese off heat.

2 lb (1kg) spinach cooked without water until barely tender, *or* ½ lb (225g) pack of frozen spinach, lightly cooked	Extra cheese 2 × 5 fl oz (150ml/²⁄₃ cup) cartons soured cream

185

To assemble the dish:

Mix the cheese sauce with the drained, chopped spinach. Put in a buttered dish approx 8 inches (20cm) in diameter and 5 inches (12.5cm) deep in alternate layers with the pancakes, sprinkling each layer of cheese sauce with extra cheese. End with a pancake and a thick layer of cheese. Spread the soured cream thickly all over the top. Bake in a moderate oven (Gas No. 4, 350°F, 180°C) for 30 minutes until golden brown.

Vegetable Moussaka (Moussakat Vegevina)

The layers of creamy fried aubergine (eggplant) blend perfectly with the creamy egg and cheese filling.

Serves 6-8

1½ lb (600-800g) aubergines (eggplants), peeled, cut in slices one finger thick, then left in salted water one hour, taken out and dried.
Dip in beaten egg, fry in 1 inch (2.5cm) oil till golden, then drain.

The filling:

7 oz (200g) each of cream cheese, salted mozzarella and grated Cheddar; or ¾ lb (350g) each Cheddar and cream cheese

2 large eggs
Plenty of black pepper
1 level teasp salt
1 level tbsp chopped parsley

The topping:

2 large eggs, beaten
½ lb (225g/2 cups) grated Cheddar cheese

Mix together the beaten eggs, seasonings, parsley and cheeses of the filling. Butter a casserole approx 12 inches (30cm) by 8 inches (20cm) by 2 inches (5cm) deep. Put the ingredients in layers as follows: 1 layer aubergine (eggplant), 1 layer cheese mix, 1 layer aubergine, 1 layer cheese mix, 1 layer aubergine. Put in a quick oven (Gas No. 6, 400°F, 200°C) for 20 minutes, then take out. Pour over the eggs for the topping and sprinkle with the grated cheese. Return to the oven for a further 10 minutes. This can be kept hot on Gas No. ½ (250°F, 120°C) for up to 1 hour.

Aubergine (Eggplant) and Cheese Casserole

This is a simpler variation on the same theme. If really fresh aubergines (eggplants) are used, there is no need either to salt or pre-fry them for this excellent supper dish.

Serves 6-8

2 lb (1kg) potatoes, boiled
2 × 8 oz (225g) aubergines
  (eggplants)
2 large onions, sliced

1½ oz (40g/3 tbsp) butter or 2 tbsp
  oil
½ lb (225g/2 cups) Cheddar
  cheese, grated
Salt and black pepper

Parboil the whole potatoes in boiling water for ten minutes, drain and slice. Slice the aubergines (eggplants) ¼ inch (0.5cm) thick and arrange a few slices in the base of a buttered ovenproof dish. Fry the onions in the oil until soft and richly golden. Now arrange the vegetables in layers – aubergines, onion, potato, etc., seasoning with salt and pepper as you do so. Sprinkle each layer with grated cheese. Cover and bake for 45 minutes at Gas No. 5 (375°F, 190°C), then uncover and brown for a further 15 minutes.

To reheat: sprinkle with additional grated cheese and dot with butter. Put in a moderate oven (Gas No. 4, 350°F, 180°C) for 30 minutes.

Noodle and Cream Cheese Puff

This can be served as a light main course with a crisp green salad or, instead of potatoes, as an accompaniment to hot fish.

Serves 6-8

½ lb (225g/3 cups) broad egg
  noodles
½ pint (275ml/1¼ cups) soured
  cream
½ lb (225g/1 cup) low or medium
  fat cream cheese

½ teasp salt
10 grinds black pepper
1 tbsp chopped fresh chives or
  parsley
3 large eggs, separated
2 oz (50g/¼ cup) butter

Boil the noodles according to packet directions and drain. Pour hot water over them to remove any excess starch. Drain again and mix with the soured cream, cheese, beaten yolks, herbs and seasonings. Fold in the egg whites, beaten until they hold stiff, glossy peaks.

Melt the butter. Pour half into the bottom of a 3 pint (1.75 litre) ovenproof gratin dish approx 12 × 10 inches (30 × 25cm) by 2 inches (5cm) deep. Add noodle mixture. Pour remaining butter over the top. Bake in a quick moderate oven (Gas No. 5, 375°F, 190°C) for 45 minutes until puffed and golden. Cut in squares to serve.

The Savoury Soufflé

Unnecessary mystique surrounds the making of this superb dish, which is in essence no more than a thick, well-flavoured sauce lightened with egg whites, then baked until it is barely set – with a crunchy brown 'top hat'. The French use the almost untranslatable word 'baveuse' to describe the quivery inside texture. Follow these pointers and you cannot go wrong.

The oven: As a soufflé needs a steady heat all round it, always preheat the oven well in advance and at a temperature 1 gas Mark (25°F, 10°C) higher than is required. This ensures that the oven is not only thoroughly heated but that there is a margin of safety to allow for the inevitable heat loss when the oven door is opened. If the baking tray is preheated at the same time, the soufflé will be further helped to rise.

The dish: For a hot soufflé, there is no need to extend the sides with a high band of paper – simply choose a deep enough dish to allow for expansion without explosion. Always butter this dish thoroughly, and for extra crunchiness, scatter its top and sides with finely grated cheese (Parmesan is ideal).

The timing: Some cookbooks recommend freezing the raw soufflé in advance but I find this interferes with the rise. One can, however, complete the soufflé (bar the baking) up to one hour in advance. This means that it can safely wait until guests have arrived before being put in the oven. As a soufflé *must* be served as soon as it is ready, it is better for the guests to wait for it, than vice versa.

The size of the soufflé: I give the quantities for three sizes, to serve 6-8, 4-6 and 1-2. In each case the lower figure is for a main dish, the higher figure when served as an entrèe or for luncheon. Although one *can* make a larger quantity to bake as individual soufflés, I would not recommend making more than 6-8 servings in one dish, as it is then extremely difficult to judge the cooking time, or indeed to ensure that the inside is cooked before the outside has overbrowned.

The cheese: It is necessary to use a cheese which will melt creamily in the oven but which has a little 'bite' to its flavour. One can use a mixture of grated Gruyère and Parmesan or Cheddar. However, if it is available there is nothing to compare with Lancashire cheese which need only be crumbled (rather than grated) into the mixture.

The extra egg white can be one you have in stock in the refrigerator, or a fresh one – in which case the unused egg should be put in a tiny airtight plastic container, refrigerated, then used within 24 hours.

Cheese Soufflé

Serves 6-8

3 oz (75g/^{1}/$_3$ cup) butter
2^1/$_4$ oz (60g/^{1}/$_2$ cup + 1 tbsp) flour
^{3}/$_4$ pint (425ml/2 cups) milk
1 level teasp salt
^{1}/$_8$ teasp white pepper *or* 15 grinds black pepper
1^1/$_2$ teasp Dijon mustard
Good pinch cayenne

Pinch nutmeg
6 egg yolks
7 egg whites
^{1}/$_4$ teasp cream of tartar or salt if not available
5 oz (150g/1^1/$_4$ cups) cheese (preferably crumbled Lancashire)

Butter a 3^1/$_2$ pint (2 litre) soufflé dish or a 4 inch (10cm) deep, 9 inch (22.5cm) wide oven glass casserole, and sprinkle with Parmesan cheese. Preheat the oven to Gas No. 6 (400°F, 200°C) and put in a baking tin.

Put the flour, butter and cold milk into a heavy-bottomed 8-9 inch (20-22.5cm) pan and bring gently to the boil, whisking with a batter-whisk or hand-held electric mixer. Add the seasonings then bubble for 3 minutes, stirring constantly with a wooden

189

spoon. Remove from the heat. Have ready the bowl in which you intend to whisk the egg whites. Separate the eggs and drop the yolks one at time into the hot sauce, stirring well after each addition, while you drop its companion white into the bowl. Whisk the whites with the cream of tartar or salt until they stand up in stiff, glossy peaks when the beaters are withdrawn.

Take a quarter of the meringue and *stir* it into the sauce, followed by all but 1 tablespoon of the grated cheese. Now drop the remaining meringue on top and, using a plastic or rubber spatula, *fold* it into the sauce as gently as possible so that the mixture becomes an even colour but remains fluffy in texture. Coax it gently into the prepared dish. With the flat of a knife, make a shallow groove round the edge of the mixture, 1 inch (2.5cm) away from the rim of the dish (this helps it to rise into a 'top hat' shape).

Put on the tray in the preheated oven, then turn it down to Gas No. 5 (375°F, 190°C). It will be ready to eat in 35 minutes, when the top will be a crusty brown.

Ingredients for 4-6

2 oz (50g/¼ cup) butter
1½ oz (40g/⅓ cup) flour
½ pint (275ml/1¼ cups) milk
½ teasp salt
10 grinds pepper
1 teasp Dijon mustard
Pinch cayenne
Pinch ground nutmeg
4 large egg yolks
5 large egg whites
3 oz (75g/¾ cup) coarsely grated cheese
Good pinch cream of tartar or salt

Ingredients for 2

Use half all quantities
but 2 large eggs only.
(If you have leftover
whites in the fridge,
add a tbsp to the other
whites. Otherwise
forget it.)

The dish:

3 in/8cm deep
8 in/20cm in diameter

2¾ in/7.5cm deep
5¾in/15cm in diameter

To bake:

Bake exactly as for larger soufflé

Bake at same
temperature as larger
soufflé, but for 30
minutes only

Mushroom Soufflé

As this is much more filling than a cheese soufflé, smaller portions can be offered and a larger number of guests served from a smaller quantity of mixture. The sauce should be highly seasoned to offset the blandness of the mushrooms.

Serves 6-8
Set the oven at Gas No. 6 (400°F, 200°C)

8 oz (225g/4 cups) mushrooms	1 oz (25g/2 tbsp) butter and a
¼ medium onion *or* 3 shallots,	squeeze of lemon juice
very finely chopped	2 tbsp medium sherry (optional)

Melt the butter, add the vegetables and lemon juice, cover and cook for 5 minutes. Uncover and allow to bubble until all the moisture has evaporated (about 3 minutes).

The sauce:

1½ oz (40g/3 tbsp) butter	2 teasp chopped parsley or
1½ oz (40g/⅜ cup) flour	scissored chives
½ pint (275ml/1¼ cups) milk	2 oz (50g/½ cup) well-flavoured
½ level teasp salt	grated cheese
Pinch each of white pepper and	4 large eggs, separated, plus an
ground mace	extra white
2 tbsp thick cream	

Put the flour, butter and cold milk into a pan, and whisk over gentle heat until a thick sauce is formed. Add the seasonings, bubble three minutes, then take off the heat and add the cream, all but 1 tablespoon of the cheese, the four egg yolks and the mushroom mixture. Whisk the whites with a pinch of salt until they hold stiff, glossy peaks. Stir a quarter of the whites thoroughly into the sauce, then gently fold in the rest.

Turn into a well-buttered, soufflé or round glass ovenproof dish of 3 pint (1¾ litre) capacity (8 in/20cm diameter, 3 in/7.5cm deep). Sprinkle with the remaining cheese. Put the soufflé into the middle of the oven and turn the heat down to Gas No. 5 (375°F, 190°C). Bake for 40 minutes until a rich brown. Serve at once.

Rice Fried Italian Style

Although the purists might consider this a second-class risotto, it

191

is in fact a well-loved peasant dish, and makes a delicious meal for the unexpected guest from left-over (or indeed freshly cooked) rice. If risotto rice is not available, use long grain rice instead, but the dish will not be as creamy.

Serves 6-8

12 oz (350g/1²/₃ cups) Italian risotto rice	6 level tbsp freshly grated Parmesan cheese
6 oz (175g/³/₄ cup) butter	Salt and black pepper to taste
	Pinch ground nutmeg

Cook rice in water or light stock according to packet instructions. Melt the butter, add the rice, toss it in butter, heating through and adding seasonings to taste. Stir the Parmesan through the mixture.

Serve with more butter and cheese for each person to stir through.

Quantities for 2-3:

2 cups left-over rice (5 oz/150g/²/₃ cup uncooked)	2 level tbsp freshly grated Parmesan cheese
2 oz (50g/¹/₄ cup) butter	Salt, pepper and a pinch of ground nutmeg

The Cheese Fondue

This deliciously-flavoured mixture of cheese, wine and spirit is surprisingly easy – and good fun to make. However, its simplicity belies a great attention to detail, both in the choice of ingredients and their preparation. There are certain specialized utensils, for instance, which are not only essential to the making and serving of the fondue, but also add greatly to the special sense of occasion. They can be purchased at any good speciality hardware shop or department store.

The cooking pot or 'caquelon'
This is simply a saucepan with rounded sides narrowing towards the top, with a short sturdy handle. It can be made variously of earthenware, a metal such as stainless steel or copper, or enamelled steel. It serves as both cooking and serving pot.

Alcohol stove with adjustable burner: This can be as simple as a camping stove, or as elaborate as the makers can produce in copper or steel. It is used to keep the fondue hot on the dining table.

A set of fondue forks: These have sharp tines set close together (to make it easy to spear cubes of bread), and long handles to prevent the diners colliding with each other's forks as they dip their speared bread into the hot fondue.

The vital ingredients: In Switzerland they prefer a mixture of Gruyère and Emmenthal. But if this is not available, any other cheese which melts easily and smoothly – or a mixture of several cheeses – can be used, either by themselves or mixed with Gruyère. For example, Cheddar, Lancashire or Gouda.

The wine: This should be both light and dry with a high acid content. As it does not need to be an expensive variety, any good supermarket brand can be used.

The spirit: This should preferably be kirsch, but if it is not available, use gin or vodka instead. However, a spirit of some kind is vital to the flavour.

The garlic: Depending on the intensity of flavour you prefer, this can either be rubbed on the surface of the caquelon, cut in half or crushed and added to the cheese mixture, but even a hint of garlic is preferable to none at all.

The bread: Dipping cubes of bread into the fondue is the central part of the fondue 'ceremony'. For this purpose a slightly stale French loaf is ideal. It should be cut into 1 inch (2.5cm) cubes – a size convenient both for dipping and eating. For any guest with a delicate digestion, the cubes can be lightly toasted in the oven beforehand.

The cornflour (cornstarch): This is used not so much to thicken the fondue as to keep all the ingredients in a smooth suspension.

And now for the recipe:

For each person (maximum of 8 for each dish of fondue)

6 oz (175g/1½·cups) cheese (see choice above), grated or cut up in thin strips

3½ fl oz (100ml/½ cup) dry white wine

1 teasp lemon juice

7 oz (200g) French bread cut in 1 inch (2.5cm) cubes

For each fondue:

2 teasp cornflour (cornstarch)

1 glass (3.5 fl oz/100ml/½ cup) kirsch, vodka or gin

10 grinds black pepper, pinch ground nutmeg (or to taste)

The fondue is prepared on a regular stove, then just before serving it is carried into the dining-room and placed on the spirit stove. Do not prepare it in advance or it will become too thick.

Spear the peeled and halved garlic clove on a fork and lightly rub round the interior of the caquelon. If, however, a stronger flavour is preferred, add the cut clove to the cheese mixture, or (stronger still) crush it before adding the cheese.

Pour the wine and the lemon juice into the caquelon and bring to steaming point over high heat. Add the cheese, reduce the heat to medium and continue to cook, stirring constantly until the mixture is smooth and has begun to bubble. Put the cornflour (cornstarch) into a small bowl and stir to a cream with the spirit, then add to the cheese mixture. Allow it to bubble for 3 minutes, stirring constantly, then season to taste with the spices.

At this point, if a first course is served, the fondue can be kept hot on a very low heat. However, I prefer to offer dips and canapés *before* the meal so that the guests can sit down at table as soon as the fondue is ready.

When ready to serve, transfer it to the spirit stove adjusted to keep it hot without further cooking. Each guest then dips a cube of bread speared on a fork into the creamy fondue, which is given an occasional stir to keep the consistency even. However, as the quantity of fondue is reduced, the portion near the bottom will thicken into the delicious 'grillon' which, as this is the best portion of all, must be shared out evenly among the guests.

Serve with wine or tea, *never* with large quantities of cold liquid such as beer or cider, as this makes a very indigestible mixture.

The Cheeseboard

A cheeseboard should be a delight to the eye as much as to the palate, so special attention needs to be paid to the display as well as to the choice, shape, texture and taste of the cheeses and the garnishes that are used.

The board: I prefer to use an undecorated platter, made of plain wood, glass or pottery, as this does not distract the eye from the beauty of the display.

The cheeses: It is important to choose a variety of textures – from the soft high fat cream cheese to hard pressed ones – as well as to make sure there is a good blend of both mild and strong flavours. For a dinner party I would serve no more than three varieties, such as Brie, Stilton and Cheddar, though if I were totally trusting of my source of supply, I would simply offer one superb variety such as Brie 'coulant' (when it's at its slightly runny peak) or Blue Stilton. However, for a cheese buffet, a wider variety can be offered but never more than eight as too much choice and mingling of flavours makes it difficult to appreciate the individual cheeses.

If possible the cheeses should be purchased on the day they are to be eaten as there is always some diminution of flavour once they have been cut. If this is not possible, however, keep well wrapped in greaseproof paper and store in a plastic container.

To arrange on the board: The Danes are the leaders in this field, and it is worth searching out an illustrated Danish cookery book to gain some insight into the art. As with a smörrebrod, a cheeseboard should be arranged in a three dimensional way, paying special attention to the juxtaposition of the different shapes and colours, and the use of garnishes such as fruit and salad vegetables.

Garnishes: These should be chosen not only for their shape and colour but also for the way in which they can be married to a particular cheese. For instance, with a highly-flavoured cheese such as Stilton, use a mild salad vegetable such as Belgian chicory or celery; with a creamy cheese such as Brie, use a slightly acid fruit such as tangerines or grapes; with a blue cheese, use a more neutral accompaniment such as walnuts or sweet black grapes;

with a hard cheese such as Cheddar, juicy apples or pears; with soft cheese such as goat's, offer fruit or vegetables with a crisp flavour or texture such as fresh strawberries or red peppers. The garnish can either be placed directly on the board as a decoration, or offered separately in small or large bowls (see below).

Suggested garnishes:

Apples	Choose crisp varieties that are not too hard. Arrange in a bowl.
Bananas	They must be fully ripe with brown spots on the skin. Offer whole.
Celery	At least an hour beforehand, wash well, then cut in 3 inch (7.5cm) strips, or the stalks from the heart can be served whole in a special celery dish or a glass tumbler.
Cherries	Put on the board in tiny bunches, or set on slightly crushed ice in one large bowl.
Belgian chicory	Cut off the end so that the leaves can be separated, wash and dry, then arrange in a wooden salad bowl or on a shallow glass platter.
Cucumber	Cut in thin slices, and arrange in overlapping rows on the board, or cut into fingers.
Grapes (green or black)	These look particularly decorative set in tiny bunches amongst the different cheeses.
Nuts (mixed, or walnuts in the shell)	These can be set in small groups on the board, or more practically in a bowl with nutcrackers.
Olives (black and green)	Serve in tiny individual soufflé dishes or cocottes placed on the board.
Peppers (red and green)	Halve the peppers, remove the white pith and seeds and cut in slices $1/4$ inch (0.5cm) thick. Use to garnish the board.
Pineapple	Use cubes of canned or fresh pineapple speared into a whole orange set on the board.
Radishes	Wash well, leaving a little stalk on for ease in handling. Arrange in a small dish or straight on the board.
Spring onions (scallions)	Cut off the roots, trim the tops down to the fleshy part then arrange in little bunches on the board.

Tangerines	Leave whole. Arrange on the board or in a bowl.
Strawberries	Wash and dab dry, then arrange on the board or in a bowl set on ice like the cherries.
Tomatoes	If cherry tomatoes are used, leave whole in a bowl, otherwise cut in wedges, de-seed and arrange on the board.
Watercress	Cut off the lower part of the stems with the roots, wash thoroughly and dry. Either arrange in tiny clusters on the board or offer with other salads such as cucumber fingers and celery.

A note on quantities: It is impossible to be specific, as much will depend on the food served beforehand. However, as a rough guide, allow 6-8 oz (175-225g) per head for a cheese party, and 3 oz (75g) after dinner. This will allow for a variety of cheeses with some left over. Always serve cheese at room temperature, which means arranging it at least one hour before it is to be served. To prevent the cheese drying out, either cover the entire board with film or leave individual cheeses in their wrapping until the very last minute.

Fish

All the recipes in this chapter have been specially selected to present fish in prime condition and with the minimum of last minute preparation. Good quality fresh fish needs only very simple – if precise-cooking to transform it into a memorable dish. As it is only the exceptional and usually expensive restaurant that is prepared to give it this kind of treatment, it makes an excellent choice for the home cook to put on an entertaining menu.

There are, however, a few 'tricks of the trade' whereby some of the more complicated restaurant-style dishes can be prepared in advance without detriment either to their texture of quality.

To Select Fish

As freshness and quality are of prime importance, there is no way one can take stale or poor quality fish and transform it into a party dish. However, one can buy less popular, cheaper varieties of fish – albeit of prime quality – and make them fit for a guest.

If possible, first choose your fishmonger, and then trust his judgement. In deciding which fish shop is likely to give you the best buy, the relationship between price, variety of fish and the quality must be understood from the start. A difference in price between two kinds of fish in the same shop usually means that one is more popular with customers than the other; halibut, for instance, is always much dearer than haddock of the same quality. However, if haddock is dearer in one shop than it is in another in the same neighbourhood, you can be almost certain that the difference in price reflects a difference in quality. Of course you must expect to pay more in the shop that dresses the fish with care.

However, the seemingly cheaper fish may well cost you dearer in the end, for if it is of second quality it is likely to be undersized or stale.

The following pointers may be helpful if self-selection is necessary. Fish must be chosen with the nose as well as the eyes. Fresh fish, no matter what the variety, looks moist and firm with a glistening skin, bright eyes and markings, and bright red gills. It should smell either of the river or the sea, but never of ammonia. Many varieties – such as herrings, smoked fish, mackerel and salmon – vary in quality according to the season and the fishing and the fishing grounds where they were caught, so the fishmonger's advice should always be sought as to the right time to buy a particular variety. Indeed, don't be too dogmatic about serving a particular variety, but follow the fishmonger's guidance on which is prime on that particular day. For this reason I have given many recipes in which several varieties of fish are interchangeable.

If possible, fish should be bought on the day it is to be cooked or within 24 hours at the latest. But as the fishmonger also buys fresh daily, it is good sense to place your order the day before it is required.

Commercial frozen fish: Frozen fish can taste no better than the fish tasted when it was fresh. So superb quality fish will freeze well, and eat well when it has been cooked. Undersized, second quality fish is likely to prove disappointing and should be avoided.

To Freeze Fish at Home

This can be good policy if a large quantity of prime fish should come your way – for example, after a fishing expedition or during the salmon season. If possible freeze fish within 24 hours of being caught.

To freeze large whole fish, e.g. salmon, salmon trout, sea bass, etc. (regular method): Remove head or not, as preferred. Remove the viscera, but do not wash. Instead wipe with a damp paper towel. Wrap each fish closely in film and then over-wrap in foil or a plastic bag.

To freeze whole large fish with head (alternative method): This method is a little more trouble than the conventional one but the perfect quality of the defrosted fish makes it really worthwhile. Do not behead or gut the fish but wipe it with a paper towel. Put uncovered in the freezer for 3 hours, or until it feels firm and rigid. Dump into a sink of warm water, then immediately put back into the freezer until a thin coating of ice has formed – about 10 minutes. Repeat the process twice more, when the fish will be completely sealed inside its coating of ice. Wrap tightly in a salmon bag or foil. This keeps extremely well.

To freeze small whole fish (e.g. trout, mackerel): Prepare as regular method above. For a large quantity, it is easiest to open freeze. Lay the well-dried fish (heads on or not, as preferred) side by side on open trays. Freeze until rigid, then place in plastic bags. They will not stick together.

For a small quantity, wrap in film, then bag or wrap in foil in quantities for 2 or 4 as preferred, and freeze.

To freeze large cuts, steaks or fillets: Prepare exactly as above, open freezing or not as convenient.

Note: Fish must be frozen quickly, so the fast-freeze switch should be put on at least 2 hours in advance. Leave on for 24 hours after the fish has been put in the freezer, and do not move fish for another 8 hours.

Storage time for frozen fish: Raw fish 6-9 months depending on time lapse after it has been caught. Longer will not affect the safety but may affect the eating quality.

Cooked fish 3 months.

To defrost fish: If possible, defrost overnight in the refrigerator. If this is not possible be sure to refrigerate if there is a time lag between defrosting and cooking the fish.

White Fish Stock

Stock made with fish bones, vegetables and perhaps a little white wine gives extra depth or flavour to any fish sauce when it is used instead of the water or to replace part of the quantity of wine recommended in the recipe. It freezes well for up to 3 months.

1 oz (25g/2 tbsp) butter
1 lb (450g) bones and trimmings
from any white fish (such as
sole, haddock, cod, whiting *or*
plaice)
1 large (8 oz/225g) onion, finely
sliced
12 stems of parsley

2 tbsp lemon juice
1/2 teasp salt
Speck white pepper
10 peppercorns
1 1/2 pints (850ml/4 cups) water *or* 5
fl oz (150ml/2/3 cup) white wine
and 1 1/4 pints (725ml/3 cups)
water

Spread the butter over the bottom of a heavy pan, then add all the ingredients (except the liquid), cover and allow to sweat over moderately high heat for 5 minutes. Add the liquid and bring to the boil, then reduce the heat until the mixture is gently bubbling, and after skimming the froth from the top cook steadily for 25 minutes.

Pour the contents of the pan through a fine sieve, pressing the solids firmly against the sieve to extract all the juices. Allow to cool, then pour into plastic cups or containers (8 oz/225ml is most convenient). Cover and freeze, or use as required.

This makes approx 1 1/4 pints (725ml/3 cups) fish stock.

Out of the Frying Pan

It is not advisable to choose a fish dish that needs to be served hot off the pan, except for an intimate occasion, when a handful of guests are either prepared to entertain themselves or join you in the kitchen. However, there are some recipes where the fish can be cooked lightly a little in advance, then kept hot in a low oven until it is married with some kind of sauce just before serving. This kind of procedure is more successful with steaks than with fillets, as the thickness of the fish prevents it drying out during the waiting period.

Fish Steaks Arbois Style

I first tasted this dish made with pike, as the rivers round the charming little town of Arbois in the Franche Comté – the Doubs, the Saône and the Loue – teem with all kinds of freshwater fish. However, I have anglicized it so that it can be made with our more easily available sea fish, and I think it is equally delectable.

Start the preparation 20 minutes before you expect the guests to arrive – or earlier, if the fish can be kept hot in a low oven (see below).

Note: In Arbois, Chef André Jeunet, who devised the recipe, used 'crème fraiche', a slightly acid thick cream. For a similar taste, use half double (heavy) cream, half soured cream.

Serves 6-8

6-8 slices haddock, hake or salmon, each 6 oz (175g) in weight
1 teasp salt
Speck white pepper
3 oz (75g/^{3}/$_4$ cup) flour
4 oz (125g/^{1}/$_2$ cup) butter and 1 tbsp oil
4 oz (125g) shallots (or mild onion), finely chopped

4 oz (125g) mushrooms, finely chopped
^{1}/$_2$ clove of garlic, crushed
^{1}/$_2$ pint (275ml/1^1/$_4$ cups) medium dry white wine (e.g. Riesling)
^{1}/$_2$ pint (275ml/1^1/$_4$ cups) whipping, soured or double (heavy) cream
To season: salt, pepper, nutmeg, chopped parsley

Wash the steaks of fish, then lightly sprinkle with salt and white pepper. Dip each steak in the flour, then pat off any excess.

Heat the butter and oil in a 9 inch (22cm) frying pan. The minute the butter starts to foam, add the fish and allow to cook steadily for 3 minutes on each side until a golden brown. Remove to a serving dish about 1 inch (2.5cm) deep, and leave in a low oven Gas No. 1, (275°F, 140°C) while completing the cooking of the sauce. (The fish can be kept hot at this stage for up to 30 minutes if covered with foil.)

To the same pan add the finely chopped shallots and mushrooms together with the crushed garlic and cook gently for 5 minutes until softened but not browned. Add the wine and bubble for 3 minutes then add the cream, a pinch of nutmeg and salt and pepper to taste.

Heat until steaming then pour over the fish and sprinkle with the parsley.

Trout in Brandy and Cream Sauce

Père Louis used to serve this dish at his hotel in Montmorillon in the heart of provincial France, where it is the custom to select the live fish from its tank then stun, gut and cook it to order. The ideal fish for this recipe weighs between 8 and 10 oz (225-275g). The butter and the lemon juice point up the flavour of a really fine trout.

This is a suitable dish to serve to 3 or 4 people, but for a larger number, either use 2 frying pans or cook in 2 batches.

For 3-4 fish
To coat the fish:

2 oz (50g/^{1}/$_2$ cup) flour	Speck white pepper
1 teasp salt	

To fry the fish:

2 oz (50g/^{1}/$_4$ cup) butter
2 teasp oil

You will need a large heavy frying pan, wide enough to hold 3-4 fish side by side.

Have the fish cleaned through the gills, leaving the head intact as this will prevent the fish from getting greasy when it is cooked.

Put the coating flour on to a square of greaseproof paper or a shallow dish as long as the fish. Wash and salt the fish, allow them to drain in a colander for 10 minutes, then lift them by the tail, and one at a time, roll them quickly in the flour, making sure each fish is coated thinly but completely. This gives a light but crisp coating. Heat the empty frying pan for 2 minutes, then put in the butter and the oil. The minute the butter starts to foam, lower in the fish side by side, making sure the underside of each fish is lying flat in the bubbling fat. Cook steadily at a gentle bubble for 5 minutes, by which time the underside should be a rich, crisp brown. Carefully turn over each fish using 2 spoons so that you do not pierce the flesh. Fry the second side for a further 5 minutes then lift out and put side by side in a shallow entrée dish, and keep hot (for up to 30 minutes) in the oven at Gas No. 2 (300°F, 150°C).

Just before serving make the following sauce:

For 3-4 fish

2 tbsp brandy
8 fl oz (225ml/1 cup) whipping
   cream
2 teasp lemon juice
Salt and black pepper

2 oz (50g/^{1}/$_2$ cup) flaked almonds
(For 6 fish use same amounts of
   ingredients, but ^{1}/$_2$ pint/275ml/
   1^1/$_4$ cups cream)

After the fish has been cooked and removed from the pan, discard all but 2 tbsp of the buttery juices. To them add the brandy, cream and lemon juice. Bubble until of a coating consistency, season, then pour over the fish and decorate with the almonds.

Hot from the Grill

Grilled fish waits for no man so these recipes are best for less formal occasions such as a special family meal or an alfresco luncheon or barbecue. Remember that unlike meat, fish does not need to be sealed by searing with high heat. Instead it needs steady moderate heat and (in the case of the less oily fish) regular basting with some kind of fat or oil.

Tremadoc Bay Grilled Mackerel

On a lucky night the weekend fisherman can catch these delicious fish by the hundred. Those not for use next day must be filleted and frozen immediately. As they are not as large as the Cornish fish, they take particularly well to grilling with this very piquant topping.

1-2 mackerel fillets per person (according to size)
Allow 6 oz (175g) filleted fish per person.

Topping:

2 oz (50g/^{1}/$_4$ cup) soft butter or 3
   tbsp corn oil
1 tbsp cider vinegar or wine
   vinegar

2 teasp French or English mustard
2 teasp Worcestershire sauce
10 grinds black pepper
Good pinch sea salt

Wash, trim and salt the fish (be sure to remove any stray bones left during the filleting), and leave in a colander for 30 minutes then dab dry with paper towels.

Beat all the topping ingredients together. Butter the grill pan and heat it under moderate heat for 3 minutes. Place the fillets on it side by side, and spread evenly with the topping. Grill under a moderate heat for 12-15 minutes until a rich brown. Serve at once.

Barbecued Mackerel with Mustard Butter

(For preparation of barbecue and pre-heating of grill see pp.87-9).
This method conserves all the flavour of the mackerel. It can also be used for any other small fish such as trout.

The fish can be cooked directly on a greased grill, or in a hinged, double-sided grill, which is especially useful for cooking small fish such as the fresh sardines now available in some parts of the country (see below).

For 3 fish allow this basting sauce:

2 oz (50g/¼ cup) melted butter mixed with 4 tbsp lemon juice and 1 tbsp
 Worcestershire sauce

Allow one fish per person. Have the heads removed, the fish split down the centre but the bone left in (more flavour). Rinse the fish under the cold tap, dab dry and salt the inside very lightly, then close up.

Brush the grill rack with oil, brush the fish all over with warm sauce, then place on the grill (or put fish in hinged grill if used, and close it). Grill about 2 inches (5cm) from the heat for 6 minutes on each side, brushing two or three times with more sauce. Season before serving with salt and pepper. Serve with lemon wedges or **Mustard Butter.**

Mustard Butter

Beat together 4 oz (125g/½ cup) soft butter; 1 level tbsp Moutarde de Dijon; 1 teasp lemon juice, and sea salt and black pepper to taste. Leave in a shallow bowl. Serve at room temperature.

205

Plaice with Crusty Cheese Topping

This is an excellent way to cook the medium plaice which are too small to make thick fillets but are nonetheless sweet and tender. The crusty topping seals in the fish juices and keeps the dish succulent.

8 fillets from 2 medium fish (3 lb/1.5kg bone-in weight)	4 heaped tbsp grated cheese (enough for a ¼ inch/0.5cm thick layer)
2 oz (50g/¼ cup) butter	
2 tbsp salad cream	Salt and white pepper

Wash the fish, sprinkle with salt and pepper, and leave in a colander to drain. 10 minutes before the fish is required, melt the butter under the grill in a dish just large enough to hold the fish tightly packed in one layer. (I use a shallow cast-iron enamelled casserole.) Dip each fillet into the melted butter, then turn it over and lay side by side in the dish. Grill for 7 minutes, basting once with the buttery juices. Spread with the salad cream, then coat thickly with the grated cheese. Continue to grill for another 3 minutes, or until the cheese has set into a crusty layer. This layer prevents these smaller fillets from drying out and at the same time makes a delicious crusty topping.

Barbecued Sardines

Unless you live near a fishing port, you are likely to buy these frozen.

Allow 6 oz (175g) fish per person.

Prepare and cook exactly as for the mackerel, but allow only 5 minutes on each side.

Serve sprinkled with sea salt, together with lemon wedges and coarse brown bread.

En Casserole

It is most convenient to cook and serve a fish dish in the same casserole. Like those made with meat or poultry, a fish casserole is particularly good-tempered and does not deteriorate if the guests are not quite on time.

Fisherman's Casserole

The chef who showed me how to make this dish used a variety of fresh and salt water fish for what he called Petite Marmite du Pêcheur. However, price permitting, I find it most delicious when made with hake fillet (though provided the fish is thick enough, I have made it with many other kinds of white fish). I think it is one of the most delicious yet simple-to-make fish dishes I know. As with all recipes for poached fish, it is important to cook it very gently so that the fish remains tender and moist. I have found that when expecting guests, provided I cook it for five minutes less than usual, I can start the dish an hour or so beforehand, then complete the cooking when the cream is added just before serving.

This method of cooking conserves all the flavour of the fish and also results in a delicious sauce. Use any filleted white fish – hake, haddock, cod, whiting or plaice.

Serves 6-8

2 oz (50g/¼ cup) butter
½ large carrot
½ medium onion
1½-2 lb (0.75-1kg) white fish
1 level teasp salt
Speck white pepper
1 small bayleaf
10 peppercorns (optional)
1 small can (6 oz/175ml/¾ cup) evaporated milk *or* 5 oz (150ml/⅔ cup) single (light) cream

2 teasp cornflour (cornstarch)
2 teasp chopped parsley
1 × 29 oz (825g) can new potatoes *or* 2 lb (1kg) scraped new potatoes boiled until tender
1 small packet frozen peas (optional)
Chopped parsley

The dish is most conveniently cooked in a stove-to-table casserole. Otherwise use an ordinary frying pan and transfer to a serving dish.

Wash and salt the fish, then cut thick fillets such as hake into 6-8 pieces, and roll up thinner fillets such as plaice or whiting.

Grate the carrot and the onion finely. Heat the butter in the chosen pan (it should be about 9 inches/22cm in diameter) and the

207

minute it has melted, but before it starts to change colour, add the grated vegetables. Stir for a minute or two to allow them to absorb some of the butter and begin to soften, then add the fish and turn it over so that it becomes coated with the buttery vegetables. Now add just enough water to cover the bottom of the pan to a depth of ¼ inch (0.5cm). Sprinkle the fish with the salt and pepper, add the bayleaf and the peppercorns at the side of the pan, cover and simmer *very* gently for 20 minutes or until the fish looks creamy right through. Remove bayleaf and peppercorns. Put the cornflour (cornstarch) in a bowl and stir in the evaporated milk or cream. Add to the fish and allow to bubble for 3 minutes.

Finally stir in the drained new potatoes, chopped parsley and cooked frozen peas (if used), and leave covered on a very low heat for 3 or 4 minutes.

Fish Gratin à La Crème

This is a superbly simple dish that looks splendid under its cheesey crust. As no liquid other than cream is used, the full flavour of the fish is conserved.

Serves 6-8

6-8 thick fillets of plaice or baby halibut (cut from fish weighing approx 1½-2 lb/675-900g each)
2 lb (1kg) new potatoes *or* 2 cans best quality new potatoes
10 fl oz (275ml/1¼ cups) whipping cream

Salt and pepper
1 medium onion, chopped
1 oz (25g/2 tbsp) butter
Butter for greasing dish
3 tbsp grated cheese

Cook the potatoes in their skins until barely tender; skin when cool, then slice ⅜ inch (1cm) thick (or drain and slice canned potatoes if used). Wash and skin the fish and salt it. Season the cream with salt and plenty of white pepper. Gently sauté the chopped onion in the butter until soft and golden. Take a dish about 1½ inches (3.75cm) deep and wide enough to hold the folded fillets in one layer. Butter it well, then arrange the sliced potatoes evenly over the bottom. Lay the folded fillets side by side on top and scatter with the onions (in a hurry, omit the sautéing and simply grate a little onion on top). Finally, pour over the seasoned cream and scatter the dish with the grated cheese. Lay a sheet of buttered greaseproof paper lightly on top. Bake in a slow moderate oven (Gas No. 3, 325°F, 160°C) for 30 minutes until the sauce is bubbling very slightly and the fish has lost its glassy appearance. Take off the paper and grill gently for 3-4 minutes until a rich golden brown, then serve at once.

Party Fish Dish with Mushrooms and Soured Cream

That's the only name I have for this simple but delicious dish because that explains all – exquisite in flavour for the most discriminating guest, yet simple and sure of success from the cook's point of view. In more plentiful days the chosen fish was Dover sole. Now lemon sole or thick fillets of plaice are more likely to be available.

Serves 6-8

Allow 2 fillets of fish per person (cut from fish weighing approx 1½ lb/675g each). Have the skin removed.
Salt and white pepper
Butter
½ lb (225g/4 cups) mushrooms sliced

1 oz (25g/2 tbsp) butter
Squeeze of lemon juice
6-8 tomatoes, sliced
2 × 5 fl oz (150ml/²⁄₃ cup) soured cream
Tomato ketchup
1 can anchovies
3 tbsp finely grated cheese

The dish can be prepared (except for cooking) earlier in the day then left under refrigeration until 25 minutes before serving.

Wash and salt the fish and leave to drain in a colander for 10 minutes. Choose an oven-to-table dish about 2 inches (5cm) deep, and wide enough to hold the rolled fillets in one layer. Generously butter the bottom and sides.

Take each fillet in turn, sprinkle with a little more salt and pepper, put a tiny knob of butter on top, roll up and lay side by side in the buttered dish. Finely slice the mushrooms and cook quickly in the butter until barely tender, then stir in a squeeze of lemon juice. Arrange around and in between the fillets with the sliced tomatoes, making sure the dish is tightly packed. Sprinkle all over with salt and pepper. Put the soured cream into a bowl, add a pinch of salt and black pepper and enough tomato ketchup to turn it a pale pink. Finally pour the cream over the contents of the dish and scatter with the grated cheese. Decorate with criss-cross pattern with the drained, washed and dried anchovy fillets.

Cover with foil. 25-30 minutes before serving, put the dish in a moderate oven (Gas No. 4, 350°F, 180°C) for 20 minutes. Uncover and grill gently for 5 minutes. Serve at once.

Sole Créole

In this very flavourful dish the fish is cooked under a delicious layer of onion, pepper and tomato, with a final topping of breadcrumbs and grated cheese. Do not use a watery fish such as haddock or cod. If sole is not available, use halibut instead.

Serves 6-8

Allow 2 fillets of lemon or Dover sole per serving, cut from fish weighing approx 1½ lb (675g) each, or 1 steak or piece of halibut weighing approx 6 oz (175g).

Créole sauce:

6 large tomatoes, skinned and chopped (or the contents of 1 × 15 oz/425g can, well drained)
2 oz (50g/¼ cup) butter
2 medium green peppers, de-seeded and cut in ¼ inch (0.5cm) cubes

1 medium clove of garlic, crushed
1 medium onion (5 oz/150g), finely chopped
1 level teasp salt
15 grinds black pepper
½ teasp dried herbes de Provence

Topping mixture:
3 heaped tbsp dry breadcrumbs tossed in 2 oz (50g/¼ cup) melted butter mixed with 3 tbsp finely grated cheese.

Melt the butter and cook the onion in it until soft and golden, then add the chopped tomatoes and the green pepper, and cook for 3-4 minutes until thick but juicy. Add the seasoning. Have the fillets (if used) skinned. Wash and salt the fish and leave in a colander to drain for 10 minutes. Roll up the fillets, then arrange the fish in one layer in a buttered casserole about 1½ inches (4cm) deep. Spread the Créole sauce over the top, then cover with the topping mixture. The dish can be refrigerated until half an hour before serving.

Bake in a quick oven (Gas No. 6, 400°F, 200°C) for 30 minutes, or until the fish flakes easily with a fork and the topping is golden.

Fillets of Sole in Provençal Sauce

This dish is equally good served hot or cold (when it makes an unusual addition to a cold buffet).

Serves 6-8

Allow 2 fillets of lemon sole per person cut from fish weighing approx 1½ lb (675g).

The sauce:

2 tbsp corn or olive oil
1 medium (5oz/150g) onion, finely chopped
1 × 28 oz (800g) can Italian tomatoes (preferably canned in juice)
1 tbsp tomato purée

3 tbsp tomato ketchup
2 medium green peppers, de-seeded and thinly sliced
2 level teasp each salt and sugar
1 tbsp lemon juice
15 grinds black pepper
1 bayleaf

Skin the fillets, wash, salt and leave in a colander to drain for 10 minutes, then roll up and lay side by side in an ovenproof casserole.

Heat the oil in a deep frying pan and cook the onion until pale golden and transparent, then add all the remaining ingredients and bubble until reduced to a thick coating consistency. Pour the sauce over the fish, and loosely cover with foil.

Bake in a quick oven (Gas No. 6, 400°F, 200°C) for 20 minutes, remove the foil and allow the sauce to reduce for a further 10 minutes. Serve just warm or quite cold.

Fish in a Creamy Sauce

A delicate sauce which has been thickened to the right creamy consistency either by reduction or a very little flour, makes the perfect partner to the more gently-flavoured fish such as plaice, sole, halibut or salmon.

Pointers to success:
If flour is used as a thickener, it should always be thoroughly cooked by bubbling the sauce for 2-3 minutes after its addition.

Wine (if used) should be neither too dry nor too acid in flavour as this would overwhelm the delicate fish flavour. Riesling, Graves and Chablis are all excellent for the purpose. However, as cider is always sweeter than wine, the driest blend available should be used.

Any kind of cream from 18%-48% (single to double – light to heavy) can be used to enrich the sauce. However, I find that whipping cream (35% butter fat) is the most practical giving the finest texture at the most economical price. If soured cream is used, add at the last moment and do not allow the sauce to boil or it may separate. As this kind of cream is acid in flavour, omit any lemon juice from the recipe.

Always taste a sauce and re-season with care as the balance of flavours will vary according to the wine and the variety of fish used.

Note: For entertaining purposes it is just not possible to cook the fish and sauce immediately before serving, as this would mean leaving the guests for an unacceptable length of time. So with each recipe I have given the most successful way to cook that particular dish in advance then reheat it just before serving. If the directions are carefully followed, there should be no loss of either flavour or texture. If a microwave oven is available, the fish can be reheated in it until bubbly and then treated as newly cooked.

Stuffed Fish Fillets in Cider Sauce

Fish fillets are spread with a mushroom stuffing, then cooked in dry cider which is thickened into a creamy sauce. As the fish is stuffed then rolled, use either thinnish fillets cut from two or three 1½ lb (675g) plaice, or six to eight 6 oz (175g) fillets of whiting. If only larger plaice is available, cut two or three wedge shapes from each large fillet.

212

Serves 6-8

Stuffing:

1/2 lb (225g/4 cups) mushrooms,
very finely chopped
3 shallots *or* 8 spring onion
(scallion) bulbs *or* 1/4 medium
onion, finely chopped

1 oz (25g/2 tbsp) butter
1 tbsp chopped parsley, good
pinch of salt, 10 grinds black
pepper

To cook the fish:

10 fl oz (275ml/11/4 cups) of dry
cider (or enough to half-cover
the fish)

Sprig of parsley, bayleaf and a
few peppercorns

For the sauce:

1 oz (25g/2 tbsp) butter and 1 oz
(25g/1/4 cup) flour (creamed
together on a plate)

Poaching liquor from the fish
8 fl oz (225ml/1 cup) single (light)
cream

First make the stuffing. Melt the butter and cook the shallots (or
spring onion (scallion) bulbs or onion if used) gently until softened
(about 5 minutes).

Add the mushrooms and cook briskly until all the moisture
evaporates, then cover and simmer very gently for 10 minutes.
Add the seasonings and the parsley, then spread on each washed
and salted fillet of fish, rolling them up and placing side by side
in a buttered shallow ovenproof dish. Pour on the cider, cover with
foil or buttered greaseproof paper, and cook for 40 minutes in a
moderate oven (Gas No. 4, 350°F, 180°C). When the fish is cooked,
pour the poaching liquid into a small pan and bring to the simmer,
then whisk in the flour/butter mixture a teaspoonful at a time.
Bubble for two minutes then stir in the cream and pour over the
fish.

(To cook ahead, coat the fish with sauce as directed then cover
with foil and refrigerate. To reheat: Put in a moderate oven (Gas
No. 4, 350°F, 180°C) for 15-20 minutes or until steaming hot.)

Put under the grill for 3 minutes until bubbly. Dust with a little
paprika and decorate with sprigs of parsley.

Haddock Mornay

This is a simpler version which is nevertheless an excellent way of turning a family meal into a party dish. If fresh haddock is not available use frozen instead – the results are equally good.

Serves 6-8

2-3 lb (1-1.25kg) fillets or 6-8 × 6 oz (175g) frozen portions
Water, plus 1 level teasp each salt and sugar

1 thick slice of lemon
Few peppercorns
Bayleaf and a sprig of parsley

Sauce:

³/₄ pint (425ml/2 cups) milk
1¹/₂ oz (40g/3 tbsp) butter and 1¹/₂ oz (40g/¹/₃ cup) flour
¹/₂ level teasp dry mustard
Good pinch of nutmeg
Pinch of cayenne pepper

2 tbsp single (light) cream or evaporated milk
2-4 oz (50-125g/¹/₂-1 cup) cheese depending on taste – a mixture of Gruyère-type with a little Parmesan is ideal, otherwise use Cheddar and Parmesan

In a lidded frying pan large enough to hold the fish in one layer, put enough water to half cover the fish when it is put in. Add the flavourings and bring to the boil. Put in the salted fish, cover the pan and simmer very gently for 20 minutes until the fish has gone opaque and flakes easily. Drain and arrange in a shallow heatproof casserole or gratin dish which has been well buttered. Keep hot in a warm oven.

To make the sauce put the flour, butter, cold milk and seasonings into a pan and bring to the boil, whisking with a balloon or batter whisk all the time, bubble to three minutes, then stir in the cream and the cheese and turn off the heat.

Pour the sauce over the fish to coat it. If possible make up some instant, or freshly mashed, potato and pipe or spoon it in a border round the fish, then scatter the centre with more cheese. Grill under medium heat for 5 minutes until bubbling through and golden brown.

This dish can be completed in advance and reheated in a moderate oven. In that case I would cover it with foil for 15-20 minutes or until the sauce is bubbly, then finish under the grill for a minute.

From the Store Cupboard

First quality canned salmon and tuna can be transformed into the most delicious and original casseroles and soufflés provided they are mixed with a very well-seasoned sauce, as in the recipes that follow.

Tuna Lasagne

A really tasty 'store cupboard' casserole that looks very appetising with its crusty golden cheese topping. There is no need to pre-cook the pasta.

Serves 6-8 **F** 3 months
12 strips of lasagne pasta

Sauce:

3 oz (75g/^{1}/$_3$ cup) butter
1 medium onion
1 medium green pepper (or 2 tbsp frozen diced pepper)
2^1/$_2$ oz (60g/^{1}/$_2$ cup + 2 tbsp) flour
1^1/$_2$ pints (850ml/4 cups) milk
1 level teasp mustard
^{1}/$_4$ teasp ground nutmeg (optional)
1^1/$_2$ level teasp salt

^{1}/$_4$ teasp white pepper
1 tbsp parsley
4 tbsp single (light) cream or top milk
4 oz (125g/1 cup) grated cheese
2 × 7 oz (200g) cans tuna, coarsely flaked
3 hard-boiled eggs, sliced

To make the sauce, finely chop the onion and the pepper. Flake the tuna and slice the eggs. Melt the butter and cook the onion in a covered pan for 5 minutes until softened, then add the pepper, cover and cook a further 3 or 4 minutes. Uncover, stir in the flour, followed by the milk and the seasonings. Whisk until bubbly, simmer 3 minutes, then stir in 3 oz (75g/^{3}/$_4$ cup) of the cheese, the cream, parsley, tuna and hard-boiled eggs.

To assemble the lasagne, butter a rectangular dish about 12 × 8 inches (30 × 20cm) and 2-3 inches (5-7.5cm) deep. Put a thin layer of sauce on the bottom, cover with 4 strips of lasagne, then sauce. Repeat twice, ending with a thin layer of sauce. Cover with the remaining cheese. Bake at Gas No. 5 (375°F, 190°C) for about 40 minutes, until a rich bubbly brown. Cut in squares to serve.

To freeze uncooked, cover with foil. Cook from frozen at Gas No. 5 (375°F, 190°C) but allow 45-60 minutes, until bubbly.

Tuna or Salmon Fish Cakes

These are excellent served both hot or cold. It is essential to allow the mashed potatoes to go cold before mixing with the other ingredients, or the mixture will not hold together in the frying pan.

Serves 6-8

4 cups cold mashed potato *or* 1 ×
   5 oz (150g) packet instant
   potato, left to go cold
2 × 7½ oz (215g) cans tuna fish *or*
   2 × 8 oz (225g) cans pink or red
   salmon
2 eggs

1 tbsp grated onion
1 tbsp chopped parsley
Salt and pepper
4 rounded tbsp porridge oats
Oil or butter for frying
Breadcrumbs for coating

Drain the fish, remove skin and any bones, and flake well with a fork. Add to the cold potato, together with the beaten eggs, onion, parsley, pinch of salt and pepper and porridge oats. Leave for half an hour to firm up. Wet palms, then form the mixture into flat fish cakes about 2½ inches (6.25cm) across and about ⅜ inch (1cm) thick. Coat with fine dry crumbs. Fry in hot, shallow oil (barely covering them) until crisp and golden brown. Drain on tissue or kitchen paper.

The Art of Salmon Cookery

Salmon and salmon trout (also know as sea trout) have such a delicately-textured flesh that they must be cooked with consummate care. In particular the liquid in which they are cooked should never be allowed to boil as this will make the flesh hard and coarse. When fish is to be served cold this can be avoided by placing the fish in cold water which is heated only until it reaches boiling point, and then leaving the fish to finish cooking in the residual heat.

A similar method can be used when baking the fish in the oven. When the fish is to be served hot, however, it is wiser to cook the fish completely (see details below). Slightly different methods are used for smaller fish such as salmon trout or with slices from larger fish, but in every case the aim is to cook the salmon at the minimum temperature and for the shortest possible time. Cooked in this way the fish will have a silky flesh that is moist on the tongue. Salmon keeps its delicate colour if lemon and vinegar are omitted from the cooking liquor.

Cooked salmon freezes to perfection, and its texture often improves in the freezer. Storage time: raw 6 months, cooked 3 months.

To poach a whole Salmon or Salmon Trout to serve hot

Ask the fishmonger to scale the fish, clean out the viscera (without slitting the belly too far) and remove the eyes (but leave on the head if it will fit into the cooking utensil). Lay the fish on the drainer of a fish kettle, and cover with cold water. To each ½ pint (275ml/1¼ cups) water used, add 2 level teasp salt and a shake of white pepper. Cover the fish kettle and bring slowly to the boil, then immediately lower the heat so that bubbles only break the surface every few seconds. Cook for 6 minutes to the pound (0.5kg), then lift out the fish, draining well, and serve.

To poach a whole Salmon or Salmon Trout to serve cold

Immediately the water has come to the boil, remove the fish kettle from the heat but leave the lid on, leaving the fish to cook in the cooking liquor. Do not refrigerate if it is to be served the same day. Otherwise foil-wrap the cold drained fish and refrigerate for up to 3 days.

To bake a whole Salmon or Salmon Trout in foil, to serve hot or cold

This is an excellent method for a large quantity of salmon for a special occasion, or if there is no fish kettle available. Take a large sheet of foil, and lightly grease with a flavourless oil such as corn oil or sunflower oil if it is to be served cold, and butter if to be served hot. Lay the fish on top and wrap so securely that no juices escape, but not so tightly that the heat cannot penetrate the fish. Bake in a moderate oven (Gas No. 4, 350°F, 180°C) 10 minutes to the pound (0.5kg) and 10 minutes over. (A 2 lb/1kg trout with head on will take 30 minutes.)

If the fish is to be served hot, test by inserting a knife into the back bone – the fish should look opaque and come away easily when lifted. Serve at once, or leave in the foil until cold, then use at once or refrigerate for up to 3 days.

217

Serve the whole salmon skinned. If it is to be served hot, garnish with parsley and serve with a warm sauce. If it is to be served cold, skin completely, decorate with overlapping cucumber slices, or remove from the bone in fillets, then portion and serve on a bed of lettuce garnished with cucumber, tomatoes and stuffed or plain hard-boiled eggs.

To poach a cut of Salmon

Take a double piece of greaseproof paper, cooking parchment or foil and butter generously. Place on it the washed and salted fish, then fold into a parcel securing it with loosely-tied string. Put in a pan just large enough to hold it, then cover it with cold water. Add 2 level teasp salt and a speck of pepper, bring slowly to the boil.

To serve a cut of Salmon hot

Reduce the heat and allow to simmer for 6 minutes to the pound (0.5kg), then lift out, drain well, unwrap and serve.

To serve a cut of Salmon cold

Remove the pan from the heat and allow the fish to cool in the covered pan for at least 12 hours. (Can be kept in liquid up to 3 days under refrigeration.)

Skin, portion and foil cover until required. Garnish as for a whole cold salmon.

To poach Salmon steaks

Proceed exactly as above, wrapping each steak in buttered paper or foil. If the steaks are to be served hot, poach for 10 minutes. Otherwise leave in the cooking liquor to go cold.

Sauce for Salmon to be served warm

5 fl oz (150ml/²/₃ cup) soured
  cream
4 oz (125g/¹/₂ cup) unsalted butter
2 egg yolks

1 teasp lemon juice
Salt and pepper
1 level tbsp chopped parsley or
  chives

Put the soured cream and cut-up butter into a double saucepan and whisk with a balloon whisk over simmering water until the mixture has blended in and the sauce has thickened slightly. Whisk in the egg yolks and continue whisking until the mixture has a pale, thick appearance. Stir in the seasonings and lemon juice. (The sauce can be kept warm over hot water until required.) Serves 6-8.

For a 'hot' tartare sauce, add 2 teasp chopped gherkins and 2 teasp chopped capers.

To grill Salmon

This delectable dish *must* be served as soon as it is cooked, or the flesh may become dry and heavy. It is particularly suitable for the more intimate dinner party.

For 2 centre steaks of salmon cut ¾-1 inch (2-2.5cm) thick, allow:

1 oz (25g/2 tbsp) butter	Salt and pepper
Juice of ½ lemon	Flour or dry breadcrumbs

Wash and salt, then dab dry the salmon. In the grill pan melt the butter until it stops foaming, then place each steak in it, and immediately turn over. Grill for 3 minutes only, turn and grill a further 7 minutes, until the flesh begins to shrink from the bones. At this stage you can dust the fish with a little flour or a few dry breadcrumbs, baste with the butter and turn up the heat for a further minute to brown the fish. Lift the fish on to a warm dish, add the juice of the lemon to the pan juices, together with a little salt and black pepper. Stir well and pour over the fish.

VARIATION
Quick Sour-Cream Sauce:
Lift the cooked fish on to a serving dish. Add 4 tbsp soured cream and 1 tbsp lemon juice to the juices in the grill pan. Stir under a gentle grill until warm, then pour over the salmon.

Baked Salmon Trout in Riesling

This superb dish comes from Alsace where it is usually prepared with pike. As it is difficult to reheat a whole fish, it must be prepared and served fresh. However, the fish can be kept hot after baking for up to 30 minutes, and the sauce finished just before serving.

Serves 6-8

One 3¹/₂ lb (1.5kg) to 4 lb (1.75kg) salmon trout or sea trout
3 oz (75g/¹/₃ cup) butter
8 fl oz (225ml/1 cup) Riesling
12 fl oz (350ml/1¹/₂ cups) whipping or double (heavy) cream

1 small onion, grated, *or* 3 shallots, finely chopped
1 level teasp salt
¹/₄ teasp white pepper
1 tbsp lemon juice (if necessary)
1 tbsp chopped parsley

Pre-heat the oven to Gas No. 5, 375°F, 190°C.

Leave the fish whole, with or without the head, as preferred. Make sure the body cavity is thoroughly rinsed, then wash the fish all over in cold water, dry with paper towels, and salt lightly inside and out.

Choose an ovenproof dish or baking tin, at least 1 inch (2.5cm) deep and as wide as the fish. Use about 1 oz (25g/2 tbsp) of the butter to grease it thoroughly, then lay the fish on top. Put the cream, wine and onion into a saucepan and bring slowly to the boil, with the salt and the pepper. Immediately it starts to bubble, pour over the fish, then cover it with a piece of buttered greaseproof paper or foil. Put into the oven and bake for 30-40 minutes, basting with the liquid every 10 minutes. When done the fish will flake easily with a fork and be a pale dull pink right to the bone. When the fish is cooked, take it out and turn the oven down to Gas No. 1, 275°F, 140°C. Carefully remove as much of the skin as possible, then lay the fish in a heatproof serving dish, re-cover with the paper or foil and return to the oven to keep hot.

To make the sauce:
Pour the cooking liquid back into the saucepan and boil down until the consistency of thin custard – it will just coat the back of a wooden spoon. Taste and add more seasonings if necessary and the lemon juice. If the sauce is tart, omit the juice. Just before serving, add the remaining butter in little pieces, heat until steaming, whisking all the time, then pour over the fish, scatter with the parsley and serve with plain boiled or mashed potatoes.

VARIATION
Use 6-8 salmon or halibut steaks, each cut ³/₄ inch (2cm) thick and weighing about 6 oz (175g). Bake in the wine and cream as above,

but for only 20 minutes. Remove the skin but leave in the bone before coating with the sauce.

Salmon Mayonnaise (for a buffet)

An excellent way of extending salmon or salmon trout, especially from the freezer.

Serves 15

2 lb (1kg) salmon or salmon trout
1/2 pint (275ml/1¼ cups) mild
   mayonnaise
1 tbsp wine vinegar
1 teasp Dijon mustard

1/2 large cucumber, cut in 3/8 inch
   (2cm) dice
9-12 hard-boiled eggs
6 tomatoes
Chives or parsley for garnish

Poach the salmon (see p.217).

   Dice the cucumber, sprinkle with salt and leave in a drainer for 30 minutes, then dry. Skin and bone the salmon, then flake roughly. Put the mayonnaise into a bowl and add the vinegar and mustard. Stir 3/4 of it into the salmon, mixed with the cucumber. The mixture should be moist but not wet. Pile into the centre of a round platter. Surround with stuffed hard-boiled eggs and vandyked tomatoes. Spoon remaining mayonnaise over the centre and garnish with snipped chives or parsley.

Egg stuffing:
Mix the yolks of the eggs with 1 oz (25g/2 tbsp) butter, 2 tbsp mayonnaise, pepper and salt and a good pinch of curry powder. The consistency should be of soft cream cheese. Pile or pipe back into the egg whites.

Two Delicate Fish Sauces

These sauces are excellent to serve as an accompaniment to hot or cold poached or baked fish such as salmon, trout or sole.

Herb Cream Sauce (to serve cold)

Serves 6-8

1 egg yolk
4 tbsp double (heavy) cream
  whipped, or 1 × 5 oz (150ml/²/₃
  cup) carton soured cream
1 tbsp wine vinegar
4 fl oz (125ml/¹/₂ cup) salad oil

Pinch of salt, dry mustard and
  white pepper
2 tbsp scissored dill or mixture of
  parsley, chives and a little fresh
  tarragon
Lemon juice if required

In blender or food processor: Put yolk, seasonings and herbs in blender and process till thoroughly mixed. Add seasonings, then oil a little at a time like mayonnaise, ending with vinegar. Add cream. Taste and add lemon juice if required. The consistency will be of a coating sauce.

By hand: Make as for mayonnaise, beating yolk, wine vinegar and seasonings, then adding the oil drop by drop. Finally add chopped herbs and cream.

Sour Cream Sauce (to serve hot)

This is similar to hollandaise, with soured cream taking the place of the majority of egg yolks.

Serves 6-8

5 fl oz (150ml/²/₃ cup) carton
  soured cream
4 oz (125g/¹/₂ cup) unsalted butter
1 egg yolk

1 teasp lemon juice
Salt and pepper
1 level tbsp chopped parsley or
  chives

Put soured cream and cut-up butter into a double saucepan and whisk with a balloon whisk over simmering water until the mixture has blended in and the sauce has thickened slightly. Whisk in the egg yolk and continue whisking till the mixture has a pale thick appearance. Stir in seasonings and lemon juice.

Meat

Choosing Meat

The most reliable way to ensure prime meat is to find a knowledgeable butcher and trust to his judgement – it is interesting that a higher percentage of meat is still bought from the small trader who gives personal over-the-counter advice than any other food, although this percentage is gradually being eroded as supermarkets and chain butchers gain a larger proportion of the trade. In many countries however, because it is almost impossible to judge meat entirely on its appearance, it has now become the practice to provide personal advice for special purchases even within the self-service meat department of a supermarket.

To help you in *your* choice of butcher – and of his meat – here are a few guidelines. However, it must be pointed out that only where there is a system of meat classification can there be a *truly* reliable guide to eating quality.

Colour: The degree of redness is no guide to quality; it simply means that the meat has been recently cut from the carcase. Best quality meat can vary from bright red to dark red-brown. The characteristic cherry red colour develops after 30 minutes' exposure to air.

Colour differences disappear when the meat is cooked, for then the final colour will depend on the degree of 'doneness' – rare, medium rare or well done.

Flavour: Although the taste of meat is affected by the way the animal has been reared (intensively-reared 'barley beef' tending to have an insipid flavour as, though the animal is heavy in weight, it is still immature), it is the method of cooking which makes the biggest difference.

The presence of fat is not always an indication of flavour, though it is good practice to buy a roasting joint marbled with fat as this keeps it juicy under high heat.

Texture: The cut surface of meat exposes the bundles of muscle fibre, or grain. Those parts of the animal which have more active use, for instance the shoulder, will have a coarser grain and will be tougher than less active, finer-grained parts such as the rib. An older animal will also have a coarser grain (and will probably produce a tougher joint) than a young animal of the same type. However, one has to strike a balance between age and flavour, which is more pronounced in an older beast.

Connective tissue: Connective tissue, which is visible as a fine silvery sheath around the outside of the muscles, or as coarse strands of gristle, is present in meat in varying amounts. It should be almost completely absent from roasting or grilling joints, when the meat is to be cooked by dry heat alone. Where a high percentage of the tissue is present, the meat must be cooked by some form of moist heat such as braising or stewing.

Tenderness: If meat is to be tender, particularly after roasting or grilling, it *must* be hung at a temperature of between 0°-2°C for a minimum of 10 days. This is also known as ageing and should be done in the butcher's cold room.

Choosing the Recipe for the Occasion

All the recipes included here are either carefully timed to allow a margin for serving times, or can be kept hot in a low oven without any loss of texture or flavour. There is also a section on outdoor cooking, though fuller instructions for a barbecue are given on pp.87-9.

The Freezing of Meat

It is advisable to consult a specialized booklet on the subject as there are so many factors to be considered. However, if you intend to freeze your own meat, or buy frozen meat from your butcher or specialist supplier, the following points may be of interest.

Recommended storage life of frozen meat

	−12°C (10°F)	−18°C (0°F)	−25°C (−13°F)	−30°C (−22°F)
		(normal running temperature of a home freezer)		
Beef	5-8 months	12 months	18 months	24 months
Lamb	3-6 months	9 months	12 months	24 months

These times can only be used as an approximate guide. Meat kept after these storage times does not have to be destroyed and is safe to eat. However, its taste will slowly but progressively deteriorate the longer it is kept.

Once storage life is used up at one temperature, no further life can be obtained by a temperature reduction. When buying meat which has already been frozen, the length of time it has been stored before purchase should be subtracted from the full storage life given in the table, whenever this information can be established.

Freezing home cooked meats: Home-cooked foods will keep in the freezer for 3 months. After that their flavour begins to deteriorate.

Thawing raw meat: Although it is possible to roast meat from frozen, it is much more difficult to judge when it is cooked, than it is with fresh meat, and a meat thermometer is therefore essential. It is consequently more reliable (and aesthically pleasing) to defrost the meat before use.

	In the refrigerator	At room temperature
Joints over 3 lb (1.25kg)	4-7 hours per lb (450g)	2-3 hours per lb (450g)
Joints under 3 lb (1.25kg)	3-4 hours per lb (450g)	1-2 hours per lb (450g)

	In the refrigerator	At room temperature
1 inch (2.5cm) thick steaks, chops, stewing steak (not cubed)	5-6 hours	2-4 hours

Slow thawing overnight in a refrigerator is recommended both for reasons of food hygiene and eating quality.

Thawing cooked meats: Follow the timetable for joints. To reheat a casserole from frozen in the oven, use a moderate temperature and reheat for 45 minutes to one hour until bubbling and heated right through. The temperature can then be turned down to Gas No. 1, 275°F, 140°C to keep the meat hot until required.

Roast and Braised Joints

A true roast is cooked by radiant heat alone – that is, it should turn on a spit in front of a glowing fire. The exact modern equivalent of this is the electric spit or rotisserie. When meat is 'roasted' in the oven, however, it is really baked – that is, cooked by a combination of radiant and convected heat. I find oven-roasting perfectly satisfactory and all the recipes in this section are cooked by this method.

Pointers to success

There is no definitive way of roasting meat, as it is impossible to allow for all the variables such as the size of the joint, how long it has been hung and the age and breed of the original animal. In recent years it has become popular to advocate roasting meat at a moderate temperature throughout the cooking period. This results in less shrinkage than when it is cooked at a higher temperature, but it is more difficult to produce the same delicious crust as with traditional methods. I suggest you try different methods yourself, bearing in mind the following general principles which apply to whatever method you choose.

The hanging period: Ask the butcher to ensure that the meat has been hung for at least 10 days. This helps enormously to produce a tender joint.

Bringing to room temperature: Whether it has been defrosted after freezer storage or stored in the refrigerator after purchase, keep the joint at room temperature for 2 hours before cooking, or the timing will not be accurate.

Pre-preparation: As a general rule, it's a good idea to rub the roast with a little flour and mustard mixed with plenty of black pepper (see individual recipes for details). This helps to promote a really crunchy brown crust. Salt the meat only as you baste it, and salt each slice again as it is carved as the salt cannot penetrate into the centre of the meat. (Salting the meat before cooking inhibits browning).

Coat the joint with 1 tbsp of oil to each 1 lb (450g) of meat.

Oven temperatures: Always pre-heat the oven (unless it is pre-set, in which case follow the manufacturer's instructions). Seal the meat by searing it at a high temperature and then lower the temperature, (see individual recipes) for the rest of the cooking period. I don't find much difference in taste between a roast cooked at a quick moderate or at a moderate temperature: it's mainly a matter of convenience – e.g. if you need a specific temperature for an accompaniment such as Yorkshire pudding.

The roasting dish: A cast aluminium roasting dish 1¹/₂-2 inches (3.5-5cm) deep is ideal. It should be large enough to hold the joint but not so large that there is an uncovered area around it which may cause the fat to overheat. Joints on the bone (such as standing rib) are placed directly in the tin. Rolled and boned joints are best put on a rack to prevent them frying in the fat at the bottom of the dish.

Basting: This should be done every half hour. At the same time the meat can be turned to simulate the action of a spit.

Testing for doneness: Either follow my timings (which have been carefully tested), or use a meat thermometer, as follows:

Meat thermometer readings:

Beef – joints under 4 lb (2kg)	–	well done 79°C (174°F)
	–	medium/rare 71°C (160°F)
Beef – joints over 4lb (2kg)	–	well done 79°C (174°F)
	–	medium/rare 71°C (160°F)
Lamb – joints under 4 lb (2kg)	–	well done 82°C (180°F)
Lamb – joints over 4 lb (2kg)	–	well done 79°C (174°F)

Spit roasting times: 20 minutes per 500g, plus 20 minutes extra (15 minutes per 1 lb and 15 minutes extra). For spit roasting in the oven, use normal oven temperatures.

The resting time: If you cut into a freshly-cooked roast you may find that though the outside is perfectly cooked, the inside is unacceptably raw, with all the juices concentrated at the centre. In order to distribute the juices throughout the meat and allow the meat fibres which have contracted in the heat of the oven to relax and become tender, let the meat *rest* for 15-20 minutes after the cooking period has been completed. This can be done in the switched off oven with the door ajar or by dishing the meat and covering with foil or a large bowl, either on the top of a ceramic hob at a low setting, or in a warming oven or on a hot plate. This has the added convenience for the hostess that the gravy can be completed before the guests sit down to dinner.

The Gravy

To produce a truly rich bown gravy without any artificial colour, add a sliced onion to the roasting dish after the initial searing. As the onion caramelizes it produces rich brown juice. Remove the onion before making the gravy – it is absolutely delicious eaten with the roast, or push it through a sieve to add to the juices.

Drain off all but a quarter of the meat fat (keep for another purpose), then add to the roasting tin twice as much water, or bouillon, as you want the finished gravy to measure (allow about 2 tbsp gravy per serving). Bring to the boil on top of the stove over direct heat, stirring well to loosen the delicious meat juices, then bubble until reduced by half. Season well. This simple gravy is the most delicious, but if you prefer a thicker one, follow the instructions in individual recipes.

Traditional Rib Roast

As a general guide allow 10-12 oz (275-350g) per person of raw meat, including the bone. In any case do not roast less than 2 ribs. Have the wing bone chined by the butcher so that the meat will stand evenly in the roasting tin.

Serves 6-8

Approx 5 lb (2.5kg) standing rib roast	Black pepper, salt, mustard powder, flour, dripping or oil

For the gravy:

1 pint (275 ml/2^1/$_2$ cups) meat stock (from cube)	2 teasp cornflour (cornstarch)

Take the meat from the refrigerator 2 hours before it is to be cooked, wipe dry with a kitchen towel and sprinkle all over with freshly ground black pepper. Just before cooking, mix together 2 teasp each of mustard powder and flour and rub it into the meat.

Stand the meat in a roasting tin and pour over it 4 or 5 tbsp of hot fat, then put in a pre-heated oven (Gas No. 8, 450°F, 230°C) for 15 minutes.

Now sprinkle lightly with salt, add a sliced onion to the tin and pour half a cup of water round the meat. Turn the oven down to Gas No. 6, 400°F, 200°C and then allow a further 20 minutes to the pound (450g). Thus a 5 lb (2.5kg) rib will take a total of 1 hour 55 minutes to be cooked to the medium-well-done stage. Baste the meat occasionally and add a little more water as it dries up.

To make the gravy:
Put the meat on a heatproof plate and leave it on a hot tray or in the oven with the door ajar for 15-20 minutes; this makes it much easier to carve. Drain as much fat as possible from the roasting tin and remove the onion to eat separately if desired. To the tin add 1 pint (575 ml) meat stock, bubble for 10 minutes until reduced by half, then (if a thicker gravy is preferred) add 2 level teasp

cornflour (cornstarch) mixed with 2 tbsp cold water. Bring to the boil, simmer for 3 minutes, then season and serve as required.

VARIATION
If you wish to complete the cooking at a lower temperature, reduce the heat to Gas No.3, 325°F, 160°C after the initial searing, and allow a further 25 minutes to the pound (450g). Thus a 5 lb (2.5kg) rib will take a total of 2 hours 20 minutes.

To Cook a Fillet of Beef in Two Stages

The timing of a fillet is so critical that the two stage method is ideal. This method was given to me by a professional cook and really does produce a superb result with a small, boneless, very tender joint.

Serves 6-8

1 × 3 lb (1.25kg) fillet	Pepper and salt
6 tbsp oil, *or* 2 oz (50g/¼ cup) margarine and 2 tbsp oil	

Note: 2 hours before the first cooking period, take the beef from the refrigerator and leave at room temperature.

Allow 12 minutes per lb (450g) plus 12 minutes for the piece, giving a total cooking time of 48 minutes divided into two cooking periods of 32 minutes and 16 minutes as follows: Early in the day or the afternoon turn on the oven at Gas No. 6, 400°F, 200°C and put in a roasting tin containing a little water (this heats the tin without allowing it to burn). Season the beef with black pepper. Run off the water from the tin, then coat the tin with a few drops of oil. Put in the fillet and pour over the fat which has been heated in a pan. Cook for 32 minutes, season with salt. Drain off the fat and allow the meat to go cold. Sixteen minutes before serving the meat, repeat the process, coating with the reheated fat and cooking as before but for 16 minutes only.
    Re-salt and serve. (The meat can be covered with foil and kept hot at Gas No. ½, 250°F, 120°C while the first course is being eaten.)

Extra Crisp Individual Yorkshire Puddings

These individual puddings can be cooked whilst the meat is resting.

Serves 6-8 (12 puddings)

2 oz (50g/^{1}/$_2$ cup) plain flour ^{1}/$_4$ pint (150 ml/^{2}/$_3$ cup) water
1 level teasp salt   2 teasp oil
1 large egg

To mix in blender or food processor: Process for 1 minute.

To mix by hand: Sieve the flour and salt into a bowl, make a well in the centre, and add the egg, oil and half the water. Stir in the flour gradually from the sides, making sure the mixture is kept smooth and free from lumps. Add enough water to make a thick batter, and beat well for 5 minutes, then stir in the remaining liquid.

With either method, leave in a cool place for 30 minutes.

To bake: Turn oven to Gas No. 7, 425°F, 220°C. Do this while the meat is resting. Put a litle nut of meat fat or ^{1}/$_4$ teasp dripping from the roast meat into 12 individual patty tins. When the fat smokes, after 5 minutes, half fill each patty tin with the batter. Return to the oven and bake for 15-20 minutes or until a rich brown.

To Roast Lamb on the Bone

As with beef, there are innumerable methods of roasting lamb. However, for a party joint this is an excellent general method (read general roasting instructions first), giving a well-done, crispy joint.

Have the meat at room temperature for 2 hours before roasting. Rub it well with black pepper, dry mustard and flour. Insert one peeled clove of garlic, cut in 4, at different parts of the joint, just under the skin (nick skin with a knife).

Pre-heat the oven to Gas No. 6, 400°F, 200°C. As lamb is fatter than beef, it does not need so much fat. Just before roasting paint the meat all over with olive oil. Cook at the same temperature all the time, allowing 30 minutes to the pound (450g). Baste frequently, turning the meat at half time. Fifteen minutes before the end of the cooking time sprinkle with soft brown sugar, or spread with a thin layer of honey, redcurrant jelly, apricot conserve or grapefruit marmalade. Sprinkle with sea salt. When the joint is done, run off the fat and make the gravy as for a wing rib (p.228). Leave the meat to stand for about 20 minutes before carving.

VARIATION
Lamb Roasted in the French Manner

The lamb is cooked until faintly pink on a bed of thinly-sliced potatoes. These absorb the juices from the meat and develop a most delicious flavour. If well-done lamb is preferred, cook a further 15-20 minutes.

Serves 6-8

1 × 4 lb (2kg) joint of lamb	3 tbsp oil
1 clove of garlic, peeled	3 lb (1.5kg) potatoes
1 teasp fresh rosemary spikes	

Pre-heat the oven to Gas No. 4, 350°F, 180°C. Prepare the lamb for roasting as above.

Peel and slice the potatoes ¼ inch (0.5cm) thick. Put in a pan, cover with cold water and 1 teasp salt and bring to the boil. Boil for 1 minute then immediately drain and dry as much as possible. Grease the roasting tin and arrange the potatoes in the centre, sprinkle with salt and pepper, then lay the meat on top, covering them as much as possible. Cook for 30 minutes to the pound (450g) plus 30 minutes over, basting occasionally and turning the potatoes.

There is no need to make a gravy as the juices have been absorbed by the potatoes.

Boned Shoulder of Lamb

Shoulder of lamb is usually cheaper than leg and is considered by butchers themselves to be the sweeter and tastier joint. But it is much more difficult to carve because of the shoulder bone. Ask the butcher to remove this and you will have a compact, easy-to-slice joint that is extremely economical and particularly delicious when it is stuffed. The butcher will either make a pocket in the shoulder or leave it flat for you to stuff and roll (see recipe for details).

The shoulder can be roasted at a high temperature (when it is especially crunchy but tends to shrink a lot) or at a lower temperature (when it will give you a higher yield but taste more like a braised joint). The slower method is generally better for more mature meat.

Always lay a boned joint on a rack (a cake rack will do) set in the roasting tin. This allows the heat to circulate underneath the meat and there is then no need to turn it once it goes into the oven.

When the gravy has been made, allow it to bubble for at least 5 minutes so that it can develop a really deep flavour. If you prefer, omit the cornflour (cornstarch) suggested in the recipe and reduce the gravy to the required thickness simply by allowing it to simmer for longer, say 10 to 15 minutes.

Roast Stuffed Shoulder of Lamb

May be stuffed and then frozen, either raw or cooked.

Serves 6-8 F 1 month raw

3¹/₂-4 lb (1.5-1.75kg) shoulder of lamb, boned and pocketed, or boned and left flat

Mint stuffing:

2 oz (50g/¹/₄ cup) margarine
1 small onion, finely chopped
6 oz (175g/2²/₃ cups) fresh
  breadcrumbs

2 teasp each finely-chopped mint
  and parsley
1 level teasp salt
¹/₄ teasp black pepper
1 egg

Apricot stuffing:

2 oz (50g/¹/₄ cup) margarine
1 small onion, finely chopped
4 oz (125g) dried apricots, soaked
  overnight in cold water to
  cover, then drained and roughly
  chopped

Grated rind of ¹/₂ lemon
¹/₂ level teasp salt
Pinch of white pepper
4 oz (125g/1¹/₃ cups) fresh
  breadcrumbs
1 egg

To make either stuffing: Melt the fat in a small frying pan and cook the onion gently until softened and golden. Put all the other ingredients into a bowl, then mix in the onion and fat until well blended, then moisten with the beaten egg. The mixture should just cling together.

To stuff a pocketed shoulder: Just pack the stuffing lightly into the pocket and sew it up into a firm compact shape.

To stuff and roll a shoulder: Lay the meat, skin side down, on a board and cut out any lumps of fat. Spread the stuffing evenly over the meat, pushing it into any little folds. Roll up neatly and sew into a compact shape. Arrange the stuffed shoulder on a rack in a roasting tin lined with foil (for ease of cleaning). Have enough foil to come up sides of meat. Lay meat on rack, sprinkle with a teasp of salt and a few grinds of black pepper and a dusting of flour, then pour over about 2 tbsps of oil. Bring up the sides of the foil to protect the ends of the meat, but don't cover it.

Very young lamb should be cooked at a high temperature. Cook at Gas No. 5, 375°F, 190°C for 30 minutes then Gas No. 6, 400°F, 200°C for 45 minutes. Remove from oven and sprinkle with 2 level tbsp demerara sugar and baste with the pan juices. Return to oven and continue to cook a further 30 minutes, until a rich brown. A 4 lb (1.75kg) shoulder will take 1 hour 45 minutes to cook.

For a less crusty meat but with less shrinkage, roast at Gas No. 3, 325°F, 160°C for 2 hours then roast at Gas No. 6, 400°F, 200°C for a further 30 minutes. Sprinkle with 2 level tbsp demerara sugar and baste with pan juices or 3 tbsp apricot soaking water. Continue to cook a further 15 minutes. A 4 lb (1.75kg) shoulder will take a total of 2 hours 45 minutes to cook.

If the stuffed joint has been frozen, pre-heat the oven to Gas No. 4, 350°F, 180°C. Sprinkle the meat with 1 teasp salt and a few grinds of black pepper. Weigh the joint. Put on a foil-covered rack (see above). Cook the meat for 40 minutes to the pound (450g) plus 40 minutes extra. After half an hour, open the oven, sprinkle the meat with a dusting of flour, and pour over 2 tbsp of oil, then continue to cook for the calculated time. Sprinkle with the sugar, as for the other methods, 15 minutes before the end of the cooking time.

At the end of the cooking time, dish the meat onto a heatproof platter and keep it hot in a low oven for 15 minutes. This 'rest' makes the meat easier to carve.

To make the gravy: Pour off all the fat except for 2 teasp. Mix 2 level teasp of cornflour (cornstarch) with ½ pint (275ml/1¼ cups) cold water and a few drops of gravy browning, then pour into the roasting tin and add half a crumbled beef cube. Bring to the boil, stirring well, then season to taste with salt and pepper. A tbsp of redcurrant jelly can be added for extra flavour. Leave the gravy to bubble very gently until the meat is carved.

Roast Shoulder of Lamb with Redcurrant Sauce

Serves 6-8

1 × 4 lb (1.75kg) shoulder of lamb (or half shoulder, depending on size)
Oil
Salt and pepper

Flour
1 onion, thinly sliced
Garlic
Demerara sugar

For the sauce:

1 teasp flour
1teasp dry mustard
2 tbsp redcurrant jelly

1/4 pint (150 ml/2/3 cup) vegetable water or meat stock

Dry the meat well, then make a nick in the thickest part of the flesh and insert a cut clove of garlic. Paint the joint all over with oil, then dust it with 1 tbsp flour, 1 teasp salt, and a speck of pepper.

In a roasting tin put 2 tbsp oil and the thinly sliced onion. Put tin in the oven and turn to moderate heat (Gas No. 4, 350°F, 180°C). When the fat is hot, put in the meat. Baste with fat. Allow 30 minutes to the pound, plus 15 minutes over. Ten minutes before the roasting time is up, open the door and sprinkle the roast with demerara sugar. Baste well and allow it to crisp and become a rich crunchy brown. Put the meat on a dish and keep it warm.

Pour off all but 2 teasp of the fat, and into that and the sediment, stir the teasp of flour. Mix well together, then add the mustard, the redcurrant jelly and the vegetable water or meat stock. Stir vigorously and allow to bubble until the sauce has become slightly thickened and glossy. Serve with the lamb.

Braised Shoulder or Other Joint of Boned Veal with Lemon and Herb Stuffing

Because veal contains no fat, it is better to cook it by braising (a combination of dry and moist heat), rather than by roasting in dry heat alone. This gives a joint with a rich brown coating but one that is tender and moist as veal should be. It is important to brown the meat thoroughly before putting it in the oven in a covered dish as no further browning will then take place.

235

1 boned out piece of veal
  weighing about 4 lb (1.75kg)
1 onion and 2 carrots, very finely
  chopped

3 tbsp oil or margarine
2 bayleaves

Lemon and herb stuffing:

6 oz (175g/2²/₃ cups) fresh
  breadcrumbs
1 level teasp salt
¹/₄ level teasp white pepper
¹/₂ level teasp dried mixed poultry
  seasoning or Italian herb
  mixture

Grated rind of ¹/₄ lemon (optional)
1 level tbsp finely chopped
  parsley
2 oz (50g/¹/₄ cup) margarine
¹/₂ large onion, finely chopped
1 egg

Put the breadcrumbs in a bowl and blend with the herbs, seasonings and lemon rind (if used). Melt the fat in a large frying pan, add the onion and simmer until tender – about 5 minutes. Pour the onion and fat over the seasoned breadcrumbs and stir well, then add the beaten egg to make a moist but not soggy mixture (don't use all the egg if it is not necessary). Lay the veal on the table and stuff the pocket. If not pocketed, simply spread with stuffing then form into a neat shape. Sew up or skewer closed. Dry well.

Melt the oil in a heavy casserole and fry the vegetables until golden. Now add the oil or margarine, put in the meat, and brown over moderate heat until richly brown on all sides. Don't rush this. Sprinkle with salt and pepper then add 2 bayleaves to casserole and the browned vegetables. Cover and put in a moderate oven (Gas No. 4, 350°F, 180°C) for 2 hours. The veal is ready when it feels soft to the touch, by which time it is a mahogany colour. If it's ready too soon, simply take it out of the oven and keep it hot on very low heat. Don't overcook or it is difficult to carve. In any case it can be dished 15 minutes before the start of the meal, then covered with foil and kept on a hot plate or in a warming oven. This makes it easier to carve.

When the meat has been removed from the casserole, skim off as much fat as possible, then put the casserole on the top of the stove. Add 1 cup of meat stock (or stock made from veal bone), and mix 1 teasp cornflour (cornstarch) with 2 tbsp water and add that. Allow to simmer until slightly thickened and rich in flavour.

Slice meat quite thickly and serve with sauce.

Note: Left-over veal can be forced into a basin and left overnight. It will then be set in a jelly and can be very thinly sliced.

Grills and Barbecues

Grilling – the modern English word, and broiling – the old English and the modern American term, are synonymous and have a very precise meaning in culinary terms. The food is cooked by radiant heat plus convection but without the use of any utensil or container. The heat source may be supplied by a gas flame, an electric element or the charcoal from a barbecue. Infra red (contact) grills use heat rays of longer wave length than those used in the more conventional method, and cooking times are therefore shorter.

A grill should always be pre-heated to its operating temperature so that the meat cooks quickly and does not dry out or become toughened. The correct degree of heat can be obtained either by adjusting a thermostat on the grill or by varying the distance of the meat from the source of the heat. Follow the manufacturer's instructions. To prevent the meat drying out under the intense heat, it is advisable to marinate it beforehand in a mixture of flavoured oil and an acid such as lemon juice, wine vinegar or wine, or to brush it with fat just before cooking (see individual recipes). The coating also prevents the meat from sticking to the grill pan, and helps it to brown, as well as acting as a medium for flavourings such as herbs and spices.

To Barbecue a Steak

For instructions on building and heating the grill, see pp.87-9.

The steak must be allowed to come to room temperature and is then brushed very lightly with olive, corn or peanut oil. The grill itself must be clean and very hot. Grease the grill bars with oil. Grill meat under fierce heat according to the following time-tables. (As salting draws the moisture to the surface and so prevent browning, it is better to salt each side after it has browned.) *Note*: Do not pierce the steak with a fork when you turn it as this will allow some of the delicious juices to escape.

A rare steak
Put the steaks on the hot grill, and seal on one side, then turn half way round to get a criss-cross pattern. After 2-3 minutes turn and brown the second side in the same way. Cook until a rich brown on both sides – allowing approx 2-3 minutes a side for a 3/4 inch (2cm) thick steak. Test – if your finger meets with very slight resistance, the steak is ready.

A medium-rare steak
The steak must either be further away from the source of the heat or in a less hot part of the fire. Cook in the same way but a little longer, until the finger meets a firmer resistance, and the top surface is covered with clear drops of blood (about 8 minutes).

A well-done steak
Cook until the beads of blood have turned to brown all over the surface. The steak now feels very firm when pressed with the finger – after 12-15 minutes. If in doubt, take a steak and nick it with a knife to see the state of the inside: apparently raw in the centre for rare steak; pink in the centre for medium rare, and barely cooked to an even colour right through for well done. Try not to overcook the steak, as it becomes progressively tougher as the juices dry up and the protein over-coagulates.

Serve plain or with barbecue sauce, some of which can be brushed on the steak as it cooks. This gives it a particularly rich brown appearance.

Barbecue Sauce
As this keeps well, it is worth making the quantity for 12.

F 3 months

Quantities for 10-12	*Quantities for 30-40*
2 tbsp oil	4 tbsp
1 medium (5 oz/150g) onion, chopped	2 large (8 oz/225g each)
2 teasp Worcestershire sauce	2 tbsp
3 tbsp wine vinegar	5 fl oz (150ml/2/3 cup)
2 teasp soy sauce	2 tbsp
1 tbsp golden (corn) syrup or honey	3 tbsp
1 tbsp tomato purée	3 tbsp
1 bouillon cube	2
3/4 pint (425ml/2 cups) water	2 pints (1 litre/5 cups)
1 tbsp cornflour (cornstarch)	3 tbsp

Sauté the onions in the hot oil until golden and tender. Add the rest of the ingredients (except the cornflour) and boil rapidly for 10 minutes (20 minutes for the larger quantity), stirring every now and again. Mix the cornflour to a cream with a little cold water and stir into the sauce. Bubble for 3 minutes – it should be as thick as ketchup.

Barbecued Lamb Chops

This is an excellent method for a large number as the chops are lightly oiled and herbed, then wrapped in foil parcels for an hour or two to allow the flavours to penetrate the meat. This avoids the need to marinate the meat, which can present problems of space when grilling a large number of chops.

Allow 1-2 chops per serving, depending on the size.
For 8 lamb chops, each cut ¾ inch (2cm) thick, you will need:
1 large clove of garlic
2 level teasp dried thyme or marjoram or mixed herbes de Provence, *or*
1 level tbsp mixed chopped fresh herbs
Oil
Black pepper, rock or sea salt

1-3 hours before you intend to cook the chops, prepare them as follows: Brush each chop with oil on both sides, then rub with a cut clove of garlic and sprinkle with the herbs and plenty of black pepper.

Arrange the chops on a large piece of foil, one on top of the other in two layers, then make into a foil package. Leave for 1-3 hours. Grill for 5 minutes on each side, 4 inches (10cm) away from the source of heat, turning once. Salt each side as it is turned, and again just before serving.

Brochettes and Kebabs

As the chunks of meat cooked on skewers are smaller than chops or steaks, it is important to prevent them drying out before they are cooked. For this reason the meat is marinated in an aromatic mixture of oil and lemon juice, and is then cooked on a pre-heated grill over a less intense fire. If vegetable pieces such as mushroom, onion and pepper are cooked on the skewer together with the meat, blanch them (bring slowly to the boil in cold water) beforehand to ensure that they become tender at the same time as the meat is cooked.

Brochettes of Lamb Provençale (Brochettes d'Agneau aux Herbes de Provence)

This is the French version, perfect with tender young lamb and the sun-drenched herbs of late summer. The same marinade can be used for barbecued lamb chops, but only half the quantity will then be needed.

Serves 6-8

2-3 lb (1-1.5kg) boned roasting lamb
3-4 red peppers, blanched

3-4 medium onions, blanched
Pepper

Marinade:

3 teasp fresh thyme and 1 teasp fresh rosemary, *or*
2 teasp herbes de Provence
2 small bayleaves
4 small cloves garlic

15 grinds black pepper
2 level tbsp chopped parsley
1/4 pint (150ml/2/3 cup) olive oil
2 tbsp lemon juice

In a mortar crush the thyme, rosemary and bayleaves. Add the garlic cloves and crush them, then add the pepper and parsley. Now add the olive oil gradually, stirring well, followed by the lemon juice. Transfer the marinade to a shallow dish.

Cut the meat into cubes about 3/4 inch (2cm) square. De-seed the peppers then cut them and the peeled onions into 8 pieces each. Bring to the boil in cold water then drain and dry.

Put the meat into the marinade. Leave for at least 2 hours, preferably 3, turning several times in the marinade.

When ready to cook, drain the meat with a slotted spoon, then thread alternately with the vegetables on 12 inch (30cm) skewers, beginning and ending with the meat. Don't pack the skewers too tightly or the food won't cook where it touches. Sprinkle with pepper.

Pre-heat the grill for 15 minutes. Lay the skewers across the grill pan so that they are resting on the sides and the food does not touch the bottom of the pan. Grill for about 10-12 minutes, basting two or three times with any remaining marinade, and turning the skewers once or twice. Salt when beginning to brown. When ready, the meat will be crusty and brown outside but still pink inside.

Serve with rice.

Souvlakia (Kebabs in the Greek Fashion)

Sprinkle the barbecue with rigani, the Greek version of oregano, and to get the best results, make sure the barbecue is really hot – it will have stopped smoking and the bricks will be covered with a fine grey ash.

The marinade which both tenderizes and flavours the food can be brushed on from 24 hours to half an hour before cooking, but the longer the better.

The quantity of meat can vary enormously depending on the rest of the menu. However, outdoor eating seems to stimulate the appetite so 8 oz (225g) per person is not too much to allow for hearty eaters, though you can get away with as little as 4 oz (125g) per serving if there are sausages, beefburgers and plenty of rice or baked potatoes on the menu.

Souvlakia can be cooked on a gas or electric grill, but it is the combination of smokey charcoal flavour and the joy of outdoor eating that provide the special quality.

To serve 6:
3-4 lb (1.25-1.75kg) boned out roasting lamb

The marinade:

3 fl oz (75ml/¹/₃ cup) olive oil
Juice of a large lemon
1 medium onion, grated or blended to a mush to extract the juice
1 large bayleaf cut in pieces
2 level teasp dry rigani (leaf oregano)

2 level teasp sea salt
Plenty of ground black pepper
Optional: tomatoes, baby onions, chunks of green pepper, whole mushrooms (brought to the boil in cold water, then drained and dried)

Cut the meat into cubes the size of a walnut. Whisk the oil and lemon juice together in a bowl large enough to hold the meat, then stir in all the seasonings and the meat. Leave until ready to grill (about 24 hours). Drain the meat from the marinade and thread on flat metal skewers (round ones cause the meat to slide about), alternately with chunks of the vegetables, if used (I wouldn't if you serve a Greek style salad that includes most of them).

Grill the kebabs three inches (7.5cm) from the source of the heat, basting with the marinade from time to time. Cook until the outside is a rich brown and the inside faintly pink – it should take about 10 minutes in all.

Serve at once as kebabs toughen if kept hot.

Special Lamb Chops

For those who do not like to carve a joint, lamb chops are an excellent choice for the menu. However, although it is quick and easy to grill them, they also need a good deal of last-minute attention. The following three recipes avoid this as they are put to cook an hour before the meal and can also be kept hot without spoiling.

I do not think these are suitable dishes for freezing, as it is difficult to reheat them without overcooking the meat.

Cumberland Cutlets

Serves 6-8

12-16 best end chops (cutlets) of lamb, chined if desired

2 eggs
Salt, pepper, dry breadcrumbs

Sauce:
8 fl oz (225ml/1 cup) chicken stock

4 rounded tbsp redcurrant jelly (about half a 12 oz/350g jar)

Juice and rind of 3 large oranges (about 8 fl oz/225ml/1 cup)

3 teasp lemon juice

Grease a roasting tin large enough to hold the cutlets side by side. If preferred, the chops can first be chined by removing the rib-bone, then formed into a neat roll and kept in shape with a cocktail stick. Otherwise simply trim off all the fat; salt and pepper the meat, then dip in egg and fine dry breadcrumbs. Arrange side by side in the roasting tin.

To make the sauce: Heat all the ingredients together until the jelly melts, then pour half over and round the cutlets. Put in a quick oven (Gas No. 6, 400°F, 200°C) for 45 minutes, then add the remainder of the sauce.

Turn down the heat to Gas No. 4, 350°F, 180°C and continue to cook for a further 25 minutes until the cutlets are a rich golden brown and the sauce is syrupy.

Lamb Chops with Barbecue Sauce

An excellent recipe for using with braising chops. If cutlets are used, they can be grilled then served with the sauce which has been bubbled on top of the stove until syrupy.

Serves 6-8

6-8 shoulder chops, well trimmed
  of fat
Salt and black pepper

1 egg
Fried breadcrumbs or medium
  matzo meal

Sauce:
4 level tbsp clear mild honey
3 level tbsp tomato ketchup
3 tbsp soy sauce
1 level teasp dry mustard
1 medium clove of garlic, crushed

½ level teasp salt
10 grinds black pepper
Juice of 1 medium orange
3 tbsp wine vinegar

Salt and pepper the chops on both sides, then brush them with the beaten egg, coat lightly with the dried crumbs and arrange in one layer in a roasting tin.

Put all the sauce ingredients into a bowl in the order given, stirring until smooth.

Bake the chops, uncovered, in a quick oven (Gas No. 6, 400°F, 200°C) for 45 minutes, then pour on the sauce and turn the oven down to Gas No. 4, 350°F, 180°C and cook for a further 20 minutes until the sauce is syrupy and the chops are richly glazed. If not to be served at once, turn right down to Gas No. 1, 275°F, 140°C to keep hot without allowing the sauce to dry up.

Lamb Chops and Potato Braise

This can be cooked in an ordinary casserole, but I like to do it in a heavy frying pan on top of the stove. This makes it ideal for bed-sitter entertaining. Use large, mature lamb chops.

Serves 6-8

6-8 large lamb chops
3 tbsp flour
2 level teasp salt
15 grinds black pepper
½ teasp paprika
4 tbsp oil
2 medium (5 oz/150g) onions,
   sliced paper-thin

½ teasp oregano
1 bayleaf
10 fl oz (275ml/1¼ cups) gravy or
   chicken stock
1 tbsp tomato purée or ketchup
2 lb (1kg) potatoes

Peel the potatoes, cut in slices about ⅜ inch (1cm) thick and leave covered with cold water. Trim the fat off the chops and dip them in the flour, seasoned with salt, pepper and paprika. Brown really well in the oil, in a wide, fairly deep frying pan. Remove and drain on tissue or kitchen paper. In the same oil, put the onion and cook until it is soft and golden (about 5 minutes), sprinkle with the oregano (instead of oregano you can use Italian seasoning or herbes de Provence) and the bayleaf and pour in the gravy or stock (made from a cube) with the purée or ketchup. Stir well together then add the drained potatoes in one layer, laying the browned chops on top of them. Cover tightly either with a lid or foil and simmer very gently for 1 hour on top of the stove.

Alternatively, the ingredients can be arranged in the same way in an oven casserole and cooked for 1½ hours at Gas No. 2, 300°F, 150°C. By the time the chops are tender the potatoes will be soft and have absorbed much of the delicious gravy.

VARIATION
Lamb Seville Style
Scatter 2 oz (50g) sliced stuffed olives over the browned chops then cook as directed.

Schnitzels and Escalopes

Although veal is an expensive meat and the schnitzels or escalopes that are cut from it are the most expensive of all, their price compares quite favourably with a roast or steak when one takes into account the fact that every ounce or grain is edible, with no fat, gristle or bone to be trimmed away. In addition, they are extremely quick and simple to cook, which can mean a big saving of effort, if not actual cash.

Where the large schnitzels are not available, excellent dishes can be made from the smaller scallops or 'scallopini' as the Italians call them. These take extremely well to a quick browning, then a gentle simmering in a light sauce. Both large schnitzels and the smaller scallops are used in the recipes below. Incidentally, all these dishes can be made using thinly-sliced and beaten chicken or turkey breast.

Wiener Schnitzel

Serves 6-8

6-8 veal schnitzel, weighing 6 oz (175g) each and cut approx ¼ inch (0.5cm) thick	3 eggs
	3 tbsp water
	Fine dried breadcrumbs
Salt and freshly ground black pepper	Oil for frying
	Lemon
3 oz (75g/¾ cup) flour	

Beat the slices of veal as thin as possible, using a cutlet bat or saucer. Sprinkle both sides well with the salt and pepper. Then dip each piece first in the flour, then in the egg beaten with the water, and finally with the dry breadcrumbs, making sure they are in an even layer. Arrange the slices side by side on a tray, and refrigerate for half and hour to set the coating.

Heat enough oil to come to a depth of ⅜ inch (1cm) in a large (approx 12 inch/30cm) frying pan. When really hot, lay the coated veal in it side by side, and cook at a gentle bubble (turn down heat after all the pieces are bubbling), for approx 4 minutes on either side until a rich brown. Serve with slices of lemon. This dish is delicious with sautéed red or green peppers, and may also be served cold for picnics.

Schnitzels in Wine and Walnut Sauce

The schnitzels for this dish can be a little smaller than for the Wiener Schnitzel, or two 3 oz (75g) pieces of veal for each serving can be used instead.

For each serving:

1 veal, turkey or chicken schnitzel	Seasoned flour
1 oz (25g/½ cup) mushrooms, whole if small, sliced if large	2 tbsp white wine
	Oil for frying
½-1 oz (15-25g/⅛-¼ cup) walnuts	

Season the schnitzel thoroughly with salt and pepper and leave for half an hour. Put 2 heaped tbsp flour in a bag and add a good pinch of salt and pepper. Put one schnitzel in the bag at a time and shake to coat thinly with the flour.

Put enough oil in a wide frying pan to cover the base to a depth of $\frac{1}{8}$ inch (0.5cm). Heat gently, then put in the floured schnitzels and cook at a gentle sizzle until a golden brown on each side. Remove from the pan and add the sliced mushrooms and halved or quartered walnuts. Toss in the fat for a minute, then add the wine. When bubbling, return the schnitzel to the pan, cover and simmer gently for 20 minutes.

To serve, remove the schnitzel to a dish, boil the sauce for a minute. Taste for seasoning, then pour over the schnitzel.

Veal Scallops with Mushrooms

Scallops can be the trimmings from the piece of veal from which schnitzels have been cut, or they can be the eye of the veal chop, thinly sliced. The best result in this dish is achieved when there is some gravy left over from a pot roast. Otherwise use a combination of white wine and strong bouillon or consommé. The dish can be completed just before dinner, then either kept hot on a low heat or reheated.

Serves 6-8 **F** 3 months

$1\frac{1}{2}$-2 lb (0.75-1kg) escalope of veal
4 tbsp oil
$1\frac{1}{2}$ lb (750g) pinky mushrooms
Seasoned flour for dredging
1 cup rich gravy (e.g. from pot roast), *or* 5 fl oz (150ml/^{2}/$_3$ cup)
dry white wine and 5 fl oz (150ml/^{2}/$_3$ cup) strong beef stock or bouillon
2 teasp tomato purée
Salt and black pepper
1 clove of garlic, crushed
Chopped parsley for garnish

Have the veal cut in very thin slices. Pound with a steak beater until as thin as possible. Slice the mushrooms finely. Heat the oil gently in a large lidded frying pan. Dip the meat in and out of the seasoned flour, then fry at a fairly brisk bubble until golden brown on both sides. Remove to a plate and add the mushrooms, cooking them for 4 or 5 minutes, until beginning to brown. Return the meat to the pan, add the garlic, and the liquid and tomato purée. Season well. Cover and simmer for 10 minutes. Serve sprinkled with parsley. Delicious with **Parsleyed Noodles** (see p.313).

246

Veal and Chicken Livers Sauté
Omit the mushrooms. For each serving, allow three 2 oz (50g)
chicken livers each cut into three. After the scallops have been
removed from the pan, fry or grill the livers quickly for three
minutes, then return the scallops to the pan, add the liquid and
proceed as described.

Party Casseroles

A superb party dish can be made from either stewed chunks or
braised slices of meat. For a stew, the meat is cut in cubes, briskly
fried to seal in some of the juices, then completely submerged in
an aromatic liquid and allowed to cook at a temperature well below
boiling point until even the toughest meat has become tenderized
and has yielded up its flavour to the sauce.

When meat is braised, however, it is also sealed first but it is
usually cut in slices rather than cubes and is only partially covered
with liquid. This means that more of the flavour of the meat is
retained, rather than all of the juice oozing out into the cooking
liquid. Braising is, therefore, an excellent way to cook meat that
is a little too tough or dry to roast, yet is too good to stew. Like
stews, braises both freeze and reheat extremely well so they are
an excellent choice for the working hostess.

The choice of dish
As well as having the right size dish, it is equally important to have
one made of the most convenient material – one that conducts the
heat evenly so that the food browns without burning, and is easily
washed up after use. The most recent developments in non-stick
finish are very satisfactory. A sauté frypan is particularly useful
for *pre-frying* of meat and chicken for casseroles as well as for *top
of stove* cooking of sautés, chops and rice dishes.

For really large quantities of stews and braises, I don't think you
can do better than choose a pot made of enamel on steel. It must
have a heavy base for even cooking, and have handles that are
heatproof up to Gas No. 10, 540°F, 280°C to make them suitable
for oven as well as top of stove cookery.

But no matter what kind of dish is used, the tenderness and
tastiness of a casserole depends mainly on long, slow cooking.
This means that the liquid in which the meat is cooked should

never come to the boil – only bubble every once in a while. Although a casserole can be simmered in this way on top of the stove, it is easier to control the heat – and the dish actually develops more flavour – if it is cooked in the oven.

Note: To cut the calories of any braise, do not brown the meat in fat or fry the vegetables, instead put them into the bubbling sauce. This seals the surface of the meat and helps to keep it juicy.

To freeze casseroles
All casseroles freeze extremely well and their flavour and texture remain excellent for up to 3 months. They may be packed in several ways.

In the cooking dish: This is fine for up to 8 servings. Freeze until solid, then dip the dish quickly in and out of a bowl of very hot water. This loosens the casserole, which can be removed en bloc, and wrapped in foil or packed in a plastic bag.

In blocks: This is excellent for a large quantity (e.g. **Harold's Hearty Casserole**). Turn the cooked casserole into a rectangular baking dish and freeze until *almost* but not quite solid. Cut up into blocks of suitable size, then foil wrap or pack in plastic bags.

Foil dishes or plastic containers: These are very convenient but expensive in large sizes. Large (4 lb/1.75kg) margarine containers make a practical and economical alternative and hold up to 8 servings.

To thaw casseroles
Turn into another casserole, cover, and reheat in a slow moderate oven (Gas No. 4, 350°F, 180°C) for 40 minutes or until bubbly, stirring once. Keep hot at Gas No. 1, 275°F, 140°C.

Boeuf Bourguignon

To most people this is the Burgundian dish par excellence, and my recipe actually comes from 'La Cloche' in Beaune. I have, however, taken the liberty of amending it slightly as chef Robert Petit's original recipe starts: 'For 8 people take two bottles of good Burgundy.' I have halved the quantity of wine and marinated the beef in it to compensate for any loss of flavour.

248

Serves 8 F 3 months

The marinade:

3 level teasp salt

20 grinds black pepper

2 medium onions, thinly sliced

Sprig of thyme, 3 bayleaves, large
  sprig parsley

3 tbsp oil

1 bottle Burgundy or similar red
  wine

3 lb (1.5kg) braising steak

3 tbsp oil

2 large onions, finely chopped

3 carrots, peeled and diced

4 level tbsp flour

1 pint (575ml/2½ cups) beef stock

Large sprig parsley

1 bayleaf

2 cloves garlic, crushed

Cut the meat into 2 inch (5cm) cubes and place in a bowl. Add all the marinade ingredients. Leave for 4 hours, stirring once or twice.

Lift the meat from the marinade with a slotted spoon and lay on paper towels to dry.

Heat the oil in a heavy frying pan and cook the onion and carrot until golden, then transfer to a large pan or oven casserole. In the same fat brown the meat, a few pieces at a time, then transfer to the casserole. Add the flour to the pan to take up the remaining fat, then add the stock, the strained marinade, herbs and garlic. Bring to the boil, stirring to make a smooth sauce, then pour over the ingredients in the casserole.

Cover, then simmer for 3 hours or for the same time in the oven at Gas No. 1, 275°F, 140°C. Serve sprinkled with parsley or with the following garnish:

½ lb (225g/4 cups) button
  mushrooms

½ lb (225g) button onions

2 oz (50g/¼ cup) oil

Chopped parsley

2 level teasp brown sugar

Cover the onions with water, bring to the boil, simmer for 7 or 8 minutes, then drain, slip off the skins, and place in the same pan with 2 tbsp oil and the sugar, cover and cook very gently for a further 15 minutes until richly glazed and tender. Cook the mushrooms quickly in the remaining fat. Arrange onions and mushrooms on top of the meat and just before serving sprinkle with parsley.

Southern Beef Casserole

This richly flavoured stew tastes even better if refrigerated overnight then reheated until bubbly before serving.

Serves 6-8 F 3 months

2¹/₂-3 lb (1-1.5kg) braising steak or stewing steak
3 tbsp oil
3 medium onions, chopped
3 green peppers, *or* 6 tbsp frozen peppers
1 15oz (425g) can tomatoes
¹/₂ pint (275ml-1¹/₄ cups) stock made with meat cube, *or* ¹/₂ pint (275ml/1¹/₄ cups) gravy, *or* ¹/₂

pint (275ml/1¹/₄ cups) dry red wine
1 fat clove of garlic
1¹/₂ level teasp mixed Italian herbs or dried basil
2 large bayleaves
3 level teasp salt
2 level teasp brown sugar
15 grinds black pepper

Heat the oil in a heavy casserole or frying pan. Slice or chop the onion and de-seed the pepper, removing the pith, and cut into ¹/₂ inch (1.25cm) squares. Cook until softened – about 10 minutes. Add the meat and continue to cook, but on a stronger heat, until the meat is sealed and richly browned on all sides. Add all the remaining ingredients, bring to simmering point, and bubble uncovered for 5 minutes to concentrate the flavour. Transfer to an oven casserole, cover and cook in a slow oven (Gas No. 2, 300°F, 150°C) for 30 minutes, then continue to cook at (Gas No. ¹/₂, 250°F, 130°C) for a further 2 hours or until the meat is absolutely tender.

Beef Braised in the Italian Style

Wine helps to tenderize the meat as well as to flavour it. Have the meat (top rib is excellent) cut into slices approx ³/₄ inch (1.75cm) thick, then cut the slices into individual servings. As no flour is used to thicken the sauce, this is a good dish for weight-watchers.

Serves 6-8 **F** 3 months

2¹/₂-3 lb (1-1.5kg) braising steak
3 level teasp salt
¹/₄ teasp freshly ground black
   pepper
1 teasp dried leaf oregano (not
   powder)
3 tbsp oil
1 large onion
2 teasp brown sugar

¹/₄ pint (150ml/²/₃ cup) dry red
   wine, *or* 2 fl oz (50ml/¹/₄ cup)
   red wine vinegar and 3 fl oz
   (75ml/¹/₃ cup) water
1 beef stock cube
2¹/₂ oz (65g) tomato purée
1 bayleaf
1 clove of garlic, crushed
Hot water

Cut the steak ³/₄ inch (1.75cm) thick. Chop the onion coarsely. Put the salt, pepper and oregano onto a piece of greaseproof or foil and turn the meat in it to coat it. Cook the onion in the oil until softened, about 5 minutes, then add the meat and cook briskly until brown on all sides, sprinkling with the brown sugar to hasten the process. Add all the remaining ingredients and enough hot water barely to cover the meat. Transfer to the oven and cook slowly (Gas No. 2, 300°F, 150°C) for 2 hours until the meat is tender and the sauce is thickened. Serve with plain boiled rice.

Paprika Beef

A very savoury dish that is not too highly seasoned.

Serves 6-8 **F** 3 months

Oil for frying
2¹/₂-3 lb (1-1.5kg) braising steak
2 level teasp paprika (sweet)
2 level teasp salt
10 grinds black pepper
2 medium onions

¹/₄ lb (125g/2 cups) mushrooms
1 large green pepper
¹/₂ pint (275ml/1¹/₄ cups) meat
   stock or thin gravy
1 tbsp tomato purée

Cut the steak ³/₄ inch (1.75cm) thick. Cut the onion in half then slice paper thin. Slice the mushrooms and halve, de-seed and slice the pepper. Lay the meat on a board. Mix the paprika, salt and pepper together, sprinkle half on the meat then pound it in using the edge of a saucer. Turn the meat over and repeat with the remaining paprika mixture. Cut the meat into 6-8 pieces.

In a frying pan, put enough oil to come to a depth of ¹/₈ inch (0.5cm). Heat for 3 or 4 minutes and when really hot, put in the meat and cook briskly until brown on both sides, turning once. Lift out the meat. In the same fat put the onion, turn down the heat and cook gently until limp – about 10 minutes, then add the mushrooms and green pepper and cook another 2 minutes or until they have absorbed the juices in the pan. Remove to a casserole and put the meat on top. Put the liquid and tomato purée into the frying pan, bring to the boil, then pour over the meat. Cover and simmer in the oven (Gas No. 2, 300°F, 150°C) for 2 hours.

Serve with plain boiled or mashed potatoes.

VARIATION

Slimmers' Paprika Beef: After the meat has been cut into 6-8 pieces, put all the remaining ingredients in a stove-to-oven casserole and bring to the boil. Lower into it the pieces of meat one at a time (to prevent the liquid going off the boil). Cover and simmer in the oven (Gas No. 2, 300°F, 150°C) for 2 hours.

Sweet and Sour Pineapple Beef

This is a particularly successful buffet dish, as the pineapple gives it a most unusual flavour. It goes well with rice.

Serves 6-8 **F** 3 months

	Quantities for 12
2½ lb-3 lb (1-1.5kg) braising or stewing steak cut into 1 inch (2.5cm) cubes	5 lb (2.25g)
2 oz (50g/¼ cup) margarine	3 oz (75g/⅓ cup)
2 tbsp oil	3 tbsp
2 medium (5oz/150g) onions, coarsely chopped	3 medium
4 sticks celery, chopped	6 sticks
1 medium can (14 oz/400g) pineapple chunks	1 × 28 oz (800g) can
½ pint (275ml/1¼ cups) beef stock made with a bouillon cube	1 pint (575ml/2½ cups)
2 level teasp salt	4 teasp
A few grinds black pepper	20 grinds
2 level tbsp cornflour (cornstarch)	4 level tbsp
1 tbsp soy sauce	2 tbsp
1 tbsp tomato ketchup	2 tbsp
2 tbsp vinegar	4 tbsp

Put the oil and margarine in a heavy pan and brown the well-dried meat on all sides. Add the onion and celery and continue to cook for a further 5 minutes, until the vegetables have wilted and absorbed most of the fat. Drain the juice from the pineapple and make it up to 10 fl oz (275ml/1¼ cups) with water (or, for larger quantity, 1 pint/575ml/2½ cups). Add with the stock and seasonings to the meat. Bring to the boil, cover and simmer for 2 hours, or until the meat is tender. Blend the cornflour (cornstarch) with the soy sauce, ketchup and vinegar, stir into the meat with the pineapple chunks. Simmer for 2 minutes. Serve piping hot. If preferred, this dish can be transferred to the oven and allowed to simmer at Gas No. 2, 300°F, 150°C for 2½ hours.

Harold's Hearty Casserole

This is a no-nonsense casserole for a large buffet supper. It has a rich satisfying flavour – a kind of poor man's Boeuf Bourguignone. As Burgundy prices are rising annually, use any medium dry red wine.

Serves 12-15 **F** 3 months

You will need a 10½ pint (5 litre) casserole or 2 smaller ones.
5 lb (2.25kg) stewing or braising steak, cut into 1 inch (2.5cm) cubes
6 tbsp oil
Plenty of black pepper
6 large onions, sliced wafer-thin
6 stalks of celery, finely sliced
6 carrots, cut in slivers
6 oz (175g/3 cups) mushrooms, sliced

3 level tbsp brown sugar
6 level teasp salt
6 bayleaves
3 pints (1.75 litres/8 cups) meat stock, or half-and-half red wine and stock (use cubes)
5 lb (2.25kg) potatoes
6 level tbsp cornflour (cornstarch) dissolved in ½ pint (275ml/1¼ cups) water

For this amount in a domestic kitchen it is best to divide the meat and vegetables into two halves and fry each half separately, then combine them in one casserole and add the remainder of the ingredients as detailed below. Heat the oil in a heavy frying pan or oven casserole, sprinkle with ½ teasp black pepper, then put in half the well-dried meat and brown briskly on all sides. Lift out and put in the casserole. To the same pan add half the vegetables and half the brown sugar and continue to cook until the mixture is a really rich brown. Add to the meat. Repeat with the second half of the oil, meat, vegetables and sugar. When the vegetables are ready, add all the wine and bubble for 5 minutes until reduced by half, then add the stock, bayleaves and salt and bring to the boil. Stir thoroughly, then add to the meat and vegetables already in the casserole. The meat should be barely covered; if not add a little more stock. Cover and simmer either on top of the stove for 1½ hours or (preferably) in a slow oven (Gas No. 2, 300°F, 150°C) for the same time.

While the casserole is cooking put the 5 lb (2.25kg) (preferably new) potatoes into a saucepan, add 2 teasp salt and cold water to cover. Bring to the boil slowly, then drain and skin. After 1½ hours, mix the cornflour (cornstarch) with the water and stir into the casserole, together with the potatoes. Leave to bubble for a further 10 minutes, then cool thoroughly.

To reheat, allow 1½ hours. Put the casserole in the oven and turn to Gas No. 6, 400°F, 200°C. It is impossible to be specific as to the exact length of time needed to reheat the meat as it depends on the oven, and also whether 2 medium or 1 large casserole is used. During the reheating of the casserole, the potatoes will finish cooking. If cooked completely beforehand they will eventually disintegrate.

Turkish Lamb Casserole

This is the Turkish equivalent of hot-pot. The aubergine (eggplant) gives it a very distinctive flavour. If you wish to freeze the casserole for later use, do not cook the aubergine (eggplant) with the meat until it is reheated. This will prevent the vegetable losing its texture.

Serves 6-8 F 3 months

2-3 aubergines (eggplants) (about 1½ lb/675g)
¼ pint (150ml/⅔ cup) oil
2½-3 lb (1-1.5kg) boned lamb shoulder or 8 shoulder lamb chops
2 medium onions, thinly sliced
1 heaped tbsp tomato purée or ketchup

½ pint (275 ml/1¼ cups) stock made from meat cube
2 level teasp brown sugar
2 level teasp salt
½ level teasp oregano or mixed Italian herbs
10 grinds black pepper

Peel the aubergines (eggplants) with a potato peeler and cut into

254

½ inch (1.25cm) cubes. Put into a bowl, cover with cold water and add 2 teasp salt. Leave for 30 minutes (brown liquid will ooze out), then drain in a sieve and dry with a paper towel. Fry gently in the hot oil until golden brown, then lift out from the pan with a draining spoon and reserve. Add 2 tbsp more oil if the aubergines have absorbed it all. To the same pan, add the trimmed chops or meat cut into 1 inch (2.5cm) cubes and brown lightly on all sides to seal the meat. If you brown the meat well before adding the liquid it will stay juicy and flavoursome and also produce a rich brown gravy. Lift the meat out and put into a casserole. To the same fat add the thinly-sliced onions, and sauté gently until golden brown, then add the tomato purée or ketchup, the seasonings and stock. Stir well, then pour the contents of the pan over the meat. Transfer to the oven and cook at Gas No. 2, 300°F, 150°C, for 1½ hours. Uncover and add the aubergines, cover and cook for a further 30 minutes until the meat is tender.

Beefburgers and Meatballs

A meatball can vary in texture from the 'chopped meat' hamburger which is first cousin to a steak, to the finely-minced sheftalia or kofte so popular in Greece and Turkey. All, however, need a tasty, gristle-free minced (ground) meat as a foundation.

It is advisable, therefore, to shop around until you find the minced (ground) meat that suits your taste. It does not necessarily have to come from a prime joint as a cheaper one such as neck can often provide the 'meatiest' mince. Be sure that it has been minced fresh on the day you buy it then use it within 24 hours, as the number of cut surfaces makes it deteriorate more quickly than other meat. It does, however, freeze to perfection, both raw and cooked. Beefburgers and meatballs can also be frozen, both cooked and raw, providing a ready meal for the barbecue or the grill.

To freeze beefburgers and meatballs
Open freeze on trays for 2 hours, then pack in plastic bags.

Meat extenders
Most people like to add some form of 'extender' to minced (ground) meat, not only because it makes it go further, but also

because it gives a more tender texture. You can take your pick of breadcrumbs, soaked bread, grated potato, matzo meal or porridge oats. I think bread gives the lightest results.

Although it is most convenient to process the eggs, extender and seasoning in a blender or food processor, it is best to mix in the meat by hand, for if it is packed too closely, as is the tendency with an electric mixer, it is not as light in texture.

General Method for Mixing Minced (Ground) Meat

By hand: Soak the bread in water to cover, then squeeze dry and add to the beaten eggs, grated onions, herbs (if used) and seasonings.

By blender or food processor: Put the fresh herbs, unbeaten eggs, slices of soaked bread, chunks of onion and seasonings into the blender or food processor, and blend for 30 seconds or until smooth.

In either case: Work together the raw meat and the egg mixture with the hands or a large fork, until smoothly blended. Leave for $1/2$ hour. The mixture can now be formed into patties or balls, and grilled, fried or stewed, as required.

Lizzie's Beefburgers

This is an excellent all-purpose beefburger which is perfect for the barbecue. Use all beef if to be served with a highly-flavoured barbecue sauce; half and half beef and veal for a lighter, more delicate flavour.

Makes 25-30 according to size and thickness
F raw 4 months, cooked 3 months

$1^1/2$ lb (675g) finely minced
  (ground) beef and $1^1/2$ lb (675g)
  finely minced (ground) veal; *or*
  3 lb (1.25kg) minced (ground)
  beef
2 large eggs
4 large slices from a toasting loaf,
  soaked in water to cover, then
  squeezed dry

1 large onion
1 clove of garlic, crushed, *or*
  pinch of garlic powder
$1/2$ teasp each mixed dry herbs and
  seasoned salt or aromat
2 level teasp salt
$1/4$ teasp freshly ground black
  pepper

Prepare the mixture as described in the General Method (p.256). Form into balls 2 inches (5cm) in diameter or patties ½-¾ inch (1-1.5cm) thick, then roll in dry breadcrumbs. Freeze or use immediately as follows:

To fry: Heat 2 tbsp of oil in a heavy frying pan for 3 minutes. Add the beefburgers in one layer and fry quickly, for 3 to 4 minutes on either side until a rich brown.

To grill: Put under a pre-heated gas or electric grill or on a charcoal grill, brush with oil or sauce. Grill for 6 minutes on one side and 4 minutes on the other, until a rich brown.

Hamburgers with Pizzaiola Sauce

The meat mixture is slightly lighter in texture than for the beefburgers, and is served with a very fresh-tasting herb and tomato sauce.

Serves 6-8 F 3 months
Meat mixture:

2 lb (1kg) minced (ground) meat	1 thick slice of bread
2 eggs	2 level teasp salt
1 medium onion	¼ teasp black pepper

Follow General Method for mixing minced (ground) meat (p.256). Leave half an hour then form into hamburgers about ½ inch (1.25cm) thick.

Whilst the meat is standing, make the Pizzaiola Sauce as follows:

1 large can (28 oz approx 800g) plum tomatoes	1 level teasp mixed dried Italian herbs
1 tbsp olive oil	2 fat cloves of garlic, crushed
1 level teasp each salt and sugar	2 level tbsp finely sliced fresh basil leaves or coarsely cut parsley
10 grinds black pepper	

If the tomatoes have been canned in tomato juice do not drain. Otherwise drain off water and put the tomatoes into a thick-based pan with all the other ingredients. Bring to the boil and bubble uncovered for 10 minutes until thick but still juicy. Taste and adjust the seasonings.

Meanwhile fry the hamburgers in shallow oil over moderate heat until a rich brown on both sides – about 5 minutes altogether. As they fry, transfer to a hot dish in a moderate oven. When all are done, pour over the sauce and leave in the oven for 5-10 minutes. Serve at once.

For convenience, hamburgers can be left in covered pan to heat through with the sauce.

Roumanian Meatballs

Serves 6-8 as a main course, 10 as an entrée or for a buffet.
F 3 months

Meat mixture:

2 lb (1kg) raw minced (ground) meat	Speck of pepper
2 eggs	1 large sprig of parsley
1/2 medium onion	1 1/2 lb (675g) aubergines (eggplants)
2 thick slices from a large loaf	1 level tbsp salt
2 level teasp salt	

Follow General Method (p.256) for mixing the minced (ground) meat. Leave meat mixture to rest for half an hour, then form into golfballs and arrange in bottom of a shallow ovenproof casserole.

While meat is resting, peel aubergines (eggplants), cut in 3/4 inch (1.5cm) slices, then cover with water plus 1 level tbsp salt. When meatballs have been formed, drain aubergines well, squeeze with hands to extract juices and dry thoroughly.

The sauce:

2 medium onions (5 oz/150g each) or 1 large	2 level tbsp brown sugar
1-2 green peppers, according to size	1 level teasp citric acid, or 2 tbsp lemon juice
3 tbsp oil	1 level teasp salt
1 large (1 lb 13 oz/825g) can tomatoes, or 2 × 14 oz (400g) cans	10 grinds black pepper
	1 crushed clove of garlic
	1 level teasp dried basil
	1 × 5 oz (150g) can tomato purée

Peel then slice the onions very finely. Halve, de-seed then cut the peppers into ³⁄₈ inch (1cm) strips.

Heat the oil in a large frying pan, then cook the onion until soft and golden – about 10 minutes. Add the strips of pepper and continue to cook for another 5 minutes. Now add all the remaining sauce ingredients, stir well and bubble for 5 minutes to thicken. Pour over the meatballs, cover, and leave in a low oven (Gas No. 2, 300°F, 150°C) for 1¹⁄₂ hours. Meanwhile fry the aubergines in 4 tbsp oil until golden. Drain on crumpled paper then add to the meatballs. Simmer uncovered for a further 30 minutes until the sauce is thick but still juicy.

This dish freezes and reheats well.

Turkish Meatballs

The meatballs are stewed in a smooth sweet and sour sauce. Pine kernels (when available) add greatly to this dish.

Serves 6-8 **F** 3 months
Meat mixture:

2 lb (1kg) minced (ground) meat	1 level teasp cinnamon
2 eggs	2 level teasp salt
1 medium onion	¹⁄₄ teasp black pepper
1 thick slice of bread	1 tbsp chopped parsley

Follow General Method (p.256) for mixing minced (ground) meat, then leave to stand for half an hour.

The sauce:

1 large onion	Juice of ¹⁄₂ large lemon
3 tbsp oil	1 level tbsp brown sugar
2 oz (50g) pine kernels (optional)	Salt and pepper
1 × 5 oz (150g) can tomato purée and 2 cans water	

Whilst the minced (ground) meat is standing, cut the onion in half and then cut in very thin slices. Heat oil in deepish frying pan or casserole, add onion and cook gently for about 5 minutes until limp, whilst you roll the meat in golfballs. Add the meat to the pan (in two lots if necessary) and cook gently until golden brown. If pine kernels are used, add them and cook for 2 minutes until golden. Now add the remaining sauce ingredients, and bring to the boil (meatballs should be barely covered – if not, add a little more water). Cover and simmer for 1 hour.

Alternatively, transfer to the oven (Gas No. 3, 325°F, 170°C) for 1 hour, then uncover and allow the sauce to reduce for a further 15 minutes. Just before serving, sprinkle with a rounded tbsp of finely chopped parsley.

Picnic Loaf

A really good meat loaf or terrine which is light-textured and well seasoned is an excellent choice for a homely get-together on a winter's night, or to eat cold with salads or in sandwiches at a picnic or barbecue. I have developed this recipe over many years to achieve a satisfying blend of flavours and a firm but tender texture.

Serves 6-8 F 3 months

2 lb (1kg) shoulder steak, minced (ground) twice
3 large slices of bread, *or* 1 cup fresh breadcrumbs
2 eggs
1 medium onion (5oz/150g)
1 teasp dry English mustard
1 generous tbsp tomato ketchup
1 tbsp prepared horseradish sauce

1 tbsp soy sauce
2 teasp chopped parsley
1 level teasp herbes de Provence
1 medium green pepper, de-seeded and chopped (optional)
2 level teasp salt
15 grinds black pepper
1 level tbsp porridge oats

In a blender or food processor put the following: bread in chunks (or crumbs), eggs, onion cut in 4, green pepper, mustard, sauces and seasonings. Blend until smooth. (If mixing by hand, grate the onion, beat the eggs, and chop the green pepper and parsley finely before adding the other ingredients.)

Turn the egg mixture into a large bowl, then add the oats and stir in the meat using a large fork until thoroughly and evenly blended. Arrange in a loaf shape about 2 inches (5cm) high and 3 inches (7.5cm) wide in centre of roasting tin just big enough to hold it with a 2 inch (5cm) margin all round.

Put in a quick oven (Gas No. 7, 425°F, 220°C) for 15 minutes, then turn to Gas No. 4, 350°F, 180°C for a further 35 minutes until richly brown. If the loaf is to be served hot, make the following gravy: fry a small, finely-chopped onion in 1 tbsp oil until soft and golden, then stir in 1 cup beef stock mixed with 2 level teasp cornflour (cornstarch). Bring to the boil, then pour round and over the meat loaf 15 minutes before it is ready. (Or use left-over roast gravy.)

Serve in slices.

Stuffed Vegetables

Stuffed vegetable dishes belong to a select group of recipes (such as strudel, meat turnovers and stuffed pancakes) in which cunning cooks have made a virtue out of the necessity of extending a meagre supply of meat, by using various delicious edible casings such as pastry, noodle dough or vegetables. In each of the following recipes there is an interchange of flavour between the meat, the vegetable and the sauce in which it is cooked which produces a glorious example of true gastronomic economics. *Note:* All stuffed vegetables taste better if left to develop flavour overnight and then reheated for 50 minutes in a moderate oven (or top of stove) until the sauce is bubbly.

Stuffed Aubergines (Eggplants) in Apricot Sauce

Slow cooking is essential to allow the aubergines to soften and the sauce to thicken in this delicious Middle Eastern dish.

Serves 6-8 **F** 3 months

3-4 large oval boat-shaped aubergines (eggplants) (¹/₂ lb/225g each)
1¹/₂ lb (675g) minced (ground) steak
1 onion (5 oz/150g)
1 egg
1 level teasp salt
10 grinds black pepper

1 thick slice bread
2-3 tbsp oil for frying
8 oz (225g/1¹/₂ cups) dried apricots soaked overnight in water to cover
To flavour the sauce: 4 level tbsp brown sugar and 1 tbsp lemon juice

To make the minced (ground) meat mixture. By hand: Soak the bread in water to cover, then after 5 minutes squeeze dry and add

261

to the meat together with the grated onion, egg and seasonings. With a blender or food processor: Put bread, onion, egg and seasonings in machine and process until smooth, then add to meat and mix well.

Cut the aubergines in half lengthwise and use a spoon to scoop out the inside, leaving ½ inch (1.25cm) flesh all the way round. Coarsely chop the scooped out flesh and fry in the oil until soft. Remove from the pan and drain, then chop to a pulp and add to the minced (ground) meat mixture.

Divide the meat mixture between the aubergine halves, press down firmly, then fry them gently in the remaining oil, on both sides, until a golden brown. (The meat mix won't stick to the pan if left until the brown crust has formed.)

Arrange in a wide, shallow ovenproof casserole (an enamel one is excellent) and surround with the soaked apricots. Pour the soaking liquid around them and sprinkle with 1 level tbsp of the brown sugar. Bring to the boil on top of the stove, then cover and transfer to the oven. Cook gently at Gas No. 3, 325°F, 160°C for 1 hour, uncover and add the remaining brown sugar and the lemon juice. Baste, then cover and cook another half hour. Uncover and continue to cook slowly for about 15 minutes to allow sauce to thicken to a syrupy consistency. Taste, and adjust seasoning if necessary.

Savoury Mince Pastries

In those countries where meat is not of a consistent quality, ordinary minced (ground) meat is cooked with special care and then used for such delicious specialities as strudel and meat pasties like the Turkish Turnovers, or 'boreks' as they are known in the Middle East. To develop the maximum flavour, the meat is first fried to seal it and then it is cooked in the minimum of liquid. Spices and herbs are also added. Ask the butcher for lean minced (ground) meat and have it put through the mincer twice. I usually make 3 lb (1.25kg) of the Savoury Meat Filling, divide it between three plastic bags and then freeze it for later use.

For a large party, I would try and freeze the raw strudel or the turnovers well ahead, then glaze and cook them fresh just before serving. Sesame and poppy seeds give a very special crunchiness to any savoury pastry dish. They are now quite freely available at health food shops, and as they are very light in weight, it is only necessary to buy an ounce or two at a time. They keep fresh for a year.

Cooking the onion and pepper in the oil before the meat is added to the pan gives the mixture a better flavour than if they are all cooked together, as the fried vegetables will become slightly caramelized and lose their acidity

Always cook puff pastry on trays which have been moistened slightly with cold water, as this helps the pastry to keep its shape as it rises. To get the maximum rise from any kind of puff or flaky pastry, follow these rules:

1. Roll it out no thicker than a knife blade.
2. Chill it for at least an hour before baking.
3. Pre-heat the oven to the given temperature.

Savoury Meat Filling

F 3 months

2 tbsp oil	2 teasp soy sauce
1 medium onion	2 teasp Worcestershire sauce
1 large green pepper *or* 4 tbsp frozen chopped pepper	2 teasp parsley *or* pinch dried parsley
1 lb (450g) lean minced (ground) meat	1 level teasp salt
	10 grinds black pepper
2 rounded tbsp tomato ketchup	2 tbsp water

Finely chop the onion, the pepper and the parsley. Heat the oil in an 8 inch (20cm) heavy saucepan or a deep frying pan and cook the onion and the pepper until soft and golden – about 5 minutes. Add the minced (ground) meat and continue to cook, stirring with a fork so that it cooks evenly. When the meat has lost its redness, add all the remaining ingredients in the order given, put on the lid and simmer for 15 minutes until the meat is tender when tasted and the mixture is juicy but not wet. If it is too liquid, simmer a few minutes without the lid. Allow to go quite cold before using.

Meat Strudel

Serves 6-8 Can be frozen uncooked
For each strudel serving 3-4:

¹/₂ lb (225g) frozen puff pastry   1 egg, beaten
¹/₂ lb (225g) **Savoury Meat Filling**   Sesame seeds
  (p.263)

Roll out the pastry into a rectangle measuring 12 × 9 inches (30 × 22.5cm). Spread the filling evenly all over leaving a 1 inch (2.5cm) border of pastry clear all the way round. Turn this border in over the filling on the short sides then roll up into a flattened Swiss roll.

Transfer to a wet baking sheet. Paint all over with the egg and scatter with the sesame seeds. Make six cuts, 2 inches (5cm) apart, through the top crust.

Bake in a hot oven (Gas No. 7, 425°F, 220°C) for 15 minutes, then reduce to Gas No. 6, 400°F, 200°C and continue to cook for a further 10-15 minutes until a rich golden brown.

Turkish Turnovers (Boreks)

Makes 24-30 Can be frozen raw or cooked

1 lb (450g) frozen puff pastry   1 beaten egg
1 lb **Savoury Meat Filling** (p.263)   Sesame seeds or poppy seeds

Roll out the pastry to the thickness of a knife blade and cut into circles about 4 inches (10cm) in diameter. Put a spoonful of filling on each round, fold over into a half moon and seal the edges firmly together. Arrange well apart on wetted baking trays. If possible refrigerate for an hour before baking.

Pre-heat the oven to Gas No. 8, 450°F, 230°C. Brush the turnovers generously with the beaten egg and scatter with the sesame seeds or poppy seeds. Bake for 15 minutes until a rich brown.

Serve hot as a main course or part of a buffet meal.

Pickled Meats

A nice piece of home-pickled brisket or tongue is supremely tasty either as a 'cold cut' or in a delectable rye bread sandwich. Many butchers will sell you a piece of their own pickled raw meat, and of course you can always buy cooked pickled meat at the delicatessen. But if you want to enjoy the genuine article with all the nuances of flavour found only in a home pickle, it's really worth preparing the pickling solution yourself. However, because the meat must be first pickled, then cooked and finally pressed, it's not worth using a joint smaller than that specified in the recipe (the yield of meat is approx half the raw weight). If there is no room in the refrigerator, the meat can be left to pickle in a cool shed or larder – the warmer the temperature the more quickly will the pickle work. The ideal temperature is about 40°F (4°C), as in a cool cellar or the least cold part of the refrigerator. Leave the meat in pickle for 14 days, 10 days in warmer weather.

Pickled Pastrami (Spiced Beef)

Serves 8-10 'as cold cut', more in sandwiches F 3 months

5-6 lb (2½-3kg) brisket, not rolled	6 oz (175g) coarse salt
1 fat clove garlic	2 level teasp saltpetre
2 teasp mixed pickling spices	3 oz (75g/⅓ cup) demerara sugar
1 level teasp crushed peppercorns	1 large onion and 2 bayleaves
2 crumbled bayleaves	

I find it convenient to pickle and cook the meat in the same dish – a cast-iron enamelled casserole, such as one would use to braise a fowl. Otherwise an earthenware dish can be used for the pickling. Put the garlic, pickling spices, bayleaves and pepper into a mortar and crush coarsely (or crush with end of a rolling pin if you do not have a mortar). Put into the chosen dish together with the sugar, salt and saltpetre. Add the meat and turn to coat with the mixture, rubbing it well into all the surfaces of the meat. Finally add cold water to come just to the top of the meat (liquid will also ooze out of it as the days go by). Refrigerate for 7-10 days or leave in the cold out-house, turning the meat daily.

To cook: Take from the liquid and wash well. Pour out the liquid from the dish and put back the meat. Cover with cold water and bring slowly to the boil on top of the stove. Remove all the scum with a spoon dipped in cold water. Now add the large onion and 2 bayleaves. Cover and simmer very gently for 4 hours. You can do this top of stove (though I find it easier to keep it at the right temperature in a very slow oven), as one would cook soup.

Lift the meat out onto a board. Part of it can now be carved rather thickly and served hot. After dinner, fit the rest into a basin, cover with a plate and several weights. Leave under pressure until quite cold. Foil wrap and refrigerate. Use as required.

VARIATION
Pickled Tongue

Serves at least 8-10 **F** 3 months

Proceed exactly as for the pickled pastrami but using 1×6 lb (3kg) or 2×3 lb (1.5kg) tongues. Cook the pickled tongue for $3^{1}/_{2}$ hours, either on the hob or in the oven, until it feels tender when pierced with a fork. Add extra boiling water if necessary to keep the tongue covered. Let the tongue cool in the stock, then remove the root and the skin. Coil the tongue round itself in a tin or casserole into which it will barely fit. Weigh down with a plate and then a weight or brick. Leave until quite cold. Unmould and refrigerate until required.

Poultry

The modern chicken can really be considered a convenience food since dressed and pre-packed birds require so little preparation before they are cooked. As they are also consistent in quality, they are certain to be tender if cooked correctly. However, with uniformity has come all too often a loss in flavour, and it is well to shop around to find a source of birds that are tasty as well as tender. In any event it is advisable to use fresh rather than frozen birds, as the flavour and quality are infinitely superior. There is in fact a significant move towards the large-scale production of fresh, chilled birds, which are now capturing a greater share of the market each year.

Choice of Bird

Fowls should be about 12 months old, when they are mature enough to make excellent stock and soup, yet still young enough to be tender and flavoursome in a casserole. A top-quality bird should have a full round breast and white skin, and if it is to be braised rather than boiled, it should be free of excessive subcutaneous fat. However, the slow cooking in liquid that is necessary to make a good pot of soup will tenderize even an over-fat grandmother hen, and render her flesh supreme for use in pies and rice or pasta dishes. Fowls should weigh between 4½-6 lb (2-3kg) ready dressed. Do not despise the fat which can be rendered down for use in pâtés and hors d'oeuvres (see p.136 for instructions).

Roasting chickens should have pliable breastbones (an indication of youth) and have a dressed weight of between 3½-4½ lb (1.5-2kg).

Frying chickens should have full compact bodies and breasts and a dressed weight of between 1½-3½ lb (0.75-1.5kg).

Grilling chickens should have a dressed weight of not more than 2½ lb (1.25kg) and they are usually split by the butcher to make two portions.

Chicken breasts can now be purchased separately (together with legs, wings and thighs), and are particularly convenient for picnics. They can also be boned, flattened and treated as schnitzel.

To Roast a Chicken, Stuffed or Unstuffed, to be Served Hot or Cold

The skin of the bird: This must be very well dried, then painted over with oil, or a mixture of oil and margarine. Seasoning with sea salt (the coarse kind) makes the flesh crisp as well as adding to flavour.

The inside of the bird: To prevent the flesh drying up before the bird is brown, it's important either to stuff the cavity or to put in a little seasoned fat.

If unstuffed, put an ounce (25g/2 tbsp) margarine on a plate and mash it with a sprig of parsley, a squeeze of lemon juice and a little salt and pepper. Put this mixture into the cavity of the bird.

One 3½ lb-4½ lb/1.5-2kg bird serves 4-6 **F** 3 months

The stuffing:

6 oz (175g/2 cups) fresh breadcrumbs	1 level teasp salt
2 oz (50g/¼ cup) margarine	Speck each of paprika and black pepper
1 small onion, finely chopped	1 beaten egg
1 level tbsp chopped parsley	

Make the crumbs either by pulling at a stale loaf with a fork, or putting chunks of bread in the blender or food processor. (I do a whole loaf at a time and keep the crumbs in the freezer.) Melt the margarine and fry the onion gently until soft and pale golden. Put the crumbs in a bowl and add the herbs and seasonings. Pour on the onions, together with the fat from the pan, and stir with a fork to moisten evenly. Add the beaten egg and mix lightly until the mixture is evenly dampened. Use to stuff the body of the bird.

To roast the bird, stuffed or unstuffed: To ensure even circulation of oven heat, it's a good idea to lay the bird on some kind of wire rack in the roasting tin, so that the heat goes all the way round. I keep a wire rack especially for the purpose – it does equally well for roasts such as shoulder of lamb or rolled rib. A small cake rack is ideal.

One 3½-4 lb/1.5-2kg chicken (net weight), stuffed or unstuffed as above

1 oz (25g/2 tbsp) margarine

1 tbsp oil (preferably olive)

½ small onion, sliced

Coarse salt

Mix the margarine and oil, spread evenly over the bird, standing breast up on a wire rack in a roasting tin just large enough to hold it. Sprinkle with sea salt or other cooking salt.

Arrange the sliced onion in the bottom of the baking tin. Put in a pre-heated oven (Gas No. 5, 375°F, 190°C) for 1½ hours (1¼ hours for a smaller bird), then baste well, and turn up the oven to Gas No. 6, 400°F, 200°C for a further 10-15 minutes, until the skin is crisp and brown. The bird can now be kept hot either in a warming oven, or by turning the oven down to Gas No. 2, 300°F, 150°C.

To make the gravy: Lift the bird on to a heatproof plate, then put the roasting tin on the cooker and add ½ pint (275ml/1¼ cups) chicken stock and 1 tbsp dry sherry (optional).

Stir well and bubble until well reduced and syrupy. If you prefer a thicker gravy, mix a teaspoon of cornflour (cornstarch) with the stock before adding to the pan. Remove the onion before serving.

Chicken en Casserole

All the recipes in this section are variations on the theme of well-browned joints cooked in an aromatic sauce. For 6-8 servings, use either two small birds (approx 3¼ lb/1.5kg each) cut into four or a large bird (4½-5½ lb/2-3kg) – a capon is excellent – cut into eight. Or buy a mixture of thigh, leg and breast portions.

All chicken casseroles taste infinitely better when allowed to mature overnight and then briefly reheated to avoid overcooking. This makes them especially convenient as a party dish. They also freeze well, for up to 3 months.

To thaw: Defrost overnight in the refrigerator, then reheat briefly (10-15 minutes on top of the stove, 30 minutes in a moderate oven) until bubbly throughout.

Note: For a party, it is most convenient to cook the joints in one layer in a roasting tin covered with foil. If necessary this can then go straight into the fridge or freezer.

Southland Barbecued Chicken

A tangy tomato sauce turns chicken into a party dish. The sauce is sufficient to cook 1 large bird cut into 8 joints or two small (3¼ lb/1.5kg) birds, each cut into four.

Serves 6-8 **F** 3 months

6-8 chicken joints
2 oz (50g/¼ cup) margarine and 2 tbsp oil
1 onion, finely chopped
2 level teasp salt
¼ teasp freshly ground black pepper
2-3 level tbsp fine brown sugar (Barbados is nice)

2 teasp prepared mustard
2-3 teasp Worcestershire sauce
Juice of ½ large lemon (about 2 tbsp)
5 oz (150g) can tomato purée, diluted with 2 cans water and a chicken stock cube

Dry the chicken joints well, then fry in the margarine and oil until golden all over. Remove to a casserole.

The sauce: Sauté the onion in the remaining fat until soft and golden, then add all the remaining ingredients. Simmer for 5 minutes, then pour over the chicken. Cover and bake in a moderate oven (Gas No 4, 350°F, 180°C) for 1 hour.

This dish is better if refrigerated overnight then heated through until bubbly in a moderate oven.

Chicken Hadassah

Cubes of aubergine (eggplant) are added towards the end of the cooking time. They add a delicious flavour to the sauce and also provide an interesting garnish.

Serves 8 **F** 3 months

Two 3^1/$_2$ lb (1.5kg) chickens (net weight), cut into a total of 12 joints

Flour

1^1/$_2$ lb (675g) aubergines (eggplants) (2-3) and oil to fry them

2 oz (50g/^{1}/$_4$ cup) margarine

The sauce:

1 large onion, finely chopped

4 skinned, ripe tomatoes

^{1}/$_2$ pint (275ml/1^1/$_4$ cups) chicken stock and ^{1}/$_4$ pint (150ml/^{2}/$_3$ cup) dry white wine, *or* ^{3}/$_4$ pint (425ml/2 cups) chicken stock

2 level teasp each of sugar and salt

^{1}/$_2$ level teasp oregano

1 crushed clove of garlic

1 tbsp chopped parsley

Start by peeling the aubergines (eggplants), then cutting into ^{1}/$_2$ inch (1.25cm) cubes. Put into a bowl of cold water to cover, with 1 tbsp of salt, and leave for half an hour until the water looks brown, then pour off the water, rinse the aubergines, squeeze to remove moisture, then dry well in a towel. Heat enough oil to come to a depth of ^{1}/$_4$ inch (0.5cm) in a large frying pan. Fry the aubergines in two lots, until golden brown. Drain on crumpled tissue paper. If oil is absorbed, then add a little more. Roll each chicken joint in well seasoned flour, add 2 oz (50g/^{1}/$_4$ cup) margarine to the oil in the pan, then brown the chicken joints on all sides. Remove to a baking tin. To the same fat, add the chopped onion and cook gently until golden brown. If there is excess fat left in the pan, carefully pour it off. To the onions add the skinned tomatoes, the stock and wine (if used), the garlic and all the seasonings. Bubble for 5 minutes until the tomatoes have softened, then pour over the chicken joints. Cover and cook slowly (Gas No 2, 300°F, 150°C) for 45 minutes. Add the aubergines, then refrigerate or freeze. Thirty minutes before serving, put in a moderate oven (Gas No 4, 350°F, 180°C) and heat through.

If the dish is reheated from frozen, allow 60 minutes.

271

Chicken Provençal

Serves 8 **F** 3 months

2 chickens (3-4 lb/1.25-1.5kg) each
  cut in four joints
1 large onion, chopped
Seasoned flour
2 medium green peppers,
  de-seeded and sliced
½ lb (225g/4 cups) button
  mushrooms, trimmed and left
  whole
2 tbsp oil
1 lb (450g) skinned tomatoes,
  chopped, *or* 6 large canned
  tomatoes
4 oz (125g) black olives in pieces

2 tbsp tomato purée
½ pint (275ml/1¼ cups) dry white
  wine
¼ pint (150ml/⅔ cup) chicken
  stock
1 fat clove of garlic, crushed
1 level teasp salt
Black pepper
2 level teasp sugar
½ teasp dried basil or 1 tbsp
  chopped fresh basil and sprig of
  fresh thyme
Chopped parsley for garnish

Drop each portion of chicken into a bag of seasoned flour, coating thinly. Fry until golden in the oil and remove. In the same fat put the onion and cook until golden, then add all remaining ingredients except the parsley. Bring to the boil.

  Arrange the chicken in a casserole and pour over the sauce. Cover and cook gently for 1½ hours at Gas No 3, 325°F, 160°C. Uncover and, if necessary, leave the lid off for a few minutes to thicken the sauce. Dish the joints and surround with the sauce. Sprinkle with chopped parsley.

Fried Chicken

Chicken can be fried on or off the bone. Use ready-cut joints, or for each four servings, use a 3-3¼ lb (1.25-2kg) bird cut into four. Or use breast portions or leg portions only, as preferred.

Wiener Backhendl

4-6 portions from each bird.

This method of frying chicken in the Viennese style can be used for chicken portions and turkey breasts. Leave yourself enough time to marinate the chicken in the lemon juice – it greatly improves the flavour. This is an excellent way to cook chicken to be served cold.

For 4-6 joints of chicken:

Juice of ½ lemon
1 level teasp salt
10 grinds black pepper
1 tbsp flour

1 large egg beaten with 1 tbsp
  water
Fine dry breadcrumbs

Put the lemon juice in a shallow dish and add salt and pepper. Turn unskinned chicken pieces in the mixture and then leave covered for half an hour, turning once. Beat the egg with water and put in a bowl. Put the flour and crumbs on two separate sheets of greaseproof paper. Take each piece of chicken in turn and shake off the excess liquid. Dip first into the flour and pat off the excess. Then brush or roll in the egg and finally coat with the crumbs.

Have ready a large heavy frying pan approximately 1 inch (2.5cm) deep in oil. (Or use a deep fryer.) Heat the oil to 375°F, 190°C. Alternatively, test by dropping in a one-inch (2.5cm) square of day-old bread. It should turn brown in 40 seconds. Gently put in the chicken and cook until golden brown on all sides. Lower the heat a little and continue to cook steadily until a rich brown – about 10 minutes in all. Drain well, then serve with a juicy vegetable, such as ratatouille or peperonata.

Sesame Chicken

This is the most convenient method for a large quantity, as it avoids smells in the kitchen and the need to stand over a hot pan of oil. For a very large number, the joints can be coated and frozen, then cooked as required.

Serves 8 F 3 months

2 young chickens, each 3¼ lb
  (1.5kg) net weight, each cut
  into 4
1 egg
2 teasp salt

15 grinds black pepper
1 level teasp paprika
3 tbsp oil
6 tbsp fine dry breadcrumbs
3 tbsp sesame seeds

Mix crumbs and sesame seeds with salt, paprika and about 15 grinds black pepper. Beat the egg and oil together. Dry the joints thoroughly, then dip first into the egg mixture then into the seasoned crumbs. This is most easily done by putting the crumbs into a paper bag and shaking the chicken joints in them one at a time. Arrange the joints on flat ungreased tins, and bake in a quick oven (Gas No. 6, 400°F, 200°C) for 45 minutes, or until the chicken is a rich golden brown and feels tender when gently pressed. The chicken can be kept hot by turning the oven to slow (Gas No. 2, 300°F, 150°C), then turn up for 2-3 minutes just before serving if the coating has gone at all limp. Can be served cold with salad, or hot with mushroom sauce (see below).

Mushroom Sauce to Serve with Chicken

Serves 6-8

2 tbsp oil and 1 oz (25g/2 tbsp) margarine

6 spring onions (scallions), or 3 shallots, finely chopped

1/4 lb (125g/2 cups) mushrooms, coarsely chopped

1 oz (25g/4 tbsp) flour

1/2 pint (275ml/1 1/4 cups) strong chicken stock (hot)

Pinch salt and black pepper

Pinch nutmeg or ground mace

2 teasp chopped parsley

2 tbsp medium dry sherry or dry vermouth

Heat the fats in a saucepan, add the onions or shallots and cook for a minute without browning, then add the mushrooms, stir well, and cook briskly for 2-3 minutes until softened but unbrowned. Add the flour and cook for a further 2 minutes then add the hot stock and seasonings. Allow to bubble for 5 minutes, stirring once or twice. Add the sherry or vermouth, taste and adjust seasonings.

Chicken (or Turkey) Schnitzel

Cooked in this way, chicken or turkey breasts taste as good as veal. It is excellent for a picnic or outdoor meal.

Freezing not recommended
For 4-6 schnitzel:

4-6 raw slices of turkey breast or chicken portions

Juice of 1/2 lemon

Flour for dredging

1 large egg

1 cup fine dry breadcrumbs

4 tbsp oil

4-6 lemon slices

Salt and pepper

Remove the skin. If chicken portions are used, it will be necessary to remove the bones with a small sharp knife. (This is not difficult.) In either case, lay the poultry meat on one piece of greaseproof paper and cover with another. Use a cutlet bat or rolling pin to beat until about ¼ inch (0.5cm) thick, just as if it were veal. Sprinkle on both sides with the lemon juice, salt and pepper and leave for 30 minutes.

Have ready two further pieces of greaseproof paper, one with flour, the other with the dry breadcrumbs. Beat the eggs in a small bowl. Dip each piece of breast first into the flour (pat off the excess) then into the egg and finally the breadcrumbs. Lay on a tin or tray and when all are ready, refrigerate until 10 minutes before cooking. (This is not absolutely necessary, but it does help to set the coating.)

Heat the oil gently for 3-4 minutes in a large heavy frying pan. Fry the breasts at a steady, moderate heat until both sides are crisp and brown. Allow 5 minutes for each side. If the pan will not hold all the schnitzels at once, keep the cooked breasts hot in a slow oven (Gas No. 2, 300°F, 150°C). Serve the schnitzels, garnished with the slices of lemon, with boiled potatoes and a green salad.

Poultry and Pastry

Left-over chicken, fowl or turkey can form the basis of a delicious filling for a variety of pies and pastries made with either shortcrust or puff pastry. It is important to ensure that the sauce is very well seasoned as the chicken itself tends to be bland in flavour. The amount of chicken used is not critical – use more or less as available and make up with extra vegetables.

Chicken pastries can be frozen uncooked, then thawed and baked just before serving.

Chicken Filling

F 3 months

2 cups (approx) cooked chicken (or turkey)
½ lb (225g) packet frozen peas or

mixed vegetables, cooked according to packet directions

The sauce:

$^1/_2$ medium onion, finely chopped
$^1/_2$ green pepper (or 1 canned pimento), thinly sliced
$^1/_4$ lb (125g/2 cups) mushrooms, thinly sliced
3 tbsp oil or $1^1/_2$ oz (40g/3 tbsp) margarine

3 tbsp (1oz/25g) flour
$^1/_2$ pint (225ml/$1^1/_4$ cups) strong chicken stock
$^1/_4$ teasp nutmeg
Salt and white pepper to taste
2 teasp parsley
2 tbsp medium sherry (optional)

Cut the poultry into chunky, bite-sized pieces and put into a bowl with the cooked vegetables. Melt the fat and cook the onion, pepper and mushrooms gently until softened (about 5 minutes); stir in the flour, then add the stock and seasonings. Whisk until smooth, then allow to bubble for 3 minutes. Add the parsley and sherry (if used). Pour over the chicken mixture and stir until blended. Allow to cool whilst you roll out the pastry.

Chicken (or Turkey) Slice

Serves 6-8 F 3 months (uncooked)

1 recipe chicken filling
1 × 8 oz (225g) packet puff pastry or home-made flaky pastry (see p.422), *or* 12 oz (350g) shortcrust pastry (see p.429)

Beaten egg
Sesame seeds

Divide the pastry into 2 pieces and roll each into a rectangle about 10 inches (25cm) long and 5-6 inches (12-15cm) wide – it should be very thin. Put one layer on to a baking tray, cover to within $^1/_2$ inch (1.25cm) of each edge with the poultry mixture, then dampen the edges, and top with the second half of the pastry. Press down firmly all round and flake the edges together with a fork. Paint all over with beaten egg and scatter thickly with sesame seeds. Make 6 cuts in the top layer. Bake in a hot oven (Gas No. 8, 450°F, 230°C) for 15-20 minutes until richly brown and well risen. Serve hot.

This dish can be frozen uncooked then thawed R overnight in the refrigerator before baking.

VARIATION 1
Chicken Plate Pie
Serves 6-8 **F** 3 months (uncooked)
Cut the pastry in half and roll out to fit the base of a 9-inch (23cm) pie plate, 1 inch (2.5cm) deep. Roll the second half slightly larger to fit the top. Spoon the chicken filling into the crust and cover with the pastry lid, pressing the edges firmly together. A little beaten egg (or yolk) brushed on the top will give a beautiful glaze. Bake the pie in a hot oven (Gas No. 8, 450°F, 230°C) for 20 minutes.

VARIATION 2
Individual Chicken Pies
Serves 6-8 (makes 9-10 pies) **F** 3 months (uncooked)
Roll the pastry out as thin as a penny and cut into 18-20 rounds each about 2½ inches (6.25cm) in diameter to fit fairly deep individual patty tins. Line 9-10 patty tins with half the rounds, then spoon the filling into them. Cover with the remaining rounds, sealing the edges well. Brush the tops with egg and scatter with sesame seeds. Bake at Gas No. 8 (450°F, 230°C) for 15-20 minutes until brown.

VARIATION 3
Chicken Turnovers
Serves 6-8 (makes 12-16) **F** 3 months (uncooked)
Roll the pastry out as thin as a penny but cut into 12-16 rounds each 3½ inches (9cm) in diameter. Divide the filling between the rounds of pastry, then turn over into half moons and seal tightly. Arrange on slightly wet ungreased baking trays, about 2 inches (5cm) apart to allow for even browning. Brush with egg and scatter with sesame seeds. Bake at (Gas No. 8 (450°F, 230°C) for 15-20 minutes or until richly brown.

Chicken (or Turkey) in Salad

Excellent salads can be made using left-over or freshly-cooked chicken, fowl, or the breast only from turkey.

To Roast a Chicken for Salad

Serves 6-8
Use a roaster weighing between 3½-4 lb (1.5-2kg) net weight. In

the body cavity put half an orange or a lemon, then spread the whole of the carcase with a thin coating of olive oil, and sprinkle with salt and pepper. Wrap *loosely* with foil, then put in a very hot oven (Gas No. 8, 450°F, 230°C) for 1 hour. Open the foil parcel and allow the bird to brown for a further 15 minutes.

Alternatively a fowl of the same size can be used. In that case, barely cover with water, add 1 whole medium (5oz/150g) onion, 2 sliced carrots, leaves and top 2 inches (5cm) from a head of celery, sprig of parsley, 2 level teasp salt, ¼ teasp white pepper.

Bring to the boil, then reduce the heat and simmer, covered, for 2½-3 hours or until the leg feels very tender when prodded with a fork. Lift the bird from the stock and allow to cool. The stock makes the basis of an excellent soup (see p.162).

Note: If preferred, a chicken can also be simmered in this way, but in that case, only half-cover it with liquid and cook for 1½ hours or until tender.

Chicken (or Turkey) and Grape Salad

Chicken marries particularly well with fruit. If Galia melon is not available use any Charentais or Cantaloup type melon that is fully ripe.

Serves 6-8

One 3½-4 lb (1.5-2kg) cooked chicken or fowl; *or* 1 lb (450g) turkey breast cut in bite-sized pieces
3 fat heads of chicory
½ lb (225g) seedless green grapes

1 small Galia melon (or half a large one) cut into balls or ¾ inch (2cm) cubes
8 of the inner stalks of a celery, cut across into ⅜ inch (1cm) slices
Chinese leaves or shredded lettuce

The dressing:

1 cup of mild mayonnaise (preferably home-made)
Juice of ½ lemon

1 level teasp curry powder
Pinch of salt and white pepper

Cut the chicory across into ½ inch (1.25cm) rings, then cut each ring in half. Mix with the chicken, the grapes and the celery. Stir the lemon juice, curry powder and seasonings into the mayonnaise

278

and stir through the chicken mixture. Half an hour before serving, halve the melon, remove the seeds then scoop out the flesh into balls, or cut into cubes. Stir into the first mixture (don't do this too soon or it will make the salad watery). Chill for half an hour, then serve on a bed of shredded Chinese leaves or lettuce.

Chicken or Turkey Second Time Round

Poultry with Rice or Pasta

Left-over poultry combines well with savoury rice, with vegetables or fruit added for extra flavour. These recipes are excellent for serving at an informal supper or teenage party.

Savoury Rice with Chicken or Turkey

Serves 10-12 Do not freeze

3 tbsp oil
2 oz (50g/^{1}/$_4$ cup) margarine
2 large onions, finely chopped
8 tbsp chopped frozen peppers, *or*
  2 medium peppers cut in ^{1}/$_2$ inch
  (1.25cm) cubes
2 cups long grain rice
4 cups hot chicken stock
4 heaped tbsp currants
Pinch each cinnamon, salt and
  cayenne pepper

Flesh from 1 cooked 3^1/$_2$-4lb
  (1.5-2kg) bird, *or* 1 lb (450g)
  cooked turkey breasts cut in
  bite-size chunks
2 oz (50g/^{1}/$_2$ cup) chopped
  almonds or cashew nuts, fried
  until golden in 1 tbsp of oil
2 tbsp soy sauce

Heat the oil and margarine in a heavy pan or casserole and fry onions with peppers until soft and golden. Add the rice and cook over moderate heat until each grain is coated with fat – about 2-3 minutes. Add the hot stock, currants, cinnamon, salt and cayenne. Bring to the boil, reduce the heat and simmer gently, covered, for 15 minutes. Uncover and add the chicken, re-cover and leave on lowest heat for a further 15 minutes. Stir in soy sauce and top with fried nuts.

Note: For 4-6 servings use ^{1}/$_2$ lb (225g) poultry meat and halve all the other ingredients.

Sweet and Sour Chicken (or Turkey) to Serve with Rice

Serves 10-12 Do not freeze

Flesh from 1 cooked 3½-4 lb (1.5-2kg) chicken or fowl; or 1 lb (450g) cooked turkey breast, cut in bite-size chunks

1 × 15 oz (425g) can pineapple titbits or chunks

2 medium onions, chopped

2 medium peppers, halved, de-seeded then cut in ½ inch (1.25cm) squares

2 tbsp oil

The sauce:

Syrup from pineapple made up to 1 pint (575ml/2½ cups) with water

5 fl oz (150ml/⅔ cup) vinegar

1 level tbsp dry mustard

4 oz (125g/½ cup) brown sugar

2 oz (50g/½ cup) cornflour (cornstarch)

2 teasp Worcestershire sauce

4 tbsp soy sauce

Salt and pepper to taste

Heat the oil and cook the onions gently for 5 minutes until softened, then add the peppers and cook for another 2 or 3 minutes until the peppers are softened but not browned.

Put the cornflour (cornstarch) in a bowl and stir in all the remaining ingredients, then add to the onion and pepper mixture. Bring to the boil and bubble for 3 minutes, then stir in the turkey and pineapple (cut each chunk into three). Cover and leave to heat through very gently for 10 minutes, or put in a covered casserole in a moderate oven (Gas No. 4, 340°F, 180°C) for 25 minutes. Serve on bed of rice.

Note: For 4-6 servings, use ½ lb (225g) left-over poultry meat and halve all the other ingredients.

Chinese Chicken Filling

Serves 6-8 F 3 months

Even a little left-over chicken can make an excellent meal if it's treated in the Chinese way. To do this it needs to be stir-fried with crunchy ingredients like peppers, almonds and bean sprouts, and seasoned with soy sauce. When it's steaming hot this mixture can be served plain with rice or boiled noodles, but it's equally delicious as the filling for a French omelette, or – my favourite – for those crispy fried pancakes the Chinese call 'spring rolls'.

For any Chinese dish the vegetables are only lightly cooked, usually for no longer than 2-3 minutes, so that they have plenty of bite left in them

2 tbsp peanuts or almonds, coarsely chopped

2 tbsp oil

1 medium onion, peeled, halved, then sliced paper-thin

1 large green pepper, halved, de-seeded, pith removed, and thinly sliced

1 small (8oz/225g) can pineapple titbits or pieces

8-10 oz (225-275g) cooked chicken or turkey breast, cut in bite-sized chunks

2 tbsp sultanas (white raisins) or raisins

1 level tbsp cornflour (cornstarch)

2 tbsp vinegar

1/4 pint (150ml/2/3 cup) syrup from pineapple

1 level tbsp soft brown sugar

2 tbsp soy sauce

Heat the oil and cook the nuts until golden. Lift out with a slotted spoon and drain on absorbent paper. In the same oil cook the onion until softened but not brown (about 5 minutes), then add the pepper and cook a further 3 minutes, stirring. Add the pineapple, chicken, sultanas (white raisins) and allow to heat gently. In a small bowl put the cornflour (cornstarch), then stir in the sugar, vinegar, pineapple syrup and soy sauce. Add to the contents of the pan, and simmer 3 minutes. Stir in the nuts. Allow to go cold.

The filling can now be used at once, or refrigerated or frozen.

Crispy Chicken Pancakes or Spring Rolls

Serves 6-8 as an entrée, 4 as a main dish **F** 3 months

These pancakes are made in a special way. First they're fried on only one side and then, when they're stuffed, the unbrowned side is fried until crisp in shallow or deep fat.

Pancakes freeze extremely well. Lay them on top of each other with a piece of film or foil in between to stop them sticking together. Defrost overnight in the refrigerator, then fill and fry them as though they were newly made.

Chinese Chicken Filling (see above)

4 oz (125g/1 cup) plain flour

2 eggs

2 teasp oil

8 fl oz (225ml/1 cup) water

2 level teasp salt

If you have a blender or food processor, the batter ingredients should be added in this order: eggs, liquid, oil, flour, salt. Process for 30 seconds or until smooth. If you make the batter, put flour and salt into a bowl. Make a well in the centre and drop in the eggs and oil. Start drawing in the flour and as the mixture gets too thick to stir, start adding the liquid until half has been stirred in. Now beat with a batter-whisk until the surface is covered with tiny bubbles. Finally stir in the remaining liquid. Pour the batter into a jug and leave to stand for one hour or longer as convenient.

Stir the batter well – it should be the consistency of single (light) cream. If too thick, add a tbsp of cold water. Have ready a board covered with a sheet of greaseproof paper, and a wad of kitchen paper for greasing the pan.

Put a 6 or 7 inch (15 or 17cm) frying pan over moderate heat for 3 minutes, then add 1 teasp of oil. Immediately smear it evenly over the bottom and sides of the pan, using the wad of paper. Hold your hand one inch above the pan. If you can feel the heat it is ready to fry the pancakes. If not, continue to heat for a minute or two longer. Now put about half a cup of batter into the pan, swirling it round the sides as well as on the bottom. A thin layer will set next to the pan. Immediately pour the remainder of the batter back into the jug. In this way you will be left with a paper-thin pancake. As soon as the pancake starts to curl away from the sides of the pan and the top looks dry (though pale), turn the pancake out on to the greaseproof paper. As soon as it has cooled a little, turn it over so that the browned side is next to the paper. Now very lightly re-grease the pan, pour in some batter and repeat the process until all the pancakes have been fried. As soon as each pancake stops steaming, lay it on top of the previous one. The pancakes are now ready to stuff.

Lay each pancake in turn, brown side uppermost, on the board. Put a spoonful of the chicken filling onto it. Turn in the sides to seal the mixture and roll over into a roll. Repeat until all twelve pancakes are stuffed. They can now be refrigerated until required (maximum 12 hours), or frozen.

To shallow fry the pancakes, 10 minutes before dinner put oil to a depth of ¼ inch (0.5cm) into the frying pan, heat for 3-4 minutes, then lay the pancakes in the oil (if it is hot enough it will sizzle as they go in). Fry, join side up, until a rich brown underneath, then turn and continue to cook until the second side is browned.

To deep fry them, put as many pancakes as will fit into a frying basket and lower into a pan one third full of oil heated until it will brown a cube of bread in 40 seconds (375°F), the same temperature as for frying chips. Fry steadily until a rich brown. Drain on kitchen paper and fry the rest of the pancakes. Serve at once.

Spaghetti with Chicken Liver Sauce

This makes a superb dish to serve for a light luncheon or as an entrée before a roast.

Serves 6-8 F 3 months

12 oz-1 lb (350-450g) fresh or
  frozen chicken livers, sliced
2 onions, finely chopped
1 clove of garlic, crushed
4 tbsp oil and 2 oz (50g/¼ cup)
  margarine
1 tbsp chopped parsley
Pinch each cayenne and black
  pepper

Italian seasoning
2 green peppers, finely chopped
½ cup stock
1 medium can Italian tomatoes
  (15oz/425g)
4 tbsp dry red wine
1 level tbsp cornflour (cornstarch)
2 tbsp water (optional)

Sauté the onion and garlic in the fat for 10 minutes, until the onion is gold (keep lid on pan). Remove lid, add the chicken livers and sauté briskly for a further 5 minutes until the livers are a rich brown. (If preferred, livers may be grilled, then added to the pan, and browning omitted.) Add all the remaining ingredients except for the cornflour and water, bring to the boil then reduce the heat, cover and simmer for 30 minutes, stirring occasionally. If the sauce is too watery, it can either be thickened by bubbling with the lid off until of coating consistency, or thickened with the cornflour (cornstarch) and water mixed to a cream, added to the sauce and bubbled for 3 minutes.

Serve on freshly boiled spaghetti. Allow 3-4 ozs (75-125g) spaghetti per serving.

Roast Stuffed Turkey

Turkey undoubtedly owes much of its present popularity to the fact that it is extremely easy to cook and is almost impossible to cook badly! However, it can be improved with a really good stuffing and gravy, so I have concentrated on giving detailed instructions for their preparation. Plan to make stock from the turkey giblets the day before. This makes it easy to remove any fat from the surface of the liquid and also means that the gravy can be made long before the bird is dished. Any delicious sediment clinging to the roasting pan after the bird has been removed, can be loosened with a little boiling water and added to the gravy at the last minute.

A little olive oil brushed on the turkey when the foil is turned back will make the skin especially brown and crisp.

What size to buy: Allow 3/4-1 lb (350-450g) per serving – the higher figure referring to the smaller bird (to allow for the higher ratio of bone to flesh). Thus an 8 lb (3.75kg) bird will provide 8 or 9 servings, a 12 lb (5.5kg) bird about 16 servings. From a 12 lb (5.5kg) bird, a family of 4 adults and 4 children could well get one hot meal, one cold meal plus another dish such as turkey pie.

Do make sure the chosen bird will fit in your oven. Too large a bird in too small an oven produces uneven browning. There should be 1 inch (2.5cm) clearance of the oven sides when the roasting tin is put in position.

To thaw a frozen bird: If the bird is frozen it is important to allow sufficient time for it to thaw before cooking. A large bird of 15 lb (6.75kg) or over may take up to 48 hours in a cool larder, garage or outhouse; a smaller bird up to 12 lb (5.5kg) will take 20 to 30 hours. If the bird has thawed completely before it is time to cook it, refrigerate it and treat it as a fresh bird.

To stuff: Stuffing the neck end gives the breast a good shape. Stuffing the body cavity helps to keep the flesh of the bird moist. However, if you do not wish to stuff the body cavity, put an onion, a bunch of parsley and a good knob of margarine inside it instead, or add 2 apples, and season well with salt and pepper, then sew or skewer closed.

For the body cavity allow approximately 1/2 lb (225g) stuffing per 5 lb (2.25kg) oven-ready weight. When the bird has been stuffed, sew or skewer the crop securely to the breast using toothpicks and then skewer or sew up the vent.

Lemon and Herb Stuffing (for the Neck)

$^1/_2$ lb (225g/$2^2/_3$ cups) fresh
  breadcrumbs
2 level teasp salt
$^1/_4$ level teasp white pepper
1 level teasp dried mixed poultry
  seasoning or Italian herb
  mixture

Grated rind of $^1/_2$ lemon
2 level tbsp finely chopped
  parsley
4 oz (125g/$^1/_2$ cup) margarine
1 large onion, finely chopped
2 eggs

Put the breadcrumbs in a bowl and blend with the herbs and seasonings. Melt the fat in a large frying pan, add the onion and simmer until tender – about 5 minutes.

Pour onion and fat over the seasoned breadcrumbs and stir well, then add the beaten eggs to make a moist but not soggy mixture (don't use all the egg if it is not necessary).

Chestnut Stuffing (for the Neck or Body)

2 lb (1kg) fresh chestnuts ($1^1/_2$
  lb/675g shelled weight) or
  equivalent canned or dried
  (*Note*: 12 oz/350g chestnuts
  soaked overnight in water to
  cover is equivalent to 2 lb/1kg
  fresh chestnuts in the shell)
Chicken stock to cover
4 oz (125g/$^1/_2$ cup) melted

margarine
1 medium (5 oz/150g) onion, finely
  chopped
6 oz (175g/2 cups) fresh
  breadcrumbs
2 level tbsp parsley
2 level teasp salt
$^1/_4$ teasp white pepper
2 large eggs

To prepare the chestnuts: With a small, very sharp knife, cut through the skin of the chestnut right round. Drop into boiling water. As soon as the cut widens to show the flesh, take out one at a time and remove the inner and outer skin (this is very easy indeed if chestnuts are fresh). Put in a pan and just cover with chicken stock. Bring to the boil and simmer gently until tender when tasted (about 30 minutes). Drain well (can be frozen at this stage).

To make the stuffing: Melt the fat without colouring it, and add the finely chopped onion. Simmer until the onion is tender and golden but not brown. Meanwhile chop the cooked chestnuts coarsely so that they still have some texture rather than being a mush. Add to the breadcrumbs in a bowl together with the parsley and seasonings. Pour on the fat and onion and mix well. Finally beat the eggs and add them, mixing with a fork until all the stuffing ingredients are evenly dampened.

To Cook the Bird

For an oven-ready packaged bird, follow the instructions given on the pack. I have found these to be very reliable for each particular brand. Otherwise use the following method which is very easy and results in a succulent, mahogany-brown bird.

Truss the bird by tying the legs together with string, then tie the wings close to the breast.

Place the trussed bird on a rack in a roasting tin, liberally paint with oil (paying particular attention to the legs which tend to dry out) then sprinkle all over with sea salt. For convenience this can be done the night before and the prepared bird refrigerated overnight.

Cover the bird completely with a double layer of butter muslin. If none is available, use two light-coloured disposable dishcloths. Paint this covering all over with more oil.

Put the bird in the over and cook at Gas No. 3, 325°F, 160°C for the entire cooking time.

To calculate the cooking time:
For a bird weighing up to 12 lbs (5.5kg), allow 25 minutes per lb (450g).
For a larger bird, allow 20 minutes per lb (450g).
For an unstuffed bird, reduce the cooking time by 20 minutes.

Note: Calculate the cooking time on the net weight of the bird before it is stuffed.

Baste the bird every hour *through* the covering, which should be kept on the bird until it is taken from the oven. Calculate the cooking time so that the bird will be ready 15 minutes before it is to be carved. If the skin is not pierced it will keep hot, loosely covered with foil.

To test for doneness: Pierce the thick part of the leg with a skewer or fork. The juice should run clear. *Or* insert a meat thermometer in the same place. It should register 185°F, 80°C.

Turkey Gravy

Pour off the fat from the baking tin and reserve for other use. Add 1 pint (575ml/2½ cups) stock (see p.162) to the tin, and stir round with a wooden spoon to release any sediment clinging to the base. A small glass of medium sherry or madeira can be poured into the tin. Mix 2 level teasp cornflour (cornstarch) with a little water and add to the mixture. Bring to the boil and simmer until thickened and clear (about 3 minutes). Taste, season and serve.

To Carve a Turkey

1. Cut off the legs and wings.
2. Separate the drumsticks from the legs, using poultry shears or the point of a knife.
3. Carve slices of meat from the legs, beginning at the bony end.
4. Carve slices of meat from the breast, starting at the neck end.

Note: Wrap left-over turkey in foil and refrigerate.

Cranberry Sauce

Serves 8 as a relish

½ lb (225g) frozen cranberries   6 fl oz (175ml/¾ cup) water
7 oz (200g/1 cup) sugar

Put the sugar and the water in a small pan, heat until the sugar has dissolved, then simmer uncovered for 5 minutes until a thick syrup has formed. Add the cranberries, cover and cook until they stop popping out of their skins. This will only take about 5 minutes. Skim off the froth with a hot, wet spoon. Put sauce in a small container and chill before use. Cranberry sauce keeps like jam.

See p.307 for **Roast Potatoes.**

To Barbecue Chicken Halves or Joints

The Bird: Splitting in two a grilling chicken weighing not more than 2½ lb (1kg) will produce a more succulent result than quarters from a larger bird, as there is less surface exposed to the fire and less chance of the flesh becoming too dry. Each half can be cut in two after cooking if desired.

The Marinade: To keep it moist, the bird can either be marinated beforehand in a mixture of oil and lemon juice or white wine, or brushed with the marinade as it cooks. Marinated birds do tend to have a richer flavour.

The Fire: This must be similar to the fire used for grilling kebabs – that is, the grill must be thoroughly hot but the fire itself less intense than for steaks. Allow the barbecue at least half an hour to heat up, and another 30-40 minutes for each chicken half to cook.

The Marinade

Enough for $1 \times 2^{1}/_{2}$ lb (1kg) bird, split in two (serves 2-4 according to appetite)

Black pepper	Olive oil
Coarse salt	Juice of 1 lemon (3 tbsp)
2 teasp fresh thyme or marjoram, chopped	

Two hours beforehand, put each halved bird into a dish, and paint all over with the lemon juice, sprinkle with black pepper and herbs, then paint all over with the olive oil. Leave in a cool place, turning once, and re-brushing with any of the marinade that has collected in the dish. When ready to cook, put the chicken on the grill and paint on one side with olive oil. Cook on one side for 10 minutes, then turn and brush with more oil and cook a further 10 minutes. Turn again, paint with oil and sprinkle with coarse salt. After 5 minutes, turn and repeat on the second side. Test to see if it is cooked by piercing the breast with a thin skewer or poultry needle – it should slide in without any resistance, and a bead of colourless liquid should seep out. If not, cook for a further 5-10 minutes.

Note: Never pierce the bird with a fork as it is turned or some of the juices will escape.

VARIATION
Omit the marinading. For each bird, mix 3 tbsp each of lemon juice (or white wine) and olive oil, with 2 teasp chopped fresh thyme and

288

marjoram, or 1 teasp dried herbes de Provence. Brush the bird with this mixture before it is cooked and at each turn.

Circassian Chicken (Cerkes Tavugu)

Strips of cold poached chicken are mixed with a most unusual creamy sauce of crushed walnuts and chicken stock. It makes a perfect buffet dish or main course for a summer luncheon.

Traditionally the nuts are pounded in a mortar but this job can now be done in seconds in a blender or food processor.

Serves 8 Do not freeze

2 × 3 lb (1kg/350g) chicken	2 teasp salt
2 carrots, sliced	10 grinds black pepper
2 stalks of celery, coarsely cut	4 sprigs of parsley
1 medium onion (5 oz/150g), left whole	

Quarter the chickens and put in a large pan. Cover with water and all the other ingredients. Bring to simmering point, then skim off any scum that has collected on the surface. Cover and simmer for 1 hour or until the chickens are tender – the legs will feel soft and waggle easily – in the joint. Allow the chicken and stock to cool, then lift out the bird, skin it, remove the flesh from the bones and cut into strips about 3 inches (7.5cm) long and ½ inch (1.25cm) wide. Pass the stock through a strainer and discard the solids.

The sauce:

½ lb (225g) broken walnut pieces	1 small clove of garlic
4 thin or 2 thick slices of bread from a large loaf, plus a little stock for soaking it	Approx ¾ pint (425ml/2 cups) chicken stock

The garnish:

2 teasp oil	Chopped parsley
½ teasp paprika	Black olives

Put the de-crusted bread in a small bowl and just cover with chicken stock. Put the walnuts in a blender or food processor, add the well squeezed bread and the garlic clove and process until it becomes a smooth paste. Add the stock gradually until it becomes a thick coating sauce. Season with salt and pepper if necessary. Stir enough of the sauce into the chicken to coat all the pieces and arrange in a mound on a shallow oval platter, preferably on a bed of cold cooked long grain rice. Cover with the remaining sauce.

In a small frying pan heat the oil and paprika until very hot, then spoon it over the chicken. Sprinkle with chopped parsley and garnish with black olives.

The dish should be served at room temperature, although it can be refrigerated until an hour before it is to be served.

Vegetables and Other Main Dish Accompaniments

When it comes to choosing vegetables there can be no compromise with quality: only the best will do, or all the effort expended in their preparation will be wasted.

Fresh v. Frozen: Although in general I prefer to use fresh vegetables in season, I would not be dogmatic, as the best frozen vegetables are very often superior to so-called 'fresh' ones which have had a long journey from farm to table. In fact some frozen vegetables, such as peas, are superior in every way to all but home-grown ones.

Freezing vegetables: Unless it is possible to purchase freshly harvested vegetables direct from farm or local market, it is not good policy to freeze bought vegetables as they start to deteriorate as soon as they have been picked. Home-grown vegetables, however, are excellent when frozen (consult a specialist book on freezing for the handling of individual varieties). Almost all vegetables will freeze for up to a year. Cook them from frozen.

Storage of vegetables: However good the quality of the vegetable, its taste and appearance on the table will depend to a large extent on the care with which it has been stored after purchase. In general all vegetables (with the exception of potatoes) keep better if tightly wrapped in film or plastic bags and refrigerated.

There are certain problems involved in cooking vegetables for an entertaining meal that do not arise in family cooking, when the vegetables can be cooked at the last minute and the family then called to sit down at the table. This system is not practical for the party cook, as not only is it difficult to leave guests for the necessary length of time, there is also a legacy of pans to be washed up after the party. So while it is best from the nutritional point of view to cook vegetables briefly and just before serving, for entertaining purposes it is probably better to compromise and follow either of two methods: choose a vegetable that can be cooked *en casserole* or reheated in a sauce; or, in the case of green vegetables, follow the French (and restaurant) method of cooking very briefly in a great deal of water early in the day. This method conserves both the colour and (if followed correctly) the texture of the vegetables, and allows them to be heated up – preferably in the serving dish – either top of stove, in the oven (in selected cases), or in the microwave, and then to present them as newly cooked.

To Cook Green Vegetables for a Party

Vegetables that can be treated in this way include any frozen or fresh green variety such as Brussels sprouts, peas, green beans, broccoli, courgettes (zucchini), cauliflower, mangetout peas, spinach or mixtures.

Quantities per serving:
Fresh vegetables:

Broad beans (in shell)	8-12 oz (225-350g)
Broccoli	4 oz (125g)
French or runner (green) beans	4-6 oz (125-175g)
Brussels sprouts, cabbage	4 oz (125g)
Spring cabbage (which has a lot of waste)	8 oz (225g)
Cauliflower	1/4 medium head
Courgettes (zucchini)	4-6 oz (125-175g)
Garden peas (in shell)	8-12 oz (225-350g)
Mangetout peas	4 oz (125g)
Spinach (fresh)	8 oz (225g)

Half fill a large pan with water and bring to the boil, then add a teasp of salt and the chosen vegetable. Cook uncovered at a vigorous boil until the vegetables are still slightly chewy (bite and see). Immediately drain through a colander, then put under the cold tap until steaming stops. Drain thoroughly.

To serve

Heat a generous ounce (25g/2 tbsp of butter – or margarine if preferred) in a small pan until it turns a pale nut-brown in colour. Immediately add the cooked vegetables and toss to coat them thoroughly. *Either* cover and reheat on top of stove until steaming through (about 5 minutes) *or* turn into a heatproof casserole, cover and reheat for 20 minutes in a moderate oven (Gas No. 4, 350°F, 180°C).

VARIATION
Sautéed Brussels Sprouts: Melt the fat, but do not allow it to change colour. Instead, add the cooked sprouts immediately and toss over gentle heat until their outside leaves turn a pale gold (2-3 minutes). Season well with salt and black pepper and serve at once.

VARIATION
Sautéed Brussels Sprouts with Chestnuts
Serves 6-8

1¹/₂-2 lb (800g-1kg) Brussels
   sprouts (cooked as above)
1 lb (450g) chestnuts (or 6 oz/175g)
   dried chestnuts soaked in cold
   water overnight)

2 oz (50g/¹/₄ cup) butter or
   margarine
1 tbsp oil
³/₄ pint (425ml/2 cups) meat or
   vegetable stock
Black pepper

Skin the chestnuts if fresh according to the directions on p.285. Put them in a pan with half the butter (or margarine) and the stock. Cover and cook until soft when pierced with a slim knife (about 20-30 minutes). Drain. Reserve the stock for other use. Melt the rest of the fat in a frying pan. When hot, add the well-drained sprouts and the cooked chestnuts. Toss over gentle heat until the sprouts are nicely browned. Season with black pepper and serve.

VARIATION
Buttered Fresh Peas
For each 6-8 servings:

3-4 lb (1kg/350g-1kg/700g) peas
   (weight in pod) cooked as above
   until not quite tender
1 tbsp sugar

2 oz (50g/¹/₄ cup) butter or
   margarine
Salt and pepper
2 teasp chopped fresh mint
   (optional)

Put the peas into an 8 inch (20cm) saucepan and shake them over medium heat for a minute to make sure all the moisture has evaporated. Then add the remaining ingredients and toss to coat the peas. Cover and cook very gently for 10 minutes, until they are absolutely tender. Turn into a dish and serve.

VARIATION
Green Beans with Toasted Nuts

Serves 6-8

This can also be done with frozen beans.
Cook 1½ lb (800g) cut or whole French (green) beans as above.
Melt 1 oz (25g/2 tbsp) butter (or margarine) and add to it 1 oz (25g) slivered almonds or chopped hazelnuts. Cook until golden, then add the beans, tossing well to coat with the nuts, and season highly with coarse salt and black pepper. Particularly delicious when used to fill a rice ring (see p.312).

To Cook Fresh Broccoli, Purple or Green

Fresh broccoli has a mass of tender heads with tougher, thicker stalks. It is, therefore, better to cook it rather like fresh asparagus; that is, to boil the stems in water, whilst the heads become tender in the steam. The vegetable can then be cooled, and reheated in the same way as other vegetables, or it can be served immediately with browned butter and a good squeeze of lemon.

Trim the stalks so that they are a similar length. If the broccoli can be stood upright in the pan further preparation is necessary. Otherwise, tie the bundles with soft string.

Bring enough water to the boil to cover the stalks. Add a teaspoon of salt and then put in the broccoli. Bring back to the boil and cover. Cook until the stalks are not quite tender if to be treated in the French manner, or fully tender if to be served at once. Drain, and cool, or serve at once with browned butter and lemon juice.

VARIATION
Broccoli Alla Parmigiana

Serves 6-8

1½-2 lb (800-1kg) broccoli cooked as above

Arrange cooked broccoli (cold or freshly cooked) in a buttered shallow ovenproof dish.

The sauce:

1 oz (25g/2 tbsp) butter
1 oz (25g/4 tbsp) flour
1/2 pint (275 ml/1 1/4 cups) milk
1 teasp salt

1/4 teasp each white pepper and
  ground nutmeg
3 oz (75g/3/4 cup) grated Parmesan
  or other well-flavoured cheese

Put all sauce ingredients (except the cheese) into a heavy-based pan and whisk over moderate heat until it thickens and bubbles. Cook 3 minutes. Turn off the heat and stir in two-thirds of the cheese. Pour over the broccoli, sprinkle with the remaining cheese and put under a hot grill until brown and bubbly.

To Cook White or Young Green-hearted Cabbage

This is better cooked freshly and in the minimum amount of water.

Serves 6-8

1 medium cabbage (1 1/2-
  2 lb/800g-1kg)
2 level teasp salt

2 oz (50g/1/4 cup) butter or
  margarine
Black pepper, salt

Quarter the cabbage head, then shred finely (if possible in a food processor), first discarding any tough outer leaves and the stalk. Half fill a large bowl with cold water and add 2 teasp salt. Put in the cabbage and leave for half an hour.

Melt the fat in a heavy-based 8 inch (20cm) saucepan. Lift the cabbage from the water and without drying it, put into the saucepan, layer with a sprinkle of salt and a few grinds of pepper. Cover and simmer in the fat and juices, shaking occasionally, until the cabbage is bite tender (10-15 minutes). Uncover and stand over a low heat to remove any excess moisture. Turn into a dish. If you need to keep it hot for 10-15 minutes, cover and put in a warm oven (Gas No. 1/2, 250°F, 120°C).

To Cook Frozen Peas and Beans

This is an alternative way of cooking frozen peas and beans which does not conserve the colour so well but does impart a most delicious flavour.

Perfect Frozen Peas

Serves 6-8

1-1½ lb (450-700g) frozen peas
1 oz (25g/2 tbsp) butter or
  margarine
3 finely chopped shallots, spring
  onion (scallion) bulbs, *or* 2 tbsp

finely chopped mild onion
1 teasp each salt, black pepper
  and sugar
5-8 fl oz (150-225 ml/¾-1 cup)
  vegetable or chicken stock

Bring the fat, seasonings, onion and liquid to the boil. Add the frozen peas, cover and simmer for 5-6 minutes, until almost tender. Uncover and simmer to evaporate any remaining liquid. The peas will be bathed in a delicious glaze.

Perfect Frozen Green Beans

Serves 6-8

1-1½ lb (450-700g) frozen beans,
  sliced or whole
2 oz (50g/¼ cup) butter, *or* 3 tbsp
  oil
½ medium onion (5 oz/150g size),

finely chopped
1 level teasp salt
Plenty of black pepper
½ teasp Italian herbs or herbes de
  Provence (dried)

Soften the onion in the fat over low heat with the lid on the pan. After 5 minutes, put in the frozen beans, add the seasonings and heat until the fat bubbles again. Cover and cook over a low heat until the beans are just tender (about 10 minutes). Serve piping hot.

Vegetable Specialities

Vegetables that blend a variety of tastes and textures can be served as a separate course or as an accompaniment to a simply-cooked main course. Beware of cooking both the main dish and the vegetables with too much elaboration or the more subtle nuances of flavour and texture may be lost.

The Aubergine (Eggplant)

Buying and keeping: Bought fresh they'll keep in the refrigerator for at least a week.

296

To salt or not before frying: You *can* fry aubergines without salting them first, but they will need *double* the quantity of oil.

On freezing: Do not freeze raw aubergine, it goes watery and bitter. However, fried, stuffed or stewed aubergine will freeze well.

Aubergine (Eggplant) Meunière

The aubergines (eggplants) need to be freshly cooked or the coating may go soggy. They can be kept hot in a shallow dish for 15 minutes in a moderate oven (Gas No. 4, 350°F, 180°C).

Serves 6-8 Do not freeze

1¹/₂-2 lb (800g-1kg) aubergines (eggplants)	6 tbsp oil (or butter plus 1 tbsp oil to prevent overbrowning)
Salt	2 tbsp chopped parsley
4 tbsp flour	15 grinds black pepper

Cut the unpeeled aubergines (eggplants) in ¹/₂-inch (1.25cm) thick slices, discarding the hard stalk ends. Put into a colander, sprinkle with salt, cover with a plate and a weight, and leave for 1 hour for the bitter juices to run out. Rinse thoroughly with cold water, then dry on paper towels or in a salad spinner. Put the flour in a plastic bag, and put in the slices a few at a time and shake them until evenly coated, brushing off excess flour before frying them, one layer at a time, in the hot fat (which should come to a depth of ¹/₄ inch/0.5cm in the frying pan). As they brown and become tender, transfer to a shallow tin in the oven. When all the slices are fried, transfer to a shallow dish and sprinkle with parsley and black pepper. Serve at once.

Courgettes (Zucchini)

As the courgette (zucchini) has a rather delicate flavour and soft texture, it can be treated very much like the aubergine (eggplant), cooked plainly but crisply or stewed in a savoury sauce. The fresh vegetable should be firm to the touch with a shiny skin. Soft dull specimens are certain to be stale. Refrigerate courgettes until required; they should keep a week.

Courgettes (Zucchini) Sauté

This is perhaps the best way of bringing out the flavour of fresh courgettes. There is no need to peel them.

Serves 6-8 Do not freeze

1½-2 lb (800g-1kg) courgettes (zucchini)	Salt
	Pepper
3 oz (75g/⅓ cup) butter *or* 4 tbsp oil	Parsley

Cut the courgettes (zucchini) into slices just over ½ inch (1.25cm) thick. Drop into a pan of cold salted water, bring to the boil and simmer for 1-2 minutes until barely tender when pierced with a fork. Drain thoroughly.

Heat butter or oil in a frying pan wide enough to hold the courgettes in one layer. As soon as it starts to bubble, lay in the slices and cook gently until golden brown and tender on both sides. Sprinkle with salt and pepper, transfer to a dish and sprinkle with chopped parsley.

Note: If you want to use whole courgettes, choose them about a finger thick. You will need to simmer them for 5 minutes before frying.

Courgettes (Zucchini) for a Slimming Diet

The courgettes (zucchini) are cooked in their own juices with the minimum of fat. They may be reheated.

Serves 6-8 F 3 months

1 ½-2 lb (800g-1kg) courgettes (zucchini)	Black pepper
	Garlic salt
1 oz (25g/2 tbsp) butter *or* 1 tbsp oil	1 tbsp fresh, *or* 2 teasp dried marjoram or oregano
1 tbsp water	

Do not peel the courgettes (zucchini), just cut off strips using a potato peeler. Cut in slices 1 inch (2.5cm) thick and sprinkle with salt. Leave for half an hour, then drain thoroughly. In a pan wide enough to hold the courgettes in one layer (about 8 inches/20cm) heat the fat with the water. Add the courgettes, sprinkle with

298

pepper, cover and cook very gently for about 10 minutes, then turn and cook the other side. Sprinkle with garlic salt and herbs. If the water has evaporated, add a further tablespoonful and swirl around the pan to release the flavourings.

Serve very hot.

Courgette (Zucchini) Crisps

If you can fry chips, this dish is easy. Serve the 'chips' with grilled chops or steaks, or with a veal dish in a sauce. An automatic deep fryer is of tremendous assistance.

Serves 6-8

1¹/₂-2 lb (800g-1kg) courgettes (zucchini), unpeeled
Salt

Flour
Oil for deep frying

Cut each courgette (zucchini) lengthwise into slices a quarter of an inch (0.5cm) thick, then cut across into 'chips' about 1¹/₂ inches (3 cm) long. Put them in a colander and sprinkle with salt. Leave for 1 hour, then dry well with paper or a tea-towel. Put a tbsp of flour into a plastic bag and toss the chips in it until they are lightly coated.

Heat a chip pan one-third full of oil until it reaches 37°F, 180°C (chip-frying temperature). Put in the floured courgettes in two batches, cooking until golden brown and crisp (about 3 to 4 minutes for each batch). Keep hot in a quick oven (Gas No. 6, 400°F, 200°C) until all are done.

Courgettes (Zucchini) in Tomato and Herb Sauce

This can be served hot or cold. It freezes well.

Serves 6-8 **F** 3 months

1¹/₂-2 lb (800g-1kg) courgettes (zucchini), cut (unpeeled) into 1 inch (2.5cm) slices
3 tbsp oil
2 medium onions, thinly sliced or chopped

1 × 15 oz (425g) can of whole tomatoes
1 teasp dried basil
1 bayleaf
1 teasp each salt and sugar and plenty of black pepper
1 clove of garlic, crushed

299

Heat the oil gently, and sauté the onions until they are pale gold, limp and transparent (5-10 minutes). Add all the remaining ingredients except for the courgettes (zucchini) and simmer, uncovered, for 5 minutes. Add the courgettes, cover and simmer until tender when pierced with a sharp knife (about 10 minutes).

If the sauce is too runny, simmer a minute or so to thicken it.

VARIATION
Courgettes (Zucchini) Niçoise: Prepare as above but with the addition of 1 tbsp chopped parsley and 12 stoned and roughly cut-up black olives.

Danish Caramelized Carrots

These are delicious served with roast or fried chicken, cold pickled brisket, or grilled fish.

Serves 6-8

1½-2 lb (800g-1kg) young carrots	1½ oz (40g/3 tbsp) butter or margarine
1½ oz (40g/3 tbsp) granulated sugar	

Scrape the carrots, and cook in boiling salted water until tender, but not soggy. Drain, and rinse in cold water. Leave in a colander while you heat the sugar in a wide frying pan until it melts and turns a pale golden brown, then add the fat. Turn the carrots in this caramel, until they are golden brown.

They may be made in advance, then carefully reheated, either top-of-stove, or for 20 minutes in a moderate oven (Gas No. 4, 350°F, 180°C).

VARIATION
Use canned baby carrots, rinsing them well, then allowing to drain before proceeding as above.

Crumbed Cauliflowerets

The cauliflower is covered with a crunchy topping of herbed crumbs.

Serves 6-8 Do not freeze

1 large or 2 medium cauliflowers, separated into flowerets	2-3 oz (50-75g/^{2}/$_3$-1 cup) fresh breadcrumbs
2 oz (50g/^{1}/$_4$ cup) butter or margarine	1 tbsp chopped parsley
	1 teasp dried fines herbes

Plunge the cauliflowerets into a pan of boiling salted water, and cook until barely tender (about 8 minutes). This can be done early in the day. Arrange in a shallow greased casserole, large enough to hold them in a layer about 1^1/$_2$ inches (3.75cm) deep. Melt the fat, then add the crumbs (use enough to absorb the butter and look moist but not wet), and mix well with the herbs. Arrange an even layer over the cauliflowerets. 15-20 minutes before required, put in a hot oven (Gas No. 7, 425°F, 220°C) to crispen the crumbs.

Crispy Fried Onion Rings

These are delicious with meat or chicken at an informal dinner (they must be cooked just before serving).

Serves 6-8
3 medium onions (1 lb/450g weight)

Batter:

3 oz (75g/^{3}/$_4$ cup) plain flour	4 fl oz (125 ml/^{1}/$_2$ cup) water
Pinch salt	1 large egg white
1^1/$_2$ tbsp corn oil	

By blender or food processor: Put the water, corn oil, flour and salt in that order into the bowl and process for 1 minute.

By hand: Put the flour and salt in a bowl, mix well and put in the oil and water. Gradually draw in the flour and stir to form a firm batter. Beat for 2 minutes.

Allow the batter to stand for ^{1}/$_2$ hour. Peel the onions and cut in slices about ^{1}/$_4$ inch (0.5cm) thick, then separate into rings and soak in cold water for half an hour.

Drain the onion and dry thoroughly. Beat the egg white until it holds stiff but glossy peaks, then fold into the batter. Heat a pan one-third full of oil until it reaches 375°F, 180°C (chip temperature, when an inch (2.5cm) cube of bread browns in 40 seconds). Dip the rings one by one in and out of the batter, twirl round to remove excess, then put into the hot oil (a frying basket is helpful in removing them). Cook until they are a crisp brown (about 2 minutes), turning if necessary. Drain and serve as soon as possible.

The Green and Red Pepper

The sweet pepper (correctly called the 'capsicum' and also known as piment doux and pimento) was much favoured by the Aztec Indians of Mexico and Peru, where it was cultivated long before it was discovered and brought to Europe by Christopher Columbus. There is little to choose in flavour between the green, red or yellow vegetable, but the red pepper is generally sweeter. Whatever the colour, the vegetable should be glossy and firm and quite free from bruises.

If the pepper is not to be used within 48 hours of purchase, it is best to store it in a plastic bag or in the vegetable container, in the least cold part of the refrigerator. Whole peppers will keep for up to 2 weeks; portions of pepper (which should be tightly wrapped in film) should be used within a week. A pepper that has been stored too long will soften and develop grey spots on the skin.

To prepare: Wash well in cold water, cut in half lengthwise, cut out the stalk, then remove the core, white pith and bitter seeds. For stuffing, cut a lid across the top, then scoop out the pith and seeds.

Fried Peppers

This is the simplest way – and one of the most delicious – to cook peppers.

Serves 6-8

6-8 large glossy green peppers	2 level teasp marjoram or oregano
3 tbsp salad oil	2 level teasp salt
1 clove of garlic, crushed with salt	15 grinds black pepper

Cut the peppers in half and remove the seeds and ribs. Wash, then slice in strips, 3 to each half. Heat the oil gently, add the peppers and cook quickly for a few minutes till beginning to soften. Stir frequently. Add the garlic, cover, reduce heat to the minimum and cook slowly (10-15 minutes) until tender but still a little crisp. Add the herbs and seasonings.

Peperonata

The peppers are stewed with onions in a savoury tomato sauce.

Do not overcook or the peppers will become limp and the dish will lose much of its charm. The dish can be served hot as a vegetable, or cold as an hors d'oeuvre or relish. It can be reheated, also frozen.

Serves 6-8 **F** 3 months

6 fine peppers, including if
   possible 3 or 4 red ones (darker
   red the better as sweeter)
3 tbsp oil
1 large onion (6 oz/175g)
1 teasp brown sugar
1 clove of garlic, crushed

1 × 14 oz (400g) can tomatoes
   (drained) *or* 8 peeled and
   chopped fresh ones
10 grinds black pepper
10 grinds (¹/₂ teasp) sea salt
1 teasp dried herbes de Provence
1 tbsp fresh chopped parsley

Halve the peppers, remove seeds and core, then cut in 1 inch (2.5cm) strips. Put the oil in a deep, wide frying pan and heat gently. Peel the onion, halve, then slice as thinly as possible and cook in the oil until limp and pale gold, sprinkling on the sugar to hasten the process (it should take about 5 minutes). Add the peppers, and continue to cook gently for 15 minutes, turning in the oil. Add the crushed clove of garlic, the tomatoes, herbs and seasonings and continue to bubble until the mixture is like a thick stew (another 10 minutes). The peppers should be soft but not soggy. Taste and add more seasonings if necessary.

Braised Red Cabbage in the Viennese Style

This hearty vegetable, with its fruity undertones, goes well with pickled meats, or meat or poultry pies. Also makes an excellent vegetarian dish.

Serves 6-8 **F** 3 months

2 lb (1kg) red cabbage, finely
   shredded
1 oz brown sugar
2 oz (50g/¹/₄ cup) butter or
   margarine
1 large (8 oz/225g) onion, finely
   chopped

2 generous tbsp crab-apple or
   redcurrant jelly
2 tbsp cider vinegar
2 tbsp water
2 teasp salt
¹/₄ teasp white pepper
1 large bayleaf

Quarter the cabbage (remove the stalk section and discard), then shred finely by hand or machine. Rinse in cold water and drain well. Melt the fat in a heavy pan large enough to hold the cabbage. Add the finely chopped onion and cook for 5 minutes, until golden brown. Add the sugar and stir until it begins to caramelize. Now add the cabbage and all the remaining ingredients, stirring well to blend, until bubbling. Transfer to an oven casserole – a covered roaster or enamelled steel dish are both excellent. Cook in a quick moderate oven (Gas No. 5, 375°F, 190°C) for 45 minutes to 1 hour. Stir twice. Taste and add more sugar if necessary: the cabbage should have an equal balance of sour and sweet. It should also have a little bite left when it is ready. It can then be kept hot at Gas No. 1, 275°F, 140°C for as long as required. It also reheats extremely well.

Potatoes

A potato that is cooked to perfection is the perfect foil for almost any main dish. However, it is essential to choose the variety of potato to suit the dish. Some bagged potatoes now are labelled with fitness for purpose, otherwise consult your greengrocer before making your choice. Here are some basic methods of cooking potatoes for party meals, together with a small selection of more specialized recipes.

Note: I do not think potatoes freeze well, with these exceptions:
1. When duchesse potatoes are piped on top of a fish casserole.
2. Parboiled potatoes that are to be roasted at a later date.

To Mash Potatoes

Freshly mashed potatoes, beaten to a creamy whip with butter and milk, make a superb accompaniment to any baked or grilled fish, or steak. If preferred, use margarine instead of butter and a little hot chicken or vegetable stock instead of milk.

Note: Mashed potatoes should not be kept hot for more than 15 minutes or they lose their fluffiness.

Serves 6-8 Do not freeze

3-4 lb (1.5-2kg) potatoes	3 oz (75g/^{1}/$_3$ cup) butter
2 level teasp salt	5 fl oz (150ml-^{2}/$_3$ cup) hot milk
^{1}/$_2$ teasp white pepper	

Peel the potatoes, cut them into quarters and put them in a pan containing sufficient boiling water to cover them. Add the salt, bring back to the boil, cover and cook at a steady boil for 15 minutes, or until a piece feels absolutely tender when pierced with a thin vegetable knife. (Do not boil vigorously, or they may become 'soupy'.) Drain the water from the potatoes, return to the stove in the same pan and shake over a gentle heat until all the moisture has evaporated.

Pour the milk down the side of the pan, and when it starts to steam, add the butter and pepper, then start whisking together with the potatoes, using either a small balloon whisk or a portable electric mixer. Continue to whisk on a very low heat until the potatoes lighten in colour and look fluffy. Add more milk if the mixture seems too dry – the texture is a matter of taste.

Pile into a warm vegetable dish and serve immediately.

Note: If preferred, omit milk and butter and use 4 oz (125g/^{1}/$_2$ cup) margarine.

VARIATION 1
Gratin Potatoes: Arrange the mashed potatoes in a shallow ovenproof dish, scatter with a thick layer of finely grated cheese and dot with 1 oz (25g/2 tbsp) butter. Grill for 5 minutes until a rich brown crust forms on the top. Serve at once.

VARIATION 2
Duchesse Potatoes: Cook only 1^1/$_2$-2 lb (800g-1kg) potatoes until tender. Mash as above but without any liquid. Instead beat in 1^1/$_2$-2 oz (40-50g/3 tbsp-^{1}/$_4$ cup) butter and 1^1/$_2$ egg yolks, seasoning very well with salt and white pepper. Pipe into large rosettes on a greased baking sheet, then brush with the remaining egg yolk diluted with 2 teasp water. (Alternatively, pipe on top of a casserole and bake as directed in that particular recipe.)

Bake in a hot oven (Gas No. 7, 425°F, 220°C) for 10-15 minutes until brown. If you wish to freeze the potatoes for later use, bake for 10 minutes only, until golden. Cool and open freeze before wrapping. To reheat, place still frozen on a baking sheet and reheat in a very hot oven (Gas No. 7, 425°F, 220°C) for 25 minutes.

To Sauté Potatoes

To achieve a really crisp, flavourful result, the potatoes should be fried slowly at first to absorb the fat, and then more quickly when they are almost ready, to make them crisp. Cold left-over potatoes can be used, but the finest results are achieved with potatoes freshly cooked in their skins.

2-3 lb (1-1.5kg) potatoes (boiled in their skins) Salt
2-3 oz (50-75g/¼-⅓ cup) butter and 3 tbsp oil (or 6 tbsp oil) Black pepper
2 teasp chopped parsley

Scrub the potatoes, then cook them whole in their skins, covered with boiling salted water for 25-40 minutes, depending on their size. Drain the potatoes and return to the empty pan to dry off on a low heat. Leave until cool enough to handle, then skin and cut into thick slices or cubes.

To fry: Put the oil and butter in a heavy frying pan. (If oil alone is used, heat for 4 minutes.) When the butter starts to foam, put in the potatoes and cook very gently, shaking the pan occasionally so that the potatoes absorb the fat rather than fry in it. This will take about 15 minutes. When the potatoes are golden all over, increase the heat to make them crisp. Drain from the fat (there should be very little, if any, left), put in a dish and sprinkle with salt, black pepper and chopped parsley.

VARIATION

Savoury Fried Potatoes (Pommes Lyonnaise): Fry potatoes for 10 minutes, then add 1 finely sliced or chopped onion to the pan. Continue to cook until the onion is soft and golden as well as the potatoes. Sprinkle with chopped parsley before serving.

To Bake Old Potatoes

This method produces a crunchy skin which is delicious to eat.

Allow 1-1½ medium potatoes per person.
Scrub well, using a non-stick panscrub, and dry thoroughly. Prick with a fork. Rub with a butter paper or brush with oil, then sprinkle with sea salt. Bake in a very hot oven (Gas No. 8, 450°F, 230°C) for 1-1¼ hours.

To serve: Cut a criss-cross in the skin, then squeeze potato to open, top with herb butter (p.491), plain butter, soured cream and chives, cottage cheeses or avocado herb topping (see below).

VARIATION
To Bake New Potatoes

These are delicious at a barbecue or buffet and can be eaten, held in the hand with a paper napkin.

Select new potatoes about 2½ inches (6cm) in diameter. (Cyprus potatoes are excellent. Don't use potatoes whose skin will rub off.) Wash well and dry. Bake at Gas No. 6, 400°F, 200°C for 1 hour.

Avocado Herb Topping

Enough for 12-15 potatoes F 3 months

1 medium (4oz/125g) avocado	2 teasp chives
4 oz (125g/½ cup) cream cheese	½ teasp salt
or cottage cheese	10 grinds black pepper
2 teasp lemon juice	

Skin the avocado, cut in half, then mash with a fork and mix with the other ingredients, or put all ingredients in a food processor and process until fluffy. Pile into a pottery bowl and cover tightly with film. Chill several hours. Left-over topping will keep under refrigeration for 3 days or may be frozen.

Roast Potatoes for a Party

I give a variety of temperatures at which potatoes can be conveniently roasted to suit the requirements of a particular menu.
   Parboil the potatoes, before you roast them. This ensures that they are tender inside with a really crunchy brown crust.

For each person you will need:

½ lb (225g) potatoes	Salt
Oil and margarine or butter	

Choose large potatoes. Peel, then cut them into slices about 1 inch (2.5cm) thick. Put into a pan of boiling water, add 1 level teasp salt, cover, bring slowly back to the boil, then cook until the potatoes are *almost* tender – the centre should feel slightly firm when pierced with a sharp knife. This should take about 15 minutes. Drain the potatoes, then return to the pan and shake over gentle heat until quite dry.

Meanwhile put a roasting tin (large enough to hold the potato slices in one layer) into the oven, covered with a ¼ inch (0.5cm) deep layer of cooking oil. The time the oil takes to heat – and the potatoes to cook – will depend on the temperature at which the oven is set. At Gas No. 3, 325°F, 160°C, the oil will take 10 minutes to heat. At Gas No. 4 or 5, 350°F or 375°F, 180°C or 190°C, it will take about 7 minutes.

Take out the tin when the oil is hot, add a nut of butter or margarine, then lay the potatoes gently into it side by side, and then immediately turn them over so they are coated on both sides. Sprinkle lightly with coarse salt and put back in the oven.

Cooking time (turn at half-time)
Gas No. 3, 325°F, 160°C: 1¼-1½ hours
Gas No. 4, 350°F, 180°C: 1 hour.
Gas No. 5, 375°F, 190°C: 1 hour

To keep hot and crisp, run off the fat when the potatoes are ready (this can be used again), and leave in tin in the oven ready to dish.

To reheat (useful if oven is full – potatoes can then be roasted in advance): Leave to go cold in the fat. Reheat under a medium grill for 7-10 minutes.

Roast Parsnips

These can be roasted in exactly the same way as potatoes. During the roasting, the starch in the parsnip is changed into sugar giving a characteristic sweet and nutty flavour.

Allow ½ lb (225g) per person

Peel using a potato peeler, then cut into wedges about 1 inch (2.5cm) thick and 3 inches (7.5cm) long. Parboil, then roast exactly as for potatoes.

To Cook New Potatoes for a Party

Serves 6-8 Do not freeze
Allow 4-5 potatoes per serving depending on size

If the skins of the potatoes are very tender, the potatoes can be well scrubbed then cooked freshly without scraping, and served with firm butter. If, however, you prefer to remove the skins of the potatoes, this is the most convenient way of preparing and cooking them.

Wash the potatoes, then put them into a pan of cold water with 2 teasp salt. Bring slowly to the boil, then cover and boil steadily until almost tender (20-30 minutes, depending on size). Drain, return to a very low heat with first a tea-towel and then the pan lid covering them for 4 minutes when they will be dry and absolutely tender. Allow to cool until they can be skinned without burning your fingers.

Just before dinner, melt 2 oz (50g-¼ cup) butter with 1 tbsp parsley, preferably in a heatproof dish. Add the potatoes, toss well to coat with the parsley butter, then allow to steam through top-of-stove or in a slow oven (Gas No. 2, 300°F, 150°C) for 15 minutes until piping hot.

Whole Fried Potatoes

New potatoes do not need to be boiled before sautéing if treated this way.

Serves 6-8 Do not freeze

2 lb (1kg) new potatoes – about 4-5 small ones per person	1 tbsp oil
1½-2 oz (40-50g/3 tbsp-¼ cup) butter or margarine	Salt

Scrape the potatoes (or simply scrub well to remove soil) and dry thoroughly in a towel.

Put the butter or margarine and oil in a lidded frying pan wide enough to hold the potatoes in one layer, and melt top of stove. The minute it starts to foam, add the potatoes and shake them gently in the fat until they are well coated on all sides. Put on the lid and cook very gently for 20-30 minutes, shaking the pan occasionally, until the potatoes are a delicious golden brown outside and very tender when pierced with a sharp knife. If required, they can be kept hot on a tiny light for up to half an hour, then re-crispened just before serving.

To serve: lift from the pan, discarding any remaining fat, and scatter with sea salt.

Rösti

This simple Swiss dish is absolutely delicious when served with cold meats or chicken. It demands a little sleight of hand which is soon developed if the instructions are carefully followed.

Serves 6-8 Do not freeze

3-3½ lb (1.25-1.5kg) potatoes (weighed before peeling)
Salt, pepper and nutmeg

Oil to come to a depth of ¼ inch (0.5cm) in a pan, plus 2 oz (50g/¼ cup) butter or margarine (for flavour)

Peel the potatoes, leave whole, then put in a pan of cold unsalted water, and bring slowly to the boil. Boil for 6 minutes until they can be pierced with a sharp knife but are still firm and waxy. Drain and allow to go quite cold. Using the coarsest grater – ½ inch (1.25cm) holes – grate the potatoes into a bowl. Put the oil and fat into a 9 inch (23cm) pan and heat until the butter or margarine melts and the foam subsides. Immediately put in the grated potatoes and pat into an even layer to form a cake that just fills the pan. Cook over moderate heat for 7 minutes until the bottom is a rich brown. Sprinkle the top with salt and pepper and nutmeg, then dribble 1 tbsp of oil over it.

Take a plate of slightly larger diameter, lay it on top of the pan, and flip the rösti into it. Then slide the rösti back into the pan so that the uncooked side is to the bottom. Continue to cook slowly but steadily for a further 5 minutes until the bottom is crisp and brown also.

Rice and Noodles

Every country that grows rice has its own way of cooking it. I have tried many of these methods and if the quality of the rice is right they all seem to work equally well. The easiest and most consistently successful, however, is the pilaff method. The rice is first fried in fat – usually with a little onion – then cooked, without stirring, in a measured amount of water, or stock. If a good quality long-grain Italian, American or Basmatti rice is cooked in this way it will always result in fluffy, separate grains. A simpler method is to wash the rice thoroughly in several lots of water, then boil it (without frying) in a measured amount of water or stock. The washing can be omitted if par-cooked, packeted rice is used.

For a salad, the pilaff method is ideal as the rice keeps its shape especially well. Always add the dressing to the rice when it is hot and absorbent.

American par-cooked rice is an excellent general-purpose rice and gives the largest yield (3½ cups of cooked rice from 1 cup of raw rice). Basmatti rice (from Pakistan) is ideal for curries. Italian rice is creamier and is excellent for making a main dish risotto with chicken or chicken livers.

To store cooked rice, put in an airtight container and refrigerate for up to a week, or freeze for up to 6 months. Always defrost rice before reheating.

To reheat rice: Cover the bottom of a pan or a casserole to a depth of ¼ inch (0.5cm) with boiling water or stock, then add the rice. Cover and reheat top of stove until steaming for 5 minutes, or for 15 minutes in the oven at Gas No. 4, 350°F, 180°C.

Quantities: For a main dish accompaniment allow 1½-2 oz (40-50g/3-4 tbsp) raw rice per serving.

Savoury Rice

This dish can be served either hot or cold.

Serves 6-8 **F** 6 months

2 tbsp oil	3 cups (1¼ pints/0.75 litre) hot
1 medium onion	chicken stock made with cubes
12 oz (350g/1½ cups) long grain	and water
Patna or Basmatti rice	2 level teasp salt
	15 grinds black pepper

In a heavy-based pan heat the oil for 2-3 minutes, add the finely chopped onion and cook for 5 minutes until softened and golden.

311

Add the well-washed rice and turn in the onion for 3 minutes. Add the hot stock, salt and pepper, and stir well. Bring to the boil, then cover tightly and cook for 20 minutes over a low heat either on top of the stove or in a quick oven (Gas No. 6, 400°F, 200°C), whichever is the most convenient. If it is to be served hot, fluff up the rice with a fork and stir an ounce (25g/2 tbsp) butter or margarine through it.

VARIATION 1
For a more assertive flavour add 1 level teasp paprika, 2 teasp tomato purée and 1 small clove of garlic, crushed.

VARIATION 2
Brown Rice Pilaff
This takes a little longer as the husk is tougher, but it has a very nutty flavour and chewy texture.
Cook as above, but boil for 20 minutes, then turn the heat almost off and allow to cook (covered) for another 30 minutes, preferably in a quick moderate oven (Gas No. 5, 375°F, 190°C).

VARIATION 3
Basmatti Rice cooked Indian Style
This is an excellent method for barbecue cookery when a measuring jug is not available.
Fry the onion and add the rice as above. After the rice has been turned in the fat for 3 minutes, cover with cold water or stock plus 1 inch (2.5cm), and add seasonings. Cover the pan with a tea-towel and then a lid. Simmer for 20 minutes, by which time the rice should have absorbed all the liquid.

VARIATION 4
Rice Ring
F 3 months
Savoury rice cooked by the basic method, or any of the variations, is packed into a well-greased ring tin. Cover with foil. With freshly cooked rice, leave in a moderate oven for 10 minutes: with cold rice, leave for 20-30 minutes or until hot to the touch. Turn out and fill the centre with green vegetables such as beans or peas.

VARIATION 5
Fried Rice
This is an excellent side dish to serve with cold meat or chicken. Left-over or frozen rice can be used.

1 recipe savoury rice	2 large green peppers
3 tbsp oil or butter	3 tbsp soy sauce
1 medium (5 oz/150g) onion	1 teasp salt
6-8 oz (175-225g/3-4 cups) mushrooms	15 grinds black pepper

Heat the oil or butter and cook the onion until it is soft and golden. Add the thinly sliced mushrooms and cook a further 3 minutes until softened. Add the peppers (quartered, de-seeded and cut into 1/4 inch/0.5cm slivers) and cook for 2 minutes until very slightly softened and coated with oil, then add the rice. Cook, stirring with a fork, until the rice is piping hot and beginning to brown. Finally add the soy sauce, salt and pepper. Stir well, taste and add more seasoning if required. Serve hot.

Can be kept hot on a low heat, or reheated.

To Cook Patna Rice in the Middle Eastern Fashion

Use Patna rice of good quality rather than par-cooked rice. Wash thoroughly until the water is clear. Put in a thick-based pan, with 1 teasp salt and 1 tbsp oil to each cup of rice, and cover to double the depth of the rice with boiling water. Boil rapidly, uncovered, until the water disappears and pockets appear in the rice, stirring occasionally. Put on the pan lid, and leave on the lowest possible heat for 30 minutes, or bake for the same length of time in a slow oven (Gas No. 2, 300°F, 150°C).

Rice Party Presentation

Rice cooked by any method can be used. Put the cooked rice on a platter, and garnish with little heaps of crisply fried onions and mushrooms, fried chicken livers, pine kernels, almonds and peas in any assortment and proportion.

Parsleyed Noodles

This is an excellent accompaniment to veal escalopes or other dishes in a light sauce. In the dairy version, it can also be served as a bed for creamed fish dishes.

Serves 6-8 Do not freeze

$^1/_2$-$^3/_4$ lb (225-350g) broad egg noodles

3 oz (75g/$^1/_3$ cup) margarine or butter

Meat stock or salted water
2 tbsp parsley
Plenty of black pepper

Cook the noodles according to the packet instructions, in water or stock. Turn into a colander and dredge with cold water to remove any excess starch. Drain thoroughly.

In the same pan, melt the fat and add the parsley and pepper. Add the noodles and continue to heat over a low light, tossing thoroughly until the noodles are well coated with the herbs and are piping hot. They may be kept hot, covered, for up to 30 minutes, either top of stove or in a low oven – Gas No. 1 (275°F, 140°C).

Salads and Their Dressings

Properly dressed, and prepared with a careful regard for texture, colour and flavour, the salad is undoubtedly one of the better modern food fashions. It is also one of the most versatile, as the range of foods that can be put into the salad bowl is almost limitless, allowing the hostess to serve the salad as an appetizer, an accompaniment, or a main dish, according to the composition of the menu.

In preparing salads it is immensely helpful to have certain specialized pieces of kitchen equipment, such as a salad spinner for drying greens, a tomato knife for cutting smooth-skinned vegetables into thin, even slices, a mandoline (which enables raw vegetables to be either sliced paper-thin or shredded into strips), and a measuring jug or spoon, since it is essential to get the proportions right when making salad dressings, together with a range of oils, vinegars and other flavourings.

Salad oil: This can be of almost any variety, ranging from the tasteless oils such as corn, peanut, sunflower and sassflower, to the more highly flavoured such as walnut (huile de noix), olive and grapeseed. I have indicated in the recipe if a specific oil is to be preferred, though it is mainly a matter of choice.

Vinegars: With the exception of coleslaw, I do not use malt vinegars in dressings. Instead, select from red and white wine vinegar, cider vinegar and any variety flavoured with herbs such as tarragon or shallots. In some cases a mixture of vinegar and lemon juice, or lemon juice alone may be preferred. Don't be afraid to experiment.

Salt and pepper: Always use sea salt and black peppercorns in

315

dressings as they are far superior to ordinary condiments, many of which are mixed with other ingredients to keep them free-flowing.

Garlic: Fresh garlic can be used either cut up to flavour the dressing and then discarded, or crushed and blended in with the other ingredients.

Mustard: Mustard powder is used in mayonnaise to help the emulsion to 'take' as well as to flavour the mixture. Prepared mustards such as English mustard, moutarde de Dijon, moutarde de Meaux and moutarde de Bordeaux, all help to add variety to the various dressings. To preserve their flavour they are best kept refrigerated.

Shallots, spring onion (scallion) bulbs and onions: These are especially useful in the dressing for cooked vegetables. Sometimes they are finely chopped; in other cases they are grated so that only the juice is used.

Herbs, fresh and dried: All French and vinaigrette dressings depend on herbs for their subtlety of flavouring. It is a good idea to experiment and develop a palate for the different varieties – parsley, chives, basil, tarragon, dill, marjoram, to name but a few. Guidance is given in individual recipes.

Sugar: A teaspoon or two of sugar is included in many of the dressings. This is not used to sweeten them but to blend the many different flavourings. It *can* be omitted if preferred.

Note: In the following recipes, salad dressings are given with salads if they have been specially balanced to suit the particular blend of ingredients. All-purpose dressings with variations are given at the end of the chapter.

Green Salads

A general guide

To ensure crisp greens, wash under the cold tap, leaf by leaf, dry in a salad spinner, then wrap loosely in a tea towel and place in a bowl in the refrigerator for 6-12 hours or overnight. Use this treatment for the following:

All lettuce varieties
Watercress (if not to be used the same day, leave with its stalks in cold water until ready for crisping)
Ordinary cress (this will keep fresh for at least 48 hours if left, refrigerated, in the growing medium)
Chicory
Endive
Chinese leaves
Shredded cabbage

Tomatoes should be cut not more than 1 hour before use.

Cucumber should be added to other greens just before use. It may be eaten freshly cut or salted by sprinkling with salt, left for 1 hour, then rinsed and dried thoroughly in a salad drier. Treated in this way it will not lose its texture, even in dressing, for a maximum of 2 days.

Do not freeze any crisp salad ingredients.

With the exception of Chinese leaves, which keep their crispness after dressing for up to 24 hours, a crisp green salad should always be dressed just before use, either in the kitchen or at the table. To make sure the dressing is mature, make it at least one hour beforehand and leave it in a jar which can be shaken just before the dressing is tossed with the salad.

Fresh herbs can be chopped and added to the dressing, or in the Greek and Italian fashion, scissored (rather than chopped) and mixed with the washed greens.

Mixed Salad

General proportions 6-8

1-2 large lettuces, washed and crisped in the refrigerator (tear leaves into bite-sized pieces)
1 bunch watercress (leaves only)
1 tbsp fresh herbs, such as scissored parsley or basil

4 tomatoes, de-seeded and cut into 4 (optional)
4 inches (10cm) cucumber, thinly sliced (optional)
6-8 red radishes, thinly sliced (optional)

317

One hour before the meal, arrange the ingredients in a bowl large enough to allow the contents to be tossed with the dressing. Cover with film or foil and leave at the bottom of the refrigerator until required.

VARIATION 1
Use thinly sliced raw courgette (zucchini) (unpeeled) instead of the cucumber.

VARIATION 2
Peel and thinly slice 1 medium avocado. Marinate in **Herb French Dressing** (p.332) for 1 hour, then drain and add to the greens just before serving. Toss the salad with additional marinade until the greens are glistening.

Chicory, Cucumber and Watercress Salad

A very crisp and crunchy salad in several shades of green.

Serves 6-8

4 pieces of Belgian chicory
1 bunch watercress
½ cucumber, thinly sliced and salted (see p.323)

1 medium green pepper, halved, de-seeded and cut in ¼ inch (0.5cm) cubes
1 recipe **Herb French Dressing** (p.332)

Cut the chicory in ½ inch (1.25cm) slices and blend with the other ingredients. Chill well. Toss at the dinner-table with herb vinaigrette.

Mixed Salad in the Greek Fashion

This is particularly delicious served with grills such as chops, steaks, kebabs or beefburgers.

Serves 6-8

1 large head crisp lettuce of any kind
½ large cucumber
1 bunch watercress
1 lb (450g) firm tomatoes
4 oz (125g) black olives

(preferably calamata)
2 tbsp shredded basil leaves (optional)
2 tbsp parsley leaves, very coarsely chopped

The dressing:

3 tbsp corn oil and 1 tbsp olive oil, or 4 tbsp corn oil if no olive available
1 tbsp lemon juice
1 tbsp white wine vinegar or cider vinegar

1/2 level teasp sea salt
1 level teasp sugar
10 grinds black pepper
1 large clove of garlic, crushed

Earlier in the day, wash the lettuce and dry in a spinner. Cut off tough lower stalks of watercress, then wash and dry. Put in a bowl and cover with a paper towel and refrigerate several hours until crisp. Peel the cucumber (or leave unpeeled if the skin seems thin and tender), then cut in 1/2 inch (1.25cm) cubes, first discarding seeds if large and coarse. Put in a colander and sprinkle with salt, then leave. Quarter or cut the tomatoes in sixths (according to size) and discard the seeds and the centre pulp. Make the dressing by combining all ingredients in a screw-top jar and shaking until thick. Refrigerate until meal-time.

   To assemble the salad, tear the lettuce into bite-sized pieces and mix with the watercress in a large bowl. Arrange the well-dried cucumber cubes and segments of tomatoes with olives on top. Sprinkle with herbs. Chill until required.

   Just before serving, shake the dressing well and toss into the salad.

Salad of Chinese Leaves, Green Pepper and Cucumber

This is an excellent side salad to serve with grills and roasts, especially in the winter months when lettuce is expensive and lacking in body. Chinese leaves have a characteristic nutty crispness and will keep up to three weeks under refrigeration. Shred off as much as you require, re-wrap in the polythene bag and refrigerate for further use. Allow approx 2-3 oz (50-75g) Chinese leaves per serving.

Serves 6-8

1-1 1/2 lb (450-700g) Chinese leaves
1 medium or 3/4 large green pepper
1/2 cucumber

First prepare the cucumber. Cut in half lengthwise, then cut in slices 1/8 inch (0.25cm) thick. Put into a colander, sprinkle with cooking salt and leave for 1 hour, then rinse off the salt and dry either in a tea towel or salad spinner (the cucumber will now keep crisp for up to 2 days).

Put the Chinese leaves on a board, and cut across in ½ inch (1.25cm) slices, producing shreds. Put into the salad bowl. Halve the pepper, remove the seeds and white pith and cut into julienne strips (approx ⅛ inch/0.25cm) either with a food processor or a sharp knife. Add to the leaves together with the salted cucumber. Cover with film and refrigerate until required.

The dressing:

5 tbsp corn oil
3 tbsp olive, sunflower or (especially nice if you can get it) grapeseed oil
3 tbsp cider (or failing that, wine) vinegar
1 tbsp lemon juice

2 teasp caster (superfine) sugar
1 rounded teasp French (Dijon) mustard
10 grinds sea salt (1 teasp)
10 grinds black pepper
1 tbsp finely chopped onion
1 small clove of garlic, crushed

Put all the ingredients into a screw-top jar and shake vigorously until thickened into an emulsion (1-2 minutes).

To serve: Add enough of the dressing to moisten the salad without soaking it.

This salad will now keep crisp under refrigeration for several hours.

Mixed Salad in the Israeli Fashion

This mixes greens with other crisp salad vegetables.

Serves 6-8

1 large Webb or iceberg lettuce (crispened as described on p.316), *or* approx 1 lb (450g) Chinese leaves
4 sticks of celery, thinly sliced
1 avocado, peeled, stoned and diced

4-6 large radishes, trimmed and thinly sliced
2 oz (50g/½ cup) raw button mushrooms, sliced
1 red or green pepper, de-seeded and sliced

320

The dressing:

1 clove of garlic, crushed
12 stuffed olives, sliced
4 spring onions (scallions), *or* 2
  shallots, chopped
2 teasp caster (superfine) sugar
  (optional but nice)

6 tbsp olive oil
2 tbsp lemon juice
1 tbsp French mustard
1 teasp salt
10 grinds black pepper

Arrange the lettuce or Chinese leaves in a large glass salad bowl. Mix all the remaining salad ingredients together, and pile in the centre of the dish. Mix the dressing ingredients together and just before serving pour over the salad and toss well. Serve at once.

Coleslaw

'Sla' is the Dutch word for salad, and was introduced to America by early settlers from the Netherlands. Not surprisingly, the best cabbage to use is the hard white variety which originates in Holland. Slaw has come to mean not only a cabbage salad, but any crisp mixture of shredded vegetables, paticularly roots. The dressing has a characteristic sweet/sour flavour. If you do not have a suitable shredder, buy commercial coleslaw and add the carrot, pepper, nuts and raisins to it: it makes a very acceptable substitute.

Coleslaw is best made 4-6 hours in advance and refrigerated. It will keep crisp for 48 hours.

Traditional Coleslaw

Serves 6-8

1 white winter cabbage (1½
  lb/700g)
1 large carrot, grated
1 green pepper, halved,
  de-seeded, white pith removed,
  then finely sliced.

Optional: 2 oz (50g/⅓ cup)
  sultanas (white raisins); 1 oz
  (25g/¼ cup) peanuts or
  hazelnuts

Discard any discoloured leaves, quarter the cabbage and remove the white core. Shred very finely with a knife, electric shredder or food processor. If the cabbage has a strong smell, soak it in a bowl of cold water (to cover) with 2 level teasp salt for 1 hour, then drain well and dry thoroughly. In either case, mix with the carrot, pepper and sultanas (if used).

Coleslaw Dressing

¹/₄ pint (150ml/²/₃ cup) mild
  mayonnaise

1 level tbsp each malt vinegar and
  caster (superfine) sugar
1 level teasp dry mustard

Blend all the seasonings with the mayonnaise in a large mixing bowl.

Add the salad ingredients and turn with a spoon and fork until well coated. Chill until required. Put into a serving bowl and top with the nuts.

VARIATION
Coleslaw of Chinese Leaves: Substitute an equal quantity of shredded Chinese leaves for the cabbage. Serves 6-8.

Red Cabbage Slaw

This looks very attractive on a buffet.

Serves 6-8

1 red cabbage (approx 1 lb/450g in weight)

The dressing:

6 tbsp oil
2 tbsp wine vinegar
1 teasp made mustard

Salt and black pepper
3 tbsp mayonnaise

Shake all dressing ingredients together for 1 minute in a screw-top jar. Shred the cabbage, either by hand or machine. Pile into a bowl or basin, sprinkle with salt, cover with a plate and weight to allow the excess bitter juices to be extracted, and to soften the cabbage. This takes about 2 hours.

Squeeze the cabbage in your hands and return to the rinsed bowl. Make the dressing and pour over the cabbage. Stir and blend the dressing well into the vegetable.

Make at least 4 hours before serving to allow the flavours to mingle.

Carrot and Raisin Slaw

A particularly refreshing yet satisfying salad.

Serves 6-8

6 large carrots
6 tbsp seedless raisins
2 oz (50g/¹/2 cup) walnuts (or
pecans if you can get them, or
even roasted peanuts), coarsely
chopped

The dressing:

5 fl oz (150ml/²/3 cup) carton
soured cream or salad cream
Juice and grated rind of ¹/2 lemon
Good pinch of salt and black
pepper
2 teasp caster (superfine) sugar

Have the carrots well chilled, then coarsely grate into a bowl and
mix with the raisins and nuts. Beat all the dressing ingredients
together and fold into the vegetable mixture.

A Variety of Cucumber Salads

Cucumber salad is extremely versatile, being mild yet crisp and
equally suitable to serve with delicate fish or a robust grill. Here
are some national variations.

Danish Cucumber Salad
*This goes particularly well with cold boiled salmon. The dressing
must be both very sweet and very tart. The herbs are essential,
together with plenty of black pepper.*

Serves 6-8

1 large cucumber
Coarse salt

The dressing:

2 level tbsp caster (superfine)
sugar
2 tbsp boiling water
4 tbsp wine vinegar
Plenty of black pepper
1 tbsp finely cut chives

Peel and slice the cucumber thinly in a soup plate, sprinkle with salt, cover with an upturned plate and a 1 lb (450g) weight. Leave for an hour. Pour off the water. Dissolve the sugar in the boiling water, then add the remaining ingredients, and pour onto the cucumber slices. Chill.

VARIATION
Swedish Cucumber Salad: Use scissored fresh dill instead of chives.

French Cucumber Salad

This is an excellent way to treat the slightly coarse outdoor cucumbers of late summer. The dressing is thickened with a little soured cream.

Serves 6-8

3 medium ridge cucumbers or 1 large cucumber	1 tbsp coarse salt

If the skin is coarse, peel, then cut the cucumbers down the centre lengthwise and remove large seeds using a teaspoon as a scoop. Slice ⅛ inch (0.25cm) thick. Place in a colander or a large sieve, mix well with the salt and let stand for 1 hour. Rinse under the cold tap, drain well, then wrap in a paper towel to remove excess moisture (or use a salad spinner).

The dressing:

4 tbsp soured cream	2 tbsp corn oil
1 tbsp wine vinegar or lemon juice	2 tbsp chopped fresh dill or
½ teasp each white pepper and caster (superfine) sugar	parsley

Put the cream, wine vinegar or lemon juice with the pepper and sugar into a bowl and whisk together then gradually whisk in the oil. Add the cucumbers and herbs, stirring well to coat them with the dressing. Arrange in a shallow oval dish.

Cyprus Cucumber Salad (Talathouri)

This can also be used as part of a summer hors d'oeuvre. It is superb served with barbecued fish.

Serves 6-8

1 large cucumber, cut in ½ inch (1.25cm) cubes
2 × 5 fl oz (150g/⅔ cup) cartons natural yoghurt
2 teasp each wine vinegar and lemon juice
1 small clove of garlic
2 level tbsp corn or (preferably) olive oil
10 grinds black pepper
1 level teasp caster (superfine) sugar (optional)
2 teasp chopped fresh mint *or* ½ level teasp dried mint

Put the cucumber in a colander and sprinkle with salt. Cover with a plate and a weight, leave for half an hour, then discard any liquid that has oozed out. Put the yoghurt in a bowl and stir in all the remaining ingredients. Finally stir in the salted cucumber. Use as a 'relish' with fish, or as a salad dressing for coleslaw salad.

VARIATION
For a richer mixture to serve with grilled salmon, use soured cream instead of yoghurt.

Swiss Potato Salad

It is important to use a waxy (rather than a floury) potato that slices without crumbling, and to dress the hot potatoes with vinaigrette, but to add the mayonnaise only when cold. Always serve this salad at room temperature, though it should be refrigerated for storage. It will keep for 2-3 days, and improves in flavour after 6 hours.

Serves 6-8 Do not freeze

2 lb (1kg) new potatoes
4 tbsp **Basic French Dressing** (p.332), *or* 3 tbsp oil and 1 tbsp vinegar mixed with ½ teasp salt and pinch each of pepper, sugar and mustard
1 level tbsp finely chopped onion
1 tbsp scissored chives, *or* the green from 1 bunch spring onions (scallions) finely chopped
1 tbsp finely chopped parsley
5-8 fl oz (150-225ml/⅔-1 cup) home-made mayonnaise (see p.335)
2 level teasp Dijon mustard
1 tbsp each of boiling water and lemon juice

Boil the potatoes in their skins until almost tender. Drain, return to the heat covered with a tea towel, then cook gently for a further 3-4 minutes until tender and absolutely dry (they will be firm). Spread on a cloth and leave until cool enough to handle, then skin and dice or slice into a bowl.

Mix the dressing with the onion and herbs, then stir gently through the potatoes. Heap into a shallow bowl.

Blend together the mayonnaise, mustard, boiling water and lemon juice. Spoon on top of the potatoes. Leave in a cool place for at least an hour. Just before serving, mix the mayonnaise through the salad and garnish with more parsley.

Tomato Salads

Because they are so refreshing, tomato salads make an excellent starter before a hearty main course. Alternatively they may be served as a side salad with highly flavoured meat and chicken dishes.

In Mediterranean countries they are made with the typical large (and often misshapen) sunripened tomatoes which are as sweet as sugar. In more temperate climates, be sure the tomatoes are fully ripe by leaving them on the kitchen windowsill for 2-3 days before use: they will turn a deep red. Do not peel tomatoes for salad unless the skin is unpleasantly coarse.

French Tomato Salad

The onion adds piquancy to the dressing.

Serves 6-8

6 large tomatoes
3 fl oz (75ml/⅓ cup) olive or salad oil
2 fl oz (50ml/¼ cup) lemon juice
1 teasp salt
1 level tbsp finely chopped onion

1 clove of garlic, crushed
1 level teasp paprika
1 teasp caster (superfine) sugar
1 level teasp fresh mint (or, if out of season, parsley)

Put all the seasoning ingredients into a screw-top jar and shake until thick (about 2 minutes). Leave 30 minutes. Slice the tomatoes into a shallow dish. Pour the dressing over and leave 1 hour in a cool place. Do not refrigerate.

Italian Tomato Salad

The fresh basil provides the distinctive flavour. This is usually served with grilled meat or chicken.

Serves 6-8

1½ lb (700g) tomatoes, really ripe but firm	2 tbsp vinaigrette dressing (see p.332)
2 tbsp snipped chives or the green from spring onions (scallions)	1 tbsp chopped fresh basil (or 1 tbsp chopped parsley and 1 teasp dried basil)
1 teasp caster (superfine) sugar	

Slice the tomatoes thinly, and lay them in a shallow dish. Sprinkle with the chives or spring onions (scallions). Add the sugar to the vinaigrette and pour over the tomatoes. Scatter with the fresh basil, or the parsley and dried basil. Leave in a cool place but do not refrigerate.

Cooked Vegetable Salads

Both canned and cooked vegetables make excellent salads. Cook the vegetables rapidly in plenty of salted water to conserve the colour, then plunge them into icy water to set it. Cook only until the vegetables are 'al dente' (that is, they still have a little bite left in them). Frozen vegetables will need hardly any cooking at all. Salads of cooked vegetables need a more highly-seasoned dressing than the typical French dressing used for green salads. Because it has a high acid content (to counteract the blandness of the vegetables), this dressing is called a 'vinaigrette'.

Cooked vegetable salads should not be frozen.

Basic Vinaigrette Dressing for cooked vegetable salads

4 tbsp any salad oil

2 tbsp wine vinegar

1 small clove of garlic, halved (less pungent) or crushed to a paste, as preferred

1 level teasp salt

10 grinds black pepper

1 level tbsp chopped parsley

Put all the ingredients into a screw-top jar and shake until thick (1-2 minutes).

Corn Salad

This is a mild salad to serve with hot or cold fish or chicken.

Serves 6-8

2 × 12 oz (350g) cans corn with peppers

1 tbsp onion, finely chopped

2 level tbsp chopped parsley

2 tbsp vinaigrette (above)

1-2 tbsp mayonnaise

Drain the corn thoroughly. In a bowl put all the remaining ingredients (reserve 1 tbsp of the mayonnaise), then add the corn and stir well together. Chill thoroughly.

Serve plain or with sliced tomatoes. Add the second tablespoon of mayonnaise if necessary to moisten just before serving.

Note: If corn with peppers is not available, use either 2 canned pimentos or 1 fresh red pepper (seeds and pith removed) and cut in ¼ inch (0.5cm) cubes.

Green Bean Salad

Serves 6-8

1 lb (450g) fresh or frozen green beans (broken into 2 or 3 pieces, or left whole, according to size)

4 tomatoes

1 medium green pepper, cubed (or 2 tbsp frozen peppers)

Basic vinaigrette dressing (above) plus:

1 level tbsp chopped onion

1 level tbsp chives (if available)

1 level tbsp chopped parsley

Boil the beans rapidly in a large pan of boiling salted water with the lid off until just bite-tender. Immediately turn into a colander and plunge into a bowl of cold water for 2 minutes to set the colour. Drain well. Mix with the dressing, the tomatoes cut in sixths and the peppers. Serve very cold.

Green and Gold Salad

An excellent winter salad that makes the best use of canned and frozen vegetables.

Serves 6-8

1 lb (450g) frozen green beans
1 × 11½ oz (315g) can corn with pimentos

2 oz (50g) black or stuffed green olives

The dressing:

3 tbsp corn or olive oil
2 tbsp wine vinegar
1 level teasp salt

10 grinds black pepper
2 teasp sugar
1 tbsp chopped onion

Drain the canned corn, slice the stuffed olives or stone the black olives and cut in four. Half fill a large pan with water, add 1 teasp salt and bring to the boil. Add the beans and cook until barely tender (about 5 minutes if sliced, 8 minutes if whole). Turn at once into a colander standing in the sink and flood with cold water to set the colour. Drain well, then put in a bowl with the drained corn and olives.

To make the dressing, put all the ingredients into a screw-top jar, seal well then shake for two minutes until thickened.

Pour over the vegetables, stir well, cover and refrigerate for several hours.

Spiced Mushrooms

A most delicious salad to serve on a cheese buffet, as a starter, or a relish.

Serves 6-8

¾ lb (350g/6 cups) very fresh small mushrooms, cut lengthwise in 4, or if button size, left whole

Basic vinaigrette dressing (see p.332) plus 2 teasp grated onion
Squeeze lemon juice
1 teasp sugar

Trim off the stalks of the mushrooms (use in a stew or other savoury dish). Rinse the mushrooms quickly then put in a pan, cover with cold water and add a squeeze of lemon juice. Cover and simmer 5 minutes, drain well then mix with the dressing. Leave for several hours or overnight before serving.

VARIATION
Mushroom, Celery and Pepper Salad
Use only ½ lb (225g/4 cups) mushrooms, but add the heart of a celery (finely sliced) and 2 fat green peppers, halved, quartered, seeds and ribs removed, and cut into very thin strips.

Leave overnight, then serve as a starter to eat with a spoon from small bowls or cocottes.

Two Fruity Salads

South Island Celery and Apple Salad

This is a variation on the classic Waldorf salad of celery and apple. It has a delicious citrus dressing and is sweetened with walnuts and raisins. It goes well with cold chicken or turkey, and also with cheese or meat strudels.

Serves 6-8 Do not freeze

8 large stalks celery	2 oz (50g/⅓ cup) seedless raisins
2 small red-skinned apples	2 oz (50g/½ cup) chopped walnuts
4 oz (125g/⅔ cup) fresh dates, stoned and roughly chopped	or salted peanuts (optional)

The dressing:

1 tbsp orange juice	¼ pint (150ml/⅔ cup) mild
1 tbsp lemon juice	mayonnaise
1 teasp fine brown sugar	

Cut the celery in ¼ inch (0.5cm) cubes. Quarter the apples, then core and cut into ¾ inch (1cm) cubes. Stone the dates and cut in four. Put in a bowl with the raisins. Stir the dressing ingredients together, then mix with the salad ingredients, stirring well. Refrigerate several hours. Turn into a salad bowl and garnish with the chopped nuts.

Omit the dates and add ¼ lb (125g) seedless grapes instead.

Pineapple Rice Salad

This is a splendid salad to add some 'body' to a barbecue meal. It is also excellent with cold cuts on a buffet.

Serves 6-8

8 oz (225g/1 cup) long-grain rice cooked according to packet instructions

Add this dressing to the hot rice:

2 tbsp wine vinegar or cider vinegar or lemon juice

½ teasp each salt and curry powder

1 level tbsp mango or other fruit chutney (optional)

4 tbsp oil

Add also:

5 level tbsp raisins (plumped by pouring on boiling water and leaving for 5 minutes, then draining).

When rice is cold add:

1 medium green and red pepper, halved, de-seeded and finely diced (or 2 canned pimentos)

4 rings pineapple or equivalent in pieces

Pile into a bowl and cover with 1-2 oz (25-50g/¼-½ cup) chopped toasted almonds, hazelnuts or peanuts.

Dressings

French Dressings for Green Salad

The dressing for a green salad is an emulsion of oil and some form of acid – lemon juice, wine vinegar or cider vinegar – delicately flavoured to complement the gentle flavour of the salad leaves. With a basic proportion of one part of acid to three parts of oil the

recipe can be endlessly permutated by using a variety of oils –
corn, peanut, olive, sassflower, sunflower, walnut, grapeseed –
and acids such as herb, wine, malt or cider vinegar or lemon juice.
In addition the seasonings can be varied with a variety of herbs,
garlic and cheeses.

To store French dressings: Leave the dressing in the screw-top jar
in which it was made in the bottom of the refrigerator, where it will
keep almost indefinitely. Perishable ingredients such as herbs and
onions should be added only on the day of use, though they will
still keep their flavour for up to 3 days.

Basic French Dressing (Vinaigrette)

6 tbsp salad oil (corn, peanut,
  sunflower)
3 tbsp olive oil
3 tbsp wine vinegar or cider
  vinegar or lemon juice

^{1}/2 level teasp each of sea salt and
  sugar
10 grinds black pepper
1 level tbsp English mustard
  powder

Place all the ingredients in a screw-top jar and shake until
thickened (2 minutes). Makes more than enough dressing to dress
a green salad for 6-8.

VARIATION 1
Herb Dressing: Add 2 level tbsp chopped mixed herbs – basil,
parsley, chives, tarragon or any combination of two or more of
them.

VARIATION 2
Garlic Dressing: Leave a peeled clove of garlic in the dressing until
dinner-time. Discard before dressing the salad.

VARIATION 3
Blue Cheese Dressing: Add 2 oz (50g/^{1}/2 cup) grated Danish blue
cheese to basic dressing.

Vinaigrette Dressing for Coleslaw

Sufficient for 1 lb (450g) shredded greens.
This is a hearty dressing for coleslaws of shredded red or white
cabbage or Chinese leaves.

¹/₄ pint (150ml/²/₃ cup) corn oil   1 level teasp salt
4 tbsp malt vinegar   ¹/₂ teasp caster (superfine) sugar
1 small clove of garlic (whole)   10 grinds black pepper
1 level teasp prepared mustard   2 teasp very finely chopped onion

Combine all the ingredients in a screw-top jar and shake thoroughly.

Mayonnaise

It is possible to buy mayonnaise as good as you can make yourself, although the flavourings tend to be bland and anonymous – a fault that is not difficult to correct with the judicious addition of salt, pepper, sugar, mustard and lemon juice. However, home-made mayonnaise is easy to make and it's possible to use exactly the oil and vinegar you like at no extra cost, so that it is really worthwhile making your own. There are only a few points to remember:

The yolks or whole egg should always be mixed with some mustard *before* the addition of any oil. This helps it to form a firm emulsion.

Use oil that is neither chilled nor warm, but at normal room temperature of approx 70°F, 21°C. If you like the flavour of olive oil, but find it expensive and a little heavy, use only a proportion to flavour the mayonnaise (say one quarter) and make up the remainder with any flavourless oil such as corn or peanut oil.

When the mayonnaise has been made, whisk in a little boiling water which will lighten it and help the emulsion to hold.

The whisking appliance to use:
1. *Rotary hand whisk*: This is excellent for making small quantities of mayonnaise. However, it takes a relatively long time because the oil must be added drop by drop.

2. *Electric whisk*: This is quicker for making large quantities of mayonnaise. However, its action is only adequate to deal with egg yolk mayonnaise. It is not possible to use it for making the more economical whole egg recipe.

3. *Blender or food processor*: These make up to 1 pint (575ml) of excellent mayonnaise, either with egg yolk or whole eggs, as preferred.

Home-made mayonnaise will keep at least 3 weeks under refrigeration. It will not freeze, as the emulsion breaks down at low temperatures.

Traditional Mayonnaise

This can be made with any of the four appliances described above. The mayonnaise is very yellow and thick.

To make ³/₄ pint (425ml)	To make 1¹/₂ pints (850ml)
2 egg yolks	4
1 level teasp dry mustard	2
2 level teasp French mustard	1 tbsp
1 level teasp each salt and sugar	2 teasp each
Pinch cayenne pepper	¹/₈ teasp
2 teasp each lemon juice and wine vinegar or cider vinegar	1 tbsp each
12 fl oz (350ml/1¹/₂ cups) oil, (half olive, half corn oil is good)	25 fl oz (700ml/3 cups)
1-2 tbsp boiling water	2-3 tbsp

If you are using a hand whisk, mix the mayonnaise in a pint measure (or 2 pint container for the larger quantity). With a mixer, use a bowl with the smallest diameter into which the beaters can fit. Have the oil and eggs at room temperature (but not too hot or the mixture will not thicken – in summer, chill the oil for an hour before use). Beat the yolks until creamy, then beat in the seasonings and a teasp of the lemon juice. Now start adding the oil. I find that the best method with an electric mixer, blender or food processor, is to dribble it down the side of the bowl so that it can be absorbed gradually. With a hand mixer it is a little more tedious, adding it drop by drop, but as soon as the sauce 'takes' – that is, thickens to the consistency of double (heavy) cream, the oil can be added in a steady stream, thinning the mixture down in between with the remaining lemon juice and the vinegar. Finally, whisk in the boiling water.

Store in a screw-top jar in the bottom of the refrigerator.

334

Whole Egg Mayonnaise

This can only be made with a blender or food processor. The mayonnaise is not quite as thick as the traditional mayonnaise but it is very satisfactory, particularly for using as the basis of one of the mayonnaise sauces (see below).

Do not freeze

1 egg (or two yolks)	1 level teasp sugar
2 level teasp dry mustard	Pinch each of cayenne and black
8 fl oz (225ml/1 cup) corn oil	pepper
2 oz (50ml/¼ cup) mild olive oil	1 level teasp salt
1 tbsp lemon juice	2 teasp boiling water

Put the whole egg or the yolks into the blender or food processor, add the salt, black pepper, sugar, mustard and cayenne pepper, and blend or process at high speed for 30 seconds. Add the lemon juice and blend for 10 seconds. Add the corn oil very slowly, trickling it in with the blender or processor at high speed. When all is in and the mayonnaise has thickened, add the olive oil and blend or process until it has been absorbed. Finally, add the boiling water to thin the mayonnaise to the consistency of thick cream.

Store in the bottom of the refrigerator in a screw-top jar or plastic container.

VARIATION

Green Herb Mayonnaise: To the egg and seasonings, add 1 tbsp each of roughly cut chives and sprigs of parsley, together with 1 small peeled clove of garlic. Proceed as for whole egg mayonnaise. The sauce will be a beautiful pale green, and is delicious with salmon and other hot or cold poached fish.

Mayonnaise Sauces

All these sauces are a blend of mayonnaise and extra flavourings.

Green Goddess Dressing

This makes a delicious dip for fish goujons or crudités. It also makes an excellent dressing for a fish salad, or to serve on hearts of lettuce.

Serves 6-8

½ pint (275ml/1¼ cups)
  mayonnaise
8 anchovy fillets, finely chopped
1 tbsp each of chopped spring
  onions (scallions) and chives

2 tbsp chopped parsley
A pinch each of salt and dry
  mustard
2 tbsp each of lemon juice and
  single (light) or soured cream

Blend all the flavourings into the mayonnaise and leave for several hours.

Mustard Mayonnaise

A Danish recipe that is excellent as a dip, or with grilled or fried fish.

Serves 6-8

½ pint (275ml/1¼ cups)
  mayonnaise
2 teasp Dijon or Bordeaux
  mustard

1 tbsp finely chopped spring onion
  (scallion)
2 teasp finely chopped parsley
Few drops of lemon juice

Blend all the flavourings into the mayonnaise and leave for several hours.

Sauce Tartare

This is a delicious variation on the classic recipe. It is excellent with grilled fish, or with poached or fried fish. It will keep for two weeks under refrigeration. Vary the fresh herbs according to what you have available.

Serves 10-12

½ pint (275ml/1¼ cups) mild
  mayonnaise
Approx 1 tbsp each lemon juice
  and single (light) cream or
  soured cream
1 small pickled cucumber (about 2
  inches/5cm), finely chopped

2 teasp each chives, tarragon and
  parsley, spring onion (scallion)
  bulb (or onion)
8 drops Tabasco sauce or a pinch
  of cayenne pepper
6 chopped stuffed olives
  (optional)

Mix all the ingredients together. Taste for sharpness. Refrigerate for several hours to allow flavours to blend.

Desserts

Dessert is derived from the French phrase meaning 'to clear the table', a tradition still followed in classic restaurants where the debris from the preceding courses – cutlery, salt, pepper, bread and crumbs – are removed before the sweet course is served. Dessert originally meant fresh fruit only, but nowadays it encompasses in addition an enormous range of hot, cold and frozen puddings, some making the final grand gesture to an elaborate dinner, others – often much more in the modern mood – offering a refreshing end to a simple hearty meal.

Almost all the recipes in this chapter contain fruit in some form, as I think it should always be an integral part of a true dessert.

Presenting Fresh Fruit

The traditional end to a classic meal is cheese followed by a bowl of fresh fruit. The following ideas are for presenting this fruit, albeit in a more dramatic guise.

Cherries on Ice

Divide dessert cherries in tiny bunches and wash in cold water. Half fill a large glass bowl or several small sundae glasses with broken cubes of ice and freeze. Just before the meal, fill up the bowl(s) with the bunches of fruit and refrigerate until required – very refreshing after a hot pudding or a tart.

The Melon

This most versatile fruit is equally at home beginning or ending a meal. The best varieties for the dessert are the cantaloup type

337

which includes Charentais, Ogen and Galia. As these are usually expensive, they can be served as part of a mixed platter of more mundane fruits such as orange and apple sections, banana slivers, pear halves and small bunches of seedless grapes.

Peel the melon, slice it thinly and sprinkle very lightly with caster (superfine) sugar and lemon juice. Chill for 1 hour before arranging with the other fruits. In mid-summer, water melon can be treated in exactly the same way, though it should be iced for longer (at least two hours), and is probably better served by itself.

Melon with Morello (Sour Red) Cherry Sauce

This is a delightful way of presenting melon halves.

Serves 6-8

3-4 Ogen or Galia melons, halved and pips removed, *or* 1 large melon, peeled and cut in circles.

Sauce:

1 can morello (sour red) cherries in syrup	(cornstarch)
	2 strips orange peel
1 tbsp caster (superfine) sugar	Juice of ½ lemon
2 level teasp cornflour	2 tbsp cherry brandy (optional)

Drain the cherries, reserving the syrup. If you have the patience, stone them. Mix the sugar and cornflour (cornstarch), then stir in the cherry syrup and strips of orange peel. Bring to the boil and simmer for 3 minutes, then remove from the heat and stir in the cherries, lemon juice and cherry brandy (if used). Chill, preferably overnight.

To serve on the half shell: Arrange melon halves on individual serving dishes, add 2 or 3 spoons of sauce. Garnish with a sprig of mint.

To serve in slices: Cut the melon in half, then cut each half in circles about ½ inch (1.25cm) thick. Carefully remove peel, then arrange each circle on individual plates and spoon the cherry sauce in the centre. Serve cold but not iced.

See also melon recipes in 'Starters' chapter.

Venetian Oranges

This is my family's traditional dessert after a turkey dinner, as it is so refreshing.

Serves any number

For each serving:
1 very large juicy orange (chilled)
Grenadine (pomegranate-
   flavoured syrup) or any other
   fruit syrup

Caster (superfine) sugar
Kirsch or any fruit brandy such as
   'marc de poires'; *or* lemon juice

Take each orange in turn and cut a thin slice off the base so that it will sit evenly on a platter. Cut a lid off the orange about two-thirds of the way up, where the fruit begins to narrow. Prepare the fruit itself as if it were a grapefruit, loosening the segments and removing the core with a special grapefruit knife. Fill the core cavity with caster (superfine) sugar and saturate it with the fruit syrup. Sprinkle the surface of the orange pulp with the lemon juice, kirsch or fruit brandy. Replace the lid and leave at room temperature for at least an hour.

The sugar will draw out the natural juices of the fruit.

Serve with a grapefruit spoon.

Whole Peaches in Wine

This is most refreshing on a hot summer's evening, as one eats the peach and drinks the wine.

Serves 6-8

6-8 fine ripe peaches
6-8 wide-mouthed glasses

1 bottle German or similar
   medium-dry white wine

Chill the peaches, wine and glasses for several hours. Half an hour before the meal, prick each peach all over with a fork and place in a chilled glass. Cover with the chilled wine and replace in the refrigerator until required (the peach skin will soften in the meantime).

Serve with teaspoons. The guests alternately sip the wine and eat the peaches, which will have absorbed much of its flavour.

Peaches in Cider: Use a medium-dry cider instead of the wine.

Pineapple Wedges

A simple but very attractive presentation of choice fresh pineapple, very refreshing after a rich meal.

Serves 6-8

1 large ripe pineapple	A few black grapes
1-2 tbsp each caster (superfine) sugar and lemon juice	6-8 glacé (candied) cherries
1 large juicy orange	Kirsch, Cointreau or Amaretto liqueur (optional)

With a large sharp knife cut the pineapple in half lengthwise including the tuft, then divide each half into three or four wedges according to the size of the fruit (each wedge should be about 1½ inches (4cm) wide). Carefully remove the core, then cut the flesh free from the skin and then cut it downwards into ¾ inch (2cm) bite-size pieces, but leave in place on the skin. Arrange on a serving dish. Lightly dust each wedge with caster (superfine) sugar and then sprinkle with the lemon juice – this helps to bring out the natural juices of the fruit. Chill for 1 hour in the refrigerator (no more or the flavour is deadened). Just before serving, divide the orange in 6-8 sections, spear on cocktail sticks and top with a grape and a glacé cherry. Use to decorate each wedge.

Pass the chosen liqueur for each guest to sprinkle on the fruit.

VARIATION

Pineapple and Orange Pyramid: Cut the pineapple into ½ inch (1.25cm) slices. Carefully remove the skin with a small serrated knife and the centre core with a small biscuit cutter. Arrange on a serving platter. Top each slice of pineapple with 3 or 4 thin slices of peeled orange, sprinkle with caster (superfine) sugar and lemon juice, and decorate as before.

Strawberries

Strawberries should be washed only if necessary – some are now grown enclosed in polythene for their entire life cycle so that they never come into contact with either atmospheric pollution or the oil. Their flavour is more intense if they are only lightly chilled (from the beginning of the meal until dessert). They can be served in any of the following ways.

2 lb (1kg) fully ripe small whole, or halved larger berries

English fashion: Arrange in individual dishes, dust with caster (superfine) sugar and mask with pouring cream.

Italian fashion: Arrange in a shallow dish. Chill for half an hour. At the table, pour over the juice of 2 oranges (for slightly tart fruit) or of two lemons (for sweet fruit). Dust with caster (superfine) sugar and serve plain or with pouring cream.

Israeli fashion: Halve the fruit and put in a heatproof dish. Dissolve 5 oz (150g/²⁄₃ cup) sugar in 5 fl oz (150ml/²⁄₃ cup) water and boil for 2 minutes. Add the juice of a lemon or lime, bring back to the boil then pour over the fruit. Chill thoroughly. Serve plain or with ice-cream.

Turkish fashion: Arrange in individual dishes. Dust with icing (confectioners') sugar, sprinkle with lemon juice, scatter with pistachio nuts and serve with whipped cream flavoured with rosewater.

Fresh Fruit Salads and Compotes

A fresh fruit salad is generally made with uncooked fruit, whilst a compote is made with fruit cooked in a syrup, but the dividing line is so nebulous that I have decided not to make any distinction between them. What is indisputable, however, is that they are one of the most refreshing desserts, as the sweetness of the fruit and syrup is counterbalanced by the tartness of the lemon or lime juice or wine. All fruits in syrup improve immeasurably if left for several hours, preferably overnight. This allows an exchange of flavours to take place between the fruit and the liquid in which it is macerating.

For compotes of cooked fruit it is useful to have a wide-lidded frying pan which allows the fruit to cook in one layer without fear of crushing or breaking. An attractive enamelled pan of this nature can also be used as a serving dish as well as for storage purposes afterwards.

Freezing: Fruit salads and compotes (with the exception of those containing bananas and strawberries) can be frozen, although (with the exception of cooked apples) there is bound to be some deterioration in texture. Freeze the mixture in a rigid polythene container, then slip it into a plastic bag and store for up to one year. Thaw overnight in the refrigerator, then add liqueur and extra fruits if desired. Refrigerate for storage for up to 48 hours. After that time the fruit tends to become soggy.

Use of canned syrup: This can be used instead of the sugar and water recommended in the recipe. Light syrups may need reinforcing with extra sugar.

Without sugar: If you do not want to use a sugar syrup for a fruit salad, either use liquid sweetener to taste in direct replacement, or sprinkle the cut-up fruits with the juice of ½ lemon and a small orange, and leave at room temperature for 1 hour or until the fruit has produced its own juice. Then refrigerate until required. The flavour will not, however, be so deep, but some people prefer it.

Winter Apple Compote

With the judicious use of fruit juice and spice, ordinary 'stewed' apples are transformed into a very special dessert.

Serves 6-8 **F** 1 year

5 large baking apples (2-2½ lb/1-1.25kg) peeled, cored and cut into 1 inch (2.5cm) slices
2-2½ oz (50-60g/½-⅔ cup) each white and brown sugar
¼ pint (150ml/⅔ cup) water
1 rounded tbsp apricot jam
1 cinnamon stick
1 teasp each grated orange and lemon rind
2 teasp lemon juice
3 fl oz (75ml/⅓ cup) orange juice

Put the sugar and the water in a wide (9-10 inch/22-25cm) pan. Add the jam, rinds and cinnamon stick. Heat gently until the sugar dissolves then boil until a syrup is formed (about 3 minutes). Add the apples in one layer, baste with the syrup, cover and cook very gently (basting once) until barely tender when pierced with a fork (about 10 minutes). Take off the heat, add the lemon and orange juices, re-cover and leave for half an hour at room temperature. Refrigerate, preferably for several hours.

Serve plain or with pouring cream, ice-cream or custard.

Fresh Apricot Fruit Salad

Unless you can pick your own sun-ripened apricots from the tree, it is best to cook them to bring out their exquisite flavour. The compote can then be used as the basis for a most delicious fruit salad.

Serves 6-8 F 1 year (without banana or liqueur)

$1^1/2$ lb (675g) fresh apricots
5 oz (150g/$^2/3$ cup) sugar
$^1/2$ pint (275ml/$1^1/4$ cups) water
Juice of $^1/2$ lemon

3 slices fresh pineapple, cut in
  bite-size pieces
3 large ripe bananas
2 tbsp apricot brandy or other
  fruit liqueur (optional)

If the apricots are large, halve (but put stones in pan for flavour). Otherwise leave whole. In a wide, shallow, lidded pan dissolve the sugar in the water over gentle heat, then bring to the boil and bubble until syrupy (about 5 minutes). Put in the apricots in one layer. Cover and simmer *very* gently until fork tender (about 15 minutes). Take off the heat, add the lemon juice and pineapple and allow to go cold. One hour before serving add the peeled and sliced bananas and the liqueur.

Bananas in White Wine

A light but satisfying sweet.

Serves 6-8 Do not freeze

6-8 stubby green-tipped bananas
$^1/4$ pint (150ml/$^2/3$ cup) each
  medium-dry white wine and
  fresh orange juice
Grated rind of $^1/2$ lemon

2 oz (50g/$^1/4$ cup) caster
  (superfine) sugar
Toasted coconut or slivered
  almonds

Peel the bananas and cut in half lengthwise.
  Put the wine, juice, rind and sugar into a wide-bottomed pan and

343

bring slowly to the boil stirring until the sugar has dissolved. Add the halved bananas in one layer, cover and simmer until tender, turning once (about 6 minutes).

Lift out the bananas and arrange in a serving, dish about 1 inch (2.5cm) deep or, if preferred, in a soufflé dish. Simmer the juices until slightly thickened (another 3-4 minutes), then pour over the bananas. Chill, preferably overnight.

Just before serving sprinkle with the toasted nuts.

Fresh Berry Fruit Salad

This is the best way to use the first expensive berries of the season.

Serves 6-8 Do not freeze

$^{1}/_{2}$-1 lb (225-450g) strawberries, raspberries or loganberries (or frozen fruit)

3 large oranges, peeled and sectioned

4 bananas, sliced

1-2 slices fresh pineapple *or* 4 slices canned in juice

Syrup:

$^{1}/_{4}$ pint (150ml/$^{2}/_{3}$ cup) water or juice from canned pineapple

5 oz (150g/$^{2}/_{3}$ cup) sugar

Juice of a large lemon or lime

2 tbsp Cointreau or Grand Marnier (optional)

Bring the sugar and water to the boil and simmer for 2 minutes until as thick as canned fruit syrup. Pour the hot syrup over the halved or whole berries in a heatproof dish, then add the lemon juice and the liqueur. When quite cold add the oranges and pineapple. Slice and add the bananas just before serving, well chilled.

Cherry Wine Compote

This started off as a cherry soup recipe, but by reducing the liquid a little it ended up as a really delicious cold compote, very suitable for serving after a grill or roast.

Serves 6-8

8 fl oz (225ml/1 cup) medium-dry red wine

3 strips orange peel

Stick of cinnamon or pinch of ground cinnamon

2 × 15 oz (425g) cans morello (sour red) or other tart cherries

1/2 pint (275ml/1 1/4 cups) water

2 tbsp cornflour (cornstarch)

Pouring cream

Put the wine, orange peel and cinnamon stick into a small saucepan and simmer gently for 5 minutes to extract the flavour and concentrate the wine. Remove the rind and stick. From the measured water, use a little to mix with the cornflour (cornstarch) until it is a smooth paste, then stir in the remainder.

Add to the pan together with the liquid from the can of cherries. Bring to the boil, simmer 2 minutes, add the cherries, then chill.

Serve plain or with pouring cream.

Note: With fresh or frozen morello cherries, use 2 lb (1kg), remove pips, and put in pan with any juice that comes out: there should be 4 fl oz (125ml/1/2 cup). If not, add a little water or syrup from other stewed fruit. Add 8 oz (225g/1 cup) sugar and simmer until tender, then use as canned.

Melon Celebration Cup

This is a light refreshing dessert with a wonderful musky melon flavour.

Serves 6-8 F 1 year (without strawberries and bananas)

3-4 medium Ogen or Galia melons

2 large, juicy oranges

3 oz (75g/1/3 cup) caster (superfine) sugar

Juice of 1 lemon

2 large bananas, sliced

1 can pineapple, drained and cut in bite-sized pieces (or 1 small fresh pineapple, diced)

1/4-1/2 lb (125-225g) fresh strawberries, sliced

Mint leaves

Liqueur, e.g. Cointreau (optional)

Cut the melon in half by vandyking with zig-zag cuts, and scoop out the fruit using a melon-ball cutter. Put into a bowl. Add all the remaining fruit, except the strawberries and bananas. Sprinkle with 3 oz (75g/1/3 cup) caster (superfine) sugar and the juice of a lemon. Leave for 2 hours until a syrup has formed. Refill the melon halves. Chill thoroughly (about 2 hours). Just before serving, stir

in the bananas and decorate with the strawberries and mint leaves.
To gild the lily a little liqueur such as Cointreau can be sprinkled
on each serving.

Marinated Melon Balls

*As melons contain a very high proportion of water, it is essential
to boil the syrup until it looks like glue before pouring it over the
fruit – otherwise it becomes too dilute and loses its flavour.*

Serves 6-8 F 1 year

For each 2 lb (1kg) melon balls (1 large or 2 medium Ogen or Galia
melons) make the following syrup:

¹/₄ pint (150ml/²/₃ cup) water	Juice of 1 lemon or large lime
5 oz (150g/²/₃ cup) sugar	2 tbsp Cointreau

Cut the melons in half, discard the seeds, and use a melon-ball
cutter to scoop out the flesh. For flesh near the skin which cannot
be cut into balls, simply remove and put in the bottom of a serving
bowl with the balls on top.

Put the sugar and water into a pan and boil until gluey (thicker
than canned syrup), then dilute with the lemon or lime juice and
the liqueur. Pour over the melon balls and leave for 1 hour at room
temperature. A great deal of liquid will come out of the melon to
dilute the syrup. Chill thoroughly. Before serving, taste and add
more lemon juice if necessary.

Quantities for 12-16:

2 large or 4 medium melons (about 4 lb/1.75kg)	(275g/1¹/₄ cups) sugar; 2 large lemons or limes; 4 tbsp
Syrup made from ¹/₂ pint (275ml/1¹/₄ cups) water; 10 oz	Cointreau

Nectarines in Apricot Sauce

*Nectarines have a very delicate flavour which is a cross between
that of a peach and an apricot.*

Serves 6-8

6-10 nectarines (depending on size, and on number of guests)
4 level tbsp apricot jam
1 teasp grated lemon and orange rind

3 level tbsp granulated sugar
8 fl oz (225ml/1 cup) water
2 tbsp apricot brandy or other liqueur (optional)
Juice of ½ lemon

Put the jam, rinds, sugar and water into a wide saucepan or lidded frying pan. Stir over gentle heat until the sugar dissolves, then cook gently for about 3 minutes or until the mixture looks syrupy. Whilst syrup cooks, skin nectarines by leaving in a pan of boiling water for 1 minute, then plunging into cold. Leave whole, or cut in halves as preferred (I like them whole). Drop skinned fruit into the syrup, cover and cook very gently until just tender (about 5 minutes). Test with a knife. Baste once or twice during this time. Take off the heat and leave covered until cool, then add the lemon juice and the liqueur (if used). Chill thoroughly before serving. Serve plain or with thick pouring cream.

VARIATION 1
Use 6-8 large peaches instead.

VARIATION 2
Peach, Berry and Pineapple Salad: Add ½ lb (225g) fresh or frozen loganberries or raspberries and one small tin of drained pineapple chunks.

Caramel Oranges Italian Style

This is the way they are served in an Italian restaurant. They look most dramatic when left whole, but for a larger number or to serve as an accompaniment, the oranges can be cut across in circles and piled on top of each other, and then covered with the caramel syrup.

To achieve the characteristic 'burnt sugar' flavour that makes this dish so distinctive, it is important to caramelize the sugar until it is a mahogany brown, then immediately cool the pan to prevent further browning. Any left over syrup makes a superb basis of another fruit salad – it will keep for weeks under refrigeration.

Serves 6-8 F 3 months.

6-8 large seedless oranges	2 tbsp lemon juice
¼ pint (150ml/⅔ cup) water	2 tbsp orange liqueur – Grand
10 oz (275g/1¼ cups) sugar	Marnier, Cointreau, Curaçao,
½ pint (275ml/1¼ cups) water	Aurum
(added ¼ pint (150ml/⅔ cup) at	
a time)	

Remove the pith from only 2 oranges, then cut into strips the width of a matchstick (total weight should be about 1 oz (25g)). Remove pith and peel from all the oranges by cutting like an apple, round and round using a serrated knife. Make sure all the pith is removed. Cut each orange across into 6 slices. Then re-form orange and put together (with a toothpick if necessary to hold in position). If not to be served whole, arrange slices in a glass serving dish. Put strips of peel into a small pan, cover with cold water and bring to the boil. Drain well, discarding the water (this removes the bitter ness of the peel).

Put the sugar and ¼ pint (150ml) of the measured water in a small thick pan and heat gently until the sugar is dissolved. Add the strips of peel and cook at the bubble for 10 minutes, then lift out with a slotted spoon and lay on a plate. Boil the syrup in the pan until it is the characteristic rich caramel brown colour, then immediately take off the heat. Cover your arm with a cloth (in case of spattering), then add the second ¼ pint (150ml/⅔ cup) water. Return to gentle heat and stir until the caramel is quite dissolved. Add the lemon juice and liqueur and pour gently over the oranges. Top with little bundles of the peel. Chill several hours.

Orange and Chestnut Salad

This is for the chestnut lover. The nuts become almost candied during the cooking period. (Fresh chestnuts can, of course, be used; if so, use 1 lb (450g), nick, bring to the boil from cold, then remove both skins. Use 1¼ pints of water (725ml/3⅓ cups) to the same amount of sugar as given below, but simmer for one hour instead of 15 minutes.)

Serves 6-8 F 3 months

1 × 9¾ oz (260g) can peeled	(extract) *or* 1 inch (2.5cm)
chestnuts	length of vanilla bean
½ pint (250ml/1¼ cups) water	Juice of a large lemon
5 oz (125g/⅔ cup) granulated	6 very large, thin-skinned juicy
sugar	oranges
Few drops vanilla essence	

Bring the water and sugar to the boil with the vanilla flavouring, then simmer gently for 5 minutes. Add the peeled chestnuts, then simmer very gently with the lid only partly on for 15 minutes until the syrup is very thick and the chestnuts look translucent. Take off the heat and add the lemon juice. Peel the oranges as though they were apples, then cut between the segments so that you have skin and pith free segments. Stir these gently into the chestnut compote together with any juice you can squeeze out of the orange 'skeleton'. Cover and chill, preferably overnight.

Spiced Pears in Cider with Cinnamon Cream (optional)

Make the dish the day before to allow the pears to soak up the flavour. They turn a beautiful gold in colour.

Serves 6-8 Do not freeze

1 pint (575ml/2$^{1}/_{2}$ cups) sweet cider
3 oz (75g/$^{1}/_{3}$ cup) caster (superfine) sugar
1 level tbsp soft dark brown sugar
Juice of a small lemon

$^{1}/_{4}$ teasp cinnamon and 3 cloves (or 1 cinnamon stick)
6-8 medium size hard pears (such as Conference), peeled and left whole with stalk
$^{1}/_{4}$ pint (150ml/$^{2}/_{3}$ cup) double (heavy) cream (whipped)

Put the cider into a pan. Add the sugar and spices with half the lemon juice, bring to the boil. Add the whole peeled pears, baste well, cover and simmer until tender but not mushy (about 15-30 minutes) – test by piercing with a sharp knife. Lift out and arrange pears, stalks up, in a dish. Bring the liquid to the boil again and simmer for 5 minutes until the flavour has intensified and the syrup has greatly reduced in volume. Add the remaining lemon juice. Pour over the pears. When cold, refrigerate overnight.

Serve with whipped cream flavoured with 2 teasp caster (superfine) sugar and a pinch of cinnamon. Pile the cream in a sauceboat and scatter lightly with cinnamon. Serve chilled.

Pears Poached in Brown Sugar

This is a simple dessert which brings out the flavour of the pears without obscuring it.

Serves 6-8 Do not freeze

6-8 Conference pears, peeled, halved and cored	¹/₄ pint (150ml/²/₃ cup) water
5 oz (150g/²/₃ cup) demerara or soft light brown sugar	Stick of cinnamon or pinch of powdered cinnamon
	Juice of ¹/₂ lemon

Put the sugar, water and cinnamon into a lidded frying pan. Heat gently until the sugar dissolves, then add the pears in one layer. Baste with the syrup, bring to the boil, then reduce heat to simmer. Cover and simmer for 15 minutes or until the pears feel tender when pierced with a small knife. Baste once or twice during the cooking time. Take off the heat, add the lemon juice. Chill for several hours.

This dish is particularly nice with pouring cream or ice-cream.

VARIATION
Substitute canned pears as follows:

1 lb 13 oz (825g) can Bartlett pears	stick of cinnamon
1 oz (25g/2 tbsp) dark brown sugar	Juice of ¹/₂ lemon
¹/₄ teasp powdered cinnamon or	

Drain the pears, reserving syrup, and put into a heatproof serving dish. Put the pear syrup together with the brown sugar and the cinnamon into a pan and bring to the boil. Simmer for 3 minutes, then add the lemon juice and pour over the pears. Cover and leave at room temperature for 1 hour, then refrigerate until required.

Fresh Pineapple Compote

This is a delightful refreshing way to serve choice fresh pineapple.

Serves 6-8

6-8 slices fresh pineapple	Juice of ¹/₂ lemon
4 fl oz (125ml/¹/₂ cup) water	2 level teasp cornflour (cornstarch)
3 oz (75g/¹/₃ cup) sugar	2 tbsp Cointreau or kirsch
Juice of 1 small orange (3 oz/75ml/¹/₃ cup)	

Slice pineapple ³/₄ inch (2cm) thick, remove the skin and core. Leave in slices or cut in wedges ¹/₂ inch (1.25cm) wide as preferred. Heat the water and the sugar until dissolved, then add the orange juice. Mix the cornflour (cornstarch) to a cream with the lemon juice and add to the hot fruit juice. Bring to the boil, simmer for 2 minutes then take off the heat and stir in the Cointreau or kirsch. Pour over the rings or mix with the sections. Allow to go quite cold. Serve with ice-cream or whipped cream.

VARIATION 1

Cut a large pineapple lengthwise through the flesh and leaves. Scoop out the flesh, remove the core, then cut the flesh in pieces. Fill the hollow with the cold compote. This can also be done with small pineapples using one half per serving.

VARIATION 2
Peach, Lychee and Pineapple Salad

1 recipe **Fresh Pineapple Compote** (using only ½ a large pineapple)

1 small tin sliced peaches in syrup
1 can lychees

Use peach syrup instead of sugar and water to make compote. When quite cold, add drained peaches and lychees, saving lychee syrup for other use (e.g. jelly).

Fruit Creams and Syllabubs

All the recipes in this section are very rich as they consist largely of fruit-flavoured cream. Serve them well chilled and in small portions.

I do not advise freezing them as they tend to lose their fluffiness when defrosted.

Avocado and Lime Syllabub
This has a most tantalizing flavour and a beautiful pale green colour.

Serves 6-8 Do not freeze

2 medium avocados
2 tbsp lemon juice
1 teasp lemon rind
8 fl oz (225ml/1 cup) double (heavy) cream

6 tbsp lime cordial
3 level tbsp icing (confectioners') sugar
For garnish: Pistachios or toasted almond nibs

Purée the peeled and stoned avocados with lemon juice and rind, using a blender or food processor. Put the cream, sugar and lime cordial into a bowl, whip until thick, then fold into the purée. Chill. Top with pistachios or toasted almond nibs.

For 4-6 use:

1 medium avocado	5 fl oz (150ml/²/₃ cup) double
4 tbsp lime cordial	(heavy) cream
1 tbsp lemon juice	2 tbsp icing (confectioners') sugar
1 teasp rind	

VARIATION
Use *fresh* lime juice and 1 extra tbsp icing (confectioners') sugar or to taste.

Strawberry Cloud of Sharon

This is a beautiful sweet to serve garnished with the first strawberries. It can be served in a trifle bowl but it is prettiest in tall flutes (glasses).

Serves 6-8 Do not freeze

Juice of 2 medium oranges and 2 lemons (8fl oz/225ml/1 cup juice altogether)	¹/₂ pint (275 ml/1¹/₄ cups) whipping or double (heavy) cream
Rind of 1 orange and 1 lemon	1¹/₂ oz (40g/¹/₃ cup) caster (superfine) sugar
2 tbsp Cointreau or sherry	¹/₂ lb (225g) strawberries
4 trifle sponges	

Combine the juices, rind and liqueur or sherry. Cut the sponges into ¹/₂ inch (1.25cm) cubes and arrange at the bottom of a trifle bowl of individual glasses. Pour over half the fruit juice mixture. Put the remaining liquid into a bowl, stir in the sugar and then the cream. Beat with a rotary whisk until the mixture stands in soft peaks. Slice the strawberries (reserving a few whole ones for decoration) and stir gently into the cream. Spoon the cream on top of the sponge and chill for at least 3 hours.

VARIATION
Raspberry, Banana or Mandarin Cloud: In place of the strawberries use ¹/₂ lb (225g) fresh or frozen raspberries, or 3 sliced bananas or 1 drained can of mandarin oranges.

Red Berry Syllabub

A little fresh or frozen fruit is marinated in a syrup which is then beaten into the cream. It is a beautiful pink in colour.

Serves 6-8 Do not freeze

$^1/_2$ lb (225g) fresh or frozen
  loganberries, raspberries or
  sliced strawberries (reserve 6-8
  berries for garnish)
Juice and grated rind of 1 lemon
4 tbsp water
2 level tbsp sugar

$^1/_2$ pint (275ml/1$^1/_4$ cups) whipping
  or double (heavy) cream
2 tbsp Crème de Framboises
  (raspberry brandy) or
  orange-flavoured liqueur
  (optional)

Put the juice and rind of the lemon, the water and sugar into a small pan and bring to the boil. Immediately pour over the fruit and leave for 1 hour.

Drain the syrup into a bowl and add the liqueur (if used) and the cream. Whisk until as thick as whipped cream. Fold in the fruit. Spoon into wine glasses. Chill thoroughly. Serve each with a sponge finger.

Strawberries in Orange Cream

In this simpler presentation, there is a higher proportion of fruit to cream.

Serves 6-8 Do not freeze

1 lb (450g) strawberries
3 large bananas
2 level tbsp caster (superfine)
  sugar

Juice of a whole medium orange
  and half a lemon
10 fl oz (275ml/1$^1/_4$ cups) whipping
  cream and 4 tbsp creamy milk

Slice the fruit into a bowl and scatter with the sugar, then pour over the fruit juices. Leave for one hour, then carefully drain off and reserve the syrup which will have formed. Put the cream into a bowl with 4 tbsp of creamy milk. Whip until it begins to thicken, then gradually beat in the fruit syrup until the mixture is thick and fluffy. Carefully stir into the fruit, then put into individual glasses or a soufflé dish.

Chill thoroughly for several hours.

Instant Lemon Syllabub

In five minutes a packet of commercial lemon mousse can be transformed into a delectable syllabub for 5-6.

Serves 5-6·Do not freeze

1 × approx 11 fl oz (313ml) frozen lemon mousse
1 tbsp lemon juice and 1 teasp of rind
2 tbsp orange liqueur (Aurum, Cointreau, Curaçao)

2 teasp icing (confectioners') sugar (optional if dry liqueur is used)
4-5 fl oz (125-150ml/$^{1}/_{2}$-$^{2}/_{3}$ cup) double (heavy) cream

For garnish:

$^{1}/_{2}$ lb (225g) sugared soft fruit *or*
1 can drained mandarin oranges *or*

2 oranges, sectioned

Defrost the mousse for 1 hour at room temperature. Put the cream, juice, rind, liqueur and sugar (if used) into a bowl and whisk until thick. Spoon onto the mousse then whisk together until smooth and creamy. Either fold the fruit through the mixture or use as a topping.

Divide between 5-6 wine glasses or individual soufflé glasses. Chill well before serving.

Fruit and Cream Gâteaux

All these cakes consist of layers of delicate fatless sponge, sandwiched with fruit and some kind of cream.

The sponge
Excellent commercial sponges are now available which have been specially formulated for this kind of presentation. However, they are expensive in relation to the ingredients they contain (though not, of course, to the labour saved). If you prefer to make your own, I give an excellent recipe which is quick and easy to prepare. It is also possible to make very acceptable sponges with a good quality sponge mix. A $^{1}/_{2}$ lb (225g) sponge mix will make one deep 9-10 inch (22.5-25cm) sponge.

Freezing

Cream gâteaux freeze extremely well which makes them an excellent choice for a large party. Add berry garnish just before serving.

Open freeze on a plate. When quite firm, wrap in film or foil. Remove wrappings then defrost in the refrigerator, allowing not less than 4 hours.

Note: It is easier to section the cakes when half frozen – this prevents the filling squeezing out at the sides.

If a plain sponge has to be split into two or three layers, do this when the cake has thawed just enough to allow a bread knife to be inserted. This makes for much more even slicing.

Storage time:
6 months plain cakes
3 months cream gâteaux

Do *not* refreeze cream cakes

Basic Dessert Sponge

This mixture makes 1 × 9-10 inch (22.5-25cm) deep layer for splitting into 3
　or 1 × 12 inch (30cm) shallow layer for topping with fruit
　or 1 × approx 15 × 10 inches (40 × 25cm) Swiss roll
　or 2 dozen little cakes for rum baba

F 6 months

3 large eggs	1/2 teasp vanilla essence (extract)
3 tbsp water	2 oz (50g/1/2 cup) self-raising flour
5 oz (150g/2/3 cup) caster (superfine) sugar	2 oz (50g/1/2 cup) cornflour (cornstarch)

Put the whites and water in a large bowl and whisk until stiff and fluffy, add the sugar a tablespoon at a time, whisking until stiff again after each addition. Stir in the vanilla and the yolks, then fold in the sifted flour and cornflour (cornstarch).

Have ready a 9-10 inch (22.5-25cm) loose-bottomed cake tin about 3 inches (7.5cm) deep; a 12 inch (30cm) shallow sponge or springform tin; or a 15 × 10 inch (40 × 25cm) Swiss roll tin greased and lined with greaseproof paper, or 2 dozen paper cases set in deep patty tins.

Bake as follows:

9-10 inch (22.5cm) tin: Gas No. 4, 350°F, 180°C; 35-40 minutes
12 inch (30cm) tin: Gas No. 4, 350°F, 180°C; 20-25 minutes
Swiss roll tin: Gas No. 5, 375°F, 190°C; 15 minutes
Small cakes: Gas No. 5, 375°F, 190°C; 20 minutes
In each case, the cake should be shrinking slightly from the sides
of the tin and should feel springy to gentle touch.

To use: The 9-10 inch (22.5-25cm) cake can be split and filled with
fruit and cream (see individual recipes).

The 12 inch (30cm) cake can be soaked in liqueur-flavoured syrup,
topped with fruit and glazed (see **Sponge Flan for a Party**,
p.478).

The Swiss roll can be trimmed to remove any crisp crust, then
rolled immediately in greaseproof paper. When cold, unroll and fill
with sliced berries and whipped cream, then dust with icing
(confectioners') sugar roll up again, and serve with ice-cream.

The little cakes can be served plain with fruit salad or syllabub,
or made into rum baba as follows:

Rum Baba

Soak the little cakes in rum syrup (see below) then glaze with warm
apricot jam and top with cream:

The syrup:

6 oz (175g/³/₄ cup) granulated sugar	8 fl oz (225ml/1 cup) water
	5 tbsp kirsch, rum or Curaçao

Simmer the sugar and water for 5 minutes then stir in the rum or
liqueur. If you want it less heady, increase the water to ¹/₂ pint
(275ml/1¹/₄ cups) and add only 2 tbsp of the spirit. Soak each cake
with the spirit, glaze with warm apricot jam (use a pastry brush),
then decorate with whipped cream.

Note: Any of the sponges can be defrosted at room temperature
in 30 minutes.

Carmel Cloud Gâteau

This is equally good with dairy or non-dairy cream. It looks superb on a buffet table.

Serves 12-15 **F** 3 months

3×9-10 inch (22.5-30cm) thin sponge layers, bought or made from one **Basic Dessert Sponge** (see p.355) split in 3 (do this when semi-frozen)

Filling:

Juice of 3 medium oranges and 2 lemons, and 3 tbsp Cointreau (optional) (12 fl oz/350ml/1½ cups liquid altogether)
Rind of 2 oranges and 1 lemon

2 oz (50g/¼ cup) caster (superfine) sugar
1 pt (575ml/2½ cups) whipping cream

To garnish:

½-¾ lb (225-450g) strawberries
Grated chocolate

Grate the peels into the juices and mix with the liqueur (if used). If possible leave for 1 hour. Use half this mixture to moisten each sponge cake. Put the remaining liquid and the cream into a bowl with the sugar, stir well then whisk until it stands in firm peaks. Put the first layer of cake onto a dish and spread with one-third of the cream mixture, put the next layer of cake on top and spread with the second third of the cream. Finally put the top layer in place and pipe with the remaining cream. Sliced strawberries can be spread on top of each layer of cream, or used to garnish the top. Sprinkle with grated chocolate. Chill well before serving.

Marron Gâteau

This is a delicious 'no bake' recipe made with a bought sponge. If you prefer to use your own, use the Super Sponge recipe (p.478) baked in an 8 inch (20cm) tin, or a sponge made from a mix.

Serves 6-8 **F** 3 months

1 × 8 inch (20cm) sponge cake, home-made or bought
1 × 8 oz (225g) can crème de marron (chestnut cream)
½ pint (275ml/1¼ cups) whipping cream
4 tbsp rum
½ oz (15g/1 tbsp) butter
Toasted almonds, or walnuts and glacé (candied) cherries for decoration

Stand the sponge layer on the serving plate and spoon 3 tbsp of the rum over it. Whip the cream, then take a tablespoon of it and add to the chestnut cream, together with the butter and the remaining tablespoon of rum. With a palette knife, spread the chestnut mixture on top of the sponge, then mask completely (including the sides) with the remaining cream, saving a little to pipe in a pattern if you feel ambitious. Decorate with the nuts or cherries. Chill for half a day before using. Serve in small portions as it is very rich.

Morello (Sour Red) Cherry Gâteau

A beautiful cake to look at and to eat. A chilled cheesecake mixture is sandwiched with a morello cherry filling between layers of light sponge.

Serves 8-10 F 3 months

1 × 9-10 inch (22.5-25cm) **Basic Dessert Sponge** (p.355) (This *must* be made in a tin with a loose base)
Icing (confectioners') sugar,

Make and bake the sponge as directed; turn out of the tin on to a cooling tray and allow to go quite cold. Split the cake in two horizontally. Whilst the cake is baking, make the cheesecake:

1 lb (450g/2 cups) cream cheese
1 lemon jelly (gelatin mix) dissolved in 3 tbsp 2 water *or* ½ oz (15g) powdered gelatine dissolved in 3 tbsp lemon juice
2 oz (50g/¼ cup) caster (superfine) sugar (plus an extra 1oz/25g/2 tbsp if lemon juice is used)
Grated rind of ½ lemon
5 fl oz (150ml/⅔ cup) soured cream

Dissolve the jelly in the water. If gelatine is used, mix with the lemon juice then stand in a bowl over kettle and heat until clear.

Put the cream cheese into a bowl, then stir in all the remaining ingredients. Put in the refrigerator to chill until the cake is ready to fill.

Cherry filling:

1 × 15 oz (425g) can morello (sour red) or other tart dessert cherries

1 level tbsp cornflour (cornstarch)
1-2 tbsp kirsch (optional)

Mix the juice from the cherries (made up with water if necessary to 8 fl oz/225ml/1 cup) with the cornflour (cornstarch). Bring to the boil and bubble for 3 minutes then stir in the kirsch (if used). Taste and add sugar if necessary. (If fresh fruit is used, allow 1 lb/450g (before stoning) stewed with 5 fl oz (150ml/^{2}/$_3$ cup) water sweetened to taste, and thickened as above.) Allow to go cold.

Wash the cake tin, then put the bottom layer of the sponge back into it, spoon the half-set cheese-cake mixture on top and cover with the cool morello cherries. Finally lay the top half of the cake lightly on the top. Put in the refrigerator and chill, preferably overnight.

To serve, pull down the sides of the tin and place the gâteau (still on the cake base) on a serving dish. Sprinkle thickly with icing (confectioners') sugar.

Persimmon Fruit Cream Gâteau

The persimmon fruit (the variety imported from Israel is known as 'Sharon fruit') should be kept until it feels as soft as a ripe plum. Carefully section, then peel off the tough skin and the fruit is ready to use to make this delectable gâteau.

Serves 8-10   **F** 3 months

1 × 9-10 inch (22.5-25cm) **Basic Dessert Sponge** (p.355) or one made from a sponge mix or 1 bought sponge of the same size

The filling:

2 Sharon fruit (persimmons)
1 banana
1 tbsp lemon juice
2 tbsp orange juice

1 tbsp caster (superfine) sugar
5 fl oz (150ml/^{2}/$_3$ cup) whipping cream
Icing (confectioners') sugar

Peel and slice the Sharon fruit (persimmons), then cover with the sugar. Add fruit juices. Leave for an hour, then drain off the juice and add it to the cream. Whisk together until thick. Fold in the fruit and sliced banana.

Slice the cake in half, fill with the cream mixture and replace the top. Sprinkle thickly with icing (confeectioners') sugar.

Refrigerate until required.

Quick Cherry/Chocolate Gâteau

This is excellent for large-scale community baking where the food is cheap and cheerful.

Serves 10-12 F 3 months

1 × 3 layer bought chocolate sponge (10-11 inches/25-27.5cm)
1 tin black cherry pie filling
10 fl oz (275ml/1¼ cups) whipping cream or non-dairy cream

2 level tbsp caster (superfine) sugar
1 level tbsp cocoa mixed with 2 tbsp milk or water
1 glass port
Grated chocolate

Spread one layer of sponge with a thin layer of cherry filling and cover with a layer of cream whipped with the cocoa and milk and sugar. Put the second layer of sponge on top and moisten well with the port. Cover with a thin layer of cherry and cream. Put top layer in place. Put a thick border of cream all around the edge and heap remaining cherry filling in the centre. Sprinkle grated chocolate over the cream and chill.

Sponge Flan for a Party

This is an excellent recipe to make when cooking for a crowd – it is particularly popular with teenagers.

Serves 12   F 3 months

For each flan use:

1 layer from a 3-layer bought 10 inch (25cm) sponge *or*
½ lb (225g) sponge mix baked in a 10 inch (25cm) tin *or*

1 **Basic Dessert Sponge** (p.355) baked in a shallow 12 inch (30cm) tin

1 tin (15oz/425g) pineapple rings
  or spears and 1 tin mandarins
  and 1 banana *or* 1½ lb (675g)

soft fruit in season
Few glacé cherries

Glaze:

8 oz (225ml/1 cup) syrup drained
  from the fruit
1 tbsp lemon juice

2 level teasp arrowroot or
  cornflour (cornstarch)

Although cornflour (cornstarch) is adequate for the glaze, arrow-root will give a clearer result.

Soaking syrup:

3 tbsp syrup drained from the
  fruit

1 tbsp liqueur or fruit brandy or
  grenadine

Mix the soaking syrup and spoon over the sponge layer arranged on its serving dish. Arrange the drained fruit in an attractive design – for example, in concentric circles.

Put the arrowroot or cornflour (cornstarch) into a small pan and gradually stir in the lemon juice and the syrup. Bring to the boil when the mixture should clear. Take off the heat and allow to cool (but not set), then spoon over the fruit or brush it over with a pastry brush to mask it completely. Allow to set for at least an hour. Serve plain or with whipped or thick pouring cream or ice-cream.

Jellied Desserts, Mousses and Cold Soufflés

All the desserts in this section consist of fruit and whipped cream, set with jelly (gelatin mix) or gelatine, with or without the addition of eggs. The aim is to use just enough 'gel' to hold these ingredients together and still have a finished texture that resembles fluffy whipped cream rather than quivery jelly. Where a recipe involves a combination of fruit purée, whipped cream and an egg-white meringue, a fluffier result will be obtained if each of the mixtures is of a similar texture. For this reason, the cream and meringue should never be beaten beyond the stage where they hold soft glossy peaks when the beater is withdrawn. Jelly (gelatin mix), regular or vegetarian gelatine, all give good results though gelatine rather than packeted jelly (gelatin mix) is better in more delicately-flavoured recipes, as there is no synthetic flavour in it. Both gelatine and jelly (gelatin mix) are most easily melted (with the liquid stated in the recipe) in the microwave at a low setting, or in a small basin, set in place of the lid, over a kettle of boiling water. Non-dairy cream may be substituted in all except the most delicately-flavoured dishes.

To freeze: Providing there is whipped cream in the mixture, the dishes will freeze well for up to 3 months. Plain jellies (gelatin mix) tend to separate at low temperatures.

Banana Bavaroise with Orange Salad

This is a superb recipe for a buffet table, as it looks very dramatic and has a light but subtle flavour.

Serves 12-16 **F** 3 months

For 6-8 halve all quantities and set in a 6 inch (15cm) tin, or in individual glass dishes.

$1\frac{1}{2}$ lb (675g) ripe bananas weighed in their skins (5 large)

4 eggs, separated

2 oz (50g/$\frac{1}{4}$ cup) caster (superfine) sugar

2 tbsp lemon juice

4 tbsp orange juice

2 teasp each grated orange and lemon rind

1 level tbsp ($\frac{1}{2}$ oz/15g) gelatine or 1 orange jelly (gelatin mix)

1 pint (575ml/$2\frac{1}{2}$ cups) whipping cream or non-dairy cream; *or* $\frac{1}{2}$ pint (275ml/$1\frac{1}{4}$ cups) each double (heavy) and single (light) cream, chilled

2 tbsp orange liqueur (Cointreau, Curaçao or Grand Marnier)

2 teasp caster (superfine) sugar

About 30 sponge fingers or boudoir biscuits (lady-fingers) (optional)

To garnish: toasted almonds

Orange salad:

6 large oranges

2 oz (50g/$\frac{1}{4}$ cup) caster (superfine) sugar

1 tbsp lemon juice

On the blender or food processor, put the egg yolks, sugar, fruit juices, rind and gelatine (if used) and blend for 40 seconds, then

362

add the peeled bananas cut in chunks and blend for a further 30 seconds or until absolutely smooth. Turn into a pan with a thick base and stir over gentle heat until the mixture is steaming *(do not let it boil)* and is thick enough to coat the back of the spoon like a custard. Add the jelly (gelatin mix) if used – and stir until dissolved. Remove from the heat, turn into a bowl or plastic container and stir until it stops steaming.

Put the chilled cream into a bowl and whisk until it is thick enough to hang on the whisk. Take out a fifth and put into a smaller bowl then continue to whisk it until it holds stiff peaks. Cover and refrigerate until needed for decoration. To the remaining four-fifths gradually add the liqueur, whisking until it holds floppy peaks only. Rinse the beaters thoroughly then whisk the egg whites until they hold very floppy peaks. Add the caster (superfine) sugar and continue to whisk until they hold soft peaks (they won't stand up straight).

Using a metal spoon fold the liqueur cream into the chilled banana mixture, followed by the whites. The mixture can now be spooned into a soufflé dish or serving bowl or moulded as follows: Select a 9 inch (22.5cm) cake tin with a loose bottom. Take the sponge fingers or boudoir biscuits (if used) and stick them side by side all round the inside. To do this most easily, moisten the sugary side of each biscuit with a dab of apricot jam and stick it to the tin. When all the biscuits are in place, gently pour in the banana mixture.

Now make the orange salad by removing the peel and pith from each orange using a sharp, serrated knife. Cut out the sections and put into a container. Scatter with the sugar and pour over the lemon juice. Cover and refrigerate with the Bavaroise.

To serve: If a tin has been used, stand it on one of smaller diameter and pull down the sides, then put the sweet (still standing on the base of the tin) on to a round plate or silver tray. Decorate the Bavaroise with some of the orange sections and the reserved cream. Scatter with toasted almonds. Serve in slices with a spoonful of orange salad.

Lemon Bavaroise

This has a delectable fresh lemon flavour which makes it especially refreshing. It is equally successful with non-dairy cream.

Serves 12 **F** 3 months

3 large eggs, separated
3 fl oz (75ml/^{1}/$_3$ cup) lemon juice
2 teasp grated lemon rind
6 oz (175g/^{3}/$_4$ cup) caster (superfine) sugar
2 level teasp gelatine (or 1 lemon jelly/gelatin mix), dissolved in 3 fl oz (75ml/^{1}/$_3$ cup) water
^{3}/$_4$ pint (425ml/2 cups) whipping cream or non-dairy cream
20 sponge fingers or packet of trifle sponges

On electric beater whisk yolks until thickened, then whisk in the sugar. Whisk in the juice and rind until mousse-like. If gelatine is used, soak in the water for 5 minutes then place over hot water until clear. If jelly (gelatin mix) is used, heat with the water until dissolved. Add to the first mixture, then put in the freezer until syrupy like unbeaten egg white – about 15 minutes (longer in refrigerator). Take out and whisk until smooth again.

Whisk cream until it hangs on the whisk then add almost all to the egg mixture (save about a quarter for decoration)

Whisk the egg whites until they hold soft peaks, then fold them in. Have ready a loose-bottomed 9 inch (22.5cm) tin which has been buttered, then line sides and bottom with fingers of sponge. Pour in the mixture, top with any remaining sponge fingers. Chill overnight.

To serve: Run a knife round the sides of the tin, then ease the cake out by standing on a tin of smaller circumference. Put on a serving dish, still on the cake tin base. Decorate with remaining whipped cream and some fruit – e.g. sliced bananas or sugared soft fruit.

Avocado Lemon/Lime Mousse

This dessert has a delicate texture and refreshing flavour. It can be set on a crumb base or presented in individual dessert glasses or demi-tasse cups. The larger number (8) can only be served when it is set on a crumb base or served with a fruit salad.

Serves 6-8 Do not freeze

1 very soft avocado
1 lemon jelly (gelatin mix)
1/2 pint (275ml/1 1/4 cups) water
2 tbsp lime cordial

1 tbsp lemon juice
4 tbsp single (light) or non-dairy
  cream

Optional crumb base:

6 oz (175g/1 1/2 cups) digestive
  biscuits (graham crackers)
3 oz (75g/1/3 cup) melted butter or
  margarine

1 level tbsp caster (superfine)
  sugar

Combine all crumb base ingredients (if used) and pack into an 8 inch (20cm) loose-bottomed cake tin. Chill until firm.

Dissolve the jelly (gelatin mix) in the water and stir in the lime cordial. Chill until it is as thick as unbeaten egg white, but not set. Halve, peel and stone the avocado. Put on blender or food processor with the cream and lemon juice, and blend until smooth. (Alternatively purée with a potato masher and add the cream and the juice. Then whisk in the half-set jelly (this may be done on blender or food processor.) Turn into individual glasses or spoon on top of the crumb base. Chill until set. Decorate with strawberries, orange segments or pipped grapes.

VARIATION
Moulded Mousse: Double the quantity. This looks beautiful set in a jelly mould and decorated with sliced strawberries or halved and pipped grapes.

Serves 12 Do not freeze

2 large, very soft avocados
2 tbsp lemon juice
2 lemon jellies (gelatin mix)
1 pint (575ml/2 1/2 cups) hot water

4 tbsp lime cordial
1/4 pint (150ml/2/3 cup) single (light)
  or non-dairy cream

Chilled Orange Soufflé

The use of concentrated frozen juice gives the soufflé a very fruity flavour.

Serves 6-8 **F** (if it contains cream)

1 can frozen orange juice (defrosted for 1/2 hour)
Rind and juice of 1/2 large lemon
1 lemon jelly (gelatin mix) *or* 1/2 oz (15g) gelatine, dissolved in 4 tbsp water
3 whole eggs and 2 yolks

3 oz (75g/1/3 cup) caster (superfine) sugar
2 egg whites plus 2 teasp caster (superfine) sugar *or* 1/4 pint (150ml/2/3 cup) double (heavy) or non-dairy cream, whipped
To garnish: grated chocolate or sugared strawberries

Put the 3 whole eggs and the 2 yolks into a basin and beat until frothy (preferably with an electric whisk). Gradually add the sugar and continue to whisk until the mixture becomes thick and mousse-like and a little of the mixture dropped from the whisk remains on the surface for a few seconds.

Put the jelly (if used) into a pan with the water and heat gently until dissolved. If gelatine is used, mix with the water and stand in a basin over steaming kettle until clear. Add the lemon juice and rind and the undiluted orange juice to the egg mixture, whisking all the time. Finally add the melted jelly or gelatine.

Either whisk the two whites until they hold stiff peaks, then beat in 2 level teasp caster (superfine) sugar and fold into the jelly mixture.

Or fold in 1/4 pint (150ml/2/3 cup) slightly whipped cream.

Spoon either mixture into a soufflé dish or individual dishes, and chill until set (2-3 hours). Serve garnished with grated chocolate or sugared strawberries.

Fruit Cream Dessert

This makes a pleasant change from the traditional jelly served at a children's party.

Serves 6-8 F 3 months

1 small (9oz/250g) can of strawberries, loganberries or blackcurrants
1 strawberry or suitable flavour jelly (gelatin mix)

1/2 pint (275ml/1 1/4 cups) milk
5 fl oz (150ml/2/3 cup) double (heavy) whipping cream or non-dairy cream
1 egg white

Drain the syrup from the strawberries, and if necessary make up to 1/4 pint (150ml/2/3 cup) with hot water. Put in a pan with the jelly and heat until dissolved. Allow to cool – this is important, otherwise it will curdle the milk. Add the milk, then put in the freezer or refrigerator while the cream is whipped until it is thick enough to hang on the whisk, and the egg white is beaten until it holds stiff but glossy peaks. Fold the white into the cream, then fold the milk mixture into it. You can either leave to set completely, then decorate with the fruit, or leave until half set, then stir in the fruit and continue setting.

Rödgröd or Kissel

There are many versions of this delightful sweet which is made in Germany, Austria and Scandinavia. The basis is always a slightly thickened fruit purée and in my version this is given added interest by the addition of raw seasonal fruits such as cherries and strawberries. I give both a summer and a winter version.

Serves 6-8 Do not freeze

Summer version

1¹/₂ lb (800g) blackcurrants
Water to cover (about ¹/₂ pint/275ml/1¹/₄ cups)
Sugar to sweeten (6-8 oz/175-225g/³/₄-1 cup)
1 slightly rounded tbsp arrowroot
or cornflour (cornstarch) to each pint (575ml/2¹/₂ cups) purée
¹/₂ lb (225g) each of stoned sweet cherries and hulled fresh strawberries

Note: Arrowroot rather than cornflour (cornstarch) is to be preferred as it gives a lighter gel.

Wash and de-stalk the blackcurrants and put into a pan. Cover with the water, and simmer until the fruit is tender – it will feel very soft when one berry is crushed between the fingers. Push through the finest sieve of a mouli (or use an ordinary fine sieve), then measure the purée to calculate the amount of thickener necessary.

Put the purée back into the pan and add the sugar to taste, dissolving it over gentle heat. Put the arrowroot or cornflour into a bowl and mix to a cream with a little water. Stir into the hot purée, bring to the boil, then simmer two minutes to cook the starch. The mixture will resemble a thick syrup. Allow to go cold, then stir in the fresh fruit.

Turn into a glass bowl and sprinkle a little sugar on top to prevent it forming a skin. Chill several hours or overnight. Serve with pouring cream.

Winter Version

1 lb (475g) can or bottle of blackcurrants	Approx 2 oz (50g/¼ cup) sugar
Blackcurrant cordial	½ lb (225g) frozen raspberries or early strawberries
1 slightly rounded tbsp arrowroot or cornflour (cornstarch)	2 medium bananas, thinly sliced

Push the contents of the can through the mouli (or a fine sieve) to make a thin purée. Pour into a measuring jug and make up to 1 pint (575ml/2½ cups) with equal quantities of blackcurrant cordial and water.

Turn into a pan, add sugar to taste, then thicken and finish as for the summer version.

Mocha Mousse

This delicious mousse may be decorated with either whipped cream or toasted almond nibs or chopped walnuts. It is also delicious when approx 3 oz (75g/¾ cup) chopped walnuts or 1 can of very well drained white peaches or morello (soured) cherries are alternated with layers of the mousse, then allowed to chill. It will then provide the larger number of servings.

Serves 8-10

6 oz (175g) plain dessert (semi-sweet) chocolate	2 tbsp Sabra liqueur (or other orange-flavoured liqueur)
6 large eggs, separated	1 tbsp caster (superfine) sugar
1 tbsp coffee syrup (see p.490) (or 2 teasp instant coffee dissolved in 1 tbsp hot water)	

Break up the chocolate and stand in a basin over very hot (not boiling) water. Heat gently until melted, then remove from the light. Immediately drop in the egg yolks and beat vigorously until the mixture begins to thicken. Stir in the coffee and the liqueur. Allow to go quite cold. Beat the whites until they just hold soft peaks, then beat in the caster (superfine) sugar. Pour the chocolate mixture into the bowl containing the egg whites and blend together. Spoon into 8 individual cups or a small soufflé dish. Leave to chill overnight.

The Pavlova Cake

Legend has it that the pavlova was created by an Australian chef in honour of the Russian ballerina, Anna Pavlova. Let me confuse the issue by saying that this marshmallow meringue is really a variation of the German Schaum Torte (foam cake)

However, in any language, a pavlova cake is absolutely delicious. Although it is usual to shape the cakes on flat trays, it is also possible to treat the mixture like an ordinary cake and bake it in two sandwich tins. All pavlovas freeze extremely well, so they are excellent desserts to make in anticipation of the party season.

If you normally keep eggs in the refrigerator, take them out an hour before you intend to make the cake. This will ensure that the whites whisk up to their maximum volume.

Add each spoonful of sugar only after the previous one has been thoroughly beaten in and the mixture stands in stiff peaks. If the sugar is added too quickly it will flatten and soften the meringue mixture and it will not rise as well.

The Pavlova Mixture

Makes two 9 inch (22.5cm) layers

Serves 8-10 F 3 months

4 large egg whites
8 oz (225g/2 cups) caster (superfine) sugar
2 level teasp cornflour (cornstarch)

¼ teasp cream of tartar or 1 teasp vinegar
1 teasp vanilla essence (extract)

Mix the cornflour (cornstarch) and the sugar in a bowl. Separate the eggs. Put the yolks into an airtight plastic container and refrigerate at once for another use. Put the whites into a large mixing bowl and add the cream of tartar (if used), otherwise add a pinch of salt. Start whisking at low speed until the mixture is frothy, then increase the speed and whisk until the mixture stands in stiff but glossy peaks. Now start adding the cornflour/sugar mixture a rounded tablespoon at a time, beating until stiff after each addition. When all the sugar has been added and the mixture is a solid meringue, beat in the vanilla. Finally beat in the vinegar (if used). The mixture is now ready to shape.

Either: Lightly grease and bottom-line with greaseproof paper two 9 inch (22.5cm) round loose-bottomed cake tins at least 1½ inches (3.75cm) deep. Spoon in the mixture and level off like any cake mixture.

Or: Draw two 8 inch (20cm) circles on greaseproof paper, then lay each piece of paper on a flat baking tin and very lightly grease (or use silicone paper that does not need greasing). Pipe or spoon the meringue into two rounds, making sure that the one to be used for the top of the cake is neat and even.

Have the oven heated to Gas No 2, 300°F, 150°C. Turn down to Gas No 1, 275°F, 140°C. Put in the cakes and bake for 45 minutes to 1 hour, changing the position of the layers at half time. They are ready when the top feels really firm and crisp to the touch.

To serve 12-16:

6 egg whites and 12 oz (350g/1½ cups) sugar

3 level teasp cornflour (cornstarch)

Generous ¼ teasp cream of tartar *or* 1½ teasp vinegar

Use two 10 inch (25cm) tins or 10 inch (25cm circles. The mixture may take a little longer to cook.

VARIATION 1
Lemon Pavlova Cake
This is very economical as it uses up the left-over yolks. The delicate sharpness of the filling contrasts perfectly with the sweet cake.

Serves 8-10 F 3 months

1 baked **Pavlova Cake** (p.369)
4 oz (125g/½ cup) caster (superfine) sugar
4 egg yolks

3 tbsp lemon juice
Grated rind of ½ lemon
8 fl oz (225ml/1 cup) whipping cream

370

Put the yolks and sugar into a small thick-bottomed pan and beat with a wooden spoon until creamy. Stir in the juice and rind. Put over gentle heat and cook, stirring constantly until the mixture thickens to the consistency of lemon curd. Do not boil. Take off the heat and keep on stirring for a minute or two. It will keep on thickening with the heat of the pan. Turn into a basin and allow to go absolutely cold. Whisk the cream until it holds firm peaks, then fold into the lemon mixture.

Put one pavlova layer on a serving dish and spread with the cream. Top with the second layer. Refrigerate overnight or freeze until required, then defrost under refrigeration.

For 12-16 servings:
Make a 6-egg-white pavlova (see p.370). For the lemon filling, use 6 egg yolks and half as much again of the remaining ingredients.

VARIATION 2
Chestnut and Liqueur Pavlova Cake
Use the canned sweetened chestnut cream or spread (crème de marron). This is one of the most delicious of all pavlova fillings which can also be used to fill ordinary sponge layers which have been moistened with a little canned fruit syrup.

Serves 8-10 **F** 3 month

1 baked **Pavlova Cake** (see p.369)
1 small (225g) can sweetened chestnut cream
10 fl oz (275ml/1¼ cups) whipping cream or non-dairy cream

1½ tbsp Tia Maria or Sabra liqueur
For decoration: 3 or 4 chestuts in syrup, angelica

Turn the chestnut cream into a bowl and stir in the liqueur. Whip the cream until it holds firm peaks, then fold into the chestnut mixture (reserve about a fifth for decoration).

Put one Pavlova layer on a serving dish and spread with the cream. Top with the second layer. Refrigerate overnight or freeze until required, then defrost under refrigeration. To decorate, pipe the remaining cream on top of cake and arrange chestnuts in syrup and angelica on it.

For 12-16:
Use a 6-egg-white pavlova (see p.370). Use the same amount of chestnut purée but ½ pint (275ml/1¼ cups) cream and 2 tbsp liqueur.

VARIATION 3
Red Berry Party Pavlova
With just half a pound of frozen berries you can make a most delicious party sweet that will serve between 8-10 or 12-16 people, depending on the size of the pavlova cake, as the same amount of filling will do for both. The secret is to pour a sugar syrup over the fruit, then use it to make a syllabub into which the berries are folded. Loganberries, raspberries and strawberries are equally delicious.

Serves 8-10 or 12-16 **F** 3 months

1 baked 4-egg- or 6-egg-white **Pavlova Cake** (see p.369)

Fill with syllabub mixture:

½ lb (225g) fresh or frozen berries (reserve 6-8 berries for garnish)
Juice and grated rind of 1 lemon
4 tbsp water
2 level tbsp sugar
½ pint (275ml/1¼ cups) whipping
or double (heavy) cream or non-dairy cream
2 tbsp Crème de Framboises or orange-flavoured liqueur (optional)

Put the juice and rind of the lemon, the water and sugar into a small pan and bring to the boil. Immediately pour over the fruit and leave for 1 hour. Drain the syrup into a bowl and add the liqueur (if used) and the cream. Whisk until as thick as whipped cream. Fold in the fruit. Use to fill the pavlova cake. Chill thoroughly for several hours or overnight.

Savarin Flavoured with Kirsch or Rum

A savarin is a rich, light yeast sponge baked in a ring tin and soaked with a flavoured syrup, then garnished with fruit and cream. It can also be served with a fruit compote without cream. It is particularly successful when frozen then reheated and treated as freshly baked. This means that only the soaking and garnishing need to be done on the day it is to be served.

372

Note: To make 1 small savarin, simply halve ingredients.

Makes 2 savarins each serving 6-8 or 1 large savarin serving 12-16 **F** 3 months

¹/₂ oz (15g/1 cake) fresh yeast or 1
  level tbsp fine dried yeast
1 level teasp sugar
2 oz (50g/¹/₂ cup) strong flour

6 tbsp milk heated – to lukewarm
  for fresh yeast; to hand hot
  (120°F, 50°C) for dried yeast

Put all the ingredients into a bowl and beat till smooth, then leave till frothy (about 10 minutes). Now add:

4 standard eggs, beaten
6 oz (175g/1¹/₂ cups) strong plain
  flour
¹/₂ level teasp salt

1 oz (25g/2 tbsp) caster (superfine)
  sugar
4 oz (125g/¹/₂ cup) soft butter or
  margarine

Beat above ingredients until mixture does not stick to spoon or mixer (5 minutes by hand or machine, 1 minute by blender or food processor).

Divide the mixture between two 1¹/₄ pint (825ml) ring tins or one 2¹/₂ pint (1.5 litre) one. Slip into plastic bag and leave till the mixture reaches the top (20-30 minutes). Bake in a hot oven (Gas No 6, 400°F, 200°C) for 25 minutes or until toast brown. Leave 5 minutes then turn out. Freeze one, if desired, as soon as cold. To use, defrost, then reheat until lukewarm in oven at Gas No 2, 300°F, 150°C, or in microwave.

The syrup:
For each small savarin (double quantities for a large one):

6 oz (175g/³/₄ cup) granulated
  sugar

8 fl oz (225ml/1 cup) water
5 tbsp kirsch or rum

While the savarin is cooking, dissolve the sugar in the water and boil gently for 5 minutes. Stir in the kirsch or rum.
    Leave the cooked savarin in the tin for 5 minutes then turn out and place, puffy side up, in a shallow round casserole. Pour the warm syrup all over, then leave until it has absorbed it completely, basting occasionally. This may take up to half an hour. Syrup should be thin enough to be absorbed but thick enough to glisten on the surface.

To serve: Turn right side up on serving dish and fill the centre with whipped cream and fruit. Particularly delicious are the following combinations: whipped cream topped with barely thawed raspberry or strawberry purée; canned pineapple folded into whipped cream into which has been whipped 2 or 3 tbsp of the pineapple syrup.

Profiteroles or Choux Puffs

You can now buy frozen profiteroles in chocolate sauce. They're certainly delicious – at a price! Yet how easy they are to make at home, with a good recipe and a little patience. Best of all, the empty puffs freeze to perfection and only need to be thawed and re-crispened for 5 minutes at Gas No. 4, 350°F, 180°C to be as good as though they had just come out of the oven.

To freeze profiteroles: Open freeze until solid, then pack in plastic bags.

I give below a large quantity of choux pastry. However, if you want only enough for 4 or 5 servings, simply divide it in half.

Serves 8-10 F 2 months

5 oz (150g/1¼ cups) plain flour
Pinch of salt
1 level tbsp caster (superfine) sugar

4 oz (125g/½ cup) butter, cut into cubes
½ pint (275 ml/1¼ cups) boiling water
4 large eggs

Measure the boiling water, put it into a thick-bottomed pan and bring back to the boil. Add the cubed butter and as soon as it has melted, add the flour, sugar and salt. Cook over gentle heat, stirring until the mixture leaves the sides and bottom of the pan quite clean and forms a ball of dough you can toss round in the pan this takes 3 or 4 minutes). Cool the dough for 10 minutes, then beat in the eggs one at a time. When the mixture has been beaten enough, it should stand up in peaks and be semi-transparent when pulled out into a ribbon.

To form the profiteroles: Put a ½ inch (1.25cm) plain nozzle into a piping bag and squeeze the mixture on to a greased sheet in little mounds, 1 inch (2.5cm) in diameter and ½ inch (1.25cm) high. (They double in size in the oven). Leave about 2 inches (5cm) space between. If no piping bag is available, drop blobs from a spoon. Bake in a quick oven (Gas No. 7, 425°F, 220°C) for 20-25 minutes. Take them from the oven and immediately make a slit in the side with a sharp knife to prevent them from going soggy. The puffs can now be cooled and filled, or frozen as required.

To fill: Whip ¼ pint (150 ml/⅔ cup) double (heavy) cream until stiff, then stir in a carton of soured cream and 2 teasp caster (superfine) sugar. I like this slightly acid cream, but if you prefer, use ½ pint (275 ml/1¼ cups) double (heavy) cream and no sugar. Pipe or spoon into the puffs through the slit. Chill until required.

To dish: Pile into a pyramid or arrange in a crystal bowl with the sauce.

Chocolate Sauce

Put 1 oz (25g/2 tbsp) butter, 8 level tbsp golden (corn) syrup and 4 oz (125g) plain chocolate into the top of a double saucepan or bowl standing in very hot water. Stir and beat until smooth and glossy. Pour over the puffs just before serving. (the sauce is nicest hot).

Fresh Raspberry Sauce: Push ¾ lb (350g) fresh raspberries through a sieve into a blender, or food processor. Add 4 oz (125g/½ cup) caster (superfine) sugar and blend for 2 minutes until thick. A little lemon juice can be added. Chill before serving.

Morello (Sour Red) Cherry Sauce

Drain the syrup from a can of pipped morello cherries and put in a saucepan with 3 tbsp redcurrant jelly. Bring to the boil, stirring, then add 1 level tbsp cornflour (cornstarch) mixed to a cream with 2 tbsp cold water. (Cherry brandy can also be used.) Bubble for 2 minutes, then add the juice and rind of a small orange. Chill.

Caramel Sauce

3 oz (75g/¹/₃ cup) soft brown sugar
3 tbsp golden (corn) syrup
1 oz (25g/2 tbsp) butter

5 tbsp unsweetened evaporated
milk

Place all the ingredients in a small strong pan and heat gently for about minutes until well blended and smooth. Do not boil. Serve hot or cold.

Hot and Fruity

These dishes are friendly and homely, easy to prepare but with the delicious flavour of hot fruit.

Rhubarb and Ginger Crumble

This is is made with 81% extraction flour which, combined with a few toasted nuts, gives it a particularly nutty flavour and texture. Ordinary white flour may be used instead.

Serves 6-8 F 3 months

1¹/₂-2 lb (675g-1kg) rhubarb
3-4 oz (75-125g/¹/₃-¹/₂ cup)
  granulated sugar

1 level teasp ginger

Crumble:

4 oz (125g/1 cup) wheatmeal 81%
  flour
1 oz (25g/¹/₄ cup) oats
1 oz (25g/¹/₄ cup) chopped walnuts
  or toasted hazelnuts (optional)

4 oz (125g/¹/₂ cup) soft brown
  sugar
3 oz (75g/¹/₃ cup) butter or
  margarine

Cut the rhubarb into 1 inch (2.5cm) lengths. Arrange in a buttered oval heatproof dish about 1 inch (2.5cm) deep. Mix the granulated sugar and ginger, then scatter on top of the rhubarb. Mix the flour, oats and nuts (if used) with the brown sugar, then gently rub in the butter until the mixture is crumbly. Arrange on top of the fruit and pat down gently into an even layer. Bake at Gas No. 6, 400°F, 200°C, for 30 minutes.

Use 1 lb (450g) each sliced apples and rhubarb. Bake at Gas No. 5, 375°F, 190°C, for 40 minutes.

Tutti Frutti Baked Apples

The juices and sweeteners combine to make a delicious fruity glaze

Serves 6-8 Do not freeze

6-8 medium Bramleys (tart cooking apples)	6 generous tbsp golden (corn) syrup
4 tbsp lemon juice	Juice of medium orange
3 oz (75g/³/₄ cup) chopped walnuts	6-8 teasp brown sugar
3 oz (75g/³/₄ cup) raisins	

Core the apples and nick the skin through the a centre. Arrange in a buttered baking dish. Mix the raisins, lemon juice and walnuts, and use to fill the centre of each apple. Top each apple with 1 teasp brown sugar. Dribble the syrup over the apples. Add enough water to cover the bottom of the dish to a depth of ¹/₄ inch (0.5cm). Add the orange juice. Bake in a slow oven (Gas No. 2, 300°F, 150°C) for 2 hours, basting several times. Serve warm or cold.

Hot Spiced Bananas

This is a really delicious dessert that can be made – and served – from a frying pan. Use a soft brown sugar, the darker the better if you like a treacly flavour. The bananas can be flamed, then served hot off the pan, or arranged in a dish and served at room temperature.

Serves 6-8 Do not freeze

6-8 large bananas

At least half an hour beforehand (earlier if convenient), slit the skin of each banana lengthwise and place on a baking sheet. Bake in a quick moderate oven (Gas No. 6, 400°F, 200°C) for 15 minutes or until the skin turns black. Leave in the skins.

The sauce:

Bare 3 oz (75g/¹/₃ cup) butter
Bare 3 oz (75g/¹/₃ cup) soft brown
  sugar

5 fl oz (150ml/²/₃ cup) orange juice
3 tbsp lemon juice
¹/₂ teasp ground cinnamon

In a heavy frying pan, melt the butter over gentle heat, then add all the remaining sauce ingredients. Bubble fiercely until a thick but juicy sauce is formed (about 3-4 minutes).

Peel the bananas and lay in the sauce, basting them well and turning until they are coated.

To serve hot: Add 4 tbsp rum, and set alight. Baste the bananas with the sauce until the flames die down, then serve at once.

To serve later: Lift the bananas on to a serving dish, and spoon over the sauce. Decorate with toasted chopped hazelnuts or almonds. Serve at room temperature, plain or with lightly whipped cream.

VARIATION
Baked Bananas with Lemon Juice and Sugar: Baked bananas are delicious served plain in their skins. Each guest 'unzips' a banana, then sprinkles it with the sugar and juice, and eats it with a spoon.

Hot Feather Sponge with Gooseberry Compote

Hot stewed gooseberries are served with a light-as-air sponge baked in individual Yorkshire pudding (patty) tins (each about 4 inches/10cm across) or heatproof saucer.

Serves 6-8 F sponge 3 months; gooseberries 6 months

Compote:

1¹/₂ lb-2 lb (675g-lkg) gooseberries
6 oz (175g/³/₄ cup) sugar

Enough water to cover the bottom
  of a wide-bottomed pan.

Put the sugar into the pan, add the water, dissolve over gentle heat. Add the topped and tailed fruit, bring to simmering, cover and simmer for 10 minutes. Allow to finish softening in the hot syrup.

378

Sponges:

4 oz (125g/^{1}/$_2$ cup) butter or
   margarine
4 oz (125g/^{1}/$_2$ cup) sugar
Grated rind of ^{1}/$_2$ lemon

4 eggs, separated
4 oz (125g/1 cup) self-raising flour
3 tbsp milk or water

Grease 6-8 heatproof saucers or individual Yorkshire pudding (patty) tins. Cream the butter and the sugar, beat in the yolks and the rind, then stir in the flour and the milk. Whisk whites until they hold floppy peaks, then fold into the other mixture. Divide between the dishes. Bake at Gas No. 5, 375°F, 190°C, for 15-20 minutes until golden brown and firm to the touch.

Serve hot gooseberries topped with hot sponges, and sprinkled with caster (superfine) sugar.

Pineapple Upside-Down Pudding

This is one of the best American culinary inventions.

Serves 6-8 F 3 months

1 medium can (approx 15 oz/425g)
   pineapple rings, spears or
   titbits
A few glacé (candied) cherries

2 oz (50g/^{1}/$_4$ cup) butter or
   margarine
2 oz (50g/^{1}/$_4$) soft brown sugar
2 level tbsp golden (corn) syrup

Grease an 8 inch (20cm) round solid-based cake tin (or a heavy non-stick frying pan makes an excellent container). Melt the butter in a heavy saucepan. Add the brown sugar and golden (corn) syrup and simmer together until the mixture is a rich brown (about 3 minutes). Pour into the cake tin. Arrange the well-drained pineapple and glaceé (candied) cherries in a design on top.

Pudding mixture:

4 oz (125g/^{1}/$_2$ cup) butter or
   margarine
4 oz (125g/^{1}/$_2$ cup) caster
   (superfine) sugar

Grated rind of ^{1}/$_2$ lemon
2 large eggs
5 oz (150g/1^1/$_4$ cups) self-raising
   flour

When using a food processor, blend eggs. lemon rind, sugar and butter (or margarine) together first until creamy in appearance, then add the flour and blend only until smooth. This gives a very light cake.

By hand: Put the soft fat and other ingredients into a bowl and beat together until smooth and creamy (2-3 minutes).

Spoon over the pudding and level with a knife. Bake in a quick moderate oven (Gas No. 5, 375°F, 190°C) for 30-40 minutes or until the pudding is golden brown and firm to the touch.

Reverse on to a serving dish and leave for 5 minutes. Lift off the cake tin. Serve plain, with custard, or with this fruit sauce.

Pineapple Sauce:

The syrup strained from the
  canned pineapple
2 tbsp orange juice or squash
Juice of ½ lemon
1 teasp each of orange and lemon
  rind, finely grated

2 level tbsp caster (superfine)
  sugar mixed with 1 level tbsp
  cornflour (cornstarch) or
2 level teasp arrowroot

Mix the cornflour (cornstarch) or arrowroot and sugar in a small pan, then stir in the juices and rinds. Bring to the boil. Simmer for 3 minutes.

Fruit Fritters

The secret of perfect fritters is a crisp coating of batter fried at exactly the right temperature. Add to that fruit that has been marinated in fruit juice or liqueurs, and you have a superb dessert that must be eaten hot off the pan.

If you use beer instead of water in the batter, the fritters will be even crisper. A perfect dessert for a cold winter's night.

Serves 6-8 Do not freeze

Batter:

4 oz (125g/1 cup) plain flour
Pinch of salt
2 tbsp corn or olive oil

8 tbsp warm water or beer
Later: 2 egg whites
Caster (superfine) sugar

Blend all ingredients, except whites, together for 1 minute, leave in the bowl.

By hand – put the flour in a bowl, make a well in the centre, then add the salt, oil and water or beer, drawing in the flour. Beat for 2 minutes until smooth.

380

Just before frying, whisk the egg whites until they stand in stiff peaks (I do this in a Pyrex measure), then fold in the batter mix. Have ready a pan of oil one-third full. Heat to 375°F, 190°C (when a cube of bread 1 inch/2.5cm square browns in 40 seconds). Spear the fruit (see below) on a fork, draining the liquid back into the bowl, then dip in and out of the batter. Fry until golden (about 3 minutes). Repeat with the remainder. Drain on crumpled tissue, and sprinkle with caster (superfine) sugar. Some like it with hot golden (corn) syrup.

To prepare the fruit:
Allow 4 pieces of fruit per person.

Liqueur is optional.

Bananas: Peel 6-8 bananas, then cut in 3 or 4 slanting slices. Sprinkle lightly with caster (superfine) sugar and the juice of 1 lemon or 2 tbsp rum. Leave half an hour to soak.

Oranges: Section choice fruit, then sprinkle with sugar and Curaçao.

Fresh pineapple: Peel, cut in slices, take out the core and cut slices in two. Sprinkle with sugar and kirsch. Canned pineapple needs acidulating with lemon juice.

Fresh apricots: Choose them slightly under-ripe, halve, stone, then sprinkle with sugar and apricot brandy.

Apples: Peel, core, cut in ½ inch (1.25cm) thick rings, sprinkle with sugar and brandy. All fruit can, of course, be simply sprinkled with sugar and lemon juice if preferred.

A Choice of Puddings

If you want to make a dried fruit pudding rich with suet, fruit and brandy, then plan to do it at least a month in advance. It will then have time to mature to perfection. However, do not despair if you cannot make it so far in advance because, if you use soft margarine instead of the traditional suet, you can make a pudding even as late as the day before it is required that will still be ready to serve. I think a plum pudding is so delicious that it can be enjoyed on any day of the year.

Leave the raw pudding mixture to stand over night so that the dried fruit can absorb some of the liquid and will therefore be extra plump and juicy.

Brandy or rum helps to mature the flavour of the pudding and that is why it is pointless to add it to the version that is made only twenty-four hours before it is eaten. However, the spirit can be added to this pudding before it receives its final steaming. Simply remove the paper cover, pour on the spirit, then re-seal and steam as directed.

If preferred, sweet sherry can be substituted for the red wine in the **Rosy Pudding Sauce**.

Ruth's Traditional Plum Pudding

This is a rich, dark, moist pudding with a superb flavour which will keep one year in a cool larder. A vegetable suet gives equally good results.

Makes 2 puddings, each serving 8-10. Do not freeze

¼ lb (125g/1 cup) plain flour
½ level teasp salt
1 level teasp mixed sweet spice
½ level teasp ground cinnamon
½ level teasp nutmeg
¼ lb (125g/1⅓ cups) fresh breadcrumbs
½ lb (225g/1½ cups) raisins
½ lb (225g/1½ cups) sultanas (white raisins)
½ lb (225g/1½ cups) currants
½ lb (225g/1½ cups) shredded suet or vegetarian suet

½ lb (225g/1½ cups) demerara sugar
¼ lb (125g/1⅓ cups) carrots, fineely grated
1 oz (25g/¼ cup) slivered almonds (optional)
¼ lb (125/1⅓ cups) cooking apple, grated
1 tbsp marmalade
Grated rind and juice of 1 lemon and 1 small orange
3 large eggs
3 tbsp rum or brandy (optional)

Sieve the flour, salt and spices into a large bowl, then add all the dry ingredients followed by the fruit rind and juice, the grated carrots, apples and marmalade, the beaten eggs and the spirit (if used). Mix really thoroughly. Cover the bowl and leave overnight for flavours to blend. Divide between two greased pudding basins and level off. Cover first with greaseproof paper and then with foil, tucking it tightly under the rim of the basin to make a moisture-proof seal. Steam for six hours. Store in a cool place. To serve – steam for a further 2 hours.

Steamed Dried Fruit Sponge Pudding

This could be made even as late as the day before it is needed and will keep for six months. However, it does need a really long steaming to ensure that it is moist and flavourful. It is not as dark or spicy as the traditional pudding but equally delicious in its own way.

Makes 2 puddings, each serving 6-8. Do not freeze

4 oz (125g/^{1}/$_2$ cup) soft margarine
4 oz (125g/^{1}/$_2$ cup) Barbados or
  Muscovado sugar
2 large eggs, beaten
Grated rind and juice of 1 small
  orange
2 oz (50g/^{1}/$_2$ cup) chopped walnuts
^{1}/$_2$ lb (225g/1^1/$_2$ cups) currants
^{1}/$_2$ lb (225g/1^1/$_2$ cups) sultanas
  (white raisins)
4 oz (125g/^{3}/$_4$ cup) raisins

2 oz (50g/^{1}/$_3$ cup) cut mixed peel
4 tbsp stout
4 oz (125g/1 cup) plain flour
^{1}/$_2$ level teasp salt
1 level teasp mixed spice
1 small apple, peeled and grated
^{1}/$_4$ lb (125g/1^1/$_3$ cups) fresh white
  breadcrumbs

Put all the ingredients into a bowl and stir until thoroughly mixed. Fill 2 basins and cook as in the traditional recipe (p.382), but if possible, allow three hours' steaming on the day it is to be served.

Rosy Pudding Sauce

This delicate pink wine sauce is lighter than a traditional white sauce. It can be made before lunch and reheated when required.

Serves 8

2 egg yolks
2 oz (50g/^{1}/$_4$ cup) caster
  (superfine) sugar
2 level teasp cornflour
  (cornstarch)

8 fl oz (225 ml/1 cup) port-type
  wine
1-2 tbsp brandy or
  orange-flavoured liqueur

Put the sugar and yolks into a bowl or the top of a double saucepan. Whisk together until they lighten in colour. This is most easily done with a portable hand or electric whisk. Now beat in the remaining ingredients. Stand mixture over a pan of boiling water and whisk until thickened. Reheat when required.

Whipped Brandy Butter

Lighter and fluffier than the traditional recipe, this is equally delicious with any steamed pudding.

Serves 8

2 oz (50g/¼ cup) butter or margarine

4 oz (125g/1 cup) icing (confectioners') sugar

1 egg

2 oz (50g/½ cup) ground almonds

2 teasp brandy

¼ pint (150ml/⅔ cup) double (heavy) cream or non-dairy cream

Cream the soft butter with the icing (confectioners') sugar and beat in the egg and almonds. Whip the cream until it holds soft peaks, then beat in the brandy. Fold into the creamed mixture. Refrigerate for at least an hour before use, but preferably overnight.

Fruit Custard Sponge Pudding

This delicious dessert is of American origin. It is especially suitable for those who want to avoid too much flour and fat in their diet, as although the baked pudding has a spongy top, it is mainly made up of egg white and air! Underneath the sponge there is a creamy fruit custard which is delicious hot or very cold. The lemon and pineapple variations are equally tasty but the pineapple one is particularly good for baking in individual dishes.

The pudding can be mixed extremely quickly with a blender or food processor. Put all the ingredients (except the egg whites and salt) into the machine and blend until smooth. This mixture can then be folded into the meringue.

Cook the pudding in a tin half full of warm water so that there is no danger of the custard overcooking and curdling before the top is sufficiently brown.

Lemon Custard Sponge Pudding

A refreshing pudding to serve after a hearty casserole.

Serves 6-8 Do not freeze

5 oz (150g/²/₃ cup) sugar
1 oz (25g/2 tbsp) butter
Juice (3 tbsp) and grated rind of 1
 large lemon

3 large eggs, separated
8 fl oz (225ml/1 cup) milk
1 oz (25g/¹/₄ cup) flour
Pinch of salt

Set the oven at Gas No. 4, 350°F, 180°C. Butter a 7-8 inch (17.5-20cm) round or oval ovenproof casserole or a soufflé dish (2-3 inches/5-7.5cm deep) and stand it in a baking tin containing 1 inch (2.5cm) of warm water. (Or use 6-8 individual soufflé dishes.)

Put the sugar, soft butter and yolks into a bowl and work together with a wooden spoon, then add the flour, juice and rind gradually stirring until smooth after each addition. Finally add the milk in the same way. Alternatively, put all the ingredients (except the egg whites and salt) into a blender or food processor and blend until smooth.

Put the egg whites into a mixing bowl, add a pinch of salt, then whisk until they hold stiff glossy peaks. Spoon on top of the first mixture then fold the two together using a metal spoon so that the air is not beaten out of the meringue. Spoon the mixture into the chosen dish or dishes.

Put the baking tin into the oven and bake for 55-60 minutes or until the top of the pudding is golden brown and firm to gentle touch. Serve straight from the oven or chill for several hours. Serve plain or with whipped cream.

Pineapple Custard Sponge Pudding

Serves 6-8 Do not freeze

15 oz (425g) can of pineapple
3 oz (75g/¹/₃ cup) sugar
1 oz (25g/¹/₄ cup) plain flour
4 fl oz (125ml/¹/₂ cup) syrup from
 the canned pineapple
2 tbsp juice and rind of an average
 lemon

3 large eggs, separated
4 fl oz (125ml/¹/₂ cup) milk
1 oz (25g/2 tbsp) very soft butter
 or margarine
Pinch of salt

Set the oven at Gas No. 4, 350°F, 180°C. Lightly butter the bottom and sides of a heatproof pudding dish or soufflé dish, 7-8 inches (17.5-20cm) in diameter and about 2-3 inches (5-7.5cm) deep, or use 6-8 individual dishes. Stand in a baking tin containing 1 inch (2.5cm) of warm water.

Into a mixing bowl put the following ingredients in the order given (alternatively put into a blender or food processor and process until smooth), stirring all the time with a wooden spoon or mixer at low speed: the sugar, flour, pineapple juice or syrup, soft butter, juice and rind of the lemon, egg yolks, milk.

Put the egg whites into a large bowl and add the pinch of salt. Whisk them until they form stiff, glossy peaks. Slowly add the liquid mixture to them folding it in with a metal spoon, so that the minimum of air is knocked out. If pineapple spears or rings are used, cut them into ½-inch (1.25cm) pieces. Arrange the cut-up fruit on the bottom of the dish, then gently spoon the custard mixture over it.

Put the baking tin into the oven and bake the pudding in exactly the same way as the **Lemon Custard Sponge Pudding** (p.385). Serve straight from the oven or chill for several hours. Serve plain or with whipped cream.

Chocolate Fondue

This is the perfect refreshment for a small teenage get-together or a campfire.

Makes about 1 cup (serves 8-10 as a dip) Do not freeze

6 oz (175g) (or 2 × 100g bars) plain dessert (semi-sweet) chocolate	1 tbsp water 2 tbsp double (heavy) cream 2 tbsp orange juice

Put the broken-up chocolate, water and cream into a sauce warmer or small pan. Stir over moderate heat on top of stove until the chocolate melts and the mixture is smooth. Remove from the heat and stir in the orange juice. Keep warm over a candle flame. Brandy may be used instead of orange juice.

Use mandarins, apple slices, bananas or marshmallows to dip into the fondue.

Frozen Desserts

The secrets of a perfect ice
With a domestic freezer it is now a practical proposition to make superb ice-cream and sorbets that are just as smooth and usually much more delicious – not to mention far less expensive – than the commercial variety.

For ice-cream
To make this successfully without a special ice-cream maker (which continually stirs the mixture as it freezes and so makes it very creamy), use a mixture based on a *mousse* of eggs, flavouring and cream rather than one based on a custard.

For sorbets
These are more difficult to make without a sorbetière (ice-cream maker), as they contain a lot of liquid which forms ice crystals when it freezes. If the mixture is frozen *slowly* the ice crystals are large and the sorbet is rough on the tongue. If, however, the mixture is frozen quickly the crystals are small and the texture is much smoother. So if your freezer has a fast freeze section it's a good idea to use it. To give the sorbet a really velvety texture, take it out of the freezer when it is still half frozen and mushy, then beat it on a mixer or (better still) a food processor until it lightens in colour (1 to 2 minutes). Be sure, however, to freeze it again as quickly as possible.

For both ice-creams and sorbets
Try and make them the day before they are needed. This gives them a chance to 'ripen' in flavour after they have frozen.

To serve

Always remove them from the freezer half an hour before dinner, and put them in the refrigerator. This gives them a chance to soften slightly, when they will be creamier on the tongue and more flavoursome to the tastebuds.

Serving suggestions

Freeze the ice-cream mixture in a glass bowl, then turn it out (dip it quickly in and out of hot water to loosen it) and decorate with whipped cream, nuts and cherries. (This can be done ahead of time then put back in the freezer.) Cut this 'bombe' like a cake.

For a special party, another delightful way is to freeze the mixture in coffee cups, then decorate with crumbled macaroons or toasted nuts just before serving.

Freeze a sorbet in a deepish container, then use an ice-cream scoop or large tablespoon to divide it between shallow wine glasses. Decorate if possible with some of the fruit from which it has been made.

Home made ice-creams and sorbets can be stored for up to four months in the freezer.

The Ingredients

Fruit Purée

The fruit for purée must be fully ripe and of a deep flavour. An electric blender purées soft fruit very quickly, but fruits with seeds (raspberries, blackberries, etc.) must also be pressed through a fine sieve or mouli to get rid of the seeds. Harder fruits, such as blackcurrants, need to be softened by cooking before they can be sieved (see p.395 for recipe).

Purées freeze well.

When using a frozen purée, thaw it overnight in the refrigerator, or allow 2-3 hours at room temperature. You can hurry it up by standing the container in cold water, or defrosting in a microwave.

Sugar

When added to a hot mixture any kind of sugar will dissolve and is therefore suitable. But when added to a cold mixture, as in a frozen mousse, icing (confectioners') sugar or caster (superfine) sugar are the only kinds that will dissolve. The proportion of sugar in an ice is important for the texture as much as the flavour. The ice will taste less sweet when frozen than when liquid.

Cream

Cream should be whisked until light and thick but not stiff and buttery, otherwise it becomes difficult to incorporate smoothly into the ice-cream mixture. Whipping cream (35% butter fat) is ideal, otherwise use equal amounts of double (heavy) and single (light) cream (48% and 18% butter fat respectively). Cream whips more readily if cold, so keep in the refrigerator until needed. Provided the ice-cream is well-flavoured, non-dairy (vegetarian) cream may be used.

Storage time

Ice-cream can be stored in the freezer for 3 months. For storage time in the ice-making compartment of a refrigerator, consult the instruction book. Never re-freeze ice-cream as the texture will be ruined and there is a danger of food poisoning, particularly with egg-based mixtures.

The Frozen Mousse

All the ice-creams in this section are based on a meringue into which is folded icing (confectioners') sugar, egg yolk, whipped cream and flavouring. Non-dairy cream may be substituted in every recipe. This mixture produces an exceptionally smooth ice-cream which is particularly successful with strong flavours such as chocolate, butterscotch, rum and liqueur. (For fresh fruit ice-creams the use of whipped cream alone gives a fresher flavour. See p.395.)

Note on quantities

For 6-8 servings, use half the quantities for 12-16, based on 2 eggs and 5 fl oz (150ml/²/₃ cup) cream.

Vanilla Ice-Cream

F 3 months

Quantities for 8-10	*Quantities for 12-16*
3 large eggs, separated	4
3 oz (75g/³/₄ cup) icing (confectioners') sugar	4 oz (125g/1 cup)
8 fl oz (225ml/1 cup) double (heavy) whipping or non-dairy cream	12 fl oz (350ml/1¹/₂ cups)
2 teasp good quality vanilla essence (extract)	1 tbsp

Put the whites into a bowl, then add a pinch of salt. Whisk until they hold stiff peaks when the beaters are withdrawn, then add the icing (confectioners') sugar a tablespoon at a time, whisking after each addition. Gently whisk in the yolks until the colour is even. Put the cream and the vanilla essence (extract) into a bowl and whip until it hangs on the whisk when it is lifted from the bowl (don't overwhip or the cream will turn buttery). Carefully fold into the meringue mixture. Turn into a plastic container (which can also be used for storage) and leave to freeze for about 6 hours.

In a refrigerator: 3★★★ – freeze as above. 1★ or 2★★ – turn refrigerator to coldest setting an hour in advance. Use 1 or 2 shallow containers. Transfer to the refrigerator half an hour before the meal.

VARIATION 1

Coffee Ice-Cream: Proceed as above but omit the vanilla. Instead flavour with strong instant coffee, coffee essence or coffee syrup (see p.490). An optional extra is a coffee-flavoured liqueur, or chopped walnuts lightly fried in butter.

Quantities for 8-10	*Quantities for 12-16*
2 tbsp instant coffee dissolved in boiling water	3 tbsp
1 tbsp coffee liqueur (optional)	3 tbsp
2 oz (50g/¹/₂ cup) chopped walnuts (optional)	3 oz (75g/²/₃ cup)
1 nut of butter or margarine	1

VARIATION 2

Chocolate Ice-Cream: Melt plain chocolate in a basin standing in a pan of simmering water or in the microwave. Stir into the meringue mixture after the yolks, with the vanilla essence, then proceed as directed.

Quantities for 8-10	Quantities for 12-16
4 oz (125g) plain (semi-sweet) chocolate	6 oz (175g)
1 teasp vanilla essence (extract)	2 teasp

VARIATION 3.

Chocolate and Rum Ice-Cream: Omit the vanilla. Mix the chocolate, melted as above, with cocoa dissolved in boiling water, then flavour with rum. Stir into the meringue after the yolks.

Quantities for 8-10	Quantities for 12-16
3 oz (75g) plain (semi-sweetened) chocolate	4 oz (125g)
1 1/2 oz (40g) cocoa	2 oz (50g)
3 tbsp boiling water	4 tbsp
2 tbsp rum	3 tbsp

VARIATION 4

Liqueur Ice-Cream: This can be made with Kirsch (to serve with stewed cherries), Cointreau, Curaçao, Grand Marnier or Aurum (to serve with peaches or raspberries), Amaretto (to serve with pears).

Omit the vanilla. Add the chosen liqueur to the meringue after the egg yolks have been added.

Quantities for 8-10	Quantities for 12-16
3 tbsp liqueur	4 tbsp

VARIATION 5

Rum and Raisin Ice-Cream: The preparation must be started 48 hours in advance when the seedless raisins are put into a small container, covered with rum, and the container closed.

Make as for vanilla ice-cream, but whisk any unabsorbed rum with a strong coffee solution into the cream. Fold the raisins into the mixture at the end.

Quantities for 8-10	Quantities for 12-16
Approx 2 tbsp rum	approx 3 tbsp
1 tbsp instant coffee dissolved in	1 1/2 tbsp
1 tbsp boiling water	1 1/2 tbsp

Butterscotch Walnut Ice-Cream

This has a glorious flavour of buttered walnut toffee.

Serves 8-10 F 3 months

1 oz (25g/2 tbsp) butter or
   margarine
2 oz (50g/¼ cup) soft brown sugar
   (the darker the better)
2 oz (50g/1 rounded tbsp) golden
   (corn) syrup
3 large eggs, separated

1 level tbsp icing (confectioners')
   sugar
2 oz (50g/½ cup) chopped walnuts
1 teasp vanilla essence (extract)
8 fl oz (225ml/1 cup) whipping,
   double (heavy) or non-dairy
   cream

Chop the walnuts; separate the eggs. Melt the butter in a small thick pan, then add the sugar, syrup and walnuts and bring to the boil. Cook for 2-3 minutes or until a rich brown. Take off the heat and add slowly to the egg yolks, stirring all the time. Add the vanilla essence (extract). Whisk the whites until they hold firm peaks, then whisk in the icing (confectioners') sugar a teaspoon at a time, whisking until firm after each addition. Whisk the cream until it stands in soft peaks, then add to the whites together with the egg yolk mixture. Use a metal spoon to fold the three mixtures together.

Put into a plastic container about 6 inches (15cm) in diameter and 6 inches (15cm) deep. Cover and freeze until firm (about 6 hours).

Chestnut Ice-Cream

This rich, smooth, deeply-flavoured ice-cream may be served in scoops, topped with chopped toasted nuts, or marrons (candied chestnuts) in brandy. For a more dramatic presentation, freeze it in a bombe mould, a basin or a 2 lb (1kg) loaf tin. To turn out, wrap for 30 seconds in a cloth wrung out in hot water, turn out and decorate with whipped cream and nuts.

Note: If the unsweetened (natural) chestnut purée is not available, use the same amount of sweetened purée, but reduce the icing (confectioners') sugar to 2 oz (50g/½ cup) and omit the vanilla essence (extract). The natural purée has a more pronounced flavour.

Serves 8-10 F 3 months

3 large eggs, separated
4 oz (125g/1 cup) icing
  (confectioners') sugar
1 small can (8½ oz/250g)
  unsweetened chestnut purée

3 tbsp rum
1 teasp vanilla essence (extract)
8 fl oz (225ml/1 cup) whipping or
  non-dairy cream

Put the whites in a large bowl and the yolks in a small one. Put the purée and the cream in two separate medium-sized bowls, and add the rum and vanilla to the purée. Whisk the whites until they hold stiff peaks, then whisk in the sugar, a tablespoon at a time, whisking until stiff again after each addition. Whisk in the yolks until the colour is even. Whip the cream until it hangs on the whisk (don't whip until stiff or it may go buttery and spoil the flavour). Fold the cream gently into the purée, then fold this mixture into the egg mixture.

Turn into a 3½ pint (2 litre) plastic container, cover and freeze for 4-5 hours. Leave a further few hours if possible for the flavours to develop.

Lemon Ice-Cream

A creamy ice-cream with a beautiful sharp lemon flavour.

Serves 8-10 F 3 months

3 large eggs, separated
Grated rind of 1 lemon
Juice of 2 large lemons (5 tbsp)

4 oz (125g/½ cup) and 1 oz (25g/2
  tbsp) caster (superfine) sugar
8 fl oz (225ml/1 cup) double
  (heavy) or non-dairy cream

Grate the lemon rind very finely, juice the two lemons and leave together in a basin. Put the whites into a bowl and add a pinch of salt. Whisk until they hold stiff peaks when the beaters are withdrawn, then add the 4 oz (125g/½ cup) sugar a tablespoon at a time, beating after each addition. Gently whisk in the yolks until the colour is even. Put the double (heavy), or non-dairy, cream and the lemon juice and rind into a bowl with the further ounce (25g/2 tbsp) sugar and immediately whisk until it is thick. (Don't leave standing or the lemon juice may curdle the cream.) When the cream is thick enough to hang on the whisk when it is lifted from the bowl, carefully fold the mixture into the meringue.

Turn into a plastic container (6 × 4 inches/15 × 10cm) and leave to freeze about 6 hours. Leave in the refrigerator half an hour to soften just before serving.

VARIATIONS
Frozen Lemon Slice
Line a deep ice tray or a long plastic container measuring about 11 × 4 × 1½ inches (27.5 × 10 × 4cm) with a strip of greased greaseproof paper, extending it above the top of the container.

For the crumb crust:

8 Digestive biscuits (Graham crackers), crumbed
2 oz (50g/¼ cup) melted butter or margarine

Pinch of cinnamon
1 level tbsp icing (confectioners') sugar

Combine all ingredients. Sprinkle two-thirds of this mixture on to the greaseproof paper, then cover with the lemon ice-cream mixture. Cover with the remaining crumbs. Freeze until firm (about 2-3 hours). To serve – lift out the greaseproof paper with the lemon slice on top (run a sharp knife round the edge first). Leave half an hour in the refrigerator to soften slightly.

Ice-cream Cups: Divide unfrozen lemon ice-cream mixture between 8-10 coffee cups. Freeze. Garnish with chopped nuts or crushed macaroons.

Honey and Banana Ice-Cream
This has a deep banana flavour with gentle undertones of honey.

F 3 months

Quantities for 8-10	Quantities for 12-16
3 large eggs	4
1½ oz (40g/3 tbsp) caster (superfine) sugar	2 oz (50g/¼ cup)
8 fl oz (225ml/1 cup) whipping or non-dairy cream	12 fl oz (350ml/1½ cups)
4½ level tbsp thin honey	6½ level tbsp
1 teasp vanilla essence (extract)	1½ teasp
3 large bananas	4
3 tbsp lemon juice	4 tbsp

Separate the eggs, putting the whites in a large bowl, the yolks in a small one. Whisk the whites until they hold stiff peaks, then whisk in the caster (superfine) sugar, whisking until stiff after each addition. Whisk in the yolks only until the colour is even.

Thoroughly mash the bananas and stir in the lemon juice. Whisk the cream until it holds soft peaks, whisk in the vanilla then gently whisk in the honey (do not overbeat – the consistency should be the same as the egg mixture). Fold the egg mixture into the cream mixture, followed by the banana mixture.

Spoon into a plastic container or loaf tin, as preferred. Cover with foil and freeze until firm. This takes about 3-6 hours depending on the depth of the mixture.

VARIATION
Honey and Brandy Ice-Cream: This has a truly superb flavour.

Omit the vanilla essence (extract), bananas and lemon juice. Instead, put the cream together with 3 tbsp brandy (for 8-10 servings; 5 tbsp brandy for 12-16) in a bowl and whisk until the mixture hangs on the whisk. Add the honey a tablespoon at a time, whisking until stiff again after each addition.

Fruit Ice-Creams

These are really frozen fools – that is, equal quantities of fruit purée and whipped cream. It is important not to whip the cream until stiff, as it is then difficult to fold evenly with the purée and may give the ice-cream a fatty flavour. Whip only until the cream hangs on the whisk when the beaters are withdrawn.

Freezing container
A loaf tin makes a useful container. The loaf of ice-cream can then be unmoulded, decorated with whipped cream and whole fruit of the same flavour, and served in slices. For scoops, use tubs or other containers about 6 inches (15cm) deep.

Blackcurrant Ice-Cream

A smooth ice-cream with a delicious blackcurrant flavour and colour.

Serves 6-8 **F** 4 month

¾ lb (350g) fresh or frozen
  blackcurrants
2 tbsp water
Juice of ½ lemon
6 oz (175g/¾ cup) granulated
  sugar

½ pint (275ml/1¼ cup) whipping
or non-dairy cream; or ¼ pint
(150ml/⅔ cup) each of single
(light) and double (heavy)
cream

Remove the stalks from the fruit. Put the blackcurrants in a pan with the water, cover and simmer for 8-10 minutes until tender. Leave until they stop steaming, then push through a sieve or 'mouli' and sweeten with the sugar and sharpen with the lemon juice. Allow to cool. Whip the cream until it just hangs on the whisk, then fold gently into the purée. Turn into a polythene container (the shallower the better for speed in freezing), and leave in the freezer or freezing compartment for about 1 hour, or until firm for ½ inch (1.25cm) round the edge.

Turn out into a chilled bowl, and beat with a rotary whisk or in a food processor, until smooth and creamy (1-2 minutes) – don't let it melt. Turn at once into the chosen container and freeze until firm.

VARIATION 1
Apricot Ice-Cream: Serves 6-8 F 4 months. Substitute ½ pint (275ml/1¼ cups) thick apricot purée (made from canned fruit) or same quantity of bottled apricot nectar, with 2 tbsp lemon juice.

VARIATION 2
Raspberry Ice-Cream: Serves 6-8 F 4 months. Substitute ¾ lb (350g) raspberries puréed and sieved then sweetened with 6 oz (175g/1½ cups) icing (confectioners') sugar. Or use ½ pint (275ml/1¼ cups) sweetened frozen purée, defrosted.

VARIATION 3
Strawberry Ice-Cream: Serves 6-8 F 4 months. In the blender or food processor, purée ¾ lb (350g/strawberries with 3 oz (75g/⅓ cup) caster (superfine) sugar for 1-2 minutes until smooth and creamy, then stir in 2 tbsp lemon juice. Or use ½ pint (275ml/1¼ cups) frozen strawberry purée, defrosted.

Frozen Raspberry Mousse

As raspberries have a strong flavour they can be made into a delicious egg-based mousse. The fruit flavour is not quite as strong as when cream alone is used, but the texture is smoother.

Serves 8-10 and 12-16 **F** 3 months

Quantities for 8-10	*Quantities for 12-16*
3 large eggs, separated	4
3 oz (75g/³/₄ cup) icing (confectioners') sugar	4 oz (125g/1 cup)
8 fl oz (225ml/1 cup) double, (heavy), whipping or non-dairy cream	12 fl oz (350ml/1¹/₂ cups)
Juice of ¹/₂ lemon	Juice of ¹/₂ large lemon
Juice of ¹/₂ small orange	Juice of ¹/₂ large orange
¹/₂ lb (225g) raspberries	12 oz (350g)
3 oz (75g/¹/₃ cup) caster (superfine) sugar	4 oz (125g/¹/₂ cup)

Put the raspberries and caster (superfine) sugar in a blender until thick (about 2 minutes). Press through a sieve to remove the pips. Whisk the whites until they hold stiff peaks, then whisk in the icing (confectioners') sugar until stiff again. Whisk in the yolks until the colour is an even yellow.

Whisk the cream until it starts to thicken, then gradually whisk in the fruit juices, whisking until thick again. Gently whisk in the raspberry purée. Fold this mixture into the egg white. Turn into a plastic container about 4 inches (10cm) deep and 6¹/₂ inches (16cm) in diameter for the smaller amount. Freeze until firm (about 4-6 hours).

Ice Cream Meringue Gâteaux

These are Pavlova cakes filled with ice-cream. They are particularly delicious after a rich main course as they are more refreshing than whipped cream Pavlovas. Take them from the freezer half an hour before the start of the meal and leave in the refrigerator until required.

Two sizes are given for each gâteau.

Chestnut Ice-Cream Meringue Gâteau

This is very quickly made as it uses ready-to-use ice-cream.

F 3 months .

Meringue

Quantities for 8-10	Quantities for 12-16
4 egg whites	6
8 oz (225g/1 cup) caster (superfine) sugar	12 oz (350g/1¹/₂ cups)
2 teasp cornflour (cornstarch)	3 teasp
¹/₄ teasp cream of tartar *or*	¹/₂ level teasp
1 teasp vinegar	1¹/₂ teasp
¹/₂ teasp vanilla essence (extract)	1 teasp

Whisk the whites with cream of tartar (if used) until they hold stiff peaks, then beat in the mixed sugar and cornflour (cornstarch) a table spoon at a time, beating until stiff after each addition. Whisk in the vanilla, and vinegar (if used). Pipe in two 9 inch (22.5cm) circles about 1 inch (2.5cm) high on greased greaseproof paper. (Pipe 10 inch (25cm) circles for larger quantity.) Have the oven set at Gas No. 2, 300°F, 150°C. Turn down to Gas No. 1, 275°F, 140°C and bake for 1 hour or until circles will lift off the paper easily. Cool completely. If not to be filled immediately, store in a tin.

Filling:

Quantities for 8-10	Quantities for 12-16
¹/₂ litre dairy ice-cream	³/₄-1 litre
Small can (225g) sweetened chestnut purée	Small can (225g)
5 fl oz (150ml/²/₃ cup) whipping cream or non-dairy cream	8 fl oz (225ml/1 cup)
2 tbsp Tia Maria or Sabra liqueur	3 tbsp

Take the dairy ice-cream from the freezer and allow to soften for 10 minutes at room temperature (or use soft scoop ice-cream). Whip the cream with the liqueur until it holds firm peaks, then blend in the chestnut purée. Gradually add the ice-cream in large spoonfuls and blend until even. Do not overbeat.

Put one layer of meringue on silver foil, cakeboard or other dish. Spread quickly with the ice-cream mixture and top with the second meringue. Put back into the freezer immediately.

Serve in wedges like a cake.

VARIATION 1

Raspberry Ice-Cream Meringue Gâteau: F 3 months. 2 meringue layers to serve 8-10 or 12-16 as required.

Filling:

Quantities for 8-10	Quantities for 12-16
¹/₂ litre vanilla ice-cream	³/₄-1 litre
¹/₂ (225g) raspberries, fresh or semi-thawed, sprinkled with	³/₄ lb (350g)
1 level tbsp icing (confectioners') sugar	1¹/₂ tbsp
2 teasp lemon juice	1 tbsp
5 fl oz (150ml/²/₃ cup) whipping or non-dairy cream	8 fl oz (225ml/1 cup)

Sprinkle the raspberries with the icing (confectioners') sugar and lemon juice and leave while you prepare the filling. Whip the cream until it hangs on the whisk. Have the ice-cream soft as thick cream. Fold the cream, the raspberries and their juice into the ice-cream. Put one meringue layer on a serving dish, spread with the raspberry filling, and arrange the other layer of meringue on top. Put in the freezer until required.

VARIATION 2

Lemon Ice-Cream Meringue Gateau: *A delectable lemon frozen mousse blends perfectly with the sweet crispy layers*
F 3 months.
2 cooked meringue layers for 8-10 or 12-16 as required.

Filling:

Quantities for 8-10	Quantities for 12-16
4 oz (125g/¹/₂ cup) caster (superfine) sugar	6 oz (175g/³/₄ cup)
4 egg yolks	6
3 teasp lemon juice	5 teasp
Grated rind from ¹/₂ lemon	1 lemon
8 fl oz (225ml/1 cup) whipping or non-dairy cream	12 fl oz (350ml/1¹/₂ cups)

Put the yolks and sugar into a small thick-bottomed pan and beat with a wooden spoon until creamy. Stir in the juice and rind. Put over gentle heat and cook, stirring constantly until the mixture thickens to the consistency of lemon curd. Do not boil. Take off the heat and keep on stirring for a minute or two. It will keep on thickening with the heat of the pan. Turn into a basin and allow to go absolutely cold. Whisk the cream until it holds firm peaks, then fold into the lemon mixture. Put one meringue layer on a serving dish and spread with the lemon mixture. Top with the second layer. Freeze.

To serve, take out of the freezer half an hour before dinner and put in the refrigerator. Serve in slices.

The Sorbet

The sorbet makes a most refreshing end to a meat or chicken dinner. To serve, arrange in scoops in wine glasses and top with a few whole fruit. A little liqueur of a matching flavour can be poured over it at the table.

Blackcurrant Sorbet

This can be made with fresh, frozen or canned fruit.

Serves 6-8 F 4 months

1 lb (450g) fresh or frozen
    blackcurrants (or 12 fl oz/350ml/
    1¹/₂ cups unsweetened purée)
6 oz (175g/³/₄ cup) granulated
    sugar

¹/₂ pint (275ml/1¹/₄ cups) water
1 tbsp lemon juice
1 large egg white, whisked until it
    holds stiff glossy peaks

Remove the stalks from the blackcurrants. Put the fruit in a pan with 2 tbsp water, cover and simmer for 8-10 minutes until tender. Leave until the mixture stops steaming then push through a sieve or 'mouli'. Put the sugar and water into a small, heavy-based pan, and heat, stirring until the sugar is dissolved. Then bring to the boil and boil steadily for 4 minutes, when a syrup will have formed. Allow to cool to room temperature. Add the purée and the lemon juice to the syrup.

Put in a shallow plastic container and chill about 3-4 hours – until softly frozen. Then put in the mixer or food processor and process until smooth (about 1 minute). Add the egg white and whisk only until blended. Re-freeze, covered, for 3 hours or overnight.

Leave in the refrigerator for 1 hour before serving to soften slightly.

VARIATION 1

Raspberry Sorbet: Substitute 1 lb (450g) raspberries or loganberries which have been puréed in a blender or food processor, then sieved to remove the seeds.

VARIATION 2

Strawberry Sorbet: Substitute 1 lb (450g) puréed strawberries. Increase the lemon juice to 2-3 tbsp.

Bottled Purée Sorbet

This uses the thin fruit purée or nectar which is bottled and sold as a drink. Flavours include passion fruit, apricot, peach and cherry.

Serves 6-8 F 4 months

12 fl oz (350ml/1½ cups) fruit purée	4 tbsp lemon juice or lime juice
5 fl oz (150ml/⅔ cup) water	1 large egg white, whisked until it holds stiff but glossy peaks
4 oz (125g/½ cup) sugar	

Put the sugar and water into a pan and dissolve over gentle heat, then simmer for 4 minutes. Stir into the fruit purée together with the fruit juice. Allow to go quite cold, then put in a plastic container in the fast-freeze section of the freezer. Freeze 2 hours until almost firm. Turn into a food processor or chilled mixer bowl and whisk until smooth. Add the stiffly whisked egg white, whisking only until evenly blended. Immediately return to the freezer and freeze until firm (about 1 hour). Put into the ordinary part of the freezer to store.

Leave half an hour in the refrigerator before serving.

Orange Liqueur Sorbet

This is a particularly refreshing sorbet. The egg white is optional; without it, the mixture is a true water ice.

Serves 6-8 F 3 months

4 oz (125g/^{1}/$_2$ cup) granulated
  sugar
^{1}/$_2$ pint (275ml/1^1/$_4$ cups) cold
  water
6 fl oz (175ml/^{3}/$_4$ cup) fresh orange
  juice and rind of 1 orange *or* 3^1/$_2$
  fl oz (100ml/^{1}/$_2$ cup)
  concentrated orange juice,
diluted with an equal amount of
  water
Juice (3 tbsp) and rind of a large
  lemon
2 tbsp orange-flavoured liqueur
1 egg white, whisked until it
  stands in stiff peaks

If fresh juice is used, grate the rind off the orange and the lemon,
add to the fresh juice and leave overnight. Alternatively, grate the
lemon rind and add to the concentrated orange juice and water.
Next day, strain and discard the rind.

Put the sugar and water into a thick-bottomed pan and heat
without boiling, stirring with a wooden spoon until the sugar is
dissolved. Simmer for 5 minutes.

Cool, add the fruit juices and liqueur. Allow to go cold, then put
in a container in the fast-freeze section of the freezer. Freeze for
2 hours until almost firm then proceed as for **Bottled Purée Sorbet**
(p.401).

Improved Commercial Lemon Sorbet

Serves 6 **F** 4 months

Grate the rind off 1 large lemon and squeeze the juice. Soften ^{1}/$_2$
litre sorbet slightly, turn into a bowl and stir in the rind and juice.
Put back into the freezer until required. This vastly improves the
flavour.

Ice-Cream Sauces

You can make these sauces and keep them for weeks in a covered
container in the refrigerator. Serve them slightly warm over
ice-cream to make a delicious 'instant' dessert, especially good for
teenage parties and large barbecues.

Caramel Sauce

*Unsalted butter is ideal for any melted butter sauce. The secret of
success is to heat the butter with the other ingredients, without*

allowing the mixture to come to the boil, until the sauce has become creamy and smooth.

Serves 12 **F** 6 months

6 oz (150g/³/₄ cup) soft brown
  sugar
4 level tbs golden (corn) syrup
2 oz (50g/¹/₄ cup) unsalted butter

Small can (6 oz/150g/³/₄ cup)
  unsweetened evaporated milk
1 teasp vanilla essence (extract)

Place all the ingredients in a small thick saucepan and heat gently until blended into a smooth cream. *Do not boil.* Serve warm or cold. This keeps for several weeks in the refrigerator. May be reheated.

Jaffa Orange Sauce

Serves 12 **F** 6 months

¹/₂ lb (225g/1 cup) unsalted butter
¹/₂ lb (225g/1 cup) caster
  (superfine) sugar

3¹/₂ fl oz (100ml/¹/₂ cup) orange
  juice
2 teasp grated lemon rind
4 oz (125g/³/₄ cup) seedless raisins

Melt the butter and the sugar in a small thick saucepan, stirring constantly until they are smoothly blended and beginning to bubble round the edges. Stir in the orange juice, lemon rind and raisins. Take off the heat. Serve warm. May be reheated. Keep under refrigeration.

Hot Chocolate Sauce

This is a well-flavoured, economical sauce, ideal for children or teenagers. Keep under refrigeration. Can be reheated.

Serves 12 **F** 6 months

3 oz (75g/¹/₃ cup) butter
8 oz (225g/2 cups) sieved icing
  (confectioners') sugar

3 oz (75g/³/₄ cup) cocoa
1 small can evaporated milk (6
  oz/175ml/³/₄ cup)

Melt the fat in a saucepan. Add the sugar and cocoa. Mix thoroughly adding a little of the milk if the mixture is very stiff.

Add the remaining milk gradually, beating well until the mixture is smooth. Bring to boiling point, stirring constantly. Continue to stir and simmer gently for 2-3 minutes. Serve warm.

Morello (Sour Red) Cherry Sauce

Serves 8-10 F 6 months

3 tbsp redcurrant jelly	2 tbsp water
15 oz (425g) can morello (sour red) cherries	Grated rind and juice of 1 small orange
1 level tbsp cornflour (cornstarch)	

Mix the redcurrant jelly with the juice drained from the can of morello cherries. Heat until melted, then stir in the cornflour (cornstarch) mixed with 2 tbsp of water. Bubble for 3 minutes, then cool a little and add the grated rind and juice of a small orange, and the morello cherries. Serve chilled.

See also: Coffee Syrup (p.490), Pineapple Compote (p.349), Bittersweet Chocolate Sauce (p.489), Pineapple Sauce for 50 (p.565), Chocolate Sauce for 50 (p.565).

Sweet Pastry

Fruit pies and flans, tarts, strudels, squares and slices – the list of memorable pastries is almost endless in its variety. Pastry-making, an art invented by the Ancient Greeks and developed by the French patissiers first in the early Middle Ages and then at the beginning of the 19th century, has been revolutionized in recent years by the advent of the electric mixer and food processor. However, although pastry-making may have been mechanized – at least where the blending of the fat and flour is concerned – the general principles of successful pastry-making remain much the same as they have always been.

The fat/flour ratio: The well-balanced pastry recipe has a high ratio of fat to flour (the fat never weighing less than half the weight of the flour) – it is the fat, be it margarine, butter or oil, that makes pastry tender, and an excess of flour that makes it tough.

The liquid content: Too much water makes it hard, while too little makes it crumbly and dry. Add just enough liquid (including beaten egg) to bind the dry ingredients together into a firm, but rollable dough.

The oven temperature: This must be high enough to cause the starch grains in the flour to burst and thus enable it to absorb the fat before it can melt and leak out of the dough.

The detailed method and ingredients for each type of pastry is given in its particular section.

Notes on the ingredients
Flour: Unless otherwise specified always use plain rather than

self-raising flour. The pastry will be crisper and stale less quickly. Self-raising flour is used only in some of the more cake-like pastries. Wheatmeal (81% extraction) flour – which is a compromise between 100% wholemeal flour that contains all the bran and nutriments of the wheat and the regular white flour (70% extraction) from which they have been mostly removed – makes excellent pastry, both sweet and savoury. Use it as a direct replacement for the white flour specified.

Sugar: Caster (superfine) and icing (confectioners') sugar only should be used to mix pastry. Granulated will overbrown and spot the pastry as it does not dissolve so readily.

Fats: I have specified the fat I consider appropriate for each pastry. Margarine may be substituted for butter, though if it is the soft variety the pastry will then be more difficult to handle.

Equipment: Electric food processors and mixers do not necessarily make better pastry, but they do make it more quickly and easily as well as making the even addition of the liquid much more simple. However, it is essential to make sure that the fat is not rubbed in too far, otherwise the pastry will not take up enough water and will be both difficult to roll and crumbly to eat.

A long rolling pin without handles is superior to a short one with handles, as it is much easier to roll the pastry into an even layer. Metal and enamel flan and pie tins help pastry to brown more evenly than heatproof pottery. This difficulty can be partly overcome by baking the dish on a metal tray which has been put in the oven at the same time as it was put on to heat.

Batch baking and freezing
Nothing is more time-saving than a stock of ready-to-roll-or-bake frozen raw pastry. This can be stored in inch (2.5cm) thick blocks or rounds, or rolled and moulded into pie and flan dishes. Ready-to-fill part-baked flan cIases are also extremely useful.

Empty flan cases can be baked without any lining if they are cooked from frozen – just prick all over with a fork before putting them into the oven.

To freeze pastry: Wrap in film or foil.

To defrost: Allow one inch (2.5cm) thick, 8 oz (225g) blocks of pastry 2-3 hours to thaw out at room temperature. (Or defrost on the microwave.) Then treat as freshly made.

Two-crust pies may be frozen raw or cooked as convenient (see recipes for detailed instructions).

Freeze fruit pies and unfilled pastry cases for up to 6 months.

Fruit Pies

The fruit pie is the universal dessert, eaten in every country and climate. It is essential to use a very short and crisp pastry that can be rolled out so thinly that it cooks in the same length of time as the fruit. To make pastry of this kind, it is necessary to use a generous amount of fat (slightly more than half the weight of the flour) and to sweeten the dough with icing (confectioners') sugar – the pastry is much easier to roll out than when caster (superfine) sugar is used. Chill the dough well before shaping it. It can then be rolled out easily without breaking or sticking to the board.

Various combinations of butter and margarine will all make successful pastry. It is best to experiment and find out which mixture suits you best (see recipe for quantities).

A little flour or cornflour (cornstarch) added to the sugar used to sweeten the fruit will produce a thick but juicy filling.

It is marginally better to freeze pies uncooked, then cook them fresh from the freezer. However, it may be more convenient to bake a batch and then reheat them.

Note: If your pie is to be frozen unbaked, brush the bottom crust with slightly whisked egg white before adding the fruit. This will stop it from becoming soggy in the freezer.

Thaw frozen cooked pies for 4 hours at room temperature, then serve or reheat in a moderate oven for 15 minutes.

Bake frozen uncooked pies straight from the freezer, but allow 15 minutes extra cooking time. If the pastry is brown before the filling feels tender (to test, pierce through the crust with a sharp knife), cover it with foil and cook until the fruit is cooked.

Fruit Pie Pastry

This is sufficient for a two-crust 8 inch (20cm) or 9 inch (22.5cm) pie.

F 6 months

8 oz (225g/2 cups) plain flour
2 level tbsp icing (confectioners') sugar
Pinch of salt
l5 oz (150g/²/₃ cup) butter, *or* 4 oz (125g/¹/₂ cup) butter and 1 oz (25g/2 tbsp) white fat, *or* 4 oz

(125g/¹/₂ cup) margarine and 1 oz (25g/2 tbsp) butter, *or* 5 oz (150g/²/₃ cup) margarine, as preferred
1 egg yolk
1 teasp vinegar
3 tbsp icy water

Put the flour, icing (confectioners') sugar and salt into a bowl and add the fat cut in 1 inch (2.5cm) cubes. Rub in gently until no pieces larger than a small pea come to the surface when the bowl is gently shaken. Using a fork, beat the egg yolk, vinegar and water to blend, then sprinkle over the flour mixture, turning it until all the dry ingredients are evenly dampened. Gather together into a dough which will be firm but pliable. The rubbing in of the fat and the mixing can of course be done in a mixer or food processor following the manufacturers' instructions. Knead gently for 30 seconds until smooth, then divide in two and press each piece into a flattened ball about 1 inch (2.5cm) thick. Wrap in film or foil and chill for at least 30 minutes.

If frozen for later use, allow 2-3 hours to defrost before rolling out.

Old-Fashioned Apple Pie (One Crust)

The apples are baked in a deep pie dish in a lemon-flavoured syrup.

Serves 6-8 **F** 6 months

The pastry:

¹/₂ lb (225g/2 cups) plain flour
Pinch of salt
4 oz (125g/¹/₂ cup) butter or margarine

2 level teasp caster (superfine) sugar
1 egg yolk
3 tbsp icy water

Mix the sugar, flour and salt, then rub in the butter until no pieces larger than a small pea come to the surface when the bowl is shaken. Beat the yolk with the water, then sprinkle on to the flour mixture and knead gently to form a firm dough. (This can of course be done in a blender or food mixer, following the manufacturer's instructions.) Chill half an hour.

Filling:

$1^1/2$ lb-2 lb (750g-1kg)
  well-flavoured baking apples
5 oz (150g/$^2/3$ cup) granulated
  sugar
Rind of 1 small lemon plus the
  juice (about 3 tbsp)

Pinch of mixed sweet spice
About $^1/2$ oz (15g/1 tbsp) butter or
  margarine
1 egg white and granulated sugar
  for glaze.

Peel and core the apples, then cut into slices $^1/8$ inch (0.25cm) thick. Put the apple peel and cores together with the lemon peel into a pan, cover with water and add the sugar and spice. Simmer uncovered for 15 minutes or until a thick syrup is formed. Strain and reserve the syrup, stirring in the lemon juice.

Put the apples into a pie dish about 2 inches (5cm) deep. (I like a Le Creuset oval dish.) Pour over the syrup and dot with the butter. Dampen the edges of the pie dish. Roll out the chilled pastry to fit, without stretching it, then lay it in place, pressing firmly to the edge of the dish.

Whisk the egg white with a fork until frothy, then paint it all over the pie. Sprinkle with the granulated sugar. Bake in a quick moderate oven (Gas No. 5, 375°F, 190°C) for 35 minutes or until the top is golden brown and the apples feel tender when the pie is pierced with a knife.

VARIATION
Add $^1/2$ lb (225g) brambles or cultivated blackberries and use only $1^1/2$ lb (800g) apples.

Streusel Apple Pie

Only one crust is made of pastry; the other is formed from a buttery crumble.

Serves 6-8 **F** 6 months
Half quantity of **Fruit Pie Pastry** (p.407)

Filling:

3 large baking apples (1¹/₂ lb/800g), peeled, cored and very thinly sliced

2 oz (50g/¹/₄ cup) sugar
1 level teasp cinnamon

Streusel:

2 oz (50g/¹/₄ cup) firm butter or margarine

3 oz (75g/¹/₃ cup) brown sugar
3 oz (75g/³/₄ cup) flour

Mix the cinnamon and sugar and sprinkle over the apple slices. Roll out the pastry to fit a 9 inch (22.5cm) pie dish, one inch (2.5cm) deep. Add the sugared apples.

Rub all streusel ingredients together and spread evenly on the top. Bake at Gas No. 7, 425°F, 220°C for 15 minutes, then at Gas No. 5, 375°F, 190°C for a further 30 minutes until a rich golden brown.

Note: It is very convenient to make an 8 oz (225g) quantity of pastry and make 2 pies at once.

Fresh Apricot or Peach Pie

Serves 6-8 F 6 months

Use a 10 inch (25cm) flan dish, 1¹/₂ inches (4cm) deep
1 recipe **Fruit Pie Pastry** (p.407)
1 egg white and 2 teasp granulated sugar for glaze

Filling:

1¹/₂-2 lb (0.75-1kg) fresh apricots
5 oz (150g/²/₃ cup) granulated sugar

1 level tbsp cornflour (cornstarch)
1 tbsp lemon juice

Halve the fruit and remove the stones. If under-ripe, cut in approx ¹/₂ inch (1.25cm) slices. Otherwise leave in halves. Put in a bowl and mix with the sugar and the cornflour (cornstarch). Roll out half the pastry to fit the bottom of the flan dish, add the fruit in an even layer, then sprinkle with the lemon juice. Roll out the top crust to fit. Sprinkle with slightly beaten egg white and granulated sugar.

Bake at Gas No. 8, 450°F, 230°C for 10 minutes, then at Gas No. 4, 350°F, 180°C for a further 40-50 minutes, until the fruit feels tender when the crust is pierced with a knife, and the crust is a rich golden brown. Nicest served just warm.

Green Gooseberry Tart

Use very hard, very green gooseberries for the maximum flavour.

Serves 6-8 **F** 6 months

1 recipe **Fruit Pie Pastry** (p.407)
1 egg white and 2 teasp granulated sugar for glaze

Filling:

1½ lb (0.75g) young green gooseberries	2 level teasp cornflour (cornstarch)
7 oz (200g/1 cup) granulated sugar	2 tbsp water

Mix the sugar and the cornflour (cornstarch) in a bowl then add the topped and tailed gooseberries and toss together gently until the fruit is coated with the sugar mixture.

Roll out one portion of chilled dough to fit either a 9-10 inch (22.5-25cm) shallow pie plate, or an 8-9 inch (20-22.5cm) flan dish. Mound the sugared fruit on top and sprinkle with the water.

Damp the edge of the pastry with cold water then roll out the second portion to fit. Press the two crusts together at the edge, trim off the excess pastry with a knife, then crimp the edges together using a fork. Beat the egg white with a fork until it is frothy, then paint all over the top crust with a pastry brush and sprinkle evenly with the sugar. Have the oven preheated at Gas No. 6, 400°F, 200°C. Put the pie in, close the door and turn the oven down to Gas No. 5, 375°F, 190°C then continue to cook for a further 35 minutes or until golden brown and crisp.

Serve only slightly warm or at room temperature, plain or with custard or cream.

Gooseberry and Strawberry Tart

An unusual blend of flavours.

Serves 6-8 **F** 6 months

1 recipe **Fruit Pie Pastry** (p.407)
1 egg white and 2 teasp granulated sugar for glaze

411

Filling:

1 lb (450g) each strawberries and gooseberries	1¹/₂ level tbsp cornflour (cornstarch)
	¹/₂ lb (225g/1 cup) granulated sugar

Mix the sugar and cornflour (cornstarch) in a bowl, then add the gooseberries and strawberries and stir gently to coat with the sugar mixture. Roll out half the pastry to fit a 10 inch (25cm) flan dish. Add the sugared fruit then cover with the top crust.

Beat the egg white until frothy, then paint all over the pastry. Scatter evenly with granulated sugar.

Bake at Gas No. 8, 450°F, 230°C for 10 minutes, then at Gas No. 4, 350°F, 180°C for a further 30 minutes or until the pastry is a rich golden brown and the fruit feels tender when the pie is pierced with a knife.

Crunchy Plum Slice

This is especially good when made with the oval free stone zwetschken plums

Serves 6-8 **F** 6 months

¹/₂ recipe **Fruit Pie Pastry** (p.407)
Roll out to fit a small Swiss roll tin or a 10 inch (25cm) sandwich tin. Scatter evenly on top:

2 lb (1kg) cooking plums halved and stoned if possible	4 oz (125g/¹/₂ cup) sugar
	1 level teaspoon cinnamon

Topping:

3 oz (75g/³/₄ cup) plain flour	3 oz (75g/¹/₃ cup) soft brown sugar
2 oz (50g/¹/₄ cup) soft butter or margarine	

Rub gently together until a crumble is formed, then sprinkle evenly on top of the plums. Bake at Gas No. 7, 425°F, 220°C for 10 minutes, then turn down to Gas No. 5, 375°F, 190°C for a further 25-30 minutes until golden brown. Serve warm or cold.

Spring Rhubarb Pie

In the oven the filling ingredients combine to make a thick juicy compote.

Serves 6-8 F 6 months

1 recipe **Fruit Pie Pastry** (p.407)
1 egg white and 2 teasp granulated sugar for glaze

Filling:

1½ lb (750g) forced rhubarb
1 oz (25g/¼ cup) flour
½ oz (15g/1 tbsp) butter or
  margarine

½ lb (225g/1 cup) granulated sugar
½ level teasp ground ginger

Use either an 8 inch (20cm) pie dish about 1 inch (2.5cm) deep, or a 10 inch (25cm) pie plate. Roll one portion of the pastry to fit the dish. Mix the flour, sugar and ginger then sprinkle a quarter of it in an even layer on the pastry. Heap the rhubarb (cut in 1 inch/2.5cm lengths) evenly on top, then sprinkle with the remaining flour mixture. Dot with butter or margarine cut into pea-sized pieces. Damp the edge of the pastry with cold water then cover with the second portion of the pastry rolled to fit. Press the top and bottom crusts together and trim the pastry with a sharp-knife. Crimp the edges with a fork. Use a fork to whisk the egg white until frothy, then paint all over the top of the pie with a pastry brush. Sprinkle with a thin layer of granulated sugar.

  Bake at Gas No. 7, 425°F, 220°C for 15 minutes, then turn down to Gas No. 4, 350°F, 180°C for another 30-40 minutes or until the rhubarb feels tender when the pie is pierced with a knife. Serve warm or cold (it's nicest warm), but not hot.

Yorkshire Fruit Tart

This is a meltingly tender pastry. The pie is cooked briefly at a very high temperature and therefore only soft, quickly-cooked fruit such as bilberries, gooseberries or red berries is suitable as a filling.

Serves 6-8 F 6 months

413

Pastry:

$1/2$ lb (225g/2 cups) self-raising flour

6 oz (175g/^{3}/4 cup) butter or margarine

4 oz (125g/^{1}/2 cup) caster (superfine) sugar

Approx 3 tbsp water to mix

Filling:

1^1/2-2 lb (750g-1kg) of the chosen fruit

4-6 oz (125g-175g/^{1}/2-^{2}/3 cup) sugar

Glaze:

A little beaten egg white

Granulated sugar

Mix the sugar and flour. Cut the butter into 1 inch (2.5cm) cubes then gently rub into the flour mixture until no pieces larger than a small pea rise to the surface when the bowl is shaken. Sprinkle with the water and when all the particles are dampened, gather into a dough. If possible chill for 1 hour.

Divide in two and roll each section into a rectangle to fit a shallow tin 12 × 8 × ^{2}/3 inch (30 × 20 × 2cm). Line with one piece of the pastry. Mix the fruit with the sugar and scatter on top. Cover with second piece of pastry, pressing it down firmly on top of the fruit. Beat the egg white with a fork until foamy then paint all over the pastry and scatter evenly with the granulated sugar. Bake in a pre-heated oven at Gas No. 8, 450°F, 230°C for 20 minutes.

Serve warm or cold. May be reheated.

Open Flans and Tarts

The flans in this section all have slightly different pastry cases – the better to blend with the particular filling. However, I also give a basic recipe for a baked sweet flan case that can be stored frozen and filled as required with fresh or canned fruit, then covered with a jam or thickened fruit glaze.

Baked Sweet Flan Case

This makes one 12 inch (30cm) flan or 2 × 7-8 inch (17-20cm) ones. The use of icing (confectioners') sugar or caster (superfine) sugar

414

is a matter of taste. Icing (confectioners') sugar makes a smoother crisper pastry, caster (superfine) sugar a crunchier one.

F 6 months
Quantities for 7-8 inch (17-20cm)

Quantities for 11-12 inch (27.5-30cm)

6 oz (175g/1¹/2 cups plain flour	8 oz (225g/2 cups)
Pinch salt	Pinch
4 oz (125g/¹/2 cup) firm butter or margarine	5 oz (150g²/3 cup)
2 level tbsp icing (confectioners') sugar	2¹/2 level tbsp
(or caster (superfine) sugar if a slightly crunchier texture is preferred)	
1 egg yolk blended with	1
2 tbsp water and	3 tbsp
1 teasp vinegar or lemon juice	1 teasp

Put the flour, salt, icing (confectioners') sugar into a bowl. Add the butter or margarine cut in one inch (2.5cm) chunks, with the egg yolk, water and vinegar. Work together either with a mixer or food processor until the dough is just formed. *Do not over-mix.* By hand: Make in the normal short pastry way – you may need a little more water in that case.

Chill 1 hour. Roll out ¹/8 inch (0.5cm) thick and carefully ease into the chosen flan case (I used a loose-bottomed metal flan case) as follows: Roll the rolling pin over the top to remove the excess pastry, then make sure the pastry comes to the top of the case all round by pushing it up a little with the fingers if necessary. Prick the bottom and sides with a fork, then line with a piece of foil sufficiently large to cover the sides and top as well as the base. Press it carefully into the shape of the flan.

Note: The flan will keep its shape without foil if frozen before it is baked. Either freeze 1 hour in regular freezer or leave overnight in the freezer compartment of refrigerator. Alternatively chill several hours before baking.

Bake at Gas No. 7, 425°F, 220°C for 10 minutes. Remove foil if used. Turn the oven down to Gas No. 4, 350°F, 180°C. Continue to cook a further 15-18 minutes until the flan is an even golden colour. Put the flan in its tin on a cooling tray. When quite cold carefully ease out and put on a flat tray or serving dish and fill.

Glazed Fruit Flan

Serves 6-8 Do not freeze

1 × 8-9 inch (20-23cm) baked
Sweet Flan Case (p.414)
1 lb (450g) fresh raspberries,
loganberries, strawberries, or a
mixture of fresh fruit *or* 1½ lb

(800g) cooked, then drained,
cherries, peaches, apricots,
plums, *or* 1 large can fruit (or a
mixture), well drained

Glaze for fresh fruit:

3 tbsp smooth apricot jam
(redcurrant jelly for red berries)

2 teasp liqueur or lemon juice

Put the jam and juice or liqueur in a pan and heat until liquid. Allow
to cool until beginning to set.

Glaze for canned or stewed fruit:

8 fl oz (225ml/1 cup) stewing or
canning syrup
2 tbsp lemon juice

2 teasp arrowroot or cornflour
(cornstarch)

Mix 2 tbsp of the syrup with the arrowroot or cornflour until it
becomes a smooth cream. Bring the remaining syrup to the boil,
stir in the dissolved thickener, and bring to the boil again, stirring
constantly. Simmer 2 minutes. Add the lemon juice and allow to
cool until beginning to set.

Put the flan case on a serving dish. Arrange the fruit in the case,
then brush on the setting glaze. You may need to do this twice to
get an even finish. Chill until required. Serve plain or with whipped
cream.

French Peach Flan

The fruit is cooked under a rich egg and cream custard.

Serves 6-8 Do not freeze
1 Sweet Flan Case (p.414), 8-9 inch (20.22.5cm), uncooked
Filling:

1 lb (450g) fresh peaches
¼ pint (150ml/⅔ cup) double
(heavy) cream

1 egg yolk
2 oz (50g/¼ cup) caster
(superfine) sugar

Glaze

2 rounded tbsp apricot jam
Juice of ½ lemon

Bake the flan case at Gas No. 6, 400°F, 200°C for 10 minutes, then remove the foil, re-prick the base, and return to the oven for 3 minutes more. It is ready when it is beginning to colour and to shrink from the sides of the tin.

Halve the peaches, stone then cut them into ½ inch (1.5cm) slices and arrange in the partly cooked flan case. Beat together the sugar, yolk and cream and pour on top. Bake for another 15-20 minutes until the fruit is tender and the custard set.

For the glaze – bring the jam and juice to the boil, then spoon over the fruit. Serve cold sprinkled with toasted almonds.

Note: If you find the base of the flan becomes soggy, sprinkle with 1 oz (25g) trifle crumbs before adding the filling.

VARIATION 1
French Apricot Flan: Use halved and stoned apricots instead of peaches.

VARIATION 2
French Apple Flan

1 lb (450g) eating apples such as
   Golden Delicious, peeled, cored
   and cut in ⅛ inch (0.25cm)
   slices

2 oz (50g/¼ cup) sugar and pinch
   of cinnamon mixed together

Toss the apples in the sugar and cinnamon mixture then arrange in overlapping circles in one layer in the flan case (unbaked). Bake at Gas No. 5, 375°F, 190°C for 25 minutes, then pour over the custard and continue as for the peaches.

Raspberry Frangipane Flan

A meltingly tender pastry case is filled with tart fruit and topped with a ground almond sponge. This flan freezes to perfection and is one of my own favourite 'entertaining' pastries.

Serves 12 or 8 **F** 6 months

Pastry:

8 oz (225g/2 cups) self-raising
  flour

5 oz (150g/²/₃ cup) butter or
  margarine

2 oz (50g/¹/₄ cup) caster
  (superfine) sugar

1 egg

Make by shortcrust pastry method (p.407). Chill 1 hour. Roll out
to fit a 12 inch (30cm) flan ring, or a deeper 10 inch (25cm) pottery
one (using left-over pastry for jam tarts). Prick lightly all over.
Chill while you prepare the filling.

12 inch (30cm)	*10 inch (25cm)*
4 oz (125g/¹/₂ cup) butter or soft margarine	3oz (75g/¹/₃ cup)
4 oz (125g/¹/₂ cup) caster (superfine) sugar	3oz (75g/¹/₃ cup)
2 large eggs	1 large egg + 1 yolk or 2 standard
4 oz (125g/1 cup) ground almonds	3 oz (75g/³/₄ cup)
Few drops almond essence (extract)	Few drops
3 level tbsp flour	1 rounded tbsp
1¹/₂lb (675g) raspberries	1 lb (450g)

A thin layer of raspberry jam spread on the base before the
raspberries intensifies the flavour. Arrange the raspberries over
the base of the flan case. Put all the filling ingredients into a bowl
and beat 2-3 minutes until smooth. Spoon over the fruit and level
off.

Bake at Gas No. 5, 375°F, 190°C for 15 minutes then at Gas No.
4, 350°F, 180°C for 30 minutes until golden brown and springy to
touch. Serve warm, dusted with icing (confectioners') sugar.
Reheats well.

Note: If pastry breaks it can be pressed into the dish with
fingers.

VARIATION

Cherry Frangipane Flan: Serves 12 or 8 **F** 6 months. Sprinkle the
base of the flan with icing (confectioners') sugar, and cover with
a single layer of raw pitted morello (sour red) or black cherries or
well-drained canned cherries.

12 inch (30cm)	*10 inch (25cm)*
2 lb (1kg) or 2 cans fruit	1¹/₂ lb (675g) or 1¹/₂ cans
1 oz (25g/4 tbsp) icing (confectioners') sugar	1 tbsp

Pastry Dessert Squares

Fresh or dried fruit which has been sandwiched between a rich sweet shortcrust pastry can be baked in a shallow rectangular tin rather than the more traditional pie shape. This makes it much easier to cut into neat portions.

These squares or fingers are delicious served either as cake or topped with cream for a special dessert. Viennese Almond Pastry is especially suitable for this kind of presentation as it is equally delicious hot or cold and it has a very tender texture. Besides the apple and mincemeat fillings for which recipes are given, try fresh rhubarb with a pinch of ginger, or ginger marmalade.

To chill the pastry so that it is easier to roll, leave it in the drip tray of the refrigerator for about an hour. It will then be just the right texture to handle.

To make it easier to transfer the pastry from the board to the tin, use the base of a large, loose-bottomed tin as an outsize spatula.

For convenience in storing, and to help keep moist any that is left over, cut only the number of squares you expect to use on a particular day and leave the rest in the baking tin. Cool, then cover with foil and refrigerate.

Viennese Almond Pastry

This pastry literally melts in the mouth.

Makes 20-24 squares **F** 6 months

9 oz (250g/2$\frac{1}{4}$ cups) plain flour
Pinch of salt
1 oz (25g/$\frac{1}{4}$ cup) ground almonds
  or hazelnuts
6 oz (175g/$\frac{3}{4}$ cup) butter

3 oz (75g/$\frac{1}{3}$ cup) caster
  (superfine) sugar
Grated rind of $\frac{1}{2}$ lemon
2 tbsp single (light) cream, top of
  milk or evaporated milk
1 egg

Separate the egg and reserve the white for glazing the pastry. Put the flour, salt, nuts, lemon rind and sugar into a bowl. Add the butter cut in $\frac{1}{4}$ inch (2.5cm) chunks and rub in gently until the mixture resembles dry breadcrumbs. Mix the egg yolk and the cream, then add to the dry ingredients and mix to a dough. Divide in two and knead each piece gently on a floured board until smooth. Flatten each piece until 1 inch (2.5cm) thick. Wrap in foil and chill for 1 hour. Use as required.

Autumn Apple Slices

These can be served warm as a dessert or cold as a cake. Covered with foil, they keep fresh in the refrigerator for several days and may also be reheated.

Makes 20-24 slices F 6 months
1 recipe **Viennese Almond Pastry** (p.419)

Filling:

4 large baking apples (about 1½ lb/675g), peeled and cored
4 oz (125g/½ cup) granulated sugar
1 level teasp cinnamon

3 tbsp raisins or sultanas (white raisins) – optional
1 egg white plus a little granulated sugar for glaze

Roll half the chilled pastry to fit a shallow tin approximately 12 × 8 inches (30 × 20cm) and ¾ inch (2cm) deep. It doesn't matter if it's a little bigger or smaller. Coarsely grate or finely slice the apples, and lay on top of the pastry in an even layer. Mix the sugar, cinnamon and raisins and scatter on top. Roll out the second half of the pastry to fit, then lay on top of the apples and press down gently to make a sandwich.

Beat the reserved egg white with a fork until it becomes frothy then paint it evenly on top of the pastry and scatter with granulated sugar.

Bake in a quick moderate oven (Gas No. 5, 375°F, 190°C) for 45 minutes until golden brown. Serve warm or cold in slices.

Brandy Mincemeat Squares

These are very quick to make. However, you can also use this pastry to make traditional mince tarts if you prefer.

Makes 40 squares F 6 months
1 recipe **Viennese Almond Pastry** (p.419)

Brandied Mincemeat Filling

2 lb (1kg) regular or vegetarian mincemeat

2 rounded tbsp apricot jam

3 tbsp brandy or rum (optional)

2 oz (50g/$\frac{1}{2}$ cup) fine biscuit (cookie) crumbs or ground nuts

Mix all the filling ingredients together. If too wet, add a few more crumbs or ground nuts. Roll out the pastry, fill, glaze and bake as for the **Autumn Apple Slices** (p.420)

VARIATION

Use the pastry and filling to make mince pies. Bake at Gas No. 5, 375°F, 190°C for 25 minutes or until golden brown.

Stuffed Monkey

Tender pastry squares with an orange-almond filling.

Makes 24 × 2 inch (5cm) squares **F** 6 months

Pastry:

8 oz (225g/2 cups) plain flour

Pinch of salt

5 oz (150g/$\frac{2}{3}$ cup) butter or margarine

4 oz (125g/$\frac{1}{2}$ cup) soft brown sugar

Small egg or $\frac{1}{2}$ large one

level teasp cinnamon

By hand: In a bowl mix together flour, salt, sugar and cinnamon. Rub in the butter until the mixture resembles fine breadcrumbs, then sprinkle with the egg and gather into a ball. Knead well until smooth.

Alternatively, put all the ingredients in the bowl of a mixer or food processor and process until a soft pliable dough is formed. Knead well. Divide in two. Roll half to fit a shallow tray 12 × 8 × $\frac{3}{4}$ inches (30 × 20 × 2cm).

Filling:

4 oz (125g/1 cup) ground almonds

1$\frac{1}{2}$ oz (40g/3 tbsp) butter or margarine

2 oz (50g/$\frac{1}{4}$ cup) caster (superfine) sugar

4 oz (125g/$\frac{2}{3}$ cup) chopped orange or citron candied peel

Yolk of an egg

Few drops of vanilla essence (extract)

Grated rind of $\frac{1}{2}$ lemon

Put the soft butter and all the remaining filling ingredients into a bowl and beat until creamy. Spread over the pastry. Cover with the remaining pastry, rolled out to fit. Mark into small squares.

Glaze:
Beat the left-over egg white until frothy, then paint over the dough. Sprinkle with granulated sugar.

Bake in a quick moderate oven (Gas No. 5, 375°F, 190°C) for 30 minutes.

Apple Slice or Jalousie

Two rectangles of delicate puff pastry or flaky pastry are sandwiched with a filling of buttered apples.

Serves 6-8 F raw 6 months

½ lb (225g) puff pastry, *or*
Quick flaky pastry (F raw 6 months):
5 oz (150g/²/₃ cup) firm butter

3 fl oz (75ml/¹/₃ cup) boiling water
8 oz (225g/2 cups) plain flour
Pinch of salt

Cut the butter into ½ inch (1.25cm) cubes, then pour on the boiling water and stir until dissolved. Add the flour sifted with the salt and mix to a soft dough. Pat into a rectangle on a sheet of foil, then wrap up and chill until firm, preferably overnight. This quantity is more than is required. The remainder can be used for any other purpose such as tartlets, or frozen for later use.

Buttered apple filling:

1 lb (450g) cooking apples (weight after peeling and coring)
1 oz (25g/2 tbsp) butter or margarine

4-6 level tbsp brown sugar
Grated rind and juice of ½ lemon
1 tbsp apricot jam (optional)

Melt the fat in a frying pan, or 8 inch (20cm) saucepan, then add the apples (cut in thick slices – about 8 to the apple), alternately with the sugar. Pour over the rind and juice and sprinkle with the jam. Cover and cook very gently for about 15 minutes until the apples are tender but still whole. Allow to go quite cold before using. Divide the pastry in half and roll each half into a very thin a rectangle measuring 11 × 6 inches (27.5 × 15cm). Place one piece of pastry on a wet ungreased baking sheet (this keeps the pastry in shape), then pile on the cooled apples, leaving a ¾ inch (2cm) margin all the way round. Dampen this margin with water. Take the second sheet of pastry, fold it lengthwise and make slanting slits down the centre, then unfold and lay in position on top of the filling. Press the edges together all the way round, then flake them together using the edge of a knife. Bake in a very hot oven (Gas No. 8, 450°F, 230°C) for 15 minutes. Take out and sprinkle with caster (superfine) sugar, then reduce the heat to Gas No. 6, 400°F, 200°C and continue to bake for further 10-15 minutes until golden brown. Serve warm in slices.

VARIATION

Apricot Slice: Serves 6 F raw 6 months.
Make exactly as for the Apple Slice (above) but spread the first layer of pastry with apricot jam to within ¾ inch (2cm) of the edge all the way round and then cover with this filling:

1 lb (450g) halved and stoned apricots, *or* 1 large can choice apricots (well drained), *or* ½ lb (225g) best dried apricots, soaked overnight in water to cover, then well drained
2 oz (50g/¼ cup) sugar for raw or dried fruit only
Squeeze of lemon juice

Tartlets

A stock of frozen baked pastry cases means that fresh fruit tartlets can be made as they're needed, literally in minutes.

Sweet Tartlet Pastry

This pastry keeps its shape merely with fork pricks, and remains crisp for hours even after filling with soft fruits. Empty tarts can be frozen, or they can be stored for up to six weeks in an airtight tin, then briefly reheated and cooled before use.

F raw 3 months; cooked 6 months: Makes 48

8 oz (225g/2 cups) plain flour
Pinch of salt
5 oz (150g/²/₃ cup) soft butter, cut in chunks

3 oz (75g/³/₄ cup) icing (confectioners') sugar
2 egg yolks, or 1 yolk and 2 teasp water (for economy)

By hand: In a bowl mix together flour, salt and sugar. Rub in the butter until the mixture resembles fine breadcrumbs, then sprinkle with the egg and gather into a ball. Knead well until smooth.

Alternatively, put all the ingredients into the mixer or food processor and mix gently until a dough is formed.

Chill for at least 1 hour. Roll out on a board sprinkled with icing (confectioners') sugar instead of flour to a thickness of ¹/₈ inch (0.25cm). Cut to fit patty tins, prick well. Bake in a moderate oven (Gas No. 4, 350°F, 180°C) for 15-20 minutes until a pale gold in colour.

VARIATION
Almond Pastry
Another version that literally melts in the mouth.

8 oz (225g/2 cups) plain flour
6 oz (175g/³/₄ cup) butter
3 oz (75g/³/₄ cup) icing (confectioners') sugar

3 oz (75g/³/₄ cup) ground almonds
1 egg

Use the same method as above, mixing the ground almonds with the flour.

Fresh Fruit Tartlets using either pastry

Brush each tartlet with warm redcurrant jelly or strawberry jam (can be omitted). Fill with whole raspberries, strawberries or loganberries, then brush with more jelly or jam. Serve plain or decorated with whipped cream.

VARIATION
Fresh Berry Tartlets on a Vanilla Cream Bed: *Sweetened and flavoured cream cheese makes an ideal foil for tart soft fruits.* 24 baked tartlets

Filling:

1 oz (25g/2 tbsp) butter	1 tbs cream
1 oz (25g/2 tbsp) caster (superfine) sugar	½ teasp vanilla essence (extract)
8 oz (225g/1 cup) rich cream cheese	1 lb (450g) whole strawberries, raspberries or loganberries
	4 tbsp warm redcurrant jelly

Beat all the filling ingredients (except the fruit and jelly) until fluffy and the texture of firm whipped cream. Spoon into the cases and level off, then arrange the choice fruit on top. Warm the jelly until liquid and then spoon over the fruit, masking it completely. Chill until required. May be made several hours in advance.

Cherry Tartlets

This method can be used with any cooked fresh fruit such as apricots, peaches, gooseberries or plums.

Makes 24 Do not freeze

Cherry filling:
1 lb (450g) fresh or frozen morello (sour red) cherries with the juice that comes out during pipping, *or* 1 × 15 oz (425g) can morello (sour red) or black cherries with their syrup

Fresh or frozen cherries will need no cooking. Strain the canned cherries (if used). To juice from frozen cherries add 6 oz (175g/¾ cup) sugar and 2 level teasp cornflour (cornstarch) slaked with a little water.

If using canned cherries, use the syrup to slake the cornflour (cornstarch). In either case bring the juice to the boil, simmer for 3 minutes. Taste and add more sugar if too sour, or a squeeze of lemon juice if black cherries have been used.

Add the cherries to the thickened juice. Chill. Use to fill tartlets and top with a blob of whipped cream.

The filling thickens up as it cools. May be made several hours in advance.

Mince Tarts

Almost any sweet pastry can be used to make mince tarts. Quick Flaky Pastry (p.422), Viennese Almond Pastry (p.419) are both excellent. Or you can use this light shortcrust pastry.

Very Short Cakey Pastry

Enough for 40 tarts F pastry or tarts 6 months

½ lb (225g/2 cups) each of plain and self-raising flour, *or* 1 lb (450g/4 cups) plain flour and 2 teasp baking powder
6 oz (175g/¾ cup) butter or margarine
4 oz (125g/½ cup) white vegetable fat

2 level tbsp icing (confectioners') sugar
6-8 tbsp icy water
2 teasp vinegar
1 egg white and a little granulated sugar or icing (confectioners') sugar, for glaze

Mix the flours and the icing (confectioners') sugar. Cut the fat into chunks then rub in by hand or machine until the mixture resembles coarse breadcrumbs but does not look damp. Sprinkle on the water and gather into a ball. Divide in two and knead each portion lightly for 30 seconds until free from cracks. Flatten into a square 1 inch (2.5cm) thick. Chill for 1 hour.

Roll out the pastry ⅛ inch (0.25cm) thick and cut into 80 circles – 40 large enough to fit the bottom of tartlet tins, and 40 slightly smaller to fit the top. Fill with mincemeat, dampen the edges of each tartlet, then cover with a circle of pastry, sealing the edges. Make a little slit in the centre. For a crisp top, brush with slightly beaten egg white and granulated sugar. For a soft top, brush with slightly beaten egg white, and sprinkle with icing (confectioners') sugar after reheating and just before serving.

Mincemeat filling: Allow ½ lb (225g) mincemeat for each dozen tarts. Use bought mincemeat or recipe for Mincemeat (p.494) or Brandied Mincemeat Filling (p.420).

Syrian Date Cakes

These delicate short pastries have a juicy date filling enclosed in a very tender short pastry. When they are made in the traditional fashion they are decorated with a pattern made by a special pincer – this can be roughly duplicated with the point of a sharp knife.

Makes 30 F 6 months

Pastry:

4 oz (125g/1 cup) plain flour	margarine
4 oz (125g/1 cup) self-raising flour	4 tbsp rosewater and 2-3 tbsp cold
6 oz (175g/³/₄ cup) butter or firm	water

Rub in the fat until the mixture resembles fine breadcrumbs.
  Mix to a dough with rosewater and water.

Filling:

12 oz (350g/2 cups) stoned dates	1 oz (25g/2tbsp) butter or
4 oz (125g/1 cup) walnuts,	margarine
chopped, *or* 1 lb (450g/2²/₃ cups)	Approx 2 tbsp water
dates	2 level teasp cinnamon
	1 tbsp lemon juice

Chop the dates coarsely and put in a pan with the fat, water, cinnamon and lemon juice. Cover and simmer, very gently, stirring occasionally until it forms a thick juicy paste. Cool. Add the walnuts (if used).
  Roll out the pastry and cut 3 inch (7.5cm) circles with a metal cutter. Put a generous spoonful of filling on each circle, then draw together into a crescent. Flatten into an oval pointed at each end. Arrange on ungreased baking trays, 2 inches (5cm) apart. Indent them with the point of a knife in herring-bone pattern. Bake at Gas No. 5, 375°F, 190°C for 20 minutes until creamy but not golden coloured. (They firm up on cooling). Remove onto a cooling tray and sprinkle with icing (confectioner') sugar. Sprinkle again when cold.

Savoury Pastry

Savoury tarts and slices can be used for a wide variety of occasions ranging from a teenage party to a rustic luncheon party to an elegant buffet. Whatever the occasion the pastry must be crisp and tender and the filling creamy and subtly seasoned. In every recipe at least part of the dish can be frozen in advance, though the complete pastry is usually nicest freshly baked.

The Quiche or Savoury Flan

The French quiche is the first cousin to the British savoury flan. However, the quiche is usually filled with a savoury custard whilst the flan is made with a savoury sauce. In my recipes I have combined the best features of both these methods by adding a little cornflour (cornstarch) to the eggs and cream. This kind of filling has more body than a quiche and is lighter in texture than a flan. Although the baked quiche can be frozen, I prefer to freeze the baked case empty and then fill and bake it freshly as required.

The addition of a teaspoon of icing (confectioners') sugar to the dry ingredients makes the pastry very crisp without noticeably sweetening it.

So that it will not shrink or lose its shape in the oven, chill the pastry case for at least half an hour before it is baked (overnight will do no harm). Better still, freeze it for several hours. If the case is lightly baked 'blind', it will not go soggy when the filling is added. Bake it only until the pastry is set but still pale in colour. It will finish browning and crispening when it is baked with the filling.

Quiches should be served warm or at room temperature, but

never hot. Unless otherwise stated, they may be reheated in a moderate oven (Gas No. 4, 350°F, 180°C) for 20 minutes or until warm to the touch.

The Pastry and the Pastry Shell

For entertaining purposes it is very useful to have raw pastry in block form, or raw or part-cooked pastry shells always in stock. This makes the actual preparation of the quiche a matter of minutes only.

To make 3 pastry shells each 8-10 inches (20-25cm) in diameter:

1 lb 2 oz (500g/4½ cups) plain flour
½ level teasp salt
3 level teasp icing (confectioners') sugar

12 oz (350g/1½ cups) butter or margarine
¼ pint cold water (150ml/⅔ cup)

By hand or machine, mix the flour, salt and icing (confectioners') sugar, then rub in the fat until each particle is the size of a small pea. Sprinkle with the water to moisten the dry ingredients evenly so that they can be gathered together into a dough – it should be moist enough to hold together without being sticky. Add a little more water if necessary. Divide the dough in three portions.

Note: for one 11-12 inch (27.5-30cm) shell use:

8 oz (225g/2 cups) plain flour
Pinch salt
1½ teasp icing (confectioners') sugar

5 oz (150g/⅔ cup) butter or margarine
3-4 tbsp cold water

To freeze raw: Flatten each portion into a rectangle about ¾ inch (1.75cm) thick. Foil or film wrap and freeze for up to 3 months. Allow 1 hour for dough to defrost before use.

To freeze as shells: Chill each portion of the dough for 1 hour, then roll out to fit the chosen flan cases – either glass, heatproof pottery or foil. (For detailed instructions see p.428.) Prick the pastry all over with a fork, then press a piece of foil into the shape, making sure the foil is wide enough to cover the edges of the pastry. (The pastry can be frozen at this stage, then cooked from frozen like the freshly made shell). If possible chill for 30 minutes to allow the pastry to relax so it will not shrink in the oven. To part-bake the shells, bake at Gas No. 7, 425°F, 220°C, for 8-10 minutes, until the pastry is set and firm to the touch, then remove the foil. Prick the base again and continue to bake a further 3-5 minutes until quite dry to the touch but unbrowned. Cool, then use the same day or freeze for up to 6 months, either in the flan dish or in a box to prevent breakage. The flan can be filled and baked straight from the freezer.

Note: If desired the complete quiche may be frozen for up to 2 months, though the texture in my opinion is not as good as when freshly baked. Reheat from frozen in a moderate oven (Gas No. 4, 350°F, 180°C) for 30-40 minutes or thaw at room temperature for 2 hours, then reheat in a moderate oven (Gas No. 4, 350°F, 180°C) for 20 minutes.

Asparagus Quiche

This has a very delicate flavour.

Serves 6-8 as a main course, 10 for a buffet

1 × 10 inch (25cm) part-baked pastry shell (p.429), set on a baking tray

Filling:

1/2 pint (275ml/1 1/4 cups) single (light) cream
3 large eggs
2 tbsp cornflour (cornstarch)
1/2 level teasp salt
Pinch nutmeg

10 grinds black pepper
1 can green asparagus tips
1 small onion, chopped and sautéed until tender in 1 oz (25g/2 tbsp) butter

Topping:

1 oz (25g/1/4 cup) grated Cheddar or Swiss cheese

1/2 oz (15g/1 tbsp) butter

Whisk the eggs with the cream, stir in the seasonings, then add gradually to the cornflour (cornstarch). Reserve 8 asparagus spears, and chop the remainder coarsely in 1/4 inch (0.5cm) slices and stir into the custard together with the onion. Fill the pastry shell with this mixture. Cover with grated cheese, dot with butter, decorate with the remaining spears of asparagus.

Bake at Gas No. 5, 375°F, 190°C for 25 minutes, then at Gas No. 4, 350°F, 180°C for 15 minutes or until golden brown and puffed.

VARIATION
Mushroom Quiche: F 3 months

¹/₂ lb (225g/4 cups) mushrooms	1¹/₂ oz (40g/3 tbsp) butter
2 tbsp spring onions (scallions), finely chopped	1 teasp each salt and lemon juice
	2 tbsp sweet sherry or port

Melt the butter, add the chopped spring onions (scallions), and cook for 1-2 minutes, add the remaining ingredients. Cover and cook gently for 5 minutes, uncover and cook briskly until all the liquid has evaporated and the mushrooms are beginning to fry in the butter. Stir the mushroom mixture into the custard and cook as for the asparagus quiche.

Asparagus Soufflé Flan

This is really a soufflé baked in a pastry case. It can be reheated but will then resemble an ordinary quiche.

Serves 6-8 as a main course, 10 for a buffet

1 × 10 inch (25cm) part-baked pastry shell (p.429), set on a baking tray

Filling:

¹/₂ small onion, finely chopped	8 or 12 oz (225 or 350g) can of green asparagus tips, whichever available
1 oz (25g/¹/₄ cup) flour	
4 oz (125g/1 cup) grated sharp cheese (e.g. Cheddar)	3 large eggs, separated
1¹/₂ oz (40g/3 tbsp) butter	1 level tbsp chopped parsley; or 2 teasp chopped fresh dill
8 fl oz (225ml/1 cup) single (light) cream	Salt and white pepper
	A little parmesan cheese

Melt the butter and sauté the onion until soft and golden, add the flour, bubble 2 minutes, then add the cream, salt and pepper. Bring to the boil, whisking, then take off the heat at once. Drop in the egg yolks, whisking well, followed by the cheese, the parsley or dill and the asparagus cut in ¹/₂ inch (1.25cm) pieces. (If more

431

convenient the sauce can now be dotted with ¹/₂ oz/15g/1 tbsp butter and left all day. An hour before serving, it can be warmed until just lukewarm, then treated as fresh.)

Whisk the egg whites with a pinch of salt until they hold stiff but still glossy peaks. Stir a third into the sauce until well mixed, then fold in the rest. Pour into the baked case and scatter with Parmesan cheese. Bake at Gas No. 5, 375°F, 190°C for 25-30 minutes, then at Gas No. 4, 350°F, 180°C for 15 minutes until golden brown. It can be kept hot at Gas No. ¹/₂, 250°F, 120°C for up to 30 minutes, although it does fall a little. Or it can be served cold.

Stuffed Olive Quiche

The olives in this quiche add an exciting flavour that contrasts with the blandness of the savoury custard.

Serves 6-8 for a main dish, 10 for a buffet
F 3 moths

1 × 9-10 inch (22.5-25cm) part-baked pastry shell (p.429) set on a baking tray

Filling:

1 tbsp cornflour (cornstarch)
10 fl oz (275ml/1¹/₄ cups) single (light) cream
3 large eggs
1 rounded teasp Dijon (French) mustard or English mustard
10 grinds black pepper

1 level tbsp fresh snipped chives or chopped parsley, or 1 teasp of either herb, dried
6 oz (175g:/1¹/₂ cups) grated sharp cheese (e.g. Cheddar)
4 oz (125g) sliced stuffed olives

Topping:

1 oz (25g/¹/₄ cup) grated cheese (preferably Parmesan)

1 oz (25g/2 tbsp) butter

Put the cornflour (cornstarch) into a bowl and slowly stir in the cream, mixing until smooth. Add the eggs and seasonings and whisk until blended. Finally stir in the grated cheese and the sliced olives. Pour into the part-baked flan case, sprinkle with the further ounce (25g/4 tbsp) of cheese and dot evenly with the butter, cut in tiny pieces.

Bake in a quick moderate oven (Gas No. 5, 375°F, 190°C) for 25

432

minutes, then at Gas No. 4, 350°F, 180°C for 15 minutes, until puffed and golden brown.

The flan will stay puffed up for up to 30 minutes and then will fall, but the texture will still be fine, though it will not look so dramatic. Serve warm or cold.

Tuna or Salmon Quiche

This is a very substantial quiche. It is also excellent when cold for a picnic or barbecue.

Serves 6-8 for a main dish, 10 for a buffet
F 3 months

1 × 10 inch (25cm) part-baked pastry shell (p.429) set on a baking tray

Filling:

1 tbsp cornflour (cornstarch)
8 fl oz (225ml/1 cup) single (light) cream
2 large eggs
½ level teasp salt
10 grinds black pepper
Few drops Tabasco sauce; or 1 teasp Worcestershire sauce

1 tbsp snipped fresh chives, dill or parsley; or 1 teasp dried herbs
4 oz (125g/1 cup) grated sharp cheese (e.g. Cheddar or Lancashire)
1 medium can (approx 7 oz/200g) tuna fish or salmon

Topping:

1 oz (25g/¼ cup) grated cheese
1 oz (25g/2 tbsp) butter

Put the cornflour (cornstarch) into a bowl and slowly stir in the cream. Add the eggs, salt, pepper, sauce and herbs, and whisk until smooth. Stir in the cheese and fish (drained and flaked roughly with a fork). Pour in to the part-baked pastry shell, sprinkle with the remaining cheese and dot with the butter, cut in tiny pieces.

Bake in a quick moderate oven (Gas No. 5, 375°F, 190°C) for 25-30 minutes, then at Gas No. 4, 350°F, 180°C for 15 minutes, until puffed and golden brown. Serve in the same way as the olive quiche (see p.432), warm or cold.

Lancashire Cheese Quiche

This makes a monster flan with a superb texture due to the special properties of the cheese. If Lancashire (mature crumbly cheese) is not available, use cheddar instead.

Serves 12 large portions, 16 smaller ones
F 3 months

1 *raw* 12 inch (30cm) pastry shell (p.429) set on a baking tray

Filling:

1 lb (450g) Lancashire cheese	¹/₂ level teasp salt
5 standard eggs	12 grinds black pepper
¹/₄ pint (150ml/²/₃ cup) single (light) cream	2 level tbsp snipped chives or chopped parsley, *or* 2 teasp dried herbs
8 fl oz (225ml/1 cup) milk	

Prick the base and sides of the pastry lightly with a fork. Put in the freezer for at least half an hour – or use a frozen raw shell. Whisk the eggs with the milk, cream, seasonings and herbs. Crumble the cheese with hands and add to the egg mixture (or stir in grated cheese). Pour into the pastry shell.

Bake in a quick oven Gas No. 7, 425°F, 220°C) for 20 minutes, then at Gas No. 4, 350°F, 180°C for a further 30-40 minutes until a rich brown and puffed. Serve warm.

Note: For a 10 inch (25cm) quiche use 3 eggs, 4 fl oz (125ml/¹/₂ cup) each of single (light) cream and milk and 10 oz (275g) cheese.

Quiche au Fromage Blanc (Cream Cheese Flan)

This Alsatian speciality has a delicate but satisfying texture quite unlike that of a custard-based quiche. It can be made from cream cheese alone, but I like the extra piquancy added by a little well-flavoured hard cheese such as grated Lancashire, Cheddar or Gruyère cheese.

Serves 6-8 Do not freeze

1 × 8 inch (20cm) pastry shell (p.429), 2 inches (5cm) deep, well chilled, set on a baking tray

Filling:

½ lb (225g/1 cup) full fat cream cheese

2 oz (50g/½ cup) grated cooking cheese (Gruyère, Lancashire or Cheddar)

3 egg yolks

1 whole egg

8 fl oz (225ml/1 cup) single (light) cream

1 tbsp each snipped chives and chopped parsley

1 teasp lemon rind

15 grinds black pepper

Mix all the filling ingredients until smooth in a blender or food processor (or mix by hand, adding the liquid ingredients and seasonings to the cheeses).

Put a baking tray in the oven and preheat to Gas No. 6, 400°F, 200°C. Put the empty shell on the hot tray, then carefully pour in the filling. Close the oven door and bake for 25 minutes until puffy and golden brown. Cool for 5 minutes then serve.

VARIATION
Arrange 3 oz (75g) smoked salmon pieces at the bottom of the shell before pouring in the filling.

In the French Manner

Although the quiche is of French origin – the 'Quiche Lorraine' is said to have been invented by Claude of Lorraine, the seventeenth-century landscape painter who was a pastrycook before he won fame as an artist – it has now been accepted into the cuisine of many other countries. The three savoury pastries in this section, however, are rarely encountered outside France. They deserve to be much better known as they are absolutely delicious and far from difficult to make.

La Tarte à l'Oignon (Alsation Onion Tart)

Also known as Zewelwaï, this tart is a speciality of the Caveau d'Eiguisheim just outside Colmar in Alsace, and has a wonderful puffy texture and a flavour unlike anything I've ever tasted before. It makes a delicious 'starter' to a fish meal, or it can be served with salads as a main dish.

Serves 6-8 Do not freeze

1 × 8 inch (20cm) part-baked pastry shell (p.429), 2 inches (5cm) deep, set on a baking tray

Filling:

1¹/₂ lb (675g) onions, finely chopped
1¹/₂ oz (40g/3 tbsp) butter and 1 tbsp oil
1 rounded tbsp flour
2 whole eggs

¹/₄ pint (150ml/²/₃ cup) whipping cream
1 level teasp salt
¹/₈ teasp pepper
Pinch nutmeg
2 oz (50g/¹/₂ cup) grated Cheddar cheese

Put the fats into a heavy frying pan, melt gently, then add the onions. Cover. Cook very slowly, stirring occasionally, until absolutely tender and golden (about ³/₄ hour): this is very important. Stir in the flour and cook for 3 or 4 minutes. Beat the eggs to blend, then stir in the cream and seasonings. Add the cooked onion and half the cheese. Pour into the tart shell. Sprinkle the remaining cheese on top and dot with the butter. Bake at the top of the oven at Gas No. 5, 375°F, 190°C for 25-30 minutes, or until a rich brown. The quiche will stay puffed for 10 minutes after the oven has been turned off. Serve very hot.

Feuilleton aux Champignons (Mushrooms in Puff Pastry)

Paper-thin layers of puff pastry are sandwiched with creamed mushrooms. Instructions are given for presenting them as a chausson (two crust puff) and as turnovers.

Serves 6-8 F raw 3 months

The chausson is most easily made in a flan dish 10 × 1 inches (25 × 2.5cm) deep or it can be made on a baking tray.
Divide the pastry in half and roll into 2 circles (about 10 inches/25 cm in diameter).

For the flan dish: Put one circle on to the base of the dish, spoon the filling on top, cover with second circle, seal together and flake the edges with a knife.

For a baking tray: Lay one circle on a baking tray. Spoon the filling on top, leaving a 1 inch (2.5cm) margin all the way round. Dampen this margin, then lay the second circle on top. Seal together and flake the edges with a knife.

For slices: Roll pastry into 2 rectangles – 6 × 12 inches (15 × 30cm) – and proceed as with circles.

For turnovers: Roll the pastry into 8 × 4¹/₂ inch (12cm) circles, top with a spoonful of the filling, fold over into a turnover. Seal together and flake edges with a knife.

14 oz (400g) puff pastry	Sesame seeds
1 egg, beaten, for glaze	

Filling:

¹/₂ lb (225g/4 cups) mushrooms, sliced thinly through cap and stalks (discard ¹/₄ inch/5cm end of stalk)
1 oz (25g/2tbsp) butter
2 teasp oil
2 tbsp chopped shallots (fresh or dried), spring onions (scallions) or mild onion
Pinch of mace

2 tbsp chopped parsley
1 level tbsp cornflour (cornstarch)
8 fl oz (225ml/1 cup) single (light) or whipping cream (or half and half cream and evaporated milk)
Pinch each of salt and white pepper
2 tbsp dry white wine (optional)

Melt the butter with the oil, then cook the shallots or onion gently for 2-3 minutes, shaking the pan well – do not overbrown as this darkens the sauce. Add the mushrooms and continue to cook for a further 4-5 minutes until softened. Add the cream (and wine if used) gradually to the cornflour (cornstarch), add to the pan and cook for a further 3 minutes until thickened. Season well.

Allow to cool, then use in any of the ways described above.

After the filling has been added to the pastry, brush with the beaten egg and sprinkle very thickly with the sesame seeds. Put in a hot oven (Gas No. 8, 450°F, 230°C) for 15 minutes, then turn down to Gas No. 6, 400°F, 200°C for a further 15 minutes or until really crisp and richly browned. Cook turnovers at the higher temperature for 20 minutes.

Serve with a salad or mixed frozen vegetables and new potatoes.

Tourte Forestière

This is also made with mushrooms, but it is quite different in character, being a shortcrust tart with a lattice top. The mushrooms are mixed with a béchamel sauce, enriched with egg yolks and cream.

Serves 6-8

1 × 9-10 inch (22.5-25cm) unbaked shell (p.429), plus left-over pastry rolled out and cut in ½ inch (1.25cm) strips

Prick the case all over, and put in the freezer.

Filling:
This must be allowed to go cold before it is used, otherwise it makes the bottom of the tart soggy and may curdle in the heat of the oven. It will come to no harm even if left overnight before use.

3 oz (75g/⅓ cup) butter
1 large onion, very finely chopped
½ lb (225g/4 cups) pinky
  mushrooms, very thinly sliced
2 oz (50g/½ cup) flour
½ teasp salt

Pinch of white pepper
Pinch of ground mace or nutmeg
½ pint (275ml/1¼ cups) milk
2 egg yolks
4 tbsp double (heavy) cream

Melt the butter and add the chopped onion, cook gently for 5 minutes until soft and golden, then add the mushrooms, cover and cook gently for 5 minutes. Uncover, bubble for 2 minutes to drive off any excess moisture, then stir in the flour. Bubble two minutes, then whisk in the milk and seasonings. Bring to the boil, stirring with a wooden spoon until thick. Cook for 2 more minutes, then take off the heat and stir in the cream mixed with the egg yolks (save 2 tbsp for glazing the tart). Allow to go quite cold. Spoon into the frozen flan case, dampen round the edge of the tart, then arrange the pastry strips across, leaving ½ inch (1.25cm) between each strip. Brush over the entire tart with the egg and cream mixture, then bake in quick oven (Gas No. 6, 400°F, 200°C) for 30 minutes until golden brown. Serve warm.

To reheat, cover the top with foil and leave in a moderate oven for 20 minutes.

Savoury Cream Cheese Strudel

A creamy herb-scented filling is encased in paper-thin puff pastry.

Note: Each strudel serves 3-4 as a main dish, 6 as a snack.

Serves 6-8 F uncooked 3 months

1/2 lb (225g) puff pastry (frozen or home-made)

Filling

1/2 lb (225g/1 cup) cream cheese or cottage cheese	1/2 level teasp salt
1/4 lb (125g/1 cup) Cheddar cheese	Few grinds black pepper
1 large egg	1 level tbsp sesame seeds (optional)
1 level tbsp fresh parsley or chives, *or* 1 teasp of either herb, dried	

Sieve the cottage cheese (if used) or put in a blender until smooth. Grate the Cheddar. Chop the parsley or snip the chives. Mix the two cheeses together in a bowl until evenly blended. Whisk the egg (saving 1 tbsp for glaze), then add to the cheeses together with the herbs and seasonings – it will be a thick but spreadable paste. On a lightly-floured board roll the pastry to the thickness of a knife blade into a rectangle about 12 inches (30cm) wide and 9 inches (22.5cm) long. The pastry should be so thin that you can see the board or counter through it.

Arrange the cheese mixture two inches (5cm) away from the long top edge in a band two inches (5cm) wide (leaving 1 inch/2.5cm clear of the filling along each short side). Turn these side edges over the filling to seal it in, then roll the pastry over about three times into a flattened Swiss roll about 3 inches (7.5cm) across. Transfer it, join down, to an ungreased baking sheet and flatten it gently with the rolling pin so that it is not more than 3/4 inch (2cm) deep. Mix six slanting cuts at equal intervals through the top crust only.

If possible chill well before cooking (pastry will be puffier) or even leave under refrigeration overnight. Just before baking, brush with the reserved tbsp of egg and scatter with the sesame seeds (if used). Bake at Gas No. 7, 425°F, 220°C for 10 minutes, then reduce the heat to Gas No. 6, 400°F, 200°C for a further 15 minutes until a rich brown. Leave for 5 or 10 minutes to cool a little, then serve in slices with a salad.

Biscuits (Cookies)

You just can't buy biscuits (cookies) as delicious as those you can make at home. Essential ingredients such as best butter, ground nuts and the finest vanilla flavouring make them too expensive to produce on a commercial scale, while it's difficult to adapt mass production methods to what has always been a domestic skill. Yet if you choose to make only those biscuits which can be mixed with speed and ease, and make up a large batch at a time, they can be one of the most delicious and versatile foods in your freezer. After all, what other food can be served equally well as an after-school snack and as the finale for an elegant dinner party?

When making biscuits in large quantities, save preparation time by avoiding biscuits that need to be rolled out and cut to shape. Instead, make those that can be rolled into balls or dropped from a spoon and will then spread into shape in the oven; alternatively shape them through a piping tube. To save baking time, shape and bake only part of the mixture and freeze the rest – it will keep as long as the baked biscuits; or shape the biscuits, but do not bake them. Instead, open freeze, pack, then bake off as required (see below).

But while good planning will save you time, there can be no economizing on the raw ingredients, for a good biscuit stands or falls by its flavour and texture-otherwise you might just as well save your energy and buy a packet instead.

Butter is essential. Even though I use margarine extensively in other baking, when it comes to biscuits I find butter gives a far better flavour and texture. Both salted and unsalted butter can be used though unsalted is preferable for melted mixtures.

Freezing butter: Normally I do not keep a stock of frozen butter, as any kind of butter will keep for at least a month in the refrigerator (at a temperature of 5°C, 41°F). However, if it is more convenient to freeze it, a lactic butter will keep up to 7 months in the freezer, while a sweetcream butter will keep up to 12 months without deterioration.

Sugar: Use caster (superfine) sugar for a crunchy biscuit, or when a melted mixture is required. Use icing (confectioners') sugar for a very fine crisp biscuit. Brown sugar is excellent in any biscuit mixture using oatmeal.

Flour: Use plain for rolled biscuits, such as shortbread, that need to keep their shape. Use self-raising for drop or moulded biscuits that need to spread into rounds during the baking time.

Nuts: Ground nuts are much used for their flavour and the delicious texture they produce. As ground almonds are so expensive, replace half the quantity with the much cheaper ground hazelnuts. Chopped hazelnuts, either plain or toasted, can also be used instead of walnuts. If walnuts are used, be sure to scald them with boiling water if they are at all dusty. Commercially prepared almond nibs and flakes are more convenient to use than those prepared at home, and cost no more.

Vanilla: Good quality vanilla essence (extract) is quite adequate for flavouring biscuits. But if you want the true continental flavour either use sachets of vanilla sugar (they weigh $^2/_3$ oz/20g each) or make up your own vanilla sugar by blending 4 oz (125g) lump sugar and 2 whole vanilla pods for about 30 seconds or until as coarse as granulated sugar. Leave in a covered container for a week then push through a fine sieve to remove the bits of pod. This has a marvellous flavour.

Freezing Biscuits: Baked and unbaked biscuits or dough will keep without deteriorating for up to 6 months (though in practice I never find they remain uneaten for anything like that time!).

Unbaked dough: Store in a plastic bag or container.

Unbaked biscuits: Open freeze until firm, then store in plastic bags.

Baked biscuits: As these are very fragile, I prefer to store them in shallow rigid plastic containers. Allow the biscuits to cool completely, then freeze at once.

Storage time: Up to 6 months, raw or cooked.

To Thaw

Baked biscuits: Remove as many as are required and leave to thaw for 15 minutes. Undecorated biscuits are improved by re-crisping in a quick moderate oven (Gas No. 5, 375°F, 190°C) for 5 minutes.

Frozen dough: Thaw for 2 hours or until pliable, then treat as freshly mixed.

Unbaked biscuits: Arrange on baking trays, allow to thaw for 15 minutes, then glaze and decorate if necessary and bake as if freshly mixed.

In this chapter you will find biscuits for children's tea parties, family and community teas and celebration teas, as well as a section of 'frivolities' to serve with cold sweets or the coffee to follow.

Biscuits that Shape Themselves

With the right kind of dough, it's possible to make perfect round biscuits without a rolling pin – you just shape them into little balls between the palms of your hand and let the heat of the oven do the rest. The simplest way to make a perfect ball is to I pinch off about a rounded tablespoon of the raw dough, put in on the palm of one hand then rotate the palm of the other hand on top of it until it becomes a sphere the size of a marble.

Treacle Crisps

Dark brown and very crisp.

Makes 48 F 6 months

5 oz (150g/²/₃ cup) dark brown
  sugar
4 oz (125g/¹/₂ cup) butter
2 rounded tbsp treacle (molasses)
1 tbsp milk
¹/₂ level teasp bicarbonate of soda

4 oz (125g/1 cup) self-raising flour
  or 4 oz (125g/1 cup) plain flour
  and 1 level teasp baking powder
3 oz (75g/1 cup) oats
1 oz (25g/¹/₂ cup) coconut
1 teasp ground ginger

Bring the sugar, butter and treacle (molasses) very slowly to the boil, stirring all the time, then stir in the bicarbonate of soda dissolved in the milk. Immediately, pour on to the flour, oats, coconut and ginger, and mix well. Leave to cool and firm up (about half an hour). Roll into marbles and arrange on greased trays, leaving room for the biscuits to spread. Bake in a moderate oven (Gas No. 4, 350°F, 180°C) for 15 minutes.

VARIATION
Syrup Crisps:
Makes 30 F 6 months Make exactly as for Treacle Crisps (above) but with these ingredients:

3 oz (75g/³/₄ cup) self-raising flour
3 oz (75g/¹/₂ cup) caster
  (superfine) sugar
3 oz (75g/1 cup) porridge oats
3 oz (75g/6 tbsp) butter

1 level tbsp golden (corn) syrup
1 tbsp milk with ¹/₂ level teasp
  bicarbonate of soda (baking
  soda)

Almond Butter Crisps

These superb Danish biscuits literally melt in the mouth. They have an irresistible flavour.

Makes 48 F 6 months

7 oz (200g/³/₄ cup + 1 tbsp) butter
6 oz (175g/³/₄ cup) caster
  (superfine) sugar
¹/₂ lb (225g/2 cups) self-raising
  flour
1 vanilla pod (use the scraped
  inside) or 2 packets vanilla

sugar, or 1 teasp vanilla essence
  (extract)
1 level teasp bicarbonate of soda
  (baking soda)
Split almonds
Glacé (candied) cherries

Work the butter into the sugar using a wooden spoon, mixer or food processor. When the sugar has been absorbed, add the vanilla flavouring and the flour sifted with the bicarbonate of soda. Roll into balls the size of a walnut and arrange on ungreased trays, leaving room for the biscuits to flatten and spread. Top with a split almond or piece of glacé (candied) cherry. Alternatively, dip the balls in a bowl of almond nibs before arranging on trays. Bake in a moderate oven (Gas No. 4, 350°F, 180°C) for 15 minutes or until golden brown.

Crunchy Hazelnut Biscuits (Cookies)

The nuts should be coarsely ground in a blender or food processor so that tiny particles are still visible (some health shops will do this for you). You do not want powdered nuts as it is the crunchiness that makes this biscuit (cookie) so different.

Makes 30 F 6 months

5 oz (150g/^{2}/$_3$ cup) butter
3 oz (75g/^{1}/$_3$ cup) caster
  (superfine) sugar
6 oz (175g/1^1/$_2$ cups) self-raising
  flour

2^1/$_2$ oz (65g/^{1}/$_2$ cup) hazelnuts,
  coarsely ground
^{1}/$_2$ teasp vanilla essence (extract)

Cut the butter into 1 inch (2.5cm) chunks and put into a mixing bowl or food processor with the sugar, flour and nuts. Rub in the fat until the mixture resembles coarse crumbs (as for pastry), then sprinkle with the vanilla and work thoroughly together into a dough, kneading well until it is like plasticine – this is best done by hand.

Pinch off pieces of the dough and roll into balls the size of a large marble. Put on greased trays two inches (0.5cm) apart. Take a large-tined fork and dip into cold water then press each ball first one way and then the other to form into a biscuit (cookie) about ^{3}/$_8$ inch (1cm) thick. Bake in a moderate oven (Gas No. 4, 350°F, 180°C) for 10-12 minutes or until golden brown. Sprinkle with caster (superfine) sugar while hot.

Lift off the trays and allow to cool. Store in an airtight container or freeze.

Orange Crisps

These delicious little biscuits (cookies) can be made by the children as they are rolled into balls rather like modelling dough. The secret is to press them into rounds with the wet tines of a fork. This also gives the biscuits a very professional touch. These are lovely to offer to guests 'dropping in'.

Makes 20 F months

5 oz (150g/1¼ cups) self-raising flour

4 oz (125g/½ cup) butter cut in 1 inch (2.5m) chunks

2 oz (50g/¼ cup) caster (superfine) sugar

Finely grated rind of 1 orange

Put the flour, sugar and rind in a bowl, add butter and rub in by hand or machine until a dough is formed which can be gathered into a ball. Pinch off pieces the size of a small walnut and roll between the palms into little balls. Arrange 2 inches (5cm) apart on ungreased trays. Take a large fork and dip it into cold water, then press down on the balls first one way and then another. Biscuits (cookies) about ⅜ inch (1cm) thick will be formed.

Bake in a moderate oven (Gas No. 4, 350°F, 180°C) for 15 minutes until a pale gold in colour. Remove from the oven and immediately sift with caster (superfine) sugar.

Brandy Snaps

These brittle curls are quite easy to make when the mixture is first cooled then rolled into balls, rather than being dropped from a teaspoon. However, to make successful brandy snaps it is essential to weigh all the ingredients with great care. This is most easily done on a scale which can be set at zero after each addition. Weigh the sugar, then pour the syrup on top and weigh that in its turn. In this way the syrup will not stick to the scales. Alternately, dust the scale pan with a little of the weighed-out flour, measure the syrup, then tip cleanly into the pan.

Children love brandy snaps plain; more sophisticated palates will relish them filled with brandy-flavoured whipped cream. (Do not fill more than an hour or two before serving or the snap may lose its crispness.)

Makes 48 F 6 months

4 oz (125g/2 tbsp) golden (corn)
  syrup
3 oz (75g/^{1}/$_3$ cup) caster
  (superfine) sugar

4 oz (125g/^{1}/$_2$ cup) butter
3^1/$_2$ oz (90g/^{7}/$_8$ cup) plain flour
1 teasp ground ginger
1 teasp grated lemon rind

Weigh all the ingredients very carefully. Put the butter into a thick-bottomed pan and heat gently until it is just melted, then stir in the sugar and syrup and continue heating and stirring until smooth. Do not allow to boil. Stir in remaining ingredients. Cool for 10 minutes until the mixture is the consistency of putty. Form into little balls each the size of a large marble by rolling a little of the mixture between the palms, then arrange 3 inches (7.5cm) apart on lightly-oiled baking trays.

Bake at Gas No. 3, 325°F, 160°C for 10 minutes until golden brown. Leave to cool for 1 minute or until the snaps can be lifted off the tray with a flexible spatula. Roll each one in turn round a wooden spoon handle, and when firm enough to hold its shape, slide off and leave to harden on a cooling tray. If they become too brittle before they can be rolled, return to the oven for 1 minute to soften again.

Serve plain or filled with brandy cream made as follows: Whip ^{1}/$_4$ pint (150ml/^{2}/$_3$ cup) whipping cream until it hangs on the whisk, then stir in 1 teasp each of brandy and sugar and continue to whip carefully until it will just hold its shape in a peak when the whisk is withdrawn.

Brandy snaps can be frozen empty or filled with whipped cream, or the uncooked mixture can be frozen.

Lemon Drops

A light-as-air biscuit (cookie) to serve with fruit sorbets or compotes.

Makes 36 F 6 months

2 eggs
^{1}/$_4$ pint (150ml/^{2}/$_3$ cup) oil
2 teasp vanilla essence (extract)
1 teasp grated lemon rind
5 oz (150g/^{2}/$_3$ cup) caster

(superfine) sugar
8 oz (225g/2 cups) self-raising
  flour
Pinch of salt
Almond nibs

Beat the eggs with a fork until well blended. Stir in the oil, vanilla and lemon rind. Blend in the sugar until the mixture thickens. Sift the flour and add to the egg mixture (the dough will be soft). Drop by rounded teaspoons on greased baking trays, 2 inches (5cm) apart. Using the bottom of a glass which has been dipped in oil and then in sugar, flatten each biscuit (cookie) into a round. Decorate with nuts. Bake in a quick oven (Gas No. 6, 400°F, 200°C) for 8-10 minutes.

Crunchy Biscuits (Cookies)

The following three biscuits (cookies) are made with oats, which gives them a particular crunchy texture.

Home-made Digestive Biscuits (Graham Crackers) (to serve with cheese)

These semi-sweet biscuits are equally delicious served with preserves at tea-time, with cheese after dinner, or at a cheese and wine party.

Makes about 30 **F** 6 months

oz (125g/1 cup) plain flour
4 oz (125g/1⅓ cup) porridge oats
4 oz (125g/½ cup) butter or
   margarine
2 level tbsp caster (superfine)
   sugar

½ level teasp each salt and
   bicarbonate of soda (baking
   soda)
2-3 tbsp milk

Mix the dry ingredients together then rub in the butter until like pastry crumbs. Mix to a firm but rollable dough with the milk mixed with the bicarbonate of soda.

Roll out ⅛ inch (0.5cm) thick on a floured board, and cut into 2½ inch (6.25cm) circles. Arrange on lightly oiled trays. Prick lightly with a fork to make a pattern on the top. Bake in a quick oven (Gas No. 6, 400°F, 200°C) for 12-15 minutes or until a rich golden brown.

Remove from the tray. When cool store in a tin.

Crunchy Date Bars

These are the ones you can buy at wholefood restaurants. A juicy date filling is sandwiched between two layers of crunch. 81% flour is creamy in colour and gives the biscuits (cookies) a nutty flavour.

Makes about 24 **F** 6 months

Filling:

12 oz (350g/2 cups) chopped and stoned fresh or packeted dates
2-4 oz (50-125g/½-1 cup) chopped walnuts

¼ pint (150ml/²/₃ cup) water
2 level teasp cinnamon
1 tbsp lemon juice

Put the dates into a pan with the walnuts and water and cook gently, stirring until they form a juicy paste. Add the lemon juice and cinnamon.

The crunch:

8 oz (225g/2 cups) 81% plain flour (or white flour if not available)
6 oz (175g/³/₄ cup) soft brown sugar

4 oz (125g/1¹/₃ cups) porridge oats
7 oz (200g/³/₄ + 2 tbsp) margarine or (preferable for the flavour) butter

Put the flour, sugar and oats into a bowl and add the melted fat, stirring until evenly moistened. Put half the crunch in a tin measuring 11 × 7 × 1¼ inches (27.5 × 17.5 × 3cm) and pat it down firmly, then spread the date mixture evenly on top. Scatter the remaining crunch on top and press into an even layer.

Bake in a moderate oven (Gas No. 4, 350°F, 180°C) for 55 minutes or until a rich brown.

Flapjacks

Simple but delicious for hearty appetites, especially out of doors.

Makes 50 **F** 6 months

½ lb (225g/2⅔ cups) breakfast or rolled oats

4 oz (125g/½ cup) butter

½ lb (225g/⅔ cup) golden (corn) syrup

4 oz (125g/½ cup) Barbados or Muscavado (very dark brown) sugar

In a pan, warm the butter until liquid then add the sugar and syrup and warm until the sugar is dissolved. Stir in the oats and mix well. Spoon into a large, flat, greased baking tin (11 × 15 × ½ inches/27.5 × 37.5 × 1.25cm), flattening with wetted fingers into a layer approx ¼ inch (0.5cm) thick.

Bake in a slow moderate oven (Gas No. 3, 325°F, 160°C) for 30 minutes or until a rich, even, deep brown – a light brown biscuit will not be as crisp. Remove from oven and after 5 minutes, when the biscuits have crispened slightly, mark into fingers 1 inch (2.5cm) wide and 3 inches (7.5cm) long, but leave in the tin until cold and really crisp.

Frivolities

In this section there are the rich and dainty biscuits (cookies) and petit fours which are so delicious served with after-dinner coffee, to accompany an ice or other delicate dessert, or to arrange in rows on a silver tray at a celebration tea-party. Each biscuit (cookie) should be barely a mouthful – no hearty tin-fillers here.

Miniature Brownies

Moist and chocolatey, just large enough to pop into the mouth! For less dainty occasions cut them into 2 inch (5cm) squares instead.

Makes 48 **F** 6 months

6 oz (175g/⅔ cup) margarine

3 level tbsp cocoa

6 oz (175g/⅔ cup) caster (superfine) or (preferably) soft dark brown sugar (Muscavado or Barbados)

2 eggs

2 oz (50g/½ cup) plain flour

2 oz (50g/½ cup) chopped walnuts

You will need a 6½-7 inch (16-17.5cm) square tin, greased and lined with greaseproof paper.

Melt 2 oz (50g/¼ cup) of the margarine in a small pan, then stir in the cocoa and set aside. Cream the remaining margarine and sugar until fluffy, then gradually beat in the eggs. Fold in the sifted flour, followed by the chopped walnuts and the cocoa mixture. Turn into the prepared tin, smooth the surface level, then bake in a moderate oven (Gas No. 4, 350°F, 180°C) for 30-35 minutes until the top springs back when gently pressed.

Sprinkle with caster sugar. Allow to cool in the tin, then cut into 48 × 1 inch (2.5cm) squares.

Almond Fingers

Fragile piped biscuits (cookies) decorated with almond flakes.

Makes 48 F 6 months

8 oz (225g/2 cups) plain flour	4 oz (125g/1 cup) ground almonds
½ level teasp baking powder	1 egg, beaten
8 oz (225g/1 cup) mild butter	1 teasp vanilla essence (extract)
3 oz (75g/⅓ cup) caster (superfine) sugar	1 oz flaked almonds

Cream the butter until it resembles mayonnaise, then beat in the sugar gradually until light and fluffy. Add the egg and the vanilla, then beat in the flour, baking powder and ground almonds. Beat well. The mixture should be the consistency of butter icing. Place in a forcing bag with a ½ inch (1.25cm) medium star tube, or put in a biscuit press. Pipe into sticks about 2 inches (5cm) long on ungreased trays. Scatter with almond flakes. Bake in a quick moderate oven (Gas No. 5, 375°F, 190°C) for 12 minutes or until a pale golden brown. Take off the tray at once and allow to cool.

Chocolate Nut Fingers

A coconut topping on a chocolate base.

Makes 24 F 6 months

6 oz (175g) milk or plain (semi-sweet) chocolate	4 oz (125g/1 cup) toasted skinned hazelnuts or walnuts, coarsely chopped

Topping:

2 oz (50g/¹/₄ cup) soft butter or margarine

4 oz (125g/1¹/₃ cups) dessicated coconut (dried and shredded)

3 oz (75g/¹/₃ cup) caster (superfine) sugar

Grated rind of ¹/₂ orange

1 large egg

If hazelnuts are used, toast these in a moderate oven (Gas No. 4, 350°F, 180°C) for 15 minutes or until they are golden brown under the skin. Put the nuts in a tea-towel and rub to remove the papery skin. Chop coarsely.

Choose a tin 7 or 8 inches (17.5 or 20cm) square or one about 10 × 7 inches (25 × 17.5cm). Grease and line with a strip of greased greaseproof paper or silicone paper. Break the chocolate into bits and scatter it over the bottom of the tin, then put in a low oven (Gas No. 1, 275°F, 140°C) for 10 minutes, when the chocolate will be soft enough to spread in an even layer. Sprinkle the chopped nuts evenly over the soft chocolate.

Put all the topping ingredients into a bowl and beat together until the mixture forms a smooth paste, then spread over the chocolate. Bake in a moderate oven (Gas No. 4, 350°F, 180°C) for 25 minutes or until golden brown. When quite cold, cut into fingers.

Golden Meringue Kisses

Unlike traditional meringues which are completely uncoloured, these little 'kisses' are a pale gold in colour because they are cooked at a slightly higher temperature in order to keep them soft inside while the outside becomes crisp and shiny. The 'kisses' can be served plain or sandwiched in pairs with whipped cream.

Note: Before making meringue kisses always wash the bowl and beaters in hot detergent, then rinse well. This will ensure that there is no grease present to prevent the egg whites beating up.

Makes 36 F 3 months

3 egg whites

6 oz (175g/³/₄ cup) caster (superfine) sugar

1 level teasp cornflour (cornstarch)

¹/₄ teasp cream of tartar or 1 teasp vinegar

Put the egg whites into a mixing bowl and add the cream of tartar. (If you are using vinegar it should be added later.) Mix the sugar and cornflour (cornstarch) together. Whisk the whites until they hold stiff but glossy peaks then start adding the sugar mixture a tablespoon at a time, beating until the meringue is stiff and glossy after each addition. Finally beat in the vinegar (if used). The meringue should now stand in stiff peaks when the beater is withdrawn.

Grease two baking sheets and line them with greased grease-proof paper. Spoon or pipe the meringue on to the paper in blobs about 1½ inches (3.75cm) across (they puff up in the oven), leaving 2 inches (5cm) between them. Have the oven pre-heated to Gas No. 2, 300°F, 150°C, put in the kisses, and immediately turn the oven down to Gas No. 1, 275°F, 140°C. Bake for 45 minutes or until the kisses feel crisp to the touch and can easily be lifted off the paper.

When quite cold, sandwich together with this cream: Whisk ¼ pint (150ml/⅔ cup) whipping cream until it starts to thicken, add 1 level teasp caster (superfine) sugar and ½ teasp vanilla essence (extract) or 1 teasp instant coffee dissolved in 2 teasp boiling water. Continue to whisk until the cream is thick enough to hold its shape. Refrigerate until required.

These kisses will keep fresh for several hours.

Nutty Butter Crisps

These butterscotch-flavoured biscuits (cookies) are ideal to serve with ice-cream or a cold sweet. Measure all the ingredients very carefully.

Makes 30 F 6 months

3 oz (75g/6 tbsp) butter
3 oz (75g/⅓ cup) caster (superfine) sugar
3 level teasp double (heavy) cream

3 oz (75g/⅔ cup) nibbed almonds
3 oz (75g/½ cup) chopped glacé (candied) cherries

Bring the butter, sugar and cream to boiling point, and simmer for 30 seconds. Add the nuts and cherries, then place in small teaspoonfuls on rice paper set on greased trays. Bake at Gas No. 4, 350°F, 180°C for 10-12 minutes until golden brown.

Remove from trays when firm and trim off rice paper.

Prelatoes

Very light and crisp sponge fingers, perfect to serve with a sorbet.

Makes 24 F 6 months

3 large eggs
$2^1/2$ oz (65g/$^1/3$ cup) caster
  (superfine) sugar
$2^1/2$ oz (65g/$^1/2$ cup + 2 tbsp) flour

Pinch of salt
2 teasp vanilla sugar *or* $^1/4$ teasp
  vanilla essence (extract)

Separate the eggs, and cream together the yolks and the sugar until white and fluffy. Beat in the flavouring. Beat the whites until they form stiff, glossy peaks. Sift together the salt and the flour. Stir a little of the egg white into the yolks and fold in the flour. Finally fold in the remaining egg white. The mixture should be firm but fluffy.

Using a $^1/2$ inch (1.25cm) plain pipe, pipe into finger lengths or rounds (or drop from a teaspoon in rounds) on a greased and floured tin. Dust with caster (superfine) sugar.

Bake in a moderate oven (Gas No. 5, 375°F, 190°C) for 5-7 minutes or until a pale golden brown.

Vanilla Kipferl

The famous Austrian speciality-crescents of almond-flavoured shortbread. I like to make them with equal quantities of almonds and hazelnuts.

Makes 36 F 6 months

6 oz (175g/$1^1/2$ cups) plain flour
6 oz (175g/$^2/3$ cup) butter
Pinch of salt
3 oz (75g/$^2/3$ cup) ground almonds
  or hazelnuts, *or* half and half

3 oz (75g/$^1/3$ cup) caster
  (superfine) sugar
1 teasp vanilla essence (extract) *or*
  2 packets vanilla sugar
Sieved icing (confectioners') or
  caster (superfine) sugar

The biscuits (cookies) can be made on the board like shortbread, or in the mixer or food processor, but in that case care must be taken not to overmix the sugar and butter.

In the mixer or food processor: Cut the butter into chunks, then mix in the sugar and vanilla until absorbed. Gradually add the flour, ground nuts and salt, until the dough leaves the side of the bowl clean. Chill for one hour.

On the board: Put the mixed salt, flour and nuts on the board, make a well in the centre, and put in the butter cut into chunks and the sugar. Work these together with the fingers, then gradually work in the surrounding dry ingredients until a dough is formed. Chill for one hour.

To form the biscuits: Try not to use any flour on the board as this will toughen the biscuits. Pinch off pieces the size of a walnut and roll between the palms into small balls. Roll each ball into a 'pencil', about ³/₄ inch (2cm) thick and 2¹/₂ inches (6cm) long, then bend into a crescent.

Arrange on ungreased baking sheets, leaving about 1 inch (2.5cm) between each biscuit (cookie), as they do spread a little. Bake in a slow, moderate oven (Gas No. 3, 325°F, 160°C) for 18 minutes or until a pale golden colour.

Carefully lift on to a cooling tray and leave for 3 minutes to firm up, then dip into a bowl, of icing (confectioners') or caster (superfine) sugar.

Stuffed Dates

Pitted dessert prunes may be substituted for dates.

Makes 24 Do not freeze **R** up to 1 week

24 fresh or dried dates	6 oz (175g/1¹/₂ cups) icing sugar
6 oz (175g/1¹/₂ cups) ground almonds	1 tbsp orangeflower or rosewater

Mix nuts, sugar and liquid and knead to a paste. Slit dates or prunes and flip out the stones, then replace with a lozenge of the almond paste.

Serve at room temperature, with coffee.

Ginger and Almond Clusters

These are crunchy little sweetmeats.

Makes 30 Do not freeze **R** 6 weeks in an airtight container

½ lb (225g) plain dessert
  (semi-sweet) chocolate
4 oz (125g) crystallised (candied)
  ginger

2 oz (50g/½ cup) toasted almond
  nibs
½ oz (15g/1 tbsp) butter or oil

Put the chocolate with the fat into a mixing bowl. Melt over hot water (or in the microwave). Stir in the roughly-chopped ginger and the toasted nuts. Put by the teaspoon into little sweet cases. Allow to set.

Frosted Grapes

These are delightful served with coffee, or used as a garnish for a cold mousse.

Do not freeze

1 egg white
Small clusters of grapes or
  individual grapes (seedless if
  possible)

Caster (superfine) sugar

Wash then dry the grapes thoroughly, or the egg white won't adhere. Beat a large egg white until it is very slightly frothy, so that it loses its 'gluey-ness'. Put the caster (superfine) sugar into a bowl. Dip each grape or cluster quickly in and out of the egg white, but make sure the surface is coated with the egg white or the sugar won't stick on. Dip immediately into the sugar, and place side by side on a cake rack. Repeat until all the grapes have been coated. They can then be left to dry in a warm place, such as the airing cupboard, but ideally they should be put into a warm oven which has just been used for baking or cooking – this gives the best 'frosted' appearance. Arrange in plastic containers or tins in layers, separated by greaseproof paper, until required, though preferably use within 24 hours.

Margaret's Shortcake Fingers

Thick, short and crumbly, these are made in minutes as they require no rolling.

Makes about 36   F 6 months

8 oz (225g/2 cups) plain flour
Pinch of salt
3 oz (75g/³/₄ cup) cornflour
  (cornstarch)
1 oz (24g/¹/₄ cup) semolina, ground
  rice or ground almonds

4 oz (125g/¹/₂ cup) caster
  (superfine) sugar
8 oz (225g/1 cup) butter

Put all the dry ingredients into a bowl. Cut the butter into ¹/₂ inch (1.25cm) chunks and then put into the bowl and rub into the flour mixture with the fingertips, or use an electric whisk at low speed, until a fine crumb is formed which looks like shortcrust pastry that has been rubbed in a little too far.

Spoon the mixture into a shallow (Swiss roll) tin approx 12 inches (30cm) by 8 inches (20cm) by ¹/₂ inch (1.25cm) deep, and press down firmly until the crumbs pack together. Prick all over with a fork, then bake at Gas No. 2, 300°F, 150°C for 55 minutes or until a very pale gold.

Remove from the oven, mark into fingers 3 inches (7.5cm) long and ³/₄ inch (2cm) wide and sprinkle with caster (superfine) sugar. When cold, remove from the tin and store in an airtight container.

Cakes

In this chapter I have included a wide selection of recipes from the simple one-stage quick-to-make cakes to the rich, expensive fruit-cakes suitable for a special occasion.

The life of a cake used to be limited to the time it would keep fresh in an airtight tin. But the advent of the freezer means that life can be prolonged for up to 3 months in the case of cream and decorated cakes and for as long as 6 months for undecorated cakes. This means that the baking for even the most elaborate tea-party or charity function can be spread over as long a period as is convenient. It also means that left over cakes (other than cream cakes) can go back into the freezer for use another time.

General storage: All cakes need airtight storage as this retards staling. In addition cream cakes should always be refrigerated or frozen until use.

To freeze: Wrap undecorated cakes in foil. Plain cakes should be loosely wrapped and left at room temperature 1-3 hours according to size. Cakes can be defrosted in the microwave, but they will then stale more quickly.

Preparation of cake tins: Unless the tin has an effective non-stick coating, it must be prepared in some way to prevent the baked cake from sticking to it. Unless specified otherwise in the individual recipe, the tin should always be lightly but thoroughly brushed with a thin coating of oil (butter or margarine may cause the mixture to stick). Richer cakes will also need either bottom-lining with a piece of oiled greaseproof paper, or, if they are to spend longer than 1½ hours in the oven, they should be completely lined with greaseproof, foil or oiled brown paper.

Cooling the cake: Place the cake in its tin on a metal cooling rack for 10 minutes to allow it to set, then gently ease it out of the tin. A spatula may be necessary to loosen the cake from the sides. Turn the cake over so that it is right side up. The easiest way to do this is to turn it on to a second cooling rack. To remove a cake from a tin with a loose bottom, stand the cake on a canister of smaller diameter, then gently ease down the sides of the cake tin. Use a spatula to transfer the cake (still on the base) from the canister to a cooling rack. Remove the base when the cake is cool enough to handle. This method is recommended for very fragile cakes or heavy fruit-cakes which might not take kindly to being turned upside down while still warm.

Notes on the ingredients:

Eggs: Most cake recipes are based on a so-called 'standard' egg (Size 3 – weighing 60g in the European Economic Community). However, for recipes using up to 3 eggs, the size of egg is not critical. After that, the use of too large an egg may upset the balance of liquid in the recipe.

Fats: Margarine produces the lightest creamed cake; butter produces the one with the best flavour. Using a mixture of both fats produces a light well-flavoured cake. For one-stage cakes, margarine alone gives a lighter result, for rich fruit-cakes (which barely rise), butter is to be preferred for its flavour.

Flour: Delicate cakes such as sponges and light creamed cakes are best made with 70% extraction white flour of the finest quality. For homelier cakes, such as the plainer fruit or spice cakes, 81% extraction flour is not only more nourishing but gives a nuttier flavour.

Sugar: Always use caster (superfine) sugar or soft brown sugar that dissolves easily in either a creamed or a one-stage cake. Granulated sugar does not give such a good result and will produce a rougher crumb.

Flavourings: Use the best quality essence (extract) you can buy.
Finely grated orange and lemon rind give a better flavour than the juice.
Add flavourings to the fat and sugar, rather than with the flour. This helps to intensify the flavour.

Quick Kuchen

Quick kuchen is a generic term that covers a wide range of cakes that can be topped either with a streusel (a sweet crumble) or with seasonal fruits. The original kuchens were always raised with yeast, but German settlers in the United States in the middle of the 19th century soon learned to use the newly-discovered 'baking powder' instead. These cakes do not have the typical flavour or savour of a yeast-raised kuchen, but are quite delicious in their own right. The cake mixture itself is an economical one, containing a low ratio of eggs and fat to flour, but a high ratio of baking powder. The resulting cake is very light, and when it is freshly baked it can also be served as a dessert.

Streusel Kuchen

F 6 months
Cake mixture:

8 oz (225g/2 cups) self-raising flour and 1 level teasp baking powder *or* 8 oz (225g/2 cups) plain flour, a pinch of salt and 3 level teasp baking powder

3 oz (75g/^{1}/3 cup) soft margarine

3 oz (75g/^{1}/3 cup) caster (superfine) sugar

1 egg

1 rounded tbsp apricot jam or ginger marmalade

^{1}/4 pint (150ml/^{2}/3 cup) milk

Put all the ingredients into a bowl and beat by hand or machine until a thick, smooth batter is formed (2-3 minutes). Turn the batter into a cake tin 12 × 9 × 2 inches (30 × 22.5 × 5cm), and level with a knife.

Streusel topping:

2 oz (50g/^{1}/2 cup) flour
2 level teasp ground cinnamon
2 oz (50g/^{1}/4 cup) butter

6 oz (175g/^{3}/4 cup) light brown sugar

Mix the flour, cinnamon and sugar. Melt the butter, then pour onto the dry ingredients and a blend with a fork until evenly moistened and crumbly. Sprinkle the streusel evenly over the cake mixture. Bake in a quick oven (Gas No. 6, 400°F, 200°C) for 25-30 minutes or until golden brown. This kuchen is soft and tender for 3 days after it has been baked. Later it can be sliced and buttered, or toasted and buttered.

Apple Kuchen with Streusel Topping

A layer of apples is laid on top of the raw cake mixture before the streusel is sprinkled on top. If preferred, omit the jam from the cake mixture and use a total of 5 oz (150g/²/₃ cup) sugar instead. This is delicious served slightly warm with sweetened whipped cream, flavoured with a pinch of cinnamon.

Makes 12 portions F 6 months
1 recipe **Kuchen Cake Mixture** (p.459)

Spoon into a greased tin measuring 12 × 9 × 2 inches (30 × 22.5 × 5cm) or into two 7 inch (17.5cm) loose-bottomed sandwich tins. Spread the batter evenly with a palette knife.
1¹/₂ lb (675g) baking apples (weight before peeling)

Peel, core and quarter the apples, then cut into slices ¹/₈ inch (0.25cm) thick. (If possible do this on the coarse slicer of a food processor.) Arrange the apple slices in overlapping rows so that the kuchen batter is completely covered. Scatter with the streusel, made as follows:

2 oz (50g/¹/₄ cup) butter, melted	6 oz (175g/³/₄ cup) soft brown
2 oz (50g/¹/₂ cup) flour	sugar
	1 teasp cinnamon

Mix the flour, sugar and cinnamon. Pour on the melted butter and mix until crumbly. Scatter evenly over the apples. Bake in a quick moderate oven (Gas No. 5, 375°F, 190°C) for 40-50 minutes, or until the cake has shrunk away from the sides of the tin, the apples feel tender when pierced with a knife, and the streusel is golden brown.

This kuchen is at its most delicious 1-2 hours after baking, when it should be cut into squares. But it is still very edible for up to 3 days. Store tightly foil-covered in the refrigerator. Freezes well. To reheat – foil cover whole kuchen or pieces and put in a moderate oven (Gas No. 4, 350°F, 180°C) until warm to the touch – about 15 minutes.

VARIATION 1
Peach Kuchen: Makes 12 portions. Peel 6 large peaches (by plunging for 1 minute into boiling water, then skinning). Slice and use to cover the kuchen instead of the apples.

Quick-Mix Cakes

These cakes are made by putting all the ingredients in a bowl together and beating them until a smooth batter is formed. It is important to use a very soft fat (preferably margarine) so that the ingredients will blend together evenly before overbeating has a chance to toughen the cake. The cakes can be made in this way by hand, electric mixer or food processor. With the latter, however, it is best to process all the ingredients (except the flour) until smooth, and then add the flour and process until evenly blended. This makes a particularly light, tender cake.

German Apfel Kuchen (Apple Cake)

A most delicious blend of flavours. Tastes very good with coffee.

F 6 months

7 oz (200g/1³/₄ cups) self-raising
   flour
5 oz (150g/²/₃ cup) soft margarine

3 oz (75g/¹/₃ cup) caster
   (superfine) sugar
1 large egg

Put all the ingredients into a bowl and beat by hand or machine until smooth (about 2 minutes). You will have a mixture which is a cross between a pastry and a cake batter. Have ready a 9 inch (22.5cm) loose-bottomed cake tin at least 2 inches (5cm) in depth. Oil it lightly, then spread two thirds of the mixture on the bottom.

The filling:

1 lb (450g) baking apples, peeled,
   cored, quartered and sliced ¹/₈
   inch (6.25cm) thick

2 slightly rounded tbsp granulated
   sugar
Squeeze of lemon juice
2 level tbsp apricot jam

Slice the apples onto the cake mixture, then sprinkle with the sugar and lemon juice and dot with the jam (apricot conserve can go straight from the tin, but ordinary jam may need to be warmed slightly). Finally, drop the remaining cake mixture by teaspoonfuls all over the apple filling.

Bake in a moderate oven (Gas No. 4, 350°F, 180°C) for 1 hour, or until the top cake mixture is golden brown, and the apple filling feels quite tender when you plunge a sharp knife into it. When cold, carefully ease from the tin.

Delicious Scones

Scones are very simple and economical to make but absolutely delicious when freshly baked and buttered. To reheat from frozen, put in a moderate oven (Gas No. 4, 350°F, 180°C) for 15 minutes, then treat as freshly baked.

Sultana (White Raisin) Scones

Makes 12-15 F 6 months

1/2 lb (225g/2 cups) self-raising flour plus 2 level teasp baking powder, *or* 1/2 lb (225g/2 cups) plain flour and 4 level teasp baking powder

1 oz (25g/2 tbsp) caster (superfine) or soft brown sugar
1 1/2 oz (40g/3 tbsp) butter
1/4 pint (150ml/2/3 cup) milk
2 oz (50g/1/3 cup) sultanas (white raisins)

Sift the dry ingredients, then rub in the fat by hand or machine until the mixture resembles coarse crumbs. Add the sultanas (white raisins).

By hand: Make a well in the centre, pour in the milk and mix to a soft but non-sticky dough with a round knife, cutting through and through the dry ingredients to moisten them evenly.

By machine: Add the milk all at once and process only until a dough is formed.

Turn out onto a lightly floured board and knead for about 30 seconds, or until no cracks remain on the underside of the dough. Roll the dough 3/4 inch (1.75cm) thick. Cut into circles 2 inches (5cm) in diameter and place on greased trays. Brush with milk and then sprinkle evenly with granulated sugar. Bake in a hot oven (Gas No. 8, 450°F, 230°C) for 12-15 minutes or until golden brown. When cool, split and butter, and serve with jam and unsweetened whipped cream.

Sugar and Spice Rings

A scone dough is rolled out and spread with a raisin filling, then formed into little rolls to eat freshly from the oven or slightly warm.

Makes 12   F 6 months
1 recipe **Scones** (p.462) without the sultanas

The filling:

1 oz (25g/2 tbsp) soft or melted
  butter
2 oz (50g/¹/₄ cup) caster
  (superfine) sugar

1 level teasp cinnamon
About 4 tbsp raisins (enough to
  cover dough)

For glaze:

2 teasp melted butter and 2 teasp brown sugar × 12

Make the scone dough in the usual way and roll out into a rectangle about 12 inches (30cm) long and 7 inches (17.5cm) wide. Spread with the 1 oz (25g/2 tbsp) butter, sprinkle with the cinnamon, sugar and dried fruit, leaving 1 inch (2.5cm) clear all the way round. Turn in the sides. Roll up tightly like a Swiss roll, then cut into rolls 1 inch (2.5cm) wide. Put the 2 teasp of melted butter and brown sugar in each of 12 patty tins and top with a roll, cut side up.

    Bake at Gas No. 7, 425°F, 220°C for 15 minutes or until a rich brown. Immediately turn out on to a cooling tray. Nicest when fresh or slightly warmed. Reheat in a foil parcel in a moderate oven until just warm to the touch – about 15 minutes.

Farmhouse Scones

These are slightly crumbly in texture. They are nicest eaten fresh, split, spread with strawberry jam and butter, or filled with cottage cheese and chives.

Makes 12 F 6 months

8 oz (225g/2 cups) 81% self-raising
  flour
2 level teasp baking powder
Pinch salt
2 oz (50g/¹/₄ cup) margarine or
  butter

1 oz (25g/2 tbsp) soft brown sugar
1 egg, beaten
5 tbsp milk
Milk to glaze, brown sugar

Set the oven to Gas No. 6, 400°F, 200°C. Lightly grease 2 baking
sheets. Place the flour, baking powder and salt in a bowl. Rub in
the margarine and add the sugar. Add the beaten egg and milk and
mix well to form a soft dough. Knead until smooth.

Place on a lightly floured board and roll out to ¹/₂ inch (1.25cm)
thickness. Cut with a 2 inch (5cm) plain or fluted cutter and place
onto the prepared baking sheet. Brush with top of milk and scatter
with brown sugar. Bake for 15-20 minutes.

Cakes with a Chocolate Flavour

Gâteau Reine de Saba (Queen of Sheba Cake)

*This delicate cake is made with potato flour (called 'fécule' in
France) which gives it a very tender, moist flavour.*

F 3 months

6 oz (175g) plain (semi-sweet)
  chocolate
4 oz (125g/¹/₂ cup) butter (unsalted
  if available)
2 oz (50g/¹/₂ cup) potato flour

4 oz (125g/¹/₂ cup) caster
  (superfine) sugar
1 level teasp baking powder
4 eggs, separated
1 teasp vanilla essence (extract)

Use an 8 inch (20cm) moule à manque (shallow tin with sloping
sides), otherwise use an 8 inch (20cm) loose-bottomed tin. In both
cases, oil the tin and bottom-line with oiled greaseproof paper. Set
the oven at Gas No. 4, 350°F, 180°C. Put the butter in a large,
thick-bottomed pan and melt it gently, then add the broken
chocolate and sugar, and stir over very gentle heat until the
chocolate and sugar have melted. Take from the heat and stir in
the egg yolks, vanilla and the sifted potato flour. Finally fold in

464

the egg whites, beaten with a pinch of salt until they hold stiff but still glossy peaks. Turn the mixture into the prepared tin and bake for 40-45 minutes until well risen and firm to a very gentle touch.

Leave on a cooling tray for 5 minutes then turn out and leave until cold. When cold, pour over the rum icing.

Rum Icing: Melt 2 oz (50g/¼ cup) butter over gentle heat, add 4 oz (125g) plain chocolate and stir until melted, then add 1 tbsp rum. Stir until smooth and gleaming, then pour over the cake and decorate with shaved chocolate or chopped nuts.

Note: If a moule à manque has been used, it will be the narrower base of the cake that is iced, rather than the top.

Marble Cake with Coffee Fudge Icing

If preferred the rum icing from the previous cake can be used to ice this tender ring cake. But the Coffee Fudge Icing, though more trouble to make, is absolutely delicious.

F 3 months

3 oz (75g/⅓ cup) butter
3 oz (75g/⅓ cup) soft margarine
7 oz (200g/1 cup) caster (superfine) sugar
8 oz (225g/2 cups) self-raising flour
3 tbsp hot water
1 teasp vanilla essence (extract)
3 large eggs
1 level tbsp cocoa and 4 level tbsp drinking (instant) chocolate
1 tbsp hot water

Cream the butter or margarine and sugar until like mayonnaise, then beat in the vanilla. Add the eggs, together with a tbsp of flour for each egg. Stir in the sifted flour, alternately with the 3 tbsp hot water, beginning and ending with flour.

Have ready a 9 inch (22.5cm) greased kugelhopf or ring tin. Drop half the mixture by spoonfuls into the tin leaving gaps between. To the remaining mixture add the cocoa, drinking (instant) chocolate and hot water and stir well until blended. Spoon into the gaps then level the cake mixture. Bake in the middle of the oven at Gas No. 4, 350°F, 180°C for 45 minutes or until firm to a gentle touch. Cool completely before icing.

Coffee Fudge Icing

¹/₂ lb (225g/1 cup) granulated sugar
2 oz (50g/¹/₄ cup) butter
5 fl oz (150ml/²/₃ cup) evaporated
  milk

2 teasp coffee essence, iced
coffee syrup or very strong
instant coffee

Put all the ingredients into a small saucepan and stir over gentle heat until the sugar is dissolved. Bring to the boil, stirring, and boil until a little dropped in cold water can be formed into a soft ball. Take from the heat and immediately stand in a bowl of cold water to stop cooking. Beat until it starts to thicken like softly whipped cream, then pour over the cake.

Mocha Sandwich

A tender milk chocolate cake with a luscious filling.

F 3 months
The cake:

4 oz (125g/¹/₂ cup) soft butter or
  margarine
4 oz (125g/¹/₂ cup) caster
  (superfine) sugar
2 eggs
1 teasp instant coffee dissolved in
  2 tbsp hot water

1 teasp vanilla essence (extract)
5 oz (150g/1¹/₄ cups) self-raising
  flour, sifted with 3 oz (75g/³/₄
  cup) drinking (instant)
  chocolate and 1 level tbsp
  cocoa
2 tbsp cold milk

Grease, then bottom-line with greaseproof paper an 8 inch (20cm) loose-bottomed cake tin (about 2 inches/5cm deep) or a moule à manque (sloping sided tin). Cream the fat and sugar until fluffy, then beat in the eggs, one at a time. Now add the vanilla and the hot coffee liquid. Add half the flour mixed with the drinking chocolate and cocoa, then the milk, followed by the rest of the flour. Do not beat, just stir to blend. (This can all be done on a food processor.) Spoon into the prepared tin and level with a knife.

    Bake in a moderate oven (Gas No. 4, 350°F, 180°C) for 40 minutes or until firm to gentle pressure. Leave on a cooling tray for 5 minutes then ease out carefully, loosening the sides with a knife if necessary. Allow to go quite cold, then carefully split through the centre and fill with the mocha cream.

Mocha cream

2 tbsp evaporated milk, *or* top milk, *or* 1 tbsp each milk and brandy, rum or Tia Maria
2 rounded tbsp drinking (instant) chocolate

1 level teasp instant coffee
3 oz (75g/¹/₃ cup) butter
3 oz (75g/³/₄ cup) icing (confectioners') sugar

Put all the ingredients except the butter and sugar into a pan and heat gently until a smooth liquid. Take off the heat. Beat the butter until it is like mayonnaise, then beat in the icing (confectioners') sugar followed by the chocolate mixture. Allow to cool until thick enough to spread, then spread between the two layers of the cake.

Serve plain sprinkled with icing (confectioners') sugar or with this mixture: Put in a pan 2 oz (50g/¹/₄ cup) butter and when melted add 4 oz (125g/1 cup) drinking (instant) chocolate. Stir over gentle heat until smooth, then pour over the cake. Decorate, if liked, with walnut halves.

Coffee Chocolate Frosting

If preferred, do not split the Mocha Sandwich but instead coat it with this delicious, smooth frosting which can also be used to coat the Marble Cake (p.465).

3 oz (75g/¹/₃ cup) soft butter
8 oz, (225g/2 cups) icing (confectioners') sugar
4 tbsp drinking (instant) chocolate

2 tbsp cocoa
2 tbsp boiling water
3 teasp instant coffee

Put the drinking (instant) chocolate, cocoa and coffee into a small bowl then pour on the boiling water and mix to a smooth cream. By hand or food processor: Cream the butter until like mayonnaise, then add half the sifted icing (confectioners') sugar, and cream again. Add the chocolate and coffee cream, and then the remaining icing sugar, beating thoroughly until smooth and glossy. Pour over the cake at once. This sets to a fudge-like consistency.

Chocolate Éclairs

I cannot pretend that these delicious little pastries are not time-consuming to make. However, they do freeze extremely well, and guests always enjoy them enormously. This recipe will not fail.

Makes 18 or 36 F empty shells 3 months: filled eclairs 1 month

Quantities for 18	*Quantities for 36*
2¹/₂ oz (65g/¹/₂ cup + 2 tbsp) plain flour	5 oz (150g/1¹/₄ cups)
Pinch salt	¹/₄ teasp
2 oz (50g/¹/₄ cup) butter	4 oz (125g/¹/₂ cup)
¹/₄ pint (150ml/²/₃ cup) boiling water	¹/₂ pint (275ml/1¹/₄ cups)
2 level teasp sugar	1 level tbsp
2 eggs	4

Put the water in a thick saucepan, add the butter cut in cubes and as soon as the fat melts and the mixture comes to the boil, add the flour, sugar and salt. Cook over gentle heat stirring until the mixture leaves the sides and bottom of the pan quite clean and forms a ball of dough you can toss around (1-2 minutes). Cool for 4-5 minutes. Beat in the eggs one at a time using an electric mixer if possible, otherwise use a wooden spoon. When the mixture has been beaten enough it should stand up in soft peaks and be semi-transparent when pulled out into a ribbon.

Put a ¹/₂ inch (1.25cm) plain piping tube into a large nylon bag and fill the bag with the mixture. Pipe the mixture into 3 inch (7.5cm) lengths on to a greased tray, cutting off each length with a sharp knife. Allow 1 inch (2.5cm) between each éclair for expansion. Bake at Gas No. 7, 425°F, 220°C for 25 minutes or until golden brown and hollow when tapped. Make slits in the sides imnmediately. Turn off the heat, return the éclairs to the oven and leave for 10 minutes with the door ajar. Cool on a rack.

The filling:

Quantities for 18	*Quantities for 36*
¹/₄ pint (150ml/²/₃ cup) whipping cream	¹/₂ pint (275ml/1¹/₄ cups)
¹/₂ teasp vanilla essence (extract)	1 teasp
2 teasp caster (superfine) sugar	1 tbsp

Whisk all the ingredients together and when the éclairs are quite cold, pipe the cream inside each one.

Chocolate icing:

Quantities for 18	*Quantities for 36*
1 oz (25g/2 tbsp) butter	2 oz (50g/¼ cup)
2 oz (50g) plain (semi-sweet) chocolate	4 oz (125g)
2 tbsp boiling water	4 tbsp
6 oz (175g/1½ cups) icing (confectioners') sugar	12 oz (350g/3 cups)

Melt the butter and chocolate together in a basin standing in a saucepan of simmering water. Remove from the heat and beat in the remaining ingredients. Beat until smooth and of a coating consistency. Use to ice the éclairs.

The shells can be frozen for up to 3 months. To re-crispen, place in the oven heated to Gas No. 7, 425°F, 220°C for 3-4 minutes. Allow to cool before filling.

Spice Cakes

There are innumerable varieties of spice cakes, the majority given a particular 'sticky' quality by the use of golden (corn) syrup, treacle (molasses) or honey. The 'stickiness' increases if the cake is left to mature, well wrapped in foil, for a period of 2 to 7 days. Always smell the spice before use to make sure it is still pungent and fresh. As spices tend to change their intensity in the freezer, if they are to be used within a month, these cakes are best kept well wrapped in an airtight tin in a larder. For a longer period – up to 3 months – they may be frozen; but they will not continue to mature in the freezer as they do at normal temperatures, so allow to mature as described above before freezing.

Ginger Loaf

A moist tender cake, studded with ginger pieces.

F 3 months. In a tin or airtight container or at room temperature, 1 month

8 fl oz (225ml/1 cup) oil

7 oz (200g/1 cup) soft brown sugar, dark if possible

1 lb (450g/1^1/2 cups) golden (corn) syrup

2 eggs

1 lb 2 oz (500g/4^1/2 cups) self-raising flour sifted with 6

level teasp ground ginger and 2 level teasp cinnamon

^{1}/2 lb (450g) jar firm ginger marmalade

The tin of syrup filled with hot water (12 fl oz/350ml/1^1/2 cups)

^{1}/2 level teasp bicarbonate of soda (baking soda)

Grease two loaf tins 9 × 5 × 3 inches (22.5 × 12.5 × 7.5cm) and line the bottoms with greaseproof paper.

Note: If two tins are not available, use a deep roasting tin approx 12 × 10 inches (30 × 25cm).

It is most convenient to use a 1 lb (450g) tin of syrup and then use it as a measure for the water. Otherwise weigh out the syrup and use a measure for the water.

Turn the oven to Gas No. 2, 300°F, 150°C. Put the *open* tin of syrup in the oven for 5 minutes to make it easy to pour, then tip the syrup into a mixing bowl. Have the flour sifted with the spices. Add the oil, sugar, eggs, marmalade and half the flour to the syrup. Stir well until smooth.

Add the remaining flour and water mixed with the bicarbonate of soda (baking soda) gradually stirring until the mixture is thoroughly blended – it will be the consistency of a pouring batter. Divide between the two tins. Bake for 1^3/4 hours until the tops are springy to gentle touch, the cakes have shrunk slightly from the sides, and a skewer comes out clean from the centres. Place both cakes on a cooling tray and leave for 30 minutes, then ease out of the tins.

The cakes can be used at once, but are better if left at least two days before cutting. Store in foil or an airtight plastic container.

Yorkshire Sponge Gingerbread

Although this does improve with keeping, I first ate it hot from the oven in a little café in the Yorkshire Dales. After a day's hike it tasted like the food of the gods! It is perfect for a picnic, as well as for a winter tea. It is equally delicious if golden (corn) syrup is used instead of treacle (molasses), but it won't be so dark in colour.

F 3 months

8 oz (225g/1 cup) butter
8 oz (225g/1 cup) soft brown sugar
8 oz (225g/³/4 cup) treacle
  (molasses)
12 oz (350g/3 cups) plain flour,
  sifted with 1 generous tbsp

ginger and 1 level teasp
cinnamon
2 eggs
¹/2 pint (275ml/1¹/4 cups) milk
2 level teasp bicarbonate of soda
  (baking soda)

Melt the butter, sugar and treacle (molasses) over low heat. Allow to cool a litle, then add to the flour, cinnamon and ginger and stir in the eggs. Warm the milk and pour on to the bicarbonate of soda (baking soda), then add to the flour mixture. Mix thoroughly (the batter will be thin). Pour into a rectangular tin approx 12 × 9 × 2 inches (30 × 22.5 × 5cm), which has been greased, then bottom-lined with greased greaseproof paper.

Bake in a slow oven (Gas No. 2, 300°F, 150°C) for 1¹/2 to 2 hours, depending on the size of the tin. (Test after 1¹/2 hours: if it springs back when lightly touched with a finger, it is ready.) Turn out on a cooling rack. When cold, store in the same tin covered with foil.

Honey and Spice Cake

Honey cakes of this kind – like all the spice cakes – were the first to be made with artificial raising agents, for the crude reagents then used left unpalatable by-products which were not readily discernible in a heavily-spiced cake. Honey was the chosen sweetener because cheap refined sugar was not widely available until the end of the 19th century

It is important to weigh the honey carefully or it will make the cake heavy and oversweet.

F 3 months

¹/2 lb (225g/2 cups) plain flour
6 oz (175g/³/4 cup) caster
  (superfine) sugar
2 level teasp each of cinnamon
  and mixed spice
10 oz (275g/³/4 cup) clear honey

4 fl oz (125ml/¹/2 cup) cooking oil
2 eggs
1 level teasp bicarbonate of soda
  (baking soda) dissolved in 4 fl
  oz (125ml/¹/2 cup) strong coffee
2 oz (50g/¹/2 cup) chopped walnuts

Mix together the flour, sugar and spices. Make a well in the centre, then add the honey, oil and eggs. Beat well together until smooth. Dissolve the bicarbonate of soda (baking soda) in the coffee and add the nuts, then stir into the mixture. Pour into a greaseproof paper lined tin approximately 10 × 8 × 2 inches (25 × 20 × 5cm).

Bake at Gas No. 3, 325°F, 160°C for 1¼ hours or until firm to the touch. Cool out of a draught. When quite cold, foil wrap and leave if possible for 1 week before using. This cake improves with keeping.

The Cheesecake

Cheesecake was first made by the ancient Greeks, but it is to present-day Americans that we owe the recipe that is most popular today. This makes a cake that is firm yet creamy, and can be baked on a base of pastry, crushed biscuits or sponge. I have given the recipe for a sponge base as I think it contrasts well with the richness of the filling. Although a topping makes the cake look particularly pretty, it can be omitted and a 5 fl oz (150ml/⅔ cup) carton of soured cream stirred into the cake instead. This makes it the richest, creamiest cheesecake of all.

It is important to use a medium or low fat cream cheese, as a high fat (double cream) cheese does not give the correct texture. It is sometimes possible to buy a special baker's cream cheese which has a fat content of 12% and undoubtedly gives the best results. If your cheesecake rises then falls, you have over-baked it – so don't be tempted to leave the cake in the oven for longer than stated. A cheesecake doesn't need to be completely set when it comes out of the oven. Like a custard, it continues to set as it cools, so providing the inch of mixture nearest to the edge of the tin is firm to the touch, the cake can be taken out of the oven.

To freeze: Cheesecake freezes extremely well. It is a good idea to portion any left over cake then open freeze it before packing in a plastic container. You can then defrost individual pieces as they are required. If you intend to use the fruit glaze, it is best to freeze the cake alone, then defrost and add the topping not more than 24 hours before it is required. The cake can be completely frozen with the glaze if absolutely necessary, but the texture of the fruit may be altered when it is defrosted.

To defrost: Take from the freezer, unwrap and put on a serving dish. Refrigerate until required. Takes about 3 hours to defrost.

Cheesecake American Style

For the base you can either use 1 packet of trifle sponges cut into slices and used to line the bottom of a buttered 7 inch (17.5cm) square tin or a 9 inch (22.5cm) loose-bottomed round cake tin; or use the following recipe:

Serves 6-8   **F** 3 months

4 oz (125g/1 cup) self-raising flour
3 oz (75g/$^1/_3$ cup) butter or margarine
2 oz (50g/$^1/_2$ cup) icing (confectioners') sugar
1 egg yolk
2 tbsp creamy milk

Put all the ingredients into a bowl and beat until smooth – about 2 minutes. Spread on the bottom of the greased loose-bottomed cake tin, bake at Gas No. 5, 375°F, 190°C for 20 minutes until golden brown. Leave in the tin but on a rack until it has cooled.

Cheesecake mixture:

2 oz (50g/$^1/_4$ cup) very soft or melted butter
2 oz (50g/$^1/_4$ cup) caster (superfine) sugar
$^1/_2$ teasp vanilla essence (extract)
2 eggs, separated
1 teasp each orange and lemon rind
Juice of half a lemon
2 teasp caster (superfine) sugar
1 lb (450g/2 cups) medium or low fat cream cheese
2 level tbsp cornflour (cornstarch)
5 fl oz (150ml/$^2/_3$ cup) soured cream

Whisk the egg whites until they hold stiff glossy peaks, then whisk in the 2 teasp caster (superfine) sugar. Put all the other ingredients, except the soured cream, into a bowl and beat until absolutely smooth. Then fold in the meringue and soured cream using a metal spoon. Spoon the mixture into the tin on top of the sponge base. Bake in a quick moderate oven (Gas No. 4, 350°F, 180°C) for 30-35 minutes until the inch (2.5cm) margin near the edge of the tin is firm to the touch. Remove from the oven. The whole cake will firm up as it cools.

The cake can now be allowed to go quite cold then refrigerated and served the next day, or it can be decorated as follows:

473

Fruit Topping: You can use any tinned fruit – sliced peaches, blackcurrants, pineapple, apricot halves, black cherries or a mixture of fresh and canned fruit.

1 lb (450g) tin fruit or 1 lb (450g) soft fruit	3 level teasp cornflour (cornstarch)
8 fl oz (225ml/1 cup) syrup from the fruit	2 level tbsp granulated sugar
	1 tbsp lemon juice

Drain the fruit thoroughly, then arrange in a design on top of the cake. Put the cornflour (cornstarch) and sugar into a pan, then gradually stir in the fruit syrup and lemon juice. Bring to the boil and simmer for 3 minutes. Cool until it has started to thicken, then spoon over the fruit. Refrigerate or freeze until required.

To serve: run a knife round the edge of the cake to loosen it from the tin. Stand it on a canister or tin of smaller size and carefully pull down the sides. The cake can then be carefully eased off the base, or the base and cake can be put onto a serving dish.

Sour Cream Topping: Omit soured cream in the cake and instead add 2 tbsp single (light) cream or top milk.

2 cartons (10 fl oz/275ml/1¼ cups) soured cream	Few drops vanilla essence (extract)
1 level tbsp caster (superfine) sugar	

Turn the oven up to Gas No. 6, 400°F, 200°C. Leave the cake to cool for 10 minutes, then mix the topping ingredients and spread over the top. Return to the oven for 8 minutes.

When cold, refrigerate or freeze as required.

Fruit-Cakes

Farmhouse Fruit-Cake

This cake requires no creaming yet it has a moist texture and a most delicious flavour. The 81% flour makes it especially tasty but ordinary white flour may be substituted.

F 6 months

6 oz (175g/³/₄ cup) soft margarine

6 oz (175g/³/₄ cup) soft dark or medium brown sugar

3 eggs

1 tbsp golden (corn) syrup

2 tbsp milk

12 oz (350g/2¹/₂ cups) mixed dried fruit

2 oz (50g/¹/₂ cups) chopped walnuts (save 6 halves)

¹/₂ lb (225g/2 cups) plain cake flour (81%)

¹/₂ level teasp baking powder

2 level teasp mixed sweet spice

Glaze: milk, demerara sugar

Grease and line a 7-8 inch (17-20cm) deep loose-bottomed cake tin with greaseproof paper.

Put all the cake ingredients, except the fruit, into a bowl and stir thoroughly until well blended – you can use an electric mixer, wooden spoon or food processor. Add the fruit. Do not mix more than is necessary to make a smooth mixture or you will toughen the cake. Spoon into the prepared tin and smooth flat. For the nicest finish, brush with milk then scatter with demerara sugar. Arrange the six walnut halves on top.

Bake at Gas No. 4 (350°F, 180°C) for ¹/₂ hour then turn down to Gas No. 3 (325°F, 160°C) and bake for a further 1-1¹/₄ hours, or until a skewer comes out clean when plunged into the centre. Leave to cool on a wire tray for half an hour then ease out of the tin.

Store in an airtight container.

Family Fruit-Cake

This is an economical fruit cake with a spongy texture and most delicious flavour. It can be made either with white or brown (81%) flour and white or brown sugar. Ideal for coffee mornings or picnics.

Makes 2 × 2 lb (1kg) loaves **F** 6 months

6 oz (175g/³/₄ cup) caster (superfine) or soft brown sugar

4 tbsp (barely rounded) golden (corn) syrup

6 oz (175g/³/₄ cup) margarine

12 oz (350g/3 cups) white or 81% (wheatmeal) self-raising flour

3 level teasp mixed sweet spice

1 level teasp cinnamon

4 level tbsp marmalade (2 each ginger and lemon is a good combination)

6 tbsp hot water

12 oz (350g/2¹/₂ cups) mixed dried fruit

2 eggs

Grease then bottom-line with greaseproof paper 2 × 2 lb (1kg) loaf tins 9 × 5 × 3 inches (23 × 13 × 7.5cm). Set the oven at Gas No. 4, 350°F, 180°C.

Put the margarine, sugar, marmalade and syrup into a saucepan and heat gently until liquid.

Put the flour and spices into a bowl then add the liquid mixture and stir thoroughly. Stir in the hot water, then the fruit and eggs. Divide the mixture between the two tins and bake at Gas No. 4, 350°F, 180°C for 30 minutes, then reduce to No. 3, 325°F, 160°C for a further 30 minutes.

Turn out of the tins and allow to cool. Can be eaten the same day but may be a little crumbly.

Fruit and Spice Loaf

A delicious moist quickbread to eat either as a cake, or buttered as a loaf. Providing the total amount remains the same, the fruit content can be varied – dates are excellent. Lovely for a family tea-party.

F 3 months

2 oz (50g/¼ cup) butter
4 oz (125g/½ cup) soft dark brown
  sugar
8 oz (225g/2 cups) mixed dried
  fruit
2 oz (50g/½ cup) chopped walnuts
  (optional)
1 level teasp bicarbonate of soda
  (baking soda)

¼ pint (150ml/⅔ cup) boiling
  water
1 egg
8 oz (225g/2 cups) self-raising
  flour, mixed with 1 level teasp
  mixed sweet spice
½ teasp vanilla essence (extract)

Lightly oil a loaf tin measuring 9 × 5 × 3 inches (23 × 13 × 8cm) then line the bottom with a strip of foil or greaseproof paper.

Put the butter (in 1 inch/2.5cm cubes) sugar, dried fruit and bicarbonate of soda into a large bowl. Pour on the boiling water and mix until the fat is dissolved. Stir to blend then add the egg followed by the flour mixed with the spice. *Do not beat* – just stir to blend. Turn into the loaf tin and bake for 45 minutes at Gas No. 4, 350°F, 180°C or until a rich golden brown. When baked the cake will have shrunk slightly from the sides of the tin.

Sprinkle with a generous layer of granulated sugar.

Raisin Spice Cake

This cake has the soft moist texture of a ginger cake but the flavour of a fruit-cake. It can be eaten fresh.

F 3 months

6 oz (175g/1 cup) seeded Valencia or ordinary raisins
4 oz (125g/1 cup) walnuts
1 level teasp bicarbonate of soda
5 fl oz (150ml/²/³ cup) boiling water
6 oz (175g/1¹/₂ cups) plain flour
Pinch of salt

6 oz (175g/³/₄ cup) caster (superfine) sugar
4 oz (125g/¹/₂ cup) butter
2 whole eggs and 1 white
1 teasp each cinnamon, vanilla essence (extract) and lemon juice

Set the oven at Gas No. 3, 325°F, 160°C.

Chop the raisins (if seedless) with the walnuts – coarsely. Add the bicarbonate of soda and the boiling water and leave.

Sieve the flour with the salt. Work the butter until creamy, then beat in the sugar gradually until fluffy. Beat the whole eggs and the white until foamy and thick. Gradually beat into the creamed mixture, followed by the cinnamon, vanilla and lemon juice. Stir in the flour and the raisin/nut mixture alternately, starting and ending with flour. Pour into a greased 9 × 5 × 3 inch (23 × 13 × 8cm) loaf tin, bottom-lined with greased paper. Bake for 1 hour 15 minutes until golden brown, risen, shrunken slightly from the sides and a skewer will come out clean from the centre. Cool. Serve in slices.

See also **Celebration Fruit-Cake**

Celebration Fruit-Cake

A very rich golden fruit-cake for the special occasion. It can be used a week after it has been baked, but the longer it is kept the moister and richer it will be. It can be covered with marzipan and iced if desired, but unless you really enjoy the work, this is usually best left to a professional patissier.

½ lb(225g/1½ cups) sultanas (white raisins) soaked overnight in 3 tbsp brandy
8 oz (225g/1 cup) butter
9 oz (250g/1 cup) caster (superfine) sugar
8 oz (225g/2 cups) plain flour
½ level teasp baking powder
4 oz (125g/⅔ cup) glacé (candied) pineapple

2 oz (50g/½ cup) ground almonds
4 eggs
Rind of 1 orange and ½ lemon, finely grated
½ lb (225g/1½ cups) glacé (candied) cherries (rinsed to remove excess sugar, then dried and halved)
4 oz (125g/⅔ cup) crystallized (candied) ginger

With a microwave the pre-soaking of the sultanas in brandy takes only an hour. Cover the sultanas with the brandy in a plastic container, cover and microwave for 1 minute, then leave 1 hour to cool before using. Otherwise leave to soak overnight.

Grease a round 9 inch (22.5cm) loose-bottomed tin, and line it sides and bottom with oiled brown paper or two layers of greased greaseproof paper. Cream the butter till like mayonnaise, then beat in the sugar until fluffy. Beat the eggs together until blended, then beat a tablespoon at a time into the creamed mixture together with the finely grated peel. Slice the ginger, chop the pineapple and halve the cherries. Mix with the ground almonds. Add to the cake mixture, alternately with the flour. Add the sultanas and any unabsorbed brandy. Pour into the prepared tin.

Bake for 1 hour at Gas No. 3, 324°F, 160°C, then for a further 30-40 minutes at Gas No. 2, 300°F, 150°C. Test. The top should spring back when touched lightly with the forefinger, and a skewer or knitting needle should come out clean from the centre.

Cool, wrap in foil then store in a tin for 1 week before use.

A Super Sponge

This is one recipe for the impatient cook – a straightforward mixture to make with an electric mixer. The recipe is based on 6 eggs, making 2 or 3 cakes depending on the size of the tins. These are excellent to have in stock for a quick dessert gâteau or to make into a jam sponge for an unexpected afternoon tea. If preferred the butter can be omitted and 3 tablespoons of oil used instead.

Note: Because of their fragile texture, invert the cooked sponges on a cooling tray while still in the baking tin, and do not attempt to ease them out until quite cold. When splitting and filling sponges, to make even cutting easier, either use a half-frozen cake or chill a fresh one well (say an hour in the refrigerator). This cake is excellent when filled with sweetened fruit and whipped cream.

F plain 6 months; cream filled 3 months

6 eggs
6 oz (175g/²/₃ cup) caster (superfine) sugar
6 oz (175g/1¹/₂ cups) self-raising flour

2 oz (50g/¹/₄ cup) butter
3 tbsp water
2 teasp lemon juice

Size of tins: Two tins, 8-9 inches (20-22.5cm) wide and 2 inches (5cm) deep; or three tins 7 inches (17.5cm) wide and 2 inches (5cm) deep.

To prepare: Lightly oil the tins all over, then bottom-line with a round of greased greaseproof paper.

Oven: Set at Gas No. 5, 375°F, 190°C. It must be well heated before the cake goes in. When you turn on the oven put the butter and water in it to heat up.

Method: Sift the flour on to a sheet of paper. Whisk the eggs until foamy, at high speed, then add the sugar and continue to whisk until thick and mousse-like – you should be able to write your initials on the surface with the mixture from the beater and see the letters clearly before they disappear.

Now whisk in the lemon juice. Take the melted butter and hot water from the oven and pour down the side of the mixture. Sift the flour on top, then, using a metal spoon, gently blend the whole mass together until it is an even fluffy mixture. Gently ease into the prepared tins. The tops of the cakes can be left plain or thinly sifted with granulated sugar.

Bake for 25 minutes until golden brown and just beginning to pull away from the sides of the tin.

Freezing Note: With such fragile cakes, it is a good idea to put them unwrapped into the freezer until they feel solid to the touch (about 1 hour). Then take them out and bag or wrap in foil. In this way the shape is not distorted by the wrapping paper. This is especially important if the cake has been split and filled with whipped cream before it is frozen.

Cakes in Miniature

Little buns may not have the dramatic impact of large gâteaux, but they are extremely practical, as they defrost much more quickly and are just the right size for children's tea-parties. As they travel well without crumbling, they are also useful for picnics.

Chocolate Cupcakes

Makes 24 **F** 6 months

4 oz (125g/¹/₂ cup) soft margarine
4 oz (125g/¹/₂ cup) caster (superfine) sugar
2 eggs
4 oz (125g/1 cup) self-raising flour

2 level tbsp drinking (instant) chocolate
1 level teasp baking powder
1 level tbsp cocoa
1 tbsp cold milk
1 teasp vanilla essence (extract)

Put 24 paper baking cases on a flat tray, or on patty tins. Set the oven to Gas No. 5, 375°F, 190°C.

Put all the ingredients into a bowl and beat by mixer or hand until smooth and creamy (about 3 minutes). With a food processor, put all ingredients (except the flour) into the bowl and process until blended. Add the flour and process just until blended (do not overbeat as this toughens the cake).

Fill the cases ²/₃ full of the mixture and bake for 15 minutes until spongy to the touch. Serve plain, sprinkled with icing (confectioners') sugar or topped with any chocolate icing.

Little Jaffa Cakes

The cakes are soaked in a citrus syrup.

Makes 20 **F** 6 months

4 oz (125g/½ cup) soft margarine

6 oz (175g/⅔ cup) caster (superfine) sugar

6 oz (175g/1½ cups) self-raising flour

Grated rind of a medium orange

2 eggs

3 tbsp milk

Syrup:

4 oz (125g/½ cup) caster (superfine) sugar

2 tbsp orange juice

2 tbsp lemon juice

Put all the cake ingredients into a bowl and beat by machine or hand until smooth (about 2 minutes). Do not overbeat or the mixture is toughened. Divide between approximately 20 little paper cases standing in patty tins – each case should be two-thirds full. Bake in a quick moderate oven Gas No. 5, 375°F, 190°C for 15 minutes until golden brown and spongy to the touch. Lift onto a cooling tray.

While the cakes are cooking, put all the syrup ingredients into a small pan and heat gently until the sugar is melted. As soon as the cakes come out of the oven, sprinkle each one with a teaspoon or two of the syrup. Allow to go quite cold before serving. These keep fresh several days and may be frozen.

VARIATION

Little Lemon Cakes: Use grated rind of 1 lemon and 4 tbsp juice when making the syrup.

Ginger Gems

Spongy little spice cakes.

Makes 24 **F** 6 months

4 oz (125g/½ cup) soft margarine

4 oz (125g/½ cup) soft brown sugar

6 oz (175g/½ cup) golden (corn) syrup

1 egg

8 oz (225g/2 cups) plain flour

2 level teasp ground ginger

½ level teasp mixed sweet spice

4 fl oz (125ml/½ cup) water

½ teasp bicarbonate of soda (baking soda) dissolved in the warm water

Set the oven to Gas No. 5, 375°F, 190°C. Arrange 24 greaseproof baking cases in patty tins.

Put the margarine, sugar, syrup and egg into a bowl or food processor. Beat until smooth. Finally add the flour sifted with the spices alternately with the water. The batter will be thin. Put a level tablespoon of mixture into each case. Bake for 20 minutes until a rich brown and spongy to gentle touch.

Foundation Recipe for Children's Birthday Cake

The traditional rich fruit-cake is too rich for most children's palates. They prefer a firm sponge, flavoured with chocolate or vanilla. They do not even like too much icing. I have found one of the most successful ideas is to bake a rectangular cake, which can then be covered with butter cream or glacé icing and decorated according to age and sex. Whatever else is put on, there must be candles and 'Happy Birthday' with the name! The two recipes below both produce light but firm cakes which are ideal for this purpose.

Chocolate Foundation Cake

Grease and bottom-line with greased greaseproof paper a rectangular tin 12 × 10 × 2 inches (30 × 25 × 5cm). Set the oven at Gas No. 4, 350°F, 180°C.

F 6 months; iced 3 months

8 oz (225g/1 cup) soft margarine	2 level teasp baking powder
8 oz (225g/1 cup) caster (superfine) sugar	4 level tbsp drinking (instant) chocolate
4 eggs	2 level tbsp cocoa
8 oz (225g/2 cups) self-raising flour	4 tbsp cold milk or water
	2 teasp vanilla essence (extract)

Put all the ingredients into a bowl and beat by mixer or hand until smooth and creamy (about 3 minutes). With food processor: put all the ingredients (except the flour) into the bowl and process until blended evenly. Add the flour and process until just blended (do not overbeat as this toughens the cake).

Spoon into the tin and smooth level with a spatula. Bake for

35-40 minutes or until firm to gentle touch and beginning to shrink from the sides of the tin. Turn out carefully on to a cooling rack. Leave until quite cold before icing.

Chocolate Bar Icing

It sets exactly like bar chocolate.

Sufficient to ice the top of a cake 12 × 10 × 2 inches (30 × 25 × 5cm).

6 oz (175g) milk or plain
   (semi-sweet) chocolate

3 oz (75g/^{1}/$_3$ cup) butter or
   margarine.

Grate or shave the chocolate with a knife and put into a small thick-bottomed pan with the fat. Heat very gently until smooth, stirring all the time, then pour over the cake and allow to set.

Quick Icing for Decoration

This can be used to pipe round the sides and also for piping a birthday greeting on the top.

F 3 months. Sufficient to decorate iced cake 12 × 10 × 2 inches (30 × 25 × 5cm).

8 oz (225g/2 cups) sifted icing
   (confectioners') sugar
4 oz (125g/^{1}/$_2$ cup) soft butter or
   margarine

1 tbsp top milk, single (light)
   cream, strong coffee, fruit juice
   or fruit cordial (orange or
   blackcurrant)

Cream the fat till like mayonnaise, then add half the icing (confectioners') sugar a tablespoon at a time. Add the liquid, then add the remainder of the sugar, gradually beating until fluffy. Add a few drops of colouring if desired. Use to decorate the cake.

Chocolate Butter Cream

This is a richer icing which can be spread on the cake instead of the Chocolate Bar Icing, (see above) and then used to pipe the greeting.

F 3 months. Sufficient to decorate a cake 12 × 10 × 2 inches (30 × 25 × 5cm).

6 oz (175g/³⁄4 cup) soft butter or margarine
8 oz (225g/2 cups) sifted icing (confectioners') sugar
4 tbsp drinking (instant) chocolate

1 tbsp single (light) cream, evaporated milk or strong coffee
1 teasp vanilla essence (extract)

Put all the ingredients into a bowl and beat by hand or machine until fluffy.

Vanilla-Flavoured Foundation Cake

F plain 6 months; iced 3 months. Makes one cake 12 × 10 × 2 inches (30 × 25 × 5cm).

9 oz (250g/1¹⁄4 cups) mixed soft butter and margarine
10 oz (275g/1¹⁄3 cups) caster (superfine) sugar
5 eggs

2 teasp vanilla essence (extract)
12 oz (350g/3 cups) plain flour
Pinch of salt
1¹⁄2 level teasp baking powder
5 tbsp hot water

Grease and bottom-line with greaseproof paper a rectangular tin 12 × 10 × 2 inches (30 × 25 × 5cm).

Beat the fats together by hand or machine until like mayonnaise. Add the sugar a tablespoon at a time, beating after each addition, until the mixture looks fluffy and has lightened in colour. Beat in the vanilla. Whisk the eggs to blend the yolks and whites, then add to the creamed mixture a tablespoon at a time. Sift the flour, salt and baking powder, then stir into the creamed mixture in three portions alternately with the water.

Turn into the prepared tin and smooth level with a spatula. Bake at Gas No. 4, 350°F, 180°C for 40-50 minutes. To test for done-ness, open the oven door gently, press the centre of the cake with the tip of the forefinger. The cake should spring back at once. If not, a faint impression will remain and the cake should be tested after a further 5 minutes.

Turn out and allow to go quite cold before icing.

Note: To make an 8 inch (20cm) round cake, halve the ingredients but use 3 eggs and no water. Bake as above.

Use either of the two icings suggested above, or the following:

Glacé Icing

Sufficient to frost the top of a cake 12 × 10 × 2 inches (30 × 25 × 5cm). Use half the ingredients for an 8 inch (20cm) cake.

12 oz (350g/3 cups) sifted icing (confectioners') sugar	3-4 tbsp liquid-water, orange juice, strong coffee

Put the icing (confectioners') sugar into a small pan (enamel if possible, as aluminium may turn white icing grey). Add half the water and a squeeze of lemon juice (omit for coffee icing). Stir well with a wooden spoon, warming over *very* gentle heat. The base of the pan should never be too hot to touch with the fingers (this can of course be done in the microwave).

To test the consistency, dip the wooden spoon into the icing – it should be thickly coated before the icing starts to run back into the pan. If too thick, add the remaining water. If too thin, add a little more icing sugar. Icing sugar varies in its power of absorbency so one cannot be exact as to the amount of liquid. However, it is better to have icing too thick than too thin. Thick icing can always be smoothed over the cake using a palette knife dipped in a jug of boiling water, whereas thin icing will just run off the cake and sit in puddles round the side.

Left-over icing can be thickened up slightly with a little extra icing sugar and used to pipe the birthday message. It will not, however, pipe rosettes like the butter-based icings.

Store Cupboard and Frozen Assets

This chapter gives recipes for some of those foods which are either in regular use or can be prepared in their season for use during the rest of the year. There is no doubt that having a stock of such 'et ceteras' as savoury and sweet sauces, preserves and purées greatly simplifies the preparations for any kind of meal.

In the Freezer

Avocado Purée

Whole avocados will not freeze, but if they are puréed with lemon juice they will do so extremely well. This can be very useful when very ripe avocados are available at a low price. Freeze them in labelled amounts, and they are then ready to use in soups, dips and cold sweets.

F 2 months
For approx 1 pint (575ml/2½ cups) purée

4 medium avocados
3 teasp lemon juice

Peel then stone the avocados and purée together with the lemon juice in the blender or food processor. Pack in rigid containers, leaving 1 inch (2.5cm) head-space to allow for expansion.

Thaw in the refrigerator overnight or at room temperature for 4 hours.

Frozen Raspberry Purée

This is extremely useful as a sauce, a topping for other fruit such as peaches, or in cold sweets and ice-cream.

F 1 year
For approx 1 pint (575ml/1½ cups) purée:

1 lb (450g) raspberries)
6 oz (175g/¾ cup) caster (superfine) sugar

Sieve the raspberries, using a mouli or fine sieve. Put in the blender or food processor with the sugar. Process for 2 minutes until thick. Freeze in plastic cups or containers.

VARIATION
Strawberry Purée: Make exactly as for raspberry purée; however, as there are no pips in the fruit, the initial sieving can be omitted.

Frozen Apple Compote

This makes an excellent filling for tarts, turnovers, slices and pancakes. The apples are just right if sliced thickly on a food processor.

F 1 year

For each 1 lb (450g) apples (weighed after peeling, 8 coring and slicing) use:
1 heaped tbsp apricot jam

Nut of butter or margarine
3 oz (75g/⅓ cup) brown sugar
Grated rind and juice of half a lemon

Grease a heavy pan with the fat, then add the peeled and cored apple slices (cut ⅜ inch/1cm thick), in layers with the sugar, jam, lemon juice and rind. Put on the lid and allow to simmer until just tender, but not completely fallen, stirring gently once or twice. Cool, pack in containers or plastic cups – allowing ½ inch (1.25cm) head-space for expansion – cover and freeze.

Chopped Fresh Herbs

R1 week **F** 6 months
These are extremely useful for both short-term (refrigerator) and long-term (freezer) storage. Chives and parsley freeze particularly well, but it's also worth freezing home-grown basil, marjoram, tarragon etc.

Although chopped herbs keep crisp for a week in the refrigerator, they tend to go limp immediately in the freezer, although they are still excellent for use in liquids such as salad dressings, sauces, soups and casseroles.

Wash and dry the herbs thoroughly, if possible in a salad dryer. Chop finely – by knife or food processor. Divide between plastic cups or make foil parcels each containing 1-2 tbsp herbs.

Note: For refrigerator storage, keep in small airtight plastic containers.

In the Refrigerator

Mint Sauce Concentrate

This is an excellent way of preserving home-grown mint. It can be made from June onwards, but do be sure the mint leaves are fresh and green. The exact amount isn't critical as long as the finished concentrate is really thick.

R 1 year

1 large bouquet of mint –
  producing a pint (575ml/2½
  cups) of leaves only, when very
  tightly packed

½ pint (275ml/1¼ cups) white
  malt distilled vinegar
6 oz (175g/¾ cup) granulated
  sugar

Strip the leaves from the stalks, wash thoroughly in a colander, using cold water, shake off as much water as possible, then wrap in a tea towel, and leave in a pottery bowl under refrigeration overnight. This facilitates chopping. (Otherwise simply wash and dry in a tea towel.) Chop either by hand, parsmint (food mill) or food processor until very fine. Put the vinegar and sugar into a pan and heat until the sugar has dissolved and the liquid has just come to the boil. Pour at once over the chopped mint and leave until cold. Spoon into a screw-top jar with a tight-fitting lid. store at the bottom of the refrigerator (or in a cool larder) for winter use.

To use: Take two or three spoonfuls and dilute to a sauce with water and a little extra sugar and vinegar if required.

Mint Sauce

If you prefer, you can make up the mint sauce for immediate use, then store the remainder. It will keep for several weeks, but will take up more storage room than the Mint Sauce Concentrate.

R 6 weeks

This is the best way to get the full mint flavour:

Strip enough leaves to half-fill a large cup when tightly packed. Add 1 tbsp caster (superfine) sugar and chop on a board until fine, or pass through a parsmint (food mill). Put in a mortar or bowl and crush with a pestle or the end of a rolling pin until the leaves are thoroughly bruised and the juices are oozing out. Stir in 5 tbsp each cider vinegar and water. Allow to stand for at least an hour before serving.

Bittersweet Chocolate Sauce

This is delicious on ice-cream and also on profiteroles. Serve hot or cold.

R 3 months

6 oz (175g) plain dark
  (semi-sweet) chocolate
6 fl oz (175ml/³/₄ cup) water
6 oz (175g/³/₄ cup) granulated
  sugar

2 teasp instant coffee
1 oz (25g/2 tbsp) butter or
  margarine
2 teasp rum or brandy

Put the broken chocolate, water and sugar into a thick-bottomed pan, bring slowly to the boil, stirring constantly until smooth. Simmer until the mixture will coat the back of the spoon, stirring all the time. Remove from the heat and add the remaining ingredients. When cold, store in an airtight container in the refrigerator.

Caramel Syrup

This is delicious on ice-cream or to pour on individual baked custards, cooked in soufflé dishes or cocottes.

R indefinitely

12 oz (350g/1½ cups) caster
  (superfine) sugar

5 fl oz (150ml/²/₃ cup) water
6 tbsp boiling water

Put the caster (superfine) sugar and water into a thick-based pan and heat, stirring until the sugar is dissolved, then boil rapidly until the water has evaporated and the sugar turns a rich mahogany brown. Immediately take the pan to the sink, cover the hand holding it with a tea towel (to avoid splashes), then add the boiling water. Return to the heat and stir until smooth. When cold, store in a glass or plastic airtight container.

Coffee Syrup

This is perfect for making iced coffee, as a sauce for ice-cream, or for flavouring icings, ice-cream and whipped cream. Use by the teaspoonful, according to the recipe or tasting until the correct coffee flavour has been achieved.

R indefinitely

For approx ½ pint (275ml/1¼
  cups):
½ oz (40g/8 level tbsp) instant
  coffee

6 oz (175g/¾ cup) granulated
  sugar
½ pint (275ml/1¼ cups) boiling
  water

Put the sugar and water into a pan, and stir over gentle heat until the sugar has dissolved, then simmer for 2 minutes. Take off the heat and stir in the instant coffee until dissolved. When quite cold, pour into a screw-top jar and refrigerate.

Herb Butter

This is delicious on grills of any kind, and also on green vegetables or baked potatoes.

F 3 months **R** 2 weeks

½ lb (225g/1 cup) unsalted butter or best margarine

4 level tbsp of chopped herbs (e.g. a mixture of parsley, chives and basil), *or* 2 tbsp chopped

parsley and 1 level teasp dried fines herbes (in winter)

2 teasp lemon juice

1 teasp lemon rind

15 grinds black pepper

Cream the butter (or margarine) until it is as creamy as mayonnaise then beat in the lemon juice, rind and herbs. Divide the mixture in two and put into greaseproof paper. Form each into a sausage about 1 inch (2.5cm) in diameter, then roll in foil and chill. To use, cut in slices.

Alternatively the mixture can be spooned into an empty plastic carton and refrigerated. Scoop out with a teaspoon as required.

VARIATION

Mustard Butter: *This is particularly delicious on grilled fish (such as mackerel or herrings) or to top baked potatoes, particularly at a barbecue. Add more mustard if you like it hot!*

½ lb (225g/1 cup) butter or best margarine

1 level teasp dry mustard

1 tbsp parsley

Pinch garlic salt

10 grinds black pepper

Squeeze lemon juice

Make exactly as for **Herb Butter** (above).

Spiced Peaches

These need 24 hours in the refrigerator to reach their full flavour, and will then keep in perfect condition for up to 4 days. They are very useful over holiday periods as they go well with cold meats and poultry.

Serves 12-16 **R** 3 days

2 large cans peach halves (16 halves)

8 fl oz (225ml/1 cup) peach syrup from can

8 fl oz (225ml/1 cup) vinegar

3 inch (7.5cm) stick cinnamon *or* pinch ground cinnamon

4 oz (125g/½ cup) sugar

Whole cloves

Stud each peach half with 3 cloves. Simmer the remaining ingredients for 3-4 minutes. Add the peach halves. Cool, then refrigerate. Serve the drained halves with meat or fish.

Preserves and Conserves

Whole Apricot Preserve

Use only the best quality dried apricots for this rich fruity jam. If whole dried apricots are used, separate into halves after soaking and before cooking.

Makes 2 lb (1 kg) **L**1 year

½ lb (225g) dried apricots

1 pint (575ml/2½ cups) water

1 lb 1 oz (½ kg/2 cups + 2 tbsp) sugar

2 tbsp lemon juice (½ very large lemon)

2 oz (50g/½ cup) slivered almonds

The night before, put the fruit in a large heavy-based pan (about 9 inches/22.5cm) and cover with the water. Next day, add extra water (if necessary) to barely cover the fruit, bring to the boil, cover then simmer until absolutely tender (about 10-20 minutes). Add the sugar, stir until it is dissolved, then add the lemon juice and the almonds and boil hard until the jam sets on a saucer. It will then be a thick viscous liquid.

(Setting test: chill a saucer in the freezer for 5 minutes, take out and put a teaspoon of jam on it, then leave a minute. If the jam has set the blob will wrinkle slightly when pushed with the forefinger.)

Pot in warm dry jars. Cover whilst hot with wax discs, with lid when cold.

Quantities for 4 lb (2kg)

1 lb (450g) apricots
2 pints (1 litre/150ml) water
2 lb 2 oz (1kg/5 cups) sugar

4 tbsp lemon juice
3 oz (75g/³/₄ cup) slivered almonds

Note: Jam will take longer to set unless made in a wide preserving pan.

Brandied Cherries

Or cherry brandy, whichever way you prefer to look at it, for the end result of this recipe is a delicately cherry-flavoured brandy with juicy, brandy-flavoured cherries. Only an acid cherry like the morello (sour red) is suitable.

L several years
Proceed with each pound (450g) of cherries as follows:

Cut off the stalks (if any) to a quarter of an inch (0.5cm). Wash the fruit thoroughly, drain, then prick five or six times all over with a darning needle. Put in a glass screw-top jar (e.g. one used for instant coffee), add enough granulated sugar to come half-way up the fruit. Cover the fruit completely with brandy (any 3-star or native brandy – e.g. Slivovitz – will do very well), making sure none of the fruit is exposed to the air. Leave at least three months, preferably six, before using the fruit in a fruit salad, and the liquid as a liqueur.

Lemon Curd

This has a truly superb flavour and texture. Yolks will make it more yellow than when whole eggs are used. Use as a spread for toast, tea cakes or tea-breads.

Makes 2¹/₂ lb (1.25kg) **R** 6 weeks

6 whole eggs (or 10 yolks)
6 oz (175g/³/₄ cup) butter

Rind and juice of 3-4 lemons (7-8
 fl oz/200-225ml/³/₄-1 cup)
1 lb (450g/2 cups) granulated sugar

Two hours before you intend to make the curd, grate the rind and juice the lemons. Leave in a jug for 2 hours, then strain thoroughly, pressing the rind against the sieve to extract all the liquid, then discard the rind.

Select the jars and wash thoroughly, then rinse and leave upside down to dry and heat in a low oven – Gas No. $^1/_2$, 200°F, 100°C for 20 minutes. Heat the sugar for 10 minutes in the same oven.

Melt the butter in a heavy pan then add the hot sugar and the strained juice. Stir over gentle heat until the sugar has dissolved completely. Whisk the eggs very thoroughly to blend the yolks and whites, then ladle a little of the hot mixture on them, stirring all the time. Return this hot egg mixture to the pan, and keep on cooking and stirring over gentle heat until the mixture thickens enough to coat the back of the spoon. (There is no need to use a double saucepan if you do not allow the mixture to boil.) As soon as the mixture has thickened, take off direct heat and keep on stirring for a minute or two. It will thicken still further but there will be no chance of curdling. Pour the hot curd into the hot jars and cover with a wax disc. Cover with foil or a lid when quite cold.

Refrigerate until required. It will keep a week at room temperature. Discard immediately if mould appears on the surface.

Mincemeat

This is made with butter instead of the traditional suet, which means that it can be served cold if desired. The butter gives it a magnificent flavour.

Makes 2$^1/_2$ lb (1.25kg) **R** months **L** 3 weeks

$^1/_2$ lb (675g/5 cups) mixed dried fruit

10 oz (275g) apples

4 oz (125g/1 cup) walnuts

2 oz (50g/$^3/_8$ cup) glacé (candied) cherries

2 tbsp each ginger marmalade and warm golden (corn) syrup

2 oz (50g/$^1/_4$ cup) soft brown sugar

1 teasp cinnamon

$^1/_2$ teasp mixed spice

$^1/_4$ teasp ground nutmeg

Rind and juice of a medium lemon

2 tbsp each brandy and port-type wine

2 oz (50g/$^1/_4$ cup) melted butter or margarine

Coarsely chop the walnuts and cherries. Coarsely grate the apples. Combine all the ingredients in the order given. Leave in the bowl for 2 days before potting or using in mince pies.

$^{1}/_{2}$ lb (225g) mincemeat will fill one dozen pies.

Mint Jelly

This can be made by itself or when making crab-apple jelly. (To make crab-apple jelly from this recipe, simply omit the vinegar, mint and colouring.) It is a beautiful green, lightly-jellied, sweet/sour preserve which is delicious with hot or cold lamb, chicken or turkey.

Makes approx 1$^{1}/_{2}$ lb (675g) **L** 1 year

2 lb (1kg) green-skinned cooking apples or crab-apples

1 pint (575ml/2$^{1}/_{2}$ cups) water

Do not peel or core the apples as these contain pectin which helps to set the jelly. Have fruit under- rather than over-ripe.

Quarter the cooking apples but leave crab-apples whole (remove stalks). Put in preserving pan with water, bring to the boil, then simmer very gently, stirring and crushing the pulp occasionally until absolutely tender. This should take about 30 minutes-1 hour (the longer period for crab-apples).

Turn the mixture into a jelly bag and leave to drain overnight. Measure the juice – there should be about a pint (575ml/2$^{1}/_{2}$ cups).

For 1 pint (575ml/2$^{1}/_{2}$ cups) the ingredients are as follows:

1 pint (575ml/2$^{1}/_{2}$ cups) juice
1 lb (450g/2 cups) sugar
  (preserving sugar makes a very clear jelly)

Juice and grated rind of $^{1}/_{2}$ large lemon
2 tbsp white wine vinegar
2 tbsp finely chopped mint
A little green colouring (optional)

Put the apple juice and sugar into a preserving pan and add the lemon rind and juice and the vinegar. Heat until the sugar is dissolved, stirring occasionally. Bring to the boil, do not stir but allow to bubble until set – about 8 minutes. (See setting test in recipe for **Whole Apricot Preserve** p.492.) The time varies according to the ripeness and variety of the fruit.

Add the chopped mint. Leave in the preserving pan for 10 minutes or until it is beginning to thicken, then stir well to distribute the mint evenly.

Turn into small pots. Put on lid when cold.

Uncooked Strawberry or Raspberry Jam

This is a marvellous jam to make if you don't like all the paraphernalia of regular jam-making. It also has the taste of fresh fruit, and is particularly delicious on scones or hot toast.

L (3 weeks when opened) **F** 9 months

Quantities for 7 lb (3kg)

Quantities for 3¹/₂ lb (1.5kg)

2¹/₂ lb (1.25kg) fruit	1¹/₄ lb (525g)
4 lb (2kg/8 cups) caster (superfine) sugar	2 lb (900g/4 cups)
8 fl oz (225ml/1 cup) liquid pectin	4 fl oz (125ml/¹/₂ cup)
(1 bottle Certo)	(¹/₂ bottle Certo)
4 tbsp lemon juice	2 tbsp

Mash the fruit gently with a fork or food processor, then put in a bowl and stir in the sugar. Leave for an hour at room temperature until the sugar has dissolved, stirring once or twice. Add the pectin and lemon juice and stir for 2 minutes.

Use a ladle or jug to fill into either jam jars, plastic cups or other waxed containers, leaving ¹/₂ inch (1.25cm) headroom, then cover in usual way. Leave for 48 hours at room temperature then refrigerate or freeze. Allow 2 hours to defrost.

Breads and Rolls

Should there be a chapter on bread-making in an entertaining cookbook? Should you even be *contemplating* making your own bread and rolls in addition to all the other delicacies that are not so readily available?

Home-made bread is not something one expects to be offered, it's just an extra special delight. And only if you really enjoy working with yeast should you attempt to make it. There is, however, a very real satisfaction to be gained from baking bread and rolls that has very little (except the smell!) to do with their eating quality. It is the quality of life that the dough possesses (for yeasts are single-celled living organisms) which I think gives it a special fascination so I have not tried to include a comprehensive list of recipes but only those which seem to me to have a particular quality of their own. For more standard recipes, and full background information, I suggest you consult one of the many specialist cookbooks on the subject.

Freezing Bread: If you do decide to bake your own bread, then it can be at a time that suits you, for bread freezes extremely well.

Storage times
White and brown bread – up to 6 months.
Enriched rolls – up to 4 months
Crisp crusted loaves and rolls (such as Vienna and French bread) – only 1 week, as after that period the crust begins to come away from the loaf.
Brioches – 2 months.
Croissants (in one layer) – 3 months.

To freeze: Wrap in aluminium foil or polythene bags.

To thaw: Loaves – leave in packaging at room temperature for 3-6 hours; leave overnight in refrigerator; or place the frozen loaf in foil in the oven at Gas No. 6, 400°F, 200°C for 45 minutes. Or defrost in the microwave.

Rolls – leave in packaging at room temperature for 1½ hours, or place frozen in foil in the oven at Gas No. 8, 450°F, 230°C for 15 minutes, or defrost in microwave.

Note: Crusty loaves and rolls thawed at room temperature should be refreshed before serving. Place unwrapped loaves or rolls in a hot oven (Gas No. 6, 400°F, 200°C) until crisp to the touch (about 5-10 minutes).

If bread or rolls are heated in any way to defrost them, they will stale much more quickly than when allowed to thaw at room temperature.

Home-made bread will stay fresh and moist for 2-3 days if wrapped loosely in a large polythene bag. Place in a bread bin or drawer kept for the purpose.

Notes on the ingredients
Flour: To achieve good results it is essential to use a strong flour which contains a high level of good quality protein. These special bread flours, which are now quite widely marketed, absorb much more liquid than the softer flour used in cake-making, and so give a good volume and a light texture to the bread.

Yeast: I prefer to use fresh yeast, if I can. It is a creamy putty colour when fresh, brown when it becomes stale. It will keep in a cool cupboard for 3-4 days, for 3 weeks in the refrigerator, and 4-6 weeks in the freezer. Dried yeast, on the other hand, does not need to be kept under refrigeration. Provided it is kept in a cool place in a tightly-closed container it will keep for up to 6 months. It is more concentrated than fresh yeast so less of it is required (about half as much as fresh yeast). However, it must be reactivated before use (see recipes). Too much dried yeast gives bread and rolls an 'off' flavour.

Salt: This is essential to give flavour to the dough, and also to prevent the yeast fermenting too quickly. However, too much will kill the yeast so do not use more than stated.

Fat: This greatly improves the flavour of the dough and the softness and colour of the crumb. It also keeps the bread fresh longer.

On kneading the dough: Kneading is essential to strengthen the dough so that there is a good rise. It can be done by hand, in a mixer fitted with a dough-hook, or (in small qualities but very effectively) in a food processor. However the dough is kneaded, it is ready when it feels firm and elastic and no longer sticks to the fingers. When I use the dough-hook of my mixer, or the food processor, I like to knead the dough according to the manufacturer's instructions, then turn it out on to a floured board and knead it for a minute or two by hand. Only by physical contact with the dough is it possible to assess whether it is ready to be put to rise.

Rising: The dough must rise at least once before baking to give the yeast time to work. It is essential to cover the dough to prevent it from drying out and forming a skin. It can be left in a large greased polythene bag, or simply put back into the greased mixing bowl, tightly covered with film and then a tea-towel. The bowl, or bag, must of course be large enough to allow the dough to expand to twice its volume.

Re-kneading or 'knocking back': This is essential to knock out any large gas bubbles which would give the dough an uneven texture. It also helps to ensure a better rise in the oven. Simply flatten the dough with the knuckles and knead into a firm dough again, using the minimum of flour on the board.

'Proving' or second rising: When the dough has been shaped ready for the oven, it must be allowed to rise again. To test: touch with a floured finger – the dough should spring back and not leave a depression where it was pressed. It is then ready for glazing and baking.

Two Lovely Brown Loaves

This bread is delicious served with cream soup, a starter such as egg mayonnaise, or a cheese buffet. The taste and texture can be varied by using different brown flours.

F 6 months

1 oz (25g/2 cakes) fresh yeast *or* 1 level tbsp dried yeast

1 lb (450g/4 cups) each white bread flour and wholemeal flour (or 2 lb/1kg/8 cups brown flour of your choice)

1½ level tbsp soft brown sugar

1 tbsp oil

4 level teasp salt

1 pint (575ml/2½ cups) warm water (blood heat)

Note: If dried yeast is used, first stir it into ½ pint (275ml/1¼ cups) of hand-hot water with a teaspoon each of the measured sugar and flour. Leave until frothy (about 15 minutes) to reactivate the yeast, then add to the remaining ½ pint (275ml/1¼ cups) lukewarm water as directed in the recipe.

Put the warm water, sugar and yeast into a large mixing bowl and add about a third of the flour, to make a batter. Mix until smooth, then cover with a tea-towel and leave for 15 minutes until frothy. Then add the salt, oil and the remaining flour and stir to a scone-like dough. Knead with a dough-hook or by hand until the dough loses its stickiness and is smooth in appearance (about 5 minutes). Oil the mixing bowl, then put back the dough, cover, and leave on the counter at room temperature for about 45 minutes or until double in bulk.

Knead again to get rid of the bubbles (2 minutes), then divide in two and shape each piece into a loaf as follows: Using floured knuckles, flatten into a rectangle 9 inches (22.5cm) wide, then roll up tightly and place, join down, in a tin measuring 9 inches (22.5cm) by 5 inches (12.5cm) by 3 inches (7.5cm). Cover and leave a further 25 minutes until risen to the top of the tin, then brush with 2 tbsp water mixed with a pinch of salt (for crustiness), and scatter with dry muesli, crushed cornflakes or granary flour.

Bake at Gas No. 8, 450°F, 230°C for 20 minutes, then at Gas No. 6, 400°F, 200°C for a further 20 minutes or until the loaf sounds hollow when the base is tapped. Leave to cool on a wire rack.

VARIATION

Two Granary Loaves: Use exactly the same ingredients except for the flour: 1½ lb (675g/6 cups) granary bread meal and 8 oz (225g/2 cups) strong plain white flour.

To shape: Instead of shaping into a rectangle, shape each half into a round 6 inches (15cm) in diameter, or into an elongated oval about 6 inches (15cm) long and 4 inches (10cm) wide. Put on 2 greased, floured baking trays, and cover with oiled film. Leave in the kitchen until puffy (about 30 minutes). Remove the film, brush with salt water (2 teasp water with ½ teasp salt) and scatter with buckwheat, oats or muesli. Bake in a hot oven (Gas No. 7, 425°F, 220°C) for 35 minutes till browned, and loaves sound hollow when tapped with the knuckles on the underside. Leave to cool on a wire rack.

Rye Bread

Rye flour has a very interesting flavour and is used a great deal in countries such as Russia and Poland which have the cold winters necessary for its cultivation. A simple way of using rye flour is to make the Two Lovely Brown Loaves (above), using half each of wholewheat flour and rye flour. However, the true continental rye bread has to be made with a 'sour dough' – that is, dough that has been allowed to ferment overnight and is then added to a freshly mixed dough. Some of the freshly mixed dough is then kept as the sour dough 'starter' for the next batch.

The bread keeps well and tastes best when it is a few days old. I have given a large recipe as it is not worth making in small quantities.

Makes 2 large loaves **F** 6 months
For the sour dough:
Yeast mixture

1 teasp sugar (brown or white) ⎫
2 tbsp hand-hot water   ⎬ mixed together, then left covered
1 teasp dried yeast   ⎭   till frothy (about 15 minutes)

Flour mixture

4 rounded tbsp wholemeal flour   4-6 oz (125-175ml/½-¾ cup) warm
  (either 100% or 89%)   water (exact quantity has to be
2 rounded tbsp rye flour   judged to give a reasonably firm
1 teasp salt   consistency)

Stir the frothy yeast liquid into the flour, salt and water. Mix to a dough. Place in a covered basin and leave to stand overnight.

501

Bread dough:

1½ lb (700g/6 cups) wholemeal flour
12 oz (350g/3 cups) rye flour
1 level teasp salt

1 heaped tbsp caraway seeds
2 tbsp oil
1 heaped tbsp malt
1 heaped tbsp molasses or treacle

For the yeast mixture:

4 teasp sugar
4 tbsp hand-hot water   } mixed together, then left covered
4 teasp dried yeast   till frothy (about 15 minutes)

Approx 1 pint (575ml/2½ cups) warm water (a little judgement has to be used for the exact quantity)

Leave the yeast liquid to rise in a basin in a warm place for 15 minutes. Mix all the other ingredients, including the sour dough and finally the yeast liquid. Knead well by hand or machine for 5-10 minutes until smooth and firm. Put in a warm place to rise, cover with a damp tea-towel or film. Allow to rise for an hour. After an hour use the dough-hook or knead again for a few minutes, remove approx 6 tbsp of the mixture and place in a basin which has a lid or firm cover for the next baking (if desired).

Knead the remainder for a few minutes and place into two warmed 2 lb (1kg) loaf tins and allow to rise for another hour in a warm place, covered with a cloth. After an hour (the centre of the loaf should peep over the sides of the tin and the sides will be ¼ inch (0.5cm) from the top), brush with a solution of 3 tbsp water and 1 teasp salt, put in a pre-heated oven, Gas No. 6, 400°F, 200°C on the middle shelf. Place a basin with water in the bottom of the cooker, as this improves the baking. Bake for 20 minutes, then reduce to Gas No. 5, 375°F, 190°C for a further 20 minutes. Finally turn out the loaves to a baking tray and bake for a further 20 minutes – this gives the loaves a good crust.

Rolls

If you want to serve hot rolls at a meal you have two alternatives: put home-baked or bought rolls into the oven straight from the freezer and reheat them, or part-bake your own rolls, freeze them, then finish off baking them just before breakfast or whenever you need them. The first method has the advantage that it can be used for both home and bought rolls, the second that the rolls really taste what they are – freshly baked. The part-baked rolls will keep for up to 4 months in the freezer, so it really makes sense to prepare a large batch at one time.

To part-bake rolls: Place shaped and risen rolls in a slow oven (Gas No. 2, 300°F, 150°C) for 20 minutes, or until set but still pale in colour, then cool and freeze.

To thaw and finish baking: Unwrap and place frozen rolls in oven to thaw and complete baking. Bake white rolls at Gas No. 6, 400°F, 200°C, brown rolls at Gas No. 8, 450°F, 230°C for 20 minutes.

To reheat baked rolls: Place frozen rolls wrapped in foil in a hot oven (Gas No. 8, 450°F, 230°C) for 15 minutes, or reheat in a microwave.

Quick-Rising White Rolls

These tender rolls are quickly made by adding ascorbic acid (Vitamin C) to the dough, which allows the rolls to be shaped as soon as the dough has been mixed. It is, however, essential to use fresh (rather than dried) yeast. Ascorbic acid tablets are available at any chemist or drugstore.

Makes 20 **F** 4 months

1 oz (25g/2 cakes) *fresh* yeast
12 fl oz (350ml/1¹/₂ cups) warm water
1 large egg and 1 yolk, *or* 2 standard eggs (reserve half of one egg for glaze)
¹/₂ × 50mg ascorbic acid tablet, crushed

1¹/₂ lb (675g/6 cups) strong plain white bread flour
3 level teasp salt
3 level teasp caster (superfine) sugar
3 tbsp oil or 1¹/₂ oz (40g/3 tbsp) very soft butter

The glaze:

1 yolk (or ¹/₂ whole egg) plus 1 teasp each salt and water

503

Heat the water until a drop on the wrist feels neither hot nor cold. Put into the mixing bowl. Add the sugar, the yeast and the crushed ascorbic acid tablet, and mix until smooth. Add one-third of the flour, and mix until smooth, then cover with film and leave for 20 minutes until it looks bubbly and frothy. Now add all the remaining flour, the salt, oil and egg, saving the yolk or half a whole egg for the glaze.

By machine: Mix with the dough-hook at minimum speed until a dough forms, then knead with the dough-hook at low speed for 3 minutes. Tip the dough onto a floured board and knead with the hands for 30 seconds to shape into a ball; the dough should have a scone-like texture.

(By hand alone, the dough should be kneaded about 10 minutes until smooth. By food processor, mix the dough in two portions according to instructions.)

To shape the rolls: Divide the dough into 20 pieces.

Dimple Rolls: Take each piece of dough and knead into a ball the size of a small apple. Roll into a round about ³/₈ inch (0.75cm) thick. Put on a floured tray to rise until puffy, as for the bread. Take two fingers and press a 'dimple' firmly into the centre of the dough. Brush with the salted egg mixture and scatter with poppy or sesame seeds (optional). Bake in a hot oven (Gas No. 7, 425°F, 220°C) for 15 minutes until a rich brown.

Knots: Roll each piece of dough into a rope 7 inches (17.5cm) long. Shape into a coil and put one end through the centre of the coil. Allow to rise until puffy. Brush with the salted egg mixture and bake as for the Dimple Rolls.

Miniature Plaits: Divide each piece of dough into three and roll into a 6 inch (15cm) rope. Plait by pressing the strands firmly together at one end, then plait tightly. Allow to rise until puffy. Brush with salted egg mixture and scatter with poppy seeds. Bake as for the Dimple Rolls.

Crusty Half-and-Half Brown Rolls

These have a really crunchy crust and are very fluffy inside.

Makes 12 F 4 months

½ lb (225g/2 cups) strong white flour	1 oz (25g/2 cakes) fresh yeast *or* 1 level tbsp dried yeast
½ lb (225g/2 cups) granary or other brown flour	2 level teasp brown sugar
¼ pint (150ml/⅔ cup) milk	2 level teasp salt
¼ pint (150ml/⅔ cup) very hot water	1 oz (25g/2 tbsp) butter

Note: If *dried* yeast is used, first stir it into ¼ pint (150ml/⅔ cup) of *hand hot* water with a teaspoon each of the measured sugar and flour. Leave until frothy (about 15 minutes) to reactivate the yeast, then add to the ¼ pint (150ml/⅔ cup) lukewarm milk and use as directed below.

If *fresh* yeast is used, proceed as follows: mix the cold milk and hot water in a mixing bowl (liquid should be blood heat) then add the yeast and the sugar.

(With dried yeast add yeast liquid to bowl and remaining teaspoon of sugar.) Now add one-third of the flour (about 5 oz (150g/1¼ cups) and beat well until a batter is formed. Cover with a tea-towel and leave for 15 minutes, while you mix the salt with the remaining flour and rub in the butter. When the yeast mixture looks frothy, add the flour mixture and mix to a dough, then knead with a dough-hook (3 minutes) or by hand (5 minutes) until a smooth, scone-like dough is formed. Grease the mixing bowl, put the dough back in it, cover with film and leave for 45 minutes or until double in volume. Knead again for 2 minutes to redistribute any large bubbles of gas, then divide into 12 pieces. Knead each little piece into a ball (or shape as for **Quick-Rising White Rolls (p.512)**) and place 2 inches (5cm) apart, on greased trays. Cover with film again and leave on the kitchen table for 30 minutes until very spongy.

To glaze:
Soft crust – dust with flour before baking, wrap in a cloth when baked.
Crisp crust – brush with 2 tbsp water and ½ teasp salt before baking.
Shiny crust – brush with milk before baking.
Golden crust – beat 1 egg with 4 tbsp milk and a brush evenly on rolls before baking.
Golden crust without milk – brush with beaten egg and 4 tbsp water.

Rolls or loaves may also be sprinkled with poppy seeds, sesame seeds or porridge oats after brushing with glaze.

Bake for 10 minutes at Gas No. 8, 450°F, 230°C then re-glaze and bake a further 5-7 minutes until a rich brown, and the base of a roll sounds hollow when tapped.

VARIATION
Wholewheat Rolls
These are darker and coarser and very filling.

Makes 12 F 4 months

Make exactly as for **Crusty Half-and-Half Brown Rolls** (above) but with the following ingredients:

A bare ounce (25g/2 cakes) fresh yeast *or* 1 level tbsp dried yeast
1 lb (450g/4 cups) wholewheat or granary flour
1 level tbsp Barbados (dark brown) sugar or honey
2 teasp oil
2 level teasp salt
½ pint (275ml/1¼ cups) warm water (blood heat)

Overnight Rolls

The dough for these tender, spongy rolls is mixed more like a cake than a regular yeast dough. For convenience it is then refrigerated overnight or for as long as four days before baking – a wonderful recipe for entertaining purposes.

If it is made with white flour the texture is somewhat similar to brioche; made with half-and-half or all brown flour it is slightly firmer but still very fine-grained. No kneading is required, but I

506

would use fresh yeast – remember it will keep for 3 weeks under refrigeration and 4-6 weeks in the freezer.

Makes 16-18 **F** 4 months

8 fl oz (225ml/1 cup) hot water
1 oz (25g/2 tbsp) sugar
3 oz (75g/¹/₃ cup) butter or
  margarine, *or* 5 tbsp oil
Generous ¹/₂ oz (15g/1 cake) fresh
  yeast mixed with 2 tbsp warm
  water

1 egg
2 level teasp salt
1 lb (450g/4 cups) white or bread
  flour, *or* ¹/₂ lb (225g/2 cups)
  each of white and brown
Little extra flour if necessary

Put the sugar and fat into a mixing bowl and pour on the hot water. Stir until the fat (if solid) is melted, then cool to lukewarm. Dissolve the yeast in the 2 tbsp of lukewarm water, then add to the cooled liquid, followed by the salt, half the flour and the beaten egg (save 2 tbsp for glazing the rolls). Beat by hand or mixer until the dough falls in sheets from the spoon or mixer, leaving it almost clean (3-4 minutes), then beat in the remaining flour. You should now have a soft, scone-like dough. If it is too wet, add a further 2 or 3 tbsp of flour, until the mixture can be gathered into a ball. Take a large plastic bag and oil the inside, drop in the dough, tie loosely and put in the least cold part of the refrigerator. Leave at least 12 hours or for as long as 4 days if required.

To shape and bake the rolls: Take out of the refrigerator. Either roll the dough on a floured board until it is ¹/₂ inch (1.25cm) thick, then cut into rounds with a 2¹/₂ inch (6.25cm) cutter, and place 2 inches (5cm) apart on greased trays, *or* divide into 16 pieces, roll each into a ball and place in a greased patty tin. Slip each baking tray into a large plastic bag, and leave for 1¹/₂ hours until the rolls feel light and spongy. To the reserved egg add ¹/₂ teasp of salt and 2 teasp water, then use to paint the top of the rolls. Leave plain or scatter with sesame seeds.

Bake in a hot oven (Gas No. 7, 425°F, 220°C) for 15 minutes until a rich brown. Serve fresh or freeze until required.

Herb Bread

This is a French or Vienna bread which is sliced down to the bottom crust but not separated. Instead, each slice is thickly spread with a herb-flavoured butter. When the bread is heated this

507

spreads through the loaf, making it fluffy and full of flavour. It makes a delicious hot accompaniment to cold meats or fish. The bread can be filled, wrapped in foil, then frozen for up to a week (after that the crust tends to come away from the loaf). The bread can also be refrigerated for up to three days before baking.

Each loaf serves 5-6 **F** 1 week

1 long French stick
4 oz (125g/$^{1}/_{2}$ cup) soft butter or margarine
2 level tbsp of a mixture of chopped fresh herbs (parsley, chives, basil) *or* 2 tbsp fresh

parsley and 1 level teasp mixed dried herbs
$^{1}/_{4}$ teasp paprika
10 grinds black pepper
2 teasp lemon juice

Cut the bread into slanting slices just under $^{1}/_{2}$ inch (1.25cm) thick, but stop at the base of the loaf so that it is left in one piece. Beat the butter to a soft cream with a wooden spoon, then beat in all the remaining ingredients. Spread this mixture thickly on one side of each slice of bread, then put the loaf onto a piece of foil large enough to enclose it completely. Spread any remaining herb butter mixture over the surface of the loaf and sprinkle with a little coarse salt (if available). Fold the foil over to seal the loaf completely. Refrigerate until required.

About 30 minutes before required, put in a quick oven (Gas No. 6, 400°F, 200°C) for 20 minutes, then fold back the foil and bake for a further 5 minutes to crispen the crust. Serve hot on a long tray or wooden platter. Each guest tears off his own portion.

If the bread has been frozen, allow an extra 10 minutes before folding back the foil.

Party Snacks and Titbits

All the recipes in this chapter are for 'finger food' – hot and cold snacks to serve at a drinks party or other informal occasion when there are no seating facilities.

It is impossible to be exact on quantities for these occasions. However, it is a good idea to provide 4-5 varieties of canapés or sandwiches, and 2-3 hot snacks, as well as assorted dips and nibbles.

See chapter on **'The Drinks Party'** (pp.109-20), and also chapter on **'Cooking for 50'** (pp.555-65).

Make your own selection from the following suggestions:

Dips with crudités and crisps

Aïoli
Aubergine Herb Dip
Avocado Dip

Cream Cheese Dip
Guacamole

Canapés

Cream Cheese Pâté or Spread
Cream Cheese and Pineapple
  Spread
Cream Cheese and Walnut Spread
Egg and Olive Butter
Gaffelbiter, Tomato and
  Cucumber

Smoked Salmon with Lemon
Smoked Salmon Sandwich Spread
Smoked Mackerel Sandwich
  Spread
Smoked Kipper Sandwich Spread
Salmon Mayonnaise

Rolled sandwiches

Asparagus Rolls
Mackerel, Kipper or Smoked
  Salmon Rolls

Egg and Olive Rolls
Smoked Salmon Rolls using Slices
  of Fish

Closed sandwiches

Pastrami or Tongue on White or
  Rye Bread
Chicken Sandwiches

Chicken Liver Pâté Sandwiches
Turkey Sandwiches
Tuna Sandwich Filling

Hot and Cheesey

Syrian Sesame Cheese Puffs
Hot Cheese Crisps

Savoury tartlets

Olive and Cheese
Petite Quiche Lorraine
Olive and Anchovy

Cheese and Onion
Miniature Pizza
Petites Gougères

Other hot snacks

Stuffed Aubergine (Eggplant) or
  Courgette (Zucchini) Slices
Chinese Chicken Bites
Fried Chicken Titbits
Liver Pâté Crisps

Pasteles
Spanish Deep-Fried Pies
Latkes on Sticks
Savoury Sausage Rolls
Goujonettes

Filling for bouchées

Sherried Chicken or Turkey Filling
Sherried Mushroom Filling

Little nibbles

Cheese and Fruit Kebabs
Stuffed Celery
Stuffed Fresh Dates

Garlic Olives
Crispy Noodles
Cheese Twists

Dips with Crudités and Crisps

It is impossible to anticipate just how much a particular group will
eat of this kind of dip, but in any case, left-overs will keep for
several days at least.

Aïoli with Crudités

A delicate garlic mayonnaise.

Do not freeze **R** 2 weeks
Blender or food processor method

To serve 12-24	*To serve 25-50*
Makes 1/2 pint (275ml/1 1/4 cups)	1 pint (575ml/2 1/2 cups)
1 egg	2
8 fl oz (225ml/1 cup) oil	3/4 pint (425ml/2 cups)
1 garlic clove	2 medium
1/2 level teasp sea salt	1 level teasp
1 tbsp lemon juice	1 1/2-2 tbsp
Few grinds black pepper	Few grinds

Peel the garlic cloves and put in blender or food processor with the salt and whole eggs and 2 tbsp of the oil. Blend or process for 30 seconds until the mixture is smooth, then add the remaining oil gradually, beating all the time. Add half the lemon juice after half the oil has been added. Taste and add the remaining lemon juice or to taste. Mixture should be like softly whipped cream. If too solid, add a teaspoon of boiling water. Serve surrounded with raw vegetables (see **Crudités** below) as a dip.

By hand
Use 1 egg yolk and 6 fl oz (175ml/3/4 cup) oil; or 2 egg yolks and 12 fl oz (350ml/1 1/2 cups) oil for larger quantity. In a mortar or bowl, crush the garlic cloves with the salt. When mushy, add egg yolks, then add the oil drop by drop, beating with a balloon or batter whisk. When half the oil has been added, stir in most of the lemon juice. Add the remaining oil more quickly and finish with the remaining lemon juice and black pepper. Keep tightly covered under refrigeration.

Crudités

Do not freeze

To serve 12-24 with *crisps and savoury* *biscuits (crackers)*	*To serve 25-50 with* *crisps and savoury* *biscuits (crackers)*
2 large carrots	4 large
2 green peppers	4
1 heart celery	2 hearts

Cut all the vegetables into strips about 2 inches (5cm) long and ³/₈ inch (1cm) wide. Wrap in film or foil and chill well.

When ready to serve, put the dip into a bowl standing on a flat plate and surround with the vegetable strips.

Crisps and savoury biscuits (crackers) also make excellent dippers.

VARIATION

Crudités in Orange Cups: *These look very attractive on a buffet or can be served with starters at a dinner party.*

Cut off and discard the top third from 8 large thick-skinned oranges and cut a thin slice from the bottom of each orange. With a curved grapefruit knife cut the pulp from each orange and put in a bowl. Scrape the juice remaining in the shells into the bowl with a small spoon and reserve the pulp and juice, covered and chilled, for another use. Chill the orange shells, covered.

Cut into 3-4 inch (7-10cm) sticks 1 bunch each of carrots, spring onions (scallions) and celery hearts, all trimmed. Make several cuts about ³/₄ inch (1.5cm) deep at one end of each spring onion (scallion) and gently spread the cut ends. Trim and score into petals 1 bunch of radishes. Chill the vegetables in a bowl of iced water until serving time. Divide between the orange cups.

Aubergine (Eggplant) Herb Dip

A gently flavoured aubergine (eggplant) pâté, whose flavour many people find hard to identify.

For 10-12 and 50. Do not freeze **R** 48 hours

To serve 10-12	To serve 50
1 large (¹/₂ lb/225g) aubergine (eggplant)	4
1 packet (3 oz/75g) Boursin (herb and garlic) cheese	4 packets
6 oz (175g/³/₄ cup) low or medium fat cream cheese	1¹/₄ lb (575g/2¹/₂ cups)
1 tbsp lemon juice	4 tbsp
2 teasp chopped parsley or chives, extra for garnish	2 tbsp
Salt to taste	1-2 teasp
Black pepper to taste	20 grinds

Using a fork, prick the surface of the aubergine (eggplant) and put it in the oven at Gas No. 5, 375°F, 190°C for 45 minutes until very soft when pierced with a skewer. Cool, then cut in half lengthways and scoop out the flesh. Chop up finely and put in a bowl with the cheeses. Blend well and stir in the lemon juice, parsley or chives and seasonings. Pile into a serving dish on a plate surrounded with crudités (see above). Garnish the dish with snipped chives or parsley.

Avocado Dip

Pale green and crunchy with green pepper, this has a most distinctive flavour.

For 12-16 and 50 F 1 month

To serve 12-16	*To serve 50*
1/4 onion, finely chopped	4 tbsp
1/2 green pepper, finely chopped	2 medium
2 medium or 1 large avocado, peeled, skinned and puréed	8 medium or 4 large
1/2 lb (225g/1 cup) low or medium fat cream cheese	2 lb (900g/4 cups)
1 level teasp salt	1 tbsp
Plenty black pepper	Plenty
2 tbsp lemon juice	6-8 tbsp
1 teasp snipped chives	2 tbsp
1 teasp chopped parsley	2 tbsp

Beat all ingredients together. Taste and add more seasoning if required. Texture should be like soft cream cheese.

VARIATION
Avocado Dip with Smoked Mackerel for 50: Thin the dip with a 5 fl oz (150ml/2/3 cup) carton soured cream and stir in 1 lb (450g) finely shredded smoked mackerel.

For 12-16: Use 2 tbsp soured cream and 1/4 lb (125g) smoked mackerel.

Guacamole

This is a more pungent version of Avocado Dip.

Do not freeze

To serve 12	To serve 50
2 × 6 oz (175g) avocados	8 × 6 oz (175g)
or	*or*
1 × 10 oz (275g)	4 × 10 oz (275g)
Sprinkle garlic salt *or*	1/2 teasp *or* 2 cloves
1/2 clove garlic, crushed	
2 tomatoes, peeled and finely chopped	8
1/4 onion, finely chopped	1 onion (5 oz/150g)
1 small green pepper, finely chopped	2 large
12 coriander seeds, crushed in a mortar or by the end of a rolling pin	1 teasp
1 tbsp olive oil	4 tbsp
Juice of 1/2 lemon (approx 2 tbsp)	5 fl oz (150ml/2/3 cup)
1/2 teasp salt	2 teasp
10 grinds black pepper	1/4 teasp

Put the peeled and stoned avocado in the blender or food processor with the lemon juice and olive oil and seasonings, and process until smooth. Add the remaining ingredients and process only until blended. Taste and add more seasoning if desired.

Put in pottery dish, closely wrap and chill for several hours or overnight. Serve with crudités (p.510) and crisps.

Cream Cheese Dip

A very tangy mixture, which needs at least 12 hours to mature in the refrigerator. Serve in a pottery bowl surrounded by crudités (p.510) and crisps.

Do not freeze **R** 4 days

To serve 12-16	To serve 40-50
1/2 lb (225g/1 cup) cream cheese	1 1/2 lb (675g/3 cups)
2 oz (50g/1/4 cup) butter	6 oz (175g/3/4 cup)
1/2 large green pepper	2 medium
6 cocktail gherkins	18
Green part of 2 spring onions (scallions) *or*	6
2 tbsp chives	6 tbsp
Sprig parsley	3 sprigs
1 tbsp mayonnaise	3 tbsp
1 tbsp French dressing	3 tbsp
1/2 teasp salt	1 1/2 teasp
1 tbsp yoghurt, soured cream *or* single (light) cream	3 tbsp

Put all the herbs and seasonings in blender or food processor and process until liquid. Add the butter and cream cheese and blend until smooth. Add sliced gherkins and green pepper. Blend only until gherkins are still visible. Stir in the yoghurt or cream. Without blender, chop finely the pepper, gherkins, spring onions (scallions) or chives, add parsley, and beat into cheese mixed with all the remaining ingredients.

Canapés

Serve canapés on crisp crackers (not cheese-flavoured) or tiny rounds of crisp French bread, well buttered. Cracker canapés should not be made more than an hour in advance as they quickly go soggy, but canapés on bread can be made up to 4 hours beforehand, provided trays or dishes are carefully wrapped in film to prevent them drying out. Make one kind of canapé at a time and put on flat trays, then arrange on large platters using a variety to make an attractive pattern.

Have ready an assortment of garnishes – cucumber and tomato slices, sliced black olives, anchovies, radish slices, pickled cucumber and gherkin slices, canned pimento, chopped parsley, paprika pepper, cress.

Cream Cheese Pâté or Spread

For 40 rounds French bread as a spread. Serves 6-8 on cheese-board F 6 weeks without garlic

$^{1}/_{2}$ lb (225g/1 cup) full fat (double) cream cheese
2 tbsp single (light) cream
2 teasp finely chopped fresh herbs (mainly parsley and chives with pinch of mint and thyme)
Pinch of salt, nutmeg
10 grinds black pepper
1 small clove garlic, finely crushed (optional)

Mix the cheese and cream and add all the remaining ingredients. Pack into a pottery bowl or individual tiny dishes and cover with film. Leave at least 24 hours before using – this is important to allow the flavours to develop.

Cream Cheese and Pineapple Spread

For 40-50 rounds French bread or crackers. Do not freeze
R 2 days

Mix ¹/₂ lb (225g/1 cup) full fat (double) cream cheese with 1 small
can crushed pineapple, drained (or the same amount of titbits,
drained and chopped) and 1 tbsp mayonnaise.

Cream Cheese and Walnut Spread

For 40-50 rounds French bread or crackers. Do not freeze
R 4 days

Mix ¹/₂ lb (225g/1 cup) full fat (double) cream cheese blended with
2 oz (50g/¹/₂ cup) finely chopped walnuts and 2 tbsp mayonnaise.

Egg and Olive Butter

For 40-50 rounds French bread or crackers. Do not freeze
R 1 day

Mash 6 hard-boiled eggs with 1 oz (25g/2 tbsp) butter, 2 tbsp salad
cream and 2 oz (50g/¹/₂ cup) finely chopped stuffed olives. Garnish
with anchovies.

Gaffelbiter, Tomato and Cucumber

For 40-50 rounds French bread or crackers
Allow 3 large cans herring titbits (Gaffelbiter). On each round of
bread put a slice of cucumber and tomato and a piece of drained
Gaffelbiter.

Smoked Salmon with Lemon

Very extravagant but delicious

For 40-50 rounds French bread or crackers
Sprinkle slices of smoked salmon with lemon juice and a little
black pepper. Cut to fit crackers or bread slices. Garnish with thin
sections of lemon or sliced fresh cucumber. Allow 1¹/₂ lb (675g)
smoked salmon.

Smoked Salmon Sandwich Spread

Very delicious and relatively economical as it can be made with smoked salmon titbits which are much cheaper than full slices.

For 40-50 rounds French bread or crackers **F** 1 month if made with fresh smoked salmon **R** 3 days

½ lb (225g) packet smoked
  salmon titbits
2 oz (50g/¼ cup) very soft butter
2 tbsp lemon juice

10 grinds black pepper
4 tbsp whipping or double (heavy)
  cream, whipped

Put all the ingredients (except the cream) in a food processor or blender and process until absolutely smooth. Turn into a container and fold in the cream which has been whipped until it holds soft peaks. Taste and add more pepper if necessary.

  Chill for several hours, well covered, to allow the flavours to blend. If frozen, allow 4 hours to defrost in the refrigerator.

VARIATION 1
Smoked Mackerel Sandwich Spread F 1 month **R** 3 days.
Substitute skinned smoked mackerel fillets for the smoked salmon. Add 2 teasp horseradish sauce or relish.

VARIATION 2
Smoked Kipper Sandwich Spread F 1 month **R** 3-4 days.
Substitute kipper fillets for the smoked salmon. If frozen cook according to packet directions. Otherwise, put in a jug, cover with boiling water and leave for 10 minutes. Drain thoroughly, flake and remove any large bones.

  Add 2 teasp Worcestershire sauce and a pinch of cayenne pepper to the other flavourings.

Salmon Mayonnaise

An excellent use for cooked frozen salmon or the shoulder portion of a whole salmon that has been frozen in joints.

For 40-50 rounds of French bread or biscuits

1 lb (450g) good weight salmon or
  salmon trout
5 fl oz (150ml/⅔ cup) mild
  mayonnaise

2 teasp lemon juice
Small teasp Dijon mustard

If necessary poach the salmon (see p.217). Skin, bone, then flake roughly. Put the mayonnaise into a bowl and add the lemon juice and mustard. Stir in the salmon – the mixture should be moist but not wet. Add salt and white pepper to taste if necessary. Garnish the canapés with cucumber twists.

Rolled Sandwiches

These delicious mouthfuls consist of a fine-textured brown bread spread with a savoury filling, then rolled and cut in three. They are particularly convenient to make as they must be prepared well ahead of time in order to 'set'.

Asparagus Rolls

Makes 60 tiny rolls. Serves 30 as part of mixed assortment of sandwiches and canapés. **F** 1 month **R** 12 hours

1 can asparagus tips	5 oz (150g/^{2}/$_3$ cup) butter
1 large sliced fine-textured brown loaf	Salad cream
	Salt

De-crust the bread, then roll each slice with a rolling pin to make the texture more compact and so facilitate rolling.

Butter, then spread thinly with salad cream. Lay 1 or 1½ asparagus tips (according to length) along the long edge of each slice, then roll up and place join side down on a tray. Repeat until all are completed, packing the rolls tightly together to stop them unrolling. Film cover and chill for not less than 2 hours, though they can be left for up to 12 hours (in which case, cover with foil as well). When ready to arrange, cut each roll into 2 or 3, and arrange standing on end in an entrée or similar dish about 1½ inches (4cm) deep.

VARIATION 1
Egg and Olive Rolls: Make the egg and olive butter on p.516. Use to spread on each slice of bread. Roll up and cut as for Asparagus Rolls.

VARIATION 2
Smoked Salmon. Mackerel or Kipper Rolls: F 1 month. Use either

the smoked mackerel, kipper or salmon sandwich spread (p.517) or smoked mackerel mousse (p.135).

Butter the bread, then spread each slice generously with the chilled fish mixture, then lay 1 or 2 long strips of pickled cucumber (about ¼ inch/0.5cm wide) down the long side of the bread in place of the asparagus. Roll and cut as for Asparagus Rolls.

Smoked Salmon Rolls using Slices of Fish

These are extravagent but quite superb for the special occasion. Frozen smoked salmon can be used, but it is not then advisable to freeze the rolls.

Serves 30 F 1 month

1 very large fresh white tin loaf, sliced	1 level tbsp chopped parsley
5 oz (150g/⅔ cup) softened butter	10-12 oz (275-350g) smoked salmon, very thinly sliced
1 tbsp lemon juice	

De-crust the bread, then roll each slice with a rolling pin to facilitate rolling.

Beat together the butter, lemon juice and parsley, then use to butter the bread. Arrange very thin slices of salmon to cover each slice. Roll up and place each roll on a tray, join side down. Film cover and chill for up to 12 hours but not less than 2. When ready to arrange, cut each roll into 2 or 3 and arrange standing up side by side in a dish about 1½ inches (4cm) deep. Makes about 60 little rolls, depending on size.

To freeze: Pack the rolls in a rigid container with greaseproof or foil between layers.

To defrost: Loosen lid and thaw at room temperature for 4 hours.

For half quantity: Use 1 small loaf; 3 oz (75g/⅓ cup) butter; 2 teasp each lemon juice and chopped parsley; 6 oz (175g) salmon.

Closed Sandwiches

F 2 months (do not freeze salads or hard-boiled eggs)

The bread, whether brown, white or rye, must be very fresh and very thinly cut and spread with some kind of fat – whether butter, best quality margarine or rendered chicken fat (delicious with roast and pickled meats and poultry). To cut even sandwiches it is a good idea to pile several up on top, and then cut through the entire pile.

Sandwiches freeze well, and they also keep splendidly under refrigeration, providing that in both cases they are wrapped first in film and then in foil. Delicious sandwiches can be made with barm cakes (round flat loaves). Any of the canapé spreads can, of course, be used for closed sandwiches. Here are some additional suggestions.

Allow 2 loaves of bread and 1-1½ lb (450-675g) meat or poultry to make 100 tiny sandwiches (large bread, quartered).

Pastrami or Tongue on White or Rye Bread

Spread the bread lightly with the chosen fat, and lay slices of cold (or hot) pastrami or tongue closely together. Top with a thin smear of any French or English mustard, and thin slices of pickled cucumber. Cover with the top slice of bread.

Chicken Sandwiches

Use a chicken cooked as on p.277 (**To roast a chicken for salad**) or simmered as for **Circassian Chicken** (p.289). 2 × 3½ lb (1.5kg) birds will make enough sandwiches for 50.

Use an enriched white bread (challah is ideal) spread with the chosen fat (preferably chicken fat), then a crisp lettuce leaf, a slice of bird and a thin topping of fruit chutney or mild mustard.

Chicken Liver Pâté Sandwiches

Use chicken liver pâté or **Pâté Maison** (p.137). Use white bread (challah again is excellent), spread with the chosen fat, with thinly sliced pickled cucumber or stuffed olives topping the pâté. Cover with a second slice of bread.

Turkey Sandwiches

Use white bread, spread with the chosen fat, then top with turkey slices spread with cranberry jelly.

Tuna Sandwich Filling

This is excellent for toasted sandwiches, and for filling barm cakes. Enough to make sandwiches for 8.

1 × 7oz (200g) can tuna	Pinch salt
1 tbsp salad dressing	Few grinds black pepper
2 tbsp vinaigrette with herbs (p.332)	Pinch of nutmeg

Drain the tuna and flake *coarsely* (do not mash). Mix with the remaining ingredients, seasoning to taste if necessary. Butter bread or toast, cover with a thick layer of tuna filling, then crisp salted lettuce. Top with buttered bread or toast. Press down firmly and cut in triangles.

Hot and Cheesey

These little snacks go particularly well with drinks as they are tasty yet more sustaining than canapés. As they must be served hot, it does require someone to be keeping an eye on their progress in the oven. Fortunately they can all be frozen at some stage in their preparation. They can all be kept warm, for up to 30 minutes, either in a special warming oven or in the regular oven at Gas No. $1/2$, 250°F, 120°C. After that they begin to dry out.

Syrian Cheese Puffs

The simple filling becomes a cheesey sponge in the oven, contrasting with the light, tender pastry. These can be frozen uncooked in advance or made and refrigerated for up to 48 hours beforehand. Serve freshly baked: do not reheat as they will go tough.

For 12 and 50 (2 puffs per person). **F** 3 months **R** 2 days

Quantities for 12	*Quantities for 50*
³/₄ lb (350g) puff pastry	2¹/₂ lb (1.25kg)
¹/₂ lb (225g/2 cups) cooking (Cheddar) cheese, finely grated	2 lb (1kg/8 cups)
2 eggs	6-7
Pinch salt	1 level teasp
Sesame seeds	

Grate cheese in food processor if available. Beat the eggs. Reserve 2 tbsp for glazing the puffs. Add remainder of the eggs to the cheese with salt to make a sticky paste. Roll the pastry to the thickness of a knife blade, then cut with 2¹/₂ inch (6cm) plain cutters into approx 25 (100) rounds. Damp the edges of each round, place a teaspoon of filling in the centre, fold over to form a half moon. Arrange on damp trays. Just before cooking brush with beaten egg. Bake in a hot oven (Gas No. 7, 425°F, 220°C) for 15 minutes. Serve warm.

Hot Cheese Crisps

These are excellent for a small group – say a teenagers' get-together. Use a good Dijon or Bordeaux mustard to add bite.

For each person allow two large rounds of bread; 1 slice of Gouda cheese large enough to cover the bread completely; some Dijon or Bordeaux mustard; very soft butter.

With each two slices of bread (no need to butter it) make a sandwich of mustard and cheese. Press the slices firmly together. Put a large, heavy-based frying pan over medium heat and allow to heat through for 3-4 minutes – or until you can feel the heat of the pan with the palm of your hand held an inch above it. Spread one side of the bread with a thin layer of soft butter, then lay butter side down in the pan. Spread the top of the sandwich with butter in the pan. (This makes it easier to handle than when both sides are buttered before cooking.) Cook steadily until the bottom of the sandwich is a rich golden brown, turn and cook until the other side is done as well. Cut each sandwich in four and serve with pickled cucumber, crisps and fresh tomatoes.

VARIATION
Liver Pâté Crisps: Spread the bread with Pâté Maison (p.137),

topped with thinly sliced pickled cucumber. Spread the outside of the bread with margarine.

Savoury Tartlets

The following three recipes are for tiny savoury tartlets. As they take so little time to bake I think it's better to do them freshly, for even if frozen ahead they would still need to be warmed up. The tartlet cases themselves can be rolled out and then frozen. This is, in fact, an advantage, since if the filling is added to the pastry cases whilst still frozen, the resulting tarts will be extra crisp.

The tartlets are better served warm rather than hot, as the flavours come through better.

Petites Quiches Lorraines

This is a creamy filling, capable of many variations.

Makes 24 (12 servings) F unbaked cases 6 months

Pastry:

½ lb (225g/2 cups) plain flour	1 level tbsp icing (confectioners')
Pinch of salt	sugar
4 oz (125g/½ cup) butter	3 tbsp icy water

Mix the flour, salt and sugar. Cut the butter into 1 inch (2.5cm) chunks, then rub in until no particles larger than a small pea rise to the surface when the bowl is shaken. Sprinkle on the water to evenly moisten the crumbs, then gather into a dough. Chill for 1 hour, then roll ¼ inch (0.5cm) thick and cut to fit 24 patty tins. Prick thoroughly. Freeze, or chill thoroughly.

The filling:

1 egg	1 level tbsp cornflour (cornstarch)
½ pint (275ml/1¼ cups) whipping cream	½ level teasp salt
	10 grinds black pepper
6 oz (175g/1½ cups) finely grated cheese	Pinch of cayenne pepper
	1 level tbsp snipped chives

(*Note*: If cream is not available, use 2 eggs and 6 fl oz (175ml/¾

523

cup) creamy milk. Divide 2 oz (50g/^{1}/$_4$ cup) butter among tartlets just before the filling is poured in.)

Beat the eggs thoroughly, then add all the remaining ingredients. When ready to bake, divide among the cases. Bake in a quick oven (Gas No. 6, 400°F, 200°C) or until the pastry is golden and the filling is puffed. May be reheated.

VARIATION 1
Olive and Anchovy: Add 2 oz (50g/^{1}/$_2$ cup) sliced black olives and 6 chopped anchovies to the filling.

VARIATION 2
Cheese and Onion: Finely chop 1 medium (5oz/150g) onion, and sauté until golden and tender in 1 oz (25g/2tbsp) butter, then stir into the filling.

Miniature Pizzas

These are baked in flaky pastry cases made with curd or cottage cheese.

Makes 24 F 1 month F cases 4 months

The pastry:

4 oz (125g/^{1}/$_2$ cup) dry curd cheese   4 oz (125g/1 cup) plain flour
  or sieved cottage cheese   Pinch of salt
4 oz (125g/^{1}/$_2$ cup) butter

Blend the butter and cheese using a wooden spoon or electric mixer at low speed. Add the flour gradually until a dough is formed. Chill for one hour. Roll out very thinly and cut to fit shallow patty tins. Prick all over the base. Bake at Gas No. 7, 425°F, 220°C for 7-10 minutes or until a pale gold in colour. Allow to cool thoroughly, then freeze, or store in an airtight container for up to a week.

The filling:
The filling can be frozen in advance as well, though I would reheat it and add the herb flavouring on the day it is used – herbs tend to 'go off' in the freezer.

2 tbsp oil	1 small clove of garlic, crushed,
1/2 large onion	or a pinch of instant garlic
1 level teasp each of sugar and	1 bayleaf
salt	1 × 15 oz (425g) can tomatoes
Plenty of black pepper	1 tbsp tomato purée
1/2 level teasp crushed basil	1/4 lb (125g/1 cup) grated cheese
	1 tin anchovies (optional)

Heat the oil, add the chopped onion and cook until softened and
golden. Add all the remaining ingredients except for the cheese
and the anchovies. Simmer uncovered until as thick as ketchup.
Put 2 teaspoons of the cooled filling into each half-baked case. Top
with a little grated cheese and a split fillet of anchovy (if used).
Bake at Gas No. 4, 350°F, 180°C for 15-20 minutes.

Alternatively, the filling and topping can be arranged in
well-pricked *unbaked* cases and then baked at Gas No. 7, 425°F,
220°C for 20 minutes.

For 50 – double all ingredients.

Petites Gougères (Little Cheese Puffs)

*These delicious puffs, miniature versions of the large Gougères
served in Burgundy, can be eaten hot or cold. They are delicious
with a glass of chilled wine.*

To freeze ahead: Allow to cool, then freeze. Just before using, put
in a hot oven (Gas No. 7, 425°F, 220°C) for 3-4 minutes to thaw
and re-crispen at the same time.

Makes 40-45 F 6 months

1/2 pint (275ml/1¼ cups) water	coarsely grated. (Cheddar can
4 oz (125g/1/2 cup) butter	be substituted if others not
5 oz (150g/1¼ cups) flour	available)
1 level teasp salt	1 additional ounce (25g/¼ cup) of
Pinch of nutmeg and white pepper	finely grated cheese (Parmesan
1 teasp Dijon mustard	is excellent)
4 eggs	1 egg mixed with 1/2 teasp water,
4 oz (125g/1 cup) Gruyère,	for topping
Jarlsberg or Emmenthal cheese,	

Bring the water to the boil with butter and seasonings. When the butter has melted and the water is bubbling, remove from the heat and add the flour all at once. Mix thoroughly with a wooden spoon, then return to moderate heat, stirring for 1-2 minutes until the mixture forms a ball, leaving the sides of the pan clean – it will resemble firm mashed potato. Remove from the heat and make a well in the centre. Add the eggs one at a time, beating after each addition to incorporate the egg thoroughly. When ready the mixture will be glossy and will fall lazily into the bowl from the lifted spoon. (*Note*: the incorporation of the eggs can be done in a mixer or food processor.) Finally beat in the coarsely grated cheese.

Using a forcing bag with a ½ inch (1.25cm) plain pipe, squeeze the pastry out on to very lightly greased trays, into little mounds about 1 inch (2.5cm) in diameter and ½ inch (1.25cm) high. Leave about 2 inches (5cm) between each puff for expansion.

Beat the egg with the water and paint a little on each puff. (Try to avoid letting it drip down the side as this stops the puffs rising.) Sprinkle with the remaining cheese. Bake in a hot oven (Gas No. 7, 425°F, 220°C) for 20-25 minutes, or until crispy to the touch and a rich golden brown.

Turn off the oven, take out the trays of puffs and pierce the side of each one with a sharp knife. Return to the oven, and leave with the door ajar for 10 minutes – this prevents the puffs going soggy. Serve hot or cold.

Other Hot Snacks

Stuffed Aubergine (Eggplant) or Courgette (Zucchini) Slices

These delicious Israeli snacks consist of vegetable slices stuffed with savoury minced (ground) meat, then fried until crisp. They can be served hot or cold.

Serves 10-12 for cocktails. Do not freeze. Can be reheated.

1 lb (450g) aubergines (eggplants) or courgettes (zucchini)

Peel and cut in lengthwise slices as thin as possible. Leave to soak in salt water for 2 hours, then drain and dry.

The stuffing:

1 lb (450g) minced (ground) meat	1 egg
1/2 onion	Thick slice of bread soaked in
2 teasp parsley	water, then squeezed dry
1/2 teasp allspice or cinnamon	

For coating: 1 egg and dry breadcrumbs.

Make the minced (ground) meat stuffing according to directions on p.256. Allow to stand half an hour.

Spread each slice of vegetable with some minced (ground) meat mixture, then roll up and squeeze closed in the palm of the hand. Dip in beaten egg and dry crumbs, then in hot shallow or deep oil until a rich golden brown. Drain on kitchen paper. Serve hot or cold.

Chinese Chicken Bites

These delicious chunks of chicken are marinated in soy sauce before being fried. They can be served hot or cold, as convenient. They are delicious served either at a drinks party, or as the first course of a meal.

2 chickens or 3 whole breasts of chicken (6 halves)

Marinade:

1 cup (approx) soy sauce	4 tbsp lemon juice
2 oz (50g/1/4 cup) sugar	

With whole birds: Cut the chickens into quarters, then chop into pieces the size of a large walnut, using a cleaver or sharp knife and rolling pin.

With breasts: Bone, then cut into 1 inch (2.5cm) chunks.

Mix the marinade ingredients. Put the chicken pieces into a shallow casserole and pour over the marinade. Leave several hours or overnight, turning as often as convenient.

When ready to fry, lift from the marinade, drain well.

To serve hot: Dip in a mixture of half-and-half cornflour (cornstarch) and plain flour. Fry in hot deep fat Gas No. 5 (375°F, 190°C) until brown and crisp.

To serve cold: Dip in flour, then beaten egg, then dry breadcrumbs and fry as above until a rich brown.

Serve on toothpicks.

Fried Chicken Titbits

These are straightforward pieces of fried chicken. Allow one joint, or two halves for each serving.

Follow method for **Sesame Chicken** (p.273), but use ready-to-cook chicken portions such as drumsticks, wings or thigh pieces.

Hot Dogs on Sticks

Allow 3 cocktail-size hot dogs per person.

Simmer frankfurters or saveloys in boiling water to cover for 5 minutes, then leave covered in steaming water until required. (Do not leave boiling or they will split.) Drain and serve on cocktail sticks, with mustard or tomato ketchup as dips.

Pasteles

This is the authentic Middle Eastern recipe. The pine kernels can be omitted, if unavailable, but they do add greatly to the charm of these little pies. It is not worth making less than this quantity.

Makes 30 individual pies **F** 3 months

Meat filling or tatbila:
This must be prepared in advance as it has to be cold when used.

1¹/₂ lb (675g) raw minced (ground) beef	1 oz (25g) pine kernels, fried until golden in a little oil
¹/₄ lb (125g) minced beef fat	¹/₂ teasp each ground cinnamon and pimento
1 large onion, finely chopped	1¹/₂ teasp salt
1 coffee cup of cold water	Black pepper

Put the beef, fat, onion and water into a heavy-based pan and cook, stirring frequently over moderate heat until the meat has lost its redness and the water has evaporated.

Stir in the pine kernels, cinnamon and pimento, salt and black pepper. Allow the mixture to cool.

Set the oven to Gas No. 6, 400°F, 200°C.

Pastry:

1 lb (450g/4 cups) plain flour	¹/₂ level teasp salt
Approx ¹/₄ pint (150ml/²/₃ cup) water	¹/₂ lb (225g/1 cup) margarine
	1 tbsp oil

Put the flour, salt and margarine (cut into small chunks) into a large bowl and sprinkle with the oil. Now rub the fat into the dry ingredients as for shortcrust pastry. Sprinkle with enough cold water to make a firm but non-sticky dough. Roll out ¹/₈ inch (0.25cm) thick on a floured board and, using plain metal pastry cutters, cut the dough into equal quantities of 3¹/₂ inch (8.75cm) and 2 inch (5cm) rounds. There should be enough for about 30 of each.

To shape the cases in the traditional way, by hand, make pleats round larger circles to form cups ³/₄ inch (2cm) deep. Fill with cooled meat, put a 2 inch (5cm) circle on top, then twist together into a piecrust edging. The cases can also be shaped in patty tins and sealed like mince tarts.

To finish:
Paint the pasteles with the beaten yolk of 1 egg, then scatter with sesame seeds (30 pasteles will need about 1 oz/25g). Bake the pies for 25 minutes until they are a rich brown.

They may be frozen baked or unbaked (in the latter case, thaw for 1 hour before baking).

Spanish Deep-Fried Pies

Crisp crescents of puff pastry filled with a savoury tuna mixture. If you intend to freeze the pies, omit the hard-boiled egg which may go watery at low temperatures.

Makes 20-24 small pies F raw (without egg) 3 months

1 lb (450g) puff pastry

Filling:

1 tbsp butter or oil	2-3 tbsp tomato ketchup
1 medium onion, finely chopped	10 grinds black pepper
¹/₂ medium green pepper, de-seeded and cut in tiny cubes	¹/₂ teasp sea salt
	Pinch nutmeg
1 × 7oz (200g) can tuna in oil	2 tbsp chopped parsley
1 hard-boiled egg, finely chopped	

Cook the onion in the fat for 3 minutes, then add the pepper and continue to cook until the onion is soft and golden. Drain the tuna and flake with a fork, then add the chopped egg (if used), the onion mixture and the seasonings. Bind with the tomato ketchup – the moist mixture should just cling together.

Roll out the pastry ⅛ inch (0.25cm) thick and cut into 20-24 3-inch (7.5cm) rounds. Put a spoonful of filling on each round, then fold over into a crescent, sealing the edges very firmly. The pies can now be frozen, or refrigerated for up to 24 hours.

Heat a pan one-third full of oil until it reaches a temperature of 360°F (180°C), or until a piece of bread browns in 1 minute. Put in the pies a few at a time, so as not to crowd the pan. Cook steadily until they puff and turn a rich golden brown, turning with a slotted spoon (this will take about 3 minutes). Drain on crumpled tissue paper.

Serve as soon as possible. The pies will keep crisp at room temperature for up to 15 minutes, or they can be kept hot in a warm oven (Gas No. 1, 275°F, 140°C) for up to half an hour.

VARIATION 1
Use ½ lb (225g) cooked chicken, fowl or turkey instead of the tuna.

VARIATION 2
Use **Savoury Meat Filling** (p.263) instead of the tuna filling.

Latkes on Sticks

These delicious little potato fritters do need to be served hot off the pan, although most of the initial cooking can be done in advance. They can, however, be pre-fried, then recrispened at the last minute.

Serves 12 for cocktails; makes 50 tiny latkes F 3 months

4 large potatoes, peeled (1 pint/575ml/2½ cup pulp when grated)	1 level teasp salt
	Pinch white pepper
	½ medium onion
2 large eggs	4 level tbsp self-raising flour

By hand: Grate the potatoes on very fine grater. Leave in a sieve to drain for 10 minutes, pressing the mixture down with a spoon once or twice to hasten the process. Whisk the eggs until fluffy, then stir in the salt and pepper, the finely grated onion and finally the flour. The mixture should be a thick batter. Blend with the grated potato.

By blender or food processor: Cut the potato into chunks and grate according to instructions. Drain for 10 minutes. Put the onion, egg, flour and seasonings into the bowl and process until smooth. Blend with the grated potato.

To fry the latkes: In a heavy frying pan, put enough oil to come to a depth of ½ inch (1.25cm). Heat until a little of the raw mixture sizzles when it is put into the hot oil. Put tablespoonfuls of the mixture into the hot oil, flattening each latke with the back of the spoon. Cook over moderate heat for 5 minutes or until the underside is a rich brown, then turn and cook the other side. The latkes should be crunchy and crisp on the outside and creamy inside. Drain on crumpled kitchen paper and serve at once on cocktail sticks.

To freeze: Fry only until light brown in colour. Drain, cool, then open freeze and bag. To recrispen plunge into hot fat (375°F, 190°C) and re-fry for 2 minutes.

Savoury Sausage Loaf

This is a delicious variation on sausage rolls using a crisp French loaf instead of pastry.

Serves 8 F up to a week before baking

1 × 18 inch (45cm) thin French stick *or* 2 smaller ones	4 tbsp cold water
1 tbsp oil	1 level tbsp chopped parsley
½ medium onion, finely chopped	1 level tbsp prepared mustard
½ lb (225g) sausage meat	½ level teasp dried oregano, basil or Italian herb mixture
½ lb (225g) raw minced (ground) beef	10 grinds black pepper
1 egg	½ level teasp salt
	A little oil

Sauté the onion in the fat until golden, then add the meats and continue to cook, stirring with a fork until the meat has lost its redness, then mix well together. Slice the bread in half and remove the loose crumb. Mix the breadcrumbs with the egg and water, then stir in the seasonings and the cooked meat mixture. If the sausage meat is very solid, it may not be necessary to use all the crumb taken from the inside of the bread. Taste and use your own judgement, as the filling should not be stodgy. Mix thoroughly with a fork, then pack back into the base of the loaf. Put the top back on and anchor firmly together. Place on a long piece of foil, then brush with oil and sprinkle with salt. Seal with a fold at the top.

Bake at Gas No. 7, 425°F, 220°C for 25 minutes, then unfold, turn oven down to Gas No. 6, 400°F, 200°C and leave to crispen for a further 5 minutes. Put on a platter and cut in 2 inch (5cm) slices.

To serve 20-24:

3 × 18 inch (45cm) French sticks	3 level tbsp chopped parsley
1½ lb (675g) each of sausage meat and minced (ground) beef	3 level tbsp prepared mustard
1 medium onion, finely chopped	The rest of the ingredients should be tripled

VARIATION

Individual Rolls: Use one crisp crusted roll per person instead of French sticks. Fill as above, taking the lid off each roll. Brush roll with oil and scatter with sesame seeds and sea salt. Bake at Gas No. 7, 425°F, 220°C for 15 minutes, then uncover and cook at Gas No. 6, 400°F, 200°C for a further 5 minutes.

Goujonettes

Piping hot morsels of fried plaice to serve with a well-chilled **Sauce Tartare** (p.336).

For 12 and 25 Do not freeze (except the raw fish)

Quantities for 12	*Quantities for 25*
2½ lb (1.25kg) thick fillets of plaice	5lb (2.25kg)
1-2 eggs	2-3
flour	
coating crumbs	
a pan of deep oil	

Have both the white and black skin removed from the fillets. Wash, arrange in a colander to drain and sprinkle with salt. Leave

532

for half an hour. Cut into strips about ¹/₂ inch (1.25cm) wide and 1¹/₂ inches (4cm) long. Have ready three shallow dishes: one with seasoned flour, one in which the eggs have been beaten with a tbsp water for each egg, and one with dried crumbs. Using a skewer or fork to hold the pieces of fish, dip first into the flour, then the egg, and then into the crumbs.

Leave them on a board for the coating to set for half an hour, or refrigerate. Heat a pan one-third full of oil (or use a deep fryer) until it reaches a temperature of 375°F, 190°C when a cube of bread browns in 30 seconds. Lower in the goujonettes half a dozen at a time and cook until a rich brown.

Drain on crumpled paper, then keep hot in a low oven (Gas No. ¹/₂, 250°F, 120°C) while the rest are cooked in relays. Pile on a serving dish and pass round with cocktail sticks and tartare sauce.

Fillings for Bouchées
(Miniature Puff Pastry Cases)

Excellent frozen bouchées can be easily purchased, and so I am not suggesting you make them yourself. However, the filling does need to be of the right consistency and carefully seasoned, so I give detailed recipes for two different varieties.

Bake the bouchées according to packet instructions, or buy baked empty cases.

Sherried Chicken or Turkey Filling

Fills 80 cocktail-size bouchées F filling 3 months; F uncooked cases 6 months

Flesh from 1 fowl or chicken (about 4 lb/2kg net weight), poached or roasted

1 medium onion (5oz/150g), finely chopped

2 large canned pimentos, thinly sliced

¹/₂ lb (225g/4 cups) mushrooms, coarsely chopped

3 oz (75g/¹/₃ cup) margarine

2 oz (50g) flour

1 pint (575ml/2¹/₂ cups) strong chicken or turkey stock

¹/₂ teasp nutmeg

Salt and white pepper to taste

1 tbsp parsley

1 glass (3¹/₂ fl oz/100ml/¹/₂ cup) dry sherry

Yolks of 2 eggs

Cut the poultry into chunky, bite-sized pieces and put into a bowl. Melt the fat and cook the onion, pimentos and mushrooms gently until softened, about 5 minutes, then stir in the flour, stock and seasonings. Whisk until smooth, then allow to bubble for 3 minutes. Add the parsley and sherry. Put the yolks in a basin and stir in some of the hot mixture, then return to the pan and cook until steaming. Do not allow to boil. Freeze, or refrigerate until required.

Sherried Mushroom Filling

Fills 80 cocktail-size bouchées **F** filling 3 months; **F** uncooked cases 6 months

1 lb (450g/8 cups) mushrooms, coarsely chopped

2 oz (50g/$1/4$ cup) butter

1 tbsp oil

4 tbsp chopped shallots (fresh or dried), spring onions (scallions) or mild onion

2 level tbsp cornflour (cornstarch)

15 fl oz (425ml/2 cups) single (light) or whipping cream

$1/2$ teasp salt

$1/4$ teasp white pepper

$1/4$ teasp ground mace or nutmeg

2 tbsp chopped parsley

1 glass ($3^1/2$ fl oz/100ml/$1/2$ cup) dry sherry

Melt the butter with the oil in a deep frying pan, then cook the shallots or onion gently for 2-3 minutes, shaking the pan well – do not overbrown as this darkens the sauce. Add the mushrooms and continue to cook for a further 3 minutes until softened. Gradually add the cream to the cornflour (cornstarch), mixing well, then add to the pan together with the seasonings and cook until thickened. Bubble for 3 minutes. Stir in the sherry and parsley.

To heat and fill the bouchées: Heat the baked pastry cases in a moderate oven (Gas No. 4, 350°F, 180°C) till piping hot (about 5 minutes). Add the hot filling (most safely reheated over boiling water), and return to the oven for a further 5 minutes. Serve at once, or turn the oven to 'warm' to keep them hot without drying out.

Little Nibbles

Stuffed Celery

One inch (2.5cm) lengths of tender crisp white celery are filled or piped with any cream mixture: for example –

½ lb (225g/1 cup) full fat (double) cream blended with 2 tbsp mayonnaise and 1 tbsp snipped chives, *or*

Aubergine Herb Dip (p.512)

Avocado Dip (p.513)

Cream Cheese Dip (p.514)

Pineapple and Cream Cheese (p.516)

Walnut and Cream Cheese (p.516)

Smoked Mackerel Mousse (p.135)

Serve chilled, speared with a cocktail stick. Allow 2 celery heads for 50 guests.

Stuffed Fresh or Dried Dates

Chilled fresh dates are particularly delicious. Otherwise use choice dried dates, but they will be sweeter. Remove the stone and replace with cream cheese flavoured with finely grated orange rind. Allow 2 dates per person. ½ lb (225g/1 cup) cream cheese and the grated rind of ½ an orange will fill 24-30 dates.

Cheese and Fruit Kebabs

Enough for 50
Use ½ lb (225g/2 cups) red cheese e.g. Cheshire or Leicester, and ½ lb (225g/2 cups) white or pale cheese – cut in ½ inch (1.25cm) cubes (this can be done the day before if the cheese is kept in an airtight container). Drain a can of mandarins and pineapple titbits; quarter 4 oz (125g/¾ cup) glacé (candied) cherries; thread alternate cubes of cheese and fruit on cocktail sticks.

Arrange on flat trays or spear, hedgehog fashion, into grapefruit.

Garlic Olives

These make a delicious appetizer served in the Spanish way with a well-chilled, very dry sherry.

1 × 10 oz (275g) jar Spanish
stuffed green olives (net
drained weight)
¹/₄ pint (150ml/²/₃ cup) oil

2 tbsp wine vinegar or cider
vinegar
1 fat clove of garlic, crushed

I find that if I use mainly corn oil (tasteless) but replace 2 tbsp of
it with olive oil, I get a richer flavour with the minimum of
expense.

Tip the olives from the jar into a sieve and discard the brine. Put
the dressing ingredients into a screw-top jar, put on the lid and
shake well. Add the olives, cover, and leave in the refrigerator for
at least 24 hours. They will keep for weeks.

When the jar of olives has been used, simply add another
crushed clove of garlic to the dressing and fill up with more drained
olives.

Crispy Noodles

Serves 12

You can make these from scratch yourself by par-boiling ¹/₂ lb
(225g/3 cups) egg noodles for 5 minutes in boiling salted water.
Drain, rinse in cold water, then dry thoroughly.

Alternatively use a 3 oz (75g) packet of par-cooked noodles.

In either case, fry a few at a time in hot oil until crispy and golden
brown. Serve, lightly salted, in bowls.

Cheese Twists

*These crisp and crunchy nibbles are both delicious and economi-
cal. They can be kept either in an airtight container for up to 3
weeks or in the freezer for 3 months. If possible 'freshen' them
for 10 minutes in a moderate oven before use.*

Serves 20 **F** 3 months **L** 3 weeks

6 oz (175g/1¹/₂ cups) plain flour
1 rounded teasp dry mustard
¹/₄ level teasp salt
Speck of cayenne pepper or few
drops of Tabasco sauce
3 oz (75g/¹/₃ cup) butter
3 oz (75g/³/₄ cup) mature, well

flavoured cooking cheese,
including about ¹/₃ Parmesan
1 large egg yolk
3 tbsp water
Beaten egg or milk to glaze
Sesame seeds (optional)

Cut the butter into ½ inch (1.25cm) chunks and put all the dry ingredients in a bowl. Rub in the butter until no chunks larger than a small pea rise to the surface when the bowl is shaken. If you rub the fat in as far as shortcrust pastry, the twists will not be so flaky. Beat the yolk with the water, then sprinkle on and knead to form a firm dough. Knead until smooth, then roll out into a rectangle ¼ inch (0.5cm) thick. Cut in strips ⅜ inch (1cm) wide and then into 2½ inch (6cm) lengths. Lay these on lightly greased trays, twisting them over once. Chill if possible for half an hour. Brush with egg or milk, then scatter with the sesame seeds (if used). Bake at Gas No. 6, 400°F, 200°C for 10-12 minutes until a rich golden brown.

Drinks

We all make tea and coffee a dozen times a day without giving it more than a passing thought: it's just a part of the daily routine. But for a special meal, the drink takes on extra significance as it is an essential complement to the food. The way you prepare tea and coffee, and the wines or other alcoholic drinks you choose to serve, is very much a matter of individual taste; there is no one correct way. So in this chapter I have simply given guidance as to what I have found to be the most effective way of preparing and serving a variety of drinks to accompany the meals and light refreshments suggested in this book. I suggest you take my ideas as a starting point, then follow your own taste.

Tea

There is an enormous variety of teas now available, ranging from the 'bread and butter' supermarket brands to the specially-blended high quality and exotically flavoured ones. I think it's important to settle on a quality 'standard' tea – probably Ceylon or Indian – for general use, and then try out other teas for more specialized use. One can get packs of assorted tea-bags that make excellent 'tasters'.

However, no matter what variety of tea is used, the way it is brewed remains the same.

Tea-bags or loose tea?
Purists will insist that only loose tea produces a perfect brew. However, for entertaining purposes, tea-bags offer many more advantages. Indeed, when more than one brew has to be made in

the same pot – for instance, at a large tea party – tea-bags are preferable from the point of view of convenience in handling and disposal. However, provided that the tea is properly brewed (see below) they should always produce an excellent cup of tea.

The teapot

China, pottery, silver and other metals all have their champions. It really doesn't seem to matter provided the pot is scrupulously clean and free from tannin deposits, and is well and truly heated before the brew is made. To do this, fill the pot one-third full of boiling water, swirl it round until all the surfaces are thoroughly heated, then discard the water and brew the tea. Alternatively the teapot and hot water can be left for ten or fifteen minutes on a hot plate or a ceramic hob at low setting (probably the most effective way of all). The brew should never come into contact with copper, brass or iron.

See p.556 for detailed instructions on brewing tea for a crowd.

Water for the tea

Whether or not the water has been freshly drawn from the tap, or reheated in the kettle, doesn't seem to affect the taste. What is vital is that the water should actually be boiling when it is poured on to the leaves, otherwise it will not infuse properly. However, once the tea has been made, it must never be allowed to boil.

Amount of tea to water

This is very much a matter of taste, but one level teaspoon of tea for each cup and one spoon 'for the pot' is a good start-off point. When making tea for a party, if a domestic-sized teapot is used, it's often a good idea to make an extra strong brew, and top each cup up with a little hot water. This also enables one to adjust the strength of the brew to individual requirements. In addition to a regular hot water jug, an insulated jug for hot water is particularly useful as it allows a 'stock' to be boiled in advance. For a small tea-party it might also be convenient to plug in an electric kettle near the serving point, so that the freshly-boiled water can be used to top up the teapot on the spot.

Brewing time

This can vary from 3-6 minutes, according to taste, during which time it is essential that the tea is kept hot, either on a hot plate, ceramic hob or under a tea cosy.

The accompaniments

Indian tea is usually served with milk (not cream) or lemon slices. China and scented or herb teas are usually served black or with lemon. Granulated sugar is fine for milk tea, but cube sugar is nicer for clear teas as it does not make them cloudy.

Orange or lemon tea

This looks most attractive in a heatproof glass. Put a thick slice of the chosen fruit in each glass, then pour a splash of boiling water directly on to it – this releases the full flavour of the fruit. Fill up with freshly made tea of slightly under average strength (this should be poured through a tea strainer so as not to spoil the appearance of the glass). Serve with a long-handled spoon (to extract the fruit juice), and cube sugar.

Mint tea

Use one sprig of fresh mint per glass, in addition to the fruit. Make in exactly the same way.

Russian tea

Although this name is given to ordinary lemon tea, there are also more exotic ways of making it for a special occasion.

Raissa Tea

For each glass, use 2 slices of lemon, 2 teasp of sugar and 1 heaped teasp of a tart cherry jam. Mix well, pressing the lemon slices to extract the juice, then add 1 inch (2.5cm) of medium-strong strained tea. Fill up with hot water to within 1/2 inch (1.25cm) of the rim of the glass, then fill up with rum. Serve at once with a biscuit or slice of sponge cake.

Iced Tea

1. *The cloudless way*: Allow double the usual amount of tea for the liquid required. Put the tea and *cold* water into a covered glass or china jug and refrigerate from 12-24 hours. When ready to serve, put one ice-cube in each glass and top up with the strained cold tea. Serve with a slice of lemon or orange, or a sprig of mint. Let each guest add sugar to taste, although the unsweetened tea is more refreshing.

2. *The traditional way*: Brew tea of the usual strength for 5 minutes. Strain and cool for 3 hours in, or out, of the refrigerator. Pour over ice-cubes and serve at once. This tea may be cloudy, but it is a convenient method for large quantities.

3. *The quick way*: Brew hot, double-strength tea in the usual way, then pour over half a glassful of ice whilst still hot. The tea will be diluted and cooled by the ice. This is the easiest way of all, though the tea may be cloudy.

VARIATION

Iced Lemon, Orange or Lime Tea: Put two teasp of fresh juice into a tall glass. Add ice-cubes to half-fill the glass then pour over double-strength hot tea. Sweeten to taste. Garnish with a slice of fruit and a sprig of fresh mint.

Special Iced Tea (serves 10): A more elaborate method which gives a more intense fruit flavour. You will need 4 sprigs of mint; 1 lemon (peeled then quartered); an inch (2.5cm) strip of lemon peel; 2 tbsp sugar; 3 pints (1.75 litres) freshly made tea, strained. Put the mint leaves, peel, sugar and 1/4 pint (150ml/2/3 cup) of the hot tea into the blender and blend for 15 seconds. Put into a jug or bowl and pour on the hot tea. Stand for 20 minutes, then strain into a jug and refrigerate until required. Serve with a twist of lemon.

Sweetener for Iced Tea

As neither granulated nor cube sugar will dissolve easily in iced tea, have a jug of sugar syrup ready prepared instead. This syrup is also excellent for cold drinks such as Citron Pressé' or for sweetening soft fruits. It will keep indefinitely in the refrigerator.

Dissolve 1 lb (450g/2 cups) sugar in 1 pint (575ml/2½ cups) water over gentle heat, then bring to the boil and bubble for one minute. Pour into a covered container, and store in the larder or refrigerator.

Coffee

A good cup of coffee depends on the use of freshly-ground coffee, but it can be brewed by any one of several methods, each of which produces a clear, full-flavoured brew. But as with making tea, there is no one combination of these different factors that will suit every palate. Here, therefore, is some general advice to guide you in your choice.

1. The beans: There are probably 100 different varieties of beans produced in the 9 main coffee producing countries, and all these different varieties may be blended before roasting, producing an incalculable number of permutations. There seems only one easy solution: when you taste a good cup of coffee anywhere, ask from what blend of coffee it has been made. Then find yourself a friendly neighborhood coffee merchant and let him guide you to your perfect blend. Or you can work your way through the different pre-packed varieties, whether beans or ready ground, until you find the one that suits you best. But whatever coffee you choose, there are certain common factors which will influence the pleasure you get from the resulting drink:

a. *The freshness*: The aroma of coffee is at its glorious peak the moment it has been roasted, gradually losing its smell until at the end of 3 weeks it will almost have disappeared. *Answer*: Never buy more than 2 weeks' supply of beans or 1 week's supply of ground coffee at a time, and keep them in an airtight container. *Exception*: If this is not possible or convenient, then freeze your stock, overwrapping the original package in a heavy duty plastic bag. Keeping-time for freshly-roasted beans is 1 year; for pre-packs, 3 months.

b. *The grind*: If possible, grind the beans fresh as you need them, to the degree of fineness required for the method you have chosen to make the coffee (see below). If not, be sure to buy the right grind or your coffee will not taste as it should.

2. Never allow coffee to boil or it becomes bitter (see note on percolated coffee below). If you need to reheat it, do so only until it steams – a microwave is ideal.

3. Always use fresh cold water, as in making tea.

4. Choose any one of the 4 coffee-making methods I give below, each of which gives a super brew.

Four Ways to Good Coffee

1. *The jug method*: The coffee is brewed in exactly the same way as tea. Use medium-ground coffee, as a fine grind will make it cloudy, while a coarse grind will result in a poorly-flavoured brew. Heat the pot, add the coffee and half water required, then stir and leave 30 seconds. Top up with boiling water, cover and leave for 5 minutes. Strain and serve.

Advantage: this is the simplest method with no special equipment required.
Disadvantage: the coffee has to be kept hot during the brewing period. This is easiest with a pot (enamel or ceramic) that can go right on the stove. Otherwise stand the pot in a pan of simmering water.

2. *Jug with metal plunger* (e.g. Melior): This is a refinement of the jug method, and makes superb coffee with the minimum of effort and reasonable initial expense. Medium to medium-fine coffee is put into the heated pot and boiling water added. The coffee is then brewed for 6 minutes before the plunger is depressed, trapping the grounds.

Advantage: no straining, no paper filters required as a fine metal filter is built in to the pot. Strength of coffee can be regulated by adjusting brewing time.
Disadvantage: equipment is more costly than an ordinary jug, and it still has to be kept hot (see jug method) unless a more expensive metal model is used.

3. *Filter paper method*: Water is poured slowly over finely-ground coffee held in a paper filter. With the original machines this had to be done by hand, but now there is a proliferation of electric models which not only pump the water over the coffee but also keep the filtered coffee hot until required. It is possible to buy a filter to fit over an ordinary coffee jug, which makes a cheap and effective method.

Advantage: no straining required, and with the electric machines the coffee is brewed automatically and kept hot until required.
Disadvantage: the initial high cost of the electric machine.

4. *Vacuum method* (e.g. Cona): Medium to fine-ground coffee is put in the upper bowl. This is placed on the lower flask which is filled with a measured amount of water. When the flask is heated the water rises through a funnel and coffee is brewed in three minutes. It is then allowed to filter back ready for serving.

Advantage: an excellent brew and a showpiece for the table. No problem about straining or keeping hot. Less expensive than electric machines.

Disadvantage: the glass parts are easily broken and are very tedious to wash up. Not for everyday use.

Note on coffee percolators: These are often attractive in design and require less coffee than any other method. But the resulting brew has a bitterness not to be found with the other methods of coffee making.

Instant Coffee

Many people claim that instant coffee is not really coffee, but just another hot drink. This is certainly true of the cheaper brands of powdered coffee. However, if you use a good brand of freeze-dried granules, it's a rare palate indeed that can tell the difference between a cup make from a freshly-opened jar and ground coffee. One secret is to make the instant coffee in a jug rather than a mug or a cup. In that way the aroma is trapped and preserved. Single (light) cream (rather than milk) also enhances the flavour.

Black or White

The high roast, slightly acid after-dinner coffee is usually served black. Coffee served at other times is usually 'whitened' with milk or cream.

If cream is used it should be single (light) cream with an 18% butterfat content. High fat creams tend to make the coffee oily. Lightly-whipped cream can, however, be used.

If milk is used, serve it cold or heat it in any of these ways:
a. Heat until steaming in a double saucepan.
b. Stand the milk in a jug in a pan of simmering water. Cover with film and heat until it steams.
c. Heat until steaming in a microwave.

Notes on curdled coffee

When milk or cream is added to coffee it sometimes seems to curdle. This is usually due to the coffee being allowed to brew too long, resulting in a high concentration of caffeines which cause the milk to curdle instead of dispersing in the coffee as a cloudy white solution. By all means make sure the milk or cream is fresh, but also ensure that the coffee is not over-brewed before it is served.

Iced Coffee

This can be both refreshing and invigorating on a hot day. It can be made in any of 3 ways – with ground coffee, instant coffee or home-made coffee syrup, whichever is the most convenient.

1. *With ground coffee*: Brew coffee by any method using 4 standard coffee measures (2 rounded tbsp of coffee) to each pint (575ml/2½ cups) of water. Brew for 4-5 minutes, then strain, cool and refrigerate in a non-metal container. Use black or with an equal quantity of milk, or in any of the combinations given below.

2. *With instant coffee*: Two hours in advance: In a large jug or bowl mix 3 heaped tbsp high roast coffee granules and 2 rounded tbsp caster (superfine) sugar, then pour on 2 pints (1 litre/5 cups) boiling water. Put 1 pint (575ml/2½ cups) cold milk into a bowl, then whisk in the coffee. Divide between two jugs and chill thoroughly.

To serve: Put a scoop of ice-cream in each glass, fill with the coffee and decorate with whipped cream. (*Note*: For the most effective presentation, whirl the coffee in the blender before pouring into the glasses. This gives it a lovely 'head', even without whipped cream.) Serves 8.

3. *With home-made coffee syrup*:
Makes ½ pint (275ml/1¼ cups); **R** indefinitely

½ oz (40g/4 rounded tbsp) instant
 coffee (preferably high roast)
6 oz (175g/¾ cup) granulated
 sugar

½ pint (275ml/1¼ cups) boiling
 water

Put the sugar and water into a pan, and stir over gentle heat until the sugar has dissolved, then simmer for 2 minutes. Stir in the instant coffee until dissolved. When quite cold, pour into a container. Refrigerate until required.

To serve:1. *Black*: Pour ½ inch (1.25cm) coffee syrup into a tall glass. Add 2 ice-cubes. Top up with cold a water.
2. *With whipped cream*: Make black iced coffee and top each serving with a blob of whipped cream (or even ice-cream).
3. *With cream*: Make in the same way, but cover the coffee syrup with the same depth of single (light) cream before adding water.
4. *White*: After the coffee and cream have been added (as in 3) top up with cold milk.

Favourite Iced Coffee

For each glass – put in ½ inch (1.25cm) coffee syrup and 2 ice-cubes. Fill two-thirds full with cold milk then top up with cold water. Finish with a tablespoon of vanilla or coffee ice-cream. Drink with a straw.

Coffee Tiberio Capri

Use a 6-inch (15cm) glass, 2 inches (5cm) in diameter. Put ½ inch (1.25cm) of coffee syrup in the bottom and 2 inches (5cm) of iced water. Top with 2 inches (5cm) ice-cream and finish with 2 inches (5cm) whipped cream, sprinkled with cocoa or drinking chocolate.

Wine

I shall not attempt to discuss this enormous subject in any depth, but merely to give some practical advice on the buying, storing and serving of wine suitable for the occasions and the menus in the book. I do believe, however, that even a superficial study of this fascinating topic will enormously repay the time spent. For wine is now no longer an esoteric subject for a specialist, a beverage only to be purchased with suitable awe. Excellent wines can be bought at supermarkets and off-licences as well as from specialist wine merchants. A glass of wine is not only a pleasure to drink in itself, but also greatly enhances the food which it has been chosen to complement.

To store wine

It is advisable always to keep wines in stock rather than to buy them for immediate consumption. There are several advantages: better wines invariably improve if correctly aged; often one is able to buy wines at advantageous prices for later use; and there is confidence in the knowledge that there will always be a suitable wine on hand to serve with even the most impromptu meal. There is, however, no need to have an actual cellar, but simply a store with the right conditions of light and heat. This could be a cupboard under the stairs, or the floor of the pantry, where the wine will not be subject to bright light, draughts, vibration or sudden changes of temperature. There should also be room for the bottles to be laid flat, preferably in some kind of wine rack or bin (or even in wooden wine crates laid on their sides), so that the cork is always in contact with the wine and therefore does not dry out and shrink, which would cause the wine to deteriorate. The ideal temperature is between 7-10°C (45-50°F). The higher the temperature, the faster the wine matures.

The serving temperature

To be enjoyed at their best, all wines must be served at the correct temperature: cool or chilled for white wines or rosés, at 'room temperature' ('chambré') – about 68°F, 20°C – for most reds.

White wines

2 hours before serving (longer on a hot day) put the wine to chill in the refrigerator (do not put to freeze, or the bottles may explode). In a bucket of ice and water this will only take 15 minutes. For a large winter party, leave the bottles outside the back door. For a large summer party, wrap each bottle in cold wet newspaper.

Red wines

These are best left in the dining-room all day (or up to 24 hours) before serving. Uncork to let the wine 'breathe' about 1 hour in advance. To judge if the wine is truly at room temperature, lay the back of your hand against the bottle: it should not feel noticeably warm nor, of course, cold.

Note: Certain light and fruity red wines such as Beaujolais, Valpolicella and Bardolino are better served lightly chilled.

Temperature guide to serving wine

Very sweet wine (including sparkling wine	8-12°C	45-55°F
Ordinary sparkling wines	10-12°C	50-55°F
Dry white wines, rosé	10-14°C	50-55°F
Young, fruity, light red wines	12-15°C	55-60°F
Red wines to be served at room temperature	16-20°C	60-68°F

To open the bottle
A corkscrew with some kind of lever attachment is the easiest to use. Avoid narrow, gimlet-like corkscrews which tend to pull out of poor corks. Be sure to wipe the mouth of the bottle with a clean cloth or paper napkin to remove any dirt, dust or sediment before pouring the wine.

To serve
Never fill a glass to the brim. If it is filled ony two-thirds full the guests will be able to savour the bouquet to the full.

Choice of glass
The true wine connoisseur prefers glasses made of thin colourless clear glass (preferably of cut or uncut crystal). After that the choice is yours, though it is advisable to use long-stemmed glasses for chilled wines to avoid warming them up by the heat of the hand. For large parties, when glasses have to be hired or borrowed, choose either tulip (tall slim glasses) or balloon (globe-shaped), both of which have rims which curve in slightly and so retain the bouquet and also the bubbles of a sparkling wine.

Matching the Wine to the Food

Over the years experience has shown that certain wines go best with certain categories of food. These should not be treated as laws that cannot be broken, but as general rules that have come about in the light of experience. For instance, one avoids heavy red wines with fish as they do not partner well with a piquant sauce. Similarly, sweet wines tend to kill the nuances of flavour in a savoury dish. So, below, I list first the category of food, and the kind of wine that suits it, and then the categories of wine, with examples in each case.

Soup, hors d'oeuvres: Dry or medium-dry sherry, dry Madeira.

Fish, shellfish, cold chicken and the like: Dry or medium-dry light white wines.

Straightforward meats (e.g. lamb, beef, roast chicken): Lighter to medium-bodied red wines.

Stronger meats (e.g. duck, goose, game, stews): Full-bodied red wines.

Dessert (sweets, ices, fruit etc.): Sweet white wines (still or sparkling).

Cheese, nuts: Port, sweet Madeira, sweet sherry. You can also finish off your red wine with the cheese – they go excellently together. Indeed, most French people have their cheese *before* the dessert, for that reason.

Chinese food: Light dry white wines, dry rosés.

Curries: Medium white wines; full-bodied dry red table wines.

Long Summer Drinks

Here is a selection of alcoholic and non-alcoholic summer coolers.

Summer Cider Cup

This is delightful for a summer luncheon.
Serves 6-8

1 litre (35.2fl oz/5 cups) bottle of medium sweet, still or sparkling cider, well chilled
4-5 tbsp Calvados

1 pint (575ml/2¹/² cups) soda water
Thin slices of orange and lemon for decoration

When ready to serve, put the cider into a glass bowl, and add the calvados and soda water. Float the fruit slices on top. Serve in glass tankards or 'highball' glasses.

High Summer Punch

This is perfect for a barbecue or alfresco lunch.
Serves 12

2 litres (10 cups) sweet or
   medium-dry cider
1 small glass dry orange Curaçao
Angostura bitters
1 green apple

Lemon juice
1 small tin pineapple cubes
Strawberries, raspberries,
   cherries

Chill the cider. When the punch is required, pour the cider into a tall jug, stir in the Curaçao and a few drops of Angostura bitters. Slice the apple and dip in lemon juice. Thread the apple, pineapple cubes, strawberries, raspberries and cherries on long skewers or kebab sticks. Plunge into the cider and serve.

Summer Wine Cup

This is especially good for a supper party. Serve in wineglasses.
Serves 10-12 (2 wineglasses each)

2 bottles white wine, such as
   Riesling or Hock
1 bottle (2½ cups) apple juice or
   sweet cider
1 lemon, peeled like an apple, but
   peel left anchored at the bottom

of the fruit
1 small can pineapple titbits
1 glass each vodka and orange
   liqueur (optional)
Fresh mint in season

Blend all the ingredients, floating the lemon in the liquid. Serve well chilled.

Sangria

There are many versions of this Spanish summer wine cup. This is particularly refreshing at a summer luncheon.
Serves 6-8

8 oz (225g/1 cup) caster
   (superfine) sugar
½ pint (275ml/1¼ cups) cold
   water
1 stick cinnamon or pinch ground
   cinnamon
1 large lemon, thinly sliced

1 large orange, thinly sliced
1 peach, thinly sliced
20 ice-cubes
1 bottle red wine (such as Rioja)
1 wineglass brandy
Soda water

Put the sugar and cinnamon and the water into a small saucepan and stir over gentle heat until the sugar has dissolved. Take off the stove and add the fruit. Leave for 4 hours (not in the refrigerator, as you want the fruit to give its flavour to the syrup). To make the sangria, put half the ice-cubes into the jug, then add half the syrup and six of the fruit slices. Top up with half the wine and fill up with soda water to taste. Repeat to make the second jugful. Float the remaining fruit slices on top of each drink.

Minty Orange Frost

This is a delicious non-alcoholic 'cocktail' or pick-me-up. The fruit sugar in the orange juice gives instant energy.

Serves 2

Juice of 2 juicy oranges or 8 fl oz (225ml/1 cup) frozen or bottled juice	4 or 5 ice-cubes
	1 teasp grenadine
	1 teasp lemon juice
Sprig of mint	

Liquidize until smooth. Serve at once.

Fhresh Lemon Cordial

This makes a very refreshing drink to serve when alcohol is not desired.

Juice of 3 large lemons	1½ lb (675g/3 cups) sugar
1 oz (25g) citric acid	2 pints (1 litre/5 cups) water

Using a potato peeler, remove the zest from each lemon. Put in the blender with ½ pint (275ml/1¼ cups) water. Blend for one minute or until the peel is in tiny bits. Put in a saucepan, together with the sugar and remaining 1½ pints (850ml/3¾ cups) water. Bring slowly to boiling point and boil for 5 minutes. Now add the lemon juice and the citric acid. Leave until quite cold, then strain to remove the lemon rind. Pour into bottles or covered jugs. This will fill two squash bottles.

To serve: Put about 1 inch (2.5cm) of the cordial in each glass. Add 2 cubes of ice, then fill up with water, soda water or tonic. Add a sprig of mint for the finishing touch.

Citron Pressé (Fresh Lemon Drink)

This is perhaps the best summer thirst quencher I know. It is a combination of freshly-squeezed lemon juice, sugar and water. It is best to have a sugar syrup ready in the refrigerator so that the drink can be made literally to order.

Sugar syrup (this keeps indefinitely in the refrigerator)

Dissolve 1 lb (450g/2 cups) of sugar in ¾ pint (425ml/2 cups) of water, stirring constantly over a low heat. When no grains of undissolved sugar remain, bring to a full rolling boil. Take off the heat immediately, cool and store in an airtight glass or plastic container.

Citron Pressé

Put a cube of ice in a tall glass and add 2 tbsp of the syrup. Add the juice of a lemon and top up with water, soda water or mineral water.

And One for Winter

Glühwein (Hot Spiced Wine Cup)

This is an excellent drink to serve instead of 'shorts' for a winter party. You'll need your largest soup pan, and if possible use an electric hot plate to keep the drink hot. The exact spicing is a matter of taste.

Quantities for 50 (2 × 4 oz (125g/½ cup) glasses each)	*Quantities for 25*
7½ litres (5 × 1½ litre bottles) any cheap red wine	4 litres
2½ litres (4½ pints/11¼ cups) water	1 litre (1¾ pints/5 cups)
2 teasp cinnamon	1 teasp
½ lb (225g/1 cup) sugar	¼-½ lb (125-225g/½-1 cup)
24 cloves	12
½ teasp ground nutmeg	¼ teasp
Peel of 3 oranges	Peel of 1 large
2 lemons, sliced	1
½ pint (275ml/1½ cups) Cointreau	¼ pint (150ml/⅔ cup)

Dissolve minimum quantity of sugar in water with the spices, peel and sliced lemon. Simmer 5 minutes then add the wine. Taste and keep on adding extra sugar until the taste is right. (This will depend on the dryness of the wine.) Cover and leave at steaming point *(do not boil)* for about an hour.

For the Very Special Occasion

Wine Cocktails

Cocktails are now back in fashion, and there are innumerable recipes and books on the subject. I am only going to suggest two unusual ones made with fruit liqueur, which I learned to love when I stayed in Burgundy.

Kir can be made with any dry white wine, but it is the Crème de Cassis (a blackcurrant liqueur) which makes it something rather special. This fruit liqueur is made from freshly picked blackcurrants blended with nothing more than sugar and a flavourless alcohol. The true Cassis connoisseur buys his year's supply at the start of the season in late summer, and plans to have it finished before the next vintage is ready the following year! This doesn't present any great difficulty, because in addition to using it in Kir, it's equally delicious served over ice-cream, or beaten into whipped cream, or added (very sparingly) to a summer fruit salad.

My version of Pink Champagne Cocktail is also made with a fruit liqueur, in this case made from raspberries.

Kir

For each glass, use four parts of a dry white wine (Aligoté is used in Burgundy) to one part of Cassis (blackcurrant liqueur).

Pink Champagne

Use enough Liqueur de Framboises (raspberry liqueur) to tinge a glass of sparkling white wine a pale pink.

Champagne Cocktail

For this, the ideal drink for a large party, use any non-vintage champagne or sparkling white wine – or dry sparkling cider.

For approx 30 (2 glasses each)

8 bottles sparkling white wine	Angostura bitters
1 bottle brandy	Sugar lumps

Put a sugar lump into each glass and add 3 drops bitters to each. Add at least 1 tbsp brandy and top up with wine immediately before serving. (Optional – add 1 slice (frozen) lemon to each glass.)

Note: To open sparkling wines, remove the foil and wire cage, wrap a cloth round the bottle, hold the bottle away from you at an angle of 45 degrees, and then twist the bottle, not the cork. In this way the gas will escape gradually, rather than with a loud 'pop' which can be wasteful.

Cooking for 50

There is a deal of unnecessary mystique attached to the techniques required when catering for a crowd. I'm not thinking of the skills involved in true *mass* catering, but of those needed to cook for up to 50 people. I like to think of catering for a group of this size in terms of cooking for an extended family whose tastes and palates haven't changed radically just because they sit down to eat with 50 rather than 5 other people. Thus all the recipes in this section are adapted from dishes first developed for 6 to 8 guests.

One must of course always bear in mind that cooking for larger numbers than usual requires not only more ingredients but also larger utensils, and much more time than usual must be allowed for even simple jobs like vegetable preparation. It is essential, therefore, to make a detailed plan of campaign, carefully calculating both the preparation time and the number of helpers that will be required. Ideally, cooking on a larger scale is best done as a team, with the tasks usually performed by one person divided among several. (Alternatively, if the job has to be done with minimal help, then it must be spread over a longer period – something that can only be achieved with adequate freezer space.) If plenty of time is allowed for the planning session, when recipes are chosen, shopping lists prepared and the time-table planned, the actual cooking can be most enjoyable – rather like playing in an orchestra instead of performing solo!

Below I give a selection of recipes for 50 which can be used for drinks parties, supper parties or community occasions. None of them needs any special expertise. In addition there is a table of quantities to help in calculating just how much food and drink to allow.

Coffee

Fresh coffee

(For 50 × 8 oz cups, or 64 coffee cups)

2 gal (8 litres/40 cups) boiling
  water

1 lb (450g/40 cups) ground coffee
8 fl oz (225ml/1 cup) cold water

Bring the water to the boil in a large pan or urn with a tap. Put the ground coffee into a muslin bag with the cold water. Put into the pan, cover and bring very slowly back to the boil (this should take 15 minutes). Do not let the coffee boil; once bubbles start to break the surface, turn off the heat. Remove bag and stir well. Coffee can now be poured into jugs and served black or with cream.

VARIATIONS
With hot milk: Use 11 pints (5½ litres/27½ cups) water to brew the coffee. Combine with 5 pints (2½ litres/12½ cups) hot milk.

With instant coffee: Use 5 oz (150g/3 cups) coffee, dissolved in 2 gal (8 litres/40 cups) boiling water.

Allow 1 lb (450g/2 cups) demerara sugar and 1½ pints (1 litre/4 cups) single (light) cream for 50-60 × 8 oz (225ml/1 cup) cups or 65-75 coffee cups.

Tea

This can be made either in several teapots or in one thermos tea dispenser. In either case, hot water will be needed to adjust the strength of the tea to individual requirements, and tea-bags are much more convenient and easier to dispose of than leaf tea. An urn with a tap in which all the necessary water can be boiled at one time is most convenient.

In teapots: Ideally these should be of catering size holding 20-25 (5 fl oz/150ml/⅔ cup) cups of tea. Make the tea in the usual way (see pp.538-40) and allow it to brew for 5 minutes before pouring.

For 100 × 5 fl oz (150ml/²/₃ cup) cups of tea (allowing 2 per person), you will need a total of 8 oz (225g) of tea bags.

In a thermos tea dispenser: This consists of an insulated metal container with a special strainer to hold the tea. After the tea has been brewed for 5 minutes, the tea bags are removed and, depending on the design, the tea will then keep hot for at least an hour without stewing.

Allow 6 oz (175g) of tea bags.

Allow 1 lb (450g/2 cups) granulated sugar and 3-4 pints (1.75-2.5 litres) milk for 50 × 2 cups of tea each.

Wine

Depending on the type of party, the amount required will vary between ¹/₃ and ¹/₂ bottle for each guest. I have therefore given amounts recommended for each occasion in the appropriate chapter

Rice

Because it reheats well, rice is more useful than potatoes when catering for a crowd. Although it can be cooked on top of the stove, it is much easier to handle if done in the oven.

Oven-Cooked Savoury Rice *(50 portions)*

3 lb (1.5kg/7 cups) long grain rice, rinsed until water runs clear	8 chicken or vegetable bouillon cubes
6 pints (3 litres/15 cups) water	4 tbsp oil

In oven roasting tins, bring water with stock cubes and oil to the boil, scatter in the rice, then bring back to the boil, stirring constantly. Cover with foil and transfer to the oven. Cook for 30-40 minutes in a moderate oven (Gas No. 4, 350°F, 180°C) or until all the moisture has been absorbed and a few grains of rice feel tender but not mushy when tasted. The oven can now be turned down to Gas No. ¹/₂, 250°F, 120°C and the rice kept hot for up to 30 minutes. If not used at once, refrigerate for up to 48 hours.

To reheat: Add a little extra water to create steam then put back in a moderate oven as above for 15-20 minutes until steaming. Keep hot as for freshly cooked rice.

Note: For parboiled long grain rice – increase the liquid by one quarter and allow 5 minutes extra cooking time. There will be a slightly larger yield.

To serve: The rice looks most attractive piled on oval platters. To garnish, arrange heaps of sliced fried mushrooms, sultanas tossed in a little fat until plump, and browned flaked almonds.

Quantities:

2 lb (1kg/16 cups) mushrooms, sliced ¹/₄ inch (0.5cm) thick	¹/₂ lb (225g/2 cups) sultanas ¹/₄ lb (125g/1 cup) almonds

The following recipes are all made in exactly the same way as for a smaller quantity. However, when frying vegetables and meat for casseroles, it is easier to divide them into two or three smaller batches to facilitate browning. Remember also that larger quantities will take longer to come to simmering point. So allow an extra half an hour – the casserole will not spoil if ready a little earlier than required. For your guidance I give here quantities for 50; the detailed instructions for preparing the dish will be found in the appropriate chapter.

Latkes *(50 servings)*

If there is help in the kitchen these can be made most successfully for a crowd. They can be kept hot and crisp for up to 15 minutes in a warm oven – Gas No. 1, 275°F, 140°C.

6 pints (3.5 litres/15 cups) grated potatoes (about 24 large) 1 dozen eggs	1 lb (450g/4 cups) self-raising flour 2 level tbsp salt ¹/₂ teasp white pepper

Follow recipe on p.530.

Savoury Rice with Chicken or Turkey *(50 portions)*

8 fl oz (225ml/1 cup) oil
$^1/_2$ lb (225g/1 cup) margarine
8 large onions, finely chopped
1 pint (575ml/2$^1/_2$ cups) chopped
   frozen peppers, or 8 medium
   fresh peppers cut in $^1/_2$ inch
   (1.25cm) cubes
1 lb (450g/3 cups) currants
3$^1/_2$ lb (1.5kg/8 cups) long grain
   rice
6$^1/_2$ pints (4 litres/16 cups) chicken

stock
1 teasp each salt, cinnamon and
   cayenne pepper
Flesh from 4 cooked 3$^1/_2$-4 lb
   (1.5-2kg) birds; or 4 lb (2kg)
   cooked turkey breasts cut in
   bite-sized chunks
$^1/_2$ lb (225g/2 cups) chopped
   almonds or cashew nuts fried in
   4 tbsp oil
8 tbsp soy sauce

Follow recipe on p.279

Chicken or Turkey Turnovers or Pies *(50 portions – makes 100 turnovers or filling for 6 pies)*

1 × 8 lb (4kg) turkey; or 2 × 4 lb (2kg) chickens

Roast the birds until just tender without stuffing but with an apple, orange or onion inside. If possible take off carcase whilst still warm and chop coarsely by hand or food processor. Make stock with giblets then make up to the quantity required in the recipe with chicken stock from cubes.

Pastry:
5 lb (2.25kg) frozen puff pastry

Sauce:
$^1/_2$ lb (225g/4 cups) mushrooms,
   thinly sliced
1 oz (25g/2 tbsp) margarine
1 tbsp oil
1 tbsp lemon juice
4 oz (125g/$^1/_2$ cup) margarine
2 medium onions, finely chopped
4 oz (125g/1 cup) plain flour
2$^1/_2$ pints (1.5 litres) stock (hot)

$^1/_4$ pint (150ml/$^2/_3$ cup) medium
   sherry or white wine
2 level tbsp chopped parsley
2 level teasp salt
$^1/_4$ teasp white pepper
Small can pimentos, chopped
1 lb (450g) frozen peas, cooked
2 beaten eggs and sesame seeds
   for glaze

Cut off then discard $^1/_4$ inch (0.5cm) stalk from each washed mushroom then slice very thinly or chop coarsely as preferred. Put in a pan with the ounce of margarine, the oil and the lemon juice. Bring to the boil then simmer covered for 5 minutes. Reserve.

Melt the 4 oz (125g/¹/₂ cup) margarine, add the onions and cook until soft and golden. Add the flour, stir well and simmer for 2 minutes, then add the hot chicken stock and whisk until the sauce thickens. Add the seasonings, sherry, pimento, peas, chopped parsley, mushrooms with their juices and finally the chopped turkey or chicken. Season well. Allow to cool.

Roll out the pastry as thin as a knife blade, then cut into 3¹/₂-4 inch (7.5-10cm) circles. Place a spoonful of filling on each circle then turn over and seal the edges well. Arrange on trays (may now be frozen).

To cook – defrost if frozen (about 2 hours at room temperature) – and brush with the beaten egg and sprinkle with sesame seeds. Have the oven heated to Gas No. 10, 500°F, 250°C. Give it time to be really heated, then put the turnovers in and bake them about 8 minutes until puffed and richly brown.

Serve hot off the pan, but allow about 5 minutes for them to cool slightly.

For pies or slices: Make 6 pies or slices according to directions on p.275. Use 2 lb (1kg) puff or flaky pastry.

Savoury Cream Cheese Strudel *(50 portions – 10 individual strudels)*

F uncooked 3 months
5 lb (2.25kg) puff pastry

Filling:

5 lb (2.25kg/10 cups) cream cheese or cottage cheese
2¹/₂ lb (1.5kg/10 cups) Cheddar cheese
9 large eggs

10 tbsp fresh parsley or chives; or 3 tbsp either herb, dried
2¹/₂ tbsp salt
¹/₄ teasp black pepper
10 tbsp sesame seeds (optional)

Follow recipe on p.439.

Roumanian Meat Balls *(50 buffet portions)*

F 3 months

Minced (ground) meat mixture:

10 lb (4.5kg) raw minced (ground) meat
10 eggs
1½ lb (675g) onions
10 thick slices from a large loaf
10 teasp salt
¼ teasp white pepper
5 large sprigs of parsley

The sauce:

3 lb (1.5kg) onions
8-10 green peppers, according to size
½ pint (275ml/1¼ cups) oil
5 large (1 lb 12oz/800g) cans tomatoes
½ lb (225g/1 cup) brown sugar
5 level teasp citric acid or 6 fl oz (175ml/¾ cup) lemon juice
5 teasp salt
½ teasp black pepper
5 cloves of garlic, crushed
5 level teasp dried basil
5 × 5 oz (150g) cans tomato purée
7 lb (3.5kg) aubergines (eggplants), cut in ¾ inch (1.5cm) slices, then soaked in water to cover with 5 level tbsp salt.

Follow recipe on p.258.

Turkish Turnovers *(50 portions – 100 turnovers)*

F raw 3 months

4 lb (2kg) frozen puff pastry
Savoury meat filling made with 4 lb (2kg) minced (ground) meat (p.255)
3 beaten eggs
Sesame seeds or poppy seeds

Follow recipe on p.264.

Corn Salad *(50 portions)*

12 × 11½ oz (315g) cans corn with pepper
1 large onion, finely chopped
6 tbsp chopped parsley
8 fl oz (225ml/1 cup) vinaigrette dressing (p.000)
5 × 8 fl oz (225ml/⅔ cup) mayonnaise

Follow the recipe on p.328.

Southern Beef Casserole *(50 portions)*

F 3 months

16 lb (7.5kg) braising steak
1/2 pint (275ml/1 1/4 cups) oil
6 lb (3kg) onions
20 green peppers or 1 1/4 pints (725ml/3 cups) frozen peppers
4 × 1 lb l2 oz (800g) cans tomatoes
3 1/2 pints (2 litres/9 cups) stock made with meat cubes; or the

same amount of dry red wine
6 fat cloves of garlic
2 tbsp mixed Italian herbs or dried basil
12 large bayleaves
4 tbsp salt
3 tbsp brown sugar
1 tbsp black pepper

Follow recipe on p.250.

Green Gold Salad *(50 portions)*

7 lb (3kg) fresh or frozen green beans
6 × 11 1/2 oz (315g) cans corn with pimentos

1 lb (450g) stoned black or green olives

Dressing:

15 fl oz (425ml/2 cups) any salad oil
8 fl oz (225ml/1 cup) wine vinegar
3 large cloves of garlic
2 level tbsp salt

1/2 teasp black pepper
7 tbsp chopped parsley
1/2 onion, finely chopped
7 tbsp snipped chives

Follow the recipe on p.329.

Coleslaw of Chinese Leaves *(50 portions)*

8 lb (4kg) shredded Chinese leaves
1 1/2 lb (675g) carrots
6 green peppers, halved, de-seeded, white pith removed, then finely sliced

3/4 lb (350g/2 1/2 cups) sultanas (white raisins) (optional)
1/2 lb (225g/2 cups) peanuts or hazelnuts (optional)

Dressing:

1 3/4 pints (1 litre/4 cups) mayonnaise
5 oz (150g/2/3 cup) sugar

5 fl oz (150ml/2/3 cup) vinegar
2 tbsp mustard powder

Follow recipe on p.322. Shred into large plastic bowl. Mix in batches with the dressing.

Easy Coleslaw *(50 servings)*

For a large quantity it is often more time-saving to buy prepared coleslaw and add extra ingredients.

7 × 12 oz (350g) cartons coleslaw
2 small heads celery, sliced across in ¼ inch (0.5cm) slices
2 green peppers, halved, de-seeded and cut in very thin strips
2 red apples, cored and cut into ½ inch (1.25cm) cubes
½ lb (225g/2 cups) sultanas (white raisins)

Mix all ingredients thoroughly.

Carrot and Raisin Slaw *(50 portions)*

10 lb (4.5kg) carrots
1 lb (450g/3 cups) seedless raisins
1 lb (450g/4 cups) walnuts, pecans, or roasted peanuts – coarsely chopped

Dressing:

1¾ pints (1 litre/4 cups) soured cream or salad cream
8 fl oz (225ml/1 cup) lemon juice and 2 tbsp grated rind
½ teasp salt
¼ teasp black pepper
7 tbsp caster (superfine) sugar

Follow the recipe on p.323.

Italian Pepper Salad *(50 portions)*

7 × 14 oz (400g) cans sweet peppers (pimentos), well drained
1 pint (575ml) olive oil
8 cloves of garlic, crushed to a paste
¼ pint (150ml/⅔ cup) finely chopped parsley
2 tbsp lemon juice
2 tbsp ground sea salt
1 teasp black pepper

Follow the recipe on p.151.

Italian Tomato Salad *(50 portions)*

10 lb (4.5kg) really ripe but firm
  tomatoes
1/2 pint (275ml/1 1/4 cups) snipped
  chives or green from spring
  onions (scallions)
2 tbsp caster (superfine) sugar

1/2 pint (275ml/1 1/4 cups)
  vinaigrette dressing (see p.332)
1/4 pint (150ml/2/3 cup) chopped
  fresh basil, *or* same amount of
  chopped parsley plus 2 tbsp
  dried basil

Follow the recipe on p.327.

South Island Celery and Apple Salad *(50 portions)*

56 large tender stalks celery
  (about 5 good celery heads)
3 lb (1.5kg) red-skinned apples
2 lb (1kg) fresh dates, stoned and
  roughly chopped

1 lb (450g/3 cups) seedless raisins
1 lb (450g/4 cups) chopped
  walnuts or salted peanuts
  (optional)

Dressing:

6 tbsp orange juice
6 tbsp lemon juice
2 tbsp fine brown sugar

1 1/2 pints (850ml/4 cups) mild
  mayonnaise (add a little more if
  necessary to coat the
  ingredients)

Follow the recipe on p.330.

Ice-Cream with Sauce *(50 portions)*

*This is an economical sweet for serving to a large number.
Especially good at a barbecue.*

Allow 1 1/2 gallons (6 litres) of ice-cream for 50 portions.

Chocolate sauce:

12 oz (350g/1 1/2 cups) butter
2 lb (1 kg/8 cups) sieved icing
  (confectioners') sugar

12 oz (350g/3 cups) cocoa
24 fl oz (700ml/3 cups) evaporated
  milk

Follow the recipe on p.403.

Melon and Satsuma Cocktail *(50 small portions)*

10 large melons (about 10 lb/4.5kg)

12 satsumas

3/4 pint (425ml/2 cups) water and

1 1/2 lb (700g) sugar, boiled together until syrupy

Juice of 3 lemons

5 tbsp lime cordial or lime juice

Follow the recipe on p.346 for **Marinated Melon Balls,** but add the peeled and sectioned satsumas.

Peach, Lychee and Pineapple Salad *(50 portions)*

Make pineapple compote with the following ingredients:

4 large fresh pineapples

Approx 1 1/2 pints (850ml/4 cups) peach syrup drained from canned fruit

1 pint (575ml/2 1/2 cups) orange juice

8 fl oz (225ml/1 cup) lemon juice

3 1/2 tbsp cornflour (cornstarch)

8 fl oz (225ml/1 cup) Cointreau or Kirsch (optional)

4 × 28 oz (800g) cans sliced peaches in syrup

6 cans lychees

Follow the recipe on p.350.

Pineapple Sauce *(50 portions)*

4 × 20 oz (575g) cans pineapple, finely chopped

12 fl oz (350ml/1 1/2 cups) orange cordial

3 tbsp lemon juice

5 oz (150g/2/3 cup) brown sugar

5 level tbsp cornflour (cornstarch)

Mix together the sugar and cornflour (cornstarch), then blend with the cordial, lemon juice and syrup strained from the fruit. Bring to the boil, stirring constantly, then simmer 3 minutes. Add the finely cut-up pineapple. Leave to go cold.

Table of Quantities to Serve 50

These must be taken as a guide only, as appetites will vary with the occasion, the time of the year, the age of the guests and the other dishes on the menu.

Food	Serving Per Person	To Order
Bread and rolls		
Crisp rolls	1-1^1/$_2$	4^1/$_2$-6^1/$_2$ doz
Large loaf	1-2 slices	2-3 loaves
Drinks		
Cocoa	8 fl oz (225ml) cup	8 oz (225g)
Coffee (ground)	6^1/$_2$ fl oz (190ml) cup	1-1^1/$_4$ lb (450-575g)
Coffee (instant)	6^1/$_2$ fl oz (190ml) cup	5 oz (150g)
Tea (amount will vary with quality and blend)	2 × 5 fl oz (150ml) cups	6 oz (175g)
Tomato juice	3 fl oz (75ml/^{1}/$_3$ cup)	7^1/$_2$ pints (3^3/$_4$ litres)
Rice and pasta		
Noodles	5 oz (150g) cooked	4 lb (2kg)
Macaroni or spaghetti	5 oz (150g) cooked	4-5 lb (2-2^1/$_2$kg)
Rice	5 oz (150g) cooked	3 lb (1^1/$_2$kg)
Dairy produce		
Butter for table	1-1^1/$_2$ pats	1-1^1/$_2$ lb (^{3}/$_4$ kg)
Butter for sandwiches	2 teaspoon	1 lb (450g)
Cream for coffee	1 tablespoon	1^1/$_2$ pints (850ml)
Cream, whipping (for garnish)	1 tablespoon	^{3}/$_4$ pint (425ml)
Cottage cheese	Scant 3 oz (75g)	10 lb (5kg)
Cheese for sandwiches	1^1/$_4$ oz (35g)	4 lb (2kg)
Eggs	1-2	50-100
Ice-cream, bulk	1 scoop	1^1/$_2$ gal (6 litres)
Ice-cream, bricks	About ^{1}/$_7$ brick	7-8 family bricks
Milk (for tea)	Approx 1 tablespoon	3 pints (1^1/$_2$ litres)
Milk (for coffee)	^{1}/$_3$ cup	5 pints (2^1/$_2$ litres)

Food	Serving Per Person	To Order
Fruit		
Prunes	3 oz (75g) cooked	5$\frac{1}{2}$ lb (2$\frac{3}{4}$kg)
Apples (stewed)	3 oz (75g) raw	15 lb (7$\frac{1}{2}$kg)
Apples (for 8 inch/20cm pie)	6-7 servings per pie	15 lb (7$\frac{1}{2}$kg)
Canned fruit	4 oz (125g)	2 × A10 cans
Fruit juice (canned)	4 fl oz (125ml)	4 × 46 fl oz (1345 ml) can

Meats	Cooked weight	Raw weight	
Chuck or bola (braised)	3 oz (75g)	5 oz (150g)	20-22 lb (10-11kg)
Minced (ground) meat for patties	3$\frac{1}{2}$ oz (90g)	4 oz (125g)	14 lb (7kg)
Standing rib roast	3 oz (75g)	8 oz (225g)	25-28 lb (12$\frac{1}{2}$-14kg)
Stew with vegetables	5$\frac{1}{2}$ oz (165g)		15 lb (7$\frac{1}{2}$kg)
Braising steak, sliced	3$\frac{1}{2}$ oz (90g)	5 oz (150g)	16 lb (8kg)
Veal chops (3 to lb/450g)	1 each		17 lb (8$\frac{1}{2}$kg)
Lamb chops (4 to lb/450g)	2 each		25 lb (12$\frac{1}{2}$kg)
Salami	2 oz (50g)		6$\frac{1}{2}$ lb (3kg)
Saveloys (12 to lb/450g)	2 each		8-10 lb (4-5kg)

Poultry		
Chicken, casseroled	$\frac{1}{4}$ chicken	40 lb (20kg) (12 chickens approx 3$\frac{1}{2}$-1.5kg each)
Chicken, fried	$\frac{1}{4}$-$\frac{1}{2}$ chicken	13-25 fryers, 2$\frac{1}{2}$-3lb (1-1$\frac{1}{2}$kg) each
Turkey, roast	2$\frac{1}{2}$ oz (65g)	35-40 lb (17-20kg)

Food	Serving Per Person	To Order
Fish		
Fish fillets	4 oz (125g)	12$\frac{1}{2}$ lb (6kg)
Fish steaks	6 oz (175g)	20 lb (9 kg)
Whole salmon, including head	8 oz (225g)	25 lb (12$\frac{1}{2}$kg)
Vegetables		
Canned	4 oz (125g)	2 × A10 cans
Frozen	2$\frac{1}{2}$-3 oz (65-75g)	7$\frac{1}{2}$-10 lb (3$\frac{1}{2}$-5kg)
Lettuce for salad	1$\frac{1}{2}$-2 oz (40-50g)	8-10 heads
Lettuce for garnish		4-5 heads
Potatoes, baked	6 oz (175g)	20 lb (10kg)
Potatoes, to mash	4 oz (125g)	12 lb (6kg)
Potatoes, chips (French fries)	About 4$\frac{1}{2}$ oz (140g)	12-15 lb (6-7$\frac{1}{2}$kg)
Potato crisps (chips)	$\frac{3}{4}$-1 oz (20-25kg)	2$\frac{1}{2}$-3 lb (1$\frac{1}{4}$-1$\frac{1}{2}$kg)
Tomatoes, sliced	3 oz (75g)	10-12 lb (5-6kg)
Miscellaneous		
Mixed nuts		1$\frac{1}{2}$ lb ($\frac{3}{4}$kg)
Honey	2 tablespoons	5 lb (2$\frac{1}{2}$kg)
Jam	2 tablespoons	5 lb (2$\frac{1}{2}$kg)
Sugar, lump	1-2 cubes	1$\frac{1}{2}$ lb ($\frac{3}{4}$kg)
Sugar, granulated	2 teaspoons	1 lb ($\frac{1}{2}$kg)
Sugar, brown	2 teaspoons	1 lb ($\frac{1}{2}$kg)
Desserts		
Cakes	2$\frac{1}{2}$ oz (65g)	2 tins, each approx 12 × 10 inches (30 × 25cm) (25 pieces each)
Fruit-cake	2$\frac{1}{2}$ oz (65g)	8 lb (4kg)
Pies, 8 inch (20cm)		8 pies
Pastry (1 crust), 6$\frac{1}{2}$ oz (190g) per pie		3$\frac{1}{4}$ lb (1$\frac{1}{2}$kg)
Pastry (2 crust), 12 oz (350g) per pie		

Food	Serving Per Person	To Order
Salads		
Vegetable (e.g. coleslaw)	5 fl oz (150ml)	1½ gal (6 litres)
Potato	4 fl oz (125ml)	1¼ gal (5 litres)
Soups		
Cream soup	5 fl oz (150ml)	1½ gal (6 litres)
Clear soup	8 fl oz (225ml)	2¼ gal (9 litres)
Gravy	3-4 tablespoons	5-6½ pints (2½ litres)
Sauce, thickened for meat	2 tablespoons	2½ pints (1¼ litres)
Mayonnaise	1½ tablespoons	2 pints (1 litre)

Appendix:
Support Systems and
Planning Techniques;
Food Storage; Stocking Up

However much or little you are prepared to cook for your guests, it is essential to equip yourself with an adequate support system of appliances, preparation machines and cooking tools. Modern equipment will not make you a better cook, but it does help to make you a more willing one, whether it is the well-sharpened knife which takes the labour out of chopping parsley, or the sophisticated food preparation machine which enables you to prepare a terrine of pâté in less than a minute, or indeed the dishwasher which does most of the clearing up after the party.

I believe it is very difficult to fit cooking for friends into today's lifestyle without a refrigerator or freezer. Indeed, in a house with central heating, low-temperature storage of some kind is absolutely essential if preparation for meals is to be spread over longer than 24 hours. The minimum allowance for *any* household is based on 2 cu feet (60 litres) of freezer space per person, plus an extra 2 cu feet, but if regular entertaining is part of your routine, then I would suggest that you could easily double this capacity, and in fact buy the largest machine which space and finance will permit. For convenience of access I would choose an upright freezer with separate baskets or drawers and good door storage rather than the cheaper chest model.

A microwave oven offers many advantages to the busy cook: cooking times can be drastically shortened, with the result that the flavour of fresh food is dramatically improved; dishes (particularly vegetables) can be cooked ahead then reheated right in the serving dish in between courses without any loss of colour and flavour; frozen foods can be thawed almost instantly to meet the contingency of unexpected guests; the ranges of baking dishes is widened to include best bone china as well as plastic and paper.

Throughout the book I have given specific suggestions for making the most of this appliance.

Some form of food preparation machine, whether it be an electric mixer with attachments or the newer food processor, is of inestimable value: the tireless machine does the job more quickly and in many cases more efficiently than human skill with a hand-held tool. Although the electric mixer with its large-capacity mixing bowl is very suitable for a household where a lot of baking is done, the food processor is far more versatile: it can mix, chop, mince, beat, knead, cream and purée, and it is easy to clean. Its main disadvantages are that it does not produce a velvety purée like a blender; it has a limited capacity for mixing cakes, biscuits and doughs, it will not whisk egg whites satisfactorily; and the blade does need to be sharpened annually.

The hand-held electric mixer is very useful even if you have the larger machine, as it is handy for beating foods like mashed potatoes or sauces at the cooker; also it will whisk anything such as cream or egg white even if it is not in a standard mixing bowl. A large-capacity blender is very useful if you make a lot of cream soups, mousses and fruit purées, although not essential since many of its functions can also be carried out by the much cheaper hand-operated food mill.

Planning is also an essential part of the support system; it involves shopping, storing fresh and frozen foods, and what I like to call 'store cupboard insurance' for canned and packeted foods, and 'chilled and frozen assets' for more perishable ones. Thus a well-stocked cupboard and bulk supplies of such perishables as breadcrumbs, chopped herbs, grated cheese, soup stocks, purées, dressings and sauces etc. in the fridge or freezer will ensure that shopping and preparations for a particular meal will be minimized.

Shopping for food is an art which is essential to anyone wishing to keep a good table with the minimum of work and expense, and detailed guidance on the selection of various foods is given in the appropriate chapter or recipe. It cannot be emphasized too strongly that all the culinary skill in the world is no substitute for quality food: *do not buy anything unless it is in prime condition*, and as far as possible buy from specialist suppliers. Since shopping is as time-consuming as cooking, I find it most convenient to divide food into categories according to the frequency with which stocks must be purchased. Here is a rough guide:

To buy a month's supply at a time

Canned foods of all kinds; frozen foods; tea; instant coffee; drinking (instant) chocolate and cocoa; sugar; flour; dried and candied fruits; nuts (whole, shredded and ground); rice; pulses; soup cereals and pasta; bottled sauces and salad dressings; salt; seasonings and dried herbs; sweet and savoury spices; oils and other cooking fats; bottled delicatessen such as olives and gherkins; packeted foods other than biscuits (cookies).

To buy a week's supply at a time

Butter; eggs; packeted and processed cheese; coffee beans; packeted sweet and savoury biscuits (crackers and cookies); durable vegetables such as potatoes, carrots, leeks, fresh herbs, onions, green peppers and cucumbers; fruits such as oranges, lemons, grapefruit, apples, bananas, tomatoes.

To buy a three-days' supply at a time

Meat and poultry (unless buying for the freezer); stoned fruits such as pears, and those which are best ripened at home such as melons and avocados; vegetables such as cauliflowers, peas, cabbages, sprouts and aubergines (eggplants); hard pressed cheeses (e.g. Cheddar); soft cheeses (e.g. Gouda); cream cheeses; yoghurt; soured and sweet cream.

To buy daily

Milk; soft fruits and berries; grapes; fresh corn; mushrooms; cakes; sweet yeast breads; bread and rolls; all fresh delicatessen (including salads, cooked meats and smoked fish); liver; raw minced (ground) meat.

Of course, with a freezer, perishable foods can be bought less frequently, but it is always preferable to use them fresh if possible.

Storing Fresh Foods

All fresh foods are perishable and must be stored under the kind of conditions which will ensure that they stay at the peak of freshness for as long as possible, whether in the refrigerator (R), the larder (L) or the larder cupboard (LC)

All perishable foods (with a few exceptions such as under-ripe fruit and potatoes – see details below) can be stored in the refrigerator (average temperature 4°C-7°C/40°F-47°F). Indeed, highly perishable foods (e.g. raw fish and meat) *must* be stored under refrigeration if they are to be safe to eat the next day. At normal refrigerator temperatures the growth of the bacteria and moulds which cause food to go bad are inhibited for a period that may vary from 2-28 days, depending on the nature of the food and its freshness when put into the refrigerator. The coldest part of the fridge (4°C, 40°F) is directly under the freezing unit, or, if there is no freezer compartment, since cold air sinks, on the bottom shelf of the cabinet. It is here that the most perishable food should be stored. The least cold part (7°C, 47°..) is farthest away from the freezing unit and in the door unit, where the less perishable foods (e.g. fruit, vegetables, butter and cheese) should be kept. Whatever the food, however, it must be covered in some way so that it does not shrivel or become discoloured in the cold dry air inside the cabinet, and also to prevent it absorbing flavours and smells from 'stronger' foods. Depending on the kind of food (details below), this covering may be plastic, foil, film or paper.

The traditional larder (average temperature 7°C-10°C/45°F-50°F) was usually sited on a north wall, and was ventilated with cold air from outside. Recent studies have shown that since the widespread installation of central heating, the average temperature in most so-called larders is 17°C (62°F), and there is no adequate ventilation. Such a larder cupboard is therefore only suitable for short-term storage (up to a week) of the less perishable fruits and vegetables, such as citrus fruits, apples and root vegetables. It can, however, be used for maturing foods like melons, avocados and pears which are actually harvested when under-ripe.

Since it is impossible to be dogmatic about how long any kind of food can be kept in prime condition – because so much will depend on the degree of freshness at the start of the storage time – it is good policy to review the contents of the fridge, the larder, and the larder cupboard every day. Any food that looks or smells even slightly unappetizing, particularly if it is of animal origin, should always be thrown away.

Meat R or L

As soon as possible after purchase meat should either be refrigerated or stored in a really cold larder (not more than 7°C, 45°F).
R position: Under freezer unit.
Wrapping: Put in special refrigerator meat container or place on plate or tray and loosely cover with film or foil.

Shrink-wrapped meat: Unless it is to be cooked the same day, remove or loosen wrapping and treat as above.
Storage time:

Joints, steaks, chops and other prime cuts	3-6 days
Minced (ground) meat, offal (*very* perishable)	1-2 days
Pickled meats, tongue, sausages (observe 'use-by' date if pre-packed)	2-6 days

Do not keep any raw meat in the *larder* longer than 24 hours.

Poultry R

Poultry is even more perishable than meat and, for safety's sake, it is advisable to refrigerate it if it is not to be used within 24 hours of purchase.

R position: In coldest part of cabinet.
Wrapping: Loosely wrap in plastic bag, film or foil (allows air to circulate and thus maintain quality).
Pre-packed birds: Open bag and remove giblets. Leave bird in bag but do not re-close.
Storage time:

Fresh birds	1-3 days

Frozen birds: Allow to defrost in refrigerator (1-3 days depending on size), then treat as fresh.

Fish R

For optimum flavour, fish should be cooked the day it is purchased or caught. It should be refrigerated as soon as it is brought into the kitchen. Handle with care to avoid bruising flesh. Do not wash until ready to cook.

R position for fresh and smoked fish: Coldest part of cabinet.
Wrapping:
Fresh fish: Wrap loosely in heavy greaseproof paper and put on plate or tray.
Smoked fish: wrap tightly in foil or greaseproof paper.
Storage time:

Fresh fish	Maximum of 1 day
Smoked salmon	3 days
Kippers and smoked white fish	10 days

Dairy foods

All dairy foods must be kept clean, cool and well covered as they easily absorb 'foreign' odours and their vitamin content is quickly diminished if exposed to light. With the exception of eggs (see below), they are best kept under refrigeration or in a very cold larder.

Eggs L (up to 10°C, 50°F) or R or LC (daily supply)

Under European Economic Community regulations, all egg cartons are stamped with the packing week (Week 1 = first week in January). To ensure the freshest eggs, always buy the highest week number available.

Position: Whether kept in L, R or LC, store with the pointed end down. This keeps the egg cell floating at the broad end and helps to conserve freshness.

Wrapping: Keep in original egg carton or in refrigerator door rack. As egg shells are extremely porous, keep well away from 'smelly' foods such as mature cheese and onions.

Storage time:

Egg yolk (in airtight container covered with cold water)	maximum 2 days
Egg white (in airtight container). *Discard if smelly*.	10 days
Whole eggs (better to buy weekly)	14 days

Fresh milk R or L

It is advisable to buy fresh milk daily and refrigerate immediately or store in cold larder.

R position: Middle of cabinet or in door rack (do not allow to freeze).

Wrapping: Keep covered, whether in the bottle (with original foil cap) or jug (foil or film) to prevent dust and other foreign bodies contaminating it.

Storage time: 1-2 days

Butter R or L

Although some sweet cream butters will keep for up to 6 months if refrigerated straight from the churn, it is advisable to buy any kind of butter on a weekly basis as it may have been in and out of the cold store before it reaches the grocer. Some butters now have a 'sell-by' date on the wrapper. Butter for daily consumption can be kept in the LC.

Position: Middle of cabinet or door storage.

Wrapping: Keep in original wrapper or in covered dish. Foil wrappers keep out the light and therefore conserve freshness and food value more effectively than paper wrappers.

Storage time: (better to buy weekly)   1 month

Cream R

Cream is particularly susceptible to high temperatures and will deteriorate in a few hours at room temperature. Storage time varies according to the time of year.

R position: Middle of cabinet (do not allow to freeze as it goes 'grainy' unless whipped).

Wrapping: Keep covered in original carton or decant into airtight plastic container.

Storage time:

Single (light), double (heavy), whipping, clotted, whipped	(summer) 2-3 days (winter) 3-4 days
Soured (cultured), yoghurt	7-10 days
Bottled	2-3 days
UHT (keep in larder)	2-3 months
Sterilized (unopened; keep at room temperature)	Indefinitely

Cheese

All cheese must be wrapped in a way that will allow it to 'breathe' without drying out, and protect it from excess heat which causes it to 'sweat'.

Hard cheese L or R

There is less likelihood of cheese drying out if it is kept in the larder rather than the refrigerator. However, for storage longer than 24 hours, refrigerate.

L position: Must be cool, dark and airy, preferably on tiled slab.

R position: Bottom shelf or door. Remove 2 hours before serving, taking off wrapping of pre-packed cheese.

Wrapping:

L Use cheese dish with ventilated lid, or place on plate covered with upturned bowl, or wrap loosely in greaseproof paper.

R Double wrap, first in greaseproof paper or special cheese paper, then put in plastic bag or container.

Storage time:

Whole cheese and very hard cheese, e.g. Parmesan (in a very cold larder and in winter, 4°C, 40°F)	Up to 6 months
Portion of cheese (use as quickly as possible)	Up to 10 days
Grated cheese (in airtight container)	Up to 2 weeks

Soft and cream cheeses R

As the moisture content is much higher than in hard cheese, these are much more perishable and should be treated in a similar way to cream. With the exception of cottage cheese, which should be served chilled, remove from refrigerator one hour before serving.

Position: Bottom of refrigerator (coldest part).

Wrapping: Wrap securely in foil or keep in airtight container.

Storage time: (depending on time of year): 4-7 days

Fruit R or L or LC (up to 3 days only)

Once it is ripe, all fresh fruit (with the exception of the banana) can be kept in peak condition by storing it in a refrigerator or a very cold larder (maximum temperature 7°C, 45°F). For short-term only (up to 3 days) they can be stored in the LC or a fruit bowl.

R position: Bottom shelf.

L and LC position: In one layer, preferably on ventilated rack.

LC wrapping: Unnecessary.

R and L wrapping: See below.

LC storage time:	Up to 3 days
R and L storage time:	See below

Note: The following instructions refer to R and L.

Apples and Pears

Both taste better if served chilled, though pears should be kept at room temperature for ½ hour before serving.

Wrapping: Unnecessary.
Storage time: Up to 10 days (may be kept longer but skin tends to shrivel).

Stoned Fruit: Peaches, plums etc.

Wrapping: Airtight plastic container in one layer.
Storage time: 3-4 days

Lemons

Wrapping: Unnecessary.
Storage time:
Whole lemons 3-4 weeks (but skins may shrivel)
Cut lemons (tightly foil-wrapped) Up to 4 days

Oranges, Tangerines, Grapefruit

Refrigerate only if to be kept for more than a week.

Melons and Pineapples

Refrigerate only when fully ripe, as they are ruined if over-chilled.
Wrapping: Unnecessary for whole fruit. Cover cut surface tightly with film or foil.
Storage time:
Whole fruit   7-10 days
Cut fruit   3-4 days
Sugared fruit   1 day

Grapes

Refrigerate only if to be kept more than 3 days in winter, 2 days in summer.
Wrapping: Place unwashed in plastic bag or airtight container.
Storage time: 4-7 days

Soft fruits

Best eaten on day of purchase but may be stored in airtight

container after being rinsed and sugared – for up to 48 hours (though they may lose their 'fresh' texture).

Bananas

Never refrigerate as the texture is ruined and the flesh may go black. Ripen (slowly) in L or (quickly) in LC.
Wrapping: Unnecessary.
Storage time: (according to ripeness):   1-7 days

Vegetables

All varieties (with the exception of potatoes) keep fresh longer if they can be stored in the refrigerator. Do not wash before storage.
R position: Bottom shelf.
L position: On ventilated rack, but no green vegetables except hard cabbage.
R wrapping: Keep each kind separately in a plastic bag. Store all the bags in special vegetable container. Keep easily-bruised varieties in special container.
L wrapping: Leave unwrapped unless special instructions are given below.

All green vegetables R

Cabbages, sprouts, cauliflowers, green beans, leeks, peas.
Storage time (according to freshness):   3-7 days

Root vegetables (except potatoes) R or L

Carrots, turnips, parsnips, swedes.
R storage time: Up to 2 weeks

Delicate vegetables R or L

Courgettes (zucchini) aubergines (eggplants), peppers, asparagus, cucumbers, artichokes.
Wrapping: Wrap tightly in film or foil.
Storage time (use as soon as possible):   Up to 5 days

Mushrooms R

Wrapping: Airtight plastic container.
Storage time (best used on day of   1-3 days
  purchase):

Tomatoes

For optimum flavour, these are best ripened at room temperature
(in LC) than used at once, though they may be stored in R.
Storage time:

R	Up to 7 days
L	Up to 4 days

Potatoes L and LC

They must be kept cool and dark, between 10°C and 16°C
(50°F-60°F). Too high a temperature causes them to sprout. Too
low a temperature gives them a sweet taste. Therefore do not
refrigerate. Unwashed potatoes keep better than washed.
L or LC position: On ventilated rack.
Wrapping: Small quantities in paper bags to protect from light.
Bulk potatoes in sack or large paper bags.
Storage time:

Old potatoes (main crop)	1-2 weeks
Bulk potatoes (up to April)	Up to 2 months
New potatoes	Up to 4 days

Salad Greens and Herbs R

These can be kept unwashed for several days either in airtight
plastic container or lidded aluminium pan. When washed, treat as
below.
Wrapping: After drying thoroughly, store in airtight plastic
container.
Storage time:

Salad greens	Up to 48 hours
Herbs (e.g. parsley)	Up to 1 week

Storing Frozen Foods (at – 18°C, 0°F – normal running temperature of a home freezer)

Here is a general guide for both raw and cooked foods. Detailed storage times are given in the different chapters and also in the individual recipe.

Note: Food *can* be kept in the freezer for longer than these recommended storage times. However, although there will be no danger to health, there may well be some loss of flavour, and fish and meat in · particular will suffer some dehydration and a consequent lessening of quality.

Baked goods

Bread	6 months
Loaves with a crisp crust such as Vienna	1 week
Rolls	4 months
Cakes (plain)	6 months
Cakes (with icing)	3 months
Pastries and pies – cooked	4 months
uncooked	1-2 months
Pastry – cooked and uncooked	4 months
Sandwiches	3 months
Breadcrumbs (fresh)	6 months

Dairy products

Butter, slightly salted	6 months
Butter, unsalted	12 months
Cheese (hard, e.g. Cheddar)	6 months
Cheese (soft e.g. Camembert, cream cheese)	3 months
Cream (specially prepared for the freezer, or home-whipped)	8 months
Ice-cream	4 months

Fruit and Vegetables (with exceptions specifically mentioned in appropriate chapter)	12 months

Fish

Raw fish (depending on time lapse after it has been caught)	6-9 months
Cooked fish	3 months

Raw Meat

Beef	Joints	12 months
	Minced (ground)	4 months
	Steaks	6 months
	Sausages	3 months
Lamb	Joints	9 months
	Chops and cutlets	6 months

Cooked Meat

Casseroles	3 months
Meat and poultry pies	3 months
Pickled meat	2 months
Sliced meat with gravy	3 months
Sliced meat without gravy	2 months
Pâté	1 month
Stock	6 months

Raw Poultry

Chicken	12 months
Duck	8 months
Goose	8 months
Turkey	8 months
Giblets	3 months
Stuffing	3 months

Cooked Poultry

	3 months

Stocking Up

If entertaining is going to fit into the pattern of everyday living, some thought must be given to it throughout the year – just like ordinary meal planning and not only when a specific occasion arises. That's why I believe you need what might be called 'store cupboard insurance' for canned and packeted foods, and 'chilled and frozen assets' for more perishable ones. These stocks of specialist food, bought or prepared on a regular basis throughout the year, can save a tremendous amount of the work – and worry – involved in preparing for any kind of special meal or occasion. They are 'background' foods, not prepared for any particular time but sure to be needed in one way or another in a wide variety of menus and recipes. They are in addition to the dishes or ingredients needed for a particular menu that can be frozen or refrigerated ahead, specific suggestions for which are given in individual menus and recipes.

In the case of canned, bottled and packeted foods, it's good policy to buy a replacement as each fresh pack is started, so that there is never any fear of running short in the middle of a cooking session. In addition, it's very useful always to keep in stock in the freezer or refrigerator, bulk supplies of those more perishable foods such as breadcrumbs, chopped herbs, grated cheese or ready-shelled chestnuts which, although they may be needed only in small quantities in a particular recipe, are nevertheless very time-consuming to prepare. This policy will ensure that the shopping for a particular meal will be restricted only to more perishable foods. Of course, all these stocks are in addition to the basic foods such as sugar, butter, eggs and flour that are used in normal everyday cooking.

In the storecupboard:
 Specialist sugars such as icing (confectioners'), caster (superfine), natural demerara, light brown and Muscavado; golden (corn) syrup; treacle (molasses).
Specialist flours including 100% wheatmeal, white bread; granary, 81% plain and self-raising.
Quality 'mixes', including bread, sponge and pastry.
Dried yeast.
Cornflour (cornstarch), arrowroot.
Bicarbonate of soda, cream of tartar.

Chicken, beef and vegetable bouillon cubes or paste.
Mustards including English (made and powdered), Dijon, Bordeaux and Meaux.

Vinegars including malt, distilled (white) malt; cider, wine; herb-flavoured.

Oil including corn oil (or other flavourless salad and frying oils such as peanut, sunflower, sassflower), virgin olive, walnut (huile de noix) – refrigerate when open.

Bottled sauces including soy, Worcestershire, Tabasco, tomato ketchup.

Garlic cloves.

Whole spices including blade mace, black peppercorns, pickling, coriander, nutmeg, cloves, cardamon

Ground spices including cinnamon, ginger, mixed, allspice, curry, mace, nutmeg, cayenne, paprika, white pepper

Dried herbs (freeze dried where possible) including basil, chives, mint, parsley, Italian mixture, herbes de Provence, fine herbes, bayleaves.

Sea salt

Canned tomato purée, juce and whole tomatoes (preferably canned in tomato juice).

Canned fish including tuna, salmon and anchovies.

Canned fruit (preferably canned in its own juice), bottled fruit including blackcurrants and cherries.

Canned 'salad' vegetables including corn, sweet red pimentos, aubergines (eggplants), asparagus tips, new potatoes, white and red beans, artichoke hearts.

Canned or bottled olives including stuffed, Queen, black, calamata (canned in Greece in wine vinegar and olive oil).

Canned or bottled pickled cucumbers and gherkins.

Pasta (white and wholemeal) including lasagne, vermicelli, egg noodles, spaghetti, macaroni.

Rice including Patna, Basmatti, brown, par-cooked long grain, Italian risotto.

Pulses, cereals and beans including pot barley, green and red lentils, butter beans, haricot beans, red and white kidney beans.

Porridge oats.

Dried coating crumbs (allow stale bread – preferably French bread – to dry out in cool oven without colouring. Reduce to crumbs in blender, food processor, mincer or by crushing with rolling pin. Store in airtight tin).

Dried fruits including raisins, muscatel (seeded raisins), currants, sultanas (white raisins), apricots, dates.

Glacé (candied) cherries.

Nuts, including walnut halves and pieces; almonds, slivered, nibbed and ground; hazelnuts, whole and ground; roasted peanuts; coconut shredded or dessicated (dried and shredded).

Sesame seeds, pine kernels.

Chocolate including drinking (instant), bittersweet dessert, coating, cocoa.

Sweet preserves including apricot (for glazes), other fruit conserves (for scones), mincemeat.

Savoury preserves including jellies such as mint, apple, redcurrant, chutney.

Gelatine (vegetable gelatin); table jellies (gelatin mix).

In the Freezer
F 1 month
Chestnuts cooked and made into stuffing (as on p.285).
Fresh yeast.

F 2 months
Herb butters (as on p.491).

Chicken meat and fish stocks – basis for soups, sauces, poaching liquids.

Soup purées – golden vegetable, borscht, mushroom, pea, tomato (follow individual soup recipe but do not add liquid).

F 3 months
Croutons (as on p.160) – reheat from frozen in hot oven (Gas No. 6, 400°F, 200°C) for 5 minutes.

Cream – but only if it contains more than 35% butter fat (e.g. whipping, double (heavy), clotted). Best policy is to buy special pack or whipping cream, or half whip fresh cream, freeze then complete whipping when defrosted.

F 4 months
Pastry. Freeze either in:
1-inch (2.5cm) thick blocks or in circles cut to fit pie, flan or tart shapes; or moulded to fit tins; or baked ready for filling.

Chestnuts peeled but uncooked for use in desserts, stuffing, vegetable dishes.

F 6 months
Herbs stored either in sprigs or chopped. A week's supply can be packed in a plastic cup and then transferred to the refrigerator as required. Or wrap enough for individual recipes in foil twists. Sprigs of parsley can be crushed between the fingers whilst still frozen. They will then have a texture similar to that if they had been chopped before freezing.

Grated cheese. Remains free-flowing even if used when frozen.

Breadcrumbs. Reduce to crumbs in blender or food processor. Can be used frozen for stuffings, puddings, gratins.

F 12 months
Seasonal fruits. If necessary, it is worth buying raspberries, blackcurrants, gooseberries and loganberries in season to freeze them for winter use. Open freeze until hard, then store in bags. Strawberries become soggy when defrosted so if you want to freeze them as berries, slice and layer with sugar (3 oz/75g) to the pound (450g). Open freeze then bag. Thaw in refrigerator for 3 hours, or until still a little icy.

Berry purées (see p.487). This is a better method for strawberries.

Uncooked berry jam. Follow recipe on p.496. Tastes like crushed sugared fresh fruit.

In the refrigerator
The average refrigerator storage time for most foods is 1-2 weeks, though certain foods containing a high proportion of sugar and vinegar have a much longer life.

R 1 week
Lemon juice. Squeeze, then keep in small airtight plastic container, invaluable when a 'squeeze' of juice is required.

Herbs. Wash, dry then store as sprigs or chopped, in airtight plastic container.

Soup and casserole vegetables. Keep an assortment of carrots, leeks, onions, squashy tomatoes, mushroom stalks, red or green peppers in season. (*Note*: to chop onion without tears, leave in freezer for 20-30 minutes beforehand.)

R 2 weeks
Grated cheese. Keep in a plastic container.
Tomato purée. Keep in opened tin covered with foil.

R 3 weeks
Partly used jars of horseradish sauce, made mustard, mayonnaise, olives, pickled cucumbers, gherkins.

R 6 months
Mint sauce concentrate (see p.488).
Sugar syrup (p.550). Keep in the summer for fruit salads and cold drinks.
Coffee syrup (p.490) for flavouring drinks, desserts, cake icings.

Keeps indefinitely
French dressing (without onion or herbs).

Index

Note: page numbers in italics refer to the menu suggestions in the earlier part of the book; page numbers in Roman type refer to the recipes

598

600